American Military Gliders of WWII

U.S.
ARMY

American Military Gliders of WWII

Development, Training, Experimentation, and Tactics of All Aircraft Types

Bill Norton

Schiffer Military History
Atglen, PA

Acknowledgments

The author would like to acknowledge the kind assistance of Gerry Balzer, Brigadier General Bob Cardenas (retired), Everett Cassagneres, Thomas Culbert, Charles Day, Bob Franz, George Larson, and Keith Thoms. Organizations that helped include Dr. Jim Young and the people of the Air Force Flight Test Center History Office; the Air Force Historical Research Agency; the fine personnel at the Air Force Materiel Command History Office; Jim Campbell of the New Haven Museum; Kase Decker and Hayden Hamilton of the American Aviation Historical Society; Jay Miller and the people of the Jay Miller Collection; archivists at the National Museum of Naval Aviation; Brett Stolle and the National Museum of the United States Air Force; the National Soaring Museum; Curtiss Utz and the staff of the Naval Aviation Archives; Amy Heidrick, John Little, and Dan Hagedorn at the Museum of Flight; Alan Renga and the folks at the San Diego Air & Space Museum; and the United States National Archives.

Book design by Stephanie Daugherty.

Library of Congress Control Number: 2012934114

Printed in China.
ISBN: 978-0-7643-4051-2

We are interested in hearing from authors with book ideas on related topics.

Published by Schiffer Publishing Ltd.
4880 Lower Valley Road
Atglen, PA 19310
Phone: (610) 593-1777
FAX: (610) 593-2002
E-mail: Info@schifferbooks.com.
Visit our web site at: www.schifferbooks.com
Please write for a free catalog.
This book may be purchased from the publisher.
Try your bookstore first.

In Europe, Schiffer books are distributed by:
Bushwood Books
6 Marksbury Avenue
Kew Gardens
Surrey TW9 4JF, England
Phone: 44 (0) 20 8392-8585
FAX: 44 (0) 20 8392-9876
E-mail: Info@bushwoodbooks.co.uk.
Visit our website at: www.bushwoodbooks.co.uk

Table of Contents

Preface ... 7

Chapter 1 Gliders Go to War ... 8
The New Weapon ... 8
The U.S. Army Reacts ... 10
Navy and Marines Vision ... 17

Chapter 2 Quick Evolution: Trainers ... 20
Numbers Game ... 21
Polyglot ... 21
Acquisition ... 22
Failed All-Wood Gambit ... 25
Troika ... 27
Navy/Marine Trainers ... 28

Chapter 3 The Training Muddle ... 32
What to Do? ... 34
Repeated Escalation ... 35
Equipment Shortfall ... 37
Relative Efficiency ... 39
Pile-Up ... 40
Even Keel ... 42
Focus Shift ... 43
Navy/Marines Training ... 47

Chapter 4 Initial Army Cargo Gliders ... 50
Frankfort Sailplane XCG-1 & XCG-2 ... 52
Waco XCG-3 & CG-3A ... 53
St. Louis Aircraft XCG-5 & XCG-6 ... 56
Bowlus Sailplane XCG-7 & XCG-8 ... 57

Chapter 5 Prevalence: Waco CG-4 and CG-15 ... 60
Development ... 61
Description ... 63
Production ... 65
Improvements ... 72
Other Operators ... 79
Waco CG-4D, XCG-15, XCG-15A, CG-15A, & G-15A ... 79

Chapter 6 Initial Amphibious Gliders ... 83
New Concepts ... 83
12-Place Glider Contracts ... 85
Bristol Aeronautical XLRQ-1 ... 85
Allied Aviation XLRA-1 ... 88
Elusive 24-Place Gliders ... 90
Production Plans ... 92

Chapter 7 The American Way ... 94
Basics ... 95
Mass Assaults ... 99
Snatch ... 105
Recovery ... 108
Pilots ... 110

Chapter 8 Advanced Army Gliders ... 112
Impulse ... 113
G & A Aircraft XCG-9 ... 114
Laister-Kauffman Aircraft XCG-10, XCG-10A, YCG-10A, CG-10A, & G-10A ... 115
Snead & Company XCG-11 ... 120
Read-York XCG-12 ... 121
Waco XCG-13, XCG-13A, YCG-13, YCG-13A, CG-13A, & G-13A ... 122
General Airborne Transport MC-1, XCG-16, & XCG-16A ... 127
60-Place Glider ... 133
Gyro-Glider ... 133
Chase Aircraft XCG-14 & XCG-14A ... 134
Airspeed AS.51 Horsa Mk. I & AS.58 Mk. II ... 138
War Wagons (Christopher XAG-1, Timm XAG-2) ... 141

Chapter 9 Navy Gliders Scuttled ... 144
Exploring Alternatives ... 145
Falling to Pieces ... 146
Proving ... 148
Decision Time ... 149
Just Won't Quit ... 151
Larger Still ... 152
Naval Aircraft Factory XLRN-1 ... 152

Chapter 10 Combat Experience ... 156
Rough Start ... 157
Main Events ... 161
Rounding Out ... 169

Chapter 11 Experimentation ... 170
Improving the Breed ... 171
Towing Service ... 172
Douglas Aircraft XCG-17 ... 176
Stopping on a Dime ... 177
Seeking Automation ... 179
Bellows Flaps ... 181
Prone Flying (MX-324, MX-334, CG-4A, XTG-33) ... 182
Man-Proven (MX-543, Northrop JB-1) ... 185
Wet Kite (Cornelius XFG-1) ... 186
Foreign Mounts ... 189

Chapter 12 Oxymoron – Powered Gliders ... 190
Fliers (XPG-1, XPG-2, XPG-2A, XPG-2B, XPG-2C, XPG-3, & XPG-3A) ... 192
Non-Fliers (XPG-4, XCG-10A, Others, Experiments) ... 196
Set Aside ... 197

Chapter 13 Sacrificial Lambs – Bomb Gliders ... 198
Navy Progress ... 199
Going Mainstream ... 294
Air Forces Parallel ... 297
Fade Out ... 211

Chapter 14 Postwar Momentum ... 212
Carrying On ... 213
Experiments Continue ... 215
Rigid Tow ... 217
Fighter-Glider Composites ... 218
Charting a Course ... 219
New Gliders ... 221
Chase XCG-18, XCG-18A, & YG-18A ... 223
Douglas XCG-19 ... 225
Chase XCG-20 & XG-20 ... 226
Extinction ... 228

Chapter 15 Retrospective ... 230
In Sum ... 231
Naval Post-Mortem ... 234
Legacy ... 234

Acronyms & Abbreviations ... 240

Appendix: Glider Summaries ... 241

Endnotes ... 248

Bibliography ... 257

Index ... 264

About the Author ... 272

Preface

In the vast literature on American military aviation of World War II the glider is rarely mentioned. Consequently, the scope and technical extent of United States glider work during the war is little appreciated. While there have been several books published previously that explored the American combat experience with military gliders of WWII, this one offers a different perspective. This volume presents more detail on the development and operation of the American gliders than previously published in popular literature, particularly with respect to experimentation and the Navy efforts. It also sheds more light on glider designs that were not taken fully to flight hardware or fielding.

German work with gliders during the war has been documented extensively, and their designs heralded as exceptionally advanced. The author hopes to counterbalance that literature and perception with this book. However, unlike many publications on American gliders of the war, this volume describes combat only in illustrating how the aircraft were employed. Combat accounts and details of such operations are well-documented in those other worthy books. Although the Americans had many glider types in development and performed numerous experiments to enhance glider utility, production of combat aircraft focused almost exclusively on the Waco CG-4A and with modest enhancement during service. The U.S. military leadership was generally less inclined to embrace the promise of "secret weapons" and to dissipate manufacturing energies, treasure, and lives on multiple types of limited added combat value. This contrasts with the German predilection. Yet, the record of U.S. glider work and achievement remains equally impressive and worthy of concise documentation made available to the general public. This book offers that insight.

Serial numbers and Bureau Numbers of the aircraft described are collected in the Appendix, along with a complete summary of gliders described in the text. Other miscellaneous serials are found in the main text within parenthesis. This book also draws more fully on official reference material than previous publications on the subject, with generous citations scattered throughout for the endnotes. The bibliography lists sources for additional reading, especially in filling out the combat account.

The author welcomes comments and additional research material. He can be contacted at williamnorton@earthlink.net.

Bill Norton
California City, California

1

Gliders Go to War

The New Weapon

World War II (WWII) is often seen as the incubator for many of the advanced weapons that followed. However, there was one military aircraft type that had its debut during the conflict, matured, and disappeared soon after. This was the combat glider that was born with the advent of airborne forces.

Glider-borne forces significantly augmented paratroopers who dropped from aircraft over-flying the battlefield. The paratroopers required time to reform and move on their target, and typically had only the equipment they dropped with for an initial assault or to beat off opposition. Conversely, the glider could, ideally, silently and precisely "airland" infantry ("glidermen") squads that did not need to reform, arrived with more gear, and were within immediate striking distance of their objectives. Such glidermen did not require the specialized parachute instruction. Alternatively, a glider could carry in significant cargo, including crew-served guns or vehicles, and thousands of pounds of ammunition and fuel. Little of such freight could then be delivered via parachute drop, and certainly with little precision. The low approach speed of the glider permitted it to land in short, unprepared fields that were inaccessible to powered transport aircraft. Hence, the glider was a significant addition to the capability of vertical envelopment or flanking of an enemy force. For the Allies, this air mobility made possible application of telling military force behind enemy lines as vital elements of large offensives that proved essential in defeating the Axis powers.

However, the Allies were not the pioneers of military glider tactics. The USSR first experimented with glider-borne forces during the 1930s, and this caught the attention

Germany focused the world's attention of the role of gliders in modern warfare with their surprise use in the opening of the Blitzkreig in the West, May 1940. While the Allies appreciated the potential, details remained sketchy for quite a while. The glider used by Germany at the time, the DFS 230, was a fairly low-capacity type, with a pilot and nine troops or 2,800 pounds of freight, but would remain in service to the end of the war. (National Museum of the United States Air Force)

of Germany who, officially constrained by the WWI armistice, collaborated with the Soviets in military development. Adolf Hitler was particularly struck by the potential of the new weapon, and employed a force of 42 10-place gliders in the initial assault on Belgium that opened his 1940 campaign in the west.

The secret of the German success in the 10 May attack on the Eben Emael fortress and River Meuse bridges was slow in being penetrated and appreciated by the British and Americans. They later had the 20 May 1941 German airborne invasion of Crete as another example of the potential of glider warfare combined with paratroops. The 74 gliders deployed a regiment to seize, in conjunction with paratroops, an airhead on the island. Although only 40 percent effective, the assault was instrumental in the German victory. The Allies were impressed with the lightly armed airborne troops playing a leading role in rapidly defeating superior, entrenched forces and capturnig strategic territory. However, the grievous personnel and aircraft losses, reducing the airborne forces to a third their strength with over 200 transports destroyed, caused the Führer to greatly diminish airborne's role thereafter. A large airborne assault on Malta and another operation in Russia, to include 250 gliders, planned for October 1942 was cancelled. Germany employed gliders only on a small scale thereafter, principally for commando raids, urgent replenishment and evacuation missions, and as mobile workshops. The Allies suffered under no such notion that gliders' usefulness had diminished.

Recognizing the glider as an element in the new tactics so successfully exploited by Germany, the Allies began or accelerated the formation, equipping and training of their own airborne units. It was clear to them that these would be essential for any return to the Continent. However, this was done without their own experience, industry prepared to manufacture the gliders, nor any established doctrine or tactics. The British created their Glider Pilot Regiment on 21 December 1941, having flown their first troop glider that June after more than a year of experimentation following a June 1940 directive from PM Churchill. For Great Britain, already staggering after defeat in France, struggling on all fronts, and preparing for a possible invasion of their island, glider warfare preparation was a notably arduous task. The United States enjoyed a period to react before being drawn into the war. For the U.S., this time was characterized by almost frantic efforts in developing suitable training and combat gliders. Still, it would be more than two years following Crete before Allied gliders were committed to a similar endeavor.

The U.S. Army Reacts

Observing the early German successes with assault gliders, General Henry 'Hap' Arnold, Chief of the U.S. Army Air Corps (U.S. Army Air Forces, USAAF, after 20 June 1941) kicked-off a "crash" program in February 1941 to acquire a glider corps for the Army's airborne forces. Army paratroops were themselves just a year old. Within months, he set progressively higher goals for number of aircraft and pilots that sent scrambling his staff in Washington, District of Columbia (D.C.), and that of Materiel Division at Wright Field in Dayton, Ohio. Material Division was responsible for the acquisition of aircraft and related systems for the Army. Its Aircraft Laboratory was the principal engineering arm. (Materiel Command was created in March 1942, headquartered in Washington, D.C., while Materiel Division continued under this organization for aircraft and related weapons work. Materiel Command was combined with Air Service Command in August 1944 to become Air Technical Services Command (ATSC)).

The U.S. Army's experience with piloted gliders had been limited to a 1922 evaluation of the GL-2, a basic model built to their specifications.[1] Thirteen gliders were

Gliders were little known to the United States military before WWII. The Army had built and evaluated 13 of these rudimentary GL-2 gliders in the first half of the 1920s, but employed them only as towed targets. It possess the high aspect ratio wing for gliding performance and low stance made possible without a propeller, but otherwise evinces the aeroplane construction techniques of the period. (National Museum of the United States Air Force)

Another Engineering Division product was the GL-3 tow target spanning 6.5 feet. It is seen on a mount attached to a Curtiss JN-4, although it is unclear from the poor image if this aircraft towed the glider upon release. The history of this type is murky, but any glider expertise derived from these 1920 experiences was meager or forgotten by the 1940s. (The Peter M. Bowers Collection/ The Museum of Flight)

subsequently built and employed through 1924 as tow targets (presumably unmanned).[2] Whether a GL-1 preceded the GL-2 is unclear, but a GL-3 succeeded it as a small towed target released from atop a biplane. As the sport of glider flying began to grow, the War Department looked in 1929 at incorporating them into the Air Corps' training program, but this was judged to add little value. Following a fatal soaring accident, a 28 December 1931 War Department fiat forbade off-duty military personnel from participating in the sport of glider flying.[3] Consequently, the military launched into their combat glider development task with essentially no experience base. Although the UK began their glider development at about the same time, it was December 1941 before the U.S. gained much insight into these efforts.

A 24 February 1941 directive from Washington set Materiel Division to the task of procuring gliders. What they should seek and how they might be employed was to be determined in a feasibility study of a "glider echelon" that Arnold requested the next day, to be delivered by 1 April. Opinions were sought from the units who would ride into combat aboard the gliders as well as the technical community. Initial considerations suggested 2-place training gliders and 8- and 15-place cargo/personnel gliders should be acquired. Arnold pressed his staff to move expeditiously. However, he insisted Dayton only engage manufacturers not already committed to significant military aircraft production. Further complicating the developers' task, Washington also directed gliders be built of "non-strategic" materials (read wood) to the extent possible, because aluminum was in short supply and committed to higher priority projects.

Even before the operational concepts and design studies requested by Arnold were ready, Materiel Command was ordered on 4 March 1941 to immediately begin the process of acquiring both training and combat gliders. Dayton responded promptly to the chief's prodding by generating two technical instructions: one for design studies and the second for procurement. Specifications were released on 8 March 1941 for 2-place training gliders, and combat gliders in the 8-place/1,900-pound useful load and 15-place/3,800-pound classes. The payload numbers were based on the metrics of a 170-pound soldier with 50 pounds of gear.

Possibly owing to this haste, documentation shows only in summer 1941 was the Army Ground Forces queried as to the size of gliders desired given the order of battle for airborne troops. The airborne forces pointed out the 14-troop glider (15-place with pilot) allowed for a pilot and typical infantry rifle squad plus two other individuals from platoon, company, or battalion headquarters. If this size glider proved impractical, "the minimum size recommended is eight, exclusive of pilot." This would accommodate a machine gun squad of five to eight soldiers.[4] Materiel Division's Chief, Brigadier General Oliver P. Echols, assured his leadership that no difficulty will be encountered in meeting expectations, as the Division "has already taken steps to incorporate provisions for carrying Airborne Task Force materiel in some of the gliders now contemplated."[5]

Rapid efforts were put into motion to acquire training gliders without the benefit of much analysis. The expedient was purchase of sport sailplanes. The two-seat high-performance designs had glide ratios of 20-30:1 (distance traveled for height lost, or best lift/drag ratio). There were few models to choose from given those then being produced inside the United States. Instead of preparing detailed military specifications, the Air Corps relied upon established Civil Aeronautics Administration (CAA) certification guidelines for Class I and II gliders. Fixed-price contracts (any overruns would be borne by the contractor alone) were common because of pre-war practice, the nature of the acquisitions, and the companies' inexperience with government contracts. However, these were for minimal sums, and it is not surprising that several firms found themselves spending beyond these values.

The handful of established sailplane manufacturers and designers were approached in spring 1941 to solicit proposals, with new designs from start-up firms also welcomed. The small size of the nation's glider industry meant that multiple sources had to be pursued to ensure enough training aircraft were delivered on an accelerated schedule for the envisioned volume of instruction. The first contracts were in place by mid-April 1941.

Having only sailplanes to test and hearsay of German operations as examples may have colored initial opinions. The concepts were that combat gliders would be built simply and inexpensively, yet ruggedly to safely deliver troops and material, and fly

General Henry 'Hap' Arnold, Chief of the U.S. Army Air Corps, stands before a CG-4A, an aircraft he strenuously championed in the face of opposition within the service. With him at Laurinburg-Maxton AAB in August 1944 is Colonel Reed Landis (right) and Colonel Y.A. Pitts, both of Troop Carrier Command. The image shows well the nylon towline and glider attachment. (United States Air Force)

at the tow speeds plus free-flight maneuvering. Undercarriage for takeoff would be released and skids employed for landing. The prevailing concept of operations was tow at up to 120 mph for a release at 12,000 feet, miles from the target and at night. This would permit a silent and surprise landing behind enemy lines. It was understood the gliders would likely be damaged beyond repair during an actual night assault landing in unprepared areas and under enemy fire. Washington made clear the aircraft should be suitable for only a few hours flying time, yet the gliders still had to be suitably airworthy.[6] Yet, although they continued to be called gliders, they were for practical purposes towed, motorless transports of unique design.

The original characteristics of the notional combat gliders are provided in the accompanying tables, the 15-place figures from a 12 February 1941 document, and the 8-place dated 21 July (possibly revised from an earlier missive). The figures were likely created via quick analysis by Wright Field engineers.

Table 01-01

Original 15-place Light Transport Glider Specifics[7]

useful load	3,800 lbs
payload	15 troops with one as pilot, 240 lbs each
landing distance, pavement	250 ft, 500 ft acceptable
THP required/lbs for 140 mph tow	0.05 hp, 0.07 hp acceptable
maximum tow speed	220 mph, 180 mph acceptable
sink rate with flaps (85 mph)	1,500 fpm, 1,100 fpm acceptable
stall speed	48 mph, 55 mph acceptable
landing, minimum speed, paved	500 ft, 250 ft acceptable
glide ratio	15:1

Table 01-02

Original 8-place Troop Glider Specifics[8]

useful load	2,100 lbs
payload	8 troops with one as pilot, 240 lbs each
maximum tow speed	120 mph
normal tow altitude	12,000 ft
stall speed (full lateral control at stall)	30 mph, 45 mph acceptable
glide ratio	15:1

The relatively efficient glide ratios of 15:1 reflected original thinking at the time that the aircraft would be released at high altitude miles from the intended landing zone (LZ). Landings were expected to be at 30 mph using only spoilers for glidepath control. However, design teams were told they could not use wing flaps or other high lift devices.[9] For a glider of the weights envisioned, this suggested a very large wing of high efficiency for exceptionally low wing loading (gross weight divided by wing area). This risked added weight that would require a tug aircraft of considerable excess horsepower to pull the glider aloft and across any appreciable range. With tow planes of higher wing loading than gliders, a compromise flight speed would have to be employed, likely to the detriment of the tug's engines, which would be run near limits if unusually high power loading (gross weight divided by engine power) was not a feature. The Douglas C-47, widely employed as a tug, normally cruised at 150 mph, whereas tow was normally at 120 mph. This foretold difficulties.

March 8th also saw Wright Field reach out to 11 manufacturers with invitations to study preliminary engineering requirements and solicit proposals of what to seek and how to proceed. Again, lacking time to write-up detailed specifications, civil aviation standards and best commercial practices were employed. Complying with Washington's direction, these were all firms involved with sailplane, light airplane, or aircraft subcontract work. Few had any significant prior experience with War Department contracting. Yet the combat gliders, although an entirely new concept, were expected to be basic in design and construction.

Only four of the 11 companies responded with expressions of definite interest. The first contracts for prototypes were let in early May 1941, and soon eight models (XCG-1 through XCG-8) were in development for delivery by the end of the year. (The X prefix to an aircraft designation represented "experimental." The C was for Cargo and G for glider.) The general glider project was identified as MX-114 (Materiel, eXperimental). The primary type designation of G for Glider was reassigned from autogiros on 5 June 1941, the latter becoming R for rotary wing.[10]

The redundant contracts for cargo glider development put several companies to work in the interest of providing a selection of aircraft to choose from and in the event some contractors failed to perform. This was a real concern given the hastily prepared requirements and immature state, plus the small size of some of the firms involved, as well as the total lack of experience designing and building large transport gliders. Even companies previously building one- or two-seat sailplanes had manufactured on the scale of tens per year, at most, and possessed no experience with high-capacity production, working on a government contract, or design and construction of large aircraft. With these and subsequent projects, some companies had more patriotic zeal than actual engineering and manufacturing potential. Firms were formed specifically to win defense contracts and, under normal circumstances, would not have been considered. Materiel Division also hoped that, even if some firms failed to bring forth competitive designs, the effort would foster organizations whose capabilities could then be employed in building other manufacturers' gliders in large numbers.

Given the nonexistent Army knowledge of gliders, General Arnold sought out experts from within America's small civilian soaring community to assist in setting the new USAAF program on the right course and filling the expertise gap within his Washington staff. These were indeed a select few, since the sport in the U.S. was made up of just a 124 registered gliders and 165 licensed pilots.[11] Those individuals who successively held the post on Arnold's staff met resistance from traditionalists in the career officer ranks, from those who disliked the glider program, and some who resented the favored status of these appointed officers. However, acting with the General's blessing, they made progress.

The first of these advisors was Lewin B. Barringer, recruited on 15 October 1941 and commissioned a Major the following May. He was a leader in the U.S. glider movement, a national soaring champion who had run a glider school, and had written on the subject. In his role as coordinator of the glider program, largely in an advisory capacity, he worked with the direct authority of Arnold and so usually got what was needed. Initially lacking an official title, he soon became Assistant in Charge of the Glider Program under the Office of the Coordinator of Air Support.[12] The cumbersome title was usually truncated in various fashions, and Barringer signed correspondence as "Head, Army Glider Program," or "Glider Specialist" before he was commissioned. The assignment of Barringer greatly helped in keeping the nascent program on course and overcoming any resistance or antipathy from unenthusiastic elements in the Air Forces.

Barringer was lost on 24 January 1943 when the transport he was flying aboard went missing. He was replaced by Richard C. Du Pont, a scion of the wealthy Du Pont family

Major Lewin Barringer (left) stands with an unknown Lieutenant besides the sole XCG-7 that the former assisted in testing. The setting is likely California's Mojave Desert during summer 1942 and the Lieutenant likely served as tow pilot. Barringer was a glider expert hired and commissioned by General Arnold to help organize the U.S. Army's glider program. (National Soaring Museum)

Richard Du Pont stands beside a TG-3 with Lieutenant Chester "Chet" Decker in the forward cockpit. Du Pont was another national leader of the national soaring scene and an aviation businessman who took over the glider specialist role on Arnold's staff after Major Barringer's death, but remained a civilian. Decker was a national soaring champion who, when inducted into the Army during 1941, became part of the team developing military gliders. (National Museum of the United States Air Force)

that, among other things, manufactured the nylon that made up glider towlines. He was another sailplane champion, past president of the Soaring Society of America, and recognized glider authority with dreams of gliders playing a role in commercial air transport. Arnold enjoined Du Pont on 12 April 1943 to take up the formally designated Office of Special Assistant on the Army Air Forces Glider Program. Du Pont took the job on the 20th but did not begin work until late May and remained a civilian. However, he was killed in the crash of an experimental combat glider on 11 September. Du Pont was replaced by his brother, Major Felix Du Pont (previously commissioned), on 5 November. However, the post of Special Assistant was abolished the same day. He then became Chief of the newly established Glider Branch within the Requirements Division of the Office of the Assistant Chief of Air Staff, Operations, Commitments, and Requirements. Felix Du Pont carried on into 1944 when his job was considered complete or the opposition finally got him reassigned. The post, which had been shuffled between different organizations within the Air Staff, was then abolished.

At the forefront of the aircraft development efforts and through the formative period was Major (soon Lieutenant Colonel, then Colonel) Fred R. Dent, Jr., assistant chief of the Aircraft Laboratory under the Experimental Engineering Section ("Engineering Division") in Dayton. He led the glider effort at Wright Field from inception and was formally assigned Director, Glider Unit, in December 1941 upon his return from a trip to Great Britain to investigate their glider efforts.[13] The formal structure had Glider Branches within the Production Engineering Section and the Aircraft Laboratory, but Dent closely led all these and experimental flying. The production branch was the responsibility of Lieutenant Colonel Ernest W. Dichman. The Glider Branch within the Laboratory had Major (soon Lieutenant Colonel) Bruce B. Price as its head. He assumed Dent's position sometime before November 1943.[14]

The political machinations in Washington, especially interaction with manufacturers by senior officers in the Chief of Staff's office, was a persistent annoyance to the engineers and contracting officials in Ohio. Dent felt the Washington crowd complicated his task with conflicting direction to contractors. This had extended to issuing separate contracts, bypassing his team entirely. Hence, the relationship between Arnold's glider advisors and the Dayton team was sometimes tense.

An example of the separate acquisition efforts in Washington was the purchase of five training gliders in May 1941 for testing and familiarization. There were no funds remaining for procurement in fiscal year 1941. (The fiscal year then ran from July through June.) However, moneys were soon found in an Experimental account.[15] An attempt to meet the immediate demand for training aircraft was appropriation of 61 privately owned sailplanes, nearly every serviceable glider in the country, under a directive dated 21 May 1942. Such was the sense of urgency following Pearl Harbor.

With agencies seeking specifics upon which to program and act on Arnold's instructions, Brigadier General Carl Spaatz, Chief of the Air Staff, submitted a 2 December 1941 plan. This envisioned that deploying one airborne division would require 500 8-place and 500 15-place gliders and, by extension, 1,000 pilots.[16] These would be towed by 292 transports with 125 as four 8-place or three 15-place gliders on en-train tow.[17] Three-quarters of the division's troops would be transported in the gliders and the remainder in the tugs.[18] The plan was to provide the means to deploy the first division by 1 July 1943 and a second soon thereafter, all in an accelerated

One of the most influential men in developing the US Army's combat glider capability was Major (later Colonel) Fred Dent, Jr. (right). He stands before the US Army's first WWII glider, a Schweizer TG-2. The event is the National Soaring Contest during September 1941 at Elmira, New York, site of the initial Army glider training. (National Soaring Museum)

Another principal figure in the Army's glider program was Bruce Price, seen here (far right) as a Lieutenant Colonel beside the XCG-13 he flew as test pilot on its maiden flight, 10 March 1943. The others are (left to right) John Parker, president of Northwest Aeronautical, Mr. Whittingham, J.B. LaMont (chief inspector), and Captain Ben West who served as Price's copilot on the flight. Price was the titular head of the Glider Branch when Dent essentially ran everything, but took over full authority when Dent was sent overseas. (National Museum of the United States Air Force)

Initial concepts for transport gliders and their operation were replete with misperceptions and over-optimism. This Air Corps art from the period illustrates the lack of knowledge and experience, with the twin-engine airplane towing aloft three medium-size gliders simultaneously. In reality, double tows were possible but with little margin on engine performance. (National Museum of the United States Air Force)

program. The Secretary of War approved the plan on 28 December, directing Arnold to include $121,869,992.00 (Spaatz's estimated cost) in a supplement to his fiscal year 1943 budget estimate to procure the airplanes and gliders, and train personnel, to transport an airborne division at the earliest possible date. However, Spaatz's materiel estimates would later be proven way off-base.[19]

Arnold directed the procurement of the projected gliders and associated equipment on 27 January 1942, by this time consisting of 150 2-place training gliders, 200-500 8-place gliders, and 500-800 15-place aircraft. At the same time he "directed that modification necessary for towing the transport gliders be incorporated in all suitable transport airplanes at the earliest practical opportunity."[20] The Douglas C-47 Skytrain, already identified as the likely paratroop jump airplane (accommodating 28 troopers or 6,000 pounds of cargo), would be the likely tug. Little prompt action appears to have been taken with respect to the transports. When on 4 February Arnold specifically directed 292 C-47s be immediately modified, there was apparently some push-back, because this was later reduced to 26 immediately required for training by 1 September.[21]

Obtaining the 1,000 pilots would be as difficult as procuring the aircraft. However, Spaatz set ambitious goals for these men, writing "Due to the degree of skill estimated to be required to pilot these large troop carrying gliders in towed formation at night, under instrument conditions and while landing in small fields it is not contemplated using other than qualified airplane pilots, preferably graduates of the Air Corps Flying Schools." He envisioned a four-week course with 50 2-place gliders to convert the men into glider pilots and 100 more for proficiency flying. Seventy O-49 (Stinson) tow planes were to be acquired for the training.[22]

Plans were also formative to haul up to four airborne divisions. Transporting three divisions (45,800 troops) would require 700 15-place and 900 30-place gliders, plus 1,250 tugs also carrying troops.[23] (Inclusion of 30-place gliders at this early date appeared to be reconsidered almost immediately, and focus remained on the 15-place machines.) On 26 March 1942, the requirements were raised to 3,000 8-place machines by 15 September 1942 to support urgent training and potential deployment. Arnold personally upped this again on 1 April to 3,700 15-place and 500 8-place gliders, adding 300 2-place trainers, plus 4,200 pilots trained by 1 July 1943, with 800 15-place and 2,000 pilots by 1 January 1943. On 22 April the 15-place requirement rose yet again to 4,700. In July 1942, Washington stated that the service needed 3,000 gliders by the end of the year, 6,000 pilots trained by 1 July 1943, and 30-place gliders were to be pursued.[24] A goal of manufacturing 350 gliders per month was espoused. Although dwarfed by fighter and bomber programs, these figures still created a sense of exasperation within commands tasked with generating these theretofore undefined resources, certain they were unattainable beginning as they were from almost nothing. However Arnold, answering also to the President and General Staff, was emphatic.

The Glider Branch performed experimental work to understand the problems inherent in glider tow and related issues that could impact design, and highlight areas for further work.[25] The early expectation of a tug dragging a flock of gliders behind was quickly dispelled by this research. Tow and glide tests of available gliders provided data for extrapolation considering the expected drag of the gliders under development. These were compared with the performance of the C-47 to understand design and operational implications.[26] (The use of bombers was not seriously pursued and, of multi-engine transports, only the C-47 was planned to be bought in numbers making them suitable for the multiple roles of glider tow, paratroop jump platform, and freight airlift.) This work showed that optimally only two 15-place gliders could be towed compared with the expected three, and four 8-placed versus six.[27] Many more C-47s would be needed for the task than originally anticipated. Additionally, the slow tug-glider combination and even slower glider in free-flight would be exposed to enemy fire for a considerable period. Even before the U.S. entered the war, foreign experience was demonstrating the high density and lethality of antiaircraft fire. Tactics developed into a tow release at low altitude for flight lasting just a few minutes. Consequently, expectations were greatly reduced.

There was by no means unanimous agreement with this course of action. As in Britain, Arnold's efforts met with resistance from within the USAAC and later USAAF, wherein many had difficulty accepting what were perceived by some as lesser aircraft and lesser pilots at a time the service had to greatly increase its capabilities. Both militaries had to address whether the pilots were foremost aviators or soldiers. The British left them as Army personnel who received considerable infantry instruction in addition to air force pilot training. Their gliders were also Army equipment, although towed by RAF bombers in what was occasionally a competition of mission priorities, training, and resources.[28] The American glider pilots and aircraft were USAAF assets servicing airborne infantry units. Although the same service, the independence of the Air Forces was growing, and there was discomfort with pilots so closely associated with ground forces. As with any military innovation, even in the progressive aeronautical field, there was inertia and bias to overcome. There were not a few officers who felt the old man was being led down the garden path, wasting effort on a misguided undertaking. Many career officers felt the enterprise a waste of resources on a wrong-headed concept. Among those to be transported in the gliders there was equal hesitation. The Chief of Infantry urged that a service test quantity of gliders first be obtained for trials at Fort Benning, Georgia, to determine suitability of the class of aircraft before committing to full-scale production. However, this cautionary approach appeared to belie his true belief that was stated bluntly as, "This office is of the opinion that gliders are an inferior as well as extremely hazardous means of transporting troops."[29]

Despite the vitriol in some quarters, others were eager to get their hands on gliders. In February 1942 Major General Davenport Johnson, commanding the Caribbean Air Force in the Panama Canal Zone, requested a service test quantity of gliders at the earliest opportunity to assist in transporting the two airborne battalions assigned to his command. Washington optimistically endorsed this request with the expectation the gliders and pilots would be available by October. As far as is known, the request was never fulfilled.[30] Commercial airlines, also reading about forthcoming Army gliders, expressed a desire to acquire such equipment that might improve their cargo load capacity.[31]

A considerable number of glider designs were funded for development by the Army during the war. Of the initial efforts generating designs for the new training and combat gliders, only half materialized as flying prototypes … as feared. Many contracts were fraught with problems—late deliveries, contractor non-performance, and business failures. With these and later efforts, the short period of execution mandated in the urgent contracts fostered considerable cost and schedule over-runs. Everything was rushed and there was much waste. Some projects had to be cancelled with little to show for the millions of dollars expended. Glider development and procurement became one of the most tumultuous Air Forces programs of the war.

Recognizing its lack of glider development experience, Materiel Command also welcomed unsolicited proposals for glider development and manufacturing from civilians and commercial entities known in the glider community. This had Glider Branch personnel busy traveling to inspect aircraft, observe demonstration flights, and study test data. Much of this came to nothing, but there was no other course, since everyone was equally ignorant about what made a successful combat transport glider.

As contractors began delivering aircraft to the Glider Branch for engineering ground and flight test evaluation, the operations tempo at Wright Field increased dramatically, as this work was added to the welter of other USAAF acquisition programs. In March 1942, the branch consisted of just Dent, Price, and five enlisted men. The enlisted personnel increased to 21 during May, and further expansions were certain.[32] Flight testing was initially undertaken at Wright Field until difficulty was experienced integrating glider operations with powered flight work. (There was also a general disdain for the gliders and the Glider Branch.) The congestion compelled establishment of Clinton County Army Air Field (CCAAF) in nearby Wilmington, about 25 miles southeast of Dayton. The move began in April 1942, and the Glider Experiment and Test Unit, 703rd Test and Experimental Base, was fully in place there during July 1943 under Major Charles H. Craig.[33] Approximately $2 million was expended in creating the base on what had been the underutilized Wilmington airport. The 190-220 assigned personnel were supported by the engineering staff at Wright Field. It became the nexus for intense military glider

After nearly 18 months of effort to acquire a combat gliders capability, the U.S. Army had little to show. Revealed to the Secretary of War during a 2 July 1942 display at Wright Field, available for display were American training glider (two TG-3s in the foreground, a TG-2 beyond, and two TG-4s), two British Hotspur 8-place machines, and two tow planes (B-23 and C-47). Elsewhere on the base the first XCG-4 airframe was being static-tested. (National Archives)

On the far side of the display line for the Secretary of War was a XCG-3 and the first examples of the CG-4A. At this time the glider activities were at Wright Field, contributing to the congestion created by prodigious wartime flight testing. The Glider Branch would soon begin their move to nearby Wilmington, Ohio, and the Clinton County Army Air Field. (National Archives)

trials in the United States. Most field trials were eventually concentrated at Laurinburg-Maxton Army Air Base (AAB), Maxton, North Carolina.

Adopting a new weapon system requires considerable experimentation during development to optimize employment and perfect tactics. The most immediate need was shakedown of new gliders, checkout with various potential tow planes, determining the best tow positions and airspeeds, finding the ideal approach speeds, and documenting loading charts. Beyond this came working with new towline material and lengths, developing new tow methods, and validating changes to gliders that corrected deficiencies or introduced improvements based on training and combat experience. And, efforts extended to exploring improvements in the overall concept and technology of combat gliders. All this kept the CCAAF and Laurinburg-Maxton teams very busy.

The recruitment and training of the U.S. glider pilots, acquisition of their aircraft, formation of the transport units for glider tow and paratroop delivery, and development of tactics in combination with other forces was a ponderous and frustrating enterprise. Slow delivery of both glider and tow aircraft, competition for training resources, and evolving doctrine were contributors. Even when committed to battle, experience dictated continuous adjustments before a truly effective and professional capability resulted.

Navy and Marines Vision

The U.S. Navy (USN) was also struck by the potential of combat gliders given the German examples. At the urging of Secretary of the Navy Frank Knox and Congress, the service began looking at gliders in April 1941 for marine landings. A silent descent and landing would be a welcome capability compared with the massive and noisy display normally accompanying a marine coastal landing. It was felt that America might be drawn into the war at any moment, and it was time for quick action based on the new paradigms of warfare evidenced by European combat. As in WWI, the U.S. appeared unprepared and so had to move quickly to respond.

The vision suggested amphibious gliders; an entirely new concept. Gliders appeared the only practical means for aircraft to complement marine seaborne assaults via landing craft and amphibious vehicles—capabilities themselves still maturing. It would require gliders to be towed aloft from the sea or hard surface runways, and then land in the water. This was a bold innovation, envisioning swarms of gliders towed into range of the objective, setting down in the shallows and beaching to deposit squads of marines ashore instead of the long and vulnerable motoring to the beach from ships offshore—albeit both followed by a fight up from the surf. It appears that inland landings were considered impractical, probably because the troops would be 'cut off' behind enemy lines with few means of near-term reinforcement.

Commandant of the Marine Corps, Major General Thomas Holcomb, had decided in October 1940 to train one marine battalion (715 men) of each regiment as "air troops." One company would be paratroopers while the rest would be lifted by airplanes to airland in combat. With Knox's subsequent direction, the Navy began exploring the potential of gliders as one means of lifting the marine air troops for both land and water delivery.[34] The latter method quickly dominated consideration. While the entire notion of United States Marine Corps (USMC) amphibious gliders was not carefully studied before program initiation, and caused many a furrowed brow, it was certainly worth exploring considering the shattering victories and new tactics of Germany and Japan.

The Navy was to develop and procure the aircraft for the Corps, as was existing procedure, while the marines trained their own pilots and airborne troops. The Commandant wrote the Chief of the Bureau of Aeronautics (BuAer) on 31 May 1941 stating the USMC's desires. He stated the envisioned need as a glider capable of:

- Takeoff from land or water as an amphibious "aquaplane"
- Transporting a minimum 12 marines at 250 pounds each with kit
- Supporting static line paratroop jumps
- Transport equipment, including light cars and 37 mm antitank guns, and light tanks if possible
- Mounting machine gun for airborne defensive fire[35]

Additionally, some documents discussed Marine gliders being towed by patrol boats, pointing out that 25 boats could tow 75 gliders to deposit troops equal to 75 such vessels alone.

The Assistant Chief of BuAer, Captain Marc A. Mitscher, had already initiated glider development when the effort was announced in April—although he made no secret of his skepticism. On 30 April, Mitscher had requested the Naval Aircraft Factory (NAF) in Philadelphia, Pennsylvania, to perform a transport glider design study. The requirements suggested machines for both land and water landings with jettisonable undercarriage, but quickly focused on a boat hull aircraft for water takeoff and landing,

After Wright Field became too crowded with the wartime pace of airplane development, the glider work was moved to nearby Wilmington, Ohio. The small Clinton Country airport was transformed to Clinton County Army Air Field as it appears in this image, 16 July 1945. Among the visible aircraft are numerous CG-4As, at least one CG-15, a few CG-13s, the sole XCG-14, XCG-16, and XCG-17, and tow planes consisting of several C-47s, a C-46, B-17, B-29, P-38, and P-51. (National Soaring Museum)

but with retractable landing gear. A small outboard motor for maneuvering on the water was also deemed necessary.[36]

The NAF assigned Lieutenant Commander (soon Commander, then Captain) Ralph S. Barnaby to supervise the design project. Among his team, participating in the eventual flight testing, were marine pilots Major Richard E. Figley, Lieutenant (later Captain) Robert V. Reilly, and Lieutenant R. Ryan. Another officer who would contribute significantly was Commander Delmar 'Del' S. Fahrney, who had just begun a glider bomb, or "GLOMB," program (Chapter 13), as an adjunct to a long-standing unmanned drone effort, and this would run coincident with the Marine transport glider work. By June 1941, towed experiments with sport sailplane were being conducted to acquaint Navy personnel with the principles of aero tow and to garner glider operational experience. Testing was principally performed in Philadelphia and later at Naval Air Station (NAS) Patuxent River in southern Maryland.[37]

Barnaby was assistant chief engineer at NAF, later chief engineer. He was a noted naval aviator and engineer in addition to being a long-time sport sailplane pilot and current president of the Soaring Society of America. He had published a book on glider design in 1930. He had been insisting transport gliders had a military role. The charismatic officer had flown the Navy's first glider experiment, dropped in a sailplane from the dirigible U.S.S. *Los Angeles*. The notion was for the glider to provide a safer means than a parachute for delivering a landing officer to the ground in the event an emergency landing and mooring of the airship was necessary. The trials at Lakehurst, New Jersey, saw Lieutenant Barnaby in a German *Prüffling* (Graduate) open cockpit, single-seat training glider (Bureau Number, BuNo, A8546). The first flight, detaching from beneath the *Los Angeles* at 3,000 feet and 40 knots, occurred on 31 January 1930. Although successful, the later in-flight mating and separation of powered aircraft and dirigibles was cause to drop the glider option.

Captain Ralph Barnaby stands beside a Pratt, Read LNE-1 training glider. Barnaby was the leading glider authority in the Navy's aircraft development and test organization, having extensive soaring experience and serving as a national leader in the sport. Consequently, he became a principal figure in the wartime project to develop combat gliders. (National Soaring Museum)

A rudimentary glider, the *Prüffling*, hangs below the dirigible U.S.S. Los Angeles in preparation for the 31 January 1930 flight with Lieutenant Ralph Barnaby in the freezing open cockpit. This was one of the few experiences with gliders for U.S. Navy before launching their WWII program, with then-Lieutenant Commander Barnaby still in the forefront. (United States Naval Institute)

At the irrepressible Barnaby's urging, six Franklin PS-2 gliders (Bureau Numbers 9401/2, 9614/7) were incorporated into naval primary pilot training to instill the skills of off-field deadstick landings in the event of engine failure. Barnaby ran this month-long portion of the program at Pensacola, Florida, from summer 1933 through 1935. However, it was not considered essential and was dropped in 1936 as a Depression-era cost-cutting measure. Barnaby continued his vocal promotion of gliders as a military asset and so was the *de facto* Navy expert on the subject.

Glider experience increased in the U.S. Navy with introduction of the Franklin PS-2 trainer. The half dozen machines were employed in the first half of the 1930s to train student pilots in deadstick landings. Although discarded to reduce costs, the experience added to the trove of knowledge possessed by Ralph Barnaby who honchoed the effort. (National Soaring Museum)

Major John Wehle, USMC, was soon assigned Glider Project Officer within the Marine Corps Division of Aviation. In the first half of 1942, Wehle spent five months in Great Britain, completing the Royal Air Force Glider Flight Training course and participating in Army glider activities. He came home convinced the Corps needed these capabilities. He was a persistent and vigorous force attempting to push the program along.

In September 1941 the USMC restructured its plans, discarding the original intentions of air troops in each regiment for a dedicated Air Infantry Battalion landing, with equipment, to augment the parachute battalion within each of its two divisions. Meetings during the latter half of August 1941 culminated with a 1 October letter from Holcomb to the Chief of Naval Operations (CNO), Admiral Harold R. Stark, setting out the basic form and purpose of the USMC glider program. The letter was subsequently endorsed by the Chief of BuAer, Rear Admiral John H. Towers, and the program approved by the CNO on 24 January 1942 and the Secretary on the 30th.

One 900-man battalion would be established on the west coast of the U.S.A. with 24-place aircraft and another on the east coast with 12-place gliders. The pilots were to be naval aviators and only the copilot a marine infantryman, so this dictated the size of the combat team to be landed. A goal for 1942 was a total of about 75 gliders, requiring 150 glider pilots. It was envisioned that lifting one battalion would require a minimum 60 12-place gliders on triple-tow behind 20 Consolidated PBY-5 Catalina twin-engine flying boats—although several successive missions might be required to haul in other equipment.

Intentions continued to coalesce as plans to moving two battalions, equating to a requirement for 100 (including 25 spares) of the 12-place and 48 (12 spares) of the 24-place gliders. After U.S. entry into the war and expansion of the USMC to four divisions in spring 1942, the glider program was expanded. By April, Corps desires had evolved to 200 12-place and 300 24-place machines to lift the two battalions in four or five missions. This was soon raised again to 600 12-place and 400 24-place gliders with 1,600 pilots. On 9 June, Holcomb wrote to the CNO recommending developing the capability to transport 12 battalions in three lifts of four, or all on a single mission. This expansion was approved by the Secretary on 30 June 1942 at a projected cost of $15,300,000.00. There were then three Air Infantry battalions in each division. On 2 July, the requirement summed to carrying 10,800 troops with 1,500,000 pounds of equipment in more than 1,271 gliders flown by 3,436 pilots and 1,041 tow planes. This broke down to 675 12-place (with 90 for training and 135 spares), 296 24-place (12 training, 59 spares), and 300 cargo gliders (60 spares). By this measure, the program already underway was woefully inadequate and a near crisis was at hand.

Glider development and pilot training moved ahead to meet the Corps' goals. Although it seemed prudent to prepare for glider combat given the uncertainties of the war, the sudden thrust of the U.S.A. into the conflict, and the examples from Europe—albeit not directly comparable to the likely theater of the Pacific islands and Far East—practicality via demonstrated marine landings remained lacking. Hence, Stark kept ambitions in check, with expenditures limited to $15 million and he forbade large-scale procurement until experimental gliders and operational training experience were in hand, and essential battlefield needs were clarified as the war progressed. Yet, the program still moved very rapidly by comparison to pre-war standards and without the methodical study so common during that period.

Schweizer Aircraft actually delivered the first USAAF military glider of the war with this XTG-2 shown being accepted by Major Fred Dent at Elmira, New York, on 15 July 1941. The machine was a minimally altered Schweizer SGS 2-8, the only licensed two-seat sailplane then in series production in the U.S.A. Delivery was less than a month after being ordered. (National Museum of the United States Air Force)

2

Quick Evolution: Trainers

Numbers Game

When planning for the glider echelon began in February 1941, the initial Army requirement was for 1,000 glider pilots. This rapidly expanded by orders of magnitude. A new Flying Training Command (FTC) curriculum had to be created from scratch while suitable training aircraft were acquired, schools formed, instructors found, and students recruited. There was not a single sailplane pilot in Army uniform and the service lacked recent experience with gliders. However, General Arnold was a tireless force propelling the glider program to meet goals supporting war planning.

From program initiation in February 1941, it was summer 1942 before training gliders became available in sufficient numbers and the Army was ready to commence large-scale instruction. Contract flight schools were employed for initial instruction, these forming all across the country. They began with a few sport gliders until the Air Forces started providing newly delivered equipment. Soaring, with ground launch and aero-tow, was the focus of training at the start. Light plane pilot skills were soon added, although focusing on unpowered and off-field landings. As the required number of glider pilots increased and course content morphed based on new perceptions of the necessary skills or the most efficient training methodology, the aircraft purchased for the program had to be adjusted. The program became chaotic, with the huge number of students and relentless pace of work precipitating much variation in instruction quality. Available aircraft always seemed to be behind demand and efforts sometimes wasteful, but the mission was accomplished.

Polyglot

At one point in 1942 the War Department planned to acquire 1,800 training gliders for the Army and Navy. This number was simply unattainable under the circumstances. The U.S. glider industry was straining to produce the contracted aircraft, yet the numbers were simply insufficient to meet the volume of instruction. Hence, while Materiel Command worked to purchase new-built training gliders, USAAF headquarters was authorized on 21 May 1942 to appropriate nearly all the serviceable civilian gliders in the country.[1]

Unlike many transport aircraft which were commandeered or impressed when the U.S. entered the conflict, the War Department paid for the sport sailplanes. However, the owners had no option of refusal and were given only what the government deemed fair compensation. Civilian flying during the war years was almost entirely forbidden anyway. Through August 1942, 61 of these machines were taken up. These are summarized in the table within the Appendix.[2]

The five gliders acquired in 1941 for experimental purposes at $12,200.00 (or at least with funds authorized for experimental purposes) included the XTG-7 and XTG-11, as subsequently designated (eXperimental Training Glider). These are also reflected in the Appendix table. The last three were identified only as "swamp gliders" from a source in Miami, Florida. Those may have been new while the XTG-11 was a famous German-built competition glider and the XTG-7 was either an import or built from an existing Polish design. However, three Briegleb BG-6s single-seaters were identified as XTG-9s, suggesting these may have been the "swamp gliders," although noted as purchased on 9 May 1942 directly from Briegleb Sailplane Corporation and counted separately in the

66. (One would have expected the service to buy new aircraft then in production.) These five were presumably added to the menagerie of sailplanes for training.[3]

The 66 gliders totaled $98,890.00, or an average $1,498.00 each, with a low of $525.00 and high of $3,340.00. Many of these were single-seat machines, some with open cockpits, and most of little real military training utility. However, with the Air Corps starting from nothing and with training doctrine still evolving, it was felt important to obtain any capability immediately.

These commercial gliders were a fantastic mixed lot of foreign and domestic products or one-off designs. Many were built by enthusiasts rather than manufacturers and so workmanship varied widely. This brought additional problems of maintaining the disparate collection of machines arriving in various states is repair. The acquisition of parts to maintain this collection must have been frustrating. Few of the appropriated machines survived their Army service; either being destroyed in mishaps or deteriorating after being set aside as uselvess. Fortunately, the Army did not long have to rely on this polyglot.[4]

An example of the appropriated civilian gliders was an elegant competition sailplane from men who would have significant roles to play in the Army glider program. The record-setting Göppingen 3 (Gö-3) Minimoa was designed by the famous German sailplane developer Wolf Hirth and built in Germany by Martin Schemp. It was acquired in 1941 for $2,000.00 from one of the test pilots and officers assigned to the Army glider program, Chester (Chet) J. Decker of Glen Rock, New Jersey. Previous owners had been Lewin Barringer and Richard Du Pont, the latter becoming national champion in the glider during 1931. Seating two, the wood and fabric glider was designated the XTG-11. Its value was felt to lie in studying foreign glider construction techniques and so was evaluated at CCAAF.[5] Laister-Kauffman Aircraft also built a new Göppingen gliders (TG-20) for the Air Forces to complement the four appropriated example, these identified as Gö-1s.[6] So, these was technically not impressed.

Acquisition

Under persistent pressure from Washington to move expediently, the first training glider was ordered on 14 April 1941. Frankfort Sailplane Company in Joliet, Indiana (originally Frankfort, Michigan), was tasked with creating a military version of their Cinema IIB two-seat competition glider. Designed by Stanley R. Corcoran, it possessed a welded steel tube airframe, wooden spar wing with plywood D-section (rounded leading edge back to the spar) and struts, spoilers, and wood frame aero surfaces, all fabric covered. Undercarriage was a single wheel with auxiliary skid.

As this was a new model, it had to be completed and CAA type certification obtained. This was done under a contract for three experimental XTG-1s[7] and trailers, the original letter contract followed by a 7 May 1941 formal document for $5,784.99. The products were delivered between 29 September and March 1942, although the contract had called for the first by 25 June 1941. These were subject to flight testing and a ground loads trial that verified the structure met requirements. (Static tests at Wright Field applied simulated flight loads on the ground. Deficient designs or manufacturing was quickly uncovered by structural failures well short of the expected maximum loads.) At least one of the machines was lost to a crash.[8]

The military felt some changes were required for production. The aircraft was stretched 1.5 inches and the all-moving tail surfaces replaced with conventional stabilizers possessing elevators and rudder. The glider was then found suitable in March 1942 and 40 TG-1As ordered on 19 May with SCR-585A radios. Deliveries ran from June through November 1942 (vice September) at a total cost was $111,016.20, or $2,775.00 per aircraft. The Air Corps also impressed six privately owned Cinema IIBs which became two TG-1As (although not matching the production configuration) and four TG-1Bs. Three single-seat Cinema IAs were also taken in plus a D-model (modified as a Model PC-2).[9]

The Air Corps bought up nearly all serviceable gliders in the United States during mid-1942 as a rapid means of acquiring training assets while contract efforts proceeded. Among the gliders swept up in this buying frenzy was this Göppingen 3 Minimoa high-performance sailplane built in Germany and flown by several notables in American soaring circles. Designated the XTG-11, the last owner was Chet Decker who became a prominent officer and test pilot of the Army's glider procurement program. (National Archives)

Frankfort Sailplane Company was the first on contract to provide Army Air Forces training gliders. Their Cinema II was the basis for the military model, the TG-1A. Here a TG-1A pilot performs an unusual low-altitude maneuver. (National Soaring Museum)"

Table 02-01	
Table Frankfort Sailplane TG-1A Specifics	
span	46.3 ft
wing area	195.3 ft^2
length	24.8 ft
height	5.1 ft
empty weight	510 lbs
maximum weight	920 lbs
tow speed	88 mph, 60 mph auto
glide speed	80 mph
stall speed	35 mph
glide ratio	20:1

Table 02-02	
Schweizer Aircraft TG-2 Specifics	
span	52.0 ft
wing area	214.0 ft^2
fuselage length	25.3 ft
height	6.8 ft
empty weight	480 lbs
gross weight	860 lbs
tow speed	72 mph, 54 mph auto
stall speed	34 mph
glide ratio	23:1

Table 02-03	
Schweizer Aircraft TG-3 Specifics	
span	54.0 ft
wing area	237.0 ft^2
length	27.6 ft
height	5.2 ft
empty weight	820 lbs
gross weight	1,200 lbs
tow speed	100 mph, 62 mph auto
stall speed	38 mph
glide ratio	24:1

Despite Frankfort being the first on contract, the first USAAF military glider delivered was from the Schweizer Aircraft Corporation of Elmira, New York. The Schweizer brothers (Ernest, Paul, and William) and their 20 employees were asked to manufacture their very reputable SGS 2-8 two-seat high-performance sailplane as the TG-2. At the time this was the first, and one of only two licensed two-place glider types under production in the country. It featured welded steel tube fuselage, strutted metal wing structure with aluminum covering forward of the spar and fabric aft, and aluminum frame control surfaces with fabric covering. It had the typical centerline wheel and skid plus spoilers.

Three XTG-2s with trailers, essentially 2-8s with minor changes, were ordered on 18 June 1941 for a fixed price of $6,510.00. Note the XTG-2 contract did not include a static article, suggesting its alterations were structurally insignificant compared with those of the XTG-1. The CAA type certificate was issued on the 28th, again suggesting very minor changes to the design. Deliveries were to be July-August 1941. The first was delivered on 15 July 1941 to Major Dent at the 12th annual National Soaring Contest in Elmira where he and General Arnold were photographed in the aircraft. (That Arnold would appear unexpectedly at the little-known event, for delivery of the smallest and least costly Army aircraft, emphasized his keen interest in the glider program.) The last XTG-2 was received in September, one later expended in a crash.[10]

An order for 18 trailered TG-2s was placed on 24 October 1941, although authorized on 29 August—the USAAF's first glider production contract and first delivered (February through July 1942). These added an electrical system for lighted night operations. It was observed that materials left from this work could be readily used in additional gliders, and so eight more TG-2s were ordered in June 1942, the last delivered in July for a total 26. Total cost was $74,461.81 or $2,864.00 per aircraft with trailer. To these were added six SGS 2-8 sailplanes impressed from civilian owners and designated TG-2s and seven examples in a slightly different configuration labeled TG-2A. Perhaps a dozen SGS-2-8s from the Navy (LNS-1, Chapter 9) were also passed to the Army in fall 1942 and designated TG-2A.

The comparatively low number of TG-2s ordered was owed to a decision to pursue a more suitable variant as the TG-3. This featured low-set, fully cantilevered wing with roomier cockpits, simplifying ingress and egress of the pilots wearing Army-issue flight gear (read parachutes), and improving rear seat instructor's visibility. It also eschewed the use of aluminum to conserve the resource for higher priority programs, but at the price of heavier weight. Lines were simplified for ease of construction with wood. The government even built Schweizer a plant in Elmira (actually Big Flats) to speed up production once they moved there in early 1943 from a former knitting factory.[11]

The work began with three XTG-3s and static test article ordered on 13 October 1941 for $13,209.00 (fixed-price contract) and December through 27 January delivery (140 days). The static article was handed over on 5 March 1942 and the flight examples by early July, the last on the 15th. Schweizer lost $19,822.73 but hoped to make this up in production. Indeed, a contract for 75 TG-3As was placed on 24 March even before

A Schweizer TG-3A is shown in the simplified silver dope finish adopted as a wartime expedient in place of the more colorful and traditional Army training scheme. The glider was an all wood and fabric variant of the TG-2, much better adapted to the USAAF role. Schweizer was among the most reliable and efficient glider manufacturers meeting the military's needs. (San Diego Air & Space Museum)

Most numerous of the sailplanes acquired for Army glider pilot training was the Laister-Kauffman TG-4A. Like many of these gliders, they were initially delivered in the pre-war training colors of blue and yellow, with red/white rudder stripes. This was soon dropped in favor of more efficient silver overall. (National Museum of the United States Air Force)

flight testing. This was increased to 160 articles, with unit price increase from $2,691.00 to $3,731.00, but 49 were cancelled in June.[12] These As included SCR-585 radio and jettisonable front canopy.[13] Production eventually reached one glider per day,[14] and all were accepted between August 1942 (June in contract) and July 1943 for $440,416.11, $4,004.00 each with trailer, but Schweizer again lost money.

The fourth production sailplane was derived from John "Jack" W. Laister's prewar *Yankee Doodle* single-seater. Laister had a very small enterprise named Universal Glider Company in Detroit, Michigan, but without production facilities. Upon hearing that the Air Corps was becoming interested in gliders, Laister traveled to Wright Field to demonstrate *Yankee Doodle* and show past work. With encouragement, Laister proposed a new design and the Army invited him in June 1941 to submit a bid. This won him a letter contract on 7 September. Laister then joined with St. Louis stockbroker John R. Kauffmann, and drawing in other glider associates, to undertake large-scale glider production. Kauffman and Mr. Whitehead had previously overseen Whitehead Aircraft Corporation which was developing a light two-place airplane. The new firm, Laister-Kauffman Aircraft, incorporated on 23 September 1941 and was based in St. Louis. It proved to be exceptionally talented and competent, in contrast to many other "start-ups" the Air Forces worked with on gliders.[15]

Laister-Kauffman's product was a two-seat glider development of the *Yankee Doodle* called the LK-10 *Yankee Doodle Two* that the Army designated TG-4. It featured a fuselage of welded steel tube and wood stringers, wooden wing with plywood leading edge and fabric aft of the spar, and wood frame aero surfaces, fabric over all. The usual wheel, skids, and spoilers were featured. The lever for the spoilers also activated the wheel brake when deployed far enough. A static test article and three XTG-4s with trailers were ordered on a 26 September 1941, valued at for $10,045.00 (final price $10,404.00). Deliveries were to be from 20 February through April 1942.

Table 02-04

Laister-Kauffman Aircraft TG-4 Specifics	
span	50.0 ft
wing area	166.0 ft^2
fuselage length	21.3 ft
height	4.3 ft
empty weight	475 lbs
gross weight	875 lbs
tow speed	103 mph, 63 mph auto
stall speed	39.5 mph
glide ratio	22:1 (ideal)

The ground test specimen was delivered ahead of schedule on 2 December (personally by Laister at 3:00 in the morning) and testing was completed on the 27th. The first flight-worth example arrived in late February.

Although the rest of the XTG-4 flight test gliders took until December 1942 to complete, the Air Forces pressed ahead with production of the glider they judged acceptable. Minor changes yielded the TG-4A that was ordered as the first large glider order, 75 requested on 4 March 1942 for $304,586.25 and 75 more on 27 May for $304,939.95, these with SCR-585 radios. This made the TG-4A the most produced American training sailplane of the war. The first production article was delivered in July 1942 and the balance by June 1943 for unit cost of $4,062.00. A single civilian example in a slightly different configuration was appropriated in 1942 as the TG-4B—apparently a commercial LK-10.

At one point in 1942 the War Department planned to acquire 646 training sailplanes of the TG-1 through -4 variety. But, this would clearly stress the production prowess of the small manufacturers beyond capacity. With directives stating that gliders were to be procured only from firms not already engaged in priority War Department tasks, many contracts went to less experienced firms. The results clearly illustrated the risk this entailed.

In searching for another source of TG-3As, a $157,620.50 15 June 1942 contract for 50 articles was given to Air Gliders, Incorporated, of Barberton, Ohio, with initial delivery in September. Air Glider was to pay Schweizer $1,000.00 plus $270.00 per glider in royalties. With Dr. Frank A. Gross as chief engineer, the firm had only just formed on 4 June. It is, then, no surprise that the Army discovered it had virtually no experience, personnel, or resources to build anything. That they got a contract at all suggests influence from "on high" and over-worked procurement officials. Suspecting the firm might have difficulty meeting terms, the contract was a cost-plus-fixed-fee type instead of the fixed-price vehicles employed with the other trainer manufacturers.[16]

Expectedly, Air Gliders' performance was very poor, with months going by before they even established production facilities. They insisted that the Schweizer plans had errors and so was given a TG-3A for reference. Their requests for contract increases were met with a $223,596.50 plus-up and another for $34,534.15. Payments totaling $408,033.68 were made. Still they failed to deliver, yet efforts to kill the contract were met with opposition from a powerful Ohio congressman. It was 11 May 1943 before the job could be cancelled, after expending $414,353.15 for a single glider taken up in July as the last USAAF WWII training glider—and perhaps the most expensive two-seat sailplane ever. Air Gliders promptly dissolved. Schweizer made a claim for $13,500.00 in support of the contract and recovery of loss on its XTG-3 work. A payment of $12,230.00 appears to have been made.

Failed All-Wood Gambit

More bad news came out of the USAAF's effort to eliminate metal from the trainers. Three contracts were let seeking all-wood designs. One of these went to Wichita Engineering Company of Wichita Falls, Texas, for their newly designed, side-by-side trainer. The firm had previously been engaged in manufacturing various mechanical devices and operating an aviation mechanics school. They had also built an experimental training glider. Three XTG-10s with plywood covering and trailers were ordered on 25 June 1942 for a fixed price of $10,500.00. Deliveries were to be August-September 1942.

Wichita Engineering fell far behind schedule and, by 1 March 1943, had expended $47,111.21. They sought a contract value increase to $65,000.00. Soon after, they asked to be released from their obligation, apparently seeing little prospect of recovering their investment. By then it was clear the Army did not require additional sailplanes and they cancelled the XTG-10 on 27 April 1943. Work was finally halted in November and what there was of the three gliders collected, final settlement being $8,500.00.

Table 02-05

Wichita Engineering XTG-10 Specifics (estimated, not built)

span	50.1 ft
wing area	204 ft^2
fuselage length	25.1 ft
empty weight	500 lbs
gross weight	900 lbs
tow speed	90 mph, 57 mph auto
stall speed	35 mph

William Hawley Bowlus, previously with Ryan Aircraft and past mechanics instructor at the Curtiss-Wright Technical Institute, had a good reputation as a sailplane designer and manufacturer. Bowlus Sailplanes Company, Incorporated, had sold some 200 gliders, many as kits, from a facility behind his home in San Fernando, California. Several dual-seat versions of the popular single-place BA-100 had been sold. This was considered the potential basis for a suitable military trainer if the cockpit dimensions were increased to accommodate men wearing regulation flight gear (parachutes). Bowlus conceived the BM-5 to meet these requirements and a mockup was completed on or about November 1941.[17]

At the end of January 1942, the country's entry into the war had dried-up Bowlus' sailplane sales. A company representative went to Dayton seeking military work. Bowlus Sailplanes was awarded a fixed-price contract for $13,175.00 on 28 April to build three XTG-12 all-wood and fabric two-seat trainers at $3,000.00 each and the fourth airframe presumably a static article at $2,500.00. All were to be delivered between June and August

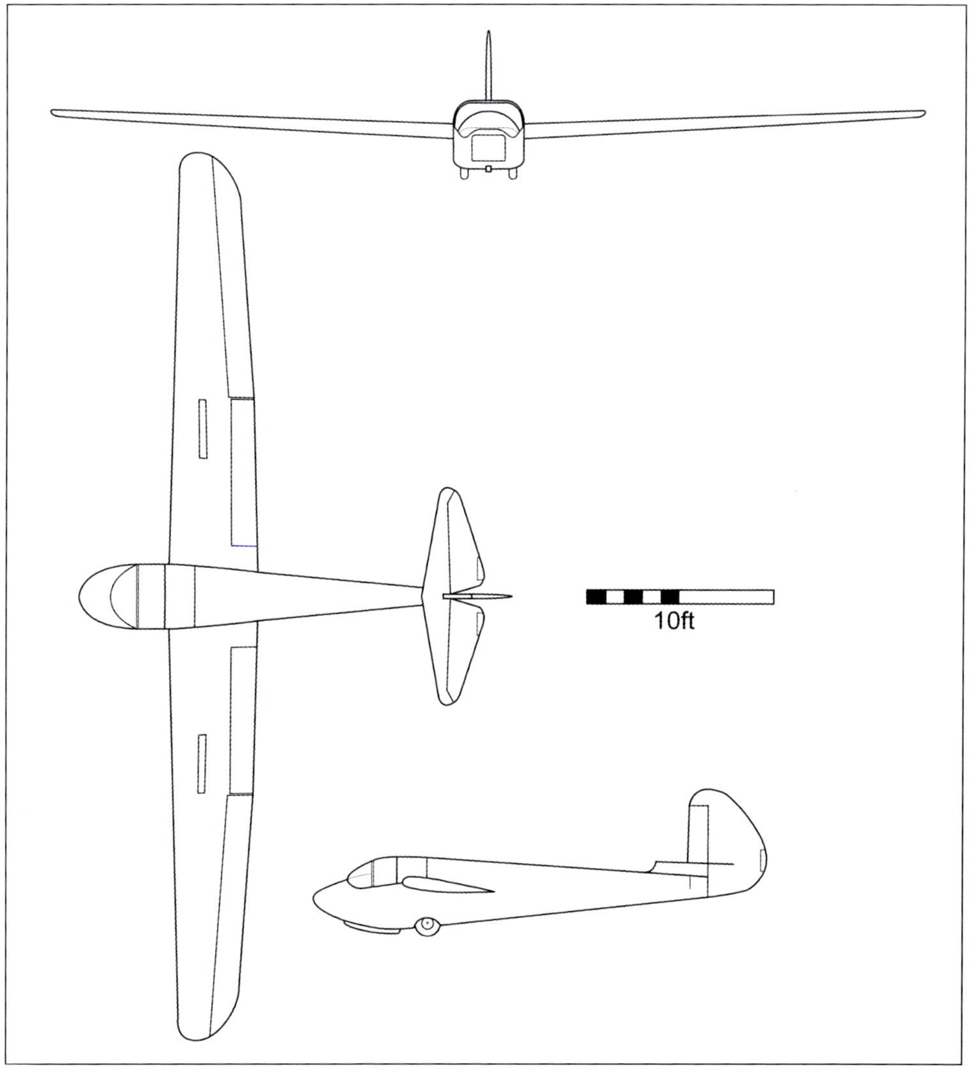

The Army sought to acquire gliders constructed almost entirely of wood to eliminate strategic materials from the non-combat aircraft. Contracting with small or inexperienced firms, this did not play out well. One failed effort was the Wichita Engineering XTG-10 that would have featured unusual line-abreast seating had it reached fruition. (Author)

1942. Materiel Command had mistakenly understood the BM-5 had already received a Class I type certificate from the CAA. It was subsequently learned that this was not the case and the certificate would likely be Class II.[18] The contract price had been based on the cost of building an existing type instead of development and certification of a new aircraft, but Bowlus had privately accepted they would lose money.

By 15 December 1942 the company had delivered nothing but requests to renegotiate the contract (for which they received just $400.00 increase). The government then dropped one of the gliders and so reduced the contract value by $3,293.72.[19] Bowlus said they had been delayed by government demands for design changes and had already expended $68,000.00 (final total was $78,564.55)[20] and were near financial collapse. In January they declared defeat and asked the government to decide their fate. After months of effort, cancellation was finally enacted on 5 August.

A single XTG-12 had flown in summer 1942 at Twenty-Nine Palms, California, and this machine was eventually taken up by the Army. A Bowlus-Du Pont *Utility* glider was also acquired to become the solitary TG-12A, although it was quite a different aircraft from the XTG-12.[21]

The third all-wood trainer, the XTG-13, was ordered on 26 June 1942 from Briegleb Sailplane Corporation of Beverly Hills, California. The $9,000.00 fixed-price contract was for three aircraft plus trailers to be delivered in August and September 1942. The firm built upon the prewar personal business of William G. "Gus" Briegleb who built and sold BG-6 single-seat gliders. The AAF would appropriate three of these sailplanes as XTG-9s.

The first of their all-wood, plywood-covered, two-seat Model BG-8 was already complete in March 1942. In pursuit of a CAA type certificate, it soon underwent static loads testing. They then moved to flight testing in June in which the aircraft was lost during a spin test. It encountered a gust and the over-speed damaged the empennage.

The prototype Briegleb TG-13A was also flown at Twenty-Nine Palms where it was reportedly wrecked. Gus Briegleb was another noted sailplane designer who appears to have stretched too far trying to serve military needs. His little firm simply could not meet the terms of the contract beyond this single late and over-budget glider. (National Soaring Museum)

Table 02-06	
Bowlus Sailplanes XTG-12 Specifics	
span	45.4 ft
fuselage length	24.8 ft
height	7.0 ft approximately
empty weight	675 lbs
gross weight	1,090 lbs
tow speed	100 mph, 70 mph auto
stall speed	39 mph

The Bowlus XTG-12 is captured during flight test at Twenty-Nine Palms during summer 1942. Hawley Bowlus had evidently built a fine sailplane, derived from a pre-war design. However, he did so far beyond allotted budget and schedule such that the project became superfluous and was cancelled. (National Archives)

The crew, including Briegleb, had to abandon the aircraft.[22] The second example was ready in September and flight tests were completed at Twenty-Nine Palms on 2 October.

By this point, Briegleb was months late delivering their first example but got their second ship to Wright Field in November 1942 (accepted 18 December), where they demonstrated its performance. They also sought additional funds. Instead, the contract was cancelled on 8 February 1943 when the remaining aircraft were still not forthcoming. Although Briegleb claimed to have spent $28,000.00, the government settlement was just $3,000.00. Yet, the company, by then renamed Sailplane Corporation of America, was left with what there was of the two other gliders. These were subsequently completed and sold to a private individual for $6,000.00. In an odd twist, the USAAF had acquired two Briegleb gliders designated TG-13A in their general sweep-up of training gliders.[23]

Table 02-07	
Briegleb Sailplane XTG-13 Specifics	
span	50.3 ft
wing area	190 ft^2
fuselage length	22.9 ft
empty weight	435 lbs
gross weight	850 lbs
tow speed	90 mph, 55 mph auto
stall speed	37 mph
glide ratio	22:1

Table 02-08	
Aeronca Aircraft TG-5 Specifics	
span	35.4 ft
wing area	158 ft^2
fuselage length	23.8 ft
height	5.9 ft
empty weight	630 lbs
gross weight	1,260 lbs
maximum speed/tow	129 mph
stall speed	45 mph
glide ratio	10:1 approximately

Table 02-09	
Taylorcraft Aviation TG-6 Specifics	
span	35.4 ft
wing area	181 ft^2
fuselage length	25.2 ft
height	6.1 ft
empty weight	615 lbs
gross weight	1,260 lbs
maximum speed/tow	140 mph
stall speed	42 mph
glide ratio	10:1 approximately

Troika

It had quickly been recognized that sailplanes were not ideal trainers for those intended to fly the combat gliders then being developed. This, along with the quantity problem, prompted Hap Arnold in summer 1942 to seek advice from his friend Charles I. Stanton, administrator of the Civil Aeronautics Administration. Working with engineer Harold D. Hoekstra, Stanton conceived in three days the conversion of light civil aircraft into gliders. The Aeronca Model 65TC Defender was the basis for the design that would remove the engine and add a third seat in an extended nose with a skid beneath, the forward two seats under a greenhouse canopy. All three seats had flight controls and basic flight instruments. The vertical stabilizers would have to be increased to ensure suitable directional stability of the altered aircraft. Reducing the stature of the landing gear allowed the glider to more resemble the stance of the envisioned combat aircraft and likely reduce the takeoff attitude angle of the wing. Each was to have wheel brakes and steerable tail wheel. The glider was squat and unattractive, but would possess the requisite low ground attitude and meager glide ratio more closely approximating that of transport gliders. Stanton then telephoned Lee Smith, president of Aeronca, to ask if his company would be willing to manufacture such gliders. Smith agreed.

Aeronca Aircraft Corporation, of Middleton, Ohio, was a long-standing light plane manufacturer of good repute. It was placed on Army contracted 8 July 1942 to build three of what was called the XTG-5, derived from their military L-3B liaison variant of the Defender. As a measure of the value of working with a highly experienced, high-volume manufacturer, Aeronca had the first example ready in just two days, nine days after the idea was first broached. Barringer himself flew the aircraft in Middleton before ferrying it on tow all the way to Washington, D.C. The XTG-5 was accepted by the Air Forces on 22 July.

Flight testing quickly showed the conversion to be a suitable training glider.[24] Consequently, the service turned to the light airplane industry to rapidly build hundreds of similar gliders based on three existing designs. With the XTG-5 as an example, Taylorcraft and Piper made similar conversions of their military liaison “Grasshopper” designs, direction given between 29 June and 8 May 1942 to procure 250 of each type.[25]

The Aeronca contract was extended to 250 TG-5s, the X contract essentially cancelled and the first machine becoming the first production article. Again, the wisdom of the approach was validated when the company delivered 50 within a month and all but one of the total between July and November 1942 (versus contractual December). Three more aircraft were built to replace three passed to the Navy as XLNR-1s. The government spent $565,681.33 for the project, or a unit price of $2,236.00. Its performance and the glider’s pudgy looks earned it the nickname “Aeronca Descender” from the trainees.[26]

The TG-6 was derived from the Taylorcraft L-2B (civil Model DC-65 “Tandem”), one of the most successful early light planes. Taylorcraft Aviation Corporation, in Alliance, Ohio, called the glider the Model ST-100 for Stanton-Taylorcraft. The alterations were similar to the XTG-5 but added spoilers. Of all these 3-seat gliders, only the TG-6 is officially credited with possessing the SCR-585 radio. The company designed, built, and flew their prototype in just nine days. Then, 18 days from the first Army request, the design was approved and full-rate production begun.[27] They received a contract for 250 (apparently including the prototype, with none designated XTG-6) on 23 July 1942 and deliveries spanned 2 August to 23 November (December in the contract). Cost was $656,754.05, or $2,596.00 per aircraft. Three more were ordered and sent on to the Navy as XLNT-1s.

Piper Aircraft Corporation of Lock Haven, Pennsylvania, supplied the third three-seat glider conversion beginning with a 15 June 1942 agreement. The aircraft was based on Piper’s very popular L-4B (civil J-3C Cub). In fact, the first example had been on their assembly line as a J-3 (s/n 9102) when it was pulled aside and finished on 17 June 1942 as a TG-8.[28] Piper’s 19 August 1942 contract was for 250 TG-8s, of which the prototype counted as the first. (It is unclear if there truly was formally an XTG-8.) Alterations were, again, akin to the others except for employing a cross axle for the wheels with individual hydraulic brakes. All were accepted between 11 September 1942 and April 1943 (instead of December 1942)[29] for $533,435.23 or $2,108.00 per aircraft. An additional three were bought to replace a trio transferred to the USN to become XLNP-1s. With over 750 of the TG-5, TG-6 and TG-8 produced by three of the country’s leading light plane manufacturers, these firms supplied three-quarters of the training gliders for half the total cost of the TG program. The problem of training glider quantity was on its way to being resolved. All this defied the early edict not to use firms already engaged in military work for glider production, but an exception was made. The overwhelming

More efficient training gliders for the Army were those converted from light planes, like the Aeronca TG-5 three-seater shown here. The engine was removed and a third seat added, in addition to lowering the stance and enlarging the vertical stabilizer. Hundreds of such gliders were built in an astonishingly short time to fill the urgent military need. (National Museum of the United States Air Force)

The TG-6 was derived from the Taylorcraft L-2 airplane. The changes were the same as for the Aeronca design except for radio and adding spoilers (evident in this contrived image). Eighteen days after the Army go-ahead, the glider was designed, built, tested, and in full-rate production. (The Peter M. Bowers Collection/The Museum of Flight)

The third of the three-seaters was the TG-8 showing its heritage with the famous Piper L-4. Carrying two students allowed for more efficient training, and the meager glide ratio was much more representative of the combat gliders to come. In just seven months the firm delivered 250 of the gliders. (The Peter M. Bowers Collection/The Museum of Flight)

success of the contracts with these well-established companies was in glaring contrast to most of the other glider development efforts and may suggest the original guidance was ill-conceived.

Table 02-10	
Piper Aircraft TG-8 Specifics	
span	35.2 ft
wing area	179 ft^2
fuselage length	23.1 ft
height	6.1 ft
empty weight	522 lbs
gross weight	1,060 lbs
maximum speed/tow	122 mph
stall speed	38 mph
glide ratio	10:1 approximately

Navy/Marine Trainers

Beginning immediate training on sport sailplanes was the most expedient means for the Navy and Marine Corps to gain knowledge of gliders and establishing a cadre of experienced glider pilots while the combat aircraft were in development. Hence, their efforts closely followed the Army example. To supply Class VLN training gliders, the USN also sought contractors not already engaged in priority powered airplane production. The aircraft were to incorporate plastic-bonded wood to the greatest extent possible, eschewing aluminum and other strategic materials required for higher-priority programs. Throughout the rest of 1941 and 1942 the Navy bought more than 150 sailplanes and Army-developed training gliders.

Since all established U.S. glider manufacturers were already fully engaged by the Army and working to the limits of their facilities, the Navy took on a new firm for mass production of a novel design. Their first glider development contract went to the Gould Aeronautical Division (later Gould Aviation Company) of Pratt, Read & Company,

The Navy developed a trainer for the Marine glider mission, employing a company new to aviation. The Pratt, Read LNE-1 (first production article shown but designated XLNE-1) featured side-by-side seating, with wood and fabric structure except for steel tubing in the fuselage. It was a worthy aircraft, but the firm fell well behind the production schedule. (National Soaring Museum)

Table 02-11	
Pratt, Read LNE-1 Specifics	
span	54.7 ft
wing area	230 ft²
fuselage length	26.2 ft
empty weight	770 lbs
maximum weight	1,150 lbs
glide ratio	26:1

Incorporated (formerly the Pratt, Read Piano Company) of Deep River, Connecticut. A manufacturer of fine piano works, the firm's president James A Gould had moved in 1940 to position his company for war-time work by attracting the likes of C.T. Ludington (formerly of Ludington Airplanes), Roger W. Griswold, II, and Lewin Barringer (before leaving to lead the Army glider program). The July 1941, $20,000.00 agreement was for a prototype to be delivered by about 1 December 1941.[30]

Pratt, Read clearly had experience in fine woodworking, but a committee of six glider enthusiasts acted as designers for the glider. Principal among these were Griswold, Parker Leonard (serving as a company vice-president), Jay Buxton, and Bob Stanley.[31] They had already designed the G-1 and so brought it to fruition as the PRG-1 which the Navy designated XLNE-1 wherein the L stood for glider, N for trainer, and E for Pratt, Read.[32] This unusual glider looked like a winged tadpole with its wide, podded fore-body of steel frame for line-abreast seating narrowing to a tubular aft fuselage of monocoque plywood. The wing was wood frame with fabric covering, the fuselage welded steel tubing covered with fabric, the control surfaces also cloth-covered. Each aileron was in two segments to avoid binding during flexure in flight. The aircraft rested with the tail on the ground until the crew climbed aboard, after which it rotated onto the nose skid. It is odd that the tradition-bound Navy would see value in side-by-side instruction that was almost unknown at the time and surely detracted from potential aircraft performance.

The civil-registered prototype PRG-1 was late, first flying on 7 March 1942 and CAA certification coming at the end of August 1942. The Navy held up production while awaiting this civil approval.[33] Aircraft weight also went up for the production configuration, increasing 185 pounds empty.[34] The service had ordered another XLNE-1 and six production LNE-1s. This was raised to 50 aircraft around the end of 1941 and then upped again to a total 100 gliders and $336,000.00 cost-plus-fixed-fee in July. All were to be delivered in eight months at a projected cost of $380,602.95. These steps were all taken before any production examples had been formally delivered.

At one point in 1942 the War Department planned to acquire 575 LNE-1 gliders at a rate of 3-10 per month. However, by July 1942 none had been delivered. The Navy was understandably dissatisfied with Pratt, Read's production difficulties. As the Army had found, sailplane manufacturers could not meet the high rate of production demanded by wartime military requirements. Also, in early 1943, the Marines had soured on use of sailplanes for their training. Consequently, production of the LNE-1 was curtailed at 75 on 5 April 1943.[35] The last was delivered in January 1943.[36] Another factor was that Pratt, Read had spent $908,000.00 to January 1943, nearly three times the contract value.[37] Final cost was $1,379,762.94 for production or a steep $18,154.78 per glider compared with an average $3,145.87 for new Army sailplanes.[38]

With Pratt, Read unable to meet training needs during 1942, the USN turned to a glider already developed for the Army to quickly put aircraft in the hands of instructors and students. They gave a $26,000.00 contract to Schweizer for 13 LNS-1s, the company's SGS 2-8. The 13th SGS 2-8 was cancelled and the final sum was $26,200.00.

Requiring trainers sooner than the LNE-1 was available, the Navy turned to Army sources, acquiring examples of many USAAF types. They bought a dozen Schweizer SGS 2-8s and designated them LNS-1s. One of these gliders is pictured at Parris Island during May 1942. (National Archives)

The Navy also acquired three each of the trio of three-place trainers derived from light planes. An example is this XLNP-1 known in the Army as the Piper TG-8. These pudgy gliders were evaluated in late 1942 and found to be effective training assets. (National Soaring Museum)

In late 1942, the Navy also acquired three each of the Army's 3-place gliders, more representative of the coming combat gliders. Ordered via the Army, these were the XLNR-1 from the Aeronca TG-5, XLNT-1 from the Taylorcraft TG-6, and the XLNP-1 from the Piper TG-8.

Three Army TG-5s became XLNR-1s. The trio of each of these three-place gliders came from the manufacturers, off the Army contracts. However, the firms then built three more to deliver the required number to the USAAF. (National Soaring Museum)

A staged photo of a civilian instructor and two Army student glider pilots was taken beside a TG-2. They are examining the parachute at the end of the towline to a ground winch, allowing a gentle descent of the cable. The civilian instructors were critical during the early stages of the instruction, yet were also rare assets that were dwindled by Selective Service. (National Soaring Museum)

3

The Training Muddle

The Army acted quickly to acquire at least some understanding of glider flying. The Combat Glider Training Program began with a dozen pilots sent for instruction at the Elmira Area Soaring Corporation School in Elmira, New York, and the Lewis School of Aeronautics in Lockport, Illinois. The first 12 students included four from Materiel Command who would be involved in the procurement and testing of gliders, and eight from the 50th Transport Wing who would help formulate plans for future training. Among these men were Major Dent and later Major Price. They trained on sailplanes of the period towed aloft by ground winch, automobile, and light plane. The 3-week/30-hour program, during June 1941, created a small cadre of knowledgeable officers who would help formulate plans for the glider echelon. Before this training could occur, on 5 June 1941 the War Department rescinded its 1931 order prohibiting active duty personnel from engaging in glider flying. Twelve flight instructors were then trained at Elmira through September.

Great Britain had at first considered making glider piloting an additional duty of bomber pilots before choosing to train Army soldiers for the duty. The American counterparts were always USAAF personnel with a unique qualification, working closely with ground troops and landing on the battlefield. Glider pilot training was an area of great uncertainty, with only guesses as to the required qualifications and proficiency. Spaatz's original intent that the pilots be fully trained USAAC airplane pilots was, after Pearl Harbor, shown to be untenable. Given the large numbers of men postulated and the huge demand for pilots, it was clear that converting power-pilots to gliders was unthinkable. However, the leadership eschewed the minimally trained "second pilot" the British employed. Consequently, by mid-February 1942 attention turned to training enlisted personnel and an aggressive recruitment program

These two officers stand beside what appears to be a pre-production Laister-Kauffman LK-10 sailplane in Elmira, New York. This famous gliding locale was site of initial training of a core cadre of glider personnel that kicked-off the program. The Army and Navy quickly saturated the few available glider flying schools in the country. (National Soaring Museum)

was launched. When the influx did not meet expectations, qualifications were reduced. Flying Training Command was frustrated trying to create a training program for a frequently changing requirement.

What to Do?

The slow pace of devising the glider program frustrated Arnold. On 7 July 1941 he requested a comprehensive plan for pilot training from his chief of staff, Brigadier General Spaatz. The fundamental doctrine of combat gliders had still not been formulated, so planning was built on a great deal of guesswork.

The envisioned program was to begin by training 150 existing Army pilots between July and October 1941 to serve as the nucleus of an instructor staff for future advanced courses once combat gliders were available. The plan suggested that at least 50 of the men would be from Air Support Command, the organization that was expected to provide tow planes. The students, 10-15 per class, would be trained at civilian pilot Elementary Schools under contract. The same scheme would be followed for glider instruction on sailplanes for 1,000 pilots. Instruction at the Advanced Army Glider Schools would continue with two-seat gliders, emphasizing tow, and provide the transition to the combat gliders then in development. Spaatz submitted his plan on 28 August and it was approved by his boss on 4 September. However, Arnold excluded the 50 pilots from Air Support Command as they could not be spared from their current duties.

Nationwide glider instruction resources would have to increase many-fold to meet Army demand. In July 1940 there had been just five gliding schools, sized for the small sport. There was soon keen competition to hire the few available instructors or those who could quickly qualify. Only 25 of the nation's glider pilots were initially judged sufficiently experienced to serve as instructors. The tremendous demand prompted formation of schools staffed by experienced pilots hastening to get commercial ratings. Most of these would be young men willing to relocate and live in sometimes spartan conditions for the opportunity to fly from dawn to dusk, six days a week. The military students would later refer to them as "legal draft dodgers." Some of the civilians who might have served as instructors were turned away because of their ties to Germany, which had been the world leader in the sailplane sport before the war.

The 150 Officer Power Pilot Program was already behind schedule when it began on 20 September 1941 with the first 9 of 21 men enrolled at Elmira. The rest were to be trained someplace in the southwest where year-round instruction was possible. This largest of the contract schools was Twenty-Nine Palms Air Academy, formed at Condor Field on the edge of a dry lakebed in the California desert. Their contract called for training 126 officers between 30 November 1941 and 21 March 1942. As it happened, while the Academy was established in November, operations did not commence until 19 January. Both locations taught 4-week courses, a new class beginning every other week. These sought 30-hours in sailplanes with ground launch via winch or automobile and aero-tow when a tug was available, and emphasis on soaring and spot landing. As purpose-built military gliders and tow planes were still lacking, the sport aircraft previously employed for civilian instruction continued to be used. The results seemed meager considering that the glider program was already a year old.

A detailed plan for mass training of the 1,000 glider pilots was finally put forth via Spaatz's original 2 December 1941 and approved on the 20th. The course would follow the four-week pattern before moving on to the Advanced course on actual transport gliders. However, the U.S. entry into the war made clear that the transfer of power pilots to the glider pilot ranks was unworkable. The burgeoning requirements for air power created tremendous demands for airplane pilots and graduates of the mainstream airplane courses were at a premium. Other sources of the 1,000 glider pilot candidates had to be considered.

By the end of December a new scheme was devised for recruiting 1,000 glider pilot trainees, from within the ranks or new recruits. The initial qualifications were completion of civilian power pilot training or at least 30-hours glider time and meeting the physical requirements of powered pilots. Unusual was the radical decision to train enlisted personnel with promotion to Staff Sergeant upon graduation (although this was slow in materializing). However, the pendulum now swung to the opposite side with the misperception that flying gliders would be easy, the pilots readily trained, and with few proficiency requirements.

The 1,000 Glider Pilot Training Program was approved with the intent of graduating the requisite number of pilots by 1 January 1943. Twenty-Nine Palms was site of a 30-hour Preliminary course. This was to be followed by an Advanced course on combat gliders at an as-yet unidentified site.

Major Fred Dent photographs the US Army's first glider, the Schweizer XTG-2 after it is loaded on its trailer for transport to Wright Field. The September 1941 event is in Elmira, New York, where Schweizer had its plant. Dent and his team were under persistent pressure to get gliders to the training fields as students flowed into the system. (National Soaring Museum)

During a press day at Twenty-Nine Palms in 1942 a pair of TG-2s stands ready for tow off by a Stinson O-49 from the dry lakebed adjacent to the field. The hot and windy conditions combined with mountains seen in the background made for good soaring conditions, although the year-round flying weather was the principal attraction for the Army. Multi-ship towing appears to have been uncommon. (National Soaring Museum)

Repeated Escalation

Even before the 1000-pilot program could get under way, Arnold threw everything into uncertainty when on 1 April 1942 he raised the glider pilot requirement to 4,200 men, with 2,000 required by 1 January 1943 and the rest by 1 July 1943. The field of potential glider pilots had to be greatly expanded.

The revised qualifications for candidates, established on 13 April, were initially quite similar to those already promulgated. Accepted were officers or enlisted personnel 18-35 years of age, volunteers from within the ranks or new recruits. The prior flying experience was measured by a pilot certificate from a powered course, or a glider pilot with 30 hours or 200 glider flights. (The Army leadership understood it had approximately 5,000 officers and enlisted men already serving with a CAA rating.[1]) No one having flunked out of a pilot program would be accepted. The individual had to complete screening and physical tests, with passing scores reduced from those for power pilots.

The U.S. Army had never before faced such a pilot training challenge. However, the curriculum adopted on 15 April 1942 to meet the 4,200-pilot requirements paralleled the earlier plan, with 30 hours in twin-gliders over four weeks plus 72-hours of ground school. Also specified were 2.5 hours instrument instruction (hooded) and 1 hour night tow. Advanced instruction was envisioned as 50 hours, but this was then tentative. Preliminary Schools were being placed on contract.

Everything was thrown into uncertainty again on 8 May 1942 when 6,000 pilots became the goal, with 3,000 needed by 1 September and the rest desired by the end of the year. Part of the motivation for this jump was early strategic plans calling for the Allies' return to Europe in 1943.

To meet the 6,000-pilot requirement, training plans were reformulated again, reducing the training period to increase the graduation rate. Light plane instruction was added as the most expedient means of training those new to flight and performing "deadstick" landings. Students would get 4 weeks/30 hours in the airplanes followed by 1 week/8 hours in sailplanes, and then 1 week/8 hours in transport gliders.

On 11 May 1942 all Army units were instructed to promote the glider pilot program within the ranks. However, owing to continuing lackluster recruitment, only about a third of the first classes, starting 1 June, were filled. Schools ran at reduced capacity. The program was again behind and a sense of desperation set in. Something dramatic had to be done.

The program was widely promoted at formations and in public media. As one measure, the Army turned to the CAA who sent letters to 85,000 certificated pilots advertising the program. Public recruitment was widespread. Even the selection of non-volunteers was considered, which would have marked a significant departure from Army tradition.[2] Instead, on 11 June, the decision was made to accept personnel with no prior flight training and promote all to Staff Sergeant upon entering the program. Students who had washed out of a pilot course were now

In addition to tow planes, the Army also procured custom-built winches for ground launch of gliders. This unit was supplied by the Glider Equipment Company and photographed during summer 1942 at Twenty-Nine Palms where it did not play a large role as the training quickly moved beyond sailplanes. A fairly rudimentary truck-towed device, the cage protects the operator from the whip-back of a snapped cable. (National Soaring Museum)

accepted provided they had not been flunked due to a flying deficiency. Physical and test score requirements were further lowered to permit those with some degraded visual acuity and color blindness. The deadline for the 3,000-pilot requirement was extended to 28 September.

Entrants lacking prior experience were labeled Class B students while those with previous training were Class A. Instruction of the former began at Preliminary Light Plane Gliding Schools with 5 weeks/40 hours (21 hours solo) of light plane day/night instruction (Phase I) then 2 weeks/15 hours of deadstick landings (Phase II). Class A students entered the program in the Preliminary Phase II with 4 weeks/30 hours. Both groups then went to an Elementary-Advanced Glider School for 1 week/8 hours in 1- or 2-place gliders, which included formation landings. Following this was a planned 1 week/8 hours in the 9- or 15-place cargo gliders then being developed, plus 60 hours ground school to include light plane maintenance.

The course content was not rigidly followed by the schools, and some altered over the coming months to meet short-term exigencies. The dual instruction paths just complicated matters, with schools running dozens of students through either phase at any given time.

The revised program was implemented on 16 May 1942, and training was back on track with a new baseline by the end of June. However, it required the rapid establishment of many more training sites all across the country to handle the massive influx of students. Civilian schools sprang up to win government contracts, with power schools now emphasized. Eighteen new Preliminary Schools had to be formed to join the two contract and five USAAF Elementary-Advanced Schools already operating. Five Advanced Schools were just being established. Thirteen glider schools were opened across the country in summer 1942. Sufficient facilities had been contracted by 1 June for the initial surge of students, and by late in the month 18 Primary Light Plane Gliding Schools were training Army students. The short timeline meant that many of the activities were operating out of tents when opened. At its peak 17 contract schools were training Army glider pilots.

Recruitment goals were finally being met by the end of June 1942. The glider pilot candidates on a whole were of a different educational and social caliber, plus older on average, than the usual mainstream aviation cadet. Many of these men were more motivated by the possibility of getting out of a dreary posting, the promise of flight pay, rapid advancement, and getting into combat assignments quickly, than they were an aviation career, although the glamour of flight was certainly a factor.

Just as the program settled into a working routine, its goals were altered again. On 10 August 1942, Washington set the pilot requirement at 7,800 by 1 March 1943, with the course to continue producing graduates at 12,000 per year with no final number stated. The program was expanded to graduate 700 pilots every two weeks through February 1943 and 462 thereafter.

An unknown pilot poses for a 'hero picture' beside an TG-5 at the John H. Wilson Glider School in Lamesa, Texas. The glider pilot wings (below) he trained to earn were worn with pride by the pilots who won them, claiming the "G" stood for "Guts." However, the very act of creating wings different from the Air Corps' traditional pilot wings meant the leadership saw these "Flight Officers" as unequal and distinct. (San Diego Air & Space Museum, below Author)

Equipment Shortfall

In July 1942, Flying Training Command had an immediate need for 934 light trainers, 144 1- and 2-place gliders (revised later to 3-place machines), and 180 cargo gliders. However, at that time Materiel Command could provide none of the promised 3-place gliders and no transport types. Liaison aircraft were transferred from other activities, with May and some June 1942 production diverted to the schools. The Stinson L-1 and Piper L-4 were prominent. Double tow of even the 3-place gliders assisted training efficiency. For sailplane triple tow, each glider was on a ¼-inch nylon line of 250 feet, 300 feet, and 350 feet, and the pilots applied rudder to maintain lateral separation until release. It was only August and September when necessary equipment was finally coming online in meaningful numbers.

Program capacity by summer 1942 was 3,336 students, with 834 entering instruction each week. However, the number of aircraft was simply inadequate for this instructional load and students were backing up in the system. It was necessary on 18 July to slow the flow of men temporarily, and some schools closed. A reduced goal of 1,500 fully qualified glider pilots by 26 September, another 1,500 by 31 December, was adopted. This may have been allowed by strategic planning that had pushed the Allies' reentry to the Continent back a year.

Efforts had begun in April 1942 to divert Stinson L-1 and L-1A liaison Vigilant aircraft to the schools for light plane preliminary instruction and sailplane towing.

Although the low glide ratio of the three-place ersatz gliders was representative of the combat gliders to come, the repeated tow and release cycles were inefficient. A TG-5 is seen under tow with two students and instructor aboard. Light panes, that could self-launch then recover deadstick after the engine was shutdown, provided more efficient training. (San Diego Air & Space Museum)

With tremendous pressure to create a combat glider force, training sailplanes were being acquired in 1942 as quickly as the nation's producers could turn them out. Unfortunately, sailplane production in the United States had been a "boutique" industry before the war and expansion to total-war capacity was problematic. An inspirational banner and American flag hang over new-built TG-1As in their trailers at Frankfort's Joliet, Indiana, plant. (National Soaring Museum)

However, these were also being delivered in numbers below requirements. Flying Training Command requested 90 new aircraft for each of July and August 1942, but only 25 per month for a total 120 would be provided. Other tow planes eventually included the Vultee BT-13 and BT-15 Valiant, and Stearman PT-17 Kaydet. Link trainers (simulators) were also introduced to the Elementary-Advanced course, with about 8 hour's instruction, although these were of limited usefulness for glider pilot training because their simulated characteristics were not those of a glider. Actual instrument flight instruction, no matter how brief, was hindered by a lack of suitable equipment that meant some students were passed without the training.

A Frankfort TG-1A was "landed out" from the pilot's base, although on a good country road. A Stinson L-1A sets up to land and tow the trainer back, illustrating the light planes that played such a crucial role in the glider pilot training program. Note the pilot parachute that was required by regulations to be worn, and forced changes to existing sailplane designs. (The Peter M. Bowers Collection/The Museum of Flight)

Aircraft were not the only deficiencies. Instructors proved difficult to secure. This problem was partially solved by keeping some graduates on as instructors. However, the quality of the ground school particularly suffered. Furthermore, standardized instructional texts were completely lacking. The individual schools created or procured what they needed, but without uniformity until draft Army manuals began to be distributed in 1943.

The hoped-for 40-hour Advanced course required 369 transport gliders to meet the graduation numbers, plus a trickle to replace an anticipated three percent attrition or supplement grounded instruction machines. This requirement compelled an expeditious decision on primary cargo glider type and rapid move to high-rate production. The winner from this process was the Waco CG-4A, as will be detailed in Chapter 5. A like number of C-47 or C-53 tugs were also essential. (The Douglas C-53 Skytrooper was a commercial DC-3 type.) But, FTC was told to expect only 90 gliders and 52 C-47s for the time being. The 9-place Waco CG-3A had been procured as a combat glider (Chapter 4), but evolving tactics had quickly determined that the 15-place CG-4A would be the principal assault glider for American forces. The 100 CG-3As were devoted to training, but these did not satisfy the requirement for advanced training on the CG-4A prior to graduation. Very few USAAF glider pilots remember the CG-3A at all, suggesting their employment as trainers was brief and very limited in locale. First conceived in May 1941, the Waco CG-4A had been frustratingly long reaching quantity production.

The complete lack of 15-place gliders through September was creating a severe backlog of students. Even instructors were not being trained. Flight Training Command requested that instructors be given training at Wright Field so as to be ready when training aircraft were delivered. However, Materiel Command insisted this was impractical. Wilmington was not yet ready to receive the large gliders, and the mix of gliders and powered aircraft at Wright Field was already becoming untenable. Increasing the number of glider flights would simply be unsafe. Also, the only two CG-4s were completely committed to flight test. However, the Glider Branch did agree to provide two pilots to train the initial cadre of instructors once production aircraft were available, this training at the Elementary-Advanced School in Lockbourne, Ohio.

The first CG-4As were delivered on 11 September 1942, a month later than planned. But the numbers were initially low and the machines suffered the usual plague of immaturity technical problems that rendered them repeatedly unserviceable. During early 1943 as much as 75 percent of the fleet was grounded at any one time for inspections and rework of manufacturing defects. These required field modifications until production changes were introduced. Other problems devolved from improper care and servicing

The move from gliders to light planes as the focus of glider pilot instruction was made with sailplanes still in the production pipeline. Many TGs were moved directly to reserve and eventually made up a serious problems with some 800 machines stored. These TG-6s, at a southwest training field, feature electric lights on the wingtips and tail. (National Soaring Museum)

of the gliders as personnel became familiar with the new machine. Also, as with any new aircraft rushed to the field, the logistics and depot support were not yet in place. By late September the chronic shortage of gliders and tow planes alike had made it impossible to attain the numerical training goals. This alone limited the graduation rate to 295 men every two weeks versus the planned 737, or 4,800 per year.

The towing of two CG-4As with a C-47 ("double tow," Chapter 7) was investigated to double the training per lift. While possible, double tow proved impractical for training. The tow plane and gliders were operated by separate units, making coordination a necessary but sometimes neglected process. Problems were also encountered with tow planes, making training progress doubly difficult. Production of C-47s was slowly ramping up and the few aircraft then available were heavily committed to other duties. It took a conference of general officers in July 1942 to assign an embryonic force of Troop Carrier Command (TCC) tow planes, the 61st Troup Carrier Group, to support initial training, with the 63rd to follow in November. The entire production run of Lockheed C-60A Lodestars through January 1943 (79 of 129 machines) were directed to the program as tow planes. These freed up one of the TCC groups, but the schools had to pilot the C-60s with their own personnel.

The first group of the 60 men remaining from the original 150 power pilots finally received their CG-4A course (about 2 hour's transition) at Lockbourne during September 1942. They were then distributed throughout the Advanced Schools as instructors. The Army formed advanced courses in five locations, although concentrated at South Plains AAB in Lubbock, Texas, after May 1943.

Relative Efficiency

With six months of experience through late summer 1942, glider pilot training became more efficient and effective. The profusion of types and models of appropriated sport gliders and contract-built 2-place trainers were a burden. The glide ratios were not representative of combat gliders in development and sortie rates were low. Auto and winch launch were poor and soaring time consuming. Consequently, the training was not ideal for military application, even when the gliders were towed aloft on double or triple aero-tows. The 3-place gliders began to displace the sailplane in fall 1942. While more representative of transport gliders, these could not be ground launched. Even with two students aboard, they were still only effective for instruction on use of spoilers for spot landings. By mid-July 1942 all ground launch had been dropped as well as soaring instruction, such as use of thermals, to be replaced by precision maneuvering.

As the rush to "do something" slowed and production combat gliders began to emerge from the drawing boards, it was clear sailplanes contributed little value in military glider pilot training beyond primary flight skill indoctrination, which was better instilled via light planes. These proved to be a more efficient training resource than gliders themselves. They could be sortied with minimal ground crew, the engine shutdown at 500 to 5,000 feet, and glided down to a spot landing off-field with roll to a stop within 15 feet of a chalked line, and then flown off again for another deadstick. They lacked only spoilers. After night instruction was added in July, around the clock, seven days a week instruction was conducted.

The CAA was operating elementary flight courses under the Civilian Pilot Training (CPT) program. They agreed to train 3,000 Class B students in the Preliminary phase by 15 September 1942 to help ease the load on the contract schools. The 10 August objectives would require around 800 students entering each phase every two weeks for the short term, which the CAA could not support. Consequently, the USAAF ran temporary courses at some Preliminary Light Airplane Gliding Schools. The CAA's elementary CPT course was 8 weeks/35-45 hours in 50-65 horsepower light planes plus 240 hours of ground school. The over 2,150 students streaming from the CPT were not always acceptable as some were physically disqualified from glider training or insufficiently trained. However, this part of the program came to an end on 15 January 1943 as the requisite number of pilots passed on.

In autumn 1942 the curriculum shifted to four separate 4-weeks stages. Class B students got 30 hours in power planes at Preliminary Schools. These and the Class A candidates then received 30-hours deadstick instruction at Elementary Glider Schools, followed by 30-hours in training gliders at Basic Glider Schools, and then a planned 40-hours in transport gliders at Advanced Glider Schools. Basic included some instrument, night, and navigation instruction, with around 17 hours solo. Each stage was at a different location, keeping the students moving across the country.

The revised program would require eight Elementary Schools, eight Basic Schools, and five Advanced Schools. But, the number of establishments in each phase fluctuated as needs changed, Basic Schools rising to twelve.

By the time students finally began flowing into the Advanced Schools in late September 1942 the course, that had been formulated for 40 hours, was then 2 weeks/15 hours, day and night, with a 25-hour ground school. Although this required 154 CG-4As and 154 tow planes, these numbers were simply unattainable. There was initially no set curriculum other than operation and maintenance. However, some fundamental content was soon established.

Glider development and tactics maturation in the U.S. and Great Britain made clear that combat gliders would most likely be simply winged trailers towed over a landing zone at no more than a few thousand feet and released for a couple minutes flight. Furthermore, the CG-4A, a comparatively simple aircraft, was found to be relatively easy to fly. Experience with the new Waco also enforced the wisdom of simplifying glider pilot training. The big transport glider's glide ratio of just around 10:1 rendered previous soaring instruction practically worthless. After February 1943, with introduction of the CG-4A in numbers permitting their use earlier in the glider pilot training, and with most of the students having flowed through the Preliminary and Elementary stages, training was streamlined again to a single stage on Wacos. This created a stable training environment in which standardized content, methods, and training materials could be developed and disseminated for the first time. However, it was still May before the CG-4A and C-47 availability and student load pressures began to ease.

Pile-Up

By autumn 1942 the program was running at full steam, but it still appeared that the mandated rate of pilot matriculation would not be met, principally because of equipment shortages. Only 300 students, 75 from each Advanced course, were moving along every two weeks. The pilot goals had to be adjusted. Only 1,300 pilots were expected to graduate by 28 September at a rate of 200 a month, or just 2,035 by 1 March 1943. Little could be done to alter the situation so these numbers were accepted. The goals were finally in consonance with real capabilities. But, on 30 September, new objectives were set at 4,000 graduates by 1 March 1943 and 400 per month afterwards through the end of that year, or a total of 8,000 men.

Towards the end of 1942 there were 10,294 trainees in the program. To that point it had been taking nine months to move a student through the 16 weeks of instruction. When students exceeded available capacity for the next schools they were moved to "replacement center pools" to await openings. At the time only 3,258 students were actively engaged in training, 1,451 *en route* via CPT, with the remaining 5,585 languishing in these "pools." An average six months was spent at these typically remote and spartan bases with poor facilities, sometimes tarpaper shacks or tents with inadequate heating. The men were given little or nothing to do and provided only meager information about what to expect. This mind-numbing idleness led to plummeting morale along with diminishing flight proficiency, AWOLs, and even suicides. While some remedial measures were taken, like half-hearted attempts at infantry training and light plane availability, the damage was done. Many of the men felt they had been misled.

Immediate measures to ease the backlog included ending the training of Class B students in early October 1942 and recruitment of new students ceased on 16 November. Basic instruction increased to two months—one month of deadstick work in light planes and one in training gliders—still at contract schools, while the Elementary phase was eliminated. Schools began to close at an increasing rate. By the time these courses ceased in March 1943, 8,520 Elementary and 6,760 Basic stage pupils had graduated, with less than five percent washout rate. Twenty-Nine Palms passed out its last class in March 1943. In 13 months of operation it instructed 1,240 glider pilots, washing out only 39. At the end it had 59 gliders and 17 tow planes.

Then, unexpectedly, Arnold directed on 12 December 1942 that the Advanced instruction be shortened again to just eight hours to accelerate training. This apparently arbitrary decision would clearly produce pilots with inadequate training and it generated discontentment throughout the program. It evolved to include three hours of solo, and two night flights with one of them solo. Flight as copilot or passenger was added in an effort to somehow supplement the meager "stick time." No one was happy with the resulting level of instruction.

It was proposed that 9,295 glider pilots would be graduated by 27 October 1943 after which the training program would probably be shut down. However, autumn 1942 had seen hesitation in buying thousands more CG-4As, suggesting that fewer pilots would be required than previously surmised. The operational commands were then able to make more educated assessments of glider needs as part of integrated airborne assaults and so expressed a need for 6,290 Wacos by 1944. As airborne divisions planned their deployment overseas in 1943 they discovered that two glider regiments, with the packed aircraft, took too much space on the transport vessels. Hence, the decision was taken to convert one of the glider regiments to paratroops.[3] The requirements for gliders and glider pilots was instantly reduced.[4] Yet, calculations showed 823 CG-4As would be required to support tactical deployment of an airborne division.[5] Additionally, gliders were being shipped to the UK in the hundreds, and then thousands, separate from the airborne units. During combat operations the number of gliders employed was decided by mission requirements, and pilots moved between units as needed, so the single regiment became somewhat meaningless. Additionally, many divisions eventually trained soldiers for both duties and so became para-glider troops.

This photo shows a flightline of Schweizer TG-2s at Condor Field, Twenty-Nine Palms Air Academy, in the California desert sometime during 1942 or 1943. At the far right is a Schweizer SGS 2-8 and an unknown type, both likely a former civil aircraft impressed into service by the Army. The apparently austere accommodation are actually comfortable compared with some training sites. (National Museum of the United States Air Force)

With combat gliders and pilots reaching operational units in early 1943, new considerations came into play. High attrition during training suggested 25 percent excess production was advisable for 1944. Airborne Command and TCC saw the need for only 6,000 gliders and a commensurate number of pilots that year, or as few as 4,000 men, with no practical means of dealing with a surplus until units began deploying overseas. Airborne Command was activated on 21 March 1942 as follow-on to creation of Army Ground Forces (AGF) under a 9 March reorganization of the War Department. The USAAF counterpart, Air Transport Command followed the next month only to be renamed Troop Carrier Command in June. These elements were only just learning how to employ their assets and were understandably hesitant to give gliders priority without better appreciation of their potential contribution. Additionally, the new TCC groups found it difficult to accommodate glider pilots and their aircraft, with suitable proficiency training, until the units were well established. Clearly some advanced planning had been lacking.

With these and other mixed signals, on 11 February 1943 new direction came that only 4,054 glider pilots were required, on hand by 31 December 1943. With the 636 already graduated, this left 3,418 to train during the year. The rate of graduation was to be slowed to 250 per month. Schools would be closed commensurate with this plan.

The upshot of all this was that thousands of students, including all those in or awaiting Elementary or Basic instruction, were to be directed to other assignments. The disposition of 7,321 excess glider pilot trainees was determined by 1 April 1943. Continuing in the program were 1,929 personnel. Of the others, those who had entered from within the service were reassigned. Those coming in from civilian life were either directed to other training or allowed to separate, although the Army believed few would choose the latter option in light of the wartime emergency. However, so was the disillusionment of many of these men that 1,147 stepped out of uniform.

Even Keel

With a focus on simply getting CG-4A pilots into the field rather than creating well-rounded airman, the program could be reduced to essentials. Glider pilots were graduating in six months with only Waco flying. All schools no longer required were closed. To pilots graduating before they could be absorbed by the TCC groups, the Advanced training on CG-4As returned to the 4 week/15-hour curriculum.

By the summer of 1943 all sailplanes were idled. Even the need for the 3-seat trainers had passed, although this time came while some 238 of the aircraft remained to be delivered. Despite the fact that they would simply be stored, Materiel Command decided to let production run its course. By fall 1943 the useless TGs had become a significant storage problem—on 30 March 1944 consisting of 800 airframes.[6]

Some semblance of stability in the program permitted concentration on effective training. Pilots who continued to linger while awaiting training would be provided light plane flight time and infantry training—both of which would later prove valuable in theater. The reduced flow of students made it possible to concentrate all Advanced training in Lubbock by mid-April 1943. By that time C-60s had taken over all the tow duties, allowing TCC elements to return to other tasks. When it was found that the C-60s could haul two CG-4As aloft, it was requested that double tows be added to the training. However, with so little time to do the other training, the Command demurred. The instruction continued to contain night, formation, and navigation training with a minimum 20 landings. Ground school was 105 hours with a good balance of military indoctrination, physical fitness, aircraft maintenance, and combat training thrown in. Many of the students also attended a 40-day (later 30 days) Technical Training Command glider mechanics course at nearby Sheppard Field, Texas.

Also in April 1943, plans were afoot to have the CAA train an additional 2,000 glider pilots in 1944, so 169 trainers and 274 L-planes were to be held onto. So, in July, all the TG-1/TG-1As and what were left of the requisitioned sport gliders were transferred to the CAA. However, nothing came of this.

Despite the change in training requirements, Lubbock still required 114 CG-4As but had only 90 due to continuing maintenance and logistical issues. Training with these precious few aircraft emphasized safety and "preservation of materiel." However, it was accepted that more tactical training had to be introduced to ensure the pilot were truly combat ready. Consequently, in August 1943, such activities as tactical landings, double towing of two Wacos, "snatching" a glider out of a short field by a passing tow plane (Chapter 7), contour cross-country (maximum 200 feet), landing over obstacles with minimum ground roll, landings on the fuselage skids, and instrument instruction in the Link were all emphasized. However, this content could only be inserted by going to 25 hours. This was approved in mid-August, but only provided the course still did not exceed a month and the graduation rate remained unchanged. The instructors finally felt satisfied with the capabilities of the pilots they were passing out of the program.

As the time for graduating the first glider pilots approached, the service had to face the discomfort felt by many traditionalists within the officer corps at the idea of enlisted personnel with "minimal" training piloting Army aircraft. Some of the men being awarded wings had as little as 46 hours of flight instruction, although the averaged later in the program was over 125 hours. As a compromise, the USAAF hit on the Flight Officer (FO) rank, established by law on 8 July 1942, with potential for promotion to 2nd Lieutenant. Similar to a present-day Warrant Officer, it was not quite a non-com and not quite an officer.[7] The FO rank emblem was 2nd Lieutenants bars with broad blue bands across the width. The benefit of the grade meant these men were not subject to the menial tasks of enlisted personnel nor the responsible for additional duties of a commissioned officer. Even the wings awarded at graduation were different; a "G" for "glider" superimposed on the center shield. Still, there were senior officers who felt the entire glider echelon scheme was misbegotten and a woeful squandering of resources. Resistance and antipathy was encountered throughout the war.

After a year of tumultuous effort, the first 20 glider pilots graduated the Advanced course at Stuttgart, Arkansas, on 23 November 1942. (This first group of pilots was commissioned upon graduation.) By 31 July 1943 the program had graduated 3,081 glider pilots. Another 1,000 were anticipated by the end of that year. On 21 August, the 1944 glider pilot requirement was set at 200 per month. This reflected continued production of combat gliders and growing appreciation of their potential role. New standards required that the trainees, still enlisted USAAF personnel, come in with power experience—such as CAA training or aviation cadet washouts—so that only the Advanced course was required.

Focus Shift

The U.S. Army eventually organized five airborne divisions, each with one glider infantry regiment, a glider artillery battalion, and other support elements transported via glider. (This was initially two regiments per division, as explained earlier, or 11 glider infantry regiments by late October 1943.) Troop Carrier Command was formed with the mission of paratroop transport, airdrop resupply, and glider tow. The transport fleet was quite small even in 1941 and had to grow by leaps and bounds to meet wartime demands. As with the gliders, transport aircraft had to be procured, aircrew trained, units formed, tactics developed, and exercises with gliders and airborne troops conducted to create a true combat potential. Their principal aircraft was the C-47 that served well, although lacking self-sealing fuel tanks, armor, or any defensive armament. The transport pilots new to the mission were given orientation flights in the copilot seat of the CG-4A. As C-47 production ramped up, the aircraft and crews (especially navigators) were in chronic short supply into 1944. The TCC was also frequently diverted to freight duties.

Operational training and tactics development were slow in coming up to speed. The mission was new and an unusual merging of Air Forces and ground combat missions that took time to coalesce. Its full maturity required combat experience and did not come without errors, the loss of good men, and destroyed aircraft.

Troop Carrier Command began receiving gliders in quantity during the first months of 1943, working toward a goal of 38 per squadron. However, it was still months before operational training came together. This was partially because the required skills were still being defined, but also because it required a new level of coordination and cooperation between ground and air elements. Airborne doctrine and tactics were still in their formative stages. Lack of aircraft had left training to little more than small unit activities. The TCC also felt the first groups of glider pilots were inadequately trained.[8] Considerable experimentation and establishment of safe practices were undertaken, although not always amicably, and with frequent changes in training content. Skeptics still had to be won over to the combat potential of the cargo glider.

Glider pilot training tapered off in 1944. But then the problem migrated to the Troup Carrier Groups which had to accommodate thousands of glider pilots while struggling with too few aircraft and too many freight missions. With 108 glider pilots per group, assigned faster than the resources were available to support them, the men were largely idle during this period. Maintaining glider pilot currency and just keeping these men occupied was a chore, with morale and proficiency suffering. (It would be 1945 before the USAAF established five landings per month as a minimal proficiency requirement for a glider pilot.) Local ground courses were devised, but there was no opportunity to log hours enough even to earn flight pay.

With lagging delivery of the CG-4A, early shortage of spares, and TCC initial focus on cargo and paratroop operations (not to mention a fuel shortage), work with glider was slow in coming up to speed. Airborne Command also had to devise tactics, advanced training courses, and mass exercises. Some TCC groups were deploying overseas without their glider echelon. Ostensibly, a group was then to be made up of four squadrons, each with 25 gliders and 50 pilots supported by 25 C-47s.[9]

One measure to address the glider pilot inactivity was creation in April 1943 of the Glider Pilot Combat Training Unit at Bowman Field, Kentucky. There comprehensive training was performed for men *en route* to their TCC assignments. Part of this included flying precision landings over an improvised 50-foot barrier—such as a wall of bamboo poles or a sheet stretched between posts—to a marked touchdown point a few hundred feet from the obstacle. The students also practiced "blitz landings" wherein the pilots approached especially fast (up to 100 mph), sometimes very low and hopping over obstructions, to get down expeditiously where field length or obstacles were not a great concern. However, a slow final approach over obstacles to a modest landing speed was favored, although an initial speedy descent was taught to avoid enemy ground fire. Instruction also sought to instill basic military skills and battlefield capabilities in addition to knowledge for combat employment of the CG-4A and liaison aircraft.

Many of the tactics and training curricula were devised by Major Mike Murphy, a highly experienced pre-war aviator who handled the CG-4A with notable finesse, to include aerobatics. In one demonstration for glider troops, with General Ridgeway aboard, commander of the 82nd Airborne Division, he did loops, slow rolls, and vertical banks, one loop ending with a landing that stopped within a few feet of a man positioned on the runway. Murphy's contribution and the tactical training went far in instilling glider pilot confidence in the Waco.

The first mass maneuvers were on 30-31 October 1942, flying resupply missions for the Second Division at Stinson Field, San Antonio, to Del Rio, Texas. A more realistic

Mike Murphy (left) became a crack glider pilot and instructor, helping to overcome bad impressions of the CG-4A. A prewar stunt pilot, he handled the Waco with amazing skill, demonstrating its handling and ruggedness. Here as a Major at Bowman Field, Kentucky, Murphy rose to the rank of Lieutenant Colonel and was among the first to land in Normandy, where he was seriously injured. (National Archives)

Diverting airplanes suitable as tugs to glider training, or periodically detailing a transport squadron to the task, became challenging. In this image Lockheed A-28 and A-29 Hudson light bombers are being employed for the task. Training of tow pilots was almost as crucial as glider pilots. (San Diego Air & Space Museum)

tactical exercise was during the week of 23 May 1943 with the 101st Airborne Division near Kershaw, South Carolina. The gliders landed infantry, combat engineers, and field artillery. With these demonstrations of glider capabilities in 1943 also came three bits of very bad news. In early June a glider crash during an exercise in Tennessee had seriously injured Major General William C. Lee, commander of the 101st Airborne Division and caused the deaths of two other men. The near disaster of the Sicily airborne operation in early July (see Chapter 10) was a severe blow. More evident was the much-publicized 1 August fatal CG-4A crash in St. Louis. Intense training during July 1943 at Laurinburg-Maxton culminated in a demonstration to brass and press on 4 August that went far in restoring confidence. Participants in the maneuvers formed a core of highly proficient aircrew who documented what had been improvised and learned, and returned to their units to pass along their experience.

Eventually, squadron training and large-scale maneuvers provided insight as to gaps in glider pilot knowledge and skills to be enforced. Those participating in exercises went back to their units and, along with field manuals that began to appear in 1943, helped guide more practical training. This process continued after units deployed and training progressed overseas, especially in concert with British airborne forces. As initial combat experience was evaluated and airborne tactics evolved, refinements to the CG-4A were introduced and new techniques taught, these instilled through continuing training and exercises. At the end of 1944 the Advanced Glider Training Base was established at Raleigh-Durham, North Carolina, where in 30 days the students were given intensive training simulating combat conditions in maneuvers. Moving from there to their assigned TCC organizations, the glider pilots would participate in further airborne training and maneuvers prior to the unit deploying overseas.

Much remained to be done in development of more effective tactics, and this came during training overseas and from combat experience. Combat operations in Europe, particularly the Normandy invasion and Holland assaults, illustrated how vital gliders were to airborne operations as part of a major offensive. Consequently, fall 1944 saw a final surge in glider orders. Most of the combat operations had been performed without copilots because many glider pilots were held in reserve for other potential short-notice assaults. This meant that one of the glidermen had to take the seat and be talked through how to fly and land the aircraft should the pilot be incapacitated by hostile fire—the

This aerial photograph shows Laurinburg-Maxton Army Air Base during the war. The North Carolina locale was the major base for airborne forces glider training and 'finishing school' for combat glider pilots. Note the liberal number of CG-4As and C-47 airplanes scattered about the installation. (National Soaring Museum)

An improvised 'bulls-eye' mowed into a field at Laurinburg-Maxton AAB served as a spot landing aid for CG-4A student pilots. The Waco proved relatively simple to fly and so this became the focus of training once the gliders became available. Spot landing and short roll-out was a vital skill developed during this phase of training. (National Soaring Museum)

success of which was generally considered wishful thinking or self-delusion. These factors raised the suggestion there were not enough glider pilots.

To meet the late requirement, the Air Forces returned to the original intent of the training program; diverting power pilot course graduates. By this time the U.S. had a surplus of newly minted airplane pilots and so could send many off for a quick glider conversion. Practice had shown that fully trained power pilots could fly the Waco proficiently after a few hours of instruction, whereas many glider pilots did not measure up this level even after passing through their entire program.[10] Additionally, they had more utility in TCC units by flying C-47s.[11] As early as June 1944, recently graduated fighter pilots were diverted to Laurinburg-Maxton after volunteering for a "special secret mission." Bomber pilots, proficient in instrument flying, followed.[12] Seventy grumbling, non-volunteer pilots were sent to Lubbock in October 1944 under Operation *Red* for two weeks training on the CG-4A. Some were given less than 10 hours flying and approximately 30 landings, before being shipped to Europe. An experiment also showed that conversion training within the TCC groups was sufficient for such men. Individual training in ATC was eliminated.[13] Subsequently, during 1945, hundreds more 8th Air Force pilots underwent conversion in-theater. These men participated in the 24 March 1945 crossing of the Rhine River that was the last large-scale glider assault in history.

Glidermen practice rapid egress from the CG-4A during a training exercise. Curiously, they are using the triangular escape hatches rather than the usual sided door. In the background an ammunition trailer is being unloaded from a glider. (National Soaring Museum)

Navy/Marines Training

As with the Army, civilian schools were engaged initially to provide introduction to glider flying for a core cadre of Navy and Marine personnel serving later in leadership and instructor roles. Lieutenant Eschol M. Mallory, USMC, was assigned to locate the interim schools. Although he felt only fully trained airplane pilots should fly the Marine's combat gliders, a view shared by Major Wehle, it was clear to their superiors that there would not be enough such men to spare for this duty. Consequently, the USMC moved in late July 1941 to recruit, within the next year, 50 officers through the grade of Captain for training as pilots and 100 noncoms to serve as copilots. Within two days the volunteers had come forward. Although thought was given to approaching Congress to establish a glider pilot rating "for officers and men as otherwise such personnel will be subject to restrictions applying to regular aviators," no such action appears to have been pursued.[14]

Beginning in November 1941, four marine pilots, including Lieutenant Colonel Vernon M. Guymon, attended the Motorless Flight Institute in Harvey, Illinois, under the oversight of Joe Stainhauser with instruction on Schweizer SGS 2-8s and Cinemas. Emphasis was on tow, cross-country flight, and landings in unfamiliar fields. In about four weeks and about $500.00 per student, these men each logged approximately 30 hours with half winch or auto tows, and half aero-tow. Eight other pilots underwent nine weeks of glider indoctrination for $775.00 each at the Lewis School of Aeronautics in Lockport, Illinois. Run by sailplane designer Stan Corcoran, the course principally employed his Cinema IIB. Other officers followed and the schools were eventually equipped with Navy-produced gliders. Service schools eventually assumed the entire training responsibility.

Following the basic instruction on sport gliders, personnel transitioned to Marine Base Parris Island, South Carolina, for advanced training. All assets were to be in place by 10 January 1942. On the 15th, the unit was designated simply the Glider Detachment and comprised 10 officers and 17 men of an authorized 14 and 56, respectively. As purpose-built sailplanes became available beginning in mid-March 1942, training and proficiency flying on LNE-1s and LNS-1s began while awaiting the combat gliders. Flying was conducted in the vicinity of Camp Lejeune and New River, and north to Cherry Point, all in North Carolina.

A formalized structure was established on 24 April as Marine Glider Group 71 (MLG-71), with Guymon as CO and authorizations for 20 or 26 officers and 218 enlisted members.[15] On 1 May was added the Marine Glider Squadron 711 (VML-711), initially commanded by then Major Mallory but Captain Barnette Robinson took over from 8 February 1943. With this reorganization came the move to Marine Corps Air Station (MCAS) Parris Island, away from powered aircraft and barrage balloon operations. The

In a less-than-realistic exercise, pilots and glidermen sprint for their aircraft at Stuttgart, Arkansas. Gliders were initially a classified development within the Army Air Forces. However, this was lifted in the interest of easing impediments to the work and so press events like this were possible. (National Museum of the United States Air Force)

Lieutenant Colonel Vernon Guymon, USMC, instructs a clutch of his student glider pilots at Parris Island, South Carolina, during May 1942. Guymon commanded Marine Glider Group 71 (MLG-71) from its formation on 24 April and through its move to Eagle Mountain Lake, Texas, where they continued to train on sailplanes while awaiting the naval transport gliders. (National Archives)

Marines also acquired for proficiency and towing a trio of Naval Aircraft Factory N3N-3 "Yellow Peril" biplanes, a North American SNJ-2, one Grumman J2F-3 Duck, a single Bellanca JE-1 Pacemaker, and even the rare NAF XN5N-1.

A Commander E.F. McDonald devised a wind generator to permit new glider pilots to gain some flight experience without achieving free-flight. An 85-horsepower Ford motor drove a 7-foot propeller, the airflow passing through a panel of stovepipe assembled like a honeycomb to straighten the flow. A glider on the far side of the panel could "fly" on short tethers just downstream. Employed at the Lewis School during September 1941, its bumps and gyrations were judged of little value and the device was set aside.[16] The Navy also acquired a Gar Wood truck-mounted winch for ground launch. The device was delivered to the NAF in February 1943 by which time it was of little use and may never have reached VML-711.

Guymon began to feel, as the Army did and Major Wehle had observed in Britain, that sailplanes were of little training value, although the promised combat gliders remained on the horizon. This view was officially enunciated in January 1943. Consequently, production of the LNE-1 was cutback. The Army's 3-place gliders had more representative flight characteristics and so were more suitable for transport glider pilot training. Seven more XLNT-1s were procured during the first half of 1943. Although

Marines prepare to launch a trio of LNS-1 trainers at Marine Base Paris Island in May 1942. These Schweizers were the same as the Army TG-2s and served until the Navy-developed LNE-1s arrived. The marine glider pilot training took much the same course as the Army program, but lack of amphibious models held them back. (National Archives)

A truck-mounted tow winch was developed by the Navy for ground launching of gliders, but was of little value by the time it was delivered in February 1943. The Gar Wood winch had actually begun as an Army contract that the Navy joined, but the USN carried on the effort after the other service withdrew when delivery fell far behind schedule. (National Soaring Museum)

The Pratt, Read LNE-1 played little role in the USMC glider training because its production was so late and drawn-out. The vast majority were simply stored after completion and then passed to the Army to be sold after the war. This is a shame as it was a fine ship. (The Peter M. Bowers Collection/The Museum of Flight)

This remarkable image shows the Navy's PBY-5 flying boat preparing to tow a CG-4A aloft. The service managed to coax 13 Wacos away from the Army to support USMC training while awaiting its own gliders. Labeled LRW-1s, the Marines reportedly never flew them. (National Soaring Museum)

the Army had found that light planes were the most efficient training resource, shutting the engine down for deadstick landings, the Marines appear never to have reached this conclusion or acted on it.

In the meantime, the USMC sought a more suitable and permanent location for Guymon's unusual unit. They finally moved to a new base at Eagle Mountain Lake, Fort Worth, Texas, on 21-24 November 1942 (commissioned 1 December). This was to have one auxiliary air field and a seaplane base. The outfit eventually achieved strength of 36 officers and 246 enlisted personnel operating 21 gliders. (This last number suggests that, while awaiting the full complement of pilots, most of the LNE-1s were stored and never flown.)

On 1 January 1943, 120 Student Naval Aviation Pilots (Glider) were undertaking instruction with the Civilian Pilot Training Program and destined for Glider Group 71. This was to continue at a pace of 60 men per month for 15.5 months, contributing to a projected total 1,534 Naval Aviator Pilots (Glider).[17] They were to be supported by 20,000 enlisted personnel, some serving as copilots. Some 4,952 tow pilots were also anticipated.[18] Two other training sites were contemplated for when the program grew to its full dimensions. Identified were Edenton, North Carolina, Shawnee, Oklahoma, plus Titusville and Addison Point, both in Florida. Construction began at all but the Florida locations, but only Eagle Mountain actually saw glider operations.

The Army passed 13 of its Waco 15-place CG-4As transport gliders to the Navy in the first half of 1943.[19] The USN redesignated those LRW-1s (R for cargo transport). This was just as these aircraft were first coming off the production lines and so particularly precious. The USMC reportedly never flew the 10 handed to them.[20] The Navy performed some evaluations with their trio, towed by an NAF-operated PBY-5A Catalina the locals fondly called *Tugboat Annie* (08065). The 300-400-foot nylon towline was attached as a bridle; an attachment to both sides of the fuselage beneath the wing aft strut attach fittings (possibly existing tiedown rings) and meeting to one line aft of the aircraft. Following release, the towline would be "hauled" or "reeled" into the "Cat" after glider release via one of the side blisters. The aircraft was also seen with a single line attached under the aft fuselage.

4

Initial Army Cargo Gliders

With Arnold fuming at delays, all four companies expressing an interest in manufacturing transport gliders for the War Department were placed on contract. Of these, three had previously built sailplanes or light airplanes in very small quantities and their manufacturing capabilities could, at best, be considered "boutique." Only Waco had built substantial airplanes in quantity and so had a well-established manufacturing capability with sizable design and production staff. However, the proposed wooden gliders and incredibly short timeline with tight budget would be a challenge even for them.

That some of the initial glider contractors failed to deliver suitable designs and hardware is not surprising. Even when successful, the evolving Army requirements led to major changes. The 8-place Waco XCG-3 was ordered as the 9-place CG-3A, but almost immediately found to be not in concert with evolving operational concepts. The order for hundreds was reduced to one hundred gliders that were relegated to training and soon after the bone yard. The 15-place Waco XCG-4 was well along when the decision was made to alter it to new requirements. In May 1942, the CG-4A was selected after brief testing and placed into immediate mass production. This glider quickly became the center of focus, with manufacturers all across the country rushing to setup production lines and deliver aircraft as quickly as possible. Some of the immature firms struggled with

This sight of glider wings (CG-4A) under manufacturing was long in being realized. Getting the materials flow established, training workers in the skills of laminated wood construction, and just developing suitable designs from small companies was extremely challenging. Only a few of the projects set in motion saw a flying glider, and fewer still of those entered production. (National Museum of the United States Air Force)

the production process while the vendors supplying parts were an even more diverse bunch. Conformance to drawings and specifications became impossible to enforce, and secondary to high production rate.

Frankfort Sailplane XCG-1 & XCG-2

Frankfort Sailplane Company (later the Aircraft Division of the Globe Corporation) offered designs against the Army's 8-place and 15-place requirements. Although these were designs far beyond the TG-1 trainer they were on contract to build, and of a type for which they had no prior experience, the government decided to proceed with these aircraft. During meetings in March and April 1942 at Wright Field the firm had also argued for a cost-plus-fixed-fee contract, but this was strenuously resisted by Dent. Frankfort then proposed doing the job for $130,000.00, but settled for $95,000.00 fixed-price after Dent stated there was only $300,000.00 for the entire 8- and 15-place experimental glider acquisition and this had to be spread amongst several companies for three or four different designs.[1]

The contract was issued on 7 May 1941 for what were designated the XCG-1 and XCG-2, the XCG-2 clearly a scale-up of the same basic design. The $21,000.00 XCG-1 document called for a wind tunnel model, a static test article, and flight test aircraft with trailer. The glider was to be delivered on 11 October 1941. The $26,000.00 XCG-2 contract did not specify a tunnel model and had a delivery date of 12 November 1941.[2]

The gliders were to have a single pilot but with provisions for dual controls. One trooper would sit beside the pilot while the rest occupied three rows of side-by-side seats for the XCG-1. The XCG-2 had six twin rows and a single seat behind the last pair, the fuselage being the same 3.5 feet width for each model. The aircraft would also feature spoilers and jettisonable undercarriage. The forward fuselage structure was welded steel tubing with fabric but all wood over the rear. The wing would be wood with plywood over the D-section and fabric covering behind. Control surfaces were wood and fabric. The manner of ingress and egress is unclear from available documentation.

Static loads ground tests of the bare airframe consists of pushing, pulling, and twisting the structure with forces representative of those to be experienced during ground operation, on tow, in free flight, and landing. Aircraft structures are normally required to carry 150 percent of these predicted design limit loads. For aircraft with so much wood for primary structure as the planned transport gliders, Materiel Division was very strict in verifying satisfactory design and construction.

Frankfort was a small company with facilities already saturated with construction of the TG-1s. As such, work on the larger models progressed slowly. Finally, the XCG-1 static test airframe arrived at Wright Field on 27 December 1941, but displayed poor workmanship and inferior design.[3] Not unexpectedly, it failed on 7 January 1943 at just 63 percent of the design limit load. An effort was also made in early 1942 to introduce the changes in the XCG-2 adopted in the CG-4A to carry a jeep (Chapter 5), but this proved impossible given the distressed state of the project.[4] In light of these issues compared with success on the TG-1 contract, manufacturing capacity, and good performance by other firms against the glider requirements, it was felt best to cancel both the XCG-1 and XCG-2 contracts. This was done on 31 March 1942 after having expended $30,478.85.

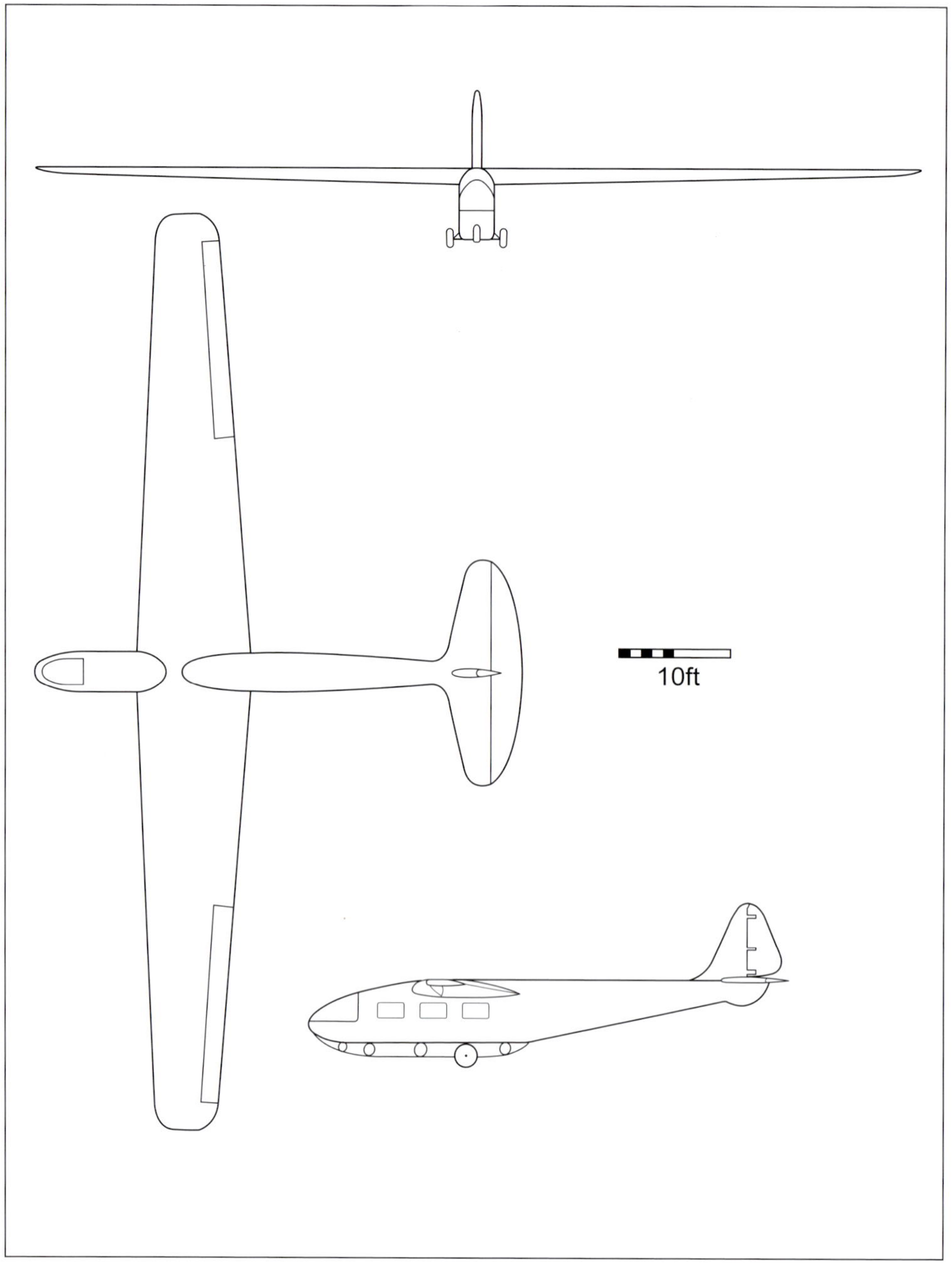

This 3-view of the XCG-1 reveals an aircraft clearly derived from the commercial glider design experience of Frankfort Sailplane Company. The simple drawing that served as the basis for the illustration had no evidence of spoilers or side doors. The cantilevered wing and centerline skid is unusual. (Author)

The XCG-1 static test article is seen rigged for loading at Wright Field. Curiously, there appears to be five rows of seats visible in the tube-frame assembly whereas the glider was to have just three rows aft of the pilots. The Frankfort airframe failed the test. (National Archives)

Table 04-01	
Frankfort Sailplane XCG-1 Specifics (estimated, not flown)	
span	85 ft
wing area	725 ft^2
fuselage length	43.5 ft
empty weight	1,600 lbs
maximum weight	3,600 lbs
tow speed	120 mph
capacity	1 pilot, 7 troops

Table 04-02	
Frankfort Sailplane XCG-2 Specifics (estimated, not built)	
span	115 ft
wing area	1322 ft^2
fuselage length	56 ft
empty weight	2,700 lbs
maximum weight	6,500 lbs
tow speed	120 mph
capacity	1 pilot, 14 troops

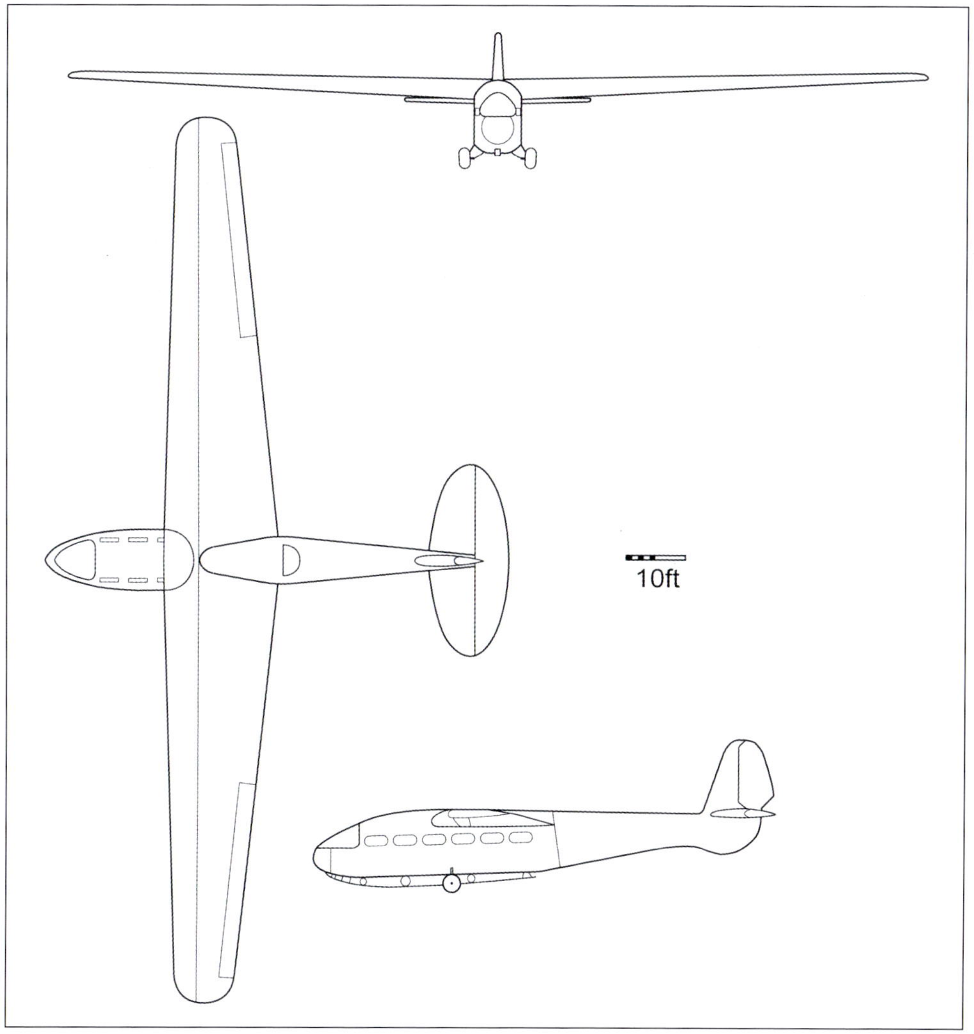

An obvious growth of the 8-place XCG-1, the Frankfort XCG-2 is unusual in carrying the sailplane features into a 15-place, 6,500-pound aircraft. Efforts during design to adopt it to carrying a jeep were not encouraging. This failure of the XCG-1 static test, and success of the XCG-4, led to contract cancellation. (Author)

Waco XCG-3 & CG-3A

Of all the companies to take on glider design and construction for the U.S. Army, Waco Aircraft Company of Troy, Ohio, was the best placed. (This was the brand name for what was originally the Weaver Aircraft Company and also seen frequently as WACO.) At the time, it was the oldest aircraft manufacturer in the country and had built a line of very worthy civil training and touring aircraft. Although new to the glider business, its other experience counted for much. Waco would become the origin for all of the USAAF's operational combat gliders produced during the war. However, their proposal for the 2-place training gliders was rejected because their cost and schedule estimates were not competitive compared with the sailplane companies.[5]

Waco responded almost immediately to the Army's queries regarding 8-place and 15-place gliders. Negotiations were nearly continuous from 11 March until award of a single $178,700.00 fixed-price contract was awarded on 5 June 1941 covering development of both the XCG-3 and XCG-4 (the XCG-3 prototype alone valued at $45,000.00). As with all such agreements, the company was to build static test airframes for government evaluation as well as a flight test aircraft of each design, with trailers.

The XCG-3 had a delivery date of 1 December 1941 and, although coming together quickly, was late. The wind tunnel testing began within a few weeks of winning the contract and was completed in September. The static test article was delivered to Dayton on 26 December. This testing ran long, through 1 May, because of a wing spar failure.[6] It passed with some modifications. The flight test prototype followed on 31 January with first flight on 3 February 1942.[7] All this progress was well ahead of the other contractors. The XCG-3 set the standard in appearance for American military gliders; brutish and ugly. It shared much in common with the CG-4A in construction techniques and general configuration. This was intentional, with the same design work applied to both the 8 and 15 seat machines—a theme followed by most of the competing companies.

Table 04-03	
Waco Aircraft XCG-3 Specifics	
span	80.5 ft
wing area	810 ft²
fuselage length	46.3 ft
empty weight	1,614 lbs
maximum weight	3,534 lbs
tow speed	120 mph
capacity	1 pilot, 7 troops

The XCG-3's lines were simple, with straight tail surfaces and high-set wing supported by external struts, boxy facets for the fuselage, and landing gear placing the fuselage low to the ground for easy egress of troops. The aircraft had what became typical equipment for such cargo gliders; spoilers, provisions for dual controls, bottom skids, and two-wheel undercarriage. The undercarriage was either fixed (training) or jettisonable (operational) for landing on the plywood skid under the keel. The interior was spartan and cramped, but could accommodate seven fully equipped troops and pilot. There were four rows of two seats, with the pilot occupying the forward left station. The wing was wood structure which plywood covering the D-section and fabric behind. The fuselage was welded steel tubing with wood stringers and fabric over all. Control surfaces were wood and fabric. It is curious that the Army permitted the use of steel tubing as the principal load-bearing structure of the CG-3 and CG-4 fuselages, plus many of the other 8- and 15-place designs, since the direction had been to employ wood to the greatest extent possible. However, it had early been determined that supply of steel tubing need not be limited if suitable priority was assigned, and this appears to have been done.[8] Interestingly, the prototype included dual controls and a full suite of flight instruments, including gyros.

The Army's rapid evaluation progressed to a favorable report in early February with suggested improvements. These were tested and documented in a 6 April report with recommendation for production. Final value was $256,391.20 for the original XCG-3/4 contract, with $59,500.00 represented by the XCG-3.[9] The USAAF promptly placed an order for what was redesignated the CG-3A.

The major change from the XCG-3 to CG-3A was in the method of emplaning and egressing. In the original design the canopy would be swung aside and the men step on the seats then crossbars and port side canopy sill longeron before leaping to the ground. Leaving through the doors should be less cumbersome and potentially quicker. The revised design had adjoining doors in both sides of the forward fuselage, plus a trio of

The Waco XCG-3 was the first American cargo glider to see the light of day, but was a baby only a mother could love. Its simple and utilitarian design set the standard for what was to follow. An over-the-side egress for combat was quickly seen as hazardous, exposing the cluster of troops to enemy fire. (National Archives)

The pilot station of the XCG-3 is interesting in revealing the welded steel tube fuselage construction Waco employed instead of the wood that had been the Army's objective from the outset of the glider program. However, using a steel bar as a backrest for the pilots appears a doubtful choice, although it was a vital step for the glidermen in quickly exiting the glider over the side. Inclusion of gyroscopic instruments like the attitude indicator and turn rate indicator reflected early thoughts the gliders would be operated at night and in weather. (National Museum of the United States Air Force)

Much effort was expended on the Waco CG-3. The CG-3A reflected changes requested by the Air Corps, to include a revised forward fuselage with side doors for easier onloading and offload. This example appears to have retained the droppable undercarriage with cross axle. (National Soaring Museum)

Only 100 CG-3As were manufactured, these by Commonwealth Aircraft and seating nine. This example lacks the cross axle and so the undercarriage appears to have been fixed. It was destroyed at CCAAF on 17 July 1944 during a severe storm but provides a close look at some of the aircraft's features. (National Archives)

Table 04-04	
Waco Aircraft CG-3A Specifics	
span	73.1 ft
wing area	740.4 ft^2
fuselage length	43.3 ft
height	7.2 ft
empty weight	2,044 lbs
maximum weight	4,400 lbs
tow speed	100 mph
maximum towing speed	120 mph 132 mph at ≤3,200 lbs
landing speed	42 mph
capacity	1 pilot, 8 troops
glide ratio	14:1

footholds beneath, and three emergency exits along the sides to the trailing edge of the wing. The changes to accommodate an eighth trooper, exclusive of the pilot, reflected the desire of the airborne forces that was stated in fall 1941 that such was the minimum practical size glider from their perspective. For production, cockpit instruments were reduced to minimal essentials, although still with a gyro horizon.

Waco's 10 March 1942, $3,905,200 contract for 200 CG-3As was the first for production tactical gliders in the United States. A 23 April production order for 100 machines, to be delivered through December, was also placed with Rearwin Aircraft and Engines, Incorporated of Kansas City, Kansas, (renamed Commonwealth Aircraft Incorporated on 7 January 1943). The USAAF quickly reconsidered Waco's priorities and converted the contract on 14 July 1942 to an order for 500 CG-4As. Rearwin's obligation increased by 200 on the 19 June at $5,895,130.50.

In this period, the War Department was planning to buy 1,063 CG-3s. However, by the time the Army accepted its first example on 26 November, the service had decided to focus on the 15-place CG-4A as its standard combat glider. The CG-3A could carry little more than the soldiers with their immediate personal kit. Even a machine gun or mortar with ammunition boxes could not be accommodated. Field experience suggested the CG-4A would be a much more practical combat mount and it was desirable to focus on a single type. On 6 November 1942, Rearwin/Commonwealth's CG-3A contract was terminated at 100 units, all coming between 15 November 1942 and 15 April 1943 for $2,791,110.01 (with a $443,379.00 overrun).

The CG-3As went to several training sites across the country for advanced pilot training and troop exercises. Eventually, this training role was supplanted by the CG-4A, and the CG-3As disappeared.

St. Louis Aircraft XCG-5 & XCG-6

Table 04-05	
St. Louis Aircraft XCG-5 Specifics	
span	89.2 ft
wing area	1,015 ft^2
fuselage length	64.6 ft
empty weight	2,310 lbs
loaded weight	4,230 lbs
tow speed	120 mph
stall speed	30 mph
capacity	1 pilot, 7 troops
glide ratio	15:1

Table 04-06	
St. Louis Aircraft XCG-6 Specifics (estimated, not built)	
span	126.5 ft
wing area	2,030 ft^2
fuselage length	76.4 ft
empty weight	3,700 lbs
loaded weight	7,500 lbs
tow speed	120 mph
capacity	1 pilot, 14 troops

St. Louis Aircraft Corporation of St. Louis, Missouri, (a subsidiary of the St. Louis Car Company) had previously manufactured the Cardinal C2 cabin-class monoplane and PT-1W biplane trainer. It, too, competed for the 8- and 15-place glider with a 15 May 1941 proposal. This resulted in a 22 May letter contract and 21 June 1941 formal document, the firm receiving a $146,402.00 obligation for both designs. The 8-seat XCG-5 was to be presented as a wind tunnel model, static test article, and flight example with trailer. It was the same for the 15-place XCG-6 but without the tunnel model. The XCG-5 was individually valued at $30,664.00 while the XCG-6 was $42,160.00.

The XCG-5 had the lines of a performance sailplane, although with enclosed cockpit and cabin. It sported a gull wing with external struts and sharply-tapering fuselage to a narrow section at the tail. There were twin doors on both sides of the forward fuselage with welded-rod step beneath the forward doors. The XCG-6 was to have been similar, albeit larger. The XCG-5 was equipped with upper-surface wing spoilers and also credited with ventilated spoiler flaps (no high-lift flaps), although the latter is not evident in photographs. There was a wooden skid plus droppable wheeled undercarriage. The wooden wing had plywood covering the D-section and fabric aft of the spar. The fuselage and fin was welded steel tubing with wood stringers and fabric covering. The horizontal stabilizer, elevators, and rudder were wood with plywood surface. Ailerons were presumably wood and fabric. With provisions for dual controls, there were two pilot stations at the front and two rows of three seats behind.[10] The XCG-6 was to have two seats in the front including the pilot, two rows of four behind, followed by a three-seat row and then two seats at the rear.

The XCG-5 model was received on 3 September 1941 and the wind tunnel work concluded on the 11th. The static test article delivery slipped from 15 October 1941 to the end of January 1942, and finally arrived on 22 February. It showed evidence of poor workmanship, and when testing commenced on 5 March the wing soon broke dramatically at 90 percent load. The fuselage also suffered repeated failures. Efforts at redesign, modification, and retest continued through the end of the year, but ultimately some issues remained. The wings also came in 430 pounds over-weight and so the specification was altered accordingly. The original specification for the XCG-5 gave an empty weight of 1,880 pounds and gross 3,800, but final values are as shown in the table.

In light of St. Louis' poor performance to that time and apparent success of the XCG-3 and XCG-4, the USAAF advised the firm on 24 January 1942 that the XCG-6 effort would be cancelled if all contracted materials were not delivered by 1 June. On 9 February the company admitted it did not have the engineering staff to undertake

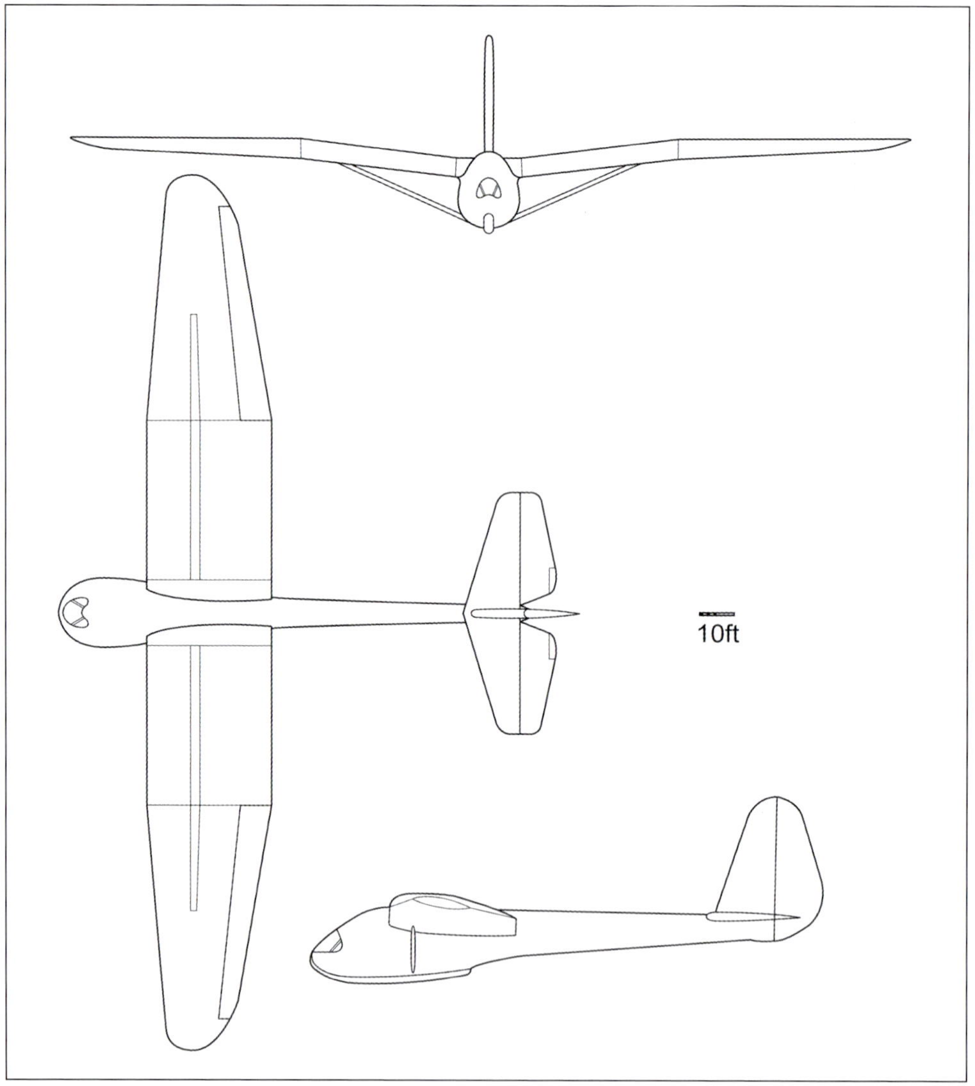

A 15-place XCG-6 was a counterpart to the XCG-5, reflecting the same general design layout but with all dimensions expanded (span 126.5 feet compared with the XCG-5's 89.2). The contractor, St, Louis Aircraft, had run well behind schedule and their XCG-6 could not be easily adopted to carry a jeep. Passed-up by Waco and their very successful XCG-4 glider, the XCG-6 was cancelled before substantial development progress had been made. (Author)

both projects within even adjusted contract terms and asked to be released from that obligation. By this time the XCG-4 was showing great promise, so it was clear St. Louis would not be receiving a production contract. Additionally, in early 1942 efforts were made to introduce changes to the XCG-6 like those adapted for the XCG-4 to accommodate a jeep. This was unsuccessful given the distressed state of the project and St. Louis' financial condition.[11] Consequently, work on the XCG-6 was halted in April with no substantial construction having been accomplished.

St. Louis Aircraft built the eight-seat XCG-5 along the lines of a sport sailplane, including gull wing. The single centerline skid and externally braces flying surfaces was typical of these glider designs. The XCG-5's wooden structure failed to pass muster and it was never flown. (National Soaring Museum)

It was hoped the XCG-5 could serve to investigate the effect of light wing loading on flight and handling characteristics, so the prototype effort proceeded. The flight test machine first flew in St. Louis on 3 October 1942. It was delivered on 4 November and accepted on 15 December, compared with a contracted 15 November 1941 and slip to 15 March 1942. Flying was delayed awaiting flutter analysis, inspection, weight and balance, and suitable towing facilities. When it was taken up on 26 March 1943 the glider proved most unsatisfactory.[12] The testers found the machine so difficult to balance properly that substantial modifications were indicated before it would be a practical operational machine.

The contract was cancelled on 1 September 1943 with St. Louis in default and $53,028.80 expended. The poor state of the XCG-5 was cause for he Army to assess it at 70 percent of the contract value. This one airframe was subsequently passed to the National Bureau of Standard's High Voltage Laboratory to test means of protecting aircraft from the effects of lightning strikes.

Bowlus Sailplane XCG-7 & XCG-8

Bowlus Sailplanes Company, Incorporated, of San Francisco, California, had a reputation for developing and producing fine sport gliders. They responded almost immediately to the Army's call for transport gliders. After March 1941 discussions, their 29 April proposals for 8- and 15-seat models were prepared with the assistance of Douglas Airplane Company, Incorporated.[13] William H. Bowlus, his company's principal designer and president, was friendly with Donald Douglas and sought the assistance of his company. Their estimate of $480,000.00 and matching schedule were well beyond those acceptable to the Army. By making the gliders essentially identical except for scale and length of cabin, the time and cost of design was cut and the bid revised to $267,050.00.

The 22 June letter contract and 29 July formal document was awarded on a fixed-price basis with $51,264.00 allotted for the XCG-7 and $132,484.00 for the 15-place XCG-8. An XCG-7 wind tunnel model (none required for the XCG-8 because of similarity), static test article of both gliders, and one flight article of each was stipulated. The XCG-7 was to be delivered on 30 December 1941 and its companion on 2 March of the following year. The gliders were to be broken down for shipment and trailers for the three large components of each were also procured.

Both Bowlus gliders had a podded cabin with a boom aft fuselage back to a simple cruciform tail. Only the length of the cabin and wing planform dimensions differentiated the two designs, cabin width remaining the same at 6.0 feet. Primary structure was spruce and birch, the cantilever wing surfaces with plywood forward of the spar and fabric aft while the fuselage was entirely wrapped in plywood. Stabilizers had plywood covering

The Bowlus Sailplanes XCG-7 was another answer to the eight-place cargo glider requirement, seen here during testing on a California dry lakebed in 1942. Developed by noted glider luminary Hawley Bowlus, the prototype was built by Douglas Aircraft. The keel of the glider appears to have been intended as the landing skid. (The Peter M. Bowers Collection/The Museum of Flight)

while movable surfaces used fabric. The wing was to feature a laminar flow airfoil for low drag and slotted flaps instead of spoilers.[14] Both models were to have provisions for dual controls and droppable alighting gear. The narrow fuselages had the pilots in tandem seating—unique among American combat gliders. The lines of the aircraft were very clean and attractive. Both lacked bottom skids, presumably the keel being considered sufficient for the single-mission aircraft. However, both were later fitted with centerline skids in Ohio. Some sources claim the XCG-7 had a single pilot and nine seats (two benches extending the length of the cabin)—eight instead of seven troops. The aircraft had troop doors on both sides of the fuselage forward of the wing. The XCG-7 could be disassembled into three components for transport. The design promised to be of low drag, potentially easing what was shaping up to be a challenging engine power and overheating issue for C-47 tugs.

The wind tunnel model was shipped on 19 November 1941. Construction of the large gliders in Bowlus' existing workspace was impossible. The intent was for firms in the Midwest to assemble the production aircraft, but some near-term expedient had to be found for construction of the prototypes. Although glider work was not supposed to be undertaken by such large firms as Douglas, already saturated with urgent War Department assignments, the company agreed to help. They performed design and wind tunnel testing for Bowlus and assembled the test article for both models at their El Segundo facilities with designer Ed Heinemann overseeing the effort. This subcontract work exceeded $500,000.00 and fell 6-12 months behind schedule. With assembly and flight testing in southern California, the center of Bowlus' activity moved to San Fernando, near Los Angeles.

Table 04-07	
Bowlus Sailplanes XCG-7 Specifics	
span	65.0 ft
wing area	700 ft^2
length	53.3 ft
empty weight	2,870 lbs
loaded weight	4,800 lbs
tow speed	120 mph sea level
capacity	1 pilot, 8 troops
glide ratio	17.7:1

Arrival of the XCG-7 static test airframe at Wright Field was on 11 February 1942, but the trials were soon halted due to structural failures. Repairs by Bowlus were prolonged, and the testing did not resume until 16 June. The airframe broke again that month under simulated towing loads of just 40 percent, and the contractor was compelled to build a new tail boom. The tests were concluded on 19 September with several deficiencies outstanding.

Despite the structural issues, a Bowlus team conducted five flights on the XCG-7 on 15-16 July 1942. After first flight from El Segundo that included Major Barringer as pilot,[15] most testing was performed at Twenty-Nine Palms. Service personnel inspected and flew the glider on 19-22 October at Muroc AAB (Rogers Dry Lake) in California's Mojave Desert. Flying continued into early 1943 and it made its way to Wright

The XCG-7 is shown under tow with its droppable undercarriage. The sleek, wooden fuselage was so narrow that the pilots were seated in tandem, but the glider still seated nine in total. Although aerodynamically sound, the structure proved difficult to bring up to requirements and so the project fell so far behind schedule as to become superfluous. (San Diego Air & Space Museum)

Table 04-08	
Bowlus Sailplanes XCG-8 Specifics	
span	85.4 ft
wing area	996 ft^2
length	61.0 ft
empty weight	3,895 lbs
loaded weight	6,800 lbs
tow speed	120 mph
stall speed	38.9 mph flaps up, 31.2 mph flaps down
capacity	1 pilot, 14 troops
glide ratio	20.3:1

The Bowlus XCG-8 grew from the XCG-7 design with greater wingspan and longer fuselage to accommodate 15 troops. Also built by Douglas, it was flown in the California desert before being shipped east. The overweight glider had a brief flight test career before it was smashed in a wind storm at Wilmington. (San Diego Air & Space Museum)

Field. The glider reportedly handled well and was even kept aloft in a thermal, but was well over the specified weight.

The XCG-8 was a scaled-up XCG-7 with modifications introduced to correct the anticipated structural deficiencies revealed by test of the former. However, XCG-8 static article (wings delivered 1 June 1942, the rest on 16 October) also failed its test when completed on 18 December. With failures as low as 35 percent design limit load, the glider was restricted in gross weight (GW) and airspeed. Awaiting decisions and actions on structural modifications, the delivery date for the flight article was slipped. Thoughts of altering the design to accommodate a jeep, as had been done with the XCG-4, were dropped given the late date and likely great added cost.[16]

During testing of the XCG-7 in October, USAAF personnel took the opportunity to inspect its sibling under construction. Like its sister design, the aircraft was flown from a dry lakebed in the desert. The Army flew it on 29 March-1 April 1943 at Mines Field, El Segundo, but it was also overweight. The aircraft was trailered and arrived at Wright Field on 17 May and eventually made its way to Wilmington.

With growing loss of confidence in Bowlus Sailplane and commitment to the CG-4A, further development was not pursued for either design. When the contract was closed out in August 1943, fully $233,929.00 had been expended on the work that yielded nothing of military value. That the effort was permitted to run so long and to such expense was a tribute to Bowlus' promotional abilities and infectious enthusiasm. Like the XCG-5, the XCG-7 was sent on 25 August to lightning tests. The XCG-8 was smashed in a 17 July 1944 windstorm at CCAAF.

A rudimentary aircraft, the Waco CG-4A cargo glider was intended to be easy to maintain and fly. What it lacked in looks it made up for in utility. However, manufacturing the big glider proved challenging in many respects. (The Peter M. Bowers Collection/The Museum of Flight)

5

Prevalence: Waco CG-4A and CG-15A

The 15-place Waco CG-4A became the centerpiece of the U.S. Army glider force during WWII and produced from 1942 through 1945. Although anything but graceful, the glider proved easy enough to fly that minimally trained pilots could handle it. A total 13,906 of the aircraft were manufactured over four years with 9,723 shipped to the war zones; numbers exceeded in the U.S. only by the B-24, P-51, and P-47, and production exceeding all other war gliders in the world combined.

The hastily assembled capability was far from ideal, but persistence and modifications allowed it to serve well with U.S. and UK forces. At the heart of this were the thousands of CG-4As that could be shipped abroad, but only by consuming voluminous cargo capacity and requiring skilled assembly at the far end. The lightweight gliders, designed for efficient generation of lift, were easily lifted in high winds. Despite aggressive tied-down efforts and tying a piece of lumber atop each wing as a spoiler, hundreds of CG-4As were destroyed in storms. Hundreds more were wrecked through rough handling, deterioration, and training accidents. During 1943, three to six gliders *per day* were being lost in training.[1] Between May 1943 and February 1944 there were 17 glidermen killed and 162 injured in glider mishaps.[2] The aircraft hulks were usually collected in enormous piles of wreckage, occasionally burned to reduce the volume. Yet, the simple airframe took a lot of punishment in action and was relatively simple to maintain and operate. Yet, despite repair capabilities, many hundreds were abandoned on the battlefield rather than recover them.

The CG-4A was never even dignified with an official USAAF name, and many of the unofficial names are not complementary. Today, only a few of the gliders remained intact for museum display. It is difficult to think of any other major warplane so little regarded that such a state of affairs was allowed to persist.

Despite strict picketing rules, the CG-4A could be damaged in high winds, even lifting sunken concrete blocks out of the ground via the tie-down lines. Hundreds of the gliders were destroyed in such mishaps, like this one. The fabric and wood elements of the structure are evident. (National Museum of the United States Air Force)

Development

The 6 June 1941, $178,700.00 contract for the XCG-3 and XCG-4 had Waco delivering a static article, a test aircraft, and trailer. Cost of the first flight article was $58,765.00. Like the other 15-place glider contracts placed in the same time period, the XCG-4 was an enlargement of its 8-place sibling, the XCG-3.

Waco again came through with performance in sharp contrast with their competition. They delivered the structural ground test example on 1 May 1942.[3] The first airworthy

This XCG-4 (possibly photographed at Waco) has yet to have the vertical tail dorsal fairing added, rudder cap extended forward, or downview windows installed, and possesses just the forward skids. However, it displays initial modifications in the aft fuselage extension closeout extension, and fixed undercarriage. The hinge tripod above the nose and more prominent joint between the nose and fuselage emphasizes this glider did have an opening nose. (National Soaring Museum)

Tab;e 05-01	
Waco Aircraft XCG-4 Specifics	
span	83.7 ft
wing area	851.5 ft^2
length	48.6 ft
height (tail on ground)	12.6 ft
empty weight	2,952 lbs
maximum weight	6,791 lbs
overload weight	9,000 lbs
maximum speed	150 mph
(including tow) (9,000 lbs)	128 mph
stall speed	44 mph
capacity	2 pilots, 13 troops
cabin length x width x height	13.2 x 5.8 x 5.4 ft height 5.0 ft at rear
glide ratio	14.7:1

This XCG-4 wheels over a camouflaged Wright Field. It possesses the fin dorsal extension but still lacks the hinged nose to accommodate a jeep (although the feature was censored from many photos of the period). The aircraft is resplendent in the blue fuselage, yellow wings, and red/white/blue rudder of the prewar Army Air Corps. (United States Air Force)

example was flown to Wright Field by Dent on 14 May 1942 where it was then officially accepted.

The second flight test glider was delayed when, in September 1941, the Army requested changes to permit a jeep to be carried within the cabin. General Arnold had expressed the desire for an armed and armored "flying jeep" that could be towed to the combat area, glide down to a controlled landing, shed its aerodynamic appendages, and carry on into combat.[4] The Aircraft Laboratory studied the concept through November 1941 and concluded it was impractical.[5] Distributing the center of gravity between the two axles was impossible. Landing loads on the tires would cause them to burst and might require structural changes to the truck frame. Likewise, the non-aerodynamic character of the ¼-ton truck would make flight precarious and likely require structural alterations. Other necessary changes to the vehicle for the flight hardware could not be defined without detailed design of the detachable components, but they could likely be extensive, adding weight and complexity of no good purpose after landing. It was far more practical to create a glider to deliver the jeep as one of many possible loads, quickly discharging it once on the ground.[6] The XCG-4, still in development, was immediately

A requirement to carry a jeep prompted significant redesign to widen the fuselage slightly and hinge the nose section. The second Waco prototype XCG-4 was delayed to execute the modification and become the XCG-4A. Note wheel ramps and how the front skids extend farther forward than for the production design. (National Soaring Museum)

identified as a likely candidate for this mission. At the beginning of October 1941, Waco suggested altering their design to accommodate airborne equipment like jeeps and guns, and asked to execute the redesign while the flying jeep study continued.

In seeking a solution, the Glider Unit worked closely with Waco engineers.[7] The changes to take the 2,320-pound road-weight jeep entailed a substantial rework of the XCG-4, widening the fuselage and hinging the nose at the top so that it, along with the pilot seats, could be raised by five men and locked into position to expose a 5.8 x 5.8-foot opening. These changes and others requested by the Army increased aircraft empty weight by 759 pounds and gross by 709 pounds. The consequence was an increase in wing loading from 4.5 psf to approximately 8.0 psf. While this sacrificed some gliding performance, it permitted a tow speed increase to 150 mph and eased C-47 engine cooling concerns. Hence, a principal mission became to carry the jeep or a 75 mm howitzer with three troopers and 25 shells.

Modifying the contract to cover the revised work and a second prototype, its final value was $111,000.00 for the XCG-4 and $256,391.20 on the joint XCG-3 and -4 contract (the second ship valued alone at $37,200.00). The revised design required modifications to the static article and extending that ground testing. The revised second flight article was delivered on 25 June 1942.[8] Its testing progressed very quickly, including a 220-mile tow from Dayton to Chanute Field, Illinois, and back again with 15 personnel onboard. The most significant changes requested by the Army were revisions to the vertical stabilizer with the rudder extended forward over the vertical stabilizer, a dorsal extension added to improve directional stability (also said to control tail flutter),[9] and an aft fuselage close-out extension matching the base of the rudder. Twin downview windows ahead of each pilot were also added. The glider could not be induced to spin under normal circumstances. Two bottom skids, all with rubber shock absorbers, were added mid-fuselage.

On 20 June 1942 the altered aircraft, the XCG-4A, was pronounced acceptable for service and the Army moved to make it their standard combat glider. This became the initial configuration for rushed production as the CG-4A.

Description

The CG-4A had wooden wings consisting of two spars and ribs covered with plywood and fabric doped over this. The tails were similarly constructed while all control surfaces were wood with fabric covering. Most wood assembly was with glue. Rather small spoilers, rotating out of the upper surface of the wings, killed lift to adjust glidepath for touchdown accuracy. The fuselage was a welded steel tube Warren truss covered with fabric and fitted with a honeycomb plywood floor possessing 216 cells. The choice of steel tubing may have been vitally important as many of Waco's competitors' all-wood airframes failed static loads testing. As it happened, a shortage of the tubing was experienced in spring 1943 to the point that a pause in CG-4A production was feared. Furthermore, as the war progressed, high quality woods like spruce were added to the nation's critical shortage list. However, Materiel Command engineers worked closely with Waco on the initial design, assisting with a major design shift to reduce the quantity of steel tubing and mahogany plywood when these experienced critical shortages.[10]

The troops would normally enter and exit via doors on each side, aft of the wing, and emergency exits were fitted under the wings. During hot and muggy conditions the glider would often be flown with doors and escape hatches removed, and the pilots in shirtsleeves. Tie-down fittings were installed in the fuselage tubing adjacent to the floor. The two pilot stations were initially fitted with a single control wheel that could be swung over before either pilot and locked with a pin. This was eventually replaced with two fixed controls. Trim tabs for all three axes of control were adjusted with overhead cranks, beside the towline disconnect lever. The towline attached via a socket atop the nose. The few electrical lights were powered by a 12-volt battery.

The CG-4A could carry more than its own empty weight. Removable wooden benches with belts were installed for 13 fully-equipped troopers. These could be removed and freight carried. It was specifically designed to accommodate a jeep with four to six troops or a 75 mm howitzer with three to five troops and up to 25 shells (these numbers apparently shifting as tactics matured). If flown empty, 300 pounds of ballast had to be installed behind each pilot seat to achieve proper trim. The pilot seats were little better than fixed plywood benches with thin padding.

The nose of the aircraft, including the pilot seats and controls, was hinged at the top and latched at the bottom so as to be raised up and locked in position to allow ready loading of wheel cargo. A pair of "two-by-fours" (lumber) and a steel cross member propped the tail up and lowered the nose for easier unloading of freight. For a jeep, a cable could be attached to the pintle at the rear of the vehicle. This was connected via pulleys to a tripod brace atop the nose so that, as the jeep rolled forward to exit, the nose automatically rose and locked. The vehicle's tires also pushed the short, hinged

A look towards the aft fuselage interior of the CG-4A, with passenger benches removed, emphasizes the short loadable volume but also displays the mix of construction materials. Exterior fabric is secured to the welded steel tube primary structure. The wooden floor and other wood elements are also evident, as are control cables, bracketry, and other accoutrements. (National Museum of the United States Air Force)

The tight troop accommodations inside the CG-4A are shown. With full combat gear it would be challenging to walk between the rows of soldiers. Note that this CG-4A has the early single control column that had to be swung into position before each pilot. (National Soaring Museum)

It required the efforts of several men to lift the nose of the CG-4A to about the 90-degree position where it locked into place. A cable attached to a jeep could allow the nose to be raised by the vehicle as it moved forward. However, the latch failed occasionally until corrected, resulting and an awful bang when the nose fell back down. (National Soaring Museum)

wheel ramps down as it moved out. The cable automatically came free after the jeep moved out, the entire process requiring just a few seconds, reducing exposure to enemy fire after landing. The pitot probe was attached to the top tripod, but with considerable airspeed and altitude error resulting.

The glider could be partially disassembled and shipped in five enormous crates weighing between 1,800 and 5,375 pounds, the total approximately 20,000 pounds. The largest crate was 24.3 feet long, 7.4 feet wide, and 8.3 feet high. These were among the largest shipping containers moved during the war. They consumed 9,000 board feet of lumber, costing an average $1,800.00 to crate, and required two railcars to move.[11] Because of the many companies building the aircraft with various levels of quality and manufacturing tolerances, only those parts matching the same individual aircraft could confidently be used together. Therefore, the matching crates had to be located in what were usually acres in which hundreds had been haphazardly deposited.

Short wheel ramps on the CG-4A allowed relatively easy roll-on and roll-off of jeeps, howitzers, and similar cargo. The aft fuselage had to be braced up for this operation, usually with a length of lumber on both sides as seen here. Note also how the tires have been chocked with sandbags. (National Soaring Museum)

Towing the big glider to a war zone was impractical, so it was designed to be broken down and packed into five enormous crates. This aft fuselage section and empennage elements are being crated at the factory. These were among the largest shipping containers moved by sea and land during the war. (National Museum of the United States Air Force)

Table 05-02	
Waco Aircraft CG-4A Specifics	
span	83.7 ft
wing area	851.5 ft²
length (tail on ground)	48.4 ft
height (tail on ground)	12.6 ft
empty weight	3,750 lbs
maximum weight	7,500 lbs
overload weight	9,000 lbs
maximum speed (including tow)	150 mph (7,500 lbs) 128 mph (9,000 lbs)
glide speed, normal	73 mph
stall speed	49 mph, 60 mph at maximum GW
capacity	2 pilots, 13 troops
cabin length x width x height	13.2 x 5.8 x 5.4 ft, height 5.0 ft at rear
glide ratio	9.25:1

Production

Even though detail design of the new XCG-4 combat glider was still underway on 7 December 1941 when the U.S. was drawn into the war, it became clear an immediate move to set up production was essential. The XCG-4 stood out as the most likely prototype to meet requirements and Waco the most capable manufacturer, so it was an easy decision to put production plans into motion.[12] The 500 15-place and 500 8-place gliders requested on 10 October now appeared much too modest.[13] Yet, Waco did not have the resources to manufacture their glider in the thousands. With an impatient General Arnold applying incessant pressure from Washington, no time was lost in seeking alternatives. The tiny Glider Branch was given authority on 12 January 1942 to seek other perspective partners to manufacturer the CG-4.[14]

As in seeking companies to develop prototypes, there were few the Wright Field team were permitted to engage on production contracts, and these generally possessed limited manufacturing experience and capacity. It became clear the contracts would have to be spread thinly amongst several manufacturers, distributing the risk of failures, with likely attendant high costs. After a review of potential producers, and personal contacts with same, a dozen firms across the country were selected to build the initial, cautionary orders for 700 CG-4As—this requirement coming down on 14 February 1942. Given that at the time there existed few specifications, drawings, or bill of materials for the CG-4, Materiel Division had to assist the inexperienced firms in preparing reasonable bids. Following Letters of Intent issued 4 through 28 February, contracts were let between 14 March and 24 April 1942 for orders of as few as 20 and as many as 230. These dozen manufacturers were Babcock Aircraft Corporation, A.G.A Aviation Corporation (soon G & A Aircraft), General Aircraft Corporation, Gibson Refrigerator Company, Laister-Kauffman Aircraft Corporation, National Aircraft Corporation, Northwestern Aeronautical Corporation, Porterfield Aircraft Company (later Ward Furniture Manufacturing Company), Pratt, Read & Company, Jenter Corporation (soon Ridgefield Manufacturing Corporation), Robertson Aircraft Corporation, and Timm Aircraft Corporation. Waco would continue refining the drawings, handle requests for alterations, and deal with other issues as they arose.

In the meantime, the required number of 15-place gliders had been upped to 3,000. At a 31 March meeting with the Chief, Materiel Division, this was raised again to 4,000 CG-4As and the schedule urgency was reemphasized. Consequently, the 12 existing contractors were persuaded to take on more work (1,590 additional), most agreeing only after expressing emphatic misgivings. Soon after, the quantity was upped again and the original 12 took on an additional 700 aircraft (to the exasperation of not a few) for a total 5,490 on order as of 2 April 1942.[15]

Concerned the CG-4A production objectives for 1942 would not be met, the USAAF violated (with concurrence) the edict from Washington and turned to large manufacturers already carrying enormous War Department jobs. Cessna Aircraft Corporation was signed up in April 1942 and The Ford Motor Company, having converted from automobile to aircraft production, signed on in June. Both committed to large orders in hopes of having 1,000 gliders in hand by 1 January 1943. Waco Aircraft Company was also asked to contribute in June after the CG-3A production was redirected. The last of 16 companies in the CG-4A manufacturing group was Rearwin (soon Commonwealth), taking a contract in November 1942. These four firms alone added 2,500 gliders to the order book (including 300 CG-3As) for a total 4,790. By September the goal had gone up again to 6,290 CG-4As by the expedient of adding 1,000 to Ford's order.[16] By such increments, the number of gliders on order by fall 1942 was 10,840 CG-4As for delivery by 1 September 1943.

Most of the 16 CG-4A manufacturers were small concerns that performed poorly while more experienced firms, such Ford, plus Boeing and Beech as subcontractors to Cessna, did expectedly well. Yet, others with no prior aircraft experience also did surprisingly well. All subcontracted to approximately 50 other firms for parts and assemblies Many of these had previously been completely uninvolved with aircraft work. Several times recommendations were made to terminate contracts to poorly performing companies, but the vast majority were allowed to continue under the supposition that it would be more costly to cancel the work than continue on. The numbers of gliders delivered from each prime contractor varied from one to 4,190, with wide variation in quality.

The first orders were especially rushed so as to get aircraft into the field as quickly as possible to support pilot training. The 1942 goal was 1,500 CG-4As by 1 October and another 1,500 by 31 December. With political plans to reenter Europe as early as

It required considerable effort, but in less than a year plants across the United States were turning out CG-4A gliders. This image is of the Ford assembly line in Iron Mountain, Michigan, that had previously handled automobiles. The Ford Motor Company eventually became the highest-volume manufacturer and with outstanding quality. (National Museum of the United States Air Force)

1942, gliders were urgently needed. Although the invasion was delayed, in July 1943 Arnold ordered the shipping of 1,441 CG-4As to England, creating additional pressure. Regardless of the angst, almost all such goals were missed. Shortages of materials and skilled manpower were a chronic problem throughout the war as highly experienced men tended to disappear into the draft. Obtaining critical material was a problem that persisted throughout the war. In some cases, the Air Forces had to waive or adjusted their specifications to permit alternative materials, methods, and hardware.

Although overtly simple, the CG-4A actually contained a little more than 70,000 parts and required nearly 7,000 hours of labor to build. Its production was not a simple undertaking. Frustrated by delays, Arnold opined that the aircraft was too complex, took too long to build, and was too expensive. Yet, every shop was working 24-hours a day, 6-days a week. Plant conversions were another issue. Even the experienced firms had trouble getting started, adopting the nontraditional materials and techniques associated with the CG-4A. What they did accomplish was remarkable under the circumstances.

The Army had estimated it would require 4,000-5,000 hours to build one of the gliders and compelled companies to bid on this basis. However, Waco estimated 5,000-7,000 and at least one bidder had predicted more than this. Likewise, Waco had estimated a unit cost of $14,000.00 based only on its incomplete experimental contract. And so, Wright Field negotiated on this number, although other manufacturers predicted higher costs. It is not surprising then that the government estimates were far from the mark and overruns on the cost-plus-fixed-fee contracts were experienced by all but one of the 16 manufacturers, to the tune of over $19 million.[17] Much wind was also passed between teeth about apparent excessive executive salaries paid on these contracts. All this was additional cause for frustrations at the Pentagon and anger on Capitol Hill, which rolled down as additional troubles for the Wright Field personnel.

The first production CG-4A was delivered by Cessna on 11 September 1942, so much later than anticipated that advanced pilot training had come to a standstill. The gamble in employing Cessna paid off and the first units delivered for vital instructor pilot training were from Cessna. In November 1942 alone this firm produced 407 gliders, although quality was criticized. The priority for raw material was shifted occasionally thereafter such that at times there were numerous incomplete gliders filling production facilities awaiting parts.

Waco provided guidance and assistance in setting up production tooling while running their own production line. Much work had to be done to develop drawings for a standard configuration all manufacturers could use at many widely separated plants. With design and construction of the XCG-4 so rushed, and production ordered before testing was complete, production was initiated based on the experimental drawings.[18] Changes were inevitable. Hence, Waco's job became a very busy and stressful one, issuing revised drawings and specifications, answering questions and requests for deviations, and responding to Air Forces' assessment of degrading quality as the production rate accelerated.

At first the USAAF intent was to provide identical tooling to each company. Bromley Engineering Company of Detroit, Michigan, was given a $534,676.60 contract to design master jigs and fixtures and a 30 July 1942 contract to fabricate 14 sets for $2,821,485.00. However, facing looming contractual delivery dates, all manufacturers struck out on their own building the required hardware. Having become superfluous, the Bromley effort was dropped in October 1942 after $647,041.08 was expended.

Building the CG-4A required some amount of large and unique tools and jigs. An example is the mount for the center fuselage assembly that permitted it to be rotated for fabric installation and other work. Although the intent was to provide identical tools to all manufacturers, time pressures forced each to build these on their own. (National Museum of the United States Air Force)

The complex wood construction inherent in the CG-4A is represented by the 'honeycomb' floor assembly. Preparing the individual elements and assembling them precisely with strong glue joints required the skills of furniture craftsman. Uncommon in aircraft manufacturing, the industry had to turn to such entities to serve as subcontractors. (National Museum of the United States Air Force)

In the interest of high production rates, the Air Forces waived or adjusted specifications. Waco revised drawings to permit alternative methods and hardware, while supervising assembly line changes to accommodate each company's unique circumstances. The service itself requested additional changes. Aircraft with these revisions were coming off the lines in early March 1943. Over 1,000 design changes were introduced in 1942 and 1943 alone, the final totaling more than 7,000. Such alterations and elements of non-standardization between manufacturers sacrificed some degree of parts uniformity and interchangeability between aircraft built by the different firms over several years. All this was a source of confusion and extra work for engineering officers and maintenance personnel at the field units. Although efforts were made to correct the problem later, it remained an annoyance through the last year of the war.

Production rate rapidly increased to meet training demands and then continued at a brisk pace to fill anticipated combat needs. Despite the earlier frenetic efforts, the fall of 1942 saw indecision, with direction that only 250 more CG-4As would be procured and all other glider purchases halted. However, by February 1943 the Army felt that 6,060 CG-4As would meet its foreseeable combat requirements. Hence, instructions changed to a reduction to 350 gliders per month through 1943. However, the tactical commands were stating requirements for 6,290 CG-4As by 1944, and so production rolled on while development of advanced models continued. In the absence of clear and consistent direction, glider production remained at breakneck speed through the final year of the war. Production was finally allowed to run down in 1944-45 when it was clear sufficient gliders had been delivered to sustain the airborne forces for the duration of the war and attention began turning to more advanced models.

Determining how many gliders to produce was a challenging calculation. It depended on the number of airborne divisions, how many airborne operations would be undertaken, projection of aircraft losses, Lend-Lease requests (aircraft passed to Great Britain), and a reserve. By June 1943 the requirement was set at 12,826 CG-4As to be delivered by June of 1944. However, within a month 600 was lopped off that total and in August the number had become 10,500. The USAAF had 1,460 in States-side storage on 1 April 1944.[19] Just shipping the thousands of enormous glider to overseas theaters was a limiting factor. By late 1943, so many of the aircraft had been built that hundreds were piling up all over the country. Some damaged in storage (usually

Behind schedule and with some initial teething troubles, CG-4As were eventually being delivered in the required numbers. In time the supply far exceeded immediate needs and huge stores of crated gliders were collecting in warehouses and depots awaiting shipment overseas where they again languished. Those that collected in outside storage like these Wacos risked deterioration in the elements. (National Museum of the United States Air Force)

water) prior to shipment were reconditioned under separate contracts. There were 1,000 stored inside, consuming 750,000 feet of floor space.[20] Shipments to theaters were based on prognostications of operations that, especially in Europe before Normandy, were based on tenuous planning. Hence, many hundreds of gliders were stored in the UK awaiting a mission need, with some deteriorating from long exposure to the damp English environment. Prior to Normandy, one officer wrote "So difficult was the storage problem in UK, and so limited was the European Theater of Operations (ETO) interest in glider operations, that serious suggestions were advanced that gliders stored in the UK be dismantled and burned."[21] Likewise, concern was expressed with shipping gliders to the Pacific too soon before use because of potential deterioration. Risks were with rust, mold, warping, and joint separation if the aircraft as not regularly inspected or the crated components aired periodically. Yet, a long service life was not to be expected in any event. One senior officer wrote, "Properly maintained, an average useful life of six months may be expected considering the deterioration factor alone."[22]

During the first half of 1944, uncertainty arose again regarding further production. Although continuity of production capability was considered, the word coming down in May was that no additional 15-place gliders were required. Plans were put in place to store at least the Ford, Northwestern, and Waco tools and jigs in the event of future production. Other manufacturers were authorized in July 1944 to dispose of such hardware and lines began to close.[23] Materiel Command advised that, if production ceased entirely, a minimum six to nine months would be necessary to bring production back up, considering lead-time in materials delivery and reconstituting the workforce.[24] That summer, requests from ETO had all reserves shipped leaving none for the Pacific if requested (which seemed likely). By fall 1944, a War Department study revealed that moving gliders between theaters would be a time-consuming and costly business, and also showed the high attrition suffered by the machines in combat, training, and storage. This prompted reconsideration of the earlier conclusion. However, with gliders being a "weapon of opportunity," it was an exercise in vague projections to anticipate large-scale airborne operations.[25] New estimates in September identified additional requirements for gliders. Suddenly it appeared there was a shortage of gliders.

Depending on how the numbers were worked, it appeared 4,450 more gliders would be required. The CBI and Far East theaters alone night need as many as 950. States-side reserves would not meet the demand. Most were anticipated to be CG-4As and CG-15As (see later) if for no other reason than evaluation and optimization of advanced models was still underway. The British alone expressed a need for 2,000 Wacos.[26] Hence, on 25 November 1944 the USAAF was directed to ensure production of 720 Wacos per month, the highest rate considered practical, yet understood to fall short of projected requirements. The effort would add 8,100 gliders in 1945. This required some scrambling to resurrect production lines that were already shutting down. All production through August 1945, some 4,500 machines, was to go to the ETO. Production of Wacos were programmed through the end of 1946 with a planned total 17,314 units.[27]

In April 1945, with the fall of Germany appearing imminent, it seemed there might be an excess of gliders and consideration was again given to cutting production. Requirements for the invasion and defeat of Japan remained an open question. By summer the numbers came up 3,941 Wacos for that theater through the end of 1946 plus 5,371 for States-side training and Lend-Lease. Plans were put in place to adjust the production rate to these requirements.[28] However, after VJ-Day production of gliders were summarily curtailed, as were almost all other aircraft production programs.

Initially the challenge was training workers to meet the skill demands of CG-4A construction, to include a large proportion of women for the first time in aircraft construction. It then became a problem of retaining the male members of the team as many disappeared into the draft. As uncertainty reigned in 1944 about continuing production, the problem was retaining these employees. (National Museum of the United States Air Force)

The summary of CG-4A production for each manufacturer, in alphabetical order, follows:

A.G.A Aviation Corporation (standing for Autogiros, Gliders and Airplanes) of Willow Grove, Pennsylvania, was so named on 11 October 1942 after previously being the Pitcairn-Larsen Autogiro Company, Incorporated. On 25 August 1942 the name was changed again to **G & A Aircraft Incorporated** because of similarity to another business and dropping Autogiros that were out of favor. After 31 May 1943 the firm was a division of the Firestone Tire and Rubber Company. During work on the XCG-9 (Chapter 8), it was proposed A.G.A. also built CG-4A gliders and so entered a bid on 14 February 1942. They immediately received a tentative Letter of Intent followed by a 9 April 1942 contract for 60 CG-4As at $1,232,288.25. This was revised upward by 120 and $2,269,496.25 on 27 June then 200 and $3,501,784.50 on 20 May 1943. A final 92 more were added on 5 September for an ultimate 472 at $14,961,168.24 and delivery by February 1944.[29] The company struggled with many difficulties and experienced a 56 percent cost overrun to produce the costliest CG-4As at an average $32,941.00. An additional 450 were ordered for 1945 but only 155 completed before cancellation. G & A's total was 627 with 295 cancelled.

Babcock Aircraft Corporation of Deland, Florida, had developed a light aircraft designed by Verne C. Babcock, but production preparation was curtailed by the war. They actively sought subcontract work and ultimately landed a 24 April 1942 agreement (14 February Letter of Intent) for 50 CG-4As at $950,187,50. This was raised by 102 at $1,887,503.88 on 19 May and then to 152 at $2,837,691.38, all for delivery by February 1943. With subsequent overruns the value rose to $3,245,602.36. The firm set up glider manufacturing in fairground buildings and a tent. This naturally introduced quality control problems, along with the usual materiel and manpower shortages, such that Babcock's progress was poor. By November 1943 the company had delivered only 54 gliders and the work was cut back on 24 June 1943 to 60 CG-4As, the last delivered on 6 July. This saved them from cancellation for default, but the government took a loss of $743,710.85.

In a bid to acquire a large number of gliders very rapidly, the Army turned in early March 1942 to a highly experienced firm with a demanding request. **Cessna Aircraft Corporation** of Wichita, Kansas, was tasked in a 4 April 1942 letter contract to build 1,000 CG-4As for $18,003,308.00 at a rate of 200 per month. This was raised in early June to 1,500 and $45,712,500.00 on a 10 June 1942 letter contract for delivery in just three months, by 1 October 1942. It would require working around-the-clock, seven days a week, but without complete tooling and jigs. The expectation was that 500 could be delivered in each of July, August and September 1942. Cessna was doubtful this could be accomplished but agreed to make its best effort. It appeared possible with the subcontract assistance of the Boeing Airplane Company's Stearman division and Beech Aircraft, both in Wichita. Cessna also built a new 108,000 square foot plant in Hutchinson, Kansas, in just over 30 days at its own expense to facilitate the program. Boeing built about half the fuselages and roughly two-thirds of the outer wing panels, and performed final assembly on those aircraft for fly-away delivery. Beech contributed approximately 50 percent of the tails and half the inner wing panels. Cessna produced all the hardware for the production in its Wichita plant and all other CG-4A manufacturing in Hutchinson. However, actual output, while impressive, did not match the lofty goals, with the first 32 machines completed in September and the monthly rate reaching 407 in November (six per day from Boeing). By that time, on 30 September, Materiel Command's Chief of Staff had advised that the contract should be cut back to 750 so as not to impede Cessna's other vital War Department commitments. The cut 750 were then distributed as additions to Commonwealth, Northwestern, and General Aircraft contracts. The total 1,500 were not achieved until April 1943 or six months later than originally intended. The cutback left Cessna with considerable surplus materials that it and the Air Forces struggled to sell and distribute to other manufacturers. The government wrote off millions in losses. Cessna's 750 CG-4As (495 crated and 255 flown away) were completed in January 1943 for $17,901,038.83. This they did exceptionally well, delivering 747 in 1942 compared with just 54 from all other manufacturers.[30] However, additional consequences was in upsetting the pooled tool design and construction, diverting materials to Cessna, and producing aircraft possessing almost certain interchangeability issues with machines produced on "hard" production jigs and tools. The service felt it worth this cost.

Ford Motor Company took on wartime aircraft production with large-scale output of such vital warplanes as the B-24 bomber. Hence, they were also approached and accepted a 19 June 1942 contract for 1,000 gliders at $18,926,470.50. This was subsequently raised to 2,200 at $49,754,164.64 for delivery by April 1944. The Iron Mountain, Michigan, plant was converted to glider manufacturing, but Ford subcontracted substantial work to Haywood-Wakefield Furniture Company. Operating three shifts a day, six days per week, their output was impressive. Ford delivered 1,000 by October 1943, reaching 130 per month, or roughly a quarter of the CG-4As rolled out that year.[31] They also uncovered Waco drawing errors and introduced efficiency innovations to the manufacturing process.[32] Ford was the only CG-4A manufacturer that did not experience a cost overrun, producing at lowest unit cost (approximately $15,000.00).[33] The USAAF turned again to Ford when 1,875 additional gliders were sought for 1945. Although completing the lions-share of these orders with 990 delivered, the rest were dropped. Total Ford production was 4,190 CG-4As.

General Aircraft Corporation of Delaware, with principal activities at Lowell Airport, South Lowell, Massachusetts, had been in business just two years and manufactured 25 copies of a light plane before being interrupted by the war. After a Letter of Intent in early February 1942, they were given a CG-4A contract on 14 March 1942 for 75 machines at $1,560,672.19. This was subsequently raised to 154 and $2,879,141.26 on 26 June, then 229 and $4,439,813.45 on 11 December, and 500 at $17,255,335.17 on 23 August 1943. The firm relocated to Astoria, Long Island, New York, to be closer to Steinway & Sons, Piano Manufacturers, who would contribute their woodworking skills to making the gliders and from whom General rented their Long Island plant. Steinway also introduced innovative production techniques to cut assembly time. General did well despite a slow start and difficult conditions. Hence, they received another order for 500 aircraft on 25 August 1943 valued at $14,950,000.00 for March 1944 delivery. Yet another was added for 1945 but cancelled after only 99 were delivered. Their total was 1,112 at $32,205,335.17.

Gibson Refrigerator Company of Greenville, Michigan, was another entrant with no prior aviation experience. Yet, within six months they had converted their plant, retrained their employees, and delivered the first aircraft. Gibson started with a 60-unit contract on 4 April 1942 at $1,272,916.80 that was raised to 363 and $6,911,688.35 then 423 for $8,184,605.15 on 22 June, and again to 632 for delivery by 4 June 1943. Their total was subsequently raised on a 22 June 1942, $29,314,892.52 contract to 1,055 CG-4As, for delivery by April 1944. Added later were 36 of which 13 were cancelled. From an initial delivery on 23 October 1942, their total was 1,078 CG-4As.

In an effort to rapidly boost CG-4A production numbers, the USAAF engaged Cessna Aircraft to build hundreds in short order. Cessna was a bit late in initial deliveries but soon reached extraordinary numbers, albeit with some complaints about quality. A principal subcontractor was Boeing's Stearman division which performed final assembly, some of their production evident outside the Wichita plant. (The Peter M. Bowers Collection/The Museum of Flight)

Laister-Kauffman Aircraft Corporation was previously introduced. On 24 March 1942, an order for 30 CG-4As at $604,526.10 was placed, but upped by 80 at $1,444,170.00 on 19 June, then 100 and $2,048,696.10 on 23 June 1943. For these 210 at $6,827,707.15, L-K applied extensive subcontracting that included Anheuser-Busch. Laister-Kauffman performance was fair, running behind their June 1943 deliver commitment. One hundred more gliders were added to the contract on 23 June 1943 and their CG-4A production reached a dozen per month. Their total was 310.

National Aircraft Corporation of Elwood, Indiana, was formed on 17 October 1941 with intent to manufactured wooden aircraft parts for the war effort. Their CG-4A contract was dated 23 March 1942 for 30 machines at $599,635.88, but quickly changed to 60 at $1,142,173.88 on 21 May then 90 and $1,741,808.68 for June 1943 delivery. Encountering severe difficulties getting production facilities up and running, National's attempt at glider production failed. The USAAF moved to cancel the contract and, despite National protesting up to Washington, it was dropped on 26 February 1943. The company completed just one CG-4A, collected in April and costing a staggering $1,515,490.34. National ceased operations in March 1943 and soon liquidated.[34]

Northwestern Aeronautical Corporation (NAC) of Minneapolis, Minnesota, was formed on 27 February 1942 by three lawyers from St. Paul; Francis Butler, Irving Clark, and Jack C. Foote. They setup John E. Parker as president, a man possessing experience in aircraft finance and with contacts in Washington, D.C. They also assumed the assets of the Columbia Aircraft Corporation of Kansas City, Missouri, plus benefited from the engineering resources of Northwest Airlines. All construction was to be undertaken by subcontractors. These "subs" were De Ponti Aviation Company of Minneapolis, experienced in rebuilding airplanes under Angelo "Shorty" De Ponti, and the Villaume Box and Lumber Company.[35] Assembly was in rented De Ponti hangars at Wold-Chamberlain Airport, Minneapolis. Their initial 31 March 1942 contract was for just 30 gliders at $626,985.60 to be delivered by year-end. However, Materiel Command had enough confidence in their capabilities to increase this by 54 and $976,118.85 on 13 May, then 216 on 7 December for a total 300. Deliveries were at first greatly impacted by materiel and labor shortages, with only two gliders completed in 1942. However, this soon picked up and deliveries went from September 1942 through July 1943. A hundred more were added on 31 May 1943 and 500 on 3 June. These 900 CG-4As were for delivery though March 1944 at $27,430.608.95. Employees peaked at 2,500 at Northwestern and an equal number for the "subs." Follow-on contracts totaled 754, of which 134 were dropped as not required. Northwestern's total was 1,510.[36]

Porterfield Aircraft Company of Kansas City, Missouri, was awarded a 20-unit CG-4A contract on 2 March 1942 after E.E. Porterfield, Jr., had actively sought Air Corps work. Lacking the resources to setup production, Porterfield then searched for a woodworking associate who might buy out his company and acquire the Army contract. On 15 May, the firm was acquired by the **Ward Furniture Manufacturing Company** of Fort Smith, Arkansas, to become the Aviation Division for which all assets were moved to Fort Smith. This was predicated on the understanding Bromley would supply the tools and jigs, so suspension of that contract greatly burdened the small company. The modest order on 31 March 1942 for 20 aircraft and $295,185.34 was increased by a still-cautionary 10 and $555,329.25 on 9 June, then 20 more at $850,514.59, all for delivery through February 1943. These 50 progressed slowly and costs rose to $3,286,200.14. Plans to add a hundred more aircraft to the order was dropped and the contract cancelled on 1 April 1943 with only seven CG-4As completed and the government writing off $1,960,540.35.

Pratt, Read & Company, Incorporated was previously introduced as manufacturing a Navy training glider. Barringer suggested they also seek a CG-4A contract.[37] The 30 March 1942 agreement was for 75 CG-4As at $1,461,204.37, but revised upward by 500 at $8,366,163.75 on 11 May then 575 and $9,827,368.12, 350 added on 11 June 1943, before ballooning to 925 and $24,059,162.11 by May 1944. Although, the company was stressed converting to aircraft production, falling behind hundreds of aircraft by November 1943 and suffering a 54 percent cost overrun, they were ultimately successful. A subsequent contract for 1,500 was curtailed at 31 as the war wound down. Their total was 956, while also repairing some 300 CG-4As damaged in training.[38]

Rearwin Aircraft and Engines, Incorporated (also introduced previously), had sold 11 models of airplanes and three models of radial engines between the wars. It took on a commitment to produce 300 CG-4As the same day, 19 June 1942, its CG-3A numbers increased by 200. However, the 200 CG-3As were converted on 6 November to 150 CG-4As. This total of 350 eventually rose to 950 for delivered by April 1944 at $26,140,122.78. The firm was renamed **Commonwealth Aircraft Incorporated** on 7 January 1943 when control of the company changed hands. A late-war contract for 520 was curtailed. Their final total was 1,470.

Jenter Corporation of Ridgefield, New Jersey, was engaged in constructing commercial displays from various materials. It approached Wright Field with an offer to build a 30-place glider designed by aeronautical engineer A.A. Gassner.[39] Instead, Colonel Dent encouraged them to bid on CG-4A production. They subsequently signed on 1 April 1942 to build 20 gliders at $413,505.50 with Gassner remaining as chief engineer. The quantity was increased by 16 for $598,364.55 on 11 May then to 56 and $1,011,870.05 on 3 June 1942, another 100 added on 2 June 1943. Jenter became **Ridgefield Manufacturing Corporation** on 22 April 1943. Their 156 were for delivery by June 1944 at $5,231,637.77 with good workmanship.

Robertson Aircraft Corporation of Robertson, Missouri, had provided aviation training and services at Lambert Field. The company president William B. Robertson (formerly a Major), approached Wright Field seeking glider work. He was granted a letter contract for 20 CG-4As at $411,603.80, formalized on 23 March 1942. This was raised by 50 at $974,572.50 on 22 June, then 70 gliders and $1,386,176.30 in early April, and 100 more at $5,996,911.06 on 27 September 1943. The 170 total at $5,996,911.06 were for delivery by February 1944. They ran behind and, although considered for cancellation, were allowed to continue to completion.

Timm Aircraft Corporation of Van Nuys, California, was a further evolution of Timm Aircraft Company created by the brothers Otto and Wallace Timm. Principally a subcontract builder of aircraft assemblies, they also designed a light trainer made of "aeromold" plasticized wood laminate that they produced for the U.S. Navy. They were also successful in the transition to gliders. Having already acquired wood aircraft construction expertise, they committed on 7 April 1942 to producing 230 CG-4As for $4,797,096.20, the largest of the original orders. This jumped to 741 at $13,105,259.31 then 971 and $17,902,355.51 gliders for completion by June 1943. They were substantially delinquent, handing over just 262 by November 1943 at $29,723,065.55. Ultimately 537 were cancelled for a total 434.

Waco Aircraft Company only came to CG-4A production after its commitment for 200 CG-3As was converted to 500 CG-4As on 14 July 1942 at $3,905,181.00. The quantity was raised a year later, 19 June 1943, by an additional 500. These thousand were to be delivered by April 1944 at $23,293,510.00. However, they did only moderately well against the delivery schedule given their burden in assisting the 15 other manufacturers. Yet, they were contracted for 75 more gliders near the end of the conflict for a total 1,075.

Improvements

The CG-4A evolved, as with all the warplanes of WWII, but without change in model number. Of the 7,000 changes mentioned previously, most were minor producibility revisions or engineering adjustments without significant operational or safety implications. However, others contributed notably to the glider's mission suitability. During the conflict the gliders were occasionally grounded to correct identified deficiencies that were a consequence of the rush to production. Despite some continuing concerns, the decision was made in October 1943 to avoid further design changes so that the manufacturers could concentrate on quantity production.

The USAAF requested notable changes early in production that contributed to the aircraft most readily recognized as the CG-4A. Among the first of these was dual pilot control columns vice the "throw-over" unit. The undercarriage was subject to major alteration.

At first the CG-4A main landing gear, without brakes or shocks, would be dropped after takeoff. Landing was then performed on plywood skids under the forward fuselage. A parachute had to be used to ensure the gear descended slowly, released above 400 feet so as not to bounce back up and strike the glider. This design evolved into a fixed gear for landing safety, the added brakes enhancing directional control and stopping distance. (A mean landing distance was 1,000 feet on the jettisonable gear, 300 feet on skids, and 150 feet on the fixed undercarriage using the technique of pitching forward onto the forward skids.)[40] The toe pedals for these brakes were on the port side pilot station only. Hence, the "operational tactical gear," as opposed to the "training gear," provided more options for landing speeds since landing on skids required a full-stall touchdown, and easier recovery of the glider. The XCG-4 and XCG-4A were initial subjects for this substitution. Although the fixed gear often failed in actual combat landings on rough fields, this would absorb some kinetic energy while the aircraft continued on the skids. The tail wheel remained nonsteerable.

As is commonly the case, difficulties were encountered with the initial production aircraft when the training organizations took them up. Serviceability rates were discouragingly low until changes were made. The most onerous of these early problems were unsuitable horizontal tail bracing wires. Failure of the wires led to two training crashes, although the crews bailed out successfully. The wires were subsequently altered, but loose wires could promoted flutter and tail failure that persisted for the life of the aircraft and was the cause of several fatal crashes.[41] Eventually, an engineering change came down to replace the wire bracing underneath the horizontal stabilizer with dual struts—a change not seen regularly until well into 1944.

Failure of the landing gear shock strut on a hard landing was also a frequent complaint, answered with a revised design.[42] Among the improvised fixes awaiting the formal fix was a metal band wrapped under the belly between the strut/undercarriage fittings to enhance their strength. This was carried over to production.[43] The locks restraining the nose in its raised position also failed with discouraging regularity, allowing this heavy structure to fall back down thunderously and dangerously. The pilots usually braced it with a piece of lumber until a reliable part was substituted across the fleet. The civilian experience and ingenuity of the GIs assisted in resolving the problems and making the glider operations more efficient.[44] It was pointed out that the aircraft was built for a one-way tactical mission and so was not necessarily suited to repeated training missions.[45]

A more dire failure received national attention. A wing separated from CG-4A (Robertson-built 42-78839) in front of the press and thousands of spectators at Lambert Field in St. Louis, on 1 August 1943. Plummeting from about 1,500-2,000 feet, the mishap took the lives of the Robertson's president and nine other persons, including local dignitaries (with St. Louis' mayor) and a service member. The gliders were temporarily grounded during the investigation and instantly branded with a bad reputation. The fault

Early CG-4As came with droppable main wheels joined by cross-axle. The aircraft was then to land on its fuselage skids. This example was assembled at Eagle Farm AB, Brisbane, Australia, on 13 February 1943. Among the first combat deployments of the aircraft, the pilots knew the gear was unsuitable and so soon improvised a fixed replacement using P-40 fighter wheels. (National Museum of the United States Air Force)

This CG-4As models a landing on skids after dropping the main wheels following takeoff. Although reducing weight and drag, the only directional control was via the rudder that rapidly lost effectiveness during deceleration. It also made for difficult recovery and reuse of the glider, reflecting the original "one-mission" intent. Note the piece of lumber bracing the nose up. (San Diego Air & Space Museum)

The in-flight failure of the starboard wing on this Robertson-built CG-4A got national attention, seen here a moment before it rolled over and dived into the ground. Many people who knew nothing about the glider program were abruptly introduced to it in an unfavorable manner. Glidermen and glider pilots were also shaken, although the fault was not endemic to the Waco design itself. (National Museum of the United States Air Force)

was a wing strut fitting provided by a subcontractor that had been machined much too thin, and the defect not caught by the inspector. This pointed up the near-impossible quality control on a project of this magnitude and pace. However, the incident aircraft had logged 233 hours and approximately 800 landings, with the landing gear replaced three times and the lift struts once owing to hard landings.[46]

In addressing the St. Louis accident and events leading to it, Materiel Command admitted that, "Generally speaking, the trouble with respect to quality control in glider plants goes back to an initial policy from higher authority to the effect that gliders were to be 'one-landing aircraft.' The initial policy required gliders be made quickly and that they be made of non-critical materials. In addition, commercial practices in the manufacture and inspection of gliders were acceptable. Moreover, gliders were designed during a rush period in the early stages of the war, when things were going against us in combat. It is generally recognized that the CG-4A is not a very refined design. Coupled with the shortcomings of design, it should be borne in mind that the standard specification, R-1800-D (which outlines our regularly accepted inspection practices), was not incorporated in the contracts for the glider. This has inevitably resulted in failure to achieve the same high quality standards as applied to aircraft. Within the past several months this matter has been considered by Air Staff, and we are now engaged in incorporating specification R-1800-D in glider contracts. Without such safeguards, it is quite apparent that the gliders would represent merely a compromise between safety and rapid output."[47]

Other refinements came by way of operational experience during training Statesside. Although a radio was part of the design specification and production drawings, availability of the battery-powered VHF radios (Bendix 3801-24) from government sources was inadequate throughout 1942. The requirement was deleted in contracts let during 1943. Consequently, radios were rare in the first mass order of CG-4As and typically only installed in the field as required. An A1A-1 interphone between the glider and tug with a cable strung along the towline was also a post-production change, helping to make the radio unnecessary. Both communication sets were not uniformly seen in the gliders throughout the war. The addition of landing and identification lights to the glider came by way of an urgent request in March 1943. Kits were produced for field installation, but these appear to have been very seldom applied. This is understandable considering the vast majority of the gliders were flown just a few times until expended in combat, and almost all in daylight.

In some cases the squadrons did not wait for folks back home to catch up with requirements and engineered their own improvements. Some of the one-off 'kluges' to Wacos seen in photographs include an emergency exit door added beside the pilot and copilot, fenders on the main gear wheels, and a welded tube frame across the nose for crash protection and ease of ground crew reaching the towline socket.

Initial operations had made clear the hazards of collision with ground objects during the off-field landings, causing a disturbingly high number of pilot injuries. Glider Branch's

This CG-4A, apparently prepared for an assault operation in ETO, models a landing light in the middle of its nose. Whether this was the kit installation or a field improvisation in unclear. Such changes to the Waco were requested by the operational units, but electrical additions were more draw on the battery. (The Peter M. Bowers Collection/The Museum of Flight)

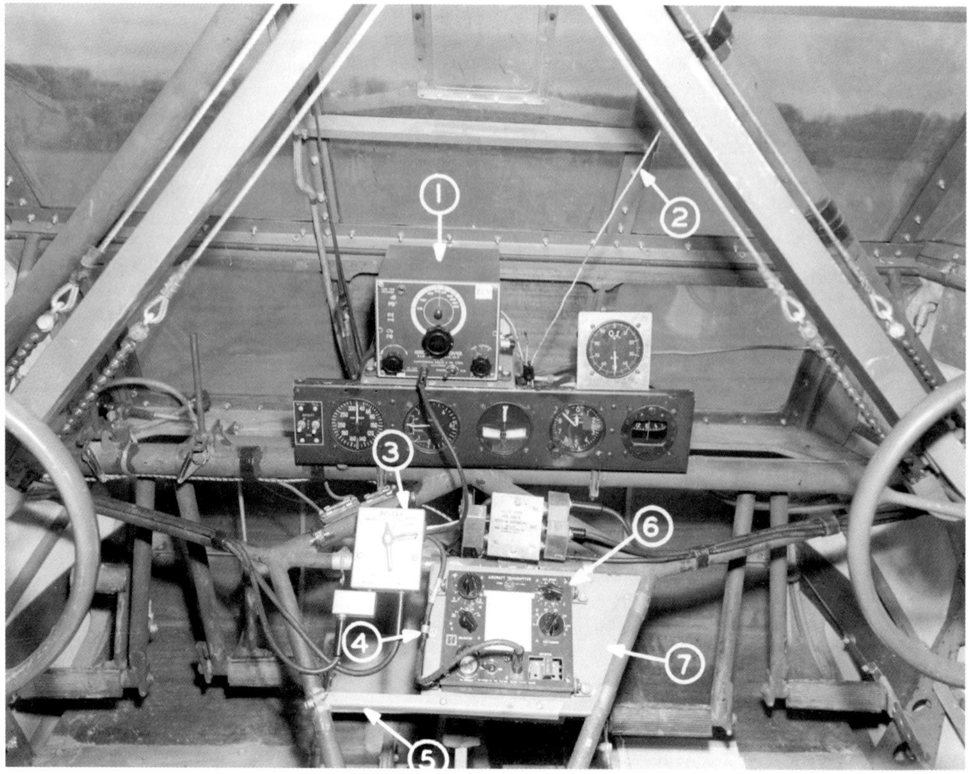

The radio installation in the CG-4A is detailed in this 10 January 1944 photograph. The gliders initial had only a 12-volt battery for a few lights, and so electrical capacity was very limited until a wind generator was added. This made equipment like a radio practical but it remained a rare installation throughout the war. (National Archives)

Captain Bob Cardenas saw an intelligence report reaching the unit suggesting glider landings in western France could end badly, with many gliders running into hedgerows. The CG-4A nose could be damaged to the extent of breaking pilots' legs and making it impossible to raise the nose and extract the cargo. A test addressing this included modifying a CG-4A with a curved nose such that impacts would be less severe. He also participated in trials with explosive charges intending to neatly separate the CG-4A into several pieces that could be man-handled off an LZ, clearing it for following gliders.[48] This may have been inspired by the explosives used to separate the British Horsa glider aft fuselage for rapid unloading. The intent was to wire the glider prior to a mission, allow the glider pilot to breakup the aircraft after landing, and rally troops to clear away the debris. It is not believed to have been fielded. It was later determined the intelligence report overstated the potential problem and so all this successful experimention went no further.

Combat units were not about to let this matter drop, and field modifications began appearing. An assembly of three larger skids on a tubular frame attached under the nose with additional internal bracing, called the "Corey skid," improved crash protection. First tested at Laurinburg-Maxton in early 1944, this was named after its inventor, the chief maintenance officer at Laurinburg-Maxton, Lieutenant Colonel Warner R. Corey. Another variant was the Parker skid with a single skid mounted under the center of the nose. These were also welcome because the pilots could rotate farther forward on landing to amplify deceleration. There was no uniform agreement on which skid was superior and so both were taken up by Wright Field, produced and fielded, competing for resources.

A parallel project had a protective steel frame added to the nose. This began with the frame inside an aerodynamic, fabric-covered fairing extending from the front of the aircraft with new windscreen plex. This was dubbed the Ludington-Griswold nose or simply "Griswold nose" after its company and designer Roger W. Griswold II and president of Ludington-Griswold Incorporated of Saybrook, Connecticut. (Griswold and C.T. Ludington apparently teamed up after their Pratt, Read experience.) After a May 1943 proposal, it was tested on 42-52802 that summer at CCAAF. The improved aerodynamics cut drag slightly and an emergency exit on the port side was most welcome. However, the original design added 83 pounds to the glider, used so many elaborate structural members that it would have been too time-consuming and costly for a field installation. The fairing was simplified but ultimately discarded, leaving just the underlying stout frame attached to the existing nose. A noteworthy feature moved the towline attachment to the apex of the nose, 17 inches farther forward than the normal nose length.[49]

On 11 October 1943, Captain Floyd J. Sweet of the Glider Branch flew the first Waco with the Griswold nose to Wright Field for evaluation.[50]

This is the original Ludington-Griswold nose modification, adding protective structure to the CG-4A within an aerodynamic fairing. It was judged too complex for a field modification. However, it had desirable features like pilot emergency exit and the towline attachment at the apex of the nose. (National Soaring Museum)

Field-developed nose protection devices for the Wacos included the Corey skid. This consisted of an external tubular frame with three skids tied to internal structure with added reinforcement. Its purpose was additional protection for pilots during impact with objects on landing—a none-too-infrequent occurrence. This image also shows the boards secured atop the wing ("mooring spoilers") to reduce lift in wind while picketed. (San Diego Air & Space Museum)

As finally selected for use, the Ludington-Griswold modification, or simply "Gris nose," added external bracing tied to internal tubing structure. It moved the towline attach point to the center of this structure and so lower on the nose in an arrangement not entirely welcome by the glider pilots. Captain Floyd Sweet stands before the aircraft that also has the Parker skid on the centerline. (National Soaring Museum)

In November 1943 a contract was being negotiated for 1,000 of the Ludington-Griswold nose modification kits at $367,256.60.[51] A central skid was sometimes added to the base of the Griswold frame to get the benefits of the Corey design—the Ludington-Corey nose.[52]

The pilots welcomed the added protection but had mixed feelings about relocating the towline. Instead of the overhead lever operating the jaws and the clear indication the jaws were closed around the ring, the nose release was via cable and the jaws invisible to the pilots. However, the lower tow point lent some enhanced tow stability and reduced the tendency for the tug to pull a fully loaded glider down onto its skids during initial takeoff acceleration (slamming down during snatch) if the pilot was inattentive. The ground crew naturally preferred the new location as it could be reached standing on the ground. Eventually configured as a field kit, the nose also had a bar extending up the front center of the windscreen to guide wires up and over. The enemy might string such wires across an LZ to decapitate glider personnel. (One account credits the Griswold nose with including a cutting blade on this bar, but it is not evident in available photographs.)[53]

The "Gris nose" modification required about 32 man-hours per glider to install, and the pace of operations meant that they were never universally applied, even when there were sufficient kits to equip every glider (rare). These frequently included either the Corey or Parker skid beneath. For summer 1944 European operations, the modifications were too much effort and too few kits were on hand to equip every glider. The design was incorporated into 1945 CG-4A production, but most of these contracts were cancelled with only a small percentage of the machines completed.

A 10-foot diameter deceleration parachute for the CG-4A was developed at Wright Field and CCAAF, and testing began in fall 1942 at both locations. Within weeks the installation and parachute dimensions had been optimized and production ordered. The chute pack was installed on the port side of the aft fuselage closeout fairing, just behind the tail wheel, and the 25-foot lead line attached to added tubular structure under this fairing. The parachute opening line ran through a tube to the cockpit and a release handle. The fairing was revised during production, beginning in 1943, to create an aft-facing 45-degree facet to which the pack was installed. The parachute was added to contracts for 1945 delivery as standard equipment, but only a small percentage of these aircraft were completed.

The "drag chute" could be deployed prior to landing (75-140 mph) to increase descent rate about 400 fpm without an increase in airspeed, or slow the glider prior to landing, and

The Corey skid was frequently seen in combination with the Gris nose. It and the Parker skid were both evaluated and judged suitable, so both were produced as kits for field installation. This example has a step welded to the skid frame, the vacuum venturi moved to the port side of the nose, and an autotow sensing arm. (National Soaring Museum)

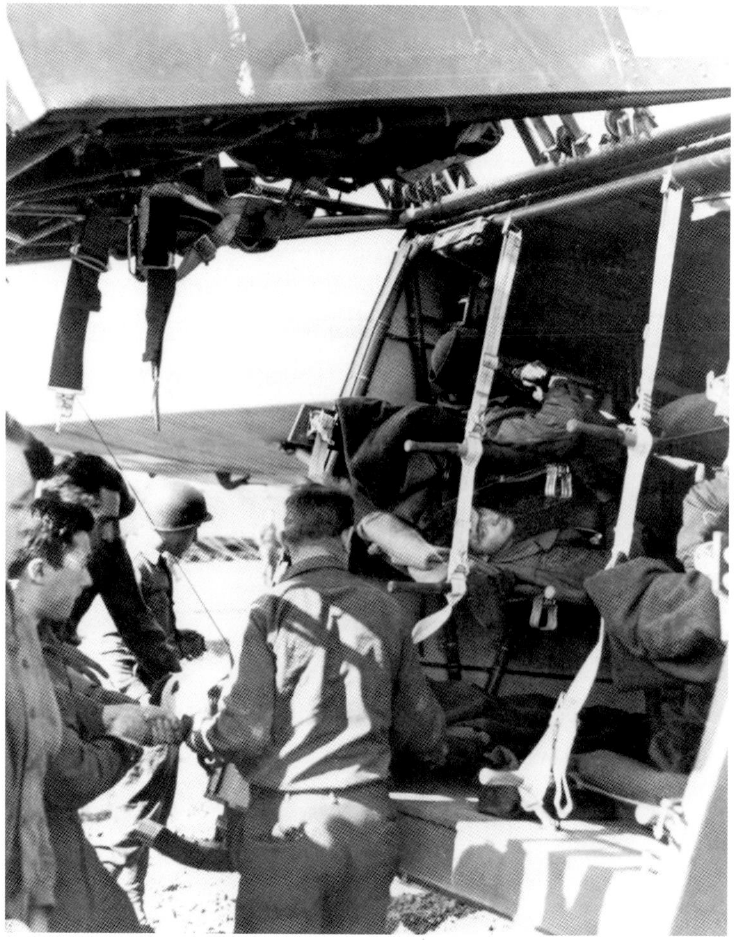

An ambulance conversion for the CG-4A was devised at CCAAF. Six litters could be mounted as shown, with aft benches retained for ambulatory patients and medical attendants. This configuration saw combat use in Europe. (National Museum of the United States Air Force)

In the interest of enhancing aircraft descent angle and deceleration, a drag parachute was developed for the CG-4A. During development of this feature, several sizes of chutes were employed, including this 24-foot example retained to the last moments of a maximum effort stop at Clinton Country AAF. Note the rather small spoilers open atop the wing. (National Museum of the United States Air Force)

to shorten stopping distance. In combination with the wheel brakes, the parachute could assist stopping a glider in 200-300 feet. It could be jettisoned if the approach appeared short. This innovation, too, was met with mixed reactions from the pilots. Large portions of the fleet were never fitted with them because of time and manpower constraints, and the typical short time allowed for glider preparation before an operation.

The nose strengthening and deceleration installations never kept up with the number of aircraft employed in operations, resulting in a mixed fleet. By the time of the Normandy invasion only 288 Wacos had the nose modification. Of the more than 1,000 CG-4As flying in September 1944 Operation *Market-Garden*, 400 carried either the Corey or Griswold noses, and about 900 the arrestor chute.

Litters could be carried in the CG-4A via a modification devised at CCAAF. Supports and straps were rigged on the inside of the forward portion of the cargo compartment, after removing the adjacent benches, to hold three litters per side. Aft benches remained for walking wounded and medical personnel.

The USAAF gave a $38,975.00 contract to Timm Aircraft on 13 May 1942 to build a CG-4A with plywood fuselage. This would provide an alternative design in the event steel tubing became scarce owing to higher priority programs. The aircraft was delivered in April 1943 as the sole XCG-4B (42-46394). It was entirely suitable, but the need for this change never arose. This aircraft was also used to test a "quadracycle" landing gear for the glider with two small struts and wheels attached to either side of the forward fuselage. The service also had several hundred of the CG-4As built in 1944 and 1945 incorporate floors consisting of a compressed wood fibers and resin product called Celluweld, although of restricted loading capacity. One such glider (42-56314) had the nose replaced with one consisting mostly of the same material.[54]

In the event the steel tubing that made up the fuselage structure of the CG-4A became scarce, Timm Aircraft was contracted to build one of the gliders with a wooden fuselage. The resulting XCG-4B was also fitted with experimental 'quadracycle' landing gear consisting of added forward struts. Note the lack of fuselage bottom skids. (National Soaring Museum)

The Waco pilots demonstrate the 10-foot diameter braking parachute for the camera during tests over CCAAF. The chute could be deployed between 80 and 140 mph to increase descent rate or reduce the landing roll, but could be jettisoned at any time. This, too, was met with mixed reactions from the line pilots. (National Soaring Museum)

After combat experience in the ETO, the glider units reported back that a modest addition of armor to protect pilots would improve mission success given the losses observed. The Clinton County team responded with a design and mockup. This would add five 0.25-inch steel plates and 150 pounds to each pilot station and additional side plates of 65 pounds. The plate and Gris-Corey nose modification increased weight of the CG-4A nose section by 365 pounds, making lift with the jeep extremely difficult and likely impossible manually without a great many men.[55] However, with no formal requirement for the armor and the war wrapping up, the idea was dropped.[56]

In the later half of 1944, as TCC and fighter squadrons began to move from base to base with the advancing battlefront, the need for rapid movement of bulky components became more urgent. Gliders offered an option to insert large equipment before the field was fully operational. The gliders could also serve as easily relocatable workshops or simply "cargo trailers" for these air units or even armor forces. The 8th Air Force converted 25 Wacos, configured for different tasks.[57] This suggested the need for a rear loading ramp and cargo floor set low to the ground.

Efforts at developing "autotow" and autopilot systems for the CG-4A is described in Chapter 11.

Other Operators

The British shelved their 15-place Hengist and acquired the CG-4A under Lend-Lease, which they named the Hadrian. These eventually numbered 746 of which five were passed to the Royal Canadian Air Force (FR580 and KH944-947) who eventually acquired 32. However, the British Army was uncomfortable with the CG-4A's fabric-covered fuselage, smaller capacity, and use of spoilers that gave a long, flat glide that made spot landings in fields lined with trees more difficult.

Records indicate an initial acquisition of 25 Hadrian Is, then 20 Hadrian IIs, and a third acquisition consisted of 1,050 Hadrian IIs, although perhaps only 746 were actually transferred.[58] The differences between Marks of Hadrians were likely only the period acquired, although Mk. Is may all have had the droppable undercarriage.

Some 519 CG-4As were delivered from storage to the UK in Fall 1944 for deployment to India.[59] The theater leadership had sought 2,000, but even the 519 found no operational use.[60]

Known serials and tie-ups are presented in the Appendix.

Waco CG-4D, XCG-15, XCG-15A, CG-15A, & G-15A

By summer 1943 the Army was gaining considerable experience with the CG-4A and large numbers were on hand. The glider met most requirements (although it had yet to be tested in combat), but had undergone only modest changes to improve on the hastily developed aircraft. Glider Branch personnel observing maneuvers in May 1943 came away with a list of more extensive refinements that included more effective spoilers, improved crash-worthiness in the nose and provide pilot emergency exits, reinforced landing skids, and more effective interior tie-down fittings. Other changes were desired that simply could not be easily accommodated in the original airframe without unacceptably disrupting production that had to continue at a high rate in meeting training and potential combat needs. Instead, the practical modifications discussed previously to the CG-4A were pursued as field kits to meet immediate needs.

Great Britain made the first combat use of the CG-4A and eventually employed hundreds of the American gliders. One such (FR579 "Voo-Doo," a Pratt, Read machine of unknown serial number) was towed between 23 June and 1 July 1943 by a RAF crew flying from Canada to Scotland in a 3,500-mile North Atlantic crossing—the only tow across the "pond." The Waco, named Hadrian by the Brits, offered a ready means to augment the glider force without extending the Horsa production. (The Peter M. Bowers Collection/The Museum of Flight)

With the CG-4A expected in some quarters to play a big role in coming combat operations, and much remaining to be done to enhance the aircraft, the decision was made in the latter half of 1943 to embark on a revised design. The $24,220.41 Contract Change Order to Waco for the work was issued on 14 October 1943, and called for glider delivery in 84 days (approximately 1 February 1944). A conference on 13-14 November 1943 resulted in a formal list of CG-4 improvements; the potential result being what was tentatively called the CG-4D.

Major Sweet led the effort. Sweet had civilian experience as a glider flight instructor before being called to active duty in December 1940. He subsequently instructed at Elmira, prepared training material in Washington, and then supervised the start-up of the Twenty-Nine Palms school. Sweet worked closely with Waco's chief engineer and designer, A. Francis Arcier. Their work yielded the XCG-15 that was very much like the CG-4A and so could be adopted with few changes to existing equipment and training, as well as being readily introduced into the existing CG-4A production lines.

Principal features of the XCG-15 included a 40 percent shorter wing with just a single strut per side and new ailerons that eliminated buffet while improving control. The higher wing loading would approach that of tug airplanes and permit higher towing speeds. Speed of 180 mph facilitated a wider selection of tow planes to include fighters, with less power required owing to lower drag. The higher wing loading and elimination of the CG-4A's small spoilers mandated addition of electrically powered slotted flaps to maintain the ability to fly the essential slow and steep landing approaches. The added electrical system was handled by charging the battery in flight with a wind generator on the port wing strut. The 30-mph increase in maximum speed also allowed a quicker descent, yet the flaps still permitted low-speed spot landings. All this naturally sacrificed glide performance, but experience had shown extended gliding would not be the norm in combat.

A more streamlined nose incorporated enhanced pilot visibility and crash protection, relocated the towline attach point to the middle of the nose, provided seats with height adjustment, and added pilot emergency exits. A hand-winch (converted C-3 bomb hoist) was employed to raise the nose. Tie-downs were built into the cargo floor. The bottom of the nose could be attached to the forward end of the cargo floor, remaining when the nose was raised and dropping down to serve as a full-width ramp. By simply swapping cables, the winch could also extend an aft fuselage jack to raise the tail for loading. Another switch of cables allowed it to be used in pulling cargo into the cabin. This one device replaced the work of several men. The wooden box troop seats of the CG-4A were replaced with fold-down canvas affairs. Two static lines could be rigged inside for paratroop jumps out the main cabin doors. The landing gear axle was incorporated within the fuselage and the shock strut under a fairing adjacent to the fuselage, eliminating the external bracing. This gave a lower profile and featured improved shock absorption and brakes. The gear was also more likely to remain on the aircraft in a rough landing. Additionally, cargo capacity was increased by 500 pounds or one additional gliderman, despite the 400-pound increase in empty weight.

The CG-15A had a hand winch to raise the nose compartment, and a drop-down nose ramp that greatly improved loading operations. The main landing gear was much more rugged, lowering the aircraft stance and eliminating external struts. Although it would have been more suitable for combat operations and 427 were built, the CG-15A did not see action. (San Diego Air & Space Museum)

The Waco CG-15A revised the CG-4A design to make it more suitable for its role following lessons learned in training and exercises. Evident here in the prototype is the more aerodynamic nose with pilot emergency exits, integral crash protection structure, relocated towline attach point, lack of main gear external struts, and shorter span wing. Note the added skids at the corners of the nose; production aircraft were devoid of skids entirely. (National Soaring Museum)

The first XCG-15 prototype was a modified CG-4A (43-37082) off the Waco line. This aircraft was redelivered on 10 January 1944 (15 February required by contract). The glider did not include all planned features and retained the CG-4A undercarriage and nose. Flight testing awaited installation of the revised nose in February. It eventually appeared with all planned improvements. Skids under the nose and forward fuselage were deleted, although fairings under the nose covering the forward mount points remained. Presumably, the presence of the under-nose ramp precluded skidding on the nose, and the main gear wheels were expected to remain on the fuselage and provide enhanced braking. These factors made removal of drag-producing skids practical. Trials proved satisfactory and two further prototypes (44-90987 and -90988) plus a static test article were ordered under a 21 September 1944 contract estimated at $270,456.00. The maiden flight of these XCG-15As occurred on 25 October. Improvements were identified, especially with respect to equipment loading. The XCG-15 was returned to Troy for upgrading to the final configuration.

The CG-15A was designed such that CG-4A production lines could be quickly converted to manufacturing the new glider with minimal disruption. Both Waco and CG-4A manufacturer Northwestern Aeronautical were initially to build the glider, the latter under a 1 August 1944 contract for 115. Ford Motor Company was also considered, but this was dropped the same month. Later, with pressure to maintain a high CG-4A delivery rate, it was thought best to restrict the work to Waco alone who could respond more quickly. Northwestern's contract was cancelled in October and supplanted with an order for additional CG-4As. The 20 September 1944 contract with Waco called for 385 CG-15s, raised the following month to 775, and then supplemented with another 225 in January 1945. This would have fielded 1,000 gliders by January 1946.

Waco's production began shifting to the CG-15A beginning on 14 October 1944. Changes were represented in the 401st Waco CG-4A to serve as the basis for production, and nine production machines were delivered by the end of the 1944, or 14 months from conception. The time required for production, shipment, and training meant that only seven CG-15As arrived in Europe on 27 March 1945, and 87 before the end of the war. Since, their tow speed was incompatible with the hundreds of other aircraft participating in the March 1945 Operation *Varsity*, the crossing of the Rhine River into Germany, they remained on the ground. Several others were shipped to the Philippines. Of the 427 CG-15As produced—the largest number of any glider other than the CG-4A—none saw combat. The last 42 manufactured added a seat for a 16th soldier.

The balance of aircraft on contract were cancelled in July 1945 and the last delivered that September. Estimated unit cost was $18,102.00, with a total $15,141,993.00 spent on the project by the USAAF.

Only Waco manufactured the CG-15A glider, a close derivative of the CG-4A. In their Troy, Ohio, plant is seen the second and third production aircraft and a XCG-15A fuselage (44-90986) awaiting conversion to the powered XPG-3. The extended flaps on 45-5278 are evidence it is a CG-15A. (National Museum of the United States Air Force)

Table 05-03	
Waco Aircraft CG-15A Specifics	
span	62.2 ft
wing area	623 ft^2
length	48.8 ft
fuselage height	12.6 ft
empty weight	4,025 lbs
gross weight	8,000 lbs
maximum speed	180 mph
stall speed	62 mph no flaps, 57 mph with flaps
capacity	2 pilots, 14 troops (16 in late production)
cabin (front) length x height x width	13.2 x 5.8 (5.0 rear) x 5.8 ft rear height x width 5.0 ft
glide ratio	10:1

The CG-15As soon sported a trio of nose skids that were faired into the profile, evident in this image. However, this machine also displays unusual and possible unique features with forward fuselage stabilizing struts and aft fuselage struts provided by fold-down elements of the fuselage. Also evident are the standard wind generator on the port wing strut, fold-down tube and canvas interior seats, and fairings around the base of the main gear hardware adjacent to the fuselage. (National Soaring Museum)

6

Initial Amphibious Gliders

The initial BuAer tasking had discussed 12-place gliders with jettisonable landing gear and possibly a watertight cabin for potential water landings. On 28 May 1941, the NAF requested permission to pursue a truly amphibious aircraft with retractable undercarriage. This was granted, especially as the USMC concept of operations had already turned in this direction. Alternative cargo of a flying boat engine was considered as the USN then had no aircraft capable of hauling such vital freight, especially to some of the remote locales frequented by these airplanes.[1]

The envisioned glider could be towed aloft from a runway by a fighter or larger aircraft, or towed off the water by a flying boat or seaplane. At the destination the glider was expected to land in the sea and maneuver in lagoons or bays with a 32-horsepower outboard motor. A landing on terrain was conceivable but more likely to result in severe aircraft damage and injuries.

New Concepts

The 12- and 24-place amphibious or "aquaplane" glider requirements were an opportunity for Barnaby's design teams to be truly innovative. After running through somewhat conventional seaplane and flying boat concepts with wing floats, the engineers hit on what Barnaby felt to be more practical candidates. Of four proposals, one was a twin-hull 'catamaran' design to carry the 6 troops in each hull, or other military freight. (The two pilots were expected to fight alongside their passengers once disembarked, and so were included in the 12 count.) Another concept possessed a high wing but 'stub-wings' sponsons at the base of the fuselage for lateral water stabilizers, as some large flying boats had featured. This prompted a more radical idea for eliminating the high wing and extending the stubs to full wings. The most promising 12-place concept was clearly this "floatwing" glider that, like the catamaran, did not require drag-generating outrigger floats that, if retractable, would required a power systems to actuate.

The concept of the floatwing envisioned an aircraft with low wing merging into a flying boat hull. Much of the flotation and stability would derive from inboard portions of the sealed, hollow wing. Dihedral would place control surfaces above the water for unimpeded lateral control during takeoff and landing. (For the eventual XLRQ-1 floatwing glider, the wingtips were normally about 5.0 feet above the water. On land, with a man standing at the tip, the clearance was still 3.0 feet overhead.) The wing was also to be equipped with spoilers and flaps.[2] The design featured a two-step planing hull, was 39.5-foot long, with 70-foot wingspan, and 13.8-foot height.[3]

On 26 July the NAF conceptual designs were submitted to BuAer. There was some disquiet with the unusual results, although it still included a landplane design that received scant attention. In addition, the Marines expressed discontent with the low-wing aquaplane glider because it would not permit rapid exit of parachute troops for static line jumps. The high-wing twin-hull design appeared more suitable in this respect and the Corps suggested it be expanded to meet the 24-place requirement. It might also be suitable for light tanks and other large articles.

The NAF was asked on 24 July to perform tests to collect validating data on the designs. Scale models of the twin-hull and floatwing aquaplanes were built for wind tunnel and towed float tank trials. These were crafted by Paul Karnow, a youthful local modelmaker. The floatwing model spanned 4.3 feet at 1/10th scale and weighed 6.05

In devising a practical concept for an amphibious transport glider, engineers at the Naval Aircraft Factory hit on the "floatwing" concept. Stability on the water would derive from the inboard portions of the low wing with substantial dihedral, while the fuselage had the normal flying boat planing hull. They had this model built for wind tunnel and water tow tank tests. (National Soaring Museum)

With uncertainty as to the suitability of the floatwing concept, other ideas were suggested. This naval glider design appears to date from the formative period of the USN glider development, yet does not conform to any of the documented projects. Its origin and fate are unknown. (Jay Miller Collection)

A large model of the 24-place amphibious glider concept was also built for scaled tests. This twin-hull 'catamaran' kept the high wing and tail clear of water spray. Note how the wing segment between the fuselages possesses a longer chord than the segments outboard of the hulls; a feature not carried to final design. (National Soaring Museum)

pounds. Tested in the NAF tank and a the National Advisory Committee for Aeronautics (NACA) Langley, Virginia, tow tank in March 1942, it demonstrated good water handling behavior, rising onto the step with excellent trim. The 1/10th scale, 12.2 pounds, 24-place twin-hull model was also tested in the tanks.

Consistent with War Department wishes, the gliders were to be built principally of wood. The exterior covering would be laminated Birch sheets impregnated with casein glue such that each layer became plasticized enough for molding under pressure and heat to more readily create compound curves. Large molds would be constructed for the primary components into which were laid the treated wood veneers for curing. The exterior surfaces were then coated with a plywood sealer and painted. The results were both watertight and insect-proof. Although some consideration was given to the NAF performing the detail design work, their non-familiarity with the preferred construction method negated this possibility.[4]

With a sense of urgency, BuAer did not wait for the test results before pressing on. A requisition for full-scale Class VLR experimental aircraft was approved on 2 August 1941. The 12- and 24-place preliminary designs were ready to be passed on to prospective manufacturers. Together, they were felt to balance technical risk from the perspectives of the floatwing and catamaran hulls. Again, in line with prevailing War Department preference, emphasis remained on firms not already committed to priority powered aircraft projects and with the gliders constructed mostly of wood.

To reduce the demand for strategic materials required by high-priority programs, the Marine gliders were to be built primarily of wood. The lamination of plasticized wood veneers into compound curves of the outer surfaces is shown in this photo of the Allied Aviation XLRA-1 under construction during 1943. The choice brought with it issues of suitable wood sources, workman training, and protection of the structure from the elements. (Naval Aviation Archives)

12-Place Glider Contracts

A few more than 19 firms were identified as potential suppliers of the amphibious gliders and sent invitation letters in July 1941. Nearly all were newly founded or with shallow experience. Invitations to bid were then sent to 17 manufacturers in mid-August, with submittals expected by the end of September. The service wanted the first glider in 180 days after contract award and the second in 210 days. For the 12-place glider, the NAF projected an empty weight of 2,814 pounds (to be guaranteed), gross 6,050 pounds, and stated $227,500.00 was a reasonable contract value that also included a static test article delivered in three months.

Four firms responded within the required 30 days to the Navy requirements for the 12-place aquaplane; Aeromold Corporation (soon renamed Greenport Aeronautical Corporation), Allied Aviation Corporation of Dundalk, Maryland, Bristol Aircraft Corporation of Bristol, Virginia, and Timm Aircraft Corporation. Allied estimated a 3,059-pound empty weight and $273,346.00 to complete the contract in the time specified. Against the same schedule, Bristol wanted $369,050.00 for their 3,169-pound design and Aeromold $322,564.00. However, Aeromold was discounted as it had just opened its doors and was not prepared to make anything but a general bid. Timm felt they needed 255 days to deliver the second article of 3,064 pounds and wanted $384,970.50.

The 8 October 1941 award went Allied, the firm with the lowest bid cost and empty weight for the XLRA-1, specifying delivery of the static article in 180 days (8 April 1942). Allied had begun operating less than a year before and had done subcontract work building airframe components for other firms. To date it had not attempted design and manufacture of an entire aircraft. None of the over-worked Navy procurement personnel visited their facility to assess ability to perform against the contract.

Engaging a second contractor was considered prudent given the uncertainty engendered in hiring such an inexperienced firm, their likely inability to manufacture gliders in quantity to a likely high-rate schedule, the general lack of experience in constructing aircraft of plasticized plywood, and the perceived urgency in the program. Even if only one design was selected for production, the other contractor could be hired to also manufacture the winning design. After BuAer proposed on 7 October letting a contract to the next lowest bidder, the decision was made to engage Greenport, in the hope that at least one would yield useful results.

Before the 15 December 1941 contract was awarded to Greenport, the firm was advised to begin work while awaiting the formal document. Delivery was to be 15 July 1942. However, it was learned the company had changed its name again to Bristol Aeronautical Corporation. Elements of Bristol Aircraft Corporation had acquired Greenport on 30 October and moved to New Haven, Connecticut.[5] The value of the contract, $283,500.00, was $10,000.00 above the Allied contract but $39,064.00 below that of the Greenport bid. And, despite being awarded later, Bristol faced a nearly identical delivery date of 20 June 1942 for the static article and first test aircraft, 20 July for the second glider. They insisted upon a 30 percent advance payment.[6]

Bristol Aeronautical XLRQ-1

The President of Bristol, George W. Warren, formerly a long-time Curtiss-Wright employee, partnering with Albert L. "Pat" Patterson. Patterson had been a naval aviator and retained close ties with service personnel, as well as having worked as an engineer at Curtiss. Warren wisely hired experienced engineers and designers, many having experience with Grumman, such as Chief Engineer J.P. Donald 'George' Garges. From a core of five individuals, Bristol grew to 750 people who would, within a year, design, develop, and build a unique military aircraft. However, their working capitol was meager and they were escutcheoned in a small lumber mill capable then of producing only small structures. Additional work space in a Ford auto dealership and a "car barn" was soon secured. Their design, the XLRQ-1, naturally accommodated an additional marine, and so was actually a 13-place glider.[7] Bristol's fiscal condition was so tenuous that it was unable to supply a bond to secure an advance payment that was necessary to finance the contract. The Navy had to step in during February 1942 and arrange financing through a service-controlled account.[8]

Closely following the NAF conceptual design, the low-wing wooden glider had flaps and spoilers, a shallow boat hull with two steps, and a vast 'greenhouse' canopy over the forward half—perhaps the largest plexiglass canopy introduced to that time. Aft panels of the canopy on both sides were hinged along the top to rise up for troop ingress and egress over the wing. Ailerons were fabric-covered. A 32-horsepower outboard motor was tested, but the bay could also accommodate a 100-horsepower Evenrude.[9] The motor could be extended through doors under the aft fuselage just forward of the aft step. It was supplied with 4 gallons of fuel and oil, another 4 gallons in reserve, and could be steered via the rudder pedals. One battery was included.

Engineering changes contributed to considerable delay in the project and weight growth. Water basin tests by NACA in spring 1942 with an 11 percent model made clear hull changes were required and so the design was altered to incorporate twin steps.[10] On 1 July 1942 the Navy specified controllable aileron and rudder trim tabs rather than the original adjustable. Bristol initially designed their aircraft with a single center landing gear, like sailplanes. The Navy judged this impractical, insisting on a retractable tricycle undercarriage in a 6 January 1943 change order. However, their decision came as the static test airframe was being finished and added to delays in the flight airframes. This change was complex, but time was saved by adopting PBY-5A oleo struts, yet only by accepting yet another

As with the Army gliders, the Navy required a static test article of each design to be tested at their facilities prior to flying an airworthy example. This appears to be the XLRQ-1 static article on its transport trailer. The setting is likely the Philadelphia Navy Yard. Note the wing root clevis fittings without evidence of landing gear mounts. (National Soaring Museum)

The Bristol XLRQ-1 static test article was turned into a flight article, seen here during water trials in Philadelphia during the last days of 1942 or perhaps early January 1943. At this time, the glider lacked any wing root fairings for the main gear, as it also lacked undercarriage. The towline attach point and fittings for other ropes assisting in securing the glider are visible on the nose. (National Soaring Museum)

weight increase.[11] Navy direction on 3 May 1943 to change from stick to yoke control, pilot overhead escape hatch altered from inward to outward opening, and instrument panel lighting alterations, all generated additional delay.[12] These change orders added $113,065.57 to the contract. These and other factors were cause for the Navy to add value to the contract on three occasions between 9 November 1942 and 30 April 1943, summing to $386,000.00.[13]

Bristol delivered their static article to the NAF on 16 October 1942. This required additional work, delaying the tests that were limited by the hull being sealed, lacking undercarriage or outboard motor bays. Trials were only made to "proof loads" of 100 percent of design versus the ultimate of 150 percent.

After completion of the limited loads tests, a decision was made to perform all necessary work, to include installation of the outboard, to permit the static airframe to serve as an initial flight aircraft for sea trials only. These preliminary tests were performed by the NAF on the Delaware River, abutting the Philadelphia Navy Yard. After delays for ice in the river, three flights were performed on 3 January 1943 with a Grumman J2F-5 Duck tug. While the lightly loaded glider performed well enough, the tug pilot noted lousy visibility and dangerously poor directional control on a takeoff that proved exceptionally long.[14] Stability of the glider on the water was "splendid."[15] Flight control and handling in flight were satisfactory. Two tows behind a PBY-5A on January 15th were much better. Two flights the following day at 6,000 pounds GW were also fine. The aircraft may not actually have been towed to height for release but simply off the water. Surface runs using the outboard motor on 20 January went well, but the crew complained of engine exhaust fumes filling the cabin and there was some water intrusion from the motor well at maximum throttle. Loading and unloading trials were also performed with fully equipped marines. Following this work the aircraft was returned for completion of static tests.

The prototype XLRQ-1 was delivered to the NAF on 5 May 1943. This had wheel controls replacing the twin sticks of the static article. The new tricycle landing gear, fitted with wheel brakes, had the mains retracting into the wing root for which wells were created with fairings added in the upper wing-fuselage junctions. This was a significant departure from the original static article, and so the machine was subjected to additional static checks

Bristol Aeronautical constructed its own model of the XLRQ-1 for wind tunnel and water tank trials (not as shown). The latter revealed the need for boat hull changes that contributed to program slips. This model sports the wing root fairings and so may not be the original configuration tested. (National Soaring Museum)

The XLRQ-1 static article, made airworthy, flies above the surface of the Delaware River during early January 1943 in one of its few test flights. This was the first amphibious glider to fly in the U.S., and little else like it was accomplished in other countries. The hull twin steps are readily evident. (National Soaring Museum)

and drop tests of the gear.[16] Three gear fairings were devised with the intention of testing each for the lowest drag. Baring completion of tests on the static article, flight restrictions were imposed that included 8,200 pounds GW and a 110 mph speed placard.[17] These made complete testing impossible, but a good shakedown was accomplished.

Surface and flight trials of the glider in Phily on 6 through 16 August 1943 had on board pilot E. K. Jaquith, observer (Bristol test pilot) Harry C. Sparks, and mechanic George Salo, all presumably Bristol employees. The PBY-5A *Tugboat Annie* was operated by Major Figley and Captain Reilly. Surface trials revealed some minor problems but were otherwise encouraging. Launching and beaching on the landing gear, water maneuvering with the outboard, and tow from shore and by a motor boat were all evaluated. Using the rudder pedals to steer the outboard was hampered by high control forces. A separate wheel for this purpose was recommended. In one case an outboard hatch door linkage failed and the door struck the propeller, damaging both. Motor boat towing was not going to work as the glider yawed badly and one wing submerged, flooding the pitot-static probe located at the wingtip. It appeared advisable to relocate the probe to above the cockpit. The crew appears to have found the glare under the expansive canopy objectionable and the overhead was soon painted a dark shade.

First flight was on 6 August and lasted 15 minutes. Tow was at 104 mph to 1,200 feet. On landing the previously damaged outboard motor well door ripped away and sank. This appears to have been the initial up-and-away flight of the XLRQ-1, becoming the first amphibious glider in the United States, if not anywhere. During the second and third flights on the 6th, each 30 minutes long with release at 2,000 feet, the gear retracted fine but the nose doors did not close completely. Tail vibrations were experienced that required subsequent minor control system rework. The fourth and fifth flights on the

Table 06-01	
Bristol Aeronautical XLRQ-1 Specifics	
span	71.2 ft
wing area	500 ft²
length	41.8 ft
height on ground	13.8 ft
empty weight	5,261 lbs
gross weight	8,603 lbs (test limit)
maximum speed	180 mph (test limit 110 mph)
glide speed	84 mph
landing speed	59 mph
capacity	2 pilots, 10 troops
glide ratio	19.9:1

The first of two formal prototype XLRQ-1s is pulled up a flying boat ramp in Philadelphia during trails in summer 1943. The wing root fillet was added for the retractable landing gear and the canopy configuration was altered several times. Note the deepened hull and step aft of the wing trailing edge, and the open outboard motor bay doors. (National Soaring Museum)

10th were each 20-minutes in duration and at heavier weights, with runway takeoff and landing. Overall, handling on the water and in flight was very good. Operations were conducted in up to four-foot swells. The landing gear was manually actuated in this glider and retraction required considerable effort by the pilot.[18] At some point a full squad of marines were loaded and unloaded for demonstration.

The water landing on the fifth flight, with 2,213 pounds of ballast, was at maximum angle of attack and about 46 mph. Some hull structural damage resulted owing to high suction loads, suggesting the need for strengthening in the areas of both steps. It was clear tests to higher weights were unsafe. Consequently, the sixth flight on the 16th was a 1.25-hour ferry from Phily back to New Haven with Sparks flying. During the mission the pilot discovered that full spoilers blanked the rudder, rendering it entirely ineffective.

While the PBY and Major Figley were in New Haven, the opportunity was taken on 16 August to fly the second XLRQ-1, completed on 30 July, to check operation of the hydraulically actuated landing gear on this example (although the accumulator had to be pumped to pressure by hand). This worked well and was judged mechanically superior to the manual system, in addition to being 200 pounds lighter. The wheel well fairings were also different than on the initial prototype, but experienced more buffeting from flow separation. A test flight was flown as late as 5 December.[19]

Allied Aviation XLRA-1

On 3 October 1941, Allied was authorized to begin work on the XLRA-1 while awaiting the final contract, signed on the 8th. This was a cost-plus-fixed-fee vehicle with 30 percent advanced payment and progress payments.[20] Delivery dates were 8 April 1942 for the static article and first test aircraft, and 8 May for the second glider. However, less than two months after contract award, these dates slipped with 15 July for the static article, and 30 days more for the first flight machine, 45 for the second. These dates soon moved farther to the right to ten months beyond the original schedule. Although the Navy admitted the ambitious delivery dates and modest contract value were merely "something to aim at," the mere fact that a company would agree to such terms for an experimental design suggested they did not understand what they were getting into.[21]

The interior of the XLRA-1 shows some troop seating and pilot stations for a total 12. The spartan instrument panel is arranged in a vertical fashion and affords excellent vision forward. The dual control wheels were a change from sticks—one of several alterations that slowed development. (Naval Aviation Archives)

The initial example XLRA-1 breaks the water off the Delaware River during flight trials in 1943. Note that the wing and aft fuselage ground stabilization struts are still in place. The towline is still in the water, offering additional drag during the acceleration to flight speed. (National Soaring Museum)

At this instant in a test flight, the XLRA-1 is still retracting its centerline landing gear and is in a low tow position. Pitot tube and sideslip vane are well above the aircraft to avoid water spray. Note the pilot sliding side windows. (National Soaring Museum)

A Grumman F4F-3 Wildcat stands ready to tow aloft the first example XLRA-1 at Mustin Field, Philadelphia. Note how the glider leans on its wing skids, these to be replaced in time with wheeled pogos. The dual centerline wheels are evident. (National Museum of Naval Aviation)

The 12-place XLRA-1 glider was unofficially named the Invader. Among the principals at Allied was president Richard E. Breed, III, executive vice-president Hugh S. Williamson, general manager Burnham Litchfield, and chief engineer Walter F. Burke. Breed had previously worked in the energy industry while Burke had a solid background in aircraft development.[22]

Showing their common heritage, the XLRA-1 looked very similar to the XLRQ-1. It was equipped with flaps and spoilers. The glider featured a dual-wheel retractable truck on the centerline, without brakes, and mid-wing outriggers. On the first aircraft the outriggers were simple skids while the second the outriggers were oleo struts with wheels and the aft fuselage featured a roller. Unlike Bristol, Allied was not immediately required to change to a tricycle gear. However, the switch from dual stick to dual wheel control cost schedule. A portion of the upper fuselage aft of the cockpit, fitted with windows, was hinged and on runners to rise up and collapse in accordion sections. Fittings were installed to support a Wright R-3350 engine in the cabin.

The static article was delivered to Philadelphia on 16 December 1942. However, the structure was incomplete and the company sent six workmen to finish construction. Weaknesses were then uncovered during test that required the wing to be rebuilt.[23] This testing was still underway in September 1943.[24] Drop tests of the landing gear were also conducted. A sample XLRA-1 wing was subjected to live gunfire testing at some point using .50 caliber and 20 mm high explosive rounds. It did not behave in a survivable manner, experiencing large areas of separated material and delaminations on both the entry and exit sides.

After delivery of the first prototype over eight months late, flight testing commenced at NAF. During the first flight on 24 March 1943, the wing was damaged. Although Allied insisted the glider had stuck a floating object, BuAer suspected design flaws, rough seas, or both.[25] The glider was repaired, including changes suggested by the static tests, but operated under restrictions because the wing was considered structurally deficient. In any event, final demonstration trials from 18 August through 9 September proved satisfactory.

Launch and recover from a seaplane ramp was good, but the trailer was less desirable than rolling on the landing gear. The 33-horsepower outboard maneuvered the craft suitably but the propeller was not the best choice and ventilation of the motor bay was

The first XLRA-1 prototype motors along at a slow speed with its outboard motor during testing in 1943. Tufts are attached to the surface of the aircraft to enable visualization of airflow in flight. The accordion doors offered over-wing egress of marines at least four at a time. (Naval Aviation Archives)

inadequate, the cabin filling with smoke and fumes. An alternative 9.7 horsepower motor propelled the glider at 4-5 knots, but just modest winds or swells impeded all movement.

Tows were performed at various times by a Grumman F4F-3 Wildcat, J2F-5 Duck, Catalina, and a motorboat. Some porpoising was experienced at the early portion of the water takeoff in light chop, and the towing seaplanes were working hard, but once on the step everything smoothed out. The wake of the tug actually smoothed out the trailing surface and quieted the glider's ride to liftoff. During the takeoff it was found that the towline dragged in the water and broke free only after both aircraft were airborne. This caused severe pitching of the glider and required considerable pilot skill to prevent a mishap. It appeared to be an endemic problem with water takeoff of a towed glider, likely also introducing additional drag for the tug to overcome.

Land takeoff and alighting were not difficult with the sailplane undercarriage, but the lack of wheel brakes was unacceptable. On one takeoff during which the glider was not aligned with the tug, the glider served sharply and dragged the port wing skid that then broke away. It appeared to be made of inferior materials. Allied replaced it with a better part. A few other minor failures occurred during the testing and were identified for correction.

The second aircraft was delivered in September.[26] Some accounts suggest the Allied glider was the better of the two competitors. Barnaby flew the XLRQ-1 and XLRA-1.

Elusive 24-Place Gliders

Following the USMC's recommendation, the NAF's catamaran glider was recast as a 24-place craft and prospective manufacturers sought. A requisition for experimental gliders was approved on 19 August 1941 and 21 firms invited to bid within 30 days. Six companies submitted proposals, but the Allied Aviation bid was rejected because it arrived after the mandated 24 September date, and Bowlus Sailplanes' because their bid was improperly based. The NAF had projected $316,000.00 as a reasonable price and empty weight of 5,728 pounds (to be guaranteed), gross 12,200 pounds. Like the 12-place program, the contractor was to deliver a static article in three months, the first flight-worthy aircraft in six months, and the second a month later. Snead & Company bid $266,510.00 and 5,728 pounds, Greenport Aeronautical Corporation $295,500.00 at 5,845 pounds, Pitcairn-Larson Autogiro Company, Incorporated, with $364,471.23 and 5,728 pounds, and Timm Aircraft Corporation at $631,897.00 with 6,092 pounds.

A contract was issued on 14 October 1941 to the lowest bidder/lowest weight—Snead & Company—although the firm also submitted good substantiating engineering data that had not been requested. The company, of Jersey City, New Jersey, had experience constructing welded steel assemblies under subcontract and steel office furnishings, but also welded aluminum assemblies such as fuel tanks and pontoons for Republic Aviation. It was entirely new to aircraft design and wood work. The company was told on 9 October to begin the XLRH-1 while awaiting the signed contract. Their delivery dates were 180 days or 14 April 1942 for the static article and initial test aircraft, 14 May for the other glider.

In the same manner as the 12-place glider, a competing project was considered in October 1941. Although Greenport was the next lowest bidder, they were being given a 12-place glider contract. Hence, the offer went to the third lowest bidder, Pitcairn-Larson. As described previously, this concern was soon renamed A.G.A. Aviation Corporation. Their design departed markedly from the NAF twin-hull concept in having an intermediate fuselage atop the wing segment between the twin hulls. This was considered an advantage to some in taking a different approach, while others saw it as a source of suspicion and noted the boat hulls appeared to be unsuitable. There was initially a desire to have A.G.A. develop the NAF design.

In meeting these doubts, A.G.A. sought assistance from Edo Aircraft Corporation who had a exemplary reputation for design and manufacturing aircraft boat hulls and floats.[27] A.G.A. also decided to demonstrate the suitability of their "twin float" design with a scaled-down flight model. This 40-percent scale wooden aircraft was built in just 35 days for $40,000.00-45,000.00, entirely company funded.[28] Captain Barnaby, along with other pilots, conducted a series of flights with this machine in Philadelphia beginning on 16 November 1941. Although some design changes were suggested, the results were satisfactory. Hence, A.G.A. was awarded a contract on 23 December for $350,941.69 ($13,529.54 less than their bid) and began work while the document was finalized. This stipulated a 30 percent advance and 6 percent fixed-fee. The contract used the vehicle of a USN-controlled account in lieu of the advance for which the resource-poor A.G.A could not secure a bank bond. They were to provide the static article in seven months on 23 July 1942 and both XLRG-1 test gliders on 23 August.

Although schedules for the 24-place contractors were admittedly little more than something on which the Navy could "hang its hat," it was optimistic in the extreme given the immaturity of the firms involved and the challenges of the undertaking. It does not appear that any of the hard-pressed USN personnel visited the competitors prior to contract award. Each of the firms was newly formed or reorganized with little or no actual airplane design and manufacturing experience. All their contracted delivery dates slipped within months of starting work.

Table 06-02

Allied Aviation XLRA-1 Specifics

span	72.0 ft
wing area	495 ft²
length	40.0 ft
height	12.3 ft
empty weight	2,800 lbs
gross weight	6,050 lbs (estimate)
tow speed	130 mph, 150 mph maximum
glide speed	83.7 mph (estimate)
stall speed	68 mph, 59 mph flaps down
capacity	2 pilots, 10 troops
landing distance	1,500 ft (pavement)
glide ratio	18.8:1 (estimate)

Table 06-03

Snead & Company XLRH-1 Specifics (estimated, not flown)

span	110.0 ft
length	48.8 ft
height	15.3 ft
empty weight	5,728 lbs (guaranteed)
gross weight	12,200 lbs
tow speed	180 mph maximum
glide speed	77.8 mph
stall speed	49.2 mph sea level
capacity	2 pilots, 22 troops
glide ratio	18.53:1

Table 06-04

A.G.A. XLRG-1 Specifics (estimated, not flown)

span	108.5 ft
length	57.0 ft
height	17.3 ft
empty weight	4,800 lbs initially, later 6,330 lbs
gross weight	12,802 lbs
tow speed	200 mph
glide speed	95 mph
stall speed	49.5 mph
capacity	2 pilots, 22 troops
glide ratio	15.75:1

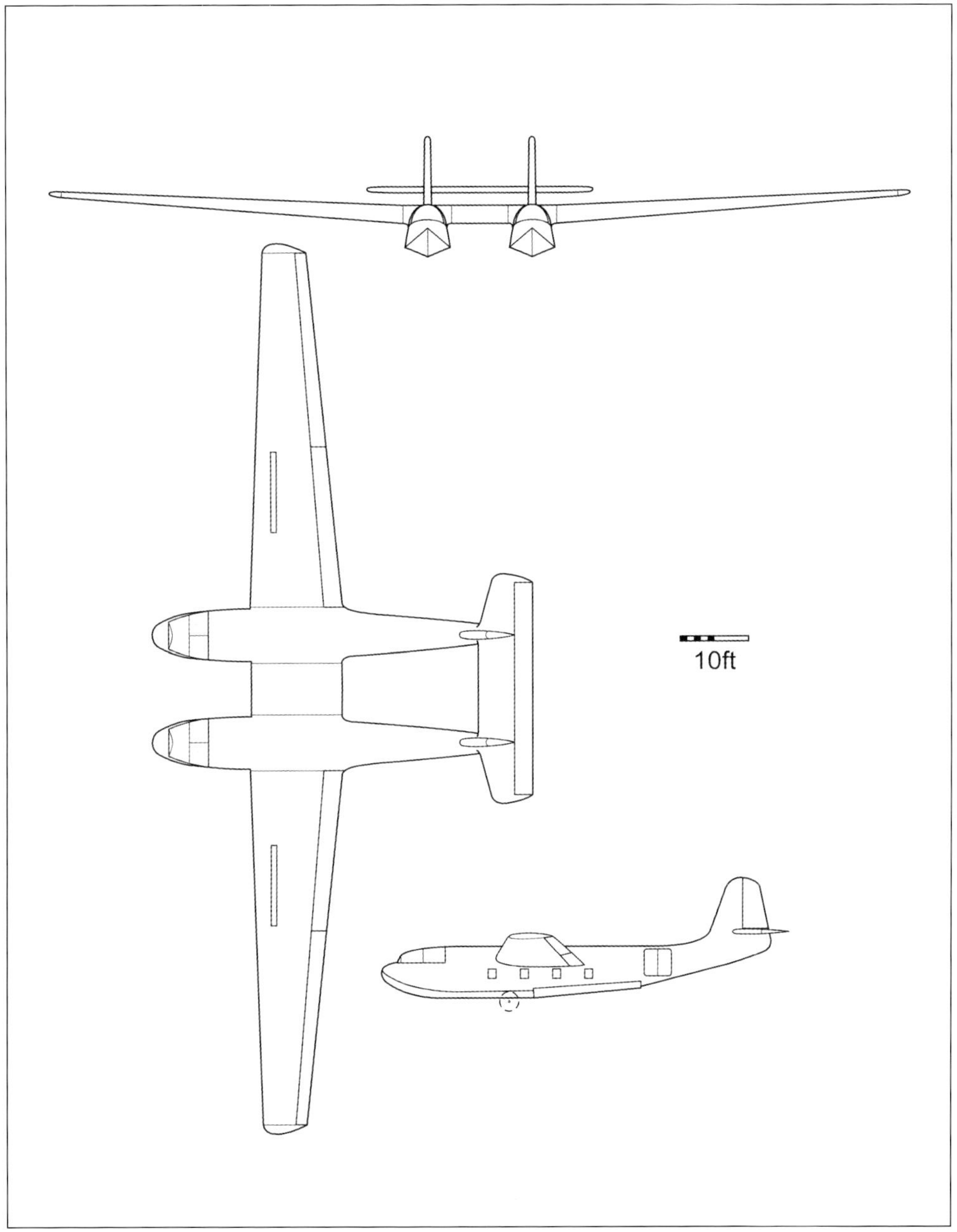

This drawing of the Snead & Company XLRH-1 is derived from the Navy report on their glider project, photos of the glider mockup, and the aircraft under construction. The twin-hull design was intended to provide stability on the water without the flight drag of wing-mounted floats. The machine was to span 110 feet and gross 12,000 pounds. (Author)

As with almost all American WWII aircraft, a mockup was constructed of the XLRH-1. This image of the nose, that contained a cockpit mockup (right), shows how the outer mold lines were altered during detailed design compared with the initial concept. Beyond is a glimpse of Snead's Orange, Virginia, plant. (National Archives)

Snead & Company was run from Jersey City, but with engineering offices in New York City and construction facilities in Orange, Virginia. Under consulting engineer Dr. Alexander Klemin, the XLRH-1 closely followed the NAF's twin hull design. Towing was to be via an attachment on the wing centersection. Two 35-horsepower outboards were to provide water propulsion. A large door was provided in the outboard side of each fuselage well aft of the wing which was equipped with spoilers and flaps. Through wind tunnel tests, it was discovered the NAF's choice of wing was unsuitable and considerable additional work had to be performed, albeit with NAF assistance. However, the firm's detailed design was judged poor, at best, by BuAer engineers. Tests at Langley's tow tank were in May 1942 and again in June with the 1/10th scale model, the main step doubled.

The competing A.G.A., previously introduced, was to create the XLRG-1. The above-wing "intermediate" center fuselage pod housed the two pilots and a dozen troops while the twin "floats," to be provided by Edo and from which the tail booms issued, would carry five marines each. Movement on the water was enabled via two 35-horsepower outboard motors. Wing flaps were featured inboard and outboard of the floats. The firm became G & A Aircraft, Incorporated in early 1942, a division of Firestone Tire and Rubber Company.

Production Plans

With the continuing pressure to get aircraft to marines for operational tests at the earliest date, required numbers expanding by leaps and bounds, and fears the Army would snatch up all remaining glider manufacturing capacity, BuAer decided to issue production contracts for 100 of each 12-place glider model.[29] The earliest exploration of production capability had been 9 February 1942 and appeared to fly in the face of the original intention to restrain the USMC glider program. Although many voices spoke against production until the value of the whole concept had been demonstrated, an order of this magnitude was still considered cautionary, ensuring resources were in place for immediate large-scale orders if such a decision was made. All the USN glider manufacturers would have had to substantially expand their facilities or find partners to meet the production commitments.

Allied was given a $2,100,000.00 Letter of Intent on 4 April 1942 for 100 units before the XLRA-1 had substantially taken form.[30] The contract was dated 8 June but not signed until the later half of August. Production was expected to commence on 15 August, although Allied lacked the space to undertake such work. The agreement included a peculiar provision by which the second flight test glider under the original contract was to count as the first production aircraft under the second cost-plus-fixed-fee contract, allowing funds to be advanced to the company ailing under the initial fixed-price contract.[31] Apparently as another concession to Allied's tottering condition, the tricycle undercarriage (modified Curtiss P-40 fighter components replacing the pogos) was to be introduced only with the 11th production machine, LRA-2.[32] This left the initial 10 with the single wheel lacking brakes, LRA-1s, that were considered unacceptable. Allied had already received a $289,800.00, 3 March 1942 contract for three XLRA-2s. Although design was complete by June 1942, no delivery date was specified.[33] The Navy anticipated a delivery rate of 10 aircraft per month and a plant was being prepared in Winston-Salem, North Carolina.

Allied had a conceptual design for a high-wing 12-place glider with traditional wingtip floats. This was to feature wing spoilers and flaps, and was noted as amphibian with a center wheel. Since there was still some doubt as to the suitability of the floatwing design, developing an alternative appeared wise to BuAer. Some in the Bureau seemed to believe Allied had the wherewithal to develop this new glider concurrent with their existing contractual obligations. A move was made on 19 March 1942 to contract for two aircraft and a static article at $289,800.00, and requisition for this XLR2A-1 was issued 28 April. However, Allied did not provide suitable quotations for contract definitization and the matter was dropped, although $1,626.47 was expended on the aborted effort.

An order for 50 gliders from Bristol was considered at the same time Allied was approached about production. However, it was 2 June 1942 before Bristol could provide a production proposal. It suggested 80-90 percent of the work would be

Table 06-05

Allied Aviation XLR2A-1 Specifics (estimated, not built)[34]

span	73.0 ft
length	41.8 ft
height on ground	14.6 ft
empty weight	3,089 lbs
gross weight	6,325 lbs
maximum speed	180 mph
glide speed	78 mph
stall speed	48.0 mph sea level
capacity	2 pilots, 10 troops
glide ratio	16.9:1

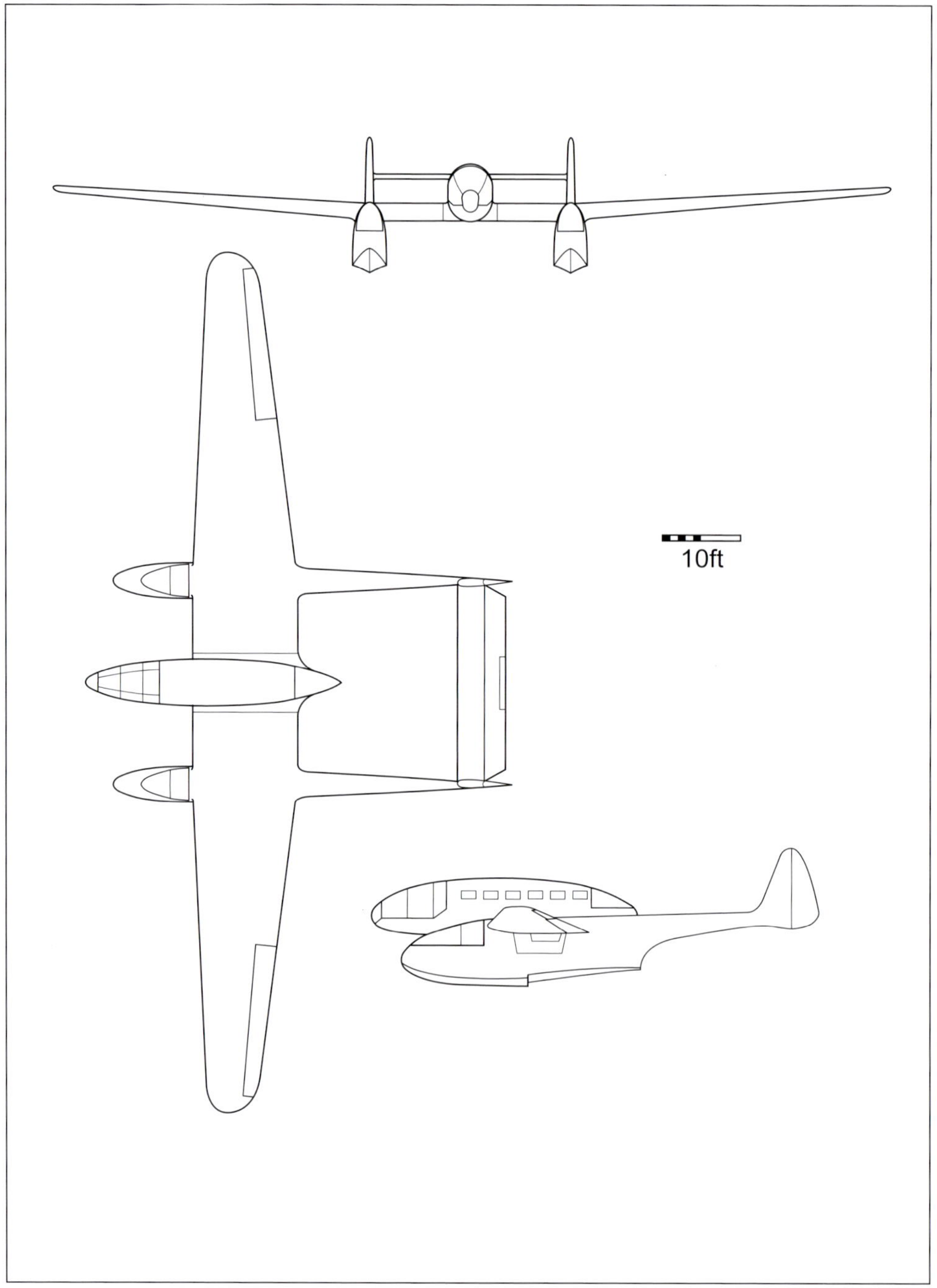

This three-view of the A.G.A. XLRG-1 was created from a drawing in the same Navy report. The infantrymen were to be distributed among the three hulls. The guns shown protruding from the hulls in early concept art were lacking in the drawing. The ambitious design was to span 108.5 feet and gross 12,802 pounds. (Author)

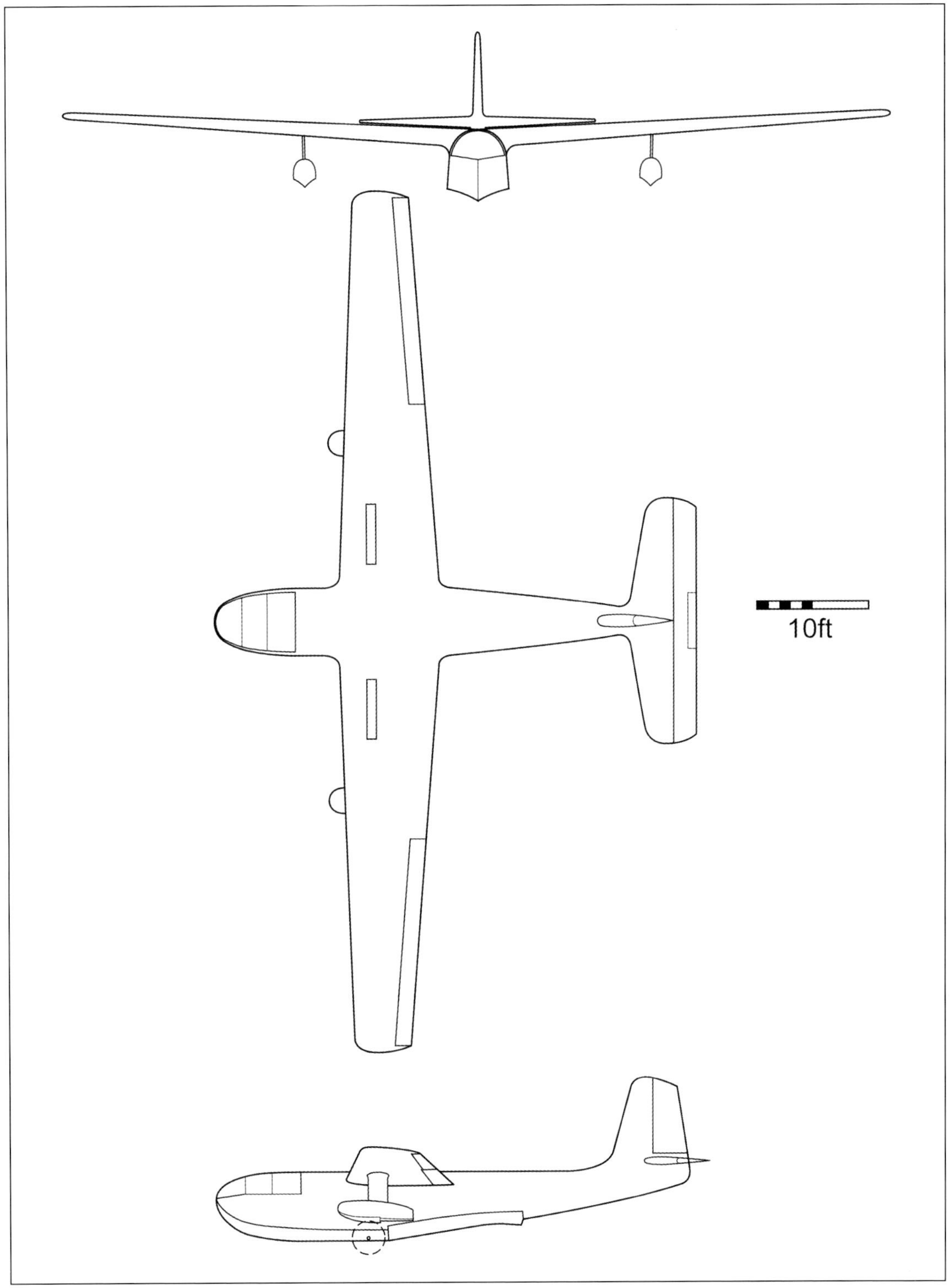

The Allied Aviation XLR2A-1 was a departure from the floatwing and twin-hull designs the Navy initially set forth to develop. It was conceived as a less technically risky alternative, one that might reach fruition sooner, and also help keep Allied financially afloat. The XLR2A-1 ultimately progressed little beyond the drawing that is the basis for this three-view. (Author)

subcontracted to experienced woodworking companies and assembled at a site still being sought. A hundred LRQ-1s were ordered from Bristol on a 4 August Letter of Intent, amended on the 19th to include ten trailers capable of hauling the gliders into and out of the water. This order came after Bristol had remarked that if it did not get a Navy production commitment it might be consumed with Army glider work.[35] The $2,878,105.00 7 September cost-plus-fixed-fee contract estimated $27,215.00 with $1,200.00 fixed-fee per aircraft. The first two gliders were to be delivered in 107 days and expectations were that, working flat out, it would be a year before the hundred gliders were completed. All this came well before substantive XLRQ-1 testing, and Mr. Warren later confessed he expected actual costs to be $43,000.00 per aircraft.[36]

The 24-place aircraft were pursued less vigorously than the 12-place models because of greater uncertainty and ambition inherent in the designs. There was residual skepticism about them, especially as they would likely be expensive to build and all conceivable landing gear or jettisonable trolley designs for a runway takeoff appeared cumbersome. However, eager to move ahead, the potential for early production was explored beginning on 9 February 1942.

Snead replied on 24 February stating it could build the suggested 50 gliders within 17 weeks of acceptance of the first XLRH-1 at a peak rate of one per day. They wanted $160,000.00 to setup the production facility and $22,785.00 per glider on a cost-plus contract. While on the face of it this proposal reflected either remarkable aplomb or extraordinary ignorance, a 50-unit production contract was prepared using the same logic as for the 12-place projects and before either contractor had accomplished much on the development contract. Snead got a $1,299,250.00 Letter of Intent on 1 April 1942. It called for production to commence 15 August. However, it soon became clear that Snead was not progressing at all well on the original experimental work, being granted a slip from 14 April to 15 September 1942 for initial delivery, and doubt about their ability to proceed to production was rife. The Letter of Intent was withdrawn on 29 August after Snead had already spent $126,233.00.[37]

Although G & A was also considered for 50-unit production, they never clearly responded to the request for information regarding potential production and their poor progress on the experimental contract did not seem to warrant such a step. No further actions were taken towards granting G & A a production contract.

A mass glider launch was a beehive of activity with many players and consuming acres of ground. Tow ropes would be carefully laid out to prevent tangling or tires crossing them. Meticulous planning and execution was always disrupted to some degree by the "fog of war." (San Diego Air & Space Museum)

7

The American Way

Through much experimentation, leveraging off prewar civilian experience and engineering analysis, equipment and operating principles were devised for America's new glider echelon. Extreme time urgency and circumstances dictated that the CG-4A would be the principal combat glider and the C-47 its tug. All else derived from this basis until operational training, combat experience, and learning from allies and enemy dictated changes. Through this evolution, dedicated personnel worked to ensure a practical war-fighting capability. As with any military undertaking, initial combat revealed inexperience and need for procedures and tactics adjustment. These were undertaken to the extent practical within materiel, time, and leadership limitations.

Basics

A tow plane had to possess sufficient excess power to pull the CG-4A aloft on a 350-foot, 11/16-inch diameter towline (15/16-inch diameter for large gliders like the CG-13A and ½-inch for the 9-place gliders). The line was initially made of hemp, but this could be readily stressed to breaking in turbulence. This left the glider pilot to find a safe landing spot over whatever terrain (if not water—and the gliders did not carry life rafts) he found himself.[1] The Americans introduced the nylon line that reduced shock loads by stretching 20-25 percent under maximum load, and up to 40 percent before parting, and so greatly reduced the likelihood of the line breaks.[2]

The common 350-foot towline weighed 95 pounds. However, it could be damaged by ultraviolet light from the sun and so had to be stored under cover. Nylon was also costly at about $1.50 per foot, or $525.00 per towline.[3] The ends of the line were looped over large metal thimbles that also captured the ring for the plug. The latter had a pin that is inserted between jaws of a coupler on the tug and glider. The jaws were opened with a lever in either cockpit and a projecting pin indicated of it was not fully closed. For the C-47, this naturally required a modification to the aft end of the fuselage.

The tow ship moved forward slowly until the line was taut, as indicated by a ground marshaller. The pilot then started the takeoff roll. A wet and muddy field could see muck thrown up by the tow plane collect on the glider windscreen and impair vision for the remainder of the flight. In North Africa and Italy the takeoffs were frequently accompanied by dust clouds that obscured the tug for the initial portion of the takeoff. At about 75 mph the glider became airborne but was held to about 15-25 feet until the tug lifted off and started its climb. Any higher and the glider could pull up the tugs tail and dangerously disturb its takeoff attitude.

A C-47 and loaded CG-4A combination normally took off at 85 mph in under 2,750 feet ground roll (4,125 feet over a 50-foot obstacle). Initial rate of climb was about 400 fpm, or less if the glider was overloaded. Service ceiling was 11,300 feet, although the combinations seldom flew to such heights. Practical radius of action was on the order of 400 miles. (These figures are for the Douglas airplanes fitted with "paddle blade" propellers. Factors such as engine wear and weather can degrade such performance.) The maximum tow speed was 150 mph, less at full load. Typical tow speed was 120 mph. Under fire, tow pilots might inadvertently or intentionally increase speed. This contributed to accidents with a couple of Wacos coming apart in flight.

The towline attach socket for the CG-4A was beyond normal reach, and so this gymnastics performance was required unless the glider had been rotated down onto its nose skids (right). The line attachment above the center of gravity had its negative aspects, but pilots like seeing the line clearly and the disconnect mechanism was a direct link. The ropes shown lack the interphone cable that was frequently strung along its length. (below National Soaring Museum, right National Archives)

"Just follow the rope" was the tongue-in-cheek instructions to those who thought flying gliders was a breeze. Holding position, high tow as seen here being favored by the Americans, required keen focus and frequent control inputs, the task only made a bit easier with three-axis trim. Especially at night or in poor visibility, the job was exhausting and the two pilots swapped off during long tows. (The Peter M. Bowers Collection/The Museum of Flight)

Once the combination was off, the glider pilot assumed the optimal tow position, usually above the tow ship. (The British favored the low-tow. This lent an indication of drifting out of position when the buffeting from the tug's wake built up.) If too high the towline could engage the tow ship elevator and force the transport's nose up to stall. Too low, the glider could also affect tow plane handling. At night the pilots held position to keep the white tail light between the wingtip navigation lights, or used lights specially installed for that purpose. In combat, it was sometimes necessary to fly in low tow so as to use a blacked-out tow ship's exhaust glow (during high-power climb) and its silhouette against the moonlit sky as a suitable reference.

Double tow took advantage of the C-47s ability to tow two normally loaded CG-4As. This used a 425-foot line (75-feet length attached to the standard 350 feet) on the right and a standard line on the left to stagger the aircraft. Each pilot had to fly off opposite wingtips of the tow plane to avoid the longer line snagging on the lead glider, and the glider on the short line always cast off first. There were a few instances of the lead glider tangling on the other line, the result being a horrific crash.

Double tow maximized transport aircraft utilization while reducing the time required deploying glidermen into the LZ. However, the strain on the C-47 under most conditions was considerable, revealed by a long takeoff run and slow climb with engine temperatures in the red, and to a ceiling of a few thousand feet at most. The Curtiss C-46 Commando was much more practical for this duty, but never available to TCC in sufficient numbers during the war. The ETO leadership, apparently seeking to increase the number of gliders towed over an LZ, considered employing Boeing B-17 bombers for the purpose. By summer 1943, the AAF had provided 400 kits for B-17 tug conversion, each requiring just two hours to install.[4] However, only the C-47 was used routinely.

If the tow plane released the line first the glider pilot had to be quick to release his end or the change in orientation and load on the jaws mechanism might make release problematic. This could be exceedingly dangerous as the elastic line would recoil back and the heavy eyelet might smash into the glider's nose or the line catch on a wheel or other part of the glider. A line trailing beneath the glider might snag on ground obstacles during a landing approach and pull the aircraft down into a crash. On rare occasions, under normal tow, the jaws refused to open and the glider had to land behind the tow ship.

Communication between the CG-4A and C-47 was supposed to be via an interphone cable strung along the towline with sufficient slack to avoid tension as the nylon stretched. However, the cable could be worn through while dragging on the ground during the initial portion of takeoff, or snapped in flight. The system failed about a third of the time. Even if this did not occur, cockpit noise made discerning anything on the headset

A double tow is seen behind a C-47 tug. One glider was on a normal 350-foot line while the other on a line extended another 75 feet, and they flew with the lateral separation shown. The combination is clearly vulnerable to attack, but could not evade easily. (National Soaring Museum)

If the tug released the towline first, the heavy end fittings could snap back and strike the glider nose, with results like that seen here, unless the pilot acted fast. If the dangling line could still not be released, the trailing end could wrap around the undercarriage or tail, causing further calamity. On approach to landing the line could also snag trees or fences, abruptly pulling the glider into the ground. (National Souring Museum)

Many potential tow planes were cleared for the task through testing at Wright Field and Clinton County. Here a Curtiss A-25 Shrike (Navy SB2C-1 Helldiver) hauls a CG-4A aloft, used only because the USAAF rejected the airplane for combat duty. Difficulties with tow planes other than the C-47 were availability, excess thrust, and the low tow airspeeds contributing to elevated engine temperatures. (National Archives)

a challenge. On tow the airstream beating on the canvas fuselage was so loud as to make conversation impossible. Glider radios began to appear in the last year of the war, but never universally or with great reliability. Consequently, the crews usually relied upon light signals from the tow ship—color filters on the Aldis lamp shown from the navigator's astrodome plexiglass bubble atop the airplane. For example, a blinking green indicated 60 seconds to release, with the tow pilot allowed to cut the glider loose after that time. Lacking even the lights, the crews relied upon signals such as lowering the landing gear or waggling the wings to indicate reaching the cast-off point. If the tow ship was flying too fast, the glider pilot flew first to one side and then the other, tugging on the airplane's tail to alert the crew to slow down. On release, everything quieted down such that one could hear the "pop" of bullets or shrapnel passing through the fabric.

Hours on tow were very tiring for the pilots and glidermen, especially if turbulence and weather were encountered, and if the altitude ensured a numbing cold (the glider was unheated). This limited flight duration, even with two pilots to permit switching off flying duty periodically. Additionally, any lights, radio, or other electrical equipment was usually battery powered, without generator to hold the charge. These factors

An Army journalist asks questions as the towline ring is inserted into the coupler jaws of the C-47. Note the interphone cable attached to the nylon line, with slack to help prevent breakage in flight. However, dragging on the ground or line stretch in flight still broke the wire often. (San Diego Air & Space Museum)

The CG-4A was utilitarian to a fault. The pilot seats consisted of thin pads over plywood and were nonadjustable—pilots adjusting their position with sandbags placed under the pad. The port pilot has his hand on the tow release level. (National Museum of the United States Air Force)

dictated that a target be within a few hundred miles and a few hours of the launch base.

The longest CG-4A tow was between 23 June and 1 July 1943 by a Royal Air Force crew flying a Hadrian I from Canada to Scotland in a 3,500-mile North Atlantic crossing—the only tow across the "pond." The longest of the four sorties was 1,000 miles in 7 hours and 20 minutes. The AAF found this interesting as they had considered tow delivery of the CG-4A to the UK. They had performed tests in January 1943 to examine its practicality. In April, a ferry of 3,560 miles was performed in Africa.[5] July saw a C-47 towed two CG-4As from Sheppard Field, Texas, to Laurinburg-Maxton for a distance of 1,243 miles, doubtfully in one hop. These arduous and hazardous missions demonstrated the possibility but impracticality of such an effort that would tie up tugs and rescue assets.

Inclement weather could make glider operations impossible. Towing, navigation, identifying the LZ, and safe landings all required a minimum of clouds and turbulence. The minimal glider instruments and blind-flying training did not facilitate safe flight on tow in zero visibility. The instruments they did have were designed for aircraft with persistent vibration from engines, and so for the smooth-flying gliders the pilots had to periodically tap the face of the instruments to ensure the needles were not sticking. The best the pilots could do was to try and maintain the correct angle on the towline until the combination broke out of the weather. A low tow position gave an indication of drifting out of position when the wake buffeting built up. Airframe icing was a killer.

As a soaring glider the CG-4A was miserable, with a glide ratio of 10:1 (5:1 with spoilers deployed). Pilots seldom took advantage of even this as they dived for the ground to reduce exposure to enemy fire, sometimes with a 90-degree turn to cut airspeed, but still coming in fast for what they called a "blitz landing." The high speed allowed low "hedge hopping" flight for a short distance along a previously visualized path to the chosen field. This could not be done into a confined field. Pilots usually sought to glide at 73 mph for 400 fpm rate of descent and touchdown at about 60 mph, depending upon aircraft weight. Typical stopping distance on dry sod with brakes was approximately 660 feet over a 50-foot tree, longer if things were wet. The emergency technique of rotating the glider up onto the nose skids facilitated stopping in as little as 150 feet.

The CG-4A was certainly unattractive and engendered little affection. The non-existent ventilation through the cabin meant glidermen frequently got sick during hot, bumpy flights. However, the glider contributed much to the war effort and had some unusual feats to its record. In one instance a pilot on a training flight found good ridge lift and, soaring, remained aloft for 4.5 hours. There were several instances of pilot performing loops in the glider and factory test flights included 3-4 g pull-ups followed by tail slides with violent pitch-outs.

The glider pilots developed skills at managing the energy of the glider to make the intended LZ while getting below ground fire quickly. The blitz landing involved making a low altitude, high speed approach, hopping over obstacles and then killing the remaining energy to land precisely but at low airspeed. Some pilots could touchdown sharply and use the rebound of the landing gear plus a bit of aft elevator to leap back into the air and clear obstacles. (The Peter M. Bowers Collection/The Museum of Flight)

Glider pilots learned how to roll the Waco up onto its nose skids to use this friction and addition to wheel braking for a quick stop—to be followed by a loud thump as the tail falls back to earth. Note that the emergency exit hatches and the troop doors have been removed to help cool the interior during a hot and dusty training day. The pilots have removed their shirts and, waiting for forward motion to cease, have focused on the cameraman. (National Museum of the United States Air Force)

Mass Assaults

Although there were trained glider mechanics, preparation for a large operation required rapid assembly of hundreds of CG-4As. There were never enough aircraft for planned operations, and so there was always a frantic effort in the weeks prior to D-Day. Men with no aircraft experience were assigned to assemble and service the gliders. The use of many marginally-skilled or untrained personnel meant the role of the inspectors was even more vital to ensure assembly had been done properly. Pilots were well advised to make their own inspection before flight. Many horror stories are told of an unsafe aircraft being discovered prior to flight or when the machine disintegrated on tow. Gliders were sometimes neglected for many weeks during which they would begin to deteriorate. The North African climate was unkind to the wood while the Asian climate promoted rust and fungus. Humidity could actually cause glue joints in the earliest gliders to debond.

Mass glider tows for the operations carried out in ETO required well-choreographed activity. The gliders and airplanes were arranged compactly, either with the tow ships on the runway and the gliders to the side or vice versa, wings overlapping. The towlines were neatly laid out in a zig-zag pattern so that they would not tangle when taken up.

Troop loading was best supervised to ensure the soldiers did not bring additional gear or ammunition aboard. This common practice could put the glider over gross and out of trim, complicating the pilot's job to the point of compromising safety. A glider ride into combat was met with mixed emotions of trading risks and benefits compared with a parachute jump. (The Peter M. Bowers Collection/The Museum of Flight)

America's sudden thrust into the war created an extreme urgency to field a combat glider capability, leading to adoption of the CG-4A and C-47 combination that would almost exclusively see the country through the war. At the end of a 350-foot nylon rope, the glider gets airborne before the tug and flies just above the runway to avoid pulling the airplane's tail up. (The Peter M. Bowers Collection/The Museum of Flight)

Glider loading was another manpower-intensive exercise. This gun crew shoves a 75 mm field gun into a much-decorated CG-4A, the short and steep wheel ramps making the task all the more difficult. Note the landing light protruding from the raised nose. (National Museum of the United States Air Force)

Positioning the gliders in the confined space was typically done with the generous supply of manpower. Even fully loaded the glider was usually easy to move about, given enough strong backs. In normal circumstances the inability of the glider to self-taxi could impede normal airplane operations unless personnel responded quickly. (National Museum of the United States Air Force)

One configurations of aircraft arrangement in preparation of a mass glider launch is evident at this field, believed to be in France during early March 1945. It permits the tug to taxi forward and the glider to be positioned behind, the towline straightened and slack taken up. In this way an entire wing of aircraft can be launched in minimum time. (San Diego Air & Space Museum)

Each combination would take off in turn, with approximately 18-30-second intervals, circling until the entire formation was aloft. It could take more than 30 minutes to get all elements of a serial off and formed up. A few reserve gliders and tow ships were maintained to replace those that fell out of the formation for whatever reason.

The aircraft manual stated a limit of 3,750 pounds of payload, but they were routinely loaded to 5,250 pounds, or 9,000 pounds gross weight. Even 10,000 pounds was seen. Glider overloading was all too common with troops sneaking extra gear and ammo aboard when the pilots were not looking. Occasionally a flying crew chief could help police the loading and prevent this practice. If the wooden floor sagged under the cargo weight or the tug got airborne before the glider, the pilots knew something was amiss. An over-weight glider could make tow difficult or impossible, over-taxing the engines of the tow plane and reducing speed dangerously. If the machine was too heavy it might not get off the ground or would wallow on tow, the combination having difficulty climbing to gaining altitude, or risked a snapped towline—especially if turbulence was encountered.

An efficient launch sequence would get combinations off in 18 to 30-second intervals. Initial climb rate might be just a few hundred feet per minute given the weight of the individual aircraft. This image dates from 8 January 1943 and was taken at South Plains AAF, Lubbock, Texas. (National Soaring Museum)

This could be dire if over water or enemy territory. Landing would be dangerously fast. Center of gravity control was also something little-regarded by the infantrymen. A misloaded glider could be impossible to trim and greatly tax the pilot's strength.

The formation was to join those from other fields in the proper order, with suitable spacing and altitude, and cross waypoints at appointed times. The Americans generally employed formations consisting of columns with four combinations in a pair of pairs echelon, a pair 100 feet apart to the right and 300 feet from the adjoining pair. One minute or 1,000-1,500 feet was maintained between echelons/elements with usually 40-48 gliders in a serial. Serials were usually separated by 4-7-minutes. The two columns might be divided into streams with 1.5-mile offset.

Ostensibly, both the American and British gliders were towed at 150 mph. However, a loaded CG-4A was typically pulled at 120 mph, and slower if overloaded. Different glider types were always assigned separate objectives. Tow ships were to pass release points with 10-second spacing and the gliders to land in an LZ with 30-second interval as tactical groups.

The formations would typically transit to the combat zone at a few thousand feet, performance ceiling of the combination, and then descend to a few hundred feet for run-in to the release point. This left few opportunities for silent and surprise landings; mass assaults being the adopted tactic. Over the combat zone the tugs would turn in pre-assigned directions after release and return at higher altitudes to avoid incoming serials. Navigation might be by dead reckoning, using special identification points like light ships and radio beam intercepts, radar beacons, or radar to identify shoreline features. Not all tugs were equipped with the appropriate receivers and scopes, so holding formation was important. Night operations usually sought periods with good lunar illumination to make LZ location easier and landings safer.

Once airborne, the combinations would assemble into formations for the trek to the objective. Various types of echelons and element were employed, with assigned spacing. With fighters and paratroop ships, a huge stream of aircraft would set out on a specified route. (The Peter M. Bowers Collection/ The Museum of Flight)

Unlike their German counterparts, the CG-4A and other Allied gliders were unarmed and so at the mercy of enemy fighters. Even if armed, gliders had to be used in an environment of friendly air superiority. Fortunately, by the time these aircraft began to be used in large numbers the Axis air arms were dying slow deaths. By the latter half of 1943, fighter support for major glider assaults was lavish, and so there is no indisputable record of any Allied glider being attacked from the air, save for a Horsa being towed to North Africa forced to ditch when its tug was attacked by a prowling Fw 200.

The fabric and wood elements of the CG-4A, with few vital systems, made it somewhat more resistant to serious damage from flak and small arms fire than airplanes. The people aboard were the most vulnerable. However, the fabric-covered fuselage and escape hatches permitted some irate glidermen to return fire while still in flight. Anti-aircraft fire could also sever the towlines.

Pathfinder teams were to drop with the paratroopers ahead of the main force to mark LZs and also place electronic navigation aids for the tug-glider formations. The Eureka radar transmitter (AN/PPN-1A) and radio beacon (CRN-4, or radio compass) emitted a coded directional signal when interrogated by the Rebecca transceiver aboard the lead tow plane.[6] The signal was displayed on a scope in the cockpit and indicated a rough bearing to the transmitter. Intersecting directional beams from SCR-717C radar signals, called Gee (stations in the UK), could also help lead navigators establish their position. Airborne radar to distinguish coastline features, rivers, and cities (with reference the maps or reconnaissance photographs), were also employed in addition to Loran navigational aids, basic pilotage, and dead reckoning.

Pathfinders marked LZs by variously means for the glider landings. They used color-coded 3x15-foot fluorescent fabric panels in a T-pattern displaying the landing direction, and a colored smoke bomb at one end to show wind direction. At night, flare pots were employed or narrow-beam, battery-powered directional Aldis lamps (Hollophane beacon lamps), often with colors and coded flashing. All these devices had their limitations but, taken as a whole, greatly aided glider delivery accuracy. However, these preparations never approached perfection. When placed properly, the LZs could still be missed. Some gliders and occupants simply disappeared without a trace, probably coming down alone far from their comrades where everyone was killed by the enemy, buried, and the aircraft burned.

The Allies flew aerial armadas during all their airborne assaults in Europe, the likes of which had not been seen before or since. The low-altitude formations, flying at just a few thousand feet to avoid anti-aircraft fire, created a resounding roar of engines and could take hours to pass overhead. This belied the original thoughts of silent glider assaults. (The Peter M. Bowers Collection/The Museum of Flight)

Night flight had the challenge of distinguishing the lights of the tow plane from stars and ground lights—provided blackout procedures permitted aircraft lights at all. The pilots could guide on the blue engine exhaust flame during climb, but at cruise power settings the flame disappeared. Night landings were exceptionally hazardous, with as little as quarter moon and only a dim oil smudge pot to mark the touchdown point. Many broken gliders, pilots, and glidermen were typically an outcome of such exercises.

Releases were usually made an a few hundred feet altitude to reduce exposure to flak, although within range of small arms fire. At these altitudes, and because of their minimal instruments, the gliders were taken to within a few miles or directly overhead their landing zone. They then had about half a minute of free flight time, leaving few options for LZ selection. The glider pilot typically had only a compass, watch, and the "Mark I eyeball" for navigation, leaving few options for LZ selection. Hence, the tow pilots had to get the gliders quite close and hold an even keel as sharp evasive maneuvering could flip the glider onto its back. Glider tow was a hazardous and difficult mission for tug and glider personnel alike, requiring challenging navigation and courage in the face of enemy fire. Experiences are related of C-47 crews keeping their burning planes on course until release, only to perish in a crash soon after.

Generally, the tow pilots were instructed to drop the valuable ropes in designated areas during egress from the combat zone for later collection. On occasion, gliders were

Glider pilots were supposed to release from the tow rope when the tug arrived at the destination, or when the tug waved them off. The pilot was then to plan the approach to the intended point of landing, hopefully with at least a base leg to set up properly. The presence of other gliders, enemy activity, and general confusion complicated the task. (National Soaring Museum)

Mass glider assaults with hundreds of gliders converging on a comparatively small area was often chaotic. Pilots jockeyed for a good landing approach in available space while trying to avoid midair collisions, then avoiding collisions on the ground with other gliders, enemy anti-glider obstacles, or those placed by Mother Nature. This photograph is an area of the battle field in March 1945 near Wesel, Germany. (National Museum of the United States Air Force)

struck by the released 95-pound towlines falling out of the sky or dangling from an airplane passing too closely overhead.

For landing, the pilot ideally setup a descending approach pattern with a downwind leg, identifying the touchdown point, and land into the wind. Combat conditions often dictated other procedures. Landings in unprepared fields were the most hazardous phase of flight, these tending to be much faster than in training as the pilots sought to get below effective ground fire or because the glider was overweight. Even the best landing could end badly given the nature of the LZs. Landing gear torn away was fairly common. The CG-4A could take punishment that a conventional aluminum aircraft could not. Films show very rough landing that caused severe damage, but from which the crew and passengers emerged to engage the enemy. However, there were also many casualties among the pilots and glidermen. Even if they emerged unscathed, they had to contend with enemy troops who might pin them down beside the glider, preventing unloading or joining up with others in their unit until after dark. It was a hazardous occupation.

To prepare for D-Day with combat landings in fields the enemy had "planted" with poles as glider obstacles, tests were performed with gliders intentionally landed between the poles to check how the wings separated.[7] The wings could also be dipped onto the surface to ground-loop, stopping before running into trees or hedgerow or swerve away for imminent collision. If impact with trees was unavoidable, the pilots were taught to aim between two trees with enough separation to admit the fuselage. The wings would be sheared off; helping to slow what remained. Many of the more serious accidents were due to over-loading and the resulting high landing speed, and not the durability of the glider.

With every combat glider assault a forced landing in an unprepared area, mishaps came with the job. Most gliders suffered some degree of damage, and the vast majority were written off. The worst was when casualties occurred or the nose was jammed and vital cargo could not be extracted. (San Diego Air & Space Museum)

Although the men frequently walked away from serious accidents, the gliders were not always considered worth repairing. The hinged nose was vulnerable as rough landings could bend the frame and prevent raising the nose to extract the cargo. Training and the elements alone consumed a great many of the aircraft. They were built for that war, not the next.

In one instance a CG-4A was able to "fight back" when the pilot intentionally ran down a German soldier firing at the landing glider. Unfortunately, there were a few incidents of unwary Allied soldiers stepping into the path of a landing glider, because of the silent approach, and being killed.

Snatch

Americans pioneered and deployed the glider "snatch" or "pickup," and the British also trained with the U.S. technique. It derived from a means of snatching mail bags by passing air mail aircraft, employed since 1939, although dating back to 1927 with marine pilots snatching dispatch bags and earlier still for trains snatching postal sacks. Richard Du Pont and All American Aviation (AAA), a firm he headed in Wilmington, Delaware, had perfected the technique. In 1941 they began using the new nylon rope for the snatch to ease shock loads. This greatly aided glider snatch when AAA conducted its first experiments. The initial test used the Model AAS-4 mailbag retrieval system in a Stinson SR-10C to snatch a 500-pound Midwest "Utility" glider with a pilot dummy.[8] In Wilmington, on 24 September 1941, Du Pont was in a propeller-less Piper J-3 Cub snatched by Camille "Cammy" Vinet in a SR-10F.

Further pickups in May 1941 prepared them for a 4-5 June demonstration at Wright Field. This included the Stinson, flown by Du Pont, snatching an XTG-3 flown by Lieutenant Chet Decker. Subsequently, 28 July tests in Wilmington demonstrated dual snatch with successive pickup of two TG-8s, each with three men aboard. Army glider development personnel decided to adopt the AAA system for the transport gliders.[9]

To accommodate the massive gliders, AAA worked through fall 1942 developing a higher-capacity system under engineer Arthur B. Schultz.[10] The Army then conducted tests in late 1942 and early 1943 with this Model 40, 4,000-pound capacity winch in a Douglas B-23 (port side of bomb bay, that bay door opened). As a safety feature, cutter blades were installed ahead of the bomber's landing gear (although snatch was not

This image depict tests with a Piper Cub (Du Pont flying from rear cockpit with Army observer in front) snatched by an All American Aviation Stinson Reliant. The Cub's propeller has been removed and replaced with a towline attachment fitting. The tail wheel has been replaced with a long skid to lower the nose on the ground, preventing a sharp pitch-over as the line suddenly pulled taut. (National Archives)

A Piper Cub demonstrates pickup of a parcel for observing Army glider personnel. This snatch technique, dating pack many years, was the basis for snatching gliders from fields too short for a normal tow-off. All American Aviation pioneered this work. (National Soaring Museum)

A B-23 bomber was modified with the Model 40 winch and snatch system. Here it snatches a CG-4A, the arm extended and the cable trailing from the bomb bay (port door open). Note the cutter blades hanging below the engine nacelles to part the cable and prevent damage to the aircraft should the operation go awry. (National Soaring Museum)

The Model 40 winch is shown installed in the port side of the B-23 bomb bay. This shared little in common with the eventual system adopted for the C-47 and routine snatch of the CG-4A. However, it illustrates the nontrivial nature of the installation, impeding the normal bombing mission. (National Soaring Museum)

performed with the gear extended) to slice the line rather than risk it snagging on the aircraft. This feature was not employed in subsequent designs. The demonstration saw Dent, in the XCG-3, snatched in December 1942.[11] All American was then placed on a fixed-price contract for 18 units. The Model 80, capacity for an 8,000-pound glider, permitted pickup of the CG-4A. The Model 120 of 12,000-pound capacity and Model 160 with 16,000 pounds were also procured, while the CCAAF team performed tests with gliders up to 25,000 pounds.[12] The Model 160 was in production during 1943 and 1944 with several hundred on orders that reached $4 million.[13]

Work continued through July 1943 at Wright and CCAAF after which the system was considered operational. The production M-80C Glider Pick-up Mechanism was finalized in the summer of 1943, technical orders written, and the system used extensively in service. Procurement and fielding of units with capacity to 12,000 pounds and higher were also done. It appears that, at least in test, all U.S. combat glider models were snatched by several types of 2- and 4-engined tugs.[14]

Snatch required a 600-700-foot long clear area (1,540 feet if there were 50-foot obstacles at each end of the field). A 225-foot, 15/16-inch diameter tow cable from the glider was coiled up in front. The free end was attached to an 80-foot line formed into a closed loop strung with spring clips as a triangle between two 12-foot tall poles. These were placed in the ground approximately 20 feet apart and about 150-300 feet ahead of the glider. The poles were sometimes painted yellow and the clips would sometimes have yellow flags attached to increase visual identification. Additionally, yellow ground stripes of about 9x3 feet were placed at the base of each pole to aid snatch pilot lineup.

The tow ship would fly just 20 feet off the deck and 130-140-mph to engage the "clothesline" with a hook in the end of a 20-foot wooden channel arm trailing 45 degrees

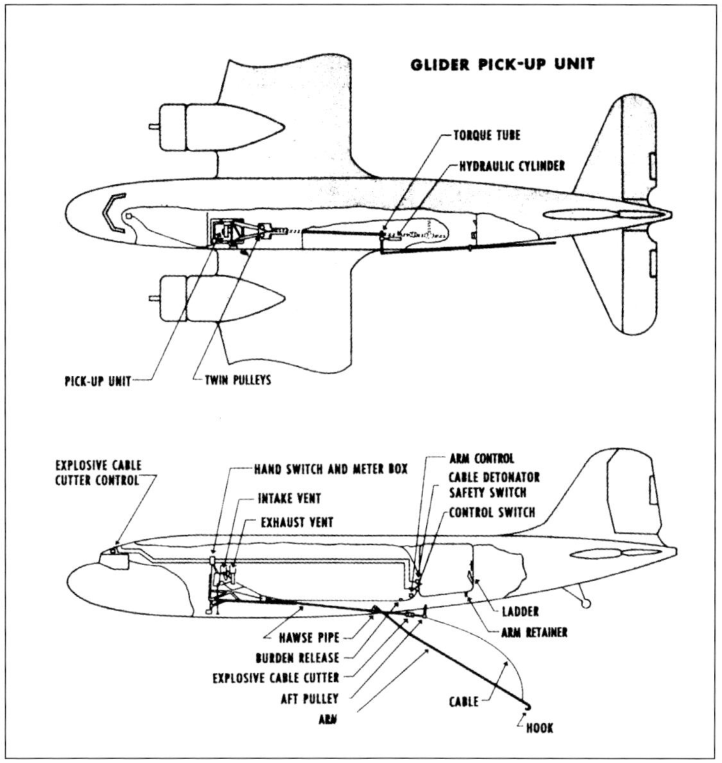

This field manual drawing details the elements of the glider snatch system employed with the C-47 during WWII. It clearly required significant modifications to the Skytrain and unique equipment demanding knowledgeable support personnel. If the equipment was not serviced properly or the snatch flown inaccurately, both tug and glider could be endangered. (Author's Collection)

A snatch operation is captured at the split second the C-47 trailing arm snags the towline loop between the upright poles. Note how the glider is offset from the airplane run-in line. The pickup cable guide and pulley suspended beneath the aircraft, near the base of the arm, is also clearly evident. (National Museum of the United States Air Force)

Although a technique was devised to transfer the tow rope from the snatch rig to the normal tail location, and another snatch performed for dual tow, this was not deployed. After snatch, the tug flew with the line off its port side and the door remaining open. (National Soaring Museum)

below the port side of the aft fuselage, raised and lowered electrically. To avoid the arm striking it, the glider was placed off-center 40 feet and angled approximately 10 degrees in towards the poles. The hook was attached to a 5/8-inch steel cable that ran through a pulley and cable guide tube, also attached to the port side, running into the cabin to a hydraulic winch with brakes. The mechanism was bolted to the deck on the port side of the cabin about 6 feet aft of the forward bulkhead. A friction clutch could be adjusted for the weight of the glider and speed of the pick-up. The heat generated by the brake was carried away through tubes leading to vents in the side of the fuselage, intake air and exhaust. When tension from the snatch caused the hook to be pulled from the channel in the arm, about 600-900 feet of cable unwound from the drum to avoid a tremendous shock tension that was also mitigated by the nylon towline. The drum was automatically slowed then braked. The pilot had applied full power before contact and so climbed away. All this happened in just seconds during which the glider accelerated rapidly at 0.7-g and became airborne in 200-feet or less, approximately three seconds, as the pilot frantically trimming nose-up. The tug initially lost 25-40 mph airspeed. The glider pilot also had to climb quickly to take up any slack in the line and prevent it snagging obstacles on the ground. The electric motor in the winch was engaged to reel in the steel cable. The glider was quickly on normal tow at 120 mph in an exciting ride, but with the towline trailing from the pulley just forward of the cargo door of the C-47 (door removed for observation) instead of from the aft-most point of the fuselage. If necessary, the tug pilot could cast the glider free by use of a cartridge-fired electric guillotine cable cutter, activated via a button in the cockpit.

The pickup technique proved surprisingly reliable and safe, and was used to collect new gliders for delivery as well as glider recovery following combat. At least experimentally, CG-4As were snatched as they rested on their skids in snow. Thousands of training and delivery snatches were performed, several hundred to retrieve gliders following training flights, and approximately 400 under combat conditions. It was even performed at night with lights atop the twin poles and lead-in markers. As suggested, conversion of a tow ship for snatch was not a trivial modification and the gear encumbered routine cargo operations.

In July 1942, the Clinton County men performed sequential snatches of two Wacos for a double tow. This required additional personnel and an elaborate 15-minute procedure for transferring the first towline to the usual aft fuselage towline attach point on the tug, and the retrieval arm rigged for another snatch.[15] This was likely considered a marginal capability and practical only under ideal conditions of aircraft light weight and good engine performance. No indications that this system was deployed have been uncovered.

Recovery

The CG-4A and other gliders were not overtly intended to be disposable, although it was understood from the beginning many would likely be damaged beyond practical repair in a combat assault landing.[16] To fly even one flight safely required airworthiness permitting any number of flights. The mission demanded they be rugged, reliable, and reusable. Still,

Moving a glider to a more suitable area for repair and recovery could be quite a chore. Necessary repairs had to be affected to make it mobile, and obstacles eliminated (brush cut). At nearly 84 feet in span, it was an enormous aircraft with fragile elements. (The Peter M. Bowers Collection/The Museum of Flight)

Following the Holland operation, a concerted effort was made to recover gliders. This photograph of a reclamation site, taken on 21 October 1944, shows the poor condition of many of the aircraft. Some that have apparently been repaired are lined up for a flight out, the area offering suitable space for a towed takeoff. (National Archives)

The Americans and Germans independently developed the concept of using gliders as rapidly repositioned repair shops for aircraft squadrons and armor units on the move. This images shows extraction of a Mobile Aircraft Repair Shop from a CG-4A, presumably equipped with the essentials for routine and field-level maintenance support of a specific aircraft type. Note the spoilers installed on the wings to defeat lift in high winds while picketed, and the pilot emergency exit door added to the port side of the nose as a field modification. (National Museum of the United States Air Force)

Field repair of gliders required some cumbersome equipment to be brought in, space to work, and means of supporting men in the field. Such resources had to wait for combat to move away from the site before they could be deployed. This image shows a glider repair unit at work at Laurinburg-Maxton on 2 September 1943. (National Museum of the United States Air Force)

the glider was comparatively inexpensive at an average $18,800.00, around $25,000.00 each once crated, shipped, assembled, and flown. Realistically, under the pressures of combat, there was little concern about recovering the typically damaged gliders from remote landing sites close to the frontlines. Few flown on operations were recovered, and the majority of CG-4As flew only one or two check flights and a ferry (a handful of hours at most) and then their one-way operational mission. Yet, machines flown in States-side training accumulated hundreds of hours, a few as many as 1,200 hours.[17]

Glider recovery typically required some disassembly, lifted with a crane onto a flatbed, transported to an airfield or large open area, preliminary repairs, and then tow to an air base for full restoration. This entailed a great deal of labor, equipment, and time. Before June 1944, the AAF had made preparations to recover gliders, including dispatching to the UK a detachment of 64 glider mechanics and 24 mobile glider repair sets designed to be transported by glider to an area with damaged gliders. Mechanics and 108 pickup installations were also sent. None of these assets were aggressively utilized.[18]

Typically near half the gliders were seriously damaged on landing or while extricating the load. It could be several days or weeks before combat conditions permitted any chance of recovering the aircraft. By then the elements, enemy action, and souvenir hunters had taken their toll. It was more practical to consider the gliders one-mission aircraft.

Repairing the wood and fabric elements of the CG-4A in the open must have been very challenging. Days of work could be required per glider. These men are hard at it, but apparently with so little equipment that they are using a wooden troop bench from the glider as a work stand. (National Museum of the United States Air Force)

One Airborne officer examining gliders following the Normandy landings concluded that 20 percent of the machines could have been snatched out immediately and another 40 percent within 30 days following repairs. In all the European landings he felt 50 percent of the gliders could have been salvaged with prior planning and determined effort. Certainly changing a wheel could be done by men pulling the opposite wing down to raise the wheel off the ground for rapid work. Most other work required a field shop, trained mechanics, and bulky equipment. However, with no action taken or instructions given, within days the gliders were pillaged in all landings for kindling and material to cover slit trenches or gun nests, picked at by souvenir hunters or locals, fabric with national markings cut away and placed atop vehicles for identification by Allied fighter planes, etc.[19] They came to be considered expendable and thousands were left on the battlefield to deterioration by vandalism and the elements.

The ideal means of recovering a glider in the field was via snatch, as shown by this pair in France soon after D-Day. However, it required up to 700 feet of clear area for the approach and climb-out, or as much as 1,500 feet if there were obstacles at each end. The small field the gliders often set down in could make this an impossible option. (San Diego Air & Space Museum)

Pilots

Many glider pilots participated in just one or two operations. Some saw no combat while a few "eager-beavers" flew in three or four assaults. Clearly, with operations months apart and all during roughly the last year of the war, the opportunities for American glider pilots to fly in combat were rarer than for many of their power counterparts. When not training, the men in Europe might serve as C-47 copilots while those in the CBI and Pacific could fly L-5 spotters, among a few other opportunities. Also unlike the power pilots and paratroopers, the glider pilots received no hazardous duty pay until this was corrected following Normandy. Once overseas, the men were prone to be transferred between TCC units in preparation for operations, undermining unit cohesion and morale.

There were sometimes no seat belts for the troops in back. There were also typically no parachutes offered to the glider pilots going into combat (despite regulations), and when provided were seldom worn because they were impractical at the altitudes usually flown (insufficient time for opening and arrested descent) and a hindrance for quick exit under fire following landing. Besides, if the pilots got up to go back and jump out of the glider they would have to pass a squad of hard-bitten infantrymen without chutes and about to be abandoned to their fate! Without the parachute seat pack, the pilots sat on sandbags and a cushion to reach the rudder pedals (seat was not adjustable while pedals had some adjustment). Additionally, circumstances often meant combat missions were flown without copilot (again contravening regulations).

After landing in the combat zone, the pilots were usually instructed to gather at the local field headquarters to await transport back to their bases for support of follow-on missions. In the meantime, they would perform such tasks as perimeter patrol or guarding prisoners. The level of infantry training for the glider pilots was most uneven, varying from intense commando training to nothing beyond basic rifle orientation. Some were sent on missions without sufficient gear to survive in the field for the few days before evacuation. So, their value once on the battlefield was marginal. A few field commanders criticized the glider pilots for wandering around encumbering operations, snapping pictures, or join up with combat squads to seek action. Most of the pilots were evacuated within a few days while some disappeared for many days as they sought diversions among the local populace. All this was in contrast to the British models in which the glider pilots were Army personnel intensely trained for infantry combat and intended to be an integral part of the squad they landed.

The pilots were better organized for *Varsity* to serve in ground combat after landing. In one action a team of glider pilots defending a crossroads defeated a German break-though attempt. This was the only time in Air Force history that a group of its officers had engaged in combat as an infantry company.

The gliders pilots were a unique interface between the Air Forces and ground forces, and it was never quite ideal. Clearly they were considered 'bastard children' in the Army Air Forces, usually living in lesser quarters than power pilots but apart from the airborne troops. Yet, when the airborne suggested the glider pilots come under their banner, the USAAF leadership would not hear of it. Many of the pilots had come directly from civilian life into glider instruction with no basic training, or had been enlisted members. It is fair to say that, in general, most were of a different character than the officers graduating power pilot training, and on average 35 versus 26 years old. Their promotions and decorations were markedly behind those of their power counterparts. Also, unlike their British counterparts, they were not assigned significant roles on headquarters and planning staffs.

Since glider pilots knew they were looked upon as 'second-class' airmen, they tended to show little regard for Army regulations. Some of the men had scant patience for military customs and courtesies, or senior personnel who did not work to earn respect. The 101st Airborne Division's history remarked that glider pilots were "... the most uninhibited individualists in the Army." Many were a hard-drinking, womanizing bunch. To these men, the "P" in their "G.P." personnel classification (Glider Pilot) stood for "Play."

Glider pilot training was almost made up as it went along, and so graduates had an uneven experience. The role was new and what it entailed, especially in combat, remained to be established. These pilots put on a show for the press, sprinting for their gliders at Stuttgart, Arkansas. (National Museum of the United States Air Force)

A typical pre-mission snapshot of pilots preparing to head into combat (although more likely wearing dungarees than khakis). These men generally went lightly armed and usually with a minimum of combat arms skills. As with all soldiers, their experiences ranged from the most dire and life-threatening to the mundane. (National Soaring Museum)

Part of a new and exclusive cadre, and an odd interface between the Air Forces and ground forces, the glider pilots were a breed apart. Only a couple rose above the rank of Lieutenant during the war and only rarely did they have roles on planning staffs. Most were content with flying, having little patience for Army protocol. (San Diego Air & Space Museum)

261100

8

Advanced Army Gliders

With American entry into the war, the alliance with Britain brought the Allies' respective airborne forces into close association. The British began delivering their Horsa plywood glider in summer 1943 to become their primary mount. The aircraft could carry more than 7,000 pounds of payload that could consist of 25 troops. This was a decidedly larger machine than the CG-4A with its 15 seats and roughly 4,000-5,000 pounds payload. The economy of placing more personnel and materiel on the ground with each landing was appealing. Both militaries decided their 8-place gliders were impractical for the operations they eventually foresaw which required relatively long tows and large invasion forces. Furthermore, testing had shown clearly that double tow of two smaller gliders was less aerodynamically efficient and economical than towing a single large glider.[1] At some point the transport glider effort came under project MX-205, with MX-285 also credited as "glider development."

Impulse

With the development of the 8- and 15-place cargo transport gliders well in hand, the Army turned its attention to larger aircraft with twice or more the payload capacity

The slight lead the British enjoyed in developing gliders within the Allied camp allowed the Americans to benefit from the their partner's approach. The Horsa was attractive because of its much greater volume compared with the U.S. Army 15-place machines, permitting up to 25 men or 7,000 pounds of materiel. These U.S. Navy personnel enjoy the spacious interior, but the narrow and steep loading ramp just behind the cockpit bulkhead on the left made onload and offload of freight a frustrating chore. (National Soaring Museum)

of the Waco CG-4A. The first officially enunciated desire for a 30-place machine were communications in December 1941 seeking the opinion of future operators.[2] Production of the Horsa itself in the U.S. was discounted from the first, after review of drawings and discussions with those who had observed the aircraft. It was judged unsuitable because of the difficulties in transporting equipment.[3] The new larger gliders were to be configured for unloading within 15 seconds of landing. Despite their size, the aircraft still had to be capable of disassembly and crating for shipment overseas. Curtiss C-46 Commando twin and Douglas C-54 Skymaster four-engine aircraft were soon to become available for tow, making such larger gliders practical, provided they had a tow speed to match.

Table 08-01	
Original 30-place Transport Glider Specifics[6]	
payload	30 troops, two as pilots, 240 lbs each
useful load	8,000 lbs
desired tow speed	150 mph
stall speed	45 mph, 55 mph acceptable
breakdown for transport	
radio for communication with tow plane and other gliders	
aerodynamically clean	

Table 08-02	
G & A Aircraft XCG-9 Specifics (estimated, not built)	
span	108.6 ft
length	63.9 ft (fuselage 44.2 ft)
height	15.3 ft
empty weight	9,901 lbs
gross weight	16,000 lbs design, 18,381 lbs maximum
tow speed	150 mph
capacity	2 pilots, 30 troops

Colonel Dent had seen the Horsas and even larger Hamilcars the British were building and, given the rapid growth of the U.S. Army airborne forces, expressed the conviction in late 1941 that gliders had to be acquired capable of transporting such cargo as 30 troops, two jeeps, a jeep towing a 75 mm gun, or other bulky cargo. The Army's 105 mm howitzer had been redesigned to fit inside the CG-4A and C-47, reducing its dimensions and cutting weight to 2,500 pounds. Additionally, General Frederick Browning, commander of the UK's airborne forces, influenced Allied thinking regarding air assaults. Concepts for massed air assaults now foresaw daylight operations with gliders descending rapidly from release at low altitude for confined area landings at low speed.[4] This "air umbrella" would be without the element of surprise.

Considerable advantages of the CG-4A was its rapid production in the many thousands, its ability to be disassembled and shipped overseas, towing by the ever-more-numerous C-47s, and ease of loading/unloading bulky cargo. It was expected any advanced glider would retain these attributes. Yet, the CG-4A's utilitarian lines made it aerodynamically inefficient. Desires for advanced gliders included a higher tow speed so that fighters could be employed in the role. Fighters were growing increasingly numerous and they could remain over the LZ to provide air cover and ground attack support after glider release.

Original concept art for the XCG-9 looked quite exciting; a radical design with defensive guns and leading edge slots. The unusual layout was "proven" through flight of a 40-percent scale glider. However, reality proved less exciting as the responsible developer, A.G.A. Aviation consistently failed to deliver on the contract terms. (National Archives)

As with the CG-15, a higher wing loading than for the 15-place machines would more closely match tug aircraft and permit high towing speeds. This, however, mandated use of wing flaps to achieve the steep approach and slow landing the mission demanded.[5]

Based upon conferences and analysis, the decision was made to develop larger gliders, specifically to carry in both a 105 mm gun and a tow vehicle, or accommodating more troops. The draft requirements are stated in Table 08-01. As with the initial contracts, only firms not involved in priority War Department work (excluding gliders) were approached.

Five contracts were let for the 30-place glider. The same desultory progress was encountered as experienced with the 8- and 15-place contracts. Work was more measured by comparison to the CG-4A's whirlwind. Additionally, the Air Forces were conducting more careful testing and evaluation before committing to production contracts. Consequently, only one of these aircraft (literally one airframe) played a combat role before the end of hostilities. Regardless, some very practical, high-utility gliders emerged from the program in the form of the Laister-Kauffman YCG-10A and Waco YCG-13A. Both underwent significant changes and extensive trials. Apart from the approximately 10,500-pounds payload capacity, features like tricycle undercarriage, low fuselage, and easy loading through cargo doors and ramp, pointed the way to postwar tactical airlifters.

G & A Aircraft XCG-9

Among the initial large glider projects was an ambitious effort calling for an armed 30-troop glider (including pilot and copilot) that was quite a departure from the conservative approaches seen in most other designs.[7] The concept art and models were exciting, having a center fuselage pod with guns at the front and rear, loading ramp folding down from the aft end of this pod, and outboard booms seating a pilot at the front of each. Ingress and egress was presumably via the canopy. The main fuselage could accommodate 20 troops and six more were fitted in each of the outer nacelles. The fuselages were to be of wood construction, and its wings would have fabric covering a monocoque wood structure.

This would have been a challenging undertaking for even an experienced team. However, after negotiations beginning in January 1942, the Army gave a Letter of Intent on the 29th to A.G.A. Aviation Corporation before it was renamed G & A Aircraft, Incorporated as previously mentioned. The $299,820.55 fixed-price contract (soon raised to $317,320.55) was signed on 27 June. It required then-A.G.A. to deliver a wind tunnel model, static article, and two XCG-9 prototypes with trailers between December 1942 and February 1943. The first airframe was valued at $100,198.87 and the second $95,880.55. The SCR 585-C radio was specified.

A.G.A had taken a Navy contract in December 1941 to build the XLRG-1 amphibious glider seating 24 marines (Chapter 6) of a layout nearly identical to the XCG-9. As previously discussed, a 40-percent scale wooden glider of this concept was prepared and flown in Philadelphia beginning on 16 November 1941. Among

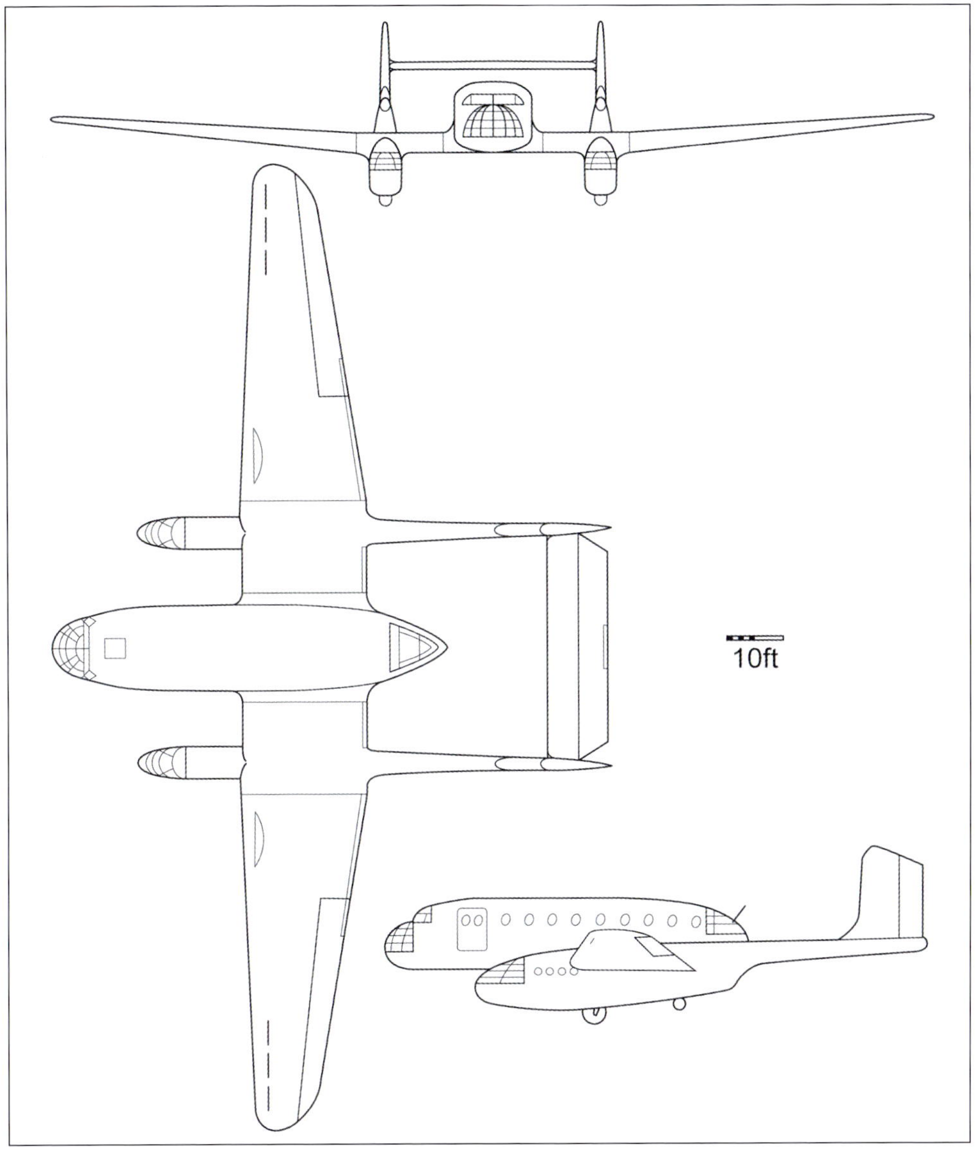

As the XCG-9 was developed it became a bit less attractive (drawing derived from an Army document) while retaining the multi-fuselage layout. A loading ramp was to fold down from the aft end of the center fuselage. Even after reorganizing and working simultaneously on a similar Navy contract (XLRG-1), the contractor went under and the XCG-9 faded into history. (Author)

the pilots was Lewin Barringer who wrote an enthusiastic report of the potential for the full-up glider.[8] The company offered design revisions that brought the Navy and Army specifications into close alignment, the concepts looking almost identical save for the outboard sponson cabins making up boat hulls in the Navy variant. This allowed A.G.A. to leverage the work of both projects.

A mockup of the XCG-9 was inspected on 1 March 1942. Despite this strong start, the XCG-9 work proved moribund. The firm consistently failed to meet schedule or show much in the way of encouraging progress on the Army airframes. A Materiel Command official visited A.G.A. on 20 July and found the firm focused on their Navy aircraft, not yet having finalized the Army glider. The tunnel model furnished on 25 October was of such poor quality that it was rejected. Another plant visit on 19 November found the new model just 10 percent complete, the static article 55 percent complete, the first glider just 5 percent along and one percent on the second. The company was also in dire financial condition.

In USAAF discussions with A.G.A., the firm sought a revised contract with payment on a cost basis, but the Army rejected this as good money after bad. The contract was cancelled on 2 December 1942. Final termination formalities took until November 1943. The government got some design documentation and construction materials to show for the $89,900.00 expended.

Laister-Kauffman Aircraft XCG-10, XCG-10A, YCG-10A, CG-10A, & G-10A

The first project to address the large glider requirement was undertaken by Laister-Kauffman Aircraft Corporation, of St. Louis. In December 1941, Dent had shown drawings of the Horsa to Jack Laister with the suggestion for U.S. production of the aircraft. However, the designer insisted he could do better, especially replacing the side cargo door of the Mk. I with more practical aft doors under the tail. This was also likely to be superior to a hinged front opening, as on the CG-4A, which could be fouled by airframe deformation on hard landings. In three days, Laister delivered concept drawings of an aircraft with a high aft fuselage to allow rear fuselage doors on the longitudinal axis for easy onload and offload. The concept so impressed that negotiations were opened in February and a letter contract issued on 18 March. A $375,000.00 formal fixed-price contract followed on 22 April 1942 calling for two test aircraft with trailers, a static article, and wind tunnel model. The airframes were to be delivered between November 1942 and April 1943.

Each glider was to seat 2 pilots and 28 troops, accommodate 8,000-pounds maximum payload, possess 150-mph tow speed, and be built of wood to the extent possible. The XCG-10 introduced features that would become common in later tactical airlifters. The high, cantilevered wing placed the bottom of the fuselage close to the ground for ease of onloading/offloading, yet high enough to protect it from damage in unprepared-field landings. Per Army request, the aircraft had a rugged tricycle undercarriage with retractable nose gear. The aircraft's rear 'clamshell' cargo doors were spring-loaded and opened from the cockpit while a short ramp beneath the doors dropped down. The short loading ramp had such a steep grade that twin wheel ramps had to be installed over them by hand for loading vehicles and guns. At the Army's insistence, cargo doors were also added at the front, although with a lower opening because of the cockpit floor overhead. This may have made the XCG-10 the first "through loading" aircraft, allowing low wheeled cargo or vehicles to load in one end and roll out the other at the destination without a need for time-consuming backing operations.

Apart from spruce and plywood, the XCG-10 design also featured some welded steel tubing and fabric construction. The truss work was found in the forward fuselage and the tail boom attachment. To keep wing structural weight down while avoiding external struts, tapered laminated wood skinning was employed on the top surface. Fabric covering was

In the search for a high-capacity glider, Jack Laister stepped forward with a concept of a tricycle-gear aircraft having loading doors at the back, the Army insisting on door in the nose as well. The Laister-Kauffmann XCG-10 was one of the largest wooden aircraft America manufactured during the war, earning the appellation "Trojan Horse." Like other Laister-Kauffmann projects, it was constructed in the St. Louis Arena, made available by wartime suspension of large sporting events. (National Archives)

When first assembled at Clinton County in fall 1943, the XCG-10 prototype (42-61099) had covers on the landing gear struts. These were soon discarded, but the fin elements below the tail boom remained as the principal means of differentiating this from later configurations of the Laister-Kauffmann glider. Note the crew door at the front and troop door ahead of the cargo doors (both sides). (National Museum of the United States Air Force)

The XCG-10 had nose cargo doors complementing the aft doors for through loading; even today an exceedingly rare feature. As can be seen, the loading ramp was short, and so individual wheel ramps had to be placed by hand. The cockpit floor made for low overhead clearance. (National Museum of the United States Air Force)

used aft of the spar. Three-axis trim was provided. The wing had slotted, hydraulically operated Fowler flaps, although supplemented by top spoilers. An electrical pump supplied hydraulic pressure for flap and nose gear operation. Electrical power was supplied by a 24 volt battery charged by a wind-driven generator. This also powered external and internal lights. A connection in the nose allowed external power to be applied. The usual glider-to-tug interphone was featured. The wing also had bays for carrying and dropping "parapacks," or parachute-recovered aerial delivery canvas bundles like those shoved out C-47 cargo doors. This feature was eventually dropped. Laister installed quad-disk hydraulic main gear brakes, and these were augmented with a parking brake. A crew door was featured in the forward port side of the glider and a troop door on each side of the aft end of the fuselage. Transparencies overhead the pilots could be jettisoned for emergency egress. Per USAAF direction, no section of the disassembled glider was to exceed 24 feet in length.

The contractor ran very late. The fuselage mockup was inspected in early May 1942 and the wind tunnel model was handed over on 27 June. Some components of the glider were passed to Wright Field for static loads testing and, these showing good qualities, permission was granted to proceed with aircraft construction before completing the full static article. However, the challenges of the design and the difficulty in obtaining materials and engineers slowed progress on the aircraft beyond the agreed delivery dates. The static test article of the XCG-10 was delivered on 26 October 1943.[9] The second flight test aircraft was to be held back to permit changes based on the static tests and early flight trials of the first ship.

By this point $497,715.50 had been spent, representing overruns covered by the government. A contract plus-up of $138,852.51 was approved on 6 May 1943 and $122,715.50 on 30 June, but money was saved by dropping the trailers. Laister-Kauffman had built his TG-4A trainers and Waco's CG-4A gliders in the St. Louis Arena and adjacent buildings. And so, the XCG-10, approximately the size of a B-17 bomber, was also born there. The XCG-10 was nearly the largest wooden military aircraft built in American during the war years, overshadowed only by the Navy's XLRN-1 glider (Chapter 9). This earned it the nickname Trojan Horse. Yet, despite the Army's dismal experience with many other wooden designs, the XCG-10 passed all strength tests.

The finished aircraft was shipped to Clinton County AAF and reassembled during 10-15 September 1943 (formally accepted 4 October). It initially had covers over the nose and main gear struts, but these seem to have been discarded early on. Flight testing began at Wilmington on 6 November 1943 with Randy Chapman and copilot Howard Blossom at the controls of the XCG-10 behind a C-47. It is also reported that during taxi tests on the 5th, the aircraft got airborne briefly. Over the following month, the aircraft proved to be a good performer, with only a few minor issues arising. The company had exceeded the USAAF specifications with a 10,000-pound payload weight. Yet, even at maximum GW, the glider handled well and landed within 300 feet thanks to the flaps and efficient brakes.

Waco's XCG-13 (see later) was already approved for production by this time, so there did not appear to be a need for pursuing the XCG-10. However, the designed showed so much promise that the USAAF acceded to Laister's urging that the requirements be increased to hauling 40 troops, in addition to the pilots, or the already-demonstrated 10,000 pounds payload. Cargo could include one of the Army's ubiquitous 2½-ton ("deuce-and-a-half") trucks, two 105 mm howitzers, a 105 towed by a ¾-ton truck, one 155 mm howitzer, among other cargo choices. Much of this could not even pass into the XCG-13. The contract was amended for the XCG-10A, raising its value to nearly $1.8 million.

The XCG-10 seated 28 troops in the comparatively cavernous cargo compartment. This shot is towards the rear of the aircraft, showing the aft cargo doors with integral windows. The heavy frames are made necessary by use of wood. (National Museum of the United States Air Force)

The company again improved on the specifications and produced a glider capable of lifting 12,650 pounds of freight. The Army agreed to deleting the nose doors, these having been found of little value, and this helped in weight control. Consequently, the nose profile became sleeker. The nose gear was moved farther forward and landing gear height reduced to bring the cargo floor to 24 inches off the ground (20 inches to the outer mold line). The lower fuselage deck and profile change in the aft fuselage permitted a longer loading ramp with lower gradient that only required 'toes' to be installed by hand at the end for wheeled freight. The fairing between the clamshell doors and tail boom could be removed to allow more clearance during cargo loading. Twin hydraulic stabilizing jacks also extended from the aft fuselage to the ground to prevent aircraft rocking and pitching during onload/offload of heavy articles. To accommodate the envisioned freight, the cabin was widened slightly. A hand-operated winch could be installed at the forward end of the compartment to aid cargo loading. In an overload capacity, 48 troops could be accommodated in 26 fold-up sidewall seats and an optional centerline row facing forward. (The sidewall seats had to be removed to fit the 155 mm howitzer.) Thirty tie-down rings could be installed in sockets within the cargo floor and ramp.

As one measure of the magnitude of the A-model changes, empty weight increased by 4,170 pounds or roughly 25 percent. The rudder was revised and ventral extension eliminated (probably to remove the loading obstruction), reducing overall length by 18 inches. A tow rope position indicator instrument was included and the specification also stated a requirement for integration of the D-1 autopilot powered by a wind-driven hydraulic pump (Chapter 11). The glider could be broken down for transport in six crates, the largest 2,160 cubic feet of 24x10x9-foot dimensions.

Once more, the Laister-Kauffman static article passed USAAF testing without difficulty. The second XCG-10 flight test aircraft was converted, beginning in early November 1943, to the XCG-10A standard before it flew. The fuselage was cut and widened, the joint lines readily evident. First flight was with this aircraft from nearby Scott Field, Illinois, on 27 April 1944 and then towed to Clinton County on the 30th where flight testing continued through 14 June. While at Scott, loading trials were performed. The first XCG-10 was returned to St. Louis for like modification.

Flight testing of the XCG-10A was very promising, its 12,650-pound capacity arousing much interest among Airborne leadership. The Army had already committed to the CG-13A, but worked to shift gears. Note that the nose gear was made retractable for this variant. (National Archives)

The redesigned XCG-10A (42-61100) widened the fuselage, deleted the nose cargo doors, lowered the stance, and lengthened the rear cargo doors for a more practical loading ramp grade. The nose profile was altered significantly, with this and deletion of the fin ventral elements making it distinct from its predecessor. It began flying in spring 1944. (The Peter M. Bowers Collection/The Museum of Flight)

These pair of images illustrate the flight deck of the XCG-10A, raised above the cargo floor. The vast transparencies were welcomed for the enhanced visibility but cursed for the radiant heating under the sun's glare.

Note the battery case and the numerous control cables that had to be protected from interference by cargo and troops. (National Archives)

Despite its enormous size (approximately that of a B-17 bomber), the XCG-10A could still be broken down for shipment. This image shows off the improved undercarriage of the A-model and the type's flaps (eschewing spoilers). The aircraft was among the first with stacked disc brakes. (National Museum of the United States Air Force)

The heavy weight of the XCG-10A meant it could only be towed by the C-47 at low gross weight. It usually required the C-46 or a four-engine aircraft as tug. However, here is seen a tandem tow by a pair of C-47s. (National Archives)

Although ostensibly a wooden aircraft, the XCG-10A glider had a welded steel tube frame in the nose for crash protection. Second Lieutenant Hutchens of the Air Technical Services Command glider unit occupies the cockpit of 42-61099. The generous downview windows for the pilots are vital for selecting a touchdown point when on the downwind leg of the landing approach. (National Archives)

The XCG-10A version added 14 centerline seats to bring normal troop capacity to 40. In overload capacity this could be 48. However, these lightly armed troops are not representative of those ready to enter combat, commonly burdened with rucksacks, squad weapons, and additional gear. (National Archives)

The XCG-10A could accommodate the Army's 2½-ton "deuce-and-a-half" trucks, albeit with the windscreen and cargo bed covering lowered and the driver hunkering down. The image shows well the sidewall fold-down seats and belts. The ability to land, open the rear doors and lower the ramp, then drive out was a tremendous added capability. (National Museum of the United States Air Force)

Table 08-03

Laister-Kauffman Aircraft XCG-10 Specifics

span	105.0 ft
wing area	1,171 ft^2
fuselage length	67.0 ft
fuselage height	26.3 ft
empty weight	7,980 lbs
loaded weight	15,980 lbs
maximum weight	17,980 lbs
tow speed	150 mph
maximum speed	180 mph (flaps up)
landing speed	50 mph
stall speed (23,000 lbs GW)	72 mph flaps up, 62 mph flaps down
capacity	2 pilots, 28 troops

Table 08-04

Laister-Kauffman Aircraft XCG-10A Specifics

span	105.0 ft
wing area	1,180 ft^2
length	67.0 ft
fuselage height	27.0 ft
empty weight	12,150 lbs
loaded weight	22,200 lbs
gross weight	23,000 lbs, 25,000 lbs alternate
maximum weight	32,000 lbs (officially 25,000 lbs)
tow speed	180 mph
power to tow	1,050 hp (150 mph, sea level, 23,000 lbs)
maximum speed	180 mph
stall speed	62 mph (maximum GW, flaps), 80 mph (no flaps)
landing speed, normal	70-75 mph
takeoff distance, average	3,504 ft (maximum GW, C-46 tug)
radius of action	560 mi (maximum GW, C-4 tug, 5,000 ft altitude)
landing distance, average	411 ft (25,000 pounds GW, full flaps) 1,238 over 50-ft obstacle
capacity	2 pilots, 40 troops
cabin length x width x height	29.7 x 7.6 fwd to 8.5 aft x 6.6 fwd to 6.7 aft ft
glide ratio	14:1

Eventually joined by the upgraded first glider, the aircraft were put through their paces, meeting or exceeding all requirements. Even given its large size, it was successfully "snatched" by a C-54 and by B-17, although the tugs were close to stall. (The first B-17 snatch was after a towline break and glider emergency landing in a cotton field. The XCG-10A was unloaded to 13,350 pounds and its ground roll made over steel landing mat laid down over the sandy ground. The B-17 was equipped with the Model 160 pick-up unit.)[10] In August, the Glider Branch declared the XCG-10A fit for production, praising the company's quality manufacturing. Some room for improvement was noted, especially correcting a violent nose-over pitch-break at heavy GW stall, empennage vibration. Elimination of the spoilers was shown acceptable. Regardless, the aircraft looked very worthy. The USAAF had paid Laister-Kauffman $774,000.00 to this point.

Operational and tactical suitability trials of the second glider were performed at Laurinburg-Maxton from 15 November through 1 December 1944, and further loading tests on 1-12 December at Camp Mackall, North Carolina. It included tows at the full 25,000-pound gross weight by C-46. The C-47 was not a suitable tow plane except at a payload weight approximately that of the CG-4A.[11] The 15,945-pound M-22 light tank was loaded but not flown. The tests also saw 62 men carried and as many as 50 paratroops in one instance; although this was ultimately limited to 40 because of unsafe crowding.[12] Payload up to 19,000 pounds was carried, bringing maximum gross weight to 32,000 pounds. Descents at 800 fpm and 130 mph were performed with a 411-foot ground roll at maximum GW. While most tests were from a runway, the unplanned cotton field landing was at near maximum GW with no glider damage suffered. However, among the long list of requested enhancements was addition of skids under the nose after a nose wheel-up landing resulted in structural damage. The Army was suitably enthusiastic about the aircraft's potential, declaring it operationally and tactically suitable.

With a sense of urgency to field large cargo gliders, the ground forces had strongly endorsed CG-10A production beginning in April 1944, and requested at least an initial quantity for service trials. In November 1944, the Airborne had recommended a 500 aircraft buy, and as many a 1,000 were contemplated. Production plans for 1945 and 1946 put into place during the last month of 1944 included 416 CG-10A, although the rate would not reach significant numbers for a year.[13] However, the AAF hesitated, struggling with competing requirements for an overstretched industry, while the AGF fumed and threatened to take the matter up with the War Department. The Air Forces estimated the greatest monthly production rate would be 80, the 500 gliders delivered in 22 months at $50 million from a standing start, but achieved by absorbing the production capacity of 240 CG-4A/CG-15As at a time the output of the 15-place gliders was below demand.[14] By 1945, CG-10A quantities in excess of 5,000 were being discussed in anticipation of support for an invasion of Japan. However, the prolonged development and evaluation of the XCG-16 (see later), championed by the glider advocates in Washington, repeatedly delayed awarding a contract. Another factor was the concern in some quarters that the aircraft was just too big. The glider community in the Army had concluded that a 10,000-pound payload was the practical limit for a tactical glider. At one point, Laister-Kauffman was told flatly there was no requirement for the glider.

Guns flown into the LZ could be increased to 105 mm with the CG-10A instead of the 75 mm brought in by the CG-4A and CG-13A. A ¾-ton truck (Jeep) pulls a 105 from the glider. Note the stabilizing struts lowered near the hinge line of the ramp. (National Soaring Museum)

A concern was voiced about the mandated wooden construction when a 200-hour inspection of the prototypes, after months of flying, revealed deterioration from moisture and fungus. With the most likely combat deployment of the aircraft being in the humid Pacific theater, a potential problem was evident.

Among this flurry of conflicting direction, authorization to purchase 500 CG-10As was finally granted on 15 February 1945.[15] On 1 March 1945, an initial $14,068,378.00 letter contract came forth for the first 100 aircraft—25 preproduction YCG-10As and 75 production CG-10As, spares and data—while tooling was to be readied for 1,000 units. Unit price was expected to be $70,000.00 plus $3,000.00 for crating to ship abroad.[16] The first delivery was expected in August with production reaching 35 units per month by March 1946, but only 395 machines by the end of 1946.[17] Once reviled, the desire for gliders had by 1945 exceed the capacity of the industry the Army had help put together from almost nothing in 1942. It was clear Laister-Kauffmann could not handle such numbers, and various additional manufacturers were considered.

By summer 1945, following VE-Day, the numbers of CG-10As to be produced were reworked to 344 for the Pacific Theater through the end of 1946 plus 384 for States-side training. The production line was set up in the Louisville, Kentucky, defense plant originally intended for the wooden Curtiss-Wright C-74 assembly. The second XCG-10A (42-61100) was bailed to Laister-Kauffman to support tooling and production setup. It was converted as the first representative CG-10A.

Snead & Company XCG-11

The first contract let against the 30-seat glider requirement went to Snead & Company (previously introduced). Discussions had begun in February and the fixed-price contract was signed on 21 April 1942 for $264,970.00. As usual, this called for a static article to be delivered on 1 September 1942, and two flight test aircraft to follow on 1 October and 1 November, plus trailers and a tunnel model.

The design featured a podded fuselage of steel tubing, wood, and fabric with plywood aft boom to the tail, and plywood-covered wing with landing flaps. The wing and control surfaces were wood covered with a mix of plywood and fabric. The available drawing suggests doors in the nose or aft end of the pod, in addition to at least one side personnel door. The contract specified that no section of the disassembled aircraft should exceed 24 feet in length, accommodating shipping requirements.[18] As with most of the large gliders that emerged after the initial surge of orders, an SCR 585-A radio was to be included (12 pounds), implying a battery and antenna as well.

A fuselage mockup was examined on 25 June 1942 and the wind tunnel model was sent to Wright Field on 24 July for testing. The latter was found unsatisfactory. On 29 August the firm sought a 110-day extension on the contract to correct the model, redesign the aircraft flaps, redo the fuselage stress analysis for a change in the steel alloy to be used, and respond to a request the fuselage width be expanded to accommodate the 105 mm howitzer. This was granted on 15 September, but on 3 November the company pressed their luck by requesting the contract be renegotiated to a cost-plus basis, expecting final costs to be $577,000.00. They still failed to perform to expectations, and on 15 November moves began to terminate the program.

The contract was cancelled on 9 June 1943 after $143,118.25 had been expended with little to show. Snead then went into receivership and defaulted, its assets acquired by Republic Aviation.

Table 08-05

Snead & Company XCG-11 Specifics (estimated, not built)	
span	112.0 ft
fuselage length	55.4 ft
forward pod	35.0 ft
height	22.0 ft
empty weight	7,767 lbs
gross weight	14,650 lbs design, 15,676 lbs maximum
tow speed	150 mph
landing speed	50 mph
capacity	2 pilots, 28 troops

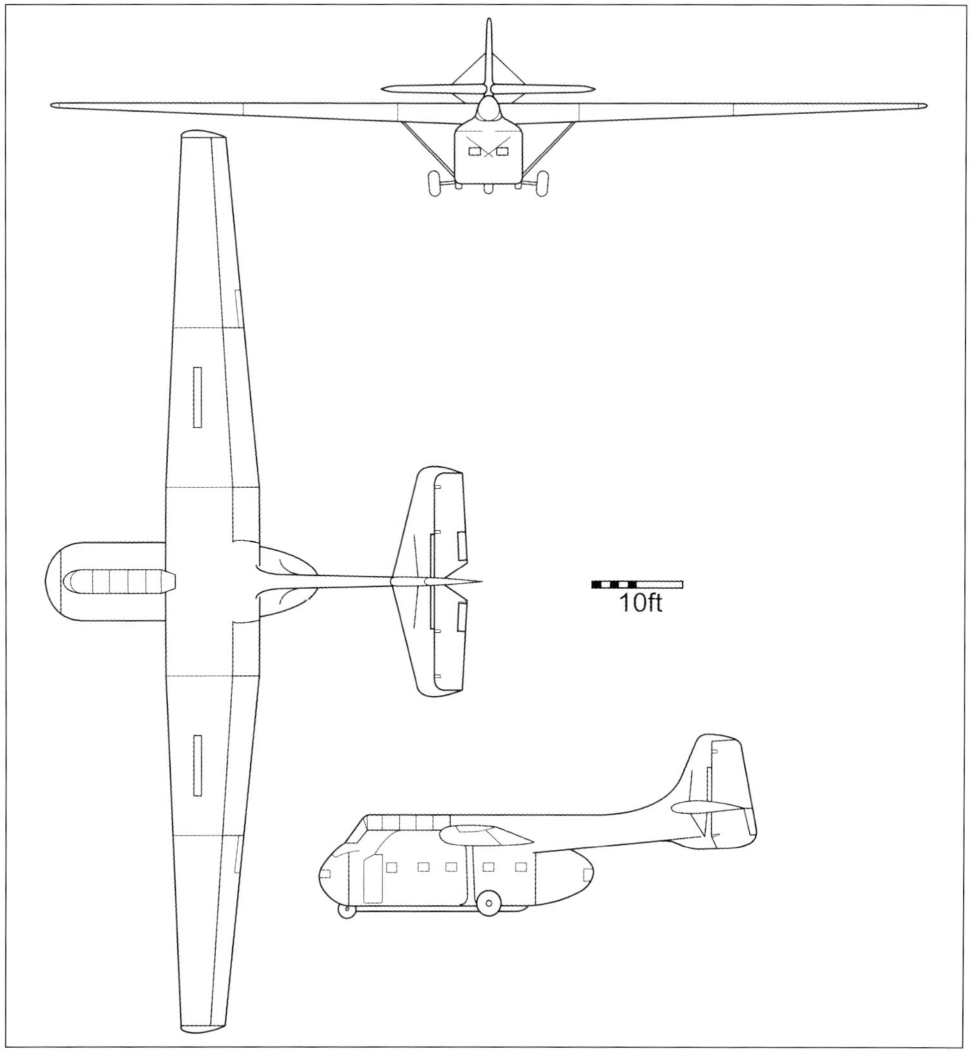

Seeking an all-wood 30-place glider under the wartime contracting constraints, the USAAF had Snead & Company developing the XCG-11 shown here. This firm had no prior aircraft experience and so, finding the development of even a motorless transport beyond their means, failed. The podded-fuselage was to have had loading doors possibly in both the forward and aft ends. (Author)

Read-York XCG-12

Aeronautical engineer Captain Hugo Sundstedt, with experience designing airplanes during WWI, heard about the Army's interest in wooden gliders during November 1941. After consulting with some officials, he began preliminary designs of same. In early spring 1942, Sundstedt set out to form a company to attract government contracts for the gliders. He associated with industrial engineer Holcomb York, industrial and production engineer Robert C. Read, and attorney Lincoln Epworth, to form the York Aircraft Corporation in New York City. The firm incorporated on 21 May 1942. Preliminary designs were in hand and Steinway Piano Company of New York agreed to be considered serving as a potential production facility.

After opening negotiations with the Glider Branch and making some suggested design changes, York Aircraft was invited in June 1942 to offer a proposal for another 30-place glider. This 23 July document earned them a 24 July Letter of Intent. The letter contract of the 25th was superseded on 17 September 1942 by the $299,830.00 formal fixed-price contract covering a tunnel model, static article, and two gliders to be delivered with trailers in March through June 1943. The contract was only approved based upon York locating the additional construction facilities of the Simmons Company in Kenosha, Wisconsin. To ensure York could gain necessary capital to setup operations, the government guaranteed 90 percent of a $60,000.00 bank loan.

A wind tunnel model was shipped on 30 September 1942 and testing completed on 23 October 1942. A fuselage mockup was inspected on the 26th or 27th and approved with minor modifications. However, this progress had run to considerable expense, with York getting generous contributions from Simmons who anticipating big returns from production. By early January 1943, Simmons foresaw an overrun of 100 to 150 percent of the contract value. After all parties met at Wright Field to discuss the situation, the contract value was increased on 18 February 1943 by $150,000.00 and one trailer eliminated.[19]

The bank loan was to be repaid in May 1943, but York was still struggling to make substantial progress. On 23 April, Simmons declared it had extended itself far enough (to the tune of some $360,000.00) and would withdraw from the deal. This would effectively scuttle the project. The Army sent an officer to Kenosha on 15 May to inspect construction progress and reported the workmanship to be good to excellent, with the static article about 80 percent complete, the first aircraft 65-70 percent and the second 55 percent.[20] Although York was still solvent, it was clear it could not continue without the assistance of Simmons. The latter agreed to continue working under some other formula that ensured it would not lose further money.

Accepting that this was all typical of "what can happen during the life of a contract," the USAAF chose to cancel the York project on 1 June 1943 with $1,200.00 expended but facing $54,000.00 to pick up on the delinquent bank note. It was reported that private capital of $636,000.00 was expended on the ineffectual effort. The work then passed to Read-York Incorporated under a 26 May 1943 agreement and 6 March 1943 contract of $426,230.00 value (same as the original contract less the cost of the model). This New York City-based company was created that month with many of the same corporate officers, on the resources in Kenosha, and some of the New York engineering staff, solely to take up the new XCG-12 contract but initially with just $100.00 in capital.

Working with government agreement to finance the work, Read-York accepted completing the contract without profit.[21] Simmons took $30,000.00 for all project materials on hand, sold raw stock, and leased its facility to Read-York. Deliveries were to be in 10 July 1943 for the static article, the first aircraft 45 days later (24 August) and the last 30 days more (23 September). Starting with a 50 percent advance of $213,115.00, Read-York was later given further advances amounting to 75 and then 90 percent of the work accomplished.

Table 08-06

Read-York XCG-12 Specifics (revised 1 November 1943) (estimated, not flown)

span	112.0 (82.0) ft
wing area	(1,157) ft^2
length	70.0 ft
height	25.0 ft
empty weight	9,349 lbs
gross weight	17,691 (21,000) lbs
tow speed	185 (180) mph (at 12,000 ft)
stall speed	(60) mph
landing speed (flaps)	48 mph
landing distance	700 ft (ground roll)
capacity	2 pilots, 28 (34) troops

The design looked like a typical transport of the period albeit with high-wing and boxy cross-section. The cockpit was above the forward cabin and the nose apparently possessed a drop-down ramp. The fuselage was to be welded steel tubing covered with fabric while the wing was wood with plywood-covered D-section and fabric aft. Control surfaces were wood with a mix of plywood and fabric covering. The fixed nose gear and strutted main gear gave the fuselage, also fitted with bottom skids, a low stance.

The static test article was delivered on 24 July 1943. However, the wings failed at 78 percent of the positive high angle-of-attack load condition. It is also reported that the wing failed at 100 percent of negative load on or about 6 September. By November it was clear a major structural redesign would be necessary and this was going to slow work on the flight articles. Consequently, Read-York did not provide the two flight test articles in August and September.

Although the first flight article was said to be 90 percent complete in November 1943 and the second 65-70 percent, the company was clearly stretched to breaking.[22] It estimated another $36,650.00 was required to complete the first flight-worthy glider, on top of the $379,794.70 already provided by the government. Read-York was desperate for another advance and contract increase, and on 1 November stated the work necessary to redesign the wing. This came with revised specifications for the glider that were significantly better (see summary), but also a $143,717.40 bill. A new loading included the jeep and 105 mm plus 1,500 pounds of ammunition and crew of six.[23] However, the government demurred, the Glider Branch recommending on 5 November 1943 the contract be terminated. The contractor had already halted work in October owing to exhausted funds. The cancellation was enacted on 6 December, the company still owing $46,435.30 for the loan guarantee. However, Read-York appealed. Their petition was denied and the company was bankrupted.

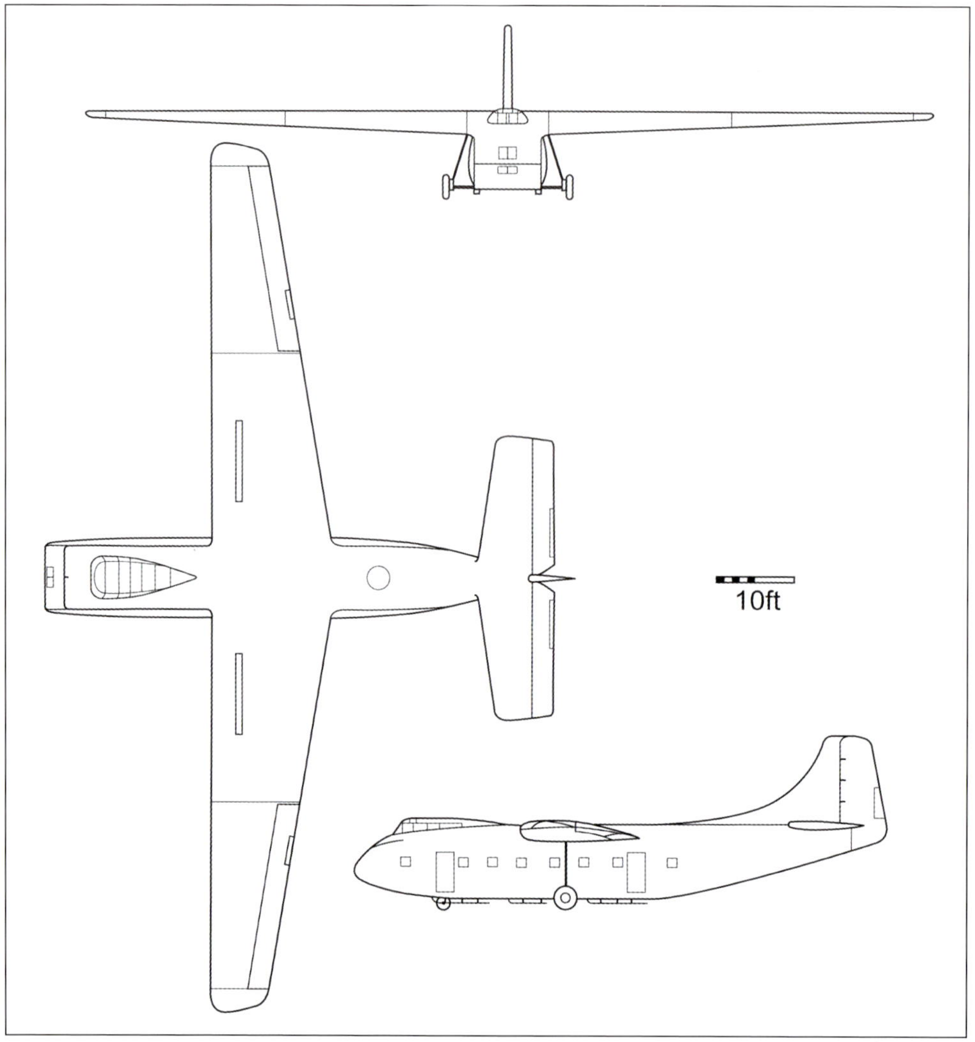

Another 30-place all-wood glider was being developed by York Aircraft, and subsequently Read-York. The design had skids supplementing the wheeled undercarriage and the nose apparently had a drop-down cargo ramp. Although a structural ground test airframe was tested (and failed), and the first flight aircraft was nearly complete, the firm ultimately collapsed. (Author)

Waco XCG-13, XCG-13A, YCG-13, YCG-13A, CG-13A, & G-13A

To meet the requirement for the 30-place glider (including pilots), the USAAF naturally welcomed efforts by Waco who had performed so well on the CG-3A and CG-4A. After initiating talks in July 1942, the XCG-13 was born from a 25 July letter contract and follow-on $352,161.00, 21 September fixed-price development contract for three airframes to be delivered between February and April 1943. The glider was a growth of the CG-4A design, initially with many similarities including conventional landing gear.

Waco developed a 30-place counterpart to the CG-4A in the CG-13. The first was this XCG-13 that, like the CG-4A, had a dorsal extension to the vertical stabilizer, tail wheel, and fuselage skids. However, all these features would be deleted. (National Museum of the United States Air Force)

A first step in the upgrade of the XCG-13 was just the tail change, performed on both prototypes but also this Northwestern YCG-13. This Waco type began as essentially an enlarged CG-4A, having the same layout and structural design. However it possessed flaps instead of the spoilers and soon evolved farther. (National Museum of the United States Air Force)

The major change first introduced into the reworked 43-28245 was the raised aft fuselage and introduction of a nose gear. The level deck aided combat loading and unloading while raising the tail reduced buffeting in flight. Note this aircraft retains a small wheel at the end of the fuselage while production machines had just a bumper. (National Archives)

The glider was to gross-out at 15,000 pounds with a useful load of 8,000 pounds, the high wing loading (18 psf) permitting tow at 175 mph and 12,000 feet. Wright Field built the wind tunnel model, completed 29 September 1942 based on Waco drawings. Waco was also permitted to complete one glider ahead of the static article.[24]

Waco did not disappoint, and the flight testing began at Wright Field on 10 March 1943 with arrival of the first of two examples. The testing was completed on the 18th with positive results. The static test article was delivered on 7 July and its tests concluded successfully soon thereafter. The second aircraft was delivered to Clinton County on 6 July incorporating several changes including hand-pumped hydraulic nose raising jacks the CCAAF troops had devised. Testing was slowed after a 17 July storm in Wilmington destroyed this second prototype, a CG-4A tossed atop it. Final contract value was $373,220.96.

The first X-plane was modified in line with the Army desire for a more durable and reusable aircraft, the XCG-13A.[25] A nose gear was adopted in place of the tail wheel. The base of the rear fuselage was angled up to raise the tail 1.5 feet and get it out of the wake of the flaps and unacceptable buffet, although some buffeting remained. The empennage was revised with deletion of the vertical tail dorsal extension, the vertical extended over the rudder instead of vice versa, and the horizontal stabilizer bottom bracing wires replaced with struts. The modification in the last sentence preceded the others, as the gliders were seen with the empennage alterations but still possessing the other XCG-13-unique features. The changes added 1,700 pounds to the empty weight and gross by 3,900 pounds, but allowed payload to be increased to 10,200 pounds.

The XCG-13 was an obvious descendent of the CG-4A, with wooden wings of similar planform but with hydraulically operated and perforated landing flaps supplementing the spoilers, retaining the external struts and boxy fuselage of fabric over welded steel tubes and wood, and with an upward hinged nose for cargo loading. This created an opening of 5.7x7.5 feet. The wing was wood with plywood-covered D-section and fabric aft. It was not exceptionally large and so the glider had an unusually high 18 psf wing loading. Many of the features of the CG-13 would appear later in the CG-15. Pilot doors were featured on both sides of the nose. Individual seats folded down from the cabin wall, and canvas seating was erected as an optional centerline row. Static lines could be rigged in the cabin for paratroop jumps out the side doors. A telescoping support tube within the aft fuselage was extended during loading to keep the glider on its nose wheel for the initial aft center of gravity movement. Doors in the bottom of the fuselage, just aft of the rear seats, permitted the drop of four parapacks arranged in a rack above within a box with release handle. This feature was deleted in production. These were to be Type A-5 or A-6 Aerial Delivery Containers of up to 75 pounds each in bomb shackles and supports weighing 60 pounds.[26] Down-view windows were provided at the pilots' feet. An observation bubble projected from the top of the glider just aft of the starboard wing root. The main landing gear had differential brakes and shock absorbers. The gear could be dropped and so fuselage skids were incorporated. The SCR-585-A radio was specified and the D-1 autopilot (Chapter 11), powered by a wind generator projecting from the starboard side of the nose, was to be standard equipment to relieve pilot workload.

This was the first of the large gliders to see the light of day, and being first in wartime circumstances was a definite advantage as the Air Forces had a tendency to order production based on early results alone. With the modifications tested on XCG-13A, the design was clearly suitable and so approved for production by June 1943.

The preproduction YCG-13A is seen in high tow. The glider was towed at much the same speed as the CG-4A but was heavier, and so remained a labor for the C-47 tow planes. Note the observation bubble atop the fuselage aft of the wing and steps for the troop doors. (National Soaring Museum)

Responding to complaints about the CG-4A, the CG-13A was a much more airplane-like glider with enhanced safety features. The nose had heavy steel tube enforcement for crash protection and with individual pilot doors. The towline attached at the apex of the nose and additional downview windows were placed at the pilots' feet. (National Museum of the United States Air Force)

The interior of the XCG-13A reveals the same construction methodology as the CG-4A. Improvements were the individual fold-down canvas and tubing seats, centerline bench for additional troops, and in-floor cargo tie-down rings. A feature that did not reach production is the aerial delivery chute behind the aft seats, with release lever for the parapacks. (National Museum of the United States Air Force)

The cockpit of the CG-13A also shared much with its "little brother." An improvement was that the seats were adjustable. The instrument panel layout is likely that of the XCG-13A as production machines had a vertically oriented panel with attitude gyro and "angle of dangle" indicators. (National Museum of the United States Air Force)

Full-rate production was initiated with a $3,095,925.00 order for 50 YCG-13s from Northwestern on 11 June 1943. This was later revised to 1 YCG-13, 2 YCG-13A, and 47 CG-13A. Ford initially begged off, pleading that it was already fully committed to War Department production. However, it was convinced to take a 50 YCG-13 ordered under a $3,468,400.00 extension on a CG-4A contract. This eventually covered 1 YCG-13, 1 YCG-13A, and 48 CG-13A built at Iron Mountain.

Northwestern's YCG-13 flew on 2 December 1943 and was towed two days later to CCAAF behind a B-23.[27] Ford's was delivered on 6 January 1944 at Dearborn, Michigan, towed off to Wilmington. The YCG-13As soon followed and these aircraft were thoroughly tested during spring 1944. The YCG-13s still had the original aft fuselage and tail wheel when delivered, but were subsequently brought up to A standard and so redesignated YCG-13A.[28] The production CG-13As also dispensed with fuselage skids.

The CG-13A offered a marked improvement in airborne attack with its ability to bring in a vehicle and gun together, an armored personnel carrier (halftrack), 1½-ton truck, and higher caliber weapons like the 105 mm gun. Despite the large size, snatch by C-47 and B-17 were demonstrated. However, criticisms of the CG-13A were myriad. Tow behind the C-47 was challenging, despite this being the most plentiful tug. Initial rate of climb of the C-47 and CG-13 combination, the glider at maximum GW, was 177 fpm and so required 37 minutes to reach the 5,000-foot service ceiling.[29] A C-46 or some four-engine aircraft was generally necessary with the glider fully loaded. The initial goal had been a stall speed of 60 mph at maximum gross weight, but 79 mph had been achieved with flaps. This meant a typical 80-mph landing speed that was roundly considered unacceptable. Landing distance on pavement at maximum GW was 640 feet.[30] A braking parachute was added and tests were being performed at the beginning of 1945 with slotted flaps to lower the stall speed, and so the landing speed. The CCAAF team also worked with deceleration rockets (Chapter 11). While Materiel Division had worked hard to increase the tow speed of gliders, achieving 135 mph for the CG-13A, this made it incompatible for tow beside the CG-4A at 120 mph. Correct loading was critical for balance, and it was found troops were doing this improperly. The floor of the cabin was approximately 2.2 feet off the ground, requiring long wheel ramps for vehicle loading. With the glider breaking down into six boxes for shipment, the largest 26.1 feet long and 9.5 feet on the sides and weighing 11,316 pounds, the shipping of CG-13s was even more cumbersome than the CG-4A, and so undesirable.

Northwestern's production number was increased by 200 in June 1944, Ford's by 300 on a letter contract. Plans existed in May 1944 to procure 1,434 of the gliders, but it was not to be.[31] After two years of development and a mass of production-representative gliders available for service trials, the decision that summer that the CG-13As "was not suitable for tactical use" came rather late, again underlining the mixed signals during the whole glider program.

The press for more Waco 15-place gliders held sway and dissatisfaction with the CG-13A resounded. Theaters expressed concern with the comparatively high landing speed, the CBI leadership rejecting the CG-13A outright. Production plans laid at the end of 1944 for the next two years included only the CG-4A/CG-15A and the CG-10A, the latter championed by the AGF. Consequently, Northwestern's order was reduced to the original 50 in November while Ford's additional was cancelled after only 37 were finished. The final two CG-13As were delivered in April 1945. This yielded two prototypes, five preproduction articles, and 132 CG-13As, or a total 139. Peak production rate was reached

A criticism of the CG-13A was the high touchdown speed, lending it a comparatively long landing distance. The Glider Branch worked to correct this with slotted flaps, deceleration rockets, and a drag parachute. Only this last was adopted, seen here at release just before touchdown. (National Museum of the United States Air Force)

in October 1944 at a modest seven per month, for a total $6,305,339.09 on the Northwestern contract. Final unit cost was $44,800.00.[32]

Some 81 CG-13As were sent to Europe, the first assembled there in November 1944. The autopilot and wind generator was standard, although most of the gliders were delivered with this as a kit for field installation. There a few non-combat flights carried balky freight like vehicles. One ditched in the Channel after the towline broke while hauling a staff car to the Continent. The British acquired six to nine of the machines (including KK790/1).[33] Twenty of the gliders were in France in time for Operation *Varsity*, but the complication of integrating them, with their higher tow speeds, into the formations was not worth the effort for such a small force. Five YCG-13As and six CG-13As were deployed to the Pacific theater. One CG-13A was towed 840 miles nonstop from Nadzab to Biak on 22 October 1944 carrying a staff car onboard for the Camalaniugan Airfield assault. That action featured this sole CG-13A in the type's only combat action. It was not recovered.

Table 08-07

Waco Aircraft CG-13A Specifics

span	85.6 ft
wing area	872.5 ft^2
fuselage length	54.3 ft
fuselage height	20.8 ft
empty weight	8,700 lbs
gross weight	15,600 lbs design, 18,900 lbs loaded
tow speed	135 mph (209 mph design)
maximum speed	195 mph
glide speed	85-95 mph
stall speed (maximum GW)	76 mph (flaps)
landing speed	59 mph
capacity	2 pilots, 28 troops
cabin length x width x height	23.8 x 7.5 x 6.0 ft aft cabin height 5.7 ft
glide ratio	12:1

Dual wheel ramps allowed for roll-on and roll-off of wheeled cargo. However, the ramp angle was steep. Note the stabilizing strut at the aft end of the fuselage and the tow rope position transmitter arm dangling from the apex of the nose with wind-driven generator on the starboard side of the nose. (National Museum of the United States Air Force)

General Airborne Transport MC-1, XCG-16 & XCG-16A

Although the Army received many unsolicited aeronautical concepts in its quest for combat gliders, most were fanciful or impractical. These received scant attention. If the offeror persisted, a closer look might be warranted, but very few were granted contracts. When an extraordinary concept originated in this manner from noted glider designer Hawley Bowlus, it was initially examined and set aside only to take on a life of its own. A formal development program was eventually born to explore the potential of the aircraft.

Bowlus' vision was of a very innovative 42-place 'span loading' glider. The proposal featured two adjacent cargo compartments, separated by the cockpit, all within a capacious 'lifting body' center section. A jeep and 105 mm gun could be carried, each in a separate compartment, as part of the 8,500-pound payload. The twin compartments were accessed via a pair of clamshell doors making up the center section leading edge and opened with hand-jacks, the lower halves forming loading ramps. The wing roots were roomy enough to accommodate defensive .50 caliber machine guns and gunners. (These were never fitted and not a part of the specifications eventually accepted for the glider.) From the center section would issue the 47-foot span swept wings with slotted flaps. The center section also had a split flap, with all flaps electrically operated. Also emerging from the center section were twin booms back to the tail. The pilots' compartment had two tandem seats under a fighter-like canopy. The tricycle undercarriage was fully retractable. The wing was to employ laminar flow airfoils. (This, too, was never mentioned again after the initial proposal.) The general design was expected to be of such low drag that the 16,000-pound gross aircraft was to be towed at 160 mph behind a C-47. The aircraft was to be made of wood with the control surfaces fabric-covered.

Bowlus embarked on his campaign to build and sell the aircraft on 10 February 1942. He built a two-seat half-scale test model on 10 September through 10 October 1942 in San Fernando, California—a remarkable 27 days for the entire design and construction at a cost of $35,000.00—and performed the initial flight tests on 13 October from Cuddyback Lake (dry), California, piloted by Bowlus. The glider handled well and ground effect was great enough to make a hard landing "impossible."[34]

Instead of competing for the 30-troops glider, the requirement released in 1942, Bowlus and partner Albert Criz approached Colonel Dent on about 15 December 1942, and subsequently lobbied other USAAF glider leadership to take an interest in their ambitious design. They were tireless in their promotion and won the interest of Richard Du Pont who had had previous business dealings with his friend, Hawley Bowlus.

With this encouragement, Bowlus and Criz formed Airborne Transport Incorporated in Los Angeles. Their 9 October 1942 preliminary type specification for what was then identified as AT2C was for a 13,000-pound gross weight glider of 8,400-pound useful load spanning 95 feet (wing sweep discarded) and landing at 45 mph with limit speed 300 mph. Maximum glide ratio was predicted to be 17.5:1 at 60 mph. Drag was anticipated to be so low that, the document claimed, a four-engine aircraft could tow four of the gliders.

The Glider Branch personnel at Wright Field were more skeptical. They were leery of Bowlus after he had failed to perform satisfactorily on the earlier XTG-12 training glider contract, and given the difficulties encountered on the

The Bowlus lifting body glider was to have two loadable compartments separated by the cockpit seating two pilots in tandem. The leading edge of the thick wind center section would open like two clam shells, the lower portions acting as twin ramps. This arrangement would allow a jeep and gun to be carried in the same glider, albeit having to be unloaded separately and hitched together. (National Archives)

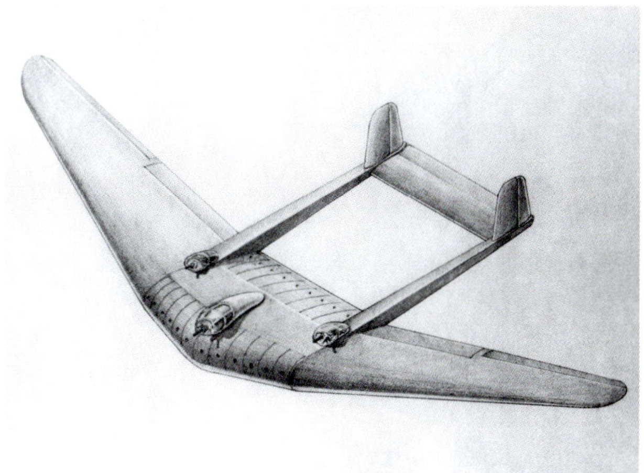

Sailplane designer Hawley Bowlus, energized as so many others were to contribute to the war effort and make a living in a wartime economy, conceived the lifting body glider of 42-place capacity. To prove out the concept and collect engineering data, Bowlus constructed a two-place sub-scale glider during 1942. This machine is shown on a southern California dry lakebed during trials in fall of that year. (National Archives)

This is the original concept for the Bowlus span-loading glider, with the cargo volume melded into the wing to added to overall lift. It was to be built of wood and possess a low-drag laminar flow wing. Note the wing sweep, square cross-section tail booms, and gun stations. (National Archives)

XCG-7 and XCG-8 projects. Review of the design suggested the pair of entrepreneurs were being exceedingly optimistic regarding performance.[35] Aircraft Laboratory analysis of the October 1942 specification calculated a B-17 bomber could tow just one, not four, of the proposed gliders. Dent visited the Los Angeles operation on about 10 January 1943 and found utterly inadequate facilities, staff, and fiscal resources to undertake even the most modest development effort.

The Glider Branch continued to be pressured by others to look more closely at the design and was criticized for a perceived "not invented here" attitude. Materiel Command finally sent three general officers out to L.A. on 6 February 1943 to investigate. They found the Airborne Transport facility to be a former dry-cleaning establishment with only the most rudimentary aircraft design and construction assets. The firm had only built a mockup of the cargo compartments for loading demonstrations, and the generals perceived loading difficulties after examining it. Engineering was "fragmentary and incomplete" and design details inconsistent. Bowlus and Criz had plans to relocate when a contract was certain, and pick up additional experienced personnel from among the area's aircraft manufacturers.[36] Suggestions that the men attempt to interest an established aviation firm with producing the glider was met with cold indifference.[37]

At an 18 March 1943 meeting, Bowlus and Criz were told by Dent and other officers that the Air Forces had sufficient large-capacity glider programs underway and the Airborne Transport design would not be taken up.[38] Undeterred, Bowlus and Criz raised money to build a full-scale MC-1 test aircraft.[39] However, they continued to find a sympathetic ear in General Arnold's office, and his glider staff appears to have provided some assistance.

Wright Field engineers inspected the prototype, built in a facility some miles from the engineering offices, and closely examined drawings, data, and plans on several occasions. They continued to express grave doubts regarding performance predictions and soundness of Airborne Transport's manufacturing practices. The internal dimensions of the cargo compartment, with maximum 15.0-foot length by 6.9-foot width and 5.1-foot height, was operationally cumbersome and did not meet the desired Air Forces measurements of 23.4 feet length, 7.7 feet width, and 6.7 feet height that was being enforced on the XCG-10 with much additional weight. There was concern expressed about unsafe stall and spin characteristics inherent in the design. Furthermore, the design appeared to infringe on a "lifting body" patent held by Vincent J. Burnelli, although a license was eventually agreed upon.

Enthusiastic about the MC-1 and championing a 1,000-aircraft contract, Du Pont and one of his colleagues, Lieutenant Colonel Ernest Gabel, went to California to observe MC-1 demonstration flights. Initial test sorties had been from Oxnard with a USAAF C-60 tow plane. On 11 September 1943, the C-60 towed the aircraft to nearby March Field. It was to be towed that night to Washington, D.C., where Arnold would inspect the craft and Du Pont would encourage interest.

During the last flights that day and its 31st, Gabel flew as pilot with Du Pont as a passenger, along with others. Unfortunately, a ballast of lead shot bags, that had not been secured, shifted aft when turbulence or wake was encountered, or due to an abrupt pilot input. The glider began a series of pitch oscillations that endangered the tow ship, but the tow pilot could not get the line to release. The glider pilots apparently dropped the line and the MC-1 entered a flat spin. Three men got out of the glider, including Du Pont. However, Du Pont's parachute had insufficient time to fully inflate and he died on impact. Three men stayed with the glider, including Gabel, Howard Morrison, and C.C. Chandler, and they also perished.

Bowlus and partner Albert Criz formed the Airborne Transport company to build their innovative glider. Although the Wright Field engineers were adamant the performance predictions were optimistic and the design overall unsuitable, the developers received encouragement and support from the glider personnel in Washington. Hence, a prototype of the MC-1 was constructed and tested. (National Museum of the United States Air Force)

Standing beside the MC-1, likely on 10 September 1943 at March Field, California, are (left to right) Captain Richard Shoop, Lieutenant Colonel Ernest Gabel, Lieutenant James Newkirk, Hawley Bowlus, unknown, and Howard Morrison. Three of these men would be dead before the following day was out and the glider destroyed. (National Soaring Museum)

The MC-1 glider, bearing civil markings, was likely photographed (this print signed by Bowlus) near March Field on 10 or 11 September 1943. There it continued flight tests during its initial shake-down, preparatory to a tow to Washington, D.C. It crashed that day on its 31st flight. (National Museum of the United States Air Force)

Despite the mishap, the designers continued to seek funding, keeping alive the notional 1,000-glider buy, and retained support from officers outside Wright Field. At the urging of Arnold's glider assistant, the renamed General Airborne Transport Company (GATC, briefly the Albert Criz Company and controlling interest held by the General American Transportation Corporation of Chicago, Illinois), submitted a draft specification and Letter of Proposal dated 8 September 1943. They proposed delivering the 1,000 aircraft between 30 November 1943 and 31 July 1944, reaching a peak 400 aircraft per month. They were then expecting a wing span of 92 feet and area of 1,176 square feet, maximum GW of 17,800 pounds for a 10,000-pound useful load.

Airborne Command stated on 4 October 1943 a requirement for 40-place gliders, needing 215 in the second quarter of 1944 and 785 in the third quarter in order to lift two divisions with reserves. Because of the urgency, they pressed for an "exploratory quantity" of 200 gliders be initiated as quickly as practicable, to be followed by 800 more if the machines proved satisfactory, bypassing experimental models. The MC-1 was specifically referenced as the most promising candidate.[40]

Material Command was instructed on 8 October to address the requirement and to specifically consider the suitability of the MC-1. They responded on the 21st advising that going immediately to production was precipitous and recommended procuring experimental ships, pointing also to the advanced features of the XCG-10 and XCG-13, and the progress made on these projects. However, Chief of Air Staff, Major General Barney M. Giles, called on 1 November 1943 for an immediate 1,000-unit production contract, as approved by General Arnold. Materiel Command, criticized for giving the project short shrift to that point, began deliberately to put events in motion to initiate production. A letter contract was drafted on 5 November and executed on the 8th in the amount of $65,182,000.00.[41]

Criz was the business face of the company, with a forceful personality and verbal talent. Regardless of his fanciful planning and enthusiastic promotion, GATC's extremely ambitious production plans flew in the face of the firm's meager facilities, personnel, and material resources and, if successful, would be "one of the most remarkable production feats in all the history of aircraft production."[42] The firm then occupied an 8,000 square foot space and had a staff of 28 engineers, 10 of whom were draftsman.[43] Additionally, Laister-Kauffmann had gotten wind of the plans to go straight to production with the Bowlus-Criz glider and protested through their Congressman.[44] Although normal and lawful competitive procurement practices were suspended during the war, the matter 'smelled foul' and this may have been a factor in reconsidering immediate production. In any event, given that GATC's production plans bordered on the fantastic and not even the most superficial tactical evaluation had been performed with the glider, Arnold wisely demurred. The contract was cancelled the same day it was enacted, and leadership consented on 9 November to a more cautionary approach.[45]

On 13 November, a Letter of Intent was issued to GATC. This covered a static test article, wind tunnel model, and two XCG-16 (Model MC-1A) flight test aircraft.[46] With an estimated value of $625,000.00, all items were to be delivered to Wright Field by 15 February 1944.[47]

GATC submitted their first model specification for the XCG-16 in December 1943. They predicted an empty weight of 9,500 pounds and gross of 19,580 pounds. They committed to a guaranteed design tow and glide speed of 220 mph against the requirement of 200 and 180, respectively. Also guaranteed was a stall speed with flaps of 58 mph and landing speed of 60 versus the requirements of 60 and 65. Likewise, 430 THP versus 700 was to be the maximum power for tow at 140 mph. GATC committed to a 600-foot landing run on pavement versus the AAF's 700. Rate of sink with full flaps and 85 mph was to be 1,100 fpm. A wind generator and battery would support an electrical system for lights and there were to be provisions for a D-1 automatic pilot. The aircraft had to be capable of being broken down for shipping, the maximum box dimension being 37 feet.[48]

The contract did not specify delivery dates, but Criz optimistically promised delivery of all gliders by 15 February 1944.[49] Sometime later, the 15th was accepted as delivery of the static article, 30 March for the first glider, and 15 April for the second.[50] However, it was mid-February when the mockup was inspected and the tunnel model handed over. Within another month GATC had already spent beyond the contract value. Tunnel tests were completed in March 1944. A month later the firm advised that expected cost at completion was approximately twice the letter contract value and deliveries would slip approximately three to four months. Expenditures to $1,264,000.00 were approved on 26 April and delivery dates established that would have the static article available on 30 April, the initial glider on 1 June 1944, and the second 15 July. The static article was delivered late, on 22 May. The contract was formally signed 14 June 1944 for $1,264,684.27.

Towed aloft by a B-17, the XCG-16's retractable gear reduced drag and it required less tug horsepower to haul aloft than the other large-capacity gliders at similar weights. However, the full gross weight of the XCG-16 and high airspeed demanded a four-engine tug. The C-47 could tow the glider at only reduced weights. (National Archives)

The sole XCG-16 is shown during early testing in southern California before relocating to Ohio. It closely resembled the MC-1 except for a revised canopy and the cargo compartment windows were actual transparencies versus the MC-1's painted rectangles. This aircraft was also given a military finish and markings. (National Soaring Museum)

The prototype XCG-16 was finally delivered to Oxnard Army Flight Strip on 25 July 1944. It was very similar to the MC-1 except for a revised canopy, installing the cargo doors' forward windows that were only painted onto the MC-1, and full rounding of the forward corners of the center section that were facetted on the MC-1. The XCG-16 was flown briefly in Oxnard before being towed by B-17 to Clinton County on 7 August (almost 2,000 miles). An inspection at that time found several unsatisfactory items. The next month GATC submitted a request for an additional $885,315.23 for overrun. This was also approved. Additionally, the company was delivering preliminary engineering data and drawings that were proving of "very good quality."[51]

Both developmental testing by Materiel Command and the Operational and Tactical Suitability testing by the Army Air Forces Board were performed at CCAAF, the latter on 16-22 October 1944. Flight testing, as always, revealed good and bad. On the positive side, the glider flew well. The very large aircraft landed at a very low speed for a 400-foot run. Stalls were benign at 57 mph with full flaps, 70 mph clean. A 1,280-fpm rate of sink with full flaps at 85 mph also bettered the guarantee and requirement.

On the negative side, in static tests the wing failed at 75 percent of design gross weight. Consequently, the flight weight was limited to this until changes could be introduced. The reinforced wing subsequently passed the static tests successfully and flight to maximum gross was permitted with the deficient wing under carefully controlled conditions and limited flight hours before the aircraft would be returned for modification.[52] Practical empty weight was 11,000 pounds, but the aircraft was flown up to 21,000 pounds gross for the 10,000-pound maximum payload. Markedly less tow aircraft power was required to pull the low-drag XCG-16 than the CG-13A, and the interior was very quiet on tow. Top tow speed was 150 mph versus the required 220 mph. Instead of 430 THP to tow at 140 mph the tug required 590. Consequently, for tow by the ubiquitous C-47, the glider was limited to 17,000-pounds gross or just 65 percent of the payload. Elevator and rudder control forces were high and large control wheel lateral displacement required to generate suitable roll response. The control forces were not harmonized and the glider tended to yaw in turbulence. Landing speed was 3 mph fast at 63.

As with many prototypes, problems were myriad. Several poor manufacturing practices were evident. Materiel Command had concluded from static testing through early July 1944 that the structure was suitably stout to provide crash protection. However, the Board judged pilot and troop crash protection and emergency exits (overhead hatch in each cargo compartment) to be inadequate. Inaccessibility of all cockpit equipment by both pilots was criticized and cockpit lighting was unacceptable for night flight. Pilot vision was so severely impaired except directly ahead that even standard landing patterns and tactical formation landings would be unacceptably hazardous. Gear and flap action was too slow. The service felt the loading ramp arrangement was unsuitable for tactical landings. The final configuration had the leading edges rotating up and a ramp aft of the lower edge rotating down. If the nose gear tore away on landing (quite probable), the ramps could not be lowered and the low opening might be inadequate to remove vehicles and guns. Separating gear components would damage the wing and flaps on landing, complicating repair and recovery. The glider was deemed unsuitable for combat landings in unprepared fields. Very significantly, the span loading made lateral c.g. critical, limited to 1,000-pounds difference between compartments.[53] This would prove difficult to manage during combat loading where soldiers had little regard for maximum weight and c.g., sneaking additional gear aboard when the crew's backs were turned.

Extensive flap surfaces contributed to a low landing speed and short roll-out of the XCG-16. While this was advantageous, the likelihood of the wheels shearing off in a tactical landing and impacting the wing and flaps was seen as a disadvantage. Pilot vision from the cockpit was also judged tactically unsuitable and unsafe. (National Archives)

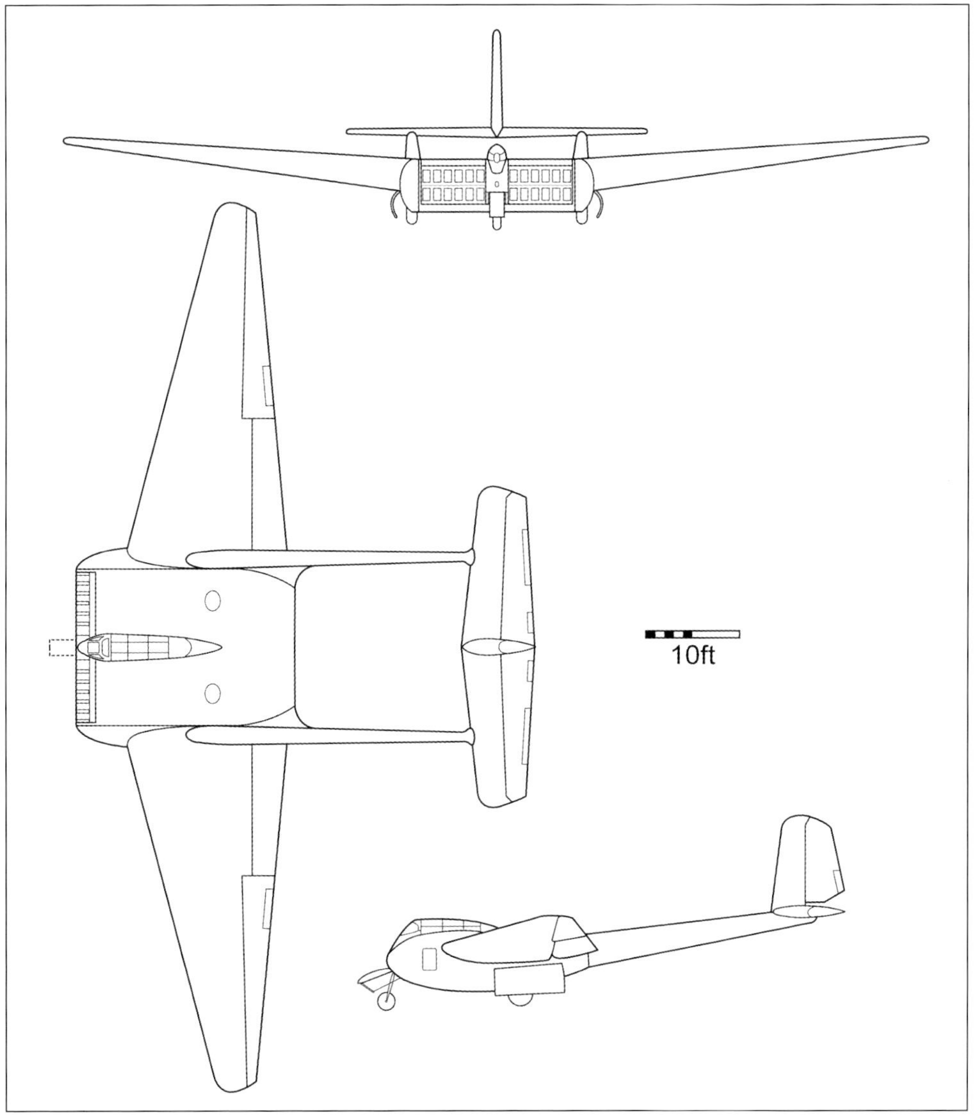

An Airborne Show at the National Airport, Washington, D.C., 2-3 November 1944, offered the opportunity to inspect the rare XCG-16. It shows how the nose of the center section opened up and a ramp lowered before each of the cargo compartments. (National Soaring Museum)

The Army Air Forces Board found the glider operationally and tactically unsuitable, and recommended no further consideration be given the XCG-16.

Some effort was made to correct deficiencies and the second glider was being built to revised specification dated 25 August 1944. On 16 November 1944, it was officially designated XCG-16A (Model MC-1B) and delivery was expected on 1 December.[54] The only obvious external differences (judged from the three-view drawing) were the forward windscreen extended to the wing leading edge, possibly reflecting a forward shift of the front seat to improve pilot view, and fairings added between the tail booms and the wing, where the latter tapered at the trailing edge, to cut drag. Empty weight had risen by 8 percent to 10,250 pounds, and design GW by 4 percent to 20,330 pounds, with no sacrifice to useful load. There were no changes to interior dimensions.[55] Given growing emphasis on crash-worthiness of gliders and protection of personnel, especially the pilot(s), GATC proposed building a metal center section at a cost of $440,000.00. This offer was rejected.[56]

Given a fairly thorough evaluation by both the engineers and Airborne, with a negative recommendation from both, Materiel Command moved on 30 November 1944 to end XCG-16 work. A telegram terminating the program was forwarded to GATC on 1 December.[57] However, this met resistance from Washington. In January 1945 Arnold's office decided the XCG-16 should undergo tactical testing, and the aircraft was ordered sent to Orlando, Florida, for service trials. However, by this time, with the CG-13A in production, the YCG-10A in the wings, and the war's end in sight, it was clear the Army did not require any new gliders. If the Army held to its own principles and regulations, the XCG-16 would need much additional work before production, making availability

A second XCG-16 was well along in construction when the program was cancelled. It was to address some of the criticisms and so was identified as the XCG-16A. This drawing shows some of the changes to include moving the canopy (and likely the cockpit) forward to improve pilot visibility and added fairings to reduce drag. (Author)

The XCG-16 (note wind generator atop fuselage) was subjected to tests by several Army organizations and all agreed it was unsuitable for the mission. However, it was championed by men high up in the "food chain" and so survived multiple challenges. Despite this, efforts at giving a production contract wavered over a long period until finally being set aside. (National Soaring Museum)

likely more than a year in the future. No additional testing appears to have been conducted and the XCG-16 sat idle in Wilmington.

The XCG-16 effort was finally closed out on 30 July 1945 without all terms of the contract fulfilled, such as delivery of the second glider, but $2,078,293.00 expended in total. The XCG-16A was well advanced in construction when work was halted. It was broken up, the XCG-16 meeting the same fate.

Table 08-08	
General Airborne Transport XCG-16 Specifics	
span	91.8 ft
wing area	1,140 ft^2
length	48.3 ft
height	18.3 ft
empty weight	9,500 lbs (11,000 lbs practical)
loaded weight	19,580 lbs (21,000 lbs demonstrated) 10,000 lbs including rolling stock
maximum speed	150 mph
stall speed	57 mph with flaps, 70 mph no flaps
landing speed	63 mph
landing distance	400 ft
capacity	2 pilots, 40 troops or 8,000 lbs
cabin length x width x height	15.0 (maximum) x 6.9 x 5.1 ft (two each)

60-Place Glider

The Aircraft Laboratory was occasionally asked to review unsolicited proposals from citizens and companies seeking to assist in the nation's defense with aeronautical developments. At least at first, these were welcome in the field of combat gliders as it was a new area with no design experience base. When Christopher Engineering Company of St. Louis, Missouri, proposed a 60-place glider of innovative layout on 1 September 1942, Materiel Division gave it due consideration. Designer Felix Nagel visited Colonel Dent's office in Dayton on 16 September. The Aircraft Laboratory dutifully reviewed the preliminary design he left behind.[58]

The all-wood aircraft was to have an empty weight of 8,000 pounds and loaded weight of 20,000 pounds. An alternative load was two jeeps and two 30 mm guns with crews. Pontoons could be fitted to make the machine amphibious, and the firm felt the design could be rescaled to smaller capacity, as desired. The aircraft was apparently like the XCG-16 in combining the fuselage and deep wing root section, and with loading doors in the leading edge. The fuselage aft to the tail was criticized as likely too short. The wing was large, yielding a wing loading of 12.0 psf that was inconsistent with trends to higher loading for combat gliders. Yet, the tapered wing aspect ratio (span divided by mean chord) was low at 6.63 compared with 9-12 for the 30-place gliders, suggesting a short and broad wing. Christopher's empty weight predictions appeared low and useful load high. The maximum tow speed of 110 mph would need to be increased, also likely to increase structural weight.[59]

The records reflect no further action on the design. Christopher was under contract for the XAG-1 glider (as Christopher Aircraft Company, see later) which went badly, so they likely did not have the means to pursue another, more ambitious aircraft project, and the equally radical XCG-16 was proving troublesome for the Air Forces.

Gyro-Glider

On 10 September 1941, Captain Frank Kowalski, Jr., sent a letter to Washington, D.C., proposing a large autogyro aircraft for landing troops. Kowalski was an infantry officer detailed to the Quartermaster Corps but with an inventor's bent, having several patents to his credit. He had spent months studying gyrocopters and preparing a preliminary design of an autogyro aircraft, also building a small operational model. The craft would be towed behind an airplane and land in an exceptionally small space. His concept was for a fuselage with tail assembly topped by an articulated unpowered rotor. Kowalski envisioned the propwash from the towplane spinning up the glider's rotor prior to flight. The craft could be towed like a fixed-wing glider.[60]

Kowlaski's "gyro-glider" idea was given due consideration and a response provided on 17 November. The 16 October summary of the evaluation shows evidence of Materiel Division involvement, but no source for the analysis is provided.[61] The analysts acknowledged that while such an aircraft was feasible, it was expected to be less efficient than a traditional glider. The auto-rotation landing might offer a bit more control than the glider, but certainly was no more limiting when committed to a landing in a narrow window of height, airspeed, and glide ratio. A glide ratio of about 6:1 was predicted; much less than the 15:1 expected of the gliders then in development. The development of the more complex rotor system would take more time and money. They dismissed the capability of the tug propwash spinning up the rotor prior to flight, especially with a twin-engine aircraft or dual tow. Some other mechanism, abroad or separate from the glider, would be required. The design was expected to possess greater drag than a winged glider, making double tow impossible. A mid-air collision between rotorcraft on double tow would likely be more catastrophic than fixed-wing gliders bumping each other. It was also pointed out that on takeoff the towline force had to act approximately through the c.g. while in flight would have to act through the center of drag force. The auto-gyro design greatly complicated this compared with a fixed-wing glider. Not discussed was the possibly greater risk of fatal combat damage to the rotor system. Gliders took a surprising amount of damage in flight from enemy fire and continued flying. An autogyro would appear to be more vulnerable.

No further action on the gyro-glider was apparently undertaken in the United States. However, in August 1941 the Germans began developing a gyro-glider based on the DFS 230 in an effort to greatly reduce the landing distance of the glider. This Focke-Achgelis Fa 225 V1 possessed a three-blade, 38.4-foot diameter unpowered rotor from the Fa 223 helicopter above a DFS 230 B-2 airframe shorn of its wings. The steep glidepath to landing made a reinforced undercarriage necessary. The rotor shaft ran through the cabin to a drum beneath the glider. A cable wound around the drum was attached to the ground such that, as the glider was pulled forward by the tug on takeoff, the unwinding cable spun the drum and the rotor. The Fa 225 was initially flown in September 1941, just seven weeks after commencing the project. It was found that glide ratio was cut to 5:1 compare with the 11:1 of the DFS 230, and tow speed was 112 mph compared with 130 mph.[62] The aircraft was also tail-heavy, requiring nose ballast. Consequently, the Fa 225 was set aside and focus remained on deceleration devices to be added to the DFS 230. However, the sole Fa 225 was employed in the rescue of Mussolini from atop a mastiff on 12 September 1943.

While Germany guilt this a Fa 225 auto-gyro by combining an unpowered helicopter rotor to a DFS 230 glider fuselage, the American's passed on such a development. An infantry officer with an inventor's inclination, Captain Frank Kowlaski, proposed the same such aircraft to his U.S. Army superiors as the "gyro-glider" to be towed to the assault area and then auto-rotate down to landing. The idea had merit, but the disadvantages outweighed these—as the German's learned. (Author's Collection)

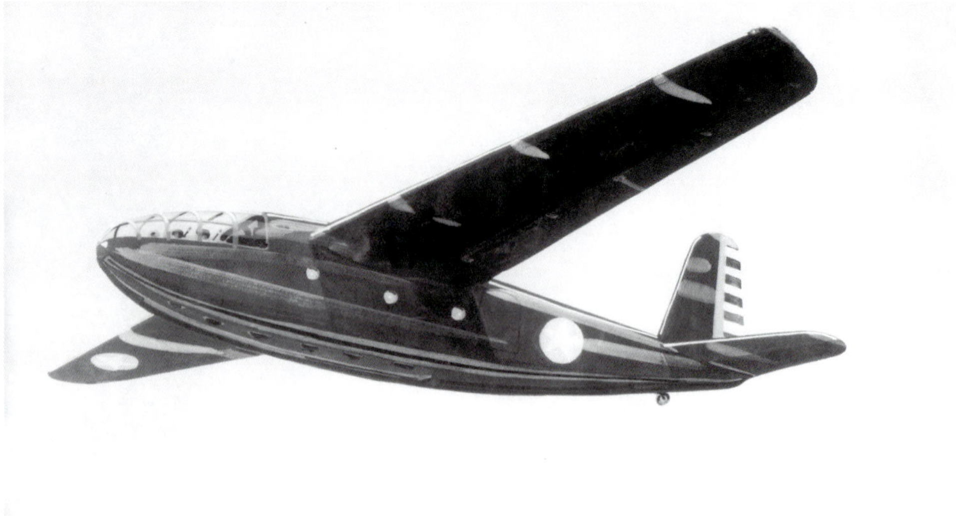

Concept art for the Chase Brothers MS glider shows the general lines of the eventual XCG-14 glider. Cantilevered wing and tail, and smooth surfaces all around, were to lend to its enhanced aerodynamic performance. However, the centerline wheels replacing skids and lack of main undercarriage did not survive to prototype. (National Archives)

Chase Aircraft XCG-14 & XCG-14A

In seeking larger gliders, a requirement was an aerodynamically clean aircraft more easily towed and at greater airspeeds, implying wing loading more closely matching that of the tugs. None of the high-capacity gliders undertaken by the Army met this requirement. The XCG-16, while appearing clean, could not be towed at mission weights without a strain on the C-47 engines. Additionally, by late 1943 the Army was seeking greater utility from cargo gliders as compared with the first "generation" of models. Experience with the CG-4A and research pointed to definite improvements possible in the transport gliders for enhanced performance. Apart from ensuring their reuse, the service wanted to tow them higher and faster, perhaps by fighters at up to 170 mph, making good aerodynamic characteristics a key design parameter. It was also desirable to use the gliders for more routine tasks such as rapid transport of high priority cargo.[63]

A formal request for the advanced glider was stated on 11 February 1943, and Materiel Command felt certain the CG-4A and derivatives could not be made to fill the role. Furthermore, experiments had demonstrated a C-47 or like aircraft could carry more freight internally and with more cruise efficiency than in combination with a loaded CG-4A that had many more operating limitations. The field commands were lukewarm on the program, but Wright Field pressed ahead.

Table 08-10

XCG-14 Specification (G = guaranteed)

maximum speed	200 mph (G)
maximum tow speed	170 mph (G), 150 mph requirement
stall speed	60 mph (G)
maximum THP 150 mph	400 hp (G), 500 hp requirement

Table 08-09

19 April 1944 15-Place Glider – Light Transport Characteristics

maximum tow speed	180 mph, 220 mph desired
stall speed	55 mph, 48 mph desired
rate of sink with flaps at 75-90 mph	1,100 fpm, 1,500 fpm desired
landing run at minimum speed, paved	500 ft, 250 ft desired
capacity, including 2 pilots	4,000 lbs, 5,000 lbs desired, or 15 troops or jeep and personnel or 37 mm anti-tank gun, crew, ammunition
communication	provisions for radio and tow line intercom
transportation	breakdown for road and overseas shipment

Characteristics of a glider with improved efficiency was issued on 19 April 1944.[64] By June the desire was for an "all metal glider of clean aerodynamic design" meeting this requirement, and crash-worthiness was taking greater emphasis at the same time following the Normandy experience.[65] However, an entirely new glider development did not appear warranted given the CG-15A work.

A firm that would contribute markedly to the advanced glider undertaking become acquainted with such work in an experimental project launched by the desire for improvements. The Chase Aircraft Company (initially Chase Brothers) first drafted a proposed specification for their 23-place MS glider dated 21 November 1942.[66] Owner of this new firm, as well as designer and chief engineer, was gifted Russian-born Michael Stroukoff who was taking his first steps into aircraft development. However, his facilities were makeshift.

To meet the requirement with a mid-size 15-place glider of 4,000-pounds useful load, the USAAF gave a $274,387.50 contract to the newly established Chase

The XCG-14 was constructed inside a city building in the Bronx, New York. The wood structure is well illustrated, including the veneer-covered rudder. Note the dual pilot controls in the uncovered cockpit. (National Archives)

Table 08-11	
Chase Aircraft XCG-14 Specifics	
span	72.2 ft
wing area	516.1 ft^2
length	42.5 ft
empty weight	4,923 lbs
loaded weight	8,923 lbs
tow speed	170 mph
capacity	2 pilots, 15 troops
cabin length x width x height	15.0 x 5.5 x 5.8 ft

This shot of the XCG-14 shows off the hydraulic landing flaps and conformal fuselage skids. While the molded canopy contributed to low drag, the optical distortion was distracting. The simple fixed landing gear is evident. (National Archives)

Aircraft Company, Incorporated, with Stroukoff as president and chief engineer, on 27 October 1943 (formalized 28 February 1944). This called for a mockup completed in 30 days, wind tunnel model delivered in 60 days, static test article in 90 days, and two XCG-14s, the first provided in 140 days and the second 30 days later. The glider was to accommodate a jeep or 75 mm howitzer. The aircraft was constructed inside a building in Manhattan, disassembled, and then reassembled inside a garage in the Bronx.

Despite the humble domain of its birth, the Chase glider was an admirable wooden construct with fabric-covered control surfaces. The fully cantilevered, high aspect ratio wing was fitted with flaps and spoilers, both hydraulically operated. It had an unusually efficient airfoil design for low drag and high lift that permitted the 170-mph maximum speed. For simplicity, the XCG-14 fuselage was made with the minimum of curvature, just rounding of corners. Contributing to the clean lines was a molded windscreen. There were dual pilot controls. The aft fuselage was to be detachable aft of the wing, perhaps with swing-aside fittings, a ramp then installed for wheeled cargo loading. However, the rear loading features were not built into the first test article. A personnel door was also located on both sides of the aft fuselage. The conventional undercarriage had detachable main gear installed in a low-drag design, and there were two integral skids under the forward fuselage. The side windows could be jettisoned to serve as firing ports. Chase bettered the requirement by seating 16 or hauling the specified 4,368-pound payload. Empty weight was anticipated to be 3,237 pounds and gross 7,607.[67]

The static test article was delivered on 17 August 1944 and did well in the trials running through 1 November, even though it deviated from the specifications. The Air Forces was eager for the flying models and urged Chase to move ahead quickly. However, Materiel Command personnel observed on 2 September 1944 that "Due to the financial difficulties and design and manufacturing discrepancies of the contractor on the XCG-14 glider it is doubtful whether a satisfactory service article can be developed from this contract."[68] Chase had been paid $190,000.00 to that time.

The first XCG-14 was inspected by the government in November 1944 and was delivered to CCAAF in December. It first flew on 1 January 1945 behind a P-47D (42-8700).[69] The molded windscreen caused some pilots to complain of optical distortion. The glider empty was 1,600 pounds overweight, or 50 percent, grossing out at 8,923 pounds or 17 percent over. The overweight condition may have contributed to unsatisfactory performance and severe fuselage damage during a landing mishap in July 1945. The aircraft was written off.

The performance promise of the XCG-14 suggested it could replace the CG-4A, and in November 1943 Wright Field was urged to move quickly on the development.[70] However, after embarking on the development, it was suggested one of the contracted XCG-14s presented an opportunity to further explore engineering solutions to meeting the 19 April 1944 requirement. Following months of discussion, Materiel Command requested in November 1944 a XCG-14 redesign to be reflected in the second prototype. This was expected to cost $160,000.00. However, it was January 1945 before a project began to take shape, 15 February before a letter contract was issued, and then 7 April for the formal agreement at an estimated $287,285.50. This would include a mockup, static test article, and one prototype. There remained a requirement that the aircraft be broken down for shipment with the largest box dimension 36 feet.

This XCG-14A was virtually a new design that Chase labeled the Avitruck. Overall dimensions were increased slightly. Fuselage construction was changed to crash-worthy welded steel tubing covered with plywood.[71] The larger wing appears to have omitted the

The sole XCG-14 came in overweight, but was still an admirable accomplishment given its mean origin. Strictly a testbed, it had no provisions for cargo loading or any tactical missions. It underwent testing during the first half of 1945 before being written off in a landing mishap. (National Soaring Museum)

A redesign of the XCG-14 was approved to explore its potential as a 'second generation' combat glider. The XCG-14A adopted a tricycle undercarriage, the nose gear retractable. An airplane cockpit enclosure addressed complaints from the original glider. (National Museum of the United States Air Force)

Table 08-12	
Chase Aircraft XCG-14A Specifics (G = guaranteed)	
span	73.9 ft
wing area	536.0 ft^2
fuselage length	45.8 ft
height	14.5 ft
empty weight	7,263 lbs
design gross weight	9,500 lbs
maximum gross weight	10,500 lbs
tow speed	170 mph (170 G)
maximum THP to tow at 140 mph	350 hp (350 G)
stall speed, no flaps	64 mph (63.5 G)
stall speed, flaps	53 mph (57.5 G)
rate of sink at 85 mph, flaps	1,100 fpm (1,100 G)
landing run at minimum speed, flaps, paved	660 ft average (450 G)
capacity	2 pilots, 18 troops
cabin length x width x height	20.0 x 7.3 x 6.3 ft

spoilers. A more conventional airplane nose improved pilot vision. It also featured a tricycle undercarriage with electrically retracted nose gear. The main wheels were equipped with brakes and the nose gear was castoring. Small wooden skids were installed ahead of the nose gear doors. The typical glider electrical system and lights were specified, powered by battery, without generator. A radio was not mandated. A rope position indicator and gyro horizon were to be standard instruments.

The entire aft fuselage pivoted up and a loading ramp dropped down for wheeled cargo onload/offload. Supporting jacks on both sides of the exit stabilized the fuselage during such operations. Troop doors were in the fuselage, ahead of the fuselage split, and the pilots were provided small doors. Seating was provided for 20, including pilots. A cargo loading winch and provisions for supporting six litters were to be included. Payload weight was increasing to 5,000 pounds and gross to 9,500 which, with the cargo compartment stretch, permitted both a jeep and 75 mm to be hauled.[72]

The mockup was inspected on 2 April 1945 and the prototype completed by 15 October. The glider flew for the first time on the 16th, reportedly towed by a P-47 to 203 mph, from the Newark, New Jersey, airport. After four flights, the aircraft was towed to Wright Field on the 18th. There were minor discrepancies, but none serious enough to prevent ferry to Air Technical Services Command.

The XCG-14A flew well but for the usual list of improvements to refine stability and control and resolve various systems issues. Tow at and above 160 mph was accompanied by very high control forces, made more objectionable by a seat that was only adjustable vertically such that many pilots had their arms fully extended to reach the control column.[73] Power to tow the aircraft appeared to exceed the specification. Landings at 80 mph had a ground roll of 1,340 feet. Full flaps stalls were at 53 mph and 62 without. Maximum rate of sink with flaps and gear down, 85 mph, was 1,070 fpm and glide ratio was measured at 16.34:1 at 89 mph. Astonishingly at this late date, the towline interphone cable was only serviceable about 20 percent of the time, yet the glider had no radio.[74]

This very worthy glider came too late in the war for production. However, the XCG-14A's wing was considered so superior that additional testing was pursued

Because of the nose of the CG-4A occasionally being jammed closed during assault landings, for the XCG-14A Chase introduced the lifting tail for cargo compartment access. Loading ramp with wheel toes, side troop doors, aft fuselage stabilizing jacks, and pilot doors are clearly visible. The glider seated 18 in back or took 5,000 pounds of freight. (National Archives)

to obtain aerodynamic data. By the time the XCG-14A flew the U.S. Army was converging on a plan for future development of combat gliders. These ambitions exceeded the capabilities of the Avitruck. Development was allowed to run its course until such time as an enlarged version, a notional XCG-14B, could be proposed (Chapter 14).[75]

Airspeed AS.51 Horsa Mk. I & AS.58 Mk. II

As another means to quickly obtained higher-capacity transport gliders, the U.S. Army looked to the British Horsa. The Airspeed Limited AS.51 Horsa I accommodated 25 troops on wooden side benches, plus the two pilots. Alternatively, it could carry 7,130 pounds of materiel including two jeeps or a jeep towing a 75 mm gun or other equipment. Cargo was loaded through a door in the forward port side of the fuselage that rotated down to form a ramp. The Mk. II glider carried 28 troops or 7,380 pounds and had a swing-aside nose for more efficient onload/offload. Initiated in December 1940, the first Horsa flew in September 1941 the following year and production commenced in June 1942. The UK had made the Horsa its principal glider, setting aside the 8-place Hotspur and 15-place Hengist, eventually building 2,238 Mk. Is and 1,561 Mk. IIs.[76] It was being manufactured in large numbers at a time comparable U.S. gliders were still in development. The Horsa was well known to the Americans, having observed it in operation with the British Army and flown it for evaluation. Several were brought to the United States for evaluation, to include flying at Clinton County and Laurinburg-Maxton after first being sought in January 1942.[77]

The glider was built almost entirely of laminated spruce and plywood. The wing was skinned in fabric aft of the main spar. The cantilevered wing possessed some internal wire tensioning, and fabric covered the wings aft of the D-section. The strutted tail unit had fabric-covered control surfaces. The fixed tricycle undercarriage could be jettisoned for landing on fuselage skids—a main skid under the belly. The flaps, wheel brakes (non-differential), and undercarriage jettison were pneumatically powered by three compressed air bottles with sufficient charge for three cycles of flaps and braking. Air brakes were created by splitting the flaps surfaces, and an arresting parachute was also installed in the rear. Lights and radio, all battery-powered, were standard equipment. The Mk. II had twin nose wheels and the tow cable attachment to the nose gear strut vice the Mk. I's 120-foot bifurcated cable that attached to the wings near the main gear strut. The angle-of-dangle indicator (Mk. II Tow Cable Angle Indicator) was standard but was useful only when the glider was in the low-tow position.

Like the CG-4A, the Horsa was not demanding to fly. They were also alike in being exceedingly noisy on tow such that the pilots had to shout to each other. In weather and heavily loaded, however, the glider was jerked about violently and was tiring to operate. Accurate landing was quite easy as the flaps (40 and 80 degrees) permitted a very steep 40-45-degree descent at 2,500 fpm or more with 100 mph on the airspeed indicator. Touchdown was 70-80 mph.

The Horsa had some unusual features. A personnel door was in the cargo ramp and a troop door on the starboard side farther aft, the latter suitable for paratroop static line jumps. Apart from doors, firing apertures were also provided for self-defense. The gear was very seldom jettisoned in action, the handle wired to prevent use, yet the 600-pound ash center skid was commonly retained. Likewise,

The UK embarked on glider development a bit earlier than the U.S. and so had a production program sooner. The primary outcome was the Airspeed Horsa Mk. I that took 25 troops or 7,130 pounds of cargo. This high-capacity wooden glider attracted the interest of the U.S. Army. (V.E.R. Blunt Collection via family)

Although the Horsa was an opportunity to quickly acquire a high-capacity glider, the effort came with problems. The British were not producing these on the scale of the CG-4A, combat onload/offload was frustrating, and the aircraft's weight made tow by the omnipresent C-47 dicey. Yet, the U.S. Army managed to acquire and operate several hundred Horsas. (National Soaring Museum)

the air brakes were rarely used and the arrestor parachute not universally installed. In addition to the Horsa's internal freight, four parachute-recovered containers could be installed in four cells within the bottom of each wing. The RAF used second-echelon bombers to tow the large aircraft.

The greatest detraction for the Horsa I was the side loading ramp. The glider deck stood more than 3.0 feet off the ground and the ramp was steep. For wheeled items and vehicles, 11.8-foot long wheel ramps were employed. However, anything man-handled up to the lip of the cargo deck then had to be laborious turned along the axis of the compartment. In combat, likely under fire, the frustrating process had to be reversed for offload. The Mk. II's hinged nose was a vast improvement, although the deck was still high. Additionally, upon landing there was risk the nose would be damaged and unable to be opened or there might be insufficient room to swing it aside.

Addressing particularly the combat offload difficulties, the idea was hatched to remove the tail of the Horsa just aft of the cargo floor. Once this structure was hauled clear, wheel ramps could be placed between the floor and ground. Initially, explosives were fitted around the rib at the aft end of the cargo compartment to blow apart the adjacent structure and separate the tail, although an ax was occasionally required to complete the job. Wirecutters were carried to sever the control cables from the cockpit to the empennage. This method presented a hazard if enemy fire prematurely set off the explosive before landing. It was then observed that the fuselage was made of three assemblies fastened together and the aft section could be removed by removing eight bolts. In the months before the invasion, the bolts were fitted with quick-release nuts, and a suitable wrench added to the aircraft equipment. Both methods were in play on D-Day, but some gliders had no such measures.

Horsa production in Britain was tapering off in 1943 and excess production capacity would be freed up. This brought forth a proposal to have the firms build gliders for the U.S. Army, with 600 in 1943 and 800 in 1944, the whole lot delivered by July 1944. At a 22 April 1943 glider conference at Wright Field, the Horsa option was specifically addressed and rejected. While carrying a great many men, the Horsa's onload/offload headaches were well known, and a jeep would barely fit only after removing items from the vehicle. Additionally, the Horsa required several times the maintenance attention of the Waco. Its all-wood construction presented deterioration issues, especially in the Asia and Pacific theaters. In any event, the enormous glider could not be broken down for shipment to those destinations. Tow with the C-47, already laboring ahead of the CG-4A, remained problematic. If acquired, the Horsa would demand additional crew training in-theater.

Despite the formal conclusions, by June 1943 efforts were put in place to acquire 600 Horsas and 100 Hamilcars from the British by the end of the year.[78] Apparently the urgency of the looming reentry onto the continent overcame broader objections. Tests in August 1943 demonstrated that a C-47 could tow a normally loaded Horsa—although just barely at 120 mph or 40 mph below the glider's recommended airspeed. Snatches by the Skytrain were also performed. These results further encouraged use of the aircraft by the U.S. Army, but not at the numbers initially contemplated. The Americans took on some 300 Horsas for the Normandy invasion, dispatching 222 with 4 aborts and losses during training certain.[79] These permitted higher capacity deliveries of the large-caliber weapons needed to deter an initial German counterattack on the Normandy beachheads. Pilots for these aircraft were initially trained in March 1944. Only Horsa Is have been observed in U.S. service. The total number of Horsas passing through U.S. Army hands has not been authoritatively established, with figures as high as 700 offered. These aircraft did not receive American designation nor serial numbers. They were apparently readily swapped between the Allied forces in the Britain Isles, with the result some aircraft were observed wearing both American and British national markings. The British Army never released any Hamilcars to American combat troops.

Many USAAF pilots felt the Horsa did not fly as well as the Waco, was almost impossible to trim, and had lower glide ratio. They liked the flaps but not the steeper glideslope that

Table 08-13

Airspeed Horsa Specifics (I = Mk. I, II = Mk. II)

span	88.0 ft
wing area	1,104 ft^2
fuselage length	67.0 ft I, 67.9 ft II
height	19.5 ft I, 20.3 ft II
empty weight	8,370 lbs
loaded weight	15,500 lbs I, 15,750 lbs II
tow speed	160 mph
maximum speed	190 mph
stall speed, no flaps	58 mph
stall speed, flaps	48 mph
capacity	2 pilots, 28 troops
side door opening	7.8 x 5.0 ft
glide ratio	7.2:1

On a whole, the U.S. Army was not entirely pleased with the Horsa. While some pilots felt it flew just fine, others complained of the poor handling, the very steep descent with landing flare, and ungainly large size. The GIs looked on the all-wood structure with suspicion and counted more serious accidents in the Horsa compared with the Waco (this example meeting a disappointing end in a 30 April 1944 training event in Great Britain). (National Museum of the United States Air Force)

gave an unnerving nose-down attitude coming over the landing threshold and made a flare necessary, unlike the CG-4A, that could be difficult to judge in smoke or darkness. It seemed more difficult to get the big glider into small fields, as demonstrated by the many accidents during their training. Mike Murphy demonstrated the Horsa to the suspicious GIs, as he had done with the CG-4A after it developed a sour reputation.[80] However, many fast landings ended badly and the glider readily breaking up. The splintering of the structure was not felt to have the same energy dissipating safety potential as the Waco, so the pilots lacked confidence in the ruggedness of the plywood construction. More American pilots and glidermen were seriously injured or killed in Horsa crash landings than in the CG-4A. This was partially due to the fact that the Americans only used the Horsa in Normandy where the LZs were particularly small and the pilots were less practiced with the aircraft. Surely their British instructors felt the aircraft were not being operated properly. An upshot of all this was that the Americans flew the Horsas only in the Normandy operation even though they still possessed 181 Horsas in the ETO on 16 September 1944,[81] with troops prepared to operate them.

The Horsa was not ideal for U.S. airborne operations and the British could never supply the number anticipated. American models of large gliders had to be pursued.

Table 08-14

Military Characteristics, Assault Gliders

capacity	1 pilot, 5 troops 2,000 lbs useful load
tow speed	200 mph, 220 mph desired
stall speed	65 mph, 55 mph desired
armament	two .50 cal firing in 90-deg forward arc two .30 cal covering rear
armor	protecting pilot from .30 cal in front and below
egress	provisions for quick exit
transport	breakdown to fit box with largest dimension 24 ft
landing deceleration	provisions for knives on skids or other means

Table 08-15

Christopher Aircraft XAG-1 Specifics (estimated, not built)

span	54.8 ft
wing area	500 ft^2
fuselage length	46.3 ft
height (on gear)	15.8 ft
empty weight	4,455 lbs
loaded weight	8,000 lbs
tow speed	240 mph
stall speed	65 mph
maximum THP for 200 mph tow	900 hp
capacity	2 pilots, 76 troops

War Wagons (Christopher XAG-1, Timm XAG-2)

Although by summer 1942 the U.S. Army was still six months from even having transport gliders for tactical training much less possessing combat experience, opinions were well advanced. Many in Airborne Command were hesitant about flying the unarmed and unarmored gliders into defended areas. Eventually the *modus operandi* became to drop paratroops first to secure the LZ prior to the gliders' arrival, although the aircraft were still certain to take some fire. However, an alternative to allow a heavily defended objective to be seized in a surprise attack appeared worth pursuing. One solution suggested was the assault glider as a virtual flying pillbox, with heavy machine guns, armor plating, and perhaps flak curtains. This would cover the deployment of troops to secure the objective, or landing field for subsequent cargo glider landings. There was, however, by no means unanimity of opinion on the wisdom of pursuing the assault glider within the combat commands and Materiel Command.

The idea of an assault glider was first raised by A.G.A. Aviation Corporation who offered an unsolicited proposal to Major Barringer in about the middle of 1942. This was passed along to Colonel Dent who transferred it to the Aircraft Laboratory for evaluation. On 25 July the Lab recommend against any action on the concept. However, Barringer also presented the concept to Army Ground Forces on 2 July 1942 who responded swiftly on the 4th, endorsing the idea in a letter to Arnold.[82] Materiel Command drew up a concept for such an aircraft in an effort to further explore its potential. A low-wing design would be necessary to reduce restrictions to field of fire from a gun turret atop the fuselage. However, the Command again recommended on 6 August that no further consideration be given the idea. Yet, given Airborne's enthusiasm for the concept, it was carried forward. Consequently, Wright Field issued the characteristics in Table 08-14 on 15 October 1942:

Materiel Command planned to acquire a static article and two assault gliders for evaluation under confidential project MX-325. They prepared preliminary type specifications and general arrangement drawings for what became an 8-place aircraft with two pilots based upon direction from Washington. The revised Military Characteristics, dated 26 October 1942, also added "If practicable, the glider should be capable of being launched from an aircraft carrier;" a requirement that received no further mention.[83]

Materiel Command contacted 17 companies between 6 November 1942 and 15 January 1943 soliciting proposals, none for which the project would interrupt vital warplane production. Only two expressed any interest, likely because the others felt eventual production was unlikely. Christopher Aircraft Company of St. Louis, Missouri, discussed the program with Materiel Command beginning in November before submitting a satisfactory proposal on 10 January 1943. Authority for Purchase was granted on the 25th for the XAG-1. Christopher was setup on the assets of National Aircraft Corporation of Elwood, Indiana, by Arthur B. Christopher and Joseph M. Brown, that company having failed on a CG-4A contract. The Elwood plant was to be employed in the XAG-1 work. A $319,250.00 fixed price contract was issued on 8 February for a wind tunnel model to be delivered in 75 days (25 April 1943), a static test article to be delivered in 180 days (8 August) and two aircraft to be delivered on in 225 days (22 September) and 255 days (21 November 1943), respectively.

Following negotiation in February and March 1943, Timm Aircraft Company entered a proposal on 19 March and Authority for Purchase was issued days later for the XAG-2. The 23 May letter contract and 6 July contract had the same requirements, including two aircraft, and was valued at $314,738.00. They were to deliver from December 1943 to March 1944.

The XAG-1 airframe was to be wood with plywood or fabric covering, the fuselage to have plywood skin. To accommodate transport, the aircraft was to break down into elements no more than 25 feet in length. The only means of entry and egress were 2.5x2.5-foot hatches available in both sides of the forward fuselage while 2.0x2.0-foot rear gunner windows could serve as emergency exists. Flaps and spoilers were featured. Tricycle landing gear was to be partially retractable, allowing landing with the gear up, yet still be jettisonable. A unique feature was that shock absorption was provided simultaneously for the landing gear and skids. Rotation of the retracted wheels would naturally create braking action against the well and the tires giving shock absorption. (The flaps, however, if extended would be destroyed in such a gear-up landing.) The specification called for a plow under the fuselage to enhance deceleration (Chapter 11).

A 116-pound Homelite HRU-28 auxiliary powerplant was to power a Martin partially retractable armored turret mounting two .50 caliber MGs with 2,000 rounds of ammunition. It would also supply electricity for the SCR-585-B radio, supplementing the battery. Two .30 caliber flexible-mounted waist guns, firing from gunner windows aft of the turret, were also provided 2,000 rounds. These were to have arcs of fire 60 degrees above and below the horizon as well as 90 degrees forward and aft. The weapons and associated gear alone weighed about 1,525 pounds. Armor plate good for up to .30 caliber rounds protected the pilots from the front and 45-degrees front-below, and weighed 360 pounds. Useful load was projected at 3,545 pounds which, subtracting the eight men accounted as 240 pounds each, left 1,625 pounds for other combat gear.[84]

Christopher received an advance payment of $95,775.00 (30 percent) in early March 1943, but found the going slow. They pointed out, when requesting a 60-day slip on all delivery dates, the delays in Wright Field engineers providing vital data on the gun mounts, turrets, and like government-furnished equipment. The contractor delivered a wind tunnel model of the XAG-1 on 10 May 1943 and all tests were completed by the 28th. The mockup was inspected on 21 June, but some changes mandated a second inspection. Aerodynamics looked good and the static article was expected in November (three months late). However, on 24 September Christopher requested another slip in aircraft deliveries to 22 February and 21 April 1944 as they struggled to acquire wood of suitable grade.[85] By late summer they were clamoring for another advance payment.

Timm's design was very similar to the XAG-1, including the structural materials and armament. Significant differences included two personnel doors in the aft fuselage. In addition to the government-required armament, Timm was going to allow the other armed men to fire from the windows after moving aside the transparencies. Timm planned slotted flaps, spoilers, and dive brakes. A trailing parachute was also to be installed in the aft fuselage. The landing gear was to be fully retractable, the nose wheel non-steerable and main wheels with brakes. The plow was to be aft of the wing trailing edge and designed to separate when drag loads exceeded 1,000 pounds. Timm did not plan to use skids under the fuselage. The mandated cockpit armor was 469.5 pounds. The firm projected a useful load of 2.870 pounds, or 950 pounds after accounting for personnel.[86]

An advanced payment of $94,421.00 was paid to Timm. Their XAG-2 mockup was inspected on 5-6 July 1943 and a wind tunnel model provided to Wright Field on 25 August with which some testing was completed. Timm was doing fairly well, it anticipating aircraft delivery in the fall, with all contract terms met by 1 March 1944.

Airborne continued to support the assault glider, asserting its requirement again in July 1943.[87] However, the USAAF opposition finally got the upper hand and the entire project was abruptly ordered suspended on 2 September 1943. This was at the

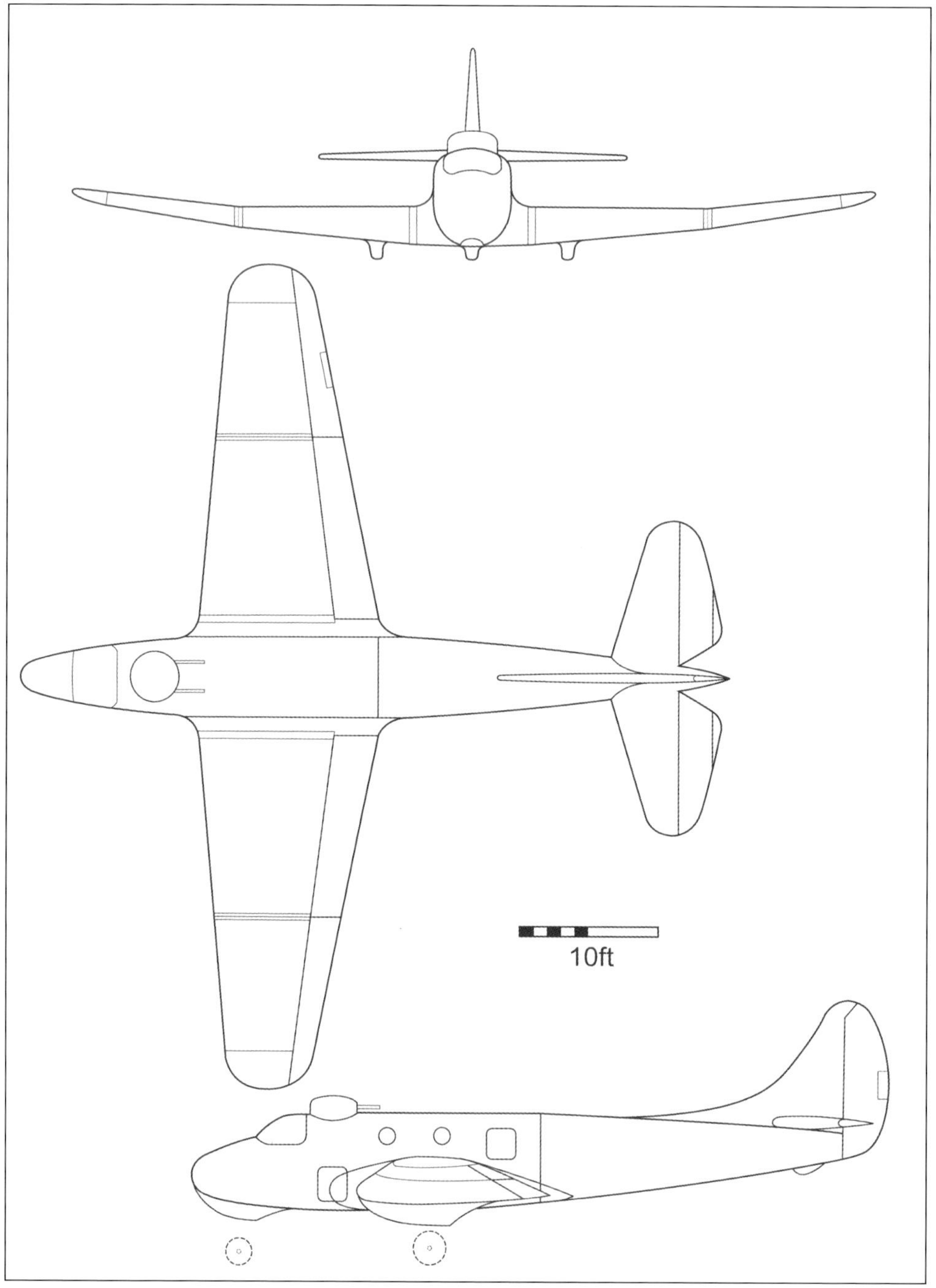

The assault glider concept differed from the cargo glider in being armored and armed for *coup de main* landings at vital objectives. The unbuilt XAG-1 was typical of this with the low wing to provide a minimally restricted field of fire for the 0.50-cal gun turret atop the fuselage. The aircraft was to be of wood and fabric but with an internal motor turning a generator providing power to the Martin turret. (Author)

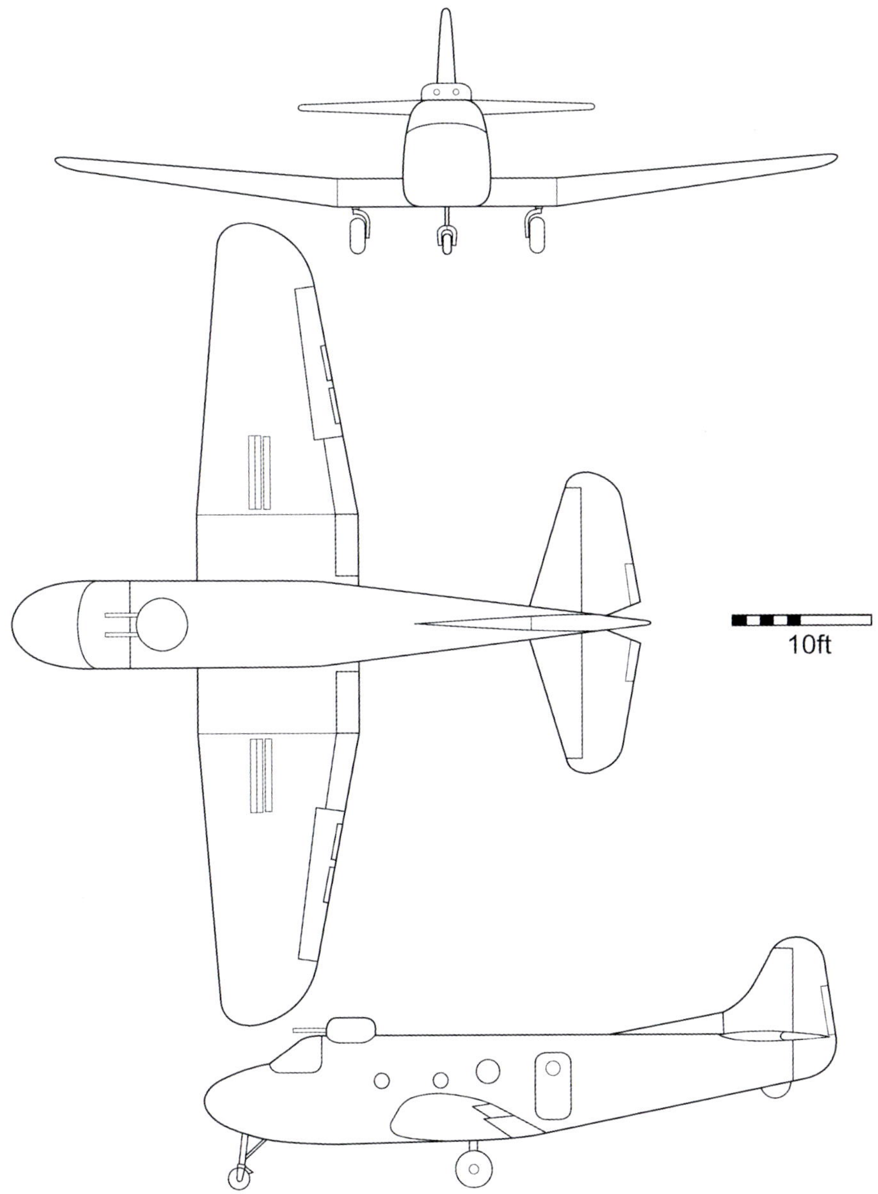

The little-known Timm Aircraft Company of Van Nuys, California, was given a contract to develop the XAG-2 assault glider shown. This was to be similar to the Christopher offering, but with fully retractable landing gear and windows doubling as firing ports. Neither assault glider progressed much beyond the drawing board due to Army indecision and finally program cancellation. (Author)

Table 08-16	
Timm Aircraft XAG-2 Specifics (estimated, not built)	
span	54.8 ft
wing area	497 ft^2
fuselage length	44.6 ft
height (on gear)	17.2 ft
empty weight	5,630 lbs
loaded weight	8,500 lbs
tow speed	240 mph
stall speed	65 mph
maximum THP for 200 mph tow	900 hp
capacity	2 pilots, 6 troops

insistence of Brigadier General Benjamin W. Chidlaw, who oversaw USAAF materiel procurement from Washington, pronouncing the scheme "nothing but a damn fool idea" and "a whim of the late Major Barringer."[88] The final verdict was a telegram from Arnold on 11 October conveying that Requirements Division advised there was no requirement for assault gliders. (This may mean there was no formally validated requirement apart from missives from Ground Forces.)

The Timm contract was cancelled on 25 October 1944 and the Christopher contract two days later. Some $160,775.00 was expended on the Christopher effort and Timm received $213,572.49. The AAF may have sought to cancel at least the XAG-1 contract by default rather than at government convenience as one missive noted that an 11 October progress inspection at Christopher's plant in Elwood found the static article only 3 percent complete and the aircraft not begun.[89] A fraud investigation was begun but the results are unclear.

The large-scale glider operations in 1944 and 1945 showed that the assault glider would have been minimally valuable for the lift slots they took away from troop carriers. With landings so scattered, they might have fought a noisy war in their immediate area but otherwise render little real value. If there were circumstances in which they would have been invaluable, none are evident from the combat history and how the Americans employed gliders.

Christopher (then Christopher-National Aircraft Products Company) inquired at the end of 1947 whether the new U.S. Air Force had found a requirement for the XAG-1. The reply was negative.[90]

The assault glider fumble was seen as an example of misguided contracting within a glider program broadly assessed as wasteful. Wright Field and the Chief of Staff's office were criticized for promoting and contracting for duplicative or advanced glider designs for which there was no clearly stated operational requirement. This is an unfair assertion given the record of responding responsibly to requirements reviewed and passed down from combat arms. Certainly the urgency of war was impetus to act given suitable direction without the unanimous and time-consuming endorsement of all concerned organizations (never a requirement in the armed forces). Results of such a policy were predictable.

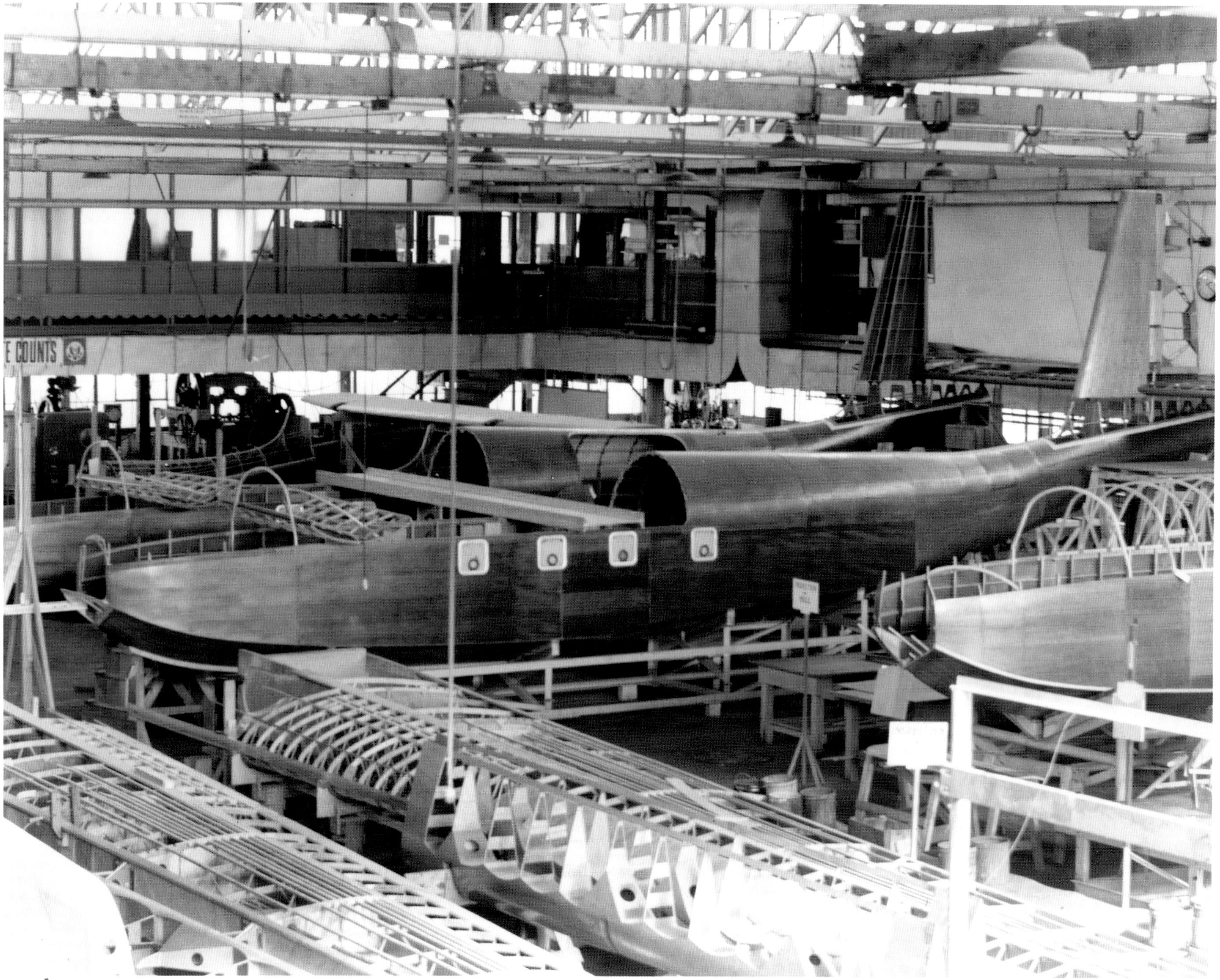

Twin hulls of the XLRH-1 are obvious in this image of the initial aircraft under construction. Note the beam joining these fuselages and the generous door opening in the aft portion, and the prodigious quantities of wood for the aircraft is evident. The weight crept intolerably over projections. (National Archives)

9

Navy Gliders Scuttled

All the USN glider work ran into difficulty, the 24-place aircraft almost immediately and especially in addressing production. The Navy was not extravagant in their funding and, with firms never before having undertaken military aircraft development, the contractors were stretched fiscally. All of them suffered delays because of their fragile financial condition, inefficient management, comparatively low priority leading to material shortages, difficulties with a relatively new construction method, vendor delays, plus difficulty hiring experienced engineers and craftsman. Design changes requested by the Navy or found prudent during the course of detail design or early laboratory tests were additional impediments. As with the Army, there was also a misconception at the beginning, on the part of all involved, that these gliders would be basic and simple aircraft, easy to design and build. In fact, they were motorless transports lacking only flight propulsion systems.

The Snead XLRH-1 static article had been delayed approximately four months to September 1942. Furthermore, by 28 May the firm appeared to be insolvent and December was the earliest practical date for delivery, if ever. At the urging of the Navy, they agreed to limit their materials purchasing supporting production to 25 percent of the Letter of Intent.[1] An inspection of Snead's manufacturing plant during early June 1942 was most disheartening, especially workmanship singled out as not up to aircraft standards. The inspectors recommended canceling production plans. Eventually the general manager was forced out and the engineering staff relocated to Orange. By October the static article was still three months away and first flying glider another month, at best.

G & A's situation appeared to be only a bit more encouraging. By 6 June 1942 their design was 1,500 pounds overweight and water tank trials indicated that substantial changes would be required to the boat hulls—likely wider and deeper—that would only add to weight problems. Their 23 July 1942 delivery date was slipped to 15 July by virtue of BuAer-imposed engineering changes, but even this was clearly optimistic. The company estimated it would require twice the negotiated contract value to reach completion. By November the XLRG-1 static test article delivery was still sometime after 1 March 1943, eight months behind schedule, and flying gliders later still.

Exploring Alternatives

As Snead and G & A thrashed in their respective quagmires during late summer 1942, Major Wehle suggested the USMC examine the possibility of having Horsa gliders manufactured in the U.S. to meet the requirement. He had flown the type and reported it was largely acceptable. Built in assemblies, this suggested some surface transportability. An order for 100 as the initial portion of a 2,000-aircraft fleet was postulated, at an eventual delivery rate of 100 per month.[2]

The USN acted quickly, looking at likely production sites. They also dispatched a 20 August 1942 missive to the British government seeking an example Horsa and complete drawings. The reply cautioned that the glider, obviously not amphibious, would likely be unsuitable for the humid conditions of the Pacific theater. Furthermore, it could barely be towed by a Douglas R4D (DC-3/C-47) and really needed a four-engine type, so the Navy and Marines might lack suitable tugs. Even if the glider could be redesigned to break down into assemblies of dimensions transportable by ship, they would consume prodigious cargo volume.

One of the Horsas (HG765) evaluated by the U.S. Navy stands ready for tow beside a LRW-1 (CG-4A). With the Navy-developed gliders faltering, this foreign model appeared a reasonable alternative by employing the same work force in building the wooden glider. The long gestation period for the Marine amphibious gliders led the Navy to consider acquiring Horsas for the role, but the British quickly disabused them of the notion. (National Soaring Museum)

Little consideration was initially given to Army types and avoiding duplicative efforts, other than to recognize that some of that service's glider manufacturers (Cessna and Pratt, Read) might be free to take on Horsa production. The assumption was that Army aircraft would naturally be inferior in meeting naval requirements. However, with the 12-place glider effort progressing discouragingly slowly, thoughts turned to the CG-4A that was transportable by sea, considering as many as 575 LRW-1s.

Rejecting the Waco, the Commandant agreed to look into the Horsa option only for training while continuing with the Navy amphibious glider development efforts.[3] When the Navy got its Horsa (H6765) it did tow tests behind a Catalina. However, circumstances would dictate that neither this nor the CG-4A proposal advanced far.

Admiral Towers expressed a desire on 13 June 1942 for an amphibious glider of capacity less than 12 for tow from a carrier deck. He felt such an aircraft, of smaller wing span than the 12-place machines, could land at lower airspeeds and in more confined spaces, and that the Marines would soon need such capabilities.[4] This and discussions with the Army may be the roots of a 26 October Army requirement that their embryonic 8-place assault gliders (Chapter 8) be capable of launch from an aircraft carrier "if practicable".[5] However, the Army's assault gliders were cancelled and no serious effort to develop any similar Navy gliders were undertaken.

Falling to Pieces

Progress on the transport gliders continued to be poor into summer 1942. Some were clearly going nowhere while even the most promising projects could offer no reliable delivery dates. A decision in June to dramatically increase procurement from 150 to 1,000 transport gliders was never acted upon. Adding to production contracts that were essentially dormant was meaningless.

It was July 1942 before thoughts turned to the issue of tugs with a proposal from Wehle to immediately acquire 72 Douglas R5D Skymaster (DC-4) transports to serve in the near-term for parachute troop operations and later as tugs. While a very worthy idea, the reality was that six dozen of the very costly four-engine transports would be exceedingly difficult to obtain in short order. The earlier notion that a Catalina could drag three 12-place gliders simultaneously was clearly misplaced. Perhaps two could be towed with difficulty. The two-engine, land-based R4D would have a radius of action of 300-400 miles towing a single 12-place glider, and so would be unsuitable for most potential amphibious operations. Adding 20 parachute troops would cut this to 100-150 miles. The R5D-1 could yield 1,300 miles, or 700 with 25 parachutists. Runway requirements were 4,000 feet for towing off a 12-place glider and 5,000 feet for the 24-place.[6] Some 200 yards of open terrain or water would be required for glider landing. In any event, this would be a small measure of the number of suitable transports required to haul the hoped for 1,000 or so operational gliders, even in multiple lifts delivering an effective and self-sustaining mass of troops in the initial assault.

Disagreements over the wisdom of pursuing the glider program had persisted from its inception. In summer 1942 the then-Lieutenant Colonel Wehle wrote a widely circulated paper suggesting the entire glider program be restudied in light of the slow progress being made and the realities of operational problems that were crystallizing. An Informal Glider Board was convened by BuAer on 9 October to review and clarify the situation. Their report on the 17th admitted that a combat-capable force would not be ready for deployment before 1 May 1944.[7] They dismissed the CG-4A as unsuitable, recommended the 24-place projects be abandoned and a single-hull design pursued. However, they suggested Letters of Intent for production of 2,200 Bristol or Allied 12-place gliders, or both, should be issued at once for delivery by 1 April 1944. All suitable tow airplanes should be fitted with the required hardware in anticipation of their use as tugs. They also adjudged that by winter 1943-1944 the USN and USMC would have 3,200 airplanes capable of towing at least one 12-place glider (presuming they all were suitably equipped and the crews trained), and so observed no additional procurement was required in this respect.[8]

These findings were followed-up by a letter from the Commandant's office cautioning against quickly expanding the present production contracts. This reflected the views of many who felt the program should not be continued beyond the initial stage until the actual combat requirements were more clearly elucidated, representative aircraft available, and operational testing completed. BuAer pointed out that delays in pursuing production until the experimental gliders had been tested and design changes identified could mean combat capability would not be attained until 1 January 1945. This suggested the entire enterprise might contribute nothing to defeating the Axis. Nonetheless, approval of the restraint came from as high as Secretary Knox on 8 December.

The second XLRQ-1 prototype is shown under tow during testing. This machine incorporated another design of the wing root fairings that also served as gear wells, seeking a low-drag configuration. Note the hatches permitting over-wing egress for marines. (Air Force Flight Test Center)

Preparing to be towed aloft from a runway on another test flight, the first XLRA-1 was the only one of these amphibious gliders to be thoroughly tested. However, the glider was not in its final configuration and structural issues limited the trials. Note the aft fuselage skid that appears to have a shock mount replacing the earlier fixed member. (National Soaring Museum)

Other reviews and discussion through January 1943 had other perspectives, some casting serious doubt on the utility of amphibious gliders for the envisioned assault mission and the ability of BuAer projects to meet requirements in a timely manner. Commanding USMC generals in the field were queried and the responses were similarly mixed, but those in the South Pacific uniformly negative. The best use would be a few for emergency replenishment of troops in the field.

By this point even the well-informed Wehle had come 180 degrees, stating emphatically that "... military gliders, amphibious or land based, are of no value to the Marine Corps."[9] He judged the weapon unproven and, seeing no real combat capability until July 1944, the money being spent on the effort was wasted. Shipment to theater was problematic, flight distances in the Pacific were too great, and weather too adverse. He recommended cancellation. Another board of BuAer program officers and NAF pilots participating in the program had to confess that glider operations appeared impractical in forward operating locations and in anything but good weather conditions. They also recommended cancellation.

The Marines were by this time committed to an island-hopping campaign in the vast reaches of the Pacific, with landings expected to commonly be beyond the range of land-based aircraft or those requiring shore-based support. It was difficult to see how gliders could meaningfully contribute to these operations. Tows lasting many hours would be exceedingly exhausting for the pilots and gliders at that time had no blind flying capabilities (and never would attain a truly operational capability).

While the Navy considered it "more defensible if we waste money than if we failed to do everything possible to get gliders,"[10] in the words of one Admiral, some of the glider efforts had reached critical mass. Snead's poor progress was cause to cancel the production contract on 29 August 1942.[11] Although their glider was beginning to come together by September, delivery still a few months out, it was 2,879 pounds over the 8,612 empty weight target. This bad news was followed by worse when a structural test wing failed at only about 50 percent of the design maximum load.[12] Furthermore, Snead facing bankruptcy and the Navy had prepared a 'get well' plan to help it recover its losses. While the situation was grim, the service still felt there was value in taking the experimental contract to completion.

The G & A situation was so bad as to appeared irrecoverable. On 15 October 1942 they stated they had spent $363,000.00, $12,000.00 in excess of the contract, and estimated they needed an additional $325,000.00 for completion with an immediate infusion of $25,000.00 to make payroll. Any deliveries were still more than two months out. The pain was ended on 13 November with a Navy stop-work order simultaneously to Snead and G & A, having expended $675,839.36 on the former and $350,741.69 on the latter.[13] The decision came from as high as the Assistant Secretary of the Navy for Air, Artemus L. Gates, and the new chief of BuAer, Rear Admiral John S. McCain. Despite both 24-place projects being terminated, the idea of developing a single-hull replacement never gelled.

Proving

To provide some of the hard data thus far lacking in the glider deliberations, BuAer issued a directive on 20 February 1943 for tests with available equipment.[14] A series of long-range flights with the Catalina (08065) and LRW-1s (42-252784/5) were planned for March 1943, and a report to be submitted during April. The Navy also had an Airspeed AS.51 Horsa borrowed from Britain and six Hotspur Mk. II gliders from the Royal Canadian Air Force for training, evaluation, and testing tug aircraft. Two Hotspur were employed at the NAF for tow test of tugs.[15]

The evaluations included towing the two Waco gliders simultaneously; one on a 350-foot towline and another on 450 feet, on 28 February 1943 from Philadelphia to Norfolk or 250 miles in four hours (due to adverse winds). Unlike the Army, the Marine pilots preferred to fly with a vertical displacement to reduce pilot workload; one above the tug slipstream and the other below.[16] The team then set out to perform a series of nonstop flights between Norfolk and Masters Field, Miami, Florida at 1,100 miles in what they called a "cargo line." This was planned to include three round trips with one glider in tow and three with dual tow. The first mission set out on 2 March with 3,190 pounds of freight in the glider, but was forced to divert to Cherry Point to wait out weather. They proceeded on the 4th. The return to Norfolk on the 8th had 1,900 pounds in the Waco and was completed in 8:10 hours. All concerned then decided the team had learned enough and the two gliders were towed back to Phily on the 17th.[17]

The PBY engines had to be operated above the recommended power setting for continuous operation when towing a fully loaded Waco LRW-1 and with double tow, but engine overheating was not experienced. Range with a single glider in trail was 1,600 miles, and 1,100 with double tow. Tow in an engine-out scenario appeared impractical, loss of altitude almost certain even with engines at maximum power and at risk of overheating. Double tow on one engine was likely impossible. Long flights were fatiguing for tug and glider pilots alike. The latter required hourly change offs, or more frequently if encountering turbulence owing to the physical strain given the high control forces and slow aircraft response. In turbulence even the tug pilots had their hands full with the glider yanking violently on the line and airplane. Because of this, dual tow was not recommended except under ideal conditions. The workload in even good weather was much more fatiguing for the glider pilot than the airplane, and towing in inclement weather remained almost impossible. The Navy men had to conclude that very long distance glider towing was operationally impractical.

The final hour of the flight from Phily was after sunset on a night of near total darkness such that the Cat pilots flew on instruments.[18] Towing on instruments proved nearly impossible because any change in glider attitude jerked on the tug, disturbing the fine control and trimming required. Night flight towing the LRW-1 was clearly impractical, the glider pilots fearing for the safety of the operation. They "complained bitterly of vertigo and extreme fatigue" owing to rough air and a particularly dark night with few tug incidental reference lights.[19]

Snead's Virginia plant was quite crammed with XLRH-1 assembly activity at its height. The dense and heavy wing structure can be seen. While construction was well underway, it was running many months behind schedule and well over budget. (National Archives)

Major Figley, in his 22 April report of the tests, also made observations of glider operational efficiency that echoed lessons learned by the Army. There was no efficiency advantage in a transport dragging cargo around in trailing gliders compared with carrying the freight itself, or even distributed between two airplanes.[20] It was recognized that gliders as towed "air trailers" had utility in cases where the bulk of the freight exceeded the volume or cargo door opening area of the airplane (but likely not the weight capability), or when the short and off-field takeoff (snatch) and landing superiority of the glider were vital to mission success. However, such cases appeared to be few and the cruise performance sacrificed by towing a glider was so severe that generating another airplane sortie to carry the additional freight *was* cost effective. The additional resources (especially personnel) required to acquire, maintain, and support the separate glider aircraft, while not great, certainly added to operating costs and resources. The added time and manpower for glider ground operations were also an unwelcome drain on

In an effort to prove the feasibility of long-endurance towing, the Naval Aircraft Factory fitted this Waco LRW-1 with autotow capability. This is evidenced by the wind-driven generator attached to the fuselage aft of the main gear and the additional venturi tubes above the cockpit. Note also the landing light installed in the starboard downview window. (National Soaring Museum)

efficiency. In windy conditions as many as ten men were required to position the Waco, in addition to the tractor operator. Furthermore, the glider movement significantly hampered powered aircraft operations on an airfield. While the Catalina could draw the towline inside, most other tugs had to drop the line somewhere on the field (a potential hazard) for later retrieval. It all simply did not sum up to any efficiency gain except in very rare circumstances offered by war.[21]

Captain Fahrney had, during the same period, worked to address the instrument flight impediment. He had focused on glider cockpit indicators of position with respect to the tug.[22] However, he learned that the NAF had an autotow device for the GLOMBs (Chapter 13) and sought tests with manned transport gliders. Clearly hastening to prop-up the faltering glider program, the NAF installed this device in an LRW-1 and a series of proving flights in April successfully conducted in Philadelphia, with a report issued on the 17th. Even during tug maneuvering and in rough weather the glider held position. Flights later that month included an autotow from Phily to National Airport, Washington, D.C., to demonstrate the capability to the Army. Two additional autotow sorties were flown there before returning.[23] Army personnel evaluated the system in Philadelphia and during a tow to Laurinburg-Maxton. While the control was sometimes jerky, it failed dramatically under heavy turbulence.[24]

Seizing upon the NAF success, a flight was conducted between 2 and 4 June 1943 and triumphantly documented by Barnaby. His report of the 12th specifically rebutted some of the Figley report, pointing out elsewhere that the CG-4A is a horrible glider and not indicative of the superior Navy models in development.[25] The LRW-1 was towed from Phily to Eglin Field (Fort Walton Beach), Florida, on 2 June 1943, or approximately 1,000 nonstop miles. Onboard the Waco were six persons and ballast equivalent of an addition four people, plus miscellaneous equipment. Flying an average 103 mph, the flight took 9.5 hours with the autotow engaged from climb-out to release, and the Cat also had its autopilot engaged for cruise. The flight included turbulence encounters, although no instrument conditions except for passing briefly through occasional clouds. The return on the 4th required 7.5 hours at 11,000 feet altitude. The team concluded that the Catalina-Waco combination operated best at 115 mph with regard to engine performance. The autotow device apparently still required some fine tuning in that the glider experienced a slight swinging on tow, slowly back and forth, in a manner that could induce airsickness. Apart from this, the glider crew had only the cold and boredom to complain about. Barnaby held this up as a solution to the reported night, inclement weather, and turbulence operational issue.

It is interesting to note that the Navy also struggled with the interphone cable strung along the towline as did its sister service, judging this unsatisfactory but never arriving at a good solution for communications between the tug and glider via this method. They made minor changes to the LRW-1s to correct perceived deficiencies, such as installing a radio and adding a landing light in the starboard pilot downview window.

Decision Time

All this speculation and summarizing came just as the floatwing glider was beginning to demonstrate its capabilities in actual tests. While grossly behind schedule, the 12-place projects had yielded flying aircraft in what was actually a remarkably short time given the complexity of the task and the nature of the organizations involved. However, more work was clearly needed to take these to production and the firms involved were suffering managerial and fiscal meltdown. The Navy was seeking a way to give Allied advanced payments to help it stave off financial collapse. The question of flight in weather was also being addressed by the Army and the GLOMB programs through the use of instruments, autotow, and autopilots systems extant or under development. It was all too little too late.

The Director of the Marine Corps Division of Aviation, General Mitchell, forwarded the most concise reports and conclusions to the Commandant on 13 March 1943, with a recommendation to liquidate the glider program. The Commandant, in turn, endorsed cancellation on 15 April in a missive to the CNO. Everyone in the chain on its way to the Chief concurred with the action. Rear Admiral Ernest J. King, Commander-in-Chief, United States Fleet, then wrote the Secretary on 18 May recommending liquidation, but that gliders on hand be used for experimental purposes. The termination decision was announced on the 18th, effective 24 June 1943. The entire operation and all contracts were closed down completely in September.

The second XLRA-1 Invader prototype shows further evolution of the canopy design. Although a true tricycle undercarriage was called for, a compromise is evident in the wheels added to the tail and wing skids. Like the XLRQ-1, the Allied glider showed promise, but the program was so beset with problems that it was ultimately cancelled. (National Soaring Museum)

When the Army and Navy set out to adopt large cargo gliders they at first appeared an outstanding means of increasing payload capacity of an airplane. However, calculations and soon practical experience showed this to be an erroneous impression. Pulling a "winged trailer" was inefficient compared with carrying the load internally or even generating a separate airplane sortie. (National Soaring Museum)

Just Won't Quit

There was some consideration of continuing the existing small-scale production contracts, or halting at the number then under substantial construction. Captain Fahrney suggested that if the USMC did not want the 200 12-place gliders, they should be built for experimental and operational test purposes, or as naval assets. He suggested they could be used as utility aircraft, such as for the flying boat support mission, towed by seaplanes and flown by any trained naval aviator. However, only the "glider enthusiasts" at BuAer seemed to believe the Navy had a requirement for gliders.

The 18 May 1943 decision by Knox and King to terminate the 12-place production contracts excluded hulls substantially along in assembly. This was assessed on 19 June as 15 aircraft each from Bristol and Allied, including their two X-planes. The initial six of each 15 would go to the Training Task Force Command and the balance, plus two Hotspurs at Eagle Mountain Lake, to the NAF for testing.[26] However, the Navy was contacted by Senator Francis Maloney on behalf of Bristol seeking to build 25, under their calculus it would cost as much to build them as cancel them, and seeking a 'promised' contract for a larger GLOMB (see later). Nothing came of all these machinations.

In the case of Bristol, its management was in a shambles, supervisors and leading engineers fleeing, and creditors strident. When the chief engineer and 11 other key engineers quit en-masse during April 1943, Warren assumed the chief engineer duties. The company was unlikely to meet even reduced contract terms. Although Bristol stated it would deliver the second glider on or around 15 July, an additional on-site review judged that the experimental contract could only be completed with an infusion of $67,435.00, this after already authorizing $499,156.00 above the original contract value or a total of $782,565.00 expended. (Another accounting has the company spending $1,400,000.00 of its advance and owing $250,000.00.[27]) At that time there were four other airframes substantially far along. The costs of the 15 production articles through 30 January 1944 could not be reliably estimated. Since procurement officials were unwilling to advance the company another nickel, there was discussion of moving the work to the NAF—more precisely having the Naval Air Modification Unit (NAMU), in Philadelphia, assume supervision of the activity. Instead, with no compelling requirement for the gliders, reason prevailed and both Bristol contracts were terminated outright on 16 September 1943, after expending nearly $4 million. Bristol again appealed to Senator Maloney, but this brought no 'stay of execution.'

Things were little better at Allied Aviation. Management clashes with the Navy in-plant inspector had BuAer insisting on personnel changes. August 1943 tests revealed the single wheel design appeared acceptable and thought was given to canceling the change to the P-40 gear that was proving troublesome, and perhaps even canceling the last five aircraft that were to receive the gear. It appeared a year might be required to produce the 15 gliders.[28] The government had already poured $2.4 million into the company, with $454,228.00 over the original experimental contract and $1,676,833.00 for production. A reasonable expectation of spending another million over the next year for the 15 production aircraft would make them exceedingly expensive gliders, indeed, at $500,000.00 over the original cost for 100. The project remained stymied by the inconclusive static tests, in progress at NAF since December 1942. By mid-September 1943 the USN leadership had stated conclusively there was no Navy requirement for the gliders. With little further consideration, the Allied contracts were cancelled on the 27th.

Final totals were $277.431.11 spent on the XLRA-1 and $793,204.30 on the XLRQ-1, plus $2,188,466.00 spent on Allied's abortive production work and $3,191,283.94 for Bristol's.[29]

In dismantling the program, the Navy agreed to transfer most or all of its glider work to the Army for evaluation, more specifically the second production articles of each type, including aircraft then under test.[30] For the XLRQ-1, this was later amended to the second flight test machine (third airframe).[31] Although Army pilots appeared in New Haven on 10 August 1943 to fly the glider to Wright Field, the Navy had yet to formally approve the transfer and the officers went home empty handed.[32] Bristol had separately approached the Army's Special Assistant to the Glider Program in hopes the USAAF could adapt the LRQ-1 to an Army mission. Some time later, on 4 August, Bristol attempted to renew this line of approach.[33] On the 16th, Wright Field made clear the Army had no requirement for a conversion of the Allied glider in any guise.[34] On 17 September, Bristol again appealed to the Army to take up the remains of the LRQ-1 project, stating they had two production LRQ-1s nearing completion, with 13 complete fuselages, parts for 18, and materials for 100.[35] Only the one operational glider remained, and the BuAer had other ideas.

The NAF took over the flight-worthy gliders and continued experimental flight testing while all other partially completed articles were destroyed. Trials of the LRQ-1 continued with a flight as late as 5 December 1943, and water operations with the second prototype.[36] Barnaby participated in many of the tests after August as pilot, along with Reilly. What was likely the only flight-worthy XLRA-1, the second ship, was destroyed on 11 December 1943 when high winds lifted an LRW-1 off the ground and deposited it atop the amphibian.[37]

What there was of the 12-place production aircraft that could possibly be of use was collected, amounting to incomplete examples of two LRA-1 (and elements of eight more) and two LRQ-1 (elements of 13 more). These were moved to the NAF for final preparation and testing. However, this work was given low priority. On 1 November 1944, one LRA-1 and one LRQ-1 were almost ready for flight, the other two being stored and

The XLRQ-1 undercarriage that was the cause of such disruption is evident on the second XLRQ-1 prototype. The strut visible towards the top trailing edge of the wing is believed to be for static ground use only. Testing of 11652 continued to at least the last month of 1943 as the navy glider program petered out. (National Museum of Naval Aviation)

canabalized for parts.[38] It is unlikely anything came of this. All of the wooden aircraft were eventually broken up.

On 5 August 1943 the Air Forces received 88 gliders from the Navy. These included 73 LNE-1s trainers which were redesignated TG-32s,[39] the two missing LNE-1s presumably lost to attrition. The vast majority of these were brand new, having never entered service. It is unclear how many of the 12 LNS-1s went to the Army. All nine original 3-place trainers were also eventually returned to the Army. The seven additional XLNT-1s had apparently been shuffled off to the NAF for use in GLOMB tests. Ten LRW-1s were also handed back to the Army on 5 August. With one lost in a wind storm, the fate of the others is unknown.[40] By that time all but the Wacos were of little value to the Army at that late date and simply joined hundreds of other trainers in storage.

Glider Group 71 was dissolved after some 372 personnel had been trained on gliders. On 30 December 1943, Marine paratroop units were also ordered disbanded. Considerable construction had been accomplished at the Titusville training base, but little preparation was done in Shawnee. Some $11,654,365.00 was spent on these bases, but other uses were found for them.[41]

Larger Still

The last Navy glider project was born of the GLOMB and transport glider programs crossing paths in 1942. The latter's cargo glider requirement was initially addressed in a BuAer planning document of 29 June 1942 that called for an aircraft that could carry either fuel, freight (including personnel), or explosives. An explosives-laden glider was to be flown onto a target via remote control as part of Fahrney's GLOMB program. As officially enunciated in a 29 September directive, three types were sought. The small glider was to carry 1,000 gallons of fuel or 6,000-8,000 pounds of explosives.[42] This was to be created by conversion of the USMC's 24-place glider, but no contract was ever let for this work given the poor state of the contractors and slow progress on the personnel glider development. The intermediate size cargo glider was to carry 2,000 gallons or a 12,000-14,000-pound explosive load. The large glider would accommodate 3,000 gallons or 18,000-20,000 pounds of explosives.

The large cargo/GLOMB gliders had already come to roost at the NAF on 18 June 1942. On 29 June, the CNO ordered the NAF to undertake the detailed design and construction of a large wooden glider to fulfill one of two requirements proposed by BuAer.[43] The Bureau had already forwarded their drawings and tentative specifications to the NAF on the 22nd. The first was an intermediate design, No. 237, that had evolved to a glider carrying 12,000-pounds of fuel or 10,000 pounds of explosives. The second of these, No. 238, was a requirement for a high-wing glider to carry 18,000-pounds of explosives or 3,000 gallons of fuel.[44] The fuel was to be delivered as cargo or transferable in flight to a long-range aircraft serving as tug.

Apparently considering two simultaneous projects too much, the NAF had initially undertaken only the top-end requirements as the XLRN-1. To meet the intermediate glider requirement, BuAer direction on 17 September 1942 was for Bristol to produce an enlarged version of their XLRQ-1.[45] It was to carry, alternatively, 24-30 passengers, 2,000 gallons of fuel, or 14,000 pounds of explosives.[46] It was also hoped that the new design challenge would keep disaffected engineering staff from departing and inject much-need funds into the failing entity. It was wisely decided on 5 December to defer this action until the NAF had tested the XLRQ-1. However, by May 1943 the dismal condition of Bristol did not bode well for such an undertaking. The idea persisted until 12 June 1943 by which time Bristol was on the ropes and procurement officials emphatically refused to contemplate issuing them another contract. Although Bristol fought for the work and had a Senator weigh in on their behalf, it was clear their credibility was depleted.[47] Captain Fahrney then proposed handing the requirement to the NAF. There it was apparently addressed as a 1944 concept labeled the XLR2N-1, but never coalesced into a program before being cancelled when the XLRN-1's fate was determined.[48]

Naval Aircraft Factory XLRN-1

The XLRN-1 was the Navy's most ambitious gliders project, America's largest glider of the war, and one of the largest aircraft the nation built of wood. Development was undertaken with tight security and apparently employed some Allied Aviation resources. The NAF set out to build a static test article and two flight test airframes. Specifications were clarified to include troops or freight like spare engines lifted to forward flying boats bases.[49] The autotow, remote pilot, and television (TV) systems from the ongoing GLOMB project were to be incorporated for test. The television camera was apparently to be mounted in a fairing under the glider's nose as such is evident in the experimental glider as built.

Work on the XLRN-1 was slowed by low priority and inevitable problems, so it was 1 October 1943 before a mockup was ready for inspection.[50] The static article was also assembled and passed its ground tests.[51] The aircraft were built at NAMU where Captain Fahrney had become CO.

With the schedule stretching out, thought was given to canceling the XLRN-1. It was no longer needed as a cargo glider and GLOMB production contracts had been issued for much smaller aircraft (Chapter 13). It was also discovered that fuel could not be safely transferred in flight with the aircraft under electronic control owing to the explosion hazard.[52] The GLOMB program, itself, was cancelled in fall 1944. However, the XLRN-1 effort was continued to glean engineering value from the investment, with the pace of construction slowed further.

The requirement for a large capacity glider to support marines ashore and to serve as a bomb glider platform yielded the XLRN-1 developed by the NAF and shown here in model form. It was to carry 18,000 pounds of cargo/explosives or 3,000 pounds of fuel. The concept included a protruding nose boom that probably was included in this model, as suggested by the ring on the nose. (National Soaring Museum)

The impressive glider had a fixed tricycle landing gear, although the main undercarriage was on a beam attached beneath the aircraft such that it could be jettisoned. The high wing was fitted with flaps plus large slotted spoiler panels that could be extended perpendicular above and below. Cargo doors or rear loading ramp are not visible in photos or discussed in the literature. However, it seems clear the low fuselage bottom and high wing were for ease of loading. Although amphibious operation is not overtly mentioned in available documentation, the lack of boat hull and wing floats may have been an expedient. The cargo missions would have required at least beaching or inland landing, if not setting down in surf. Provisions were made for two types of auxiliary power units, with a gasoline motor in the fuselage and a wind-driven generator in the starboard wing leading edge. These would generate electrical current plus power vacuum and hydraulic pumps, and a defueling pump. A 50-gallon fuel tank was provided for starting only on the ground. The generator would also charge batteries capable of providing 30-minutes of electrical power. Apart from radio and lights, these would also power servos, radio altimeter, remote control receiver, and television for the autopilot and remote controlled flight system. Empty weight had crept up during detail design and assembly with 3,121 pounds overweight from about 11,000 pounds, depending on mission configuration, to 18,000 pounds in the flight test configuration. The Navy considered that a follow-on aircraft of magnesium might reduce the overweight condition.[53] The wing outer panels, each weighing 1,750 pounds, could be detached for transport. The center panel contained fuel tanks and lines for the fuel transfer mission.

The initial design had a tapered boom extending 5-8 feet ahead of the nose.[54] This was referred to as a "tow boom," but the test glider was towed from a fitting at the apex of the flattened nose which may have been a base for the boom.[55] During tests of the refueling concept (Chapter 12) the hose was "stopped along the towline."[56] The refueling was said to be via a 2.5-inch diameter hose.[57] If the XLRN-1 fuel transfer was to be done similarly, it is possible the boom played a role in the refueling.

Prototype assembly continued into early 1944, with costs exceeding a million dollars. One source of the delay was a reworking of the control system to reduce friction and yoke/pedal forces. Flight testing was to be conducted at NAS Patuxent River. The glider was delivered there by barge with the outer wing panels removed in early October 1944 and then assembled by the 19th.

Taxi tests and brief lift-offs behind *Tugboat Annie* on the 24 October had the glider at 19,200 pounds GW with Major Figley and Captain Barnaby at the controls. On the third run they experienced a mishap when a crosswind gust caused the glider to veer off the runway and destroy a runway light with a gear bogey. Handling qualities were good, although aileron and rudder responsiveness was sluggish. Testing continued the following day with brief liftoffs and short flights at various flap settings, the final four included release and flight reaching 100 feet altitude in hops up to 30 seconds. Between run 4 and 5, the top slat in each top spoiler was removed to correct an over-balance condition and false trailing edges added to the elevator. Between 6 and 7, half the elevator static balance was removed. The eighth run was the first true flight, performed with Lieutenant Ryan replacing Barnaby as copilot, then-Major Reilly flying the Cat.[58] The XLRN-1 was at 19,400 pounds and the sortie lasted 24 minutes, reaching just 300 feet altitude.

The pilots found the longitudinal stability to be poor, with oscillations due to over-control owing to poor harmony in pitch and yaw. Internal and external control

The XLRN-1 is shown on 19 October 1944 after assembly at NAS Patuxent River. The aircraft was clearly a proof-of-concept as it lacked troops or cargo doors, the aircrew apparently coming and going via the steps below the cockpit windows. Note the protruding mount for the electrical generator on the starboard leading edge. (National Museum of Naval Aviation)

Unlike the troop transport gliders, the XLRN-1 showed no evidence of being intended for water operations, lacking a boat hull, although this may have been merely an expedient for an initial design. This view emphasizes the thick wing with 'picket fence' spoilers top and bottom, and the cross-beam main landing gear. Note the fairing for a television camera beside the nose gear and the wing flaps and the three protruding members atop the aircraft (purpose unclear). (The Peter M. Bowers Collection/The Museum of Flight)

system changes were necessary. A 7-inch false trailing edge was applied to the rudder, the elevators rebalanced, and the elevator tabs locked out. The second flight was not until 7 November after two more "taxi" events. Testing proceeded into November with Barnaby again doing much of the flying. Flight three was on the 9th, was performed after altering the elevator trailing edge again. The 55-minute sortie reached 5,000 feet and 120 mph, and included a stall. Directional control was inadequate and rudder pedal forces remained prohibitively high.

Testing continued until 1 January 1945 with various rudder and elevator false trailing edges attempted. Flights included a full-up weight of 36,000 pounds for which the glider had to be towed by the R5D-1. Herein lay another limitation. This four-engine transport, numbers spread thinly across the services, was one of the few aircraft that could tow the fully loaded glider. The PBY-5A could pull the XLRN-1 only at light weight.

The handling deficiencies finally ended the project. All required modifications could not be supported for a mere demonstration effort. Barnaby himself recommended terminating the project, concluding that wooden aircraft of such size were impractical and might not standup well in some theaters.[59] It seems doubtful that autotow trials or remote control flights with a TV camera were performed, although the equipment was reportedly installed to include the TV camera in the nose.[60] The second aircraft was never completed and both gliders were ordered dismantled and salvaged in February 1945.[61] No total cost for the program has been uncovered.

Table 09-01	
Naval Aircraft Factory XLRN-1 Specifics	
span	110.0 ft
wing area	1,200 ft^2
length	67.5 ft
height	18.4 ft
empty weight	19,764 lbs
loaded weight	37,764 lbs
overload weight	40,000 lbs
maximum tow speed	180 mph
stall speed	60 mph (no flaps)

The enormous size of the XLRN-1 is indicated in this team picture, it being the largest American glider of the war and amongst the largest aircraft the nation built of wood. The stout structure with beefy main gear (no cross-shaft) is apparent as well as the towline attachment at the nose. Captain Barnaby is the shorter man wearing a baseball cap in the middle of the second row. (National Soaring Museum)

The NAF XLRN-1 had some handling qualities difficulties requiring changes during test that are evident in the empennage (along with propeller on the generator extension at the starboard leading edge). The corrections were never entirely resolved satisfactorily. By the time it flew in fall 1944, the glider was clearly excess to needs and so not pursued further. (National Soaring Museum)

The great mass of the XLRN-1, at 36,000 pounds fully loaded, meant that only a four-engine tug was suitable to tow it aloft at anything but nearly empty weight. This alone would have greatly limited its combat practicality. A Douglas R5D-1 hauls the glider across the NAS Patuxent River backdrop. (National Soaring Museum)

Formations of tugs and gliders were reliant upon the navigation and guidance of the lead planes. In the first combat experiences this was shown to still be developing. Combinations became lost or missed their LZ by many miles. (National Museum of the United States Air Force)

10

Combat Experience

The CG-4A was the heart of the airborne operations employing gliders during WWII, progressively modified to improve its ruggedness and utility. It was flown into combat by Americans and British forces alike. These Allies became mutually reliant and they made a good if sometimes contentious team. The USAAF frequently lifted British paratroopers and gliders into battle. The American materiel and manpower contributions were always more than twice that of their partner.

Rough Start

The British were the first of the Allies to employ gliders in combat. Operation *Freshman* on 19 November 1942 employed two Horsas for a commando raid in Norway to destroy a facility connected with German nuclear research. It ended with the team disappearing. It was learned later the glider/tow plane combinations could not find the objective due to weather and failure of navigation equipment. The men were killed in crashes or captured and murdered by the Nazis.

The American glider team's first deployment was to North Africa in early 1943, following with the initial American ground combat of the war. They did not support the initial airborne operations, and their lack was sorely felt. Once deployed, the glider team slowly moved across Tunisia, training and transporting gear for Army units.

When the British planned for the airborne portion of Operation *Husky*, the 9 July 1943 invasion of Sicily from North Africa, a late decision was made to employ British glider troops in a night assault, in concert with U.S. and British paratroops, to help ensure the success of the shore landings. Despite this being the first large-scale Allied combat experience with gliders (three years after the German introduction) and the largest airborne operation in history to that time, everything was thrown together hastily with inexperienced personnel. Reconnaissance photographs showed the proposed LZs to be quite small, rocky or wooded. However, the decision was irrevocable.

The British Army had only 27 Horsas in theater, these having been towed a perilous 1,400 miles from Great Britain to Morocco, in the longest operational tow of the war by any nation. Consequently, the decision was made to use many of the 500 CG-4As arriving in the theater by sea. Assembly was delayed by some of the crates for individual gliders being delivered to different ports. Time had grown so short that glider assembly became an "extreme emergency," and the training of U.S. glider pilots in mechanics' duties proved invaluable. Their work was interrupted by many of the assembled Wacos being destroyed or severely damaged in an 18 December 1943 wind storm, then the rest being grounded for mandatory tail bracing wire inspections.

The CG-4As would be towed mostly by the USAAF crews and C-47s. The British pilots were recent graduates with little experience and no prior night flying exposure. Their U.S. counterparts gave these men a brief course in the Waco. The three weeks' instruction comprised bare essentials, amounting to an average 4.5 hours per pilot, with approximately 1.2 at night and around 16 lifts per pilot. The C-47 teams were also undergoing quick training as few had any previous gliders tow experience. No large night formation flights, approaches over water, or landings simulating combat conditions were conducted. Nineteen of the U.S. Army pilots "volunteered" to fly as copilots during the invasion.

Predictably, things did not go well. For Operation *Ladbroke*, 136 Wacos and 8 Horsas were committed for the first strike followed by 10 Horsas and 8 CG-4As of *Fustian*

The Horsa could not be broken down for practical transport by sea, so had to be towed to distant theaters. This proved impractical and so the British Army acquired CG-4As they named Hadrians. Their first employment was in the invasion of Sicily, July 1943. Shown is the well-known "Voo-Voo" arriving in Britain. (The Peter M. Bowers Collection/The Museum of Flight)

released three days later targeted to seize a vital bridge. The 240-mile, 3-hour over-water flight was flown at just 200 feet altitude to avoid radar detection. Unexpectedly, salt spray raised by the tow ships collecting on glider windscreens and degraded forward vision. As would become common in all such operations, several tow ships turned back with mechanical trouble, and 1-2 percent of the gliders cut loose with their own mechanical difficulties, loads shifting dangerously, or towlines parting in turbulence because the pilot drifted down into the tow plane's slipstream or due to glider overloading.

Although the Sicily invasion was successful and the glider troops contributed significant value, on the whole the airborne mission was little short of disastrous. The route was a very challenging navigational exercise at that time in the war. The inexperience of the TCC crews was evident when many in the first lift released their gliders too far off-shore because they became lost or misjudged the distance given an unanticipated headwind and blowing dust. The navigation for dropping American paratroopers was equally dismal, pointing up grave deficiencies for future night glider lifts. Added to this was their first exposure to enemy searchlights and flak—actually comparatively light and inaccurate. Some 69 gliders landed in the sea with 326 men drowning, including 57 glider pilots of which five were American. Those that made it over land had difficulty finding their LZs owing to incorrect release points, smoke from combat, or simply the darkness (quarter moon). Only 49 CG-4As and five Horsas landed in Sicily, four within their assigned LZ and 22 within 1 mile.

The second glider lift and the troop planes that flew inland were badly shot up by nervous Navy gunners in the invasion fleet. Four gliders were probably shot down. Many of the landings ended badly in the rough terrain, but few men were severely injured. However, only 1 in 15 of these soldiers reached their objectives that night.

The Sicily experience offered many lessons for future improvement. However, military leadership was close to disbanding airborne forces altogether or limiting them to smaller affairs. At this time other events were also shedding an unfavorable light on the U.S. glider program. The pilot training program was in a bad state and glider production lagging. The St. Louis CG-4A accident also made the papers and became well known to the glidermen. The revelation that some components were made by a firm previously

The combat debut of the CG-4A looked very bad, but principally because of circumstances and poor execution by leadership. The aircraft that made it to landings faired only as well as expected. There were some severe crackups and casualties, as suggested by this image, somewhere in European combat. (National Museum of the United States Air Force)

The droppable undercarriage for the CG-4A came in handy when three of the gliders had to land in snow in Yugoslavia. The landing in snow on skids was exceptionally short, and the glider not expected to be recovered. Shown is not this event, but where the GIs appear to be rigging the glider for tow off on the skids. (National Soaring Museum)

manufacturing coffins contributed to glidermen christening the Waco with the "flying coffin" moniker, in addition to the "manned tow-target" already granted.

Ultimately, after further study and successful exercises, the U.S. Army carried on with gliders. However, this history and just the unusual nature of the aircraft and its mission made soldiers hesitant to ride in gliders. Also, unlike paratroopers, the glidermen received no hazardous duty pay until this was corrected following Normandy. As it was, they were assigned to the role; not asked to volunteer like the pilots. They also bore in mind Hitler's pronouncement that any captured commandos would be immediately shot. With this background, the pilots were proud of telling those who asked that the "G" emblazoned on their glider pilot wings stood for "Guts!"

A glider base and training center was established on Sicily. Many more operations in Italy were planned, with various levels of preparation—including gliders loaded and ready to launch—but all were cancelled due to the rapidly advancing front. The British flew a three-glider mission from Italy into Yugoslavia, towed by Americans, on 19 February 1944 to deliver Russian advisors to Marshall Tito's partisans. Operation *Bunghole* was the first daylight glider operation for the Allies and involved CG-4A landing in snow, marking the only time the jettisonable undercarriage was employed. The UK conducted several other small-scale glider operations on the Continent in support of resistance fighters. The Americans never did the same, but did soon gained valuable experience of their own prior to mass-glider operations in western Europe.

A team of American glider pilots and mechanics with 27 gliders were deployed to Australia in January and February 1943 to participate in the New Guinea campaign. During August, 25 of the gliders were towed 400 miles across the Coral Sea to Port Moresby. They were then hauled over the Owen Stanley Mountains to Dobodura in preparation for the opening assaults on Lae. Eleven were loaded with engineering equipment for their 5 September mission to establish an airhead at Nadzab airfield. However, the mission was cancelled when Nadzab was captured and the field found to be in good condition. This was much to the relief of the glider crews who did not feel comfortable with the prospect of flying 320 miles over jungle in gliders of questionable airworthiness. One of the aircraft had shed its tail in flight from Australia and the crew was killed in

Among the first deployments of the glider force was a small team sent to Australia in anticipation of contributing in New Guinea. Here the first CG-4A assembled at Eagle Farm Air Base, Brisbane, is towed up for its check flight (with droppable undercarriage). The gliders had suffered damage in transport and so there was some relief on the part of the pilots when the combat operation was cancelled. (National Museum of the United States Air Force)

Glider pilots of the 1st Air Commando are photographed during preparations for their actions behind Japanese lines in Burma. Given a choice of aircraft to take, the leaders chose the unproven Wacos and their pilots. But, fired by determination, they created a unique combat capability. (United States Air Force)

the resulting plunge to the sea. All the machines had suffered deterioration during their transit to Australia.[1] The glider pilots instead flew spotter planes while the gliders rotted to scrap from neglect.

The airborne troops participating in the retaking of the Philippines also did not employ gliders until the end of the war. It was a different story in the China-Burma-India (CBI) theater although conditions were not ideal for gliders. The long-distance tows over high mountains and dense forests were stressful. But, they had the potential for greatly contributing to the operations in the area that included the only airborne missions conducted without paratroops.

A force of 150 CG-4As, 25 TG-5 trainers, and 100 handpicked glider pilots, was established in India by December 1943. Their principal action was Operation *Thursday*, from 5 March to mid-May 1944. This provided insertion and logistics support of British "Chindit" commandos hundreds of miles behind Japanese limes in Burma. It began with the seizure of airheads in jungle clearings; dozens of CG-4As bringing in engineering troops and equipment to clear landing strips for C-47s. This was the first combat use of double tow, although it did not go well. The strain on the C-47s' engines and fuel reserves climbing over 8,000-foot mountains was considerable. Another lesson was not to leave tow ropes out on the soggy ground for days prior to an operation and allow trucks to drive over them. Overloading of the gliders was also epidemic. Several gliders were lost over the jungle when the lines snapped. Double tows were discontinued for the remainder of the operation. The initial landings were also messy, with most gliders being

Clockwise from Top Left: 1. Tows over the 8,000-foot Chin Hills, Burma, encountered turbulence that snapped some tow ropes. Much was learned that was helpful in planning the Normandy airborne landings. This image likely shows a glider in high tow above a tug below the aircraft whose tail is visible. (United States Air Force) 2. A training glider that made it into a war zone was 25 of the Aeronca TG-5s. These "Air Knockers" served to maintain pilot currency (plus flight pay) and provided low-volume, high priority combat transport. These gliders were usually towed by the Noorduyn UC-64 Norseman. (National Soaring Museum) 3. Troops discuss the day's activities the morning after the combat assault landings at "Broadway" in Burma, 5 March 1944. Beyond them are the remains of two gliders that collided in the chaotic night landings. The results led to use of dawn and dusk land assaults that followed in Europe. (United States Air Force) 4. Special reduced-size tractors, bulldozers, graders, scrappers, and rollers were developed for carriage aboard the gliders. These combat engineers demonstrate the equipment that could be used to prepare an airstrip for powered aircraft after landing by glider. Water and possibly fuel bladders were also developed for CG-4A carriage. (VER Blunt Collection via family)

The glider snatch was widely practiced but seldom used in combat. The occasions when it was used were generally to extract a glider bearing wounded personnel, transporting them to rear aid stations in a fraction the time of overland travel. The usual sight was as seen here; a C-47 snagging a CG-4A. (The Peter M. Bowers Collection/The Museum of Flight)

wrecked and casualties suffered. However, the missions were successful, the airheads allowing airlanding of thousands of troops, hundreds of tons of materiel, and hundreds of pack animals. Very useful but temperamental mules and ponies were carried three per CG-4A, tethered to an installed crossbar. A shallow fence of padded bamboo was secured at the sidewalls to prevent the animals from kicking through the fabric.

In the weeks after *Thursday*, gliders provided on-call delivery of vital materiel like ammunition, medical supplies, provisions, and even collapsible motorboats for river crossings. They landed in unprepared jungle clearings, on sand bars, and dried rice paddies, sometimes under fire. They also inserted troops and extracted wounded via snatch. This last undoubtedly saved many lives under the extremely difficult CBI conditions. The CG-4As flew 96 flights carrying in 1,059 troops, 155 tons of cargo, plus invaluable animals. The cost was 54 gliders destroyed, most of the others lost to a typhoon. There were dozens of casualties from crashes and enemy fire, including 19 glider pilots killed. Operations through May consumed the majority of the gliders but were counted largely successful, the CG-4A proving its worth in the difficult circumstances of the theater. The campaign was instrumental in weakening Japans hold on Burma and easing pressure on the supply routes into China. The lessons learned were transferred to those preparing for the largest airborne operation of the war.

Main Events

With the time for the invasion of Western Europe approaching, American airborne forces were collected in Great Britain. They and the British forces were honed to a fine edge, with the Sicily and CBI lessons taken to heart. Apart from glidermen, jeeps and field guns with crews were to be flown in the Wacos, albeit in separate aircraft that needed to land near each other. Because none of the higher-capacity U.S. gliders were immediately available, the Americans operated hundreds of Horsas that could lift a jeep and towed gun together. The British, for their part, operated hundreds of CG-4A Hadrians. They also added their enormous Hamilcar glider which could load a light tank as part of its 17,500-pound cargo.

The Americans returned the Anglo favor by adopting hundreds of Horsas while awaiting the larger capacity U.S. gliders that ultimately never entered combat. The Horsas were never counted clearly or given Army serial numbers. The Horsas and Hadrians were swapped between the Allies without accounting, unlike all other aircraft. (National Soaring Museum)

Unlike the Germans who had used gliders to insert airborne troops ahead of the paratroop force, the Allied did the reverse. If Crete was a measure of the success of the German approach, the Allies may have saved many lives in choosing the opposite approach. The paratroops dropped in first to seize the landing zone in preparation for glider landings. Once on the ground, the glidermen were to assist paratroopers in holding the LZ to facilitate unloading and regrouping before moving on their objectives. At first the intent to perform night landings were met with much trepidation, but senior commanders insisted that gliders would be little use if this was not possible. Although exercises proved the general potential for successful night assaults with an acceptable number of accidents, a concession was made to perform the missions at dawn or dusk. By the end of 1944, night landings were considered suitable only for emergency circumstances, and where moonlight and navigational aids were adequate.[2]

As with pathfinders, combat engineers were also to be inserted ahead of the landings to remove obstacles. Field Marshal Rommel's troops on the English Channel coast had prepared likely landing fields with poles, 8-12-foot long and 4-12-inches in diameter, sometimes wired together and to mines, for what were dubbed "Rommel's Asparagus" (*Rommel-spargel*). Some areas were intentionally flooded to discourage landings.

In the few months before the invasion, State-side training was accelerated and pilots shipped to England, among those transferred from other theaters, to bring the total to more than 950 men. Between May 1943 and February 1944, 2,100 CG-4As were transported to Britain and collected at Crookham Common. Just assembling this staggering number of aircraft was a daunting task that was at first not appreciated.

Progress from November 1943 was initially so slow owing to inexperience, meager resources, and working outside in foul weather that a crisis developed. Initial attempts to employ untrained civilian workers were a failure, with their output slow and many gliders unflyable. Air Forces personnel then took over, but on-the-job training of the undermanned unit was still too slow. Only a few hundred gliders were ready by the end of 1943, and 100 of these were destroyed in a violent storm during March. By early 1944, the rate of assembly was so low that it was feared, with attrition, there were too few to support training. The invasion also loomed with a real possibility of insufficient Wacos. The Army went into crisis mode. Trained glider mechanics and engineering staff were rushed to the job and worked around-the-clock to avert a shortfall. They were soon erecting 30 gliders per day, with 910 in April 1944 alone.[3] However, there were barely enough glider pilots to fly aircraft on hand, and these without copilots. On 31 May the USAAF had 1,118 CG-4As and 301 Horsas ready for action.

The Normandy invasion was to be the first experience in which three entire airborne divisions (two American, some 13,350 men) would be delivered to combat in a single day. This meant hundreds of gliders descending simultaneously into congested LZs. Large exercises, one approaching the level of a rehearsal (unique during the war), built the skills for these large formations to gather following takeoff, navigate to an objective, and perform mass glider landings with the minimum of confusion and hazard. However, for such training the gliders were usually brought down in large, clear spaces where they could be readily towed out again. Actual landings in confined fields, with trees or stone walls, were considered too dangerous and glider recovery too cumbersome.

Unlike Sicily, the airborne portion of the 6-7 June invasion, Operation *Neptune*, was meticulously planned, aircraft in excellent shape, and personnel in top form. The gliders sortied from fields in southern England to reduce flight time to 2.5-3 hours. Getting the hundreds of aircraft off and formed up into orderly streams from multiple bases, and passing over objectives in an organized and safe manner, was exceedingly challenging. Route planning, reconnaissance photography to familiarize the crews with the LZs, and briefings were excellent. The airborne forces sought to seize vital bridges and crossroads, destroy key defensive facilities, and generally disrupt German communications and reinforcement efforts as the coastal bridgehead was won and consolidated. These attacks were part of the largest military operation in history.

On D-Day and D+1, during dawn and dusk landings, the Americans released 291 Wacos and 218 Horsas following paratroop drops. The Horsas were reserved for the afternoon to give additional daylight as they were more difficult to land in small fields. As usual, some gliders dropped out for various reasons. It all proved a messy affair in execution, but fortunately the enemy was the most confused.

Not all the airplanes were equipped with the electronic navigational aids or the crews trained, and it was only in later operations that this was remedied. Many times the pathfinders did not drop accurately and could not find the LZ in time, or their equipment did not operate properly. Some tow pilots got lost and did not arrive within range of the LZ, leaving the glider pilot to decide whether to cast off. Radio silence was observed and many combinations lacked the interphone between glider and tug.

Ideal interval and formation were not always possible, but there were few midair or ground collisions. Many LZs were contested and the afternoon lifts received a "warmer" welcome from the defenders. The selected fields were at the minimal limit of size, especially as they were generally encircled by 40-foot trees that had been indiscernible

The pilot is pressing the towline release lever while a GI outside inserts the towing ring-plug into the jaws at the top of the glider's nose. In combat, the copilot station was typically manned by a nervous infantryman whom the pilot provided a quick verbal course in flying should he become a casualty during the mission. Parachutes were supposedly mandatory as well, but these were also frequently ditched because of shortages. (National Soaring Museum)

Until June 1944, the concept of mass glider assault and the practicality of the CG-4A for the role had been little tested in combat, despite thousands of gliders purchased and thousands of men trained. Yet, the airborne forces (also little tested in combat) relied in great measure on the glider to execute D-Day landings successfully. This image emphasizes the close quarters for the 13 infantrymen and relatively small loadable volume of the Waco. (National Museum of the United States Air Force)

This is like thousands of similar pre-mission snapshots from D-Day of glidermen preparing to board their Waco. Few such men came to welcome a ride into combat in the CG-4A. However, they appreciated the ability to land together and with more combat potential than scattered paratroop landings. (San Diego Air & Space Museum)

in reconnaissance photographs. Perhaps half the gliders were destroyed or badly smashed on landing, and many of the rest suffered some damage—typically running into the anti-glider obstacles, hedgerows, or cattle. Unloading frequently had to wait until nightfall because of enemy sniping or mortar fire.

In many cases during *Neptune*, the glider pilots had difficulty locating their LZ and, with less than 30 seconds of free flight and only 1-2 miles reach, had to choose any suitable site not already crowded with gliders. Accuracy of the glider landings was poor, only 19 percent ending within the assigned LZs and another 18 percent within 2 miles. This left guns without jeeps to tow them in addition to troops without their leaders. Fortunately, this scattering lent the appearance to the Germans that there were airborne troops everywhere, and they grossly overestimated their numbers. A vast number of small unit actions sufficed in absence of consolidated engagements.

The gliders performed as well as had been expected, and certainly better than many had feared. Over 20 percent of the materiel delivered to the beachheads during D-Day was landed via gliders, with 40-50 percent of the equipment within 2 miles of the objective. Of these 95 guns, 290 vehicles, and 238 tons or gear, only 50 percent made it into action. The gliders also landed nearly 4,000 men of whom 463 were casualties, or 12 percent. Of the 1,034 American glider pilots sent off on 6-7 June, 44 were killed, 122 wounded, and 33 captured or missing. Subsequent lifts were planned but ultimately cancelled as unnecessary. Ten Wacos flew urgent resupply missions on 10 and 13 June. Weeks after Normandy only 13 Wacos had been snatched and flown to England; all the Horsas were written off.

The collecting of gliders preparatory to a major assault created storage and maintenance challenges. The gliders had no utility besides their typically single combat mission, yet were made of materials that could deteriorate comparatively quickly if left to the elements. This problem is illustrated by these Wacos assembled and awaiting a mission at a poorly drained airfield. (The Peter M. Bowers Collection/The Museum of Flight)

Glider undercarriage was a frequent casualty of the combat landings, as exemplified by this CG-4A equipped with the Corey skid shown in this invasion snapshot during D-Day. Collision with an anti-glider pole may have created the hole in the port wing leading edge. Note the Waco beyond with the aft fuselage propped up with lumber to facilitate cargo unloading. (San Diego Air & Space Museum)

Following Normandy, all subsequent glider assaults were in daylight. Experience suggested casualties would be about the same, balancing the hazards of night landings and scattered gliders with more accurate ground fire, while troops would assemble and attack in force more quickly. Sixteen major airborne operations were planned but subsequently cancelled due to the rapid advance of Allied troops following the breakout from the Normandy beachhead or due to the commitment of TCC to aerial supply operations. Some of these operations progressed to the point of loading aircraft and even engines running before the stand-down order came. This contributed to a dramatic drop-off in training and exercises, but without impacting performance.

The invasion of southern France, 15 August 1944, followed the same theme as Normandy although the airborne missions flew from Italy. As before, the commanders found they were short of gliders and hundreds had to be shipped in as priority cargo. This was followed by crisis-mode assembly with too little time for satisfactory training or glider modifications. No dress rehearsal was performed. (Training was sometimes minimized just to ensure against glider attrition.) Some 600 glider pilots were transferred from Britain to support the operation.

Dawn pathfinder missions were only marginally successful but release accuracy was good. A morning lift of 33 American CG-4As and 36 Glider Pilot Regiment Horsas found ground fog. Despite this, the Americans, flying with copilots, made good landings after circling for an hour while the British serial was recalled. The main lift in the afternoon included seven serials for 332 USAAF Wacos towed by C-47s and aircrew turned after the AM paratroop drops. These were among the longest combat tows of

A different airfield arrangement is illustrated, compared with that shown in Chapter 7, for a TCC wing preparing for a mass glider tow operation. The tremendous resources the United States brought to the fight is evident in the many dozens of aircraft, matched by many dozens more at other fields. The C-47 in the foreground is fitted with parapacks underneath. (San Diego Air & Space Museum)

A small segment of a glider serial—a pair of C-47 and CG-4A combinations—crosses a flooded Normandy countryside on D-Day. As shown, the flight to the Landing Zone (LZ) was typically at just a few hundred feet altitude. The gliders were towed on a 350-foot, 11/16-inch diameter nylon line and cast off on a signal from the transport, usually right over the LZ. (National Soaring Museum)

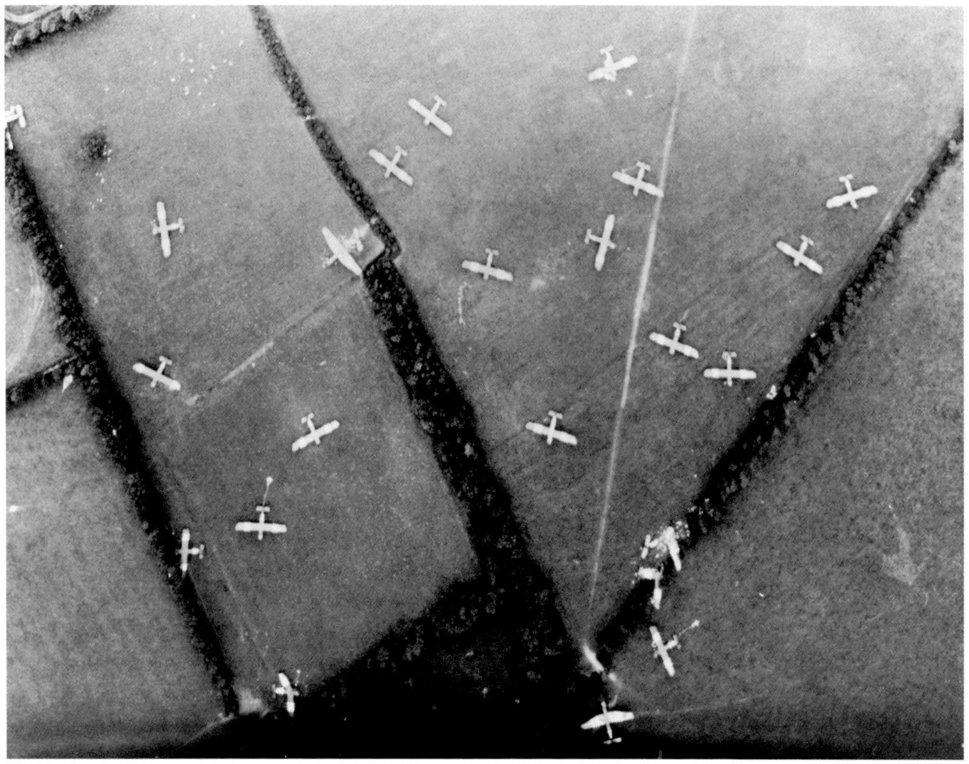

This image of a Normandy landing zone is revealing. It includes CG-4As as well as Horsas. Some of the Wacos are trailing braking parachutes. Those that encountered the hedgerows are clearly badly damaged or destroyed, with the pilots lucky if they escaped without injury. The fields look shockingly small, and efforts to avoid collisions with other gliders must have been stressful. (National Archives)

The cost of a mass glider assault is easily visible in these aircraft collected afterwards for reclamation. Nearly every glider has suffered some manner of damage, some severe. The manpower and materiel effort required to repair these machines would clearly be prodigious, especially considering this is but a small portion of the gliders that participated in the operation. (National Archives)

the war at around four hours and with the first double tows in Europe. The landings were largely unopposed. The greatest hiccup was bunching when the 10-minute interval between formations broke down. At one point approximately 150 gliders were in free flight, wheeling in slow-motion over the close LZs. A few midair collisions had men and materiel raining through the swarm. Still, 90-95 percent of the gliders landed on or near their assigned LZs.

The Wacos brought in 2,611 troops, 213 anti-tank guns and mortars, 221 vehicles, and 500 tons of heavy cargo. The cost was 11 glider pilots killed and 30 wounded, and more than 100 glidermen injured. As usual, many gliders were damaged in landing or by *Rommel-spargel*. Not one of the over 400 gliders in Operation *Dragoon* was recovered.

With more confidence in airborne operations and gliders, they were made central in a bid to accelerate the collapse of German defenses by seizing a deep salient into Holland and across three key bridges, the farthest spanning the Rhine River. Airborne divisions would be inserted as a "carpet" (Operation *Market*), seizing key transportation nodes, across which assaulting ground forces would roll (Operation *Garden*). The Americans were assigned the capture of bridges in the Eindhoven and Nijmegen areas while the British drew the farthest objective at Arnhem. The tremendous flak threats at Arnhem led to some LZs and DZs being set relatively far from the objective. Lacking sufficient number of tow planes and deciding to forego the precarious double tow for the long mission, the lift had to be planned for three periods on consecutive days. This naturally yielded the element of surprise and prevented maximum offensive effort from the start, made more acute by troops remaining to hold LZs for follow-on lifts.

Another concerted effort at Crookham Common was necessary to add 1,500 CG-4As to the fleet, assembling 60 aircraft per day—and even 100 on one occasion.[4] The U.S. still had 104 Horsas but, having acquired a dislike for the type, chose not to employ them. There were 2,060 glider pilots on hand, but the Wacos still flew without copilots for the three-hour flight. The divisional commanders preferred to fill the seat with an infantryman ... who had to be talked through how to fly and land the aircraft if the pilot was incapacitated! The airborne divisions also suffered a shortage or parachutes for the paratroops, directing these soldiers to gliders.[5]

The enormous *Market* began on 17 September 1944 with 1,545 troop ships and 451 tug/glider combinations lifting from 24 English airfields, with more than 1,000 fighter escorts. This thunderous aerial armada alone, stretching back over 50 miles, emphasized to the

Gliders as far as the eye can see in Holland, spied from a passing B-24. This one operation over six days saw 1,618 American and 697 British gliders towed nearly 300 miles in a bid that ultimately failed to achieve its objective and proved exceedingly costly for the British Glider Pilot Regiment. (National Archives)

Glider assaults in Europe were part of huge airborne operations that included the dropping of thousands of paratroopers, although usually into different areas (Landing Zones versus Drop Zones). This image (likely from Holland) shows paratroops dropping into a prior LZ. Note the low drop altitude and the hundreds of canopies already on the ground amid the gliders. (National Soaring Museum)

Other than paratroops, airdrop for combat delivery of materiel and aerial resupply remained in its infancy, making gliders invaluable assets. Only relatively light articles could be dropped by parachute out the airplane's cargo doors or released from racks under the belly. Loads are "kicked" out the door in a postwar image. (San Diego Air & Space Museum)

Soldiers prepare airdrop bundles for installation on racks under a C-47 in preparation of a mission to Guadalcanal. (National Archives)

German defenders the growing tenuousness of their situation. Increased skill permitted a reduction in the interval between serials. Once again, a few disruptions of the elaborate formations resulted in congestion over the LZs. Some elements had to climb above their assigned altitude, and this resulted in gliders descending through other formations. In some cases the intensity of enemy fire made it necessary to withdraw immediately upon landing, setting the gliders alight to prevent their cargo falling into enemy hands.

As fate would have it, the second and third glider lifts and paratroop drops were postponed, recalled, or rerouted due to appalling weather. The final lifts were not made until D+6. Resupply via airdrop was maturing but still very inaccurate and of comparatively low volume. It could not deliver large items or exceptionally heavy cargo like fuel and shells. The ground attack was also slowed and failed to break through to relieve the British paras on the Arnhem bridge. All this left under-strength and lightly armed airborne troops fighting for days against superior defenders.

The glider missions were about as successful as could be expected under the difficult circumstances. German gunners found the Allied formations exceptional targets and 132 gliders were lost to ground fire and accidents, with a like toll in transports. Still, about 90 percent of the glider sorties were effective. The 1,618 Wacos brought in almost 9,500 troops, 140 guns, 710 vehicles and 465 trailers, and 1,135 tons of other cargo. The Americans lost 12 glider pilots killed, 37 wounded, and 65 missing. The CG-4A reinforced noses, still not universally installed, were instrumental in reducing landing casualties. By comparison, the British landed 621 gliders with 4,215 troops, 105 guns, and 1,026 vehicles.

In the end, despite executing all glider lifts and dangerous airdrop missions, the Arnhem assault failed, and so the ultimate objective of the enormous and costly operation was not secured. The Allied troops were cut off and the Germans blew the bridge. Only a quarter of the more than 10,000 men managed to extricate themselves. Of those remaining behind were half of the glider pilots—nearly 700 men. The British airborne forces and Glider Pilot Regiment never quite recovered from their attempt at the "bridge too far."

On General Arnold's insistence, considerable airlift, replenishment, and almost 1,000 men were dedicated over three months to recovering CG-4As in Holland. Despite this, only 281 of the 1,736 American gliders dispatched were recovered. Yet, the hard-used aircraft were shunned—hardly worth the effort.

Despite the Holland failure, airborne was mature and considered a vital element of a major offensive. Consequently, in October 1944 there was a reenergizing of glider production in the U.S. To ensure rapid and high-quantity deliveries, these were almost entirely more CG-4As instead of the newer, more advanced models that had been in development and were ready for high-rate production. Also, it was only in the last months of the war that C-46s and C-54s, more suitable for towing larger gliders, were available in numbers to support the mission.

Following *Market*, several airborne missions were planned but dropped. With liberation of French territory, it was possible to move squadrons to the continent. Gliders were occasionally used to insert engineers and airfield control parties into airfields recently evacuated by the Luftwaffe. When the Allies moved into Greece from Italy during mid

Despite initial intentions, almost all combat glider missions were performed in daylight and good weather. Glider tow just could not be done effectively otherwise without exhausting the pilots. Autotow and autopilot systems to hold the tow position, while effective in tests, were deployed operationally only in small numbers and not used in combat. (National Soaring Museum)

A squad of 277th Parachute Field Artillery, 101st Airborne, awaits the signal to board their glider for the trip into combat that is clearly going to involve flight over water (note the Mae West floatation vests). The event is probably the assault into Holland that involved a lot of waiting for weather to clear. The chalked aircraft markings were common for combat missions. (National Soaring Museum)

Urgent replenishment missions could include such hazardous cargo as these 60mm mortar shells stacked inside a CG-4A. A hit from anti-aircraft fire while carrying such freight turned the aircraft into a funeral pyre. Note the pilots are not wearing the parachutes demanded by regulations—these occasionally in short supply. (National Museum of the United States Air Force)

October 1944's Operation *Manna*, gliders and airdrop were essential in moving materiel into air bases being made ready for airlift. Twenty CG-4As were employed by British troops for the airlanding that seized an Athens airfield and return the exiled Greek government.

During the Battle of the Bulge, in December 1944, gliders flying out of French airfields permitted resupply of the encircled American forces at Bastogne as Operation *Repulse*, bringing in materiel that could not be airdropped and with much greater effectiveness. The most immediate need was for combat surgeons and corpsmen, and a single glider brought in a team of 13 such personnel on the morning of 26 December. Later that day 10 Wacos brought in 16 tons of badly needed medical supplies, fuel and artillery rounds, plus personnel. Although Allied ground forces broke through to Bastogne late on the 26th, the supply situation remained tenuous with paradrops only partially effective. Consequently, a 50-glider lift on the 27th carried in 53 tons of desperately needed fuel, shells, and medical supplies; cargo that could not be dropped. But, the mission was costly with 15 gliders and 17 tow planes downed.

Gliders were employed for casualty evacuation at the isolated bridgehead opposite Remagen on 22 March 1945. Two Wacos configured for litter carriage supported evacuation of critically wounded personnel. In a short time the pair of gliders were loaded and snatched out, landing 30 minutes later near a field hospital. This was a fraction of the time for ground transport over rough roads.

The Rhine River crossing into Germany at Wesel, 24 March 1945's Operation *Varsity*, was the single most concentrated airborne assault of the war, although still smaller in scope than the drawn-out *Market*. Two divisions of 17,000 men and gear were inserted into a small area during a single lift in just 2.5 hours. The force sortied from 12 bases in France and 11 in Britain. Two-thirds of the gliders were on double tow. This was possible because all of the U.S. gliders were launched from French fields with a 2.5-hour flight behind C-47s fitted with long-range fuel tanks in their cabins. With 2,875 jump and tow planes, 1,346 gliders, and 1,400 fighters, this 500-mile long triple stream of aircraft required approximately three hours to pass over a point on the ground.

Separate pathfinder drops were eliminated because the navigation was comparatively easy and the drop was so close to concentrated enemy forces. In another change for surprise effect, the assault followed, not preceded, the start of the ground offensive. The airborne mission was to seize high ground commanding the river crossing. The gliders also went in before the paratroops to increase the surprise factor. Another innovation was early insertion of combat control teams of glider pilots, radio operators, and gear to inform headquarters and approaching serials of the LZ situation.

Unlike *Market*, a training program was conducted in preparation for *Varsity*. With glider pilots held in reserve for another potential assault, there were again too few to fill all copilot requirements. Instead, 70 exceedingly unhappy power pilot graduates back in the States were given a quick CG-4A course and shipped to join 8th Air Force pilots converted locally. These men filled approximately half the copilot seats.

There were no glider obstacles erected at Wesel, but nearly 75 percent of the gliders suffering some damage from flak and ground fire, with about a dozen CG-4As shot down. Landing damage was still high at 50 percent due primarily to fast landings to avoid the enemy fire. One unanticipated factor was drifting smoke from shelling and bombing, plus smoke generated to screen the river crossing. This reduced visibility to about half a mile and made locating LZs difficult. However, approximately 90 percent of the gliders landed in or near their assigned LZ. The 883 CG-4As brought in 4,810 troops, 645 vehicles, 43 heavy guns, and 1,036 tons of cargo. Their role also included two successful *coup de main* assaults on bridges. Of the 1,770 American glider pilots landing in Germany, 35 were killed, 106 wounded, and 55 went missing. Although ten CG-4As were flown in configured as ambulances and with medical personnel, all casualties were evacuated overland.

Recovery teams sent just two days after the *Varsity* assault still found vandalism in addition to the landing damage, and only 148 of the Wacos were recovered. Even this took the efforts of 600 men. Horsas had to be disassembled and hauled out on lorries.

Despite several planned larger operations, *Varsity* proved to be the last glider employment in Europe. Germany capitulated little more than a month later.

An improved CG-4A, the Waco CG-15A, was optimized to match the combat conditions and demonstrated needs of the airborne forces. Many of the nagging problems of the earlier, hastily-developed, machine were corrected. Although available in sufficient numbers to join the final assaults of the war, the desire not to complicate the lifts with gliders towed at different airspeeds meant they remained behind and did not see combat. (The Peter M. Bowers Collection/The Museum of Flight)

A double tow is seen behind a B-17 tug. This is what the tow ship crew saw from their astrodome with gliders in trail. Dual tow was initially expected to play a big role in combat, but was employed only sparingly because of the strain on the C-47 engines. (National Soaring Museum)

At a formerly enemy airfield on the Continent, American troops launch tug-glider combinations for Operation *Varsity*, 24 March 1945. A C-47 moves up as a towline lies ready to be attached, already connected to the next CG-4A in its line. Beyond, Gooneybirds extend into the distance as do Wacos on both sides of the runway. (San Diego Air & Space Museum)

Rounding Out

Back in Burma, gliders continued to be used for resupply and to rapidly secure airfields. In the Pacific, gliders were also used to move equipment and supplies. As elsewhere, combat operations were planned but cancelled. Their only assault in the theater was also the final one in history, 23 June 1945. Six CG-4As and a single CG-13A were towed three hours from Lipa to support an unopposed landing at Camalaniugan Airfield on northern Luzon, the Philippines, with jeeps and guns. An unnecessary preparatory bombing raid left craters that claimed one of the CG-4As.

Army glider acquisitions for 1945 anticipated their use in the final act of the struggle with Japan, and many glider pilots expected transfers to the Pacific. Yet, planning for invasion of the Japanese islands, as it stood when that nation surrender on 15 August, had airborne forces only as reserve elements. The exceedingly long tows over vast ocean distances, and launch from the few already congested island airfields, would have been enormously difficult and hazardous. Only after airfields had been secured in the initial landings would glider operations in support of subsequent Japan assaults have been practical.

States-side engineers and procurement personnel worked long and hard to develop high-capacity aircraft like this XCG-13A in answer to demands from the field. This advanced glider had flaps, nose gear for a level deck facilitating onload and offload, large cabin for vehicles and towed artillery together, and this example models the autotow sensor arm on the nose plus wind-driven generator on the starboard side. To ensure high numbers of CG-4As for large-scale operations, assets like the CG-13A were not employed during the final airborne operations of the war. (National Archives)

A poor but rare image depicts a tandem tow by C-47s of CG-4As on double tow behind the rear Gooneybird. While such capabilities were demonstrated in flight test, they were not employed operationally. It would have permitted exceptionally heavy gliders to be taken up, but such was never necessary in combat. (National Archives)

11

Experimentation

The U.S. military began their glider programs with little in-house knowledge of such aircraft, how best to train glider pilots, or the most effective means of deploying gliders in combat. Hence, there were many missteps and wrong turns in developing the initial aircraft and tactics. Once experience was gained with the purpose-built military gliders, improvements to techniques or hardware were undertaken. This work required a whole stable of training and transport gliders conceived, developed, and subjected to experimental flight testing.

Improving the Breed

The 'bread and butter' flight test work was the shakedown of the new gliders, developing the best tow speeds and towline lengths, clearance with each tow plane type, and creating loading charts. Improvements based upon field experience were developed and evaluated. Modifications to the ubiquitous CG-4A, in particular, were thoroughly evaluated. However, efforts extended beyond these, to features ultimately never adopted. Perfecting multiple tow capability, with two or three gliders dragged aloft by a single tug, provided an important capability. Tow by fighters was especially pursued for those gliders that could be tugged at the higher speeds. Snatching a glider off the ground vice towing it off also had to be perfected and then demonstrated with most new glider types and likely tow planes. Apart from this 'routine' work, many experiments and long-term trials, especially in response to field experience or desires, were performed as well.

Paratroopers jumping from both the tow plane and gliders could concentrate infantry power more quickly. Although jumping from the glider was cumbersome and would require aircraft modifications to be entirely suitable, testing showed the concept to be practical. In September 1943, jumps from the tug and CG-4As on double tow were successfully demonstrated.[1] However, the range of such combinations with a full load of paratroopers was quite limited, and jumping from gliders negated their value in landing heavy ordnance and munitions. It went no further. There were instances in which paratroopers jumped from tow planes in combat, but not gliders.

Evaluations on 30 July 1944 at Laurinburg-Maxton by Mike Murphy examined CG-4A behavior in water landings. This was done more to learn the emergency ditching characteristics of the aircraft than to explore any amphibious capability. It was observed that the glider could float for as long as two hours, or indefinitely if buoys (empty barrels) were placed under at least the wings.[2]

Numerous potential tow planes were evaluated throughout the war. The most commonly employed of these were the C-46, C-47, C-54, C-60, A-25, B-17, B-24, B-25, PBY-5, P-38, and P-47. All were practical, and suitable instructions were published for all combinations of tow ship and glider. Double tow was pioneered by the Glider Branch in September 1943. An experiment with a C-54 towing three CG-4As simultaneously was successful.

The fighter tow capability was extensively evaluated, to include snatch. Bob Cardenas felt the P-38 was particularly suited to these activities because its tricycle gear and twin engines with counter-rotating propellers made the glider pilot's task during the launch phase particularly easy. The P-38 tow modifications included a line release socket installed at the trailing edge of each horizontal tail extension outboard of the vertical stabilizer. A sling between these two sockets joined the single towline. Cardenas was convinced the fighter's potency was not impaired by the tow modifications, and its ability to provide

This pair of images depict the experimental ditching of a CG-4A (42-62007) at Laurinburg-Maxton on 30 July 1943 to determine the water behavior of the glider. Touchdown and floatation were good, the glider eventually settling onto its wings were it would float indefinitely, especially if buoys such as the 50-gallon drums were placed under them. Swimmers are lashing the drums to the aircraft as the crew paddle away in the emergency life raft. (National Soaring Museum)

Tow by fighter was extensively tested as transports were in chronic short supply and also required for paratroop drops and aerial resupply. This Republic P-47D-5 Thunderbolt (42-8700) has been modified for glider tow with a towline attachment under the aft fuselage. A release cable is almost certainly strung to a handle in the cockpit, as well as an intercom cable. (National Soaring Museum)

ground attack support following glider combat landings could be of tremendous value. He went so far as to tow fully loaded gliders from Minneapolis to Florida, and flew the modified P-38 in mock combat with a standard Lightning. However, Fighter Command would not hear of fighters being diverted to tow tasks.

Towing Service

A long-term effort attempted to improve the natural trailing stability of gliders on tow to relieve pilot workload. Depending on conditions like lighting and turbulence, the task of holding position on the tow ship could be quite fatiguing, requiring a relief pilot to take over periodically. One means at remedy was to find the 'sweet spot' for towline attachment to the glider, with respect to the aircraft's center-of-gravity (c.g.), that minimized aircraft disturbance from gusts. Natural stability of towed targets had been achieved with two and three towline attach points, the lines meeting at a bridle ahead of the nose and then down to a single line to the tug. The glider required permanent nose-down trim so as to trail below the tug's slipstream.[3] The Army also observed that the British routinely towed the Horsa from dual points.

Experiments with two (bifurcated) and three (trifurcated) towline attach points were performed using the XTG-6, XCG-4A, and XCG-15A glider prototypes. The multiple lines met for a single line a dozen feet or so in front of the aircraft, without a bridle. The specially modified TG-6, called the XTG-33, and the CG-4A had a "dihedral tow bar;"[4] twin attach points above the cockpit (and c.g.) on outriggers like insect antennae. Trifurcated tow used these high points in addition to the normal nose fitting, but trials were also performed with lines attached to each wing, outboard of the fuselage, and the nose, this last of shorter length that placed the apex of the three lines above and a specific distance ahead of the glider on low tow.

In general, the outcome of these trials was favorable. Flight on tow was much more stable than on a single line attachment. This reduced glider pilot fatigue for long flights, but retrimming was still required as flight conditions changed. However, the results were not judged worth the effort of modifying a fleet of thousands of gliders flown only infrequently on long missions. It would also have complicated autopilot tow using angle-of-dangle (see later).

For service and maintenance, engines were some of the most time-consuming and parts-intensive elements of WWII aircraft. Often an airplane was airworthy apart

Seeking to improve glider stability on tow as a means of reducing pilot workload, various methods of attaching the towline were explored. This unknown unmanned glider, possibly a tow target or purpose-built article, displays a bifurcated line attachment high above the glider's center of gravity. (National Museum of the United States Air Force)

Another glider tow target, possibly used for multipoint line attachment tests, has come to a bad end. It appears to have a triangular cross-section and landing skid with a spring for impact load damping. (National Soaring Museum)

from one or more engines being unserviceable, and sometimes the location where the machine was grounded awaiting engine work was unsuitable to affect the repairs. With these observations, both the Army and Navy explored towing unserviceable, unpowered airplanes with another airplane.

This activity began with towing small single-engine aircraft like trainers and fighters. The propeller was removed and a towline attachment installed on the prop shaft, secured so as not to turn, and a release cable run to the cockpit. Trials were also performed snatching these aircraft. Released over the destination, the aircraft would be glided down to landing. The Army experiments were performed with at least a Vultee BT-13, All American Aviation's Stinson (XC-81D), Republic P-47, and North American P-51. The tests with fighters were performed at Muroc AAB in October 1944 under project MX-200.

The Naval Aircraft Factory also undertook such tests, including a 16 May 1943 flight using the Army design to haul a Curtiss XSBC-3 (9225) via their PBY-5A (08065) on a 300-foot, 5/8-inch nylon rope from Akron, Ohio, to Philadelphia. To compensate for the removed propeller, 80 pounds of lead shot bags were placed in the aircraft's nose. Preparation for the flight required just 1.5 hours. The NAF reportedly performed several more such tows at the request of nearby units with stranded aircraft.[5] In 1944, NACA used a P-61A (42-5572) to tow a waxed P-51, sans propeller, to altitude where it was released and piloted down to landing, collecting aerodynamic data for comparison with wind tunnel results.

During tests of shortened tow ropes in January 1943, the singular Naval Aircraft Factory XN5N-1 (1521) trainer towed an LNE-1 (31506) glider. The NAF normally used ¼-inch nylon line 300-450-foot long, but had previously operated with lines as short as 130 feet. This last had found "the glider to be subjected to more severe buffeting during takeoff, and in flight the glider pilot must maintain position more accurately." This could

Seeking to improve tow stability and reduce pilot effort in holding the proper tow position, multiple towline attachments to the glider were tested. This CG-4A has been rigged at CCAAF with a bifurcated towing arrangement, each of the two towline attachment points at the end of the structures projecting from the nose. Although successful, such arrangements were not adopted as standard. (National Soaring Museum)

A much-modified Taylorcraft TG-6 became the sole XTG-33 and was fitted with bifurcated tow attachment for a separate flight test project. The design required two line release mechanism. Although these were fairly reliable, the consequences of one line failing to release could be dramatic. (National Soaring Museum)

Towing a fighter or trainer with an ailing engine to a suitable repair facility could prove useful in combat theaters, so this capability was perfected. Among the earliest tests of the technique used this Stinson Reliant SR-10F NX2311 (UC-81D 43-7280, c/n 5810) shown being snatched at CCAAF by their B-23 tug. The towline was attached to a fitting that replaced the propeller and a cable strung to the cockpit for line release. (National Soaring Museum)

Army tests of fighter tows in October 1944 included this P-47B at Muroc AAB. Lack of engine power to operate the hydraulic pump, the gear was left down. Snatched by a B-17, the towline was later released and the aircraft glided in to a landing. (Air Force Flight Test Center)

accelerate fatigue, although at night the pilot had more chance to keep sight of the tug.[6] For the NAF project, the tow rope was progressively shortened from 50 to 25 feet. They found the pilot could hold tow position with no more effort than flying formation in a powered aircraft, although both the tug and glider pilots had to be experienced.[7] The glider encountered more buffeting on takeoff and had to hold position more accurately, demanding more skill from the pilot who was more rapidly fatigued.

Shortening towline length to a minimum on a solid link would greatly reduce glider pilot workload in holding a position, especially when flying in bad weather or for long cruise flight. That close to the tug, the glider was naturally above the greatest portion of the airplane's wake, which descended as downwash. The Navy developed this tow bar and acquired 35 CG-4As in 1944 to employ this device through conversion to what the Army would call CG-4Cs (soon G-4Cs). Nothing more of this activity has come to light.

Tow was investigated as a means of extending the range of aircraft operating over the vast distances in the Pacific theater, particularly fighters trying to stay with bombers throughout their mission. This included inflight snatch of the ersatz glider. The first such experiment was by the Navy in late 1941 under Barnaby's direction, with a Grumman F4F Wildcat fighter towed by a Grumman TBF torpedo bomber. On 10 May 1942, two F4Fs flown by Lieutenant Commander W.H. McClure and Lieutenant Commander R.W. Denbo, snagged lines trailing behind a Douglas BD-1 (A-20A Havoc). They were towed for an hour at 7,000 feet and 180 mph.[8] The Curtiss Electric propellers could be feathered after the engine stopped and then, using battery power, the pitch coarsened to begin turning for engine restart when desired.[9] This success was later repeated with a Boeing B-17C Flying Fortress bomber borrowed from Wright Field for an eight-hour tow.[10] Also during 1942, an F4F towed an Army Cessna UC-77 Airmaster from Philadelphia to the nation's capital.[11]

The Army's B-17C towed a Bell P-39 Airacobra for over 10 hours on 31 August 1942.[12] The P-39 pilot engaged a hook at the tip of his wing to the towline, stabilized with a drogue or streamer, and drew away until the hook set against a stopper at the end of the line. The hook was attached to a pendant that ran through spring clamps to an attachment on the spar near the root of the wing and outside the propeller arc. When the pendant released under towing load the aircraft was towed slightly to one side and needed only slight rudder trim to maintain position to one side of the tug. Once on tow, the fighter engine could be shutdown and the propellers feathered, later restarted via

The U.S. Navy also performed fighter tow tests, leveraging off experience gleaned from their short-lived glider program. Here a Curtiss XSBC-3 is under tow in May 1943 using a line fitting identical to the Army's (National Soaring Museum)

The fighter tow experiments led to the idea of an airplane snagging an aircraft in flight for towing assist, especially ailing B-29 bombers returning to an island base over vast Pacific distances. Shown under testing with two C-47s, the tow subject closes on the line stabilized by two sleeves, trailing from the tow ship. (National Soaring Museum)

windmilling. A cockpit control released the pendant and line. A second hookup could be made using a pendant on the opposite wing.

The fighter tow capability was never carried forward to field use. For the Navy, the tests served to collect data supporting their glider bomb program (Chapter 13). For the Army, the work gave encouragement to an even more ambitious application of towing a B-29 suffering engine trouble or other malady. The idea was to get a towline on the stricken aircraft in flight and assist it in reaching its destination—in this case Tinian island over the very long over-water route following a bombing strike on Japan. The tests in spring 1945 used two C-47s before being successfully executed with two B-29s. It proved practical and was deployed just as the first atomic bomb was dropped. The system was apparently set aside postwar.

The trailing Gooney Bird pilot has snagged the towline with his wingtip hook during tests in spring 1945. He could then shut down his engines and feather the propeller. The aircraft glided easily in trail to one side of the tug, requiring only slight rudder trim. (National Soaring Museum)

Douglas Aircraft XCG-17

The experience towing airplanes with inoperative engines, and the continuing perception that towed transports were an efficient means of moving freight, was inspiration for an engineless cargo airplane-turned-glider experiment. A potential was perceived in towing transport aircraft with their engines removed as a means of moving materiel. The immediate need was flying supplies over the Himalayas, or 'hump,' from India to China, after the Japanese cut the "Burma Road." Existing gliders would not be towed along the route because of the altitude, turbulence, and small additional payload. However, an unpowered transport could be towed at higher speeds and, on account of the relatively high wing loading, would better ride the mountain turbulence.

After a suggestion from Lieutenant Chet Decker of the Glider Branch, the Aircraft Laboratory performed a study in fall 1943 that suggested modification of a C-47 to become a glider held merit. Payload weight could be between 11,000-15,500 pounds and towing speed 150-170 mph. Part of the freight capacity could be 42 troops, or the 'glider' could carry such loads as 49 personnel, 2,200 gallons of fuel, or three jeeps, a 4x4 truck, and eight men. Fuel carried in the aircraft's tanks would be pumped out at the destination. With a 15,500-pounds useful load, the aircraft could transport 3.75 times a CG-4A's maximum load. The drag under tow at 150 mph was the same as a CG-4A at 7,500 pounds. Expected cost of developing and executing the modification was $80,000.00.

The notion was explored further through flight testing that included C-47 deadstick landings followed by takeoff under partial power while being towed by another C-47. The data indicated an unpowered C-47 could be towed and successfully landed. Alteration of a C-47 to the XCG-17 glider was approved.

The notion that one transport aircraft towing another would provide more efficient cargo delivery gave birth to the XCG-17 conversion of the Douglas C-47. Engines were replaced with ballast and domes, the interior reduced to essentials, and a tow fitting installed on the belly (visible in this image). The concept was developed and built by Glider Branch personnel at Clinton County AAF. (The Peter M. Bowers Collection/The Museum of Flight)

The first XCG-17 example was actually a mobilized DC-3, 41-18496. It was moved to modification in April 1944 and completed on 12 June. The personnel at Clinton County AAF performed all design and conversion work. This included aerodynamic shells and ballast fastened to the firewalls in place of the engines and nacelles. Initially, a bifurcated towline was considered, with attachment to the engine mounts.[13] Ultimately, a single line was attached to a fitting added under the fuselage just aft of the wing leading edge. Unnecessary interior gear was removed to lighten the empty weight and provide more cargo space. Eliminating the radio operator and navigator spaces, and removing bulkheads, expanded the loadable cabin length to 30.4 feet. The floor was beefed-up to handle heavier cargo. The XCG-17 was still very large, with a four-engine Douglas C-54 Skymaster the desired tow plane of several attempted (including a Consolidated B-24 Liberator), behind which the XCG-17 could be flown to 270-290 mph.

Flight trials took place at Wilmington beginning in June and running through the latter half of 1944, initially with Major D.O. Dodd at the glider's controls. Experiments were conducted towing the glider with two C-47s in tandem—a concept proven earlier with otherwise-unmodified C-47s. While practical, the middle C-47 was difficult to handle because of the influences of the glider as well as the lead airplane. The XCG-17 configuration demonstrated a glide ratio of 14:1, superior to all U.S. military transport gliders. The research and testing yielded a kit for converting a C-47 to CG-17 relatively quickly, or back again, in a matter of hours.

The XCG-17 was a fascinating experiment showing what creative thinking motivated by urgent need could produce from an Army made up of people drawn from all walks of life. However, the improving situation in the CBI theater made such measures unnecessary. It had also become clear that, despite initial assumptions, it was not efficient for one transport to tow another, either or both hauling freight.

The sole XCG-17 remained at CCAAF until November 1945 and was retired to the Tucson, Arizona, "bone yard" in August 1946. It was eventually bought and rebuilt as a commercial DC-3.

Another CG-17 was created in 1946 as an exercise for a field maintenance team in Manila and towed by C-54 on a long over-water mission. "The Nez Pèrcé" had faceted firewall domes, unlike the States-side example. This aircraft was restored to a powered flight configuration while the original XCG-17 was sent to the "bone yard" before being bought and also restored. (National Museum of the United States Air Force)

Towing the XCG-17 required a four-engine bomber or transport, although tests were performed with a tandem tow of two C-47s, as seen here. This rare flight configuration also used experimentally for other heavy gliders. Analysis and testing demonstrated that the idea was not efficient. (National Soaring Museum)

Some field trials were conducted with another converted C-47 (43-16229) nicknamed "The Nez Pèrcé," beginning in January 1946. This modification was apparently done as an exercise for a maintenance unit at Nichols Field, near Manila, the Philippine Islands. The nacelle domes were faceted instead of the perfectly hemispherical units fabricated at Wright Field. An auxiliary power unit taken from a B-24 allowed operation of a radio and other electrical equipment. Towing was by C-54, the first flight on 17 June. It was later towed to Tokyo via Okinawa carrying 5,000 pounds of cargo over the 1,750-1,800 miles, making it one of the longest over-water tows. Each of the two legs was 6.5 hours, the second coming close to a bad end when a storm was encountered. This aircraft was eventually restored to powered configuration.

Table 11-01	
XCG-17 Specifics	
span	95 ft
wing area	987 ft^2
empty weight	11,000 lbs
loaded weight	26,000 lbs
tow speed	255 mph, maximum 290 mph
capacity	49 passengers or rolling stock
cabin length x width x height	37.7 x 7.3 x 6.1 ft

Stopping on a Dime

During the initial American glider assault in Normandy, a glider carried Brigadier General Don Pratt, Assistant Divisional Commander of the 101st Airborne Division, was piloted by then Lieutenant Colonel Mike Murphy. Both men were the highest ranking personnel in their perspective roles participating via gliders. Some overzealous subalterns installed 1/4 inch steel plate under the cockpit seats and on the cargo floor. Murphy learned of this just before the flight, but chose to proceed. The results were predictable. The glider was grossly over-weight and out of trim. It was difficult to control during the 2.5-hour flight across the Channel. Despite the excessive weight, Murphy made a good landing in the assigned LZ with the deceleration chute deployed, but the glider touched down with a tailwind at 80 mph vice the normal 60 and slid 800 feet down hill on wet alfalfa with locked brakes and the glider on its nose skids. It impacted a hedgerow and tree at 72 mph. Even the Griswold nose on the glider was inadequate protection. Murphy's legs were broken, his copilot killed, and Pratt perished from a whiplash-induced broken neck. This completely avoidable outcome again cast the safety of gliders in doubt and, in typical Army fashion, prompted an order to find a means to rapidly slow gliders landing on wet vegetation and to more safely land the glider in small fields.

Apart from the existing deceleration parachute, others means explored included attaching rocket boosters firing forward. These had been in test as rocket-assisted takeoff to allow the glider to be towed off at higher gross weights or extend a dragged-in approach over obstacles. In that application, a Jet-Assisted Take-Off (JATO) rocket motor bottle[14] was attached under each wing adjacent to the strut fittings. Aimed forward for deceleration, these motors (including the Aerojet A8AS-1000) were attached under the wings adjacent to the strut fittings, beside the wheel struts, or on the nose. For the XCG-13, four rockets were attached under the nose. However, to avoid a violent ground loop and potential damage, the motors had to fire simultaneously, but no reliable method for guaranteeing this was found. Firing before touchdown risked a stall. These limitations, the prodigious clouds of smoke produced, the strict rocket storage requirements found

The wreckage of Lieutenant Colonel Mike Murphy D-Day CG-4A lies where it barreled into a hedgerow and tree in Normandy. It has been further pulled apart to extract bodies of those who died, and a trooper has cut away the fabric markings as a souvenir. This mishap, that took the life of a general officer, prompted additional testing of glider deceleration devices. (National Museum of the United States Air Force)

daunting for field units, and fire hazard made JATO impractical. A British #5 Mk. 1/n rocket was tried and had advantages over JATO, but the concept was not fielded.

After a general challenge was issued to glider personnel for deceleration schemes, two Laurinburg-Maxton pilots, Arthur Lee and Rovel S. Houghton came forward. Their idea was mounting spring-loaded plow blades just inboard of each wheel, deployed immediately after touchdown. Their design was taken up and expanded upon at Wright Field.[15] Small plow blades were employed, either released at the end of a nylon rope or rotating down from the bottom of the glider (as observed on the German Go 242), in both cases digging into the soil. Stops as short as 100 feet were demonstrated, but the plow tended to grab and throw up an impressive 'rooster tails' of dirt, and half the time broke away from the glider. A configuration called the Chase Plow progressed to tactical trials at Laurinburg-Maxton in June 1945 where it continued to be met with praise, substantially reducing landing distance with little to criticize.[16] One configuration was found suitable and kits were shipped to Europe. This was also specified as standard equipment for some late-war glider projects. The end of the war halted all such work.

Also tested was a "bazooka" fastened vertically to the side of the glider and firing a spike on a line straight into the ground beneath the aircraft. A line extended from the spike to the glider. Although described as a bazooka in the literature, photographs show a tube narrower and longer than that used with the weapon employed to fire a rocket-propelled antitank round. Images suggest the bazooka round rocket charge alone may have been adopted and electrically fired. Testing of this device was resurrected well after the war.

A potential solution to the glider landing deceleration problem was the solid-propellant rocket motors already being tested as means to get a heavy glider off more easily or extend a dragged-in landing approach. This CG-4A has two such JATO motors firing from the root of each wing strut for an assisted takeoff at CCAAF. Use as aft-firing propulsion units was never fielded. (National Soaring Museum)

Experiments were performed employing the motors as forward-firing "retrorockets" to slow a cargo glider on landing. Here a rocket at the top of each wing strut fires forward as a CG-15A touches down. Achieving symmetrical firing was important to avoid loss of directional control and a ground loop, but was not always successful. (National Soaring Museum)

In this pair of photos, the retrorockets are on a XCG-4A. The enormous smoke cloud (not fully developed in this photo) was characteristic of the JATO motors commonly used. British rockets were also included in the trials. (top: National Soaring Museum, bottom: The Peter M. Bowers Collection/The Museum of Flight)

Other deceleration devices attempted included plow blades rotating down from beneath the fuselage, from behind each main wheel, or detaching on an elastic nylon line.

This pair of images shows the results of landing a CG-15A and CG-4A with a centerline plow blade at CCAAF. Each has been abruptly stopped in less than 100 feet by a plow blade that cut a distinct furrow. (top: National Museum of the United States Air Force, bottom: National Soaring Museum)

Another experimental deceleration device was this spike propelled from the tube attached to the fuselage. Although described in literature as a "bazooka," this arrangement appears to have a small, electrically fire charge at the top of the spike. A steel cable secured the spike to the nylon line held by frangible strings beneath the fuselage. (National Soaring Museum)

Seeking Automation

Except for very brief periods, glider tow and free flight through clouds, and other "blind flying" conditions, was impractical. Only a few blind flying instruments could be practically introduced to the glider that lacked engine-driven electrical and vacuum systems. Usually the pilots simply tried to keep the vertical and horizontal angle of the visible portion of the tow rope extending away from the glider at what appeared to be normal. Additionally, extended flights on tow, even in smooth air, could be very fatiguing for the glider pilots as they had to make constant control adjustments. These considerations were motivation to investigate introducing an autopilot into the gliders in what became a long and complex effort.

The Americans observed the Tow Cable Angle Indicator instrument in the Hotspur and Horsa displaying what the British euphemistically called the "angle-of-dangle". This indicated the cable angle relative to a nominal value for correct tow position, permitting the pilot to make corrections if the vertical and horizontal pointers indicated a deviation. Experimenting with their own version of this instrument under MX-296, the mechanical input to what the Americans called the Tow Rope Position Indicator was provided by a "feeler" rod protruding from the glider's nose and resting on the towline rope a few feet out from the attach point. The pilot worked to keep vertical and horizontal bars centered in the instrument. This, in combination with an attitude gyro (artificial horizon), provided suction via a venturi mounted on one side of the nose or above the cockpit, allowed a pilot to hold the proper tow position on the tug and a wings-level attitude. All necessary power was from the battery, and so operating time was limited.

The equipment developed was inadequate for sustained instrument flight as vertigo and pilot fatigue problems persisted, but worked well enough for intermittent flying into clouds. By mid-1943 it was widely evaluated by operational units and plans were afoot to deploy it to the field. This did not occur.

Seeking an autotow system that would allow hands-off flying, the Glider Branch worked with a modified airplane A-3A Automatic Pilot during June 1943. Installed in CG-4A 42-52852, it required a wind-driven hydraulic and vacuum pumps. The gains for the bank and climb gyros had to be manually adjusted for the glider to hold proper tow position, especially during turns. In free-flight the aircraft was also flown with these two knobs. In both conditions, rudder control was not required and so this element of the system was considered for removal.[17]

For follow-up tests, it seemed that for truly automatic control employing the tow rope angle changes during tow to "thumb" the control gains was possible. This employed gimbals and the hydraulic actuators moving the flight control cables, powered by the ram air-driven pump. The system sought to maintain the "dangle" at the proper angle by driving any error that developed to zero by suitable automatic control input via servos.[18] Tests were conducted on a CG-4A, CG-13A (43-43927), and a CG-15A. The CG-4A work bore fruit in September 1944 using a further modified airplane A-3 autopilot, called the D-1 autopilot, from the Jack & Heintz Company of Cleveland, Ohio (a subsidiary of General Electric). It worked reasonably well, as verified that month during a 110-minute flight from Cleveland to CCAAF in moderate turbulence. Flight under actual instrument conditions was also conducted. This still required the pilot to make manual trim adjustment as flight conditions changed. However, the system was ultimately deemed operationally unsuitable, principally because it could not perform cross-control

The input rod was lightly attached to the tow rope as seen in this photo of a CG-4A (45-14663) on tow. In this case of the glider fitted with the "Griswold nose," the position feed into the hydraulic servos must have been mechanically simpler. The input fed the glider angle-of-dangle, autotow, and autopilot systems developed during the war. Note the Corey skid under the nose and the deceleration parachute release frame at the aft end of the glider. (National Soaring Museum)

The angle-of-dangle system is seen in a CG-4A installation. The cables from the tow rope sensor are seen entering the box as is the vacuum line to the artificial horizon. Many pilots were exposed to this system and judged it quite suitable, but it did not become standard kit. (National Soaring Museum)

The original "angle-of-dangle" input rod is shown on a CG-4A. The rod would be attached to the tow rope via the clips at the end. Damaging movement of the rod on line release was prevented by the springs at the base. (National Soaring Museum)

This image of the CG-15A "angle-of-dangle" system shows the Tow Rope Position Indicator, an attitude gyro, and trim selectors—these last to center the rope crosshairs to the pilot's satisfactory tow position. The device, in combination with the artificial horizon and battery power, permitted some measure of tow in instrument conditions. (National Soaring Museum)

An airplane A-3 autopilot was adopted to an autotow application for the American cargo gliders. The cockpit installation is shown for the CG-4A, the three hydraulic cylinders for the three-axis control visible just under the windscreen on the starboard side. This system required the pilot to adjust the roll and pitch gyros with the dials provided, and so was not fully automatic until the D-1 version was devised and tested. (National Museum of the United States Air Force)

The "feeler" that would rest on the tow rope is seen protruding from the nose of a CG-15A. This rod provided the "angle-of-dangle" reading to the autotow Tow Rope Position Indicator or the error signal to the developmental autotow system. This glider is fitted with a trio of faired nose skids that were common after the war on these gliders. (National Archives)

inputs, such as roll with opposite yaw. Yet, the British conducted similar trials in 1946 with the D-1 installed aboard a Horsa and judged the results quite satisfactory.

Ultimately, the cost of introducing any such equipment in the manned glider fleet appeared impractical given the late stage of the war and how the CG-4As were being employed as 'expendable materiel' in daylight operations. It seemed, even in 1944, few in command saw much future for the military transport glider.

Bellows Flaps

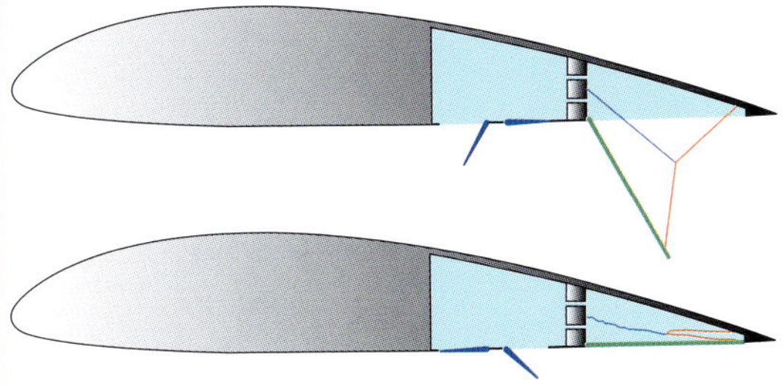

This drawing depicts a section view of a wing with the bellows flaps that would allow flaps on gliders lacking motive power. In the top section the forward-opening scoop permits passing air to pressurize the bellows and extend the flap, while in the bottom view shutting the forward and opening the aft facing scoop creates an internal low pressure to suck the flap closed. The design was to be installed on a modified XTG-3 for flight testing, but is unclear if this was accomplished. (Author)

One of the three XTG-3s was designated to receive experimental bellow flaps under project MX-294. Initiated in January 1943, it was to permit testing with the device that might find application on combat gliders. The increasing wing loading of cargo gliders suggested the advantage of adding flaps to keep approach and landing speeds low. Being unpowered, the gliders lacked hydraulics and had very limited battery power for extending the flaps, and a mechanical system would add undesirable weight. Using the energy in the passing airflow to extend the flaps appeared practical.

The idea was the pilot need only to open a small forward-facing scoop under each wing to admit the air rushing past. This would flow into a cavity above the flap and inflate a bag of gas-impervious doped fabric that would expand to push the hinged split flap down and hold it against the airstream. The design could have hinged panels or fabric above and at the aft end of the flaps to prevent over-extension, yet fold up when the flap stowed. Otherwise, the balloon would belly out and reduce the flap deflection unless stiffener strips or retraining line were attached internally. The pilot needed only to open an aft-facing scoop behind which the passing air flow would create a low pressure in the flap cavity to suck the surface back up. The degree of scoop opening controlled the rate of deflection, although degree of deflection was apparently limited to full.

The concept and a model had been offered to the Air Corp in 1933 by the L.P.R. Corporation, but had languished with no action. It came to Materiel Division's attention during 1941-1942 that the British were experimenting with similar mechanisms. Tests with the 1933 model were conducted earlier in 1942, under the general cargo glider project MX-114, in a wind tunnel and mounted on a jeep speeding down the highway. Some deficiencies were identified, so a new model was tested in August with superior results. Consequently, full-scale tests were sought.

By 7 December 1942 the Aircraft Laboratory had a design for the XTG-3 bellows flaps 75 percent complete. It was felt the concept might also be applied to airbrakes on powered aircraft.[19] The balloon was discarded for a simple plenum pressurized by the airflow and made up of the aircraft structure and gas-impervious fabric panels restrained by a cord (see drawing). The proposed flaps were 10 feet long and of 1 foot chord with a maximum 75 percent deflection. A lever in the front and rear cockpits operated the scoops of which various sizes were to be tested. Although the installation was authorized on 24 April 1943 with an expected completion date of 1 June, no record was located indicating that it was accomplished and flown.[20]

Prone Flying (MX-324, MX-334, CG-4A, XTG-33)

The XP-79 project had its conception in a 15 September 1942 unsolicited proposal from Northrop Aircraft Incorporated in response to USAAF interest in high-speed interceptors. John A. "Jack" Northrop, on a life's quest to realize all-wing aircraft, envisioned a tailless rocket plane with a novel prone pilot position that research suggested would permit the pilot to tolerate greater maneuvering g-forces than a seated pilot. It also allowed for smaller aircraft frontal and side area to reduce drag and vulnerability to enemy gunners. The earliest idea was for the Model 14 Jet-Driven Interceptor to be an expendable point-defense fighter. Once the rocket and kinetic energy had been expended and the mission completed, explosives would blow the ship apart and the pilot recovered via parachute.

The primary XP-79s fighter development project was initiated on 12 January 1943. At a loaded weight of 11,400 pounds, the aircraft was to be powered by the Aerojet XCALR-2000A 2,000-pounds force (lbf) motor employing two primary combustion chambers and a pair of auxiliary chambers. These consumed a total 8,400 pounds of propellant for 35.5-minutes endurance. The aircraft was expected to be assisted aloft with two to six JATO rockets units, dropped after takeoff, providing near-zero takeoff distance. The formal NS-14 specification of 1 April 1943 dropped the expendable fighter notion for a proper aircraft with four retractable landing skids. In this case takeoff would have used a droppable trolley or other means.

The "flying wing" concept was so radical that Materiel Division decided three mockups would be created for wind tunnel and flight testing, collecting data to reduce technical risk, under project MX-334.[21] A powered research version of the mockup would be MX-324 while the parent program was MX-365. Northrop was so saturated with work that the Engineering Division at Wright Field assumed responsibility for much of the analysis and drawing preparation. This ran several weeks late and the project fell behind schedule. Under a contract that eventually totaled $149,542.50, Northrop constructed these Model N-12 mockups/aircraft beginning in November 1942. They were fabricated primarily of plywood over a steel tube centersection frame. It was found the wing cross-section alone was inadequate to contain the prone pilot in a configuration permitting suitable operation of the aircraft, so an extended canopy had to be added and the centersection thickened 20 percent. Like the conceptual XP-79, the glider would use skids with rubber disk shock absorbers for undercarriage. Testing of the MX-334s would include glides and flights propelled by the rocket motor.[22]

A CG-4A was modified in early 1943 for trials with the pilot lying face down. This would provide experienc in designing the necessary controls, pilot couch and restraints, and provide lessons on how best to optimize the configuration for pilot functioning in

A TG-6 three-place training glider was modified into the XTG-33 accommodating a prone pilot in an extended nose while the rearmost pilot station was retained for safety pilot.

This featured a pilot couch, revised controls, and wide starboard side hatch allowing relatively easy emergency egress. The pilot (Bernie Driscoll) appears to have chin support, a yoke control with trim wheel below, and instruments placed below his longitudinal axis for easier reading. (top: National Museum of the United States Air Force, bottom: National Soaring Museum)

such a position. The CG-4A starboard pilot station was altered to accommodate a prone position couch and revised controls while a safety pilot occupied the unmodified port station.[23] The flying with the modified Waco began in late 1943 at Clinton County, and prospective MX-334 pilots were given introductory sorties in the aircraft. However, the control forces, particularly aileron, were too great and the so the aircraft was misrepresentative. Instead, a TG-6 was modified by Taylorcraft in 1944 for trials of the prone piloting position to become the odd-ball XTG-33.[24] The nose and controls were altered to allow the pilot to fly in the prone position while the aft-most control station was retained for a safety pilot. This was tested in summer 1944 at CCAAF and served as a transitional trainer for the XP-79.

The MX-334 possessed 21.8° wing sweep and basic flying wing controls. Elevons operated symmetrically with fore-aft motion of the pilot's control bar to produce pitch, and asymmetrically with differential motion of the bar for roll. Further inboard, combination rudders/speedbrakes ("brudders") split to rotate both above and below the wing for directional (yaw) control. Force to deploy the brudders was provided by bellows fed by ram air from intakes under the wing root leading edges. This directional control was originally to be manipulated via "bobsled steering motion" of the control bar. However, to permit single-hand control of the bar, ultimately the brudders were modulated by pilot pedals for rudders and a handle for brakes. A means of supporting and counterbalancing the pilot's head under g-loading had to be devised, but the pilots requested a simple chin rest. Completed initially as gliders while awaiting the rocket motors, the MX-334s were fitted only with a radio (although frequently nonfunctional).

The first glider was completed in May 1943 and subjected to ground loads and vibration tests. Northrop was then preparing to begin glider tests when the government directed they send the aircraft to NACA Langley for full-scale wind tunnel trials that summer. At Langley, roll authority near stall was found deficient. Fixed leading edge slats were added near the wingtips to improve elevon roll effectiveness as stall was approached. Much to Mr. Northrop's frustration, analysis and tunnel testing made clear the aircraft required a vertical surface for minimal directional stability. The offending appendage was added without rudder, held erect with guy wires. A final change was the addition of small wheels to the landing skids. The bifurcated towline attached to the skids.

The MX-334 gliders began flight testing from Muroc, within reach of the Northrop's Hawthorne plant. Commencing with glider No. 2, likely without the vertical stabilizer, it was initially towed by a Cadillac automobile on 27 August 1943, with Harry Crosby (contract test pilot) at the glider controls. Attempting low-speed hops off the surface, the aircraft porpoised badly on its undercarriage. After removing the skid wheels, another attempt at up to 35 mph found the porpoising only reduced and the skids' steel rub strips wearing rapidly. There may have been a third "flight" on the 28th before taking the glider back to Hawthorne. There a quadracycle arrangement of four wheels were attached to the skids and the bifurcated towline attachments moved to the wing leading edge, both sides, outboard of the pilot.

Table 11-02

Northrop Aircraft MX-324/334 Specifics

span	32.0 ft
wing area	244 ft^2
length	14.3 ft
height	7.0 ft
maximum speed (demonstrated)	350 mph
stall speed	75-80 mph
gross weight (MX-334)	approximately 2,600-2800 lbs
gross weight (MX-324)	3,300-4,252 lbs (unfueled to fueled)

Testing resumed at Muroc on 14 September with good results at up to 55 mph. Crosby then attempted to take off. The glider lifted at 60-65 mph but began severe pitch oscillations that ended with ground impact and bounce back into the air. The glider yawed about 45 degrees and the towline slipped on the bridle after which the aircraft was pulled back to the ground in a sideslip to suffer grave damage.

Feeling the aircraft was too near stall with auto-tow, the team moved to aero-tow behind a Lockheed P-38 Lightning fighter previously modified for glider tow. Testing began 30 September with ground tows on a 300-foot towline and John Meyers in glider No. 3. The vertical stabilizer was installed for more ground runs on 2 October to 70 mph and with small hops off the lakebed. These showed good results, so a flight followed that day with tow to 170 mph and release at 6,300 feet. Only a problem with the towline release had to be corrected and additional flight instruments were added subsequently. Further flights were suspended when the two test pilots became unavailable. In the meantime, a droppable quadracycle dolly was devised for attachment to the skids to replace the high-drag wheels. (In subsequent flights with the dolly it was not dropped.)

The flying continued with a 9 November sortie by Crosby. The following day, upon release at 13,000 feet, he may have flown through the wake of the Lightning. The glider nosed over into a dive that steepened beyond the vertical, experienced several tumbling gyrations, and ended in an inverted spin at 9,500 feet. Flow from the slats blanked the elevons entirely and negated roll authority. With no response to the controls, Crosby chose to abandon the glider. The bottom escape hatch (now overhead) needed some persuasion to release. The pilot then scrambled out, sat for a few seconds on the leading edge, and then slid off to open his parachute. The aircraft circled him, descending at the same rate and impacted just 150 feet from where he alighted. Only the undercarriage could be salvaged for ship No. 1. It was subsequently determined that the top escape hatch probably departed the aircraft at the point of towline release and this was later shown to generate a strong nose-down moment.

Aircraft No. 1 was returned from Virginia and prepared to take up the test flying. The slats were removed and the skids modified to take the dolly. The 2,000-lbf thrust rocket motor development was running exceptionally long. However, a reduced system with just one 200-lbf XCALR-200A auxiliary thrust chamber was fitted. The installation of propellant cells, pressurization tanks, and electrical gear added 427 pounds to the glider's weight. This brought typical flight weight (unfueled) to 3,495-3,600 pounds based on ballast used to establish the desired c.g. location. All flights were to be initially unpowered, continuing to examine stability and control of the craft under MX-324.

Flights of glider No. 1 began on 30 November. Crosby chose to keep the wheel dolly attached. This was repeated on 2 December but the glider bounced badly on landing with the dolly and the skids were partially destroyed. The MX-324 escaped harm and so aircraft No. 3's original gear was substituted. However, the arrival of the rainy season flooded Muroc's lakebed and the Lightning tow ship required maintenance attention, so a pause again beset the project.

The hiatus permitted time to look again at the undercarriage and the decision was made to replace the skids and wheels with fixed oleo struts and wheels enclosed in fairings. The main wheels were fitted with brakes and the shock struts were held in a fully compressed state to reduce drag until just before landing when they were unlocked and extended. The nose gear was offset 1.2 feet to port so it could mount to stout structure. The fairings must also have enhanced the glider's directional stability. A tank was installed at this point or later for water ballast that could be dumped prior to landing. Radio telemetry of data from onboard the aircraft was also introduced—among the first uses of this technology.

The testing resumed in April 1944 at Roach Lake, on the California-Nevada border, with ground runs behind a car to check out the new undercarriage. The next glide flight was on the 19th with Crosby in ship 3, and seven more followed through 19 May, the last three from Harpers Lake, near Barstow, California. The aircraft typically required full back elevator to leave the ground and climb above the tow's wake. Flying speeds were from stall at 75-80 mph to 305 mph in dives and with up to 6.1-g pull-ups performed. Most free-flights lasted 5-8 minutes of busy test maneuvers and data recording. Release was from as high as 16,500 feet after about 15 minutes tow, the pilot breathing oxygen from a bottle via a tube in held between his teeth. Landings were typically at 100 mph. Three different fin sizes were also flight tested, of 5, 10 and 15 square feet. The larger was the standard as only it provided suitable directional stability. The pilot couch was also adjusted to reduce pilot fatigue. It was observed that, lying in the cockpit, the backpack parachute weighed uncomfortably on the pilot. Dust kicked up by the tug would collect on the glider windscreen, obscuring the pilot view. This was minimized by oiling a takeoff strip on the lakebed.

Resting on the wheeled skids, this MX-334 has a full-size 15 square foot tail and pilot in cockpit. The venturi under the cockpit surely provided suction to vacuum gyro instruments. The vertical surface under the wingtip is presumably a skid to protect the wing should it drag during takeoff or landing. (Gerald Balzer Collection)

One of the MX-334 gliders rests on the lakebed surface between flights. Wheels have been attached to the landing skids and a radio aerial protrudes from atop the vehicle. This example is fitted with the small tail of 5 square feet, clearly a plywood sheet held erect with wires. (Gerald Balzer Collection)

The 14th flight on 19 May was at aft c.g. Glider No. 2 easily left the ground but after release again experienced what appeared to be an incipient inverted spin. Although recovering, landing was very difficult and the controls largely ineffectual. The glider bounded violently several times before the nose gear collapsed. The glider was severely damaged and Crosby suffered two teeth knocked out on the chin support, his shoulder harness having slipped off earlier during the inverted event. There were clearly serious stability and handling issues with MX-324.

The testing had been instructive in addition to being eventful. Plans to restore No. 2 in a configuration to take the large engine were shelved because of workload on higher priority projects. Additionally, studies suggested making the modifications required to match the configuration of the XP-79 as it had developed and to install the entire propulsion system in the glider would be prohibitive. Northrop lacked excess resources to undertake the effort in any case. Yet, there was value in continuing the glider program, so ship 2 was fitted with the 200-lbf rocket motor and prepared to resume the testing.

The XCALR-200A was secured with the pilot's legs straddling the unit. It was not throttleable and had just five-minutes burn time. The motor mixed two liquid propellants, monoethylaniline ("aniline") and red fuming nitric acid, that combust spontaneously. The propellants were separated by the cockpit, one component in each wing root. Accidental mixing of these corrosive fuels or contact with the pilot had to be prevented at all costs, so neoprene shields separated the center section from the tanks. The pilot chin support had also been replaced with a V-support that supported the head in all maneuvers.

The engine was first run installed at Harpers Lake on 22 June 1944 and the following day the aircraft was allowed to roll on the lakebed under this thrust and Crosby's control. The MX-324 No. 2 "Rocket Wing" still had to be towed aloft and released for airborne firing of the motor. This was first to be performed on 1 July with Alex Papana at the controls. However, the pilot mistakenly pulled the lever jettisoning the top and bottom hatches instead of the towline release. Consequently, upon release, the glider became sharply nose-heavy and it required considerable pilot skill to get back on the

Seen from below is the XCALR-200A rocket motor installed in a MX-324 along with the two fuel cells. The pilot couch is visible through the bottom escape hatch opening, the pilot's legs to extend back on either side of the engine's centerline components. This was just one element of the long-delayed ultimate motor and so provided such meager thrust that it only permitted a few minutes of level flight at modest airspeed. (Gerald Balzer Collection)

Harry Crosby poses with one of the MX-324s, standing with his legs out the lower hatch and his torso out the upper hatch. This example of the glider had proper undercarriage and a very low thrust rocket engine. By this time the work had been reduced to a research project and the flying-wing configuration continued to offer dangerous surprises. (Gerald Balzer Collection)

The MX-324 performed several powered flights during July 1944. By this point the rocket propulsion had been abandoned and the XP-79 had become turbojet-powered, so the gliders were shelved. Soon after the war the XP-79B flew one flight that ended in a crash that took Crosby's life.

(National Museum of the United States Air Force)

ground safely. The hatches were recovered, repaired, and reinstalled. This appeared to demonstrate dramatically that loss of one or both hatches likely precipitated the 9 November 1943 mishap.

Finally, the first MX-324 powered flight occurred on 5 July 1944 after Crosby was towed by the P-38 to 15,000 feet. After a series of test maneuvers, Crosby started the engine at 150 mph, becoming America's first rocket plane. The meager thrust only slowed the rate of descent during its brief burn. The motor was operated for most of the next 13 flights though 27 July at both Harpers and Muroc lakes, either Crosby or Papana piloting. Under power, the aircraft could fly level at 120-130 mph. The glider work was concluded at the end of the month.

Despite progress with the gliders, with $403,187.00 expended and approximately 11 flight hour accumulated in 29 sorties, the XP-79 rocket propulsion was abandoned for twin turbojets and retractable undercarriage, the aircraft redesignated XP-79B. The project had lost its military urgency and was continued only for engineering studies. Its one flight, soon after the war, ended in a crash that took Harry Crosby's life and the project was cancelled. In subsequent decades the prone flying position remained tantalizingly attractive but problematic. It is a good position, but not necessarily for flying aircraft.

Man-Proven (MX-543, Northrop JB-1)

As the Americans came up to speed for the total-war effort, they explored almost all weapon concepts. The USAAF followed-up on Navy "aerial torpedo" work with their own missile projects. The potential of combining the new jet engine technology with an autonomous flying bomb was attractive. The earliest engines appeared too large for this application. Subsequently, the Air Forces approached Northrop for an airframe concept while seeking a suitable powerplant from General Electric (GE). Northrop could move quickly as they employed the same wing design as the MX-324/334, albeit scaled down, and GE built on their cutting-edge turbosuperchargers. Initially designated MX-543 and secret, this was soon named the JB-1. The USAAF ordered two prototypes in September 1944 and Don Smith served as project engineer.[25]

Northrop again applied its flying wing ambitions to the JB-1, with a modestly swept wing, vertical tail, and center body to house two engines. An inlet fed the engines that exhausted at the wing trailing edge. Outboard of the center body was a fairing within each wing root to enclose one 2,000 pound bomb. Flight controls appear to have consisted of only elevons and rudder. The missile was to be launched from a rocket-propelled sled riding on a 400-foot track. The two engines were to be derived from GE Type B-31 turbosuperchargers, used with bomber engines. Each was to be connected to a combustion chamber and nozzle. This became the Type B1 turbojet engine. Producing 200 lbf each, a 200-mile range at 427 mph and 5,000 feet altitude was expected.[26] The pre-programmed guidance system was to be provided by the Hammond Instrument Company of Chicago, Illinois.

To prove-out the aerodynamics and flight controls of the JB-1, Northrop assembled the first prototype as an unpowered version of the missiles with three wheels and an enclosed pilot station within the center body (pilot seated upright). This JB-1A glider would be towed to altitude and released for flight test maneuvering with data telemetered to the ground.[27] The airframe was build of aluminum outer wing panels with magnesium tips, but the center section used magnesium joined by Northrop's heliarc

Another Northrop flying wing aircraft (albeit with vertical tail) was the JB–1A missile tested as a glider. This JB-1a airframe with open cockpit and headrest sits on the Muroc lakebed awaiting a test flight during late summer 1945, the large antenna associated with a telemetry system while the fittings at the nose of the wing root fairings were for a bifurcated tow rope. Initial flight testing revealed severe buffeting from the open-cockpit design of the JB-1A, so an enclosed cockpit was created with taller canopy and turtledeck fairing back to the trailing edge of the aircraft. (top: National Archives, bottom: Gerald Balzer Collection)

The JB-1 sits posed for launch at Eglin Field, Florida, on 7 December 1944. Unlike the glider, the center body houses two small turbojet engines, inlet and exhausts, while fuel is contained in the outer wing panels. The one and only flight was unsuccessful. (National Archives)

Table 11-03

Northrop Aircraft MX-543 glider Specifics

span	28.3 ft
wing area	155 ft^2
length	10.5 ft
height	4.5 ft
maximum speed (missile)	427 mph (5,000 ft altitude)
gross weight (missile)	7,080 lbs

welding technique. Like the MX-324/334, the glider was given no markings or serial number—the JB-1 being a "missile."

Harry Crosby took the tiny glider up behind a P-38 at Muroc for the first time on 27 August 1944.[28] Stability and control data could be obtained as the pilot performed maneuvers during brief free flight. The aircraft initially had just a windscreen ahead of the pilot opening with a headrest on a shallow fairing behind. However, the buffeting from turbulated air behind the windscreen was so severe that flight control was dangerously impaired. Consequently, an enclosed canopy was added with turtle deck fairing back to the tail.[29] The Hammond guidance system may also have been tested aboard the glider, no earlier than October 1944.[30] The flying qualities were apparently good enough that the pilot also performed slow rolls.[31] Crosby found the glider difficult to land because of the powerful ground effect cushion of air under the wings close to the surface. The aircraft would floated 8-10 feet above the lakebed until airspeed bled off to the point of stall and it plopped jarringly onto the surface. The only alternative was to fly it onto the ground at high speed and hold it there during deceleration.

The glider flights went well, but first flight of the powered JB-1 on 7 December 1944 at Eglin Field was a failure. The engines were only producing about half the expected thrust so the missile had to be flown at reduced weight. Upon launch one engine was already failing. At nine degrees nose-up attitude and elevons set nine degrees trailing edge up, the JB-1 climbed steeply and stalled, then crashed. A second JB-1 had been built and the contract had been extended to 11 production articles. Despite this, the USAAF chose to cancel the program and have Northrop introduce a pulsejet engine in the redesigned JB-10.

Wet Kite (Cornelius XFG-1)

The vast distances in the CBI and Pacific theaters made support missions for offensives against Japanese forces exceedingly challenging for the U.S. during the first two years of the war. This would be especially true for the new B-29 bomber units about to take to the field, but operating at the limits of their range for roundtrip bombing missions until bases closer to Japan's home islands were captured. Thoughts on how to improve the situation led to the idea of an unmanned fuel glider towed behind a transport or bomber. Fuel would be transferred from the glider through a "tow hose" via a wind-driven pump. Once the fuel was drained the glider would be released and discarded.

The USAAF conducted a feasibility study of the concept as MX-151 and decided it had merit.[32] A 4 October 1943, $273,420.00 Army cost-plus-fixed-fee contract for two expendable fuel gliders and static article was then placed with The Cornelius Aircraft Corporation of Dayton, Ohio, under project MX-416.[33] Cornelius was to deliver a static test article and the first of two aircraft in March 1944.

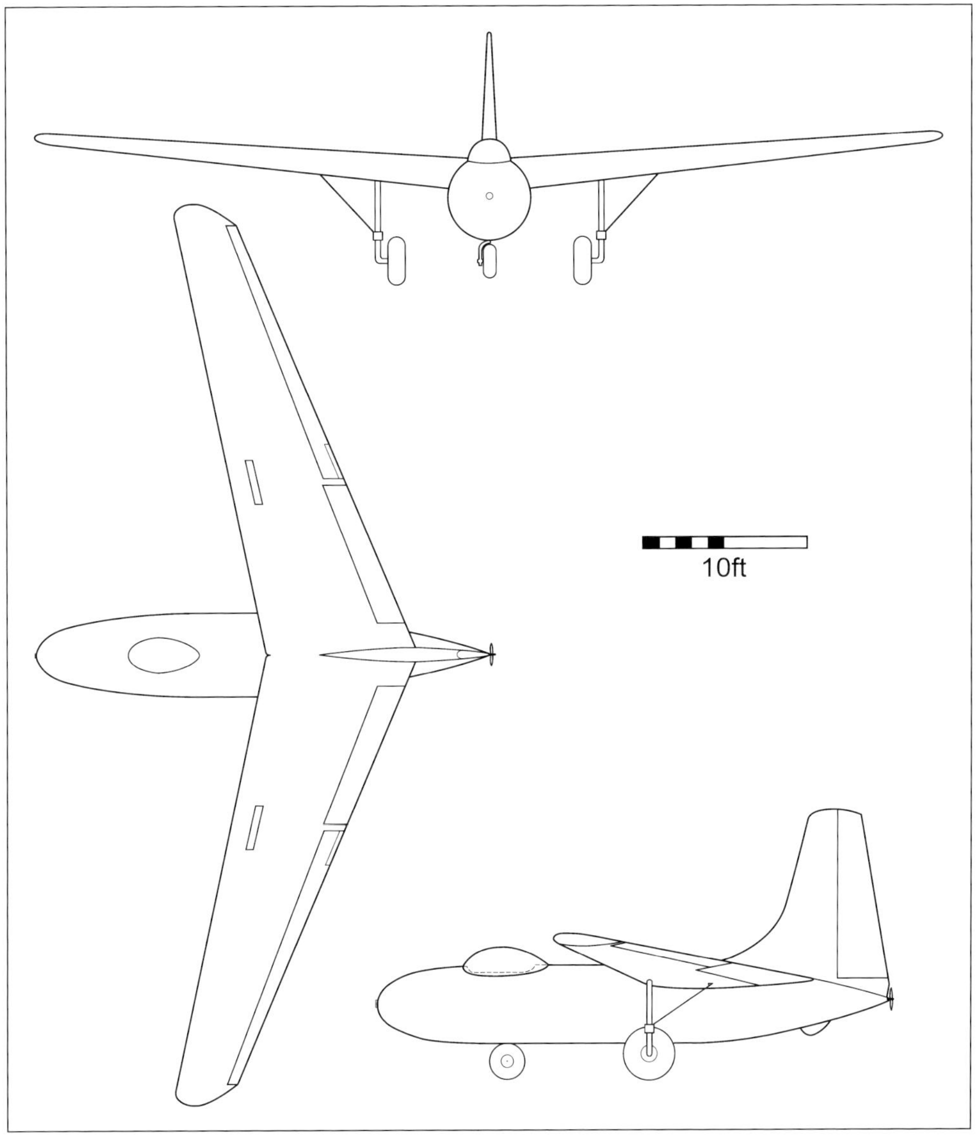

This three-view drawing of the FG-1 unmanned towed fuel glider reveals differences from the two manned flight test articles that were assembled and flown. The bubble fairing in the area where a cockpit would lay may indicate intention for it to be optionally manned for the purpose of ferrying the aircraft to its launch point or for flight test after assembly. Note the propeller for a wind-driven generator and/or fuel pump at the aft and of the fuselage. (Author)

The company's leader, George W. Cornelius, was a longtime promoter of aircraft innovations. The XFG-1 was a tailless aircraft that was essentially the same as their cancelled XBG-3 bomb glider (Chapter 13). It was intended to supply 764 gallons (4,584 pounds) of fuel from two tanks as part of the 8,000-pound all-up weight. The undercarriage would serve only for takeoff, after which it was to be jettisoned. The wing had 15° forward sweep at quarter chord and dihedral could be set between 2 and 8 degrees prior to flight. The design was expected to be naturally stable on tow and for basic free flight, and so did not need an autopilot.[34]

Development saw wind tunnel testing and static loads trials during summer 1944. Langley looked especially at the spin characteristics in their 20-foot Vertical Spin Tunnel with a 5.6 percent model during July 1944, subsequently offering very specific techniques for recovery from the unconventional spinning behavior that was observed.[35] With Cornelius lacking construction facilities, Spartan Aircraft Company in Tulsa, Oklahoma, built the two gliders under subcontract. The fuselage was constructed of steel tubing and wood fvraming. The nose and tail cones were poplar plywood and the rest of the fuselage covered in fabric. The wings were wood structure with plywood covering, the aft spar being steel tubing. These were manned aircraft with fixed gear to support flight testing.

Initial flight of the XFG-1 in a manned configuration for testing was in October 1945. The glider flew quite well despite its unusual tailless configuration. Note the wind turbine protruding from the port nose. (The Peter M. Bowers Collection/ The Museum of Flight)

The first XFG-1 was lost in a spin accident that claimed the life of test pilot Alfred Rietherman. The crumpled remains are shown in an Ohio field, the cockpit largely intact. The wood frame and laminate structure with some fabric is evident. (National Soaring Museum)

The initial XFG-1 took to the air the first time on 11 October 1944, probably in Tulsa before being moved to CCAAF. Although it flew quite well, it was lost on 14 March 1945 at Wilmington. During spin tests it entered a flat spin from which Spartan test pilot Alfred Rietherman did not recover. He did not employ NACA's recommended procedure. Rietherman bailed out at too low an altitude and was killed.

By this time $249,990.00 had been spent on the project. Long range C-46 and C-54 transports were being introduced in ever-increasing numbers, and bases seized or built for the B-29 bombers were making its missions less hazardous. So, the day was late for the fuel glider concept and the project appeared ripe for cancellation. Additionally, it had been learned that static electric build-up on the aircraft or radio transmissions could ignite fuel vapors during any in-flight transfer. Yet, the glider was likely the first large aircraft with a forward swept wing flown outside Germany. Indeed, the design had been selected partially because it could provide data on a configuration that might serve a future fighter development program. Consequently, the project continued.

Table 11-04

Cornelius Aircraft XFG-1 Specifics

span	54.0 ft
wing area	350 ft²
length	29.4 ft
height	14. 8 ft
empty weight *	3,362 lbs
gross weight	8,000 lbs
maximum speed (tow/free)	250 mph
stall speed	74.5 mph
maximum THP to tow 200 mph	340 hp

* 3,275 expected in unmanned configuration

To address the spin problem, Captain Adam J. Stolzenberger constructed a quarter-scale free-flight model of the XFG-1 at Wright Field. During August 1945, the glider was dropped from an M-Type Navy blimp flying from NAS Lakehurst, New Jersey, and flown via radio control. This permitted the spin modes and recovery techniques to be safely investigated, and the model recovered with a parachute. Motion picture film of the model motion was compared with film from the Rietherman tests that led to his death, and NACA performed additional spin tunnel work at Langley. With the insight provided, the spin characteristics of the XFG-1 were judged safe to resume flight testing.

The second prototype XFG-1 was flown at CCAAF where the servicemen dubbed it "The Goose." A "spin chute" at the aft end of the fuselage would be deployed in the event a recovery-resistant spin developed. Parachute inflation could cause the aircraft nose to drop, breaking the stall and allowing recovery. The testing began initially with three flights to refamiliarize the pilot, Spartan's Alex Papana, with the craft. The fourth flight on 5 September 1945 then moved to spins. After a few cautionary spin entries and recoveries, the aircraft departed into a spin with a flat-oscillating pitch phase and fast-steep phase. Although eventually recovering, Papana observed that, "It seems to the pilot that the timing, the sequence, and the amount of controls to be used are so critical and of such importance in being successful in stopping the spin, that any variation in these elements would result in total ineffectuality."[36] This might suggest something beyond the skills of the average pilot.

The next flight, on 6 September, continued the spin investigation. Again, the aircraft entered its adverse spin behavior but this time Papana's efforts proved fruitless and he deployed the spin chute at 10,500 feet after a wild descent from 18,000 feet. He wrote, "It is the Pilot's opinion that the spin is unconventional, unpredictable, vicious and dangerous. ... Aside from the poor spinning characteristics and the difficulty of the recovery procedures, the glider has very good flying qualities and is not in the least dangerous."[37] The Army concluded that a spin chute would always be necessary. It is unclear what if any additional testing was performed with the glider.

The development was abandoned after the expenditure of $237,420.00. However, the design was deemed to have superior stability and control to other tailless concepts. So, the Army may have felt the expense worthwhile. One can learn even from failures. The configuration found application in the jet-powered Convair XA-44 bomber-attack aircraft project, despite the unacceptable spin characteristics, but died postwar. The XFG-1 was ordered salvaged on 22 November 1946.[38]

A quarter-scale model of the XFG-1 was built for free-flight spin tests. Dropped from a Navy blimp in August 1945, it provided data supporting flight of the second XFG-1 following the fatal spin mishap with the first article. Note the antennae protruding from the top of the model supporting remote radio control of the model for commanding spin recovery procedures, and the removable forward covering that may enclose a recovery parachute. (National Archives)

A second XFG-1 was completed (here at a display with spin chute assembly on aft fuselage), but flight awaited additional spin recovery investigation. By the time it flew the war had ended and the notion of a fuel glider had been abandoned. The development was subsequently dropped because the spin characteristics proved too hazardous. (National Museum of the United States Air Force)

Foreign Mounts

The Army and Navy both sought insights from the British glider experience as that country was slightly ahead in development and manufacturing during 1941. Examples of Britain's three principal transport gliders were obtained for evaluation and as training aids.

Even before the first CG-4A was built, two 8-place General Aircraft Limited (GAL.48) Hotspur (likely Mk. IIs) and two 30-place Airspeed AS.51 Horsa gliders were in Ohio. Dent reported on 9 December 1941, following his exploratory trip to Britain, that arrangements had been made for two Hotspurs to be sent to the U.S.[39] The Marines are also reported to have obtained six Hotspurs Mk. IIs as these were more representative of the 12-place gliders they were developing. The Navy had a Horsa (HG765) and did tow tests behind a PBY-5A. A giant GAL Hamilcar glider was brought across in 1944 and run through tests at CCAAF.[40]

A captured Gotha Go 242 was on hand at CCAAF by at least summer 1944, but in a non-flyable state. It was subsequently rebuilt by the Technical School, Sheppard Field, Texas. This required a broken left wing spar to be replaced, Chase Aircraft doing this work in the Bronx. The rebuild was apparently completed in spring 1945 before the aircraft was delivered to Wilmington. The glider was then flown on several evaluation missions.[41]

A few examples of British gliders were acquired for evaluation and training by the U.S. Army and Navy, including this GAL Hotspur photographed at Wright Field. Like the CG-3A, this was the UK's first transport glider, but employed strictly as a trainer. It first flew in November 1940. (The Peter M. Bowers Collection/The Museum of Flight)

The Navy also considered the British Horsa glider to fill the Marine assault glider requirement. However, the type was hardly suitable for their mission and towing by available naval aircraft was questionable. The Catalina ready here to take up an example Horsa had difficulty with the task. (National Soaring Museum)

An example GAL Hamilcar heavy glider was brought to the United States from Great Britain for evaluation. Obtained before June 1944, it was as late as October before it had been assembled and readied for flight tests at CCAAF. As the American high-capacity gliders were already well-along in development by that point, anything learned was unlikely to have had large implications. (National Soaring Museum)

Captured German gliders were tested by Great Britain, and surely the reports were made available to the Americans. However, one example made its way to the United States late in the war in the form of the Gotha Go 242, dubbed "Fabric Fortress" by its GI evaluators. It had to be assembled and repaired, making it 1945 before this glider was flown at Clinton Country AAF. (Ray Wagner Collection)

The XPG-2 engine nacelle was designed to fit neatly as a unit under the inboard wing of a CG-4A. The installation contained oil and fuel tanks as well as the engine. The two nacelles and related gear added 2,980 pounds to the aircraft empty weight. (San Diego Air & Space Museum)

12

Oxymoron — Powered Gliders

Powcred gliders seem a contradiction in terms, However, the Army saw value in the concept of gliders designed for easy installation of engines. This would permit the gliders to be readily delivered to different locations in preparation for an attack or more easily recovered following an airborne operation. The power could be used to get a heavy glider off during a normal tow or extend the glide range following release, albeit sacrificing some payload. The modified aircraft could also be used for routine movement of freight and personnel, relieving the tasking on the over-stretched transport aircraft fleet. It might put thousands of idle CG-4As and glider pilots to good use between airborne operations, but readily returned to their engineless glider configuration.

Waco suggested added engines to improve the utility of the hundreds of CG-4As collecting in distribution centers. The larger, more expensive gliders being developed during 1943 and 1944 particularly made the economics of power attractive. Lacking true tactical airlifters at the time; a stopgap appeared better than nothing.

Although a powered glider seems an oxymoron, the idea of quickly installed "power packs" could allow easier pre-positioning of gliders, permit them to perform some freight missions, and support tow at higher weights, appeared to have merit. This XPG-1 was one of three models subjected to flight testing, all conversions of the CG-4As and CG-15A. However, the compromised payload of the glider and performance of the "airplane" remained to be determined. (The Peter M. Bowers Collection/The Museum of Flight)

There seemed as many proponents of powered gliders as those decrying the entire notion as daft. Nonetheless, with the worthy goals in mind, the application of twin engine packages ("packs") or "power eggs" on the ubiquitous CG-4A was explored. The program was initiated at Materiel Command in early 1943, as usual with issuance of several contracts against the same requirement. This was for the engines, fuel tanks, and associated controls to be installed or removed in a matter of hours with the minimum of heavy equipment. The PG or Powered Glider designation was assigned.

Fliers (XPG-1, XPG-2, XPG-2A, XPG-2B, XPG-2C, XPG-3, & XPG-3A)

The earliest powered glider effort in the Army was installation of a 65-horsepower engine on the port wing of a the XCG-4. This was arranged in a "pack" containing the engine, six gallons of fuel, and two gallons of oil. For the added weight of 350 pounds, the glide range was doubled. The next step was duplicating the installation on the starboard wing but with more powerful engines. Power remained too low to permit unaided takeoff at full weight, but the promise was evident.[1]

Table 12-01	
XPG-1 Specifics	
empty weight	5,800 lbs
gross weight	7,500 lbs
maximum speed	150 mph
maximum range speed	80 mph
maximum range	300 mi
maximum rate of climb	100 fpm
stall speed	50 mph
fuel/oil capacity	100/? gal

The first contract was let in April 1943 under which one CG-4A was converted for $52,000.00 by Northwestern with a pair of Franklin 6AC-298-N3 125-horsepower horizontally opposed, four cylinder engines to become the XPG-1. (All horsepower values are given at takeoff power.) The packs, with two-blade fixed propellers, were installed on the wing struts. They added 2,050 pounds to the empty weight and so dramatically cut allowable payload weight from the usual 3,750-5,250 pounds.

Testing of the XPG-1 began with first flight on 13 May 1943 at Wold-Chamberlain Field. While test results were encouraging, it was clear the aircraft was woefully underpowered and experienced high engine temperatures. It could get off unassisted only in favorable conditions, cruise speed was 80 mph, typical climb rate about 100 fpm, and range around 300 miles. It was towed to CCAAF for further testing, but it was destroyed there in the 17 July storm. The poor performance of the airplane did not encourage creating another XPG-1. The "PG" designation and the anemic performance had immediately earned it the moniker "pig" by the Army personnel.

Another CG-4A producer, Ridgefield Manufacturing, was given $27,100.00 to create the XPG-2. Their proposal dated from 8 March 1943.[2] They added a pair of 175-horsepower L-440-1 (commercial 6-440C-2) Ranger inline engines with 86-inch

An XPG-2 is shown in flight. The aircraft barely touched 100 mph top speed empty, 81 mph with payload, had a ceiling of just 3,000 feet, and a range of 250 miles. This unimpressive performance, as a generous definition, would have greatly limited any operational utility. (National Archives)

Northwestern developed such an installation employing 125-horsepower Franklin engines to create the XPG-1 during 1943. The neat installation used engines of low weight and so modest power in an effort to retain the highest payload fraction. Mechanically praise-worthy, the performance results were uninspiring. (The Peter M. Bowers Collection/The Museum of Flight)

Table 12-02	
XPG-2 Specifics	
gross weight	8,500 lbs
maximum speed	100 mph
maximum range speed	81 mph
maximum range	270 mi
endurance	3.6 hrs
maximum rate of climb	290 fpm at sea level (8,500 lbs GW)
service ceiling	approximately 3,000 ft
takeoff over 50-foot obstacle	2,750 ft (7,500 lbs GW)
fuel/oil capacity	120/10 gal

Another "powered glider" design was undertaken by Ridgefield as the XPG-2 using 175-horsepower Ranger inline engines. Nearly all the PGs used fixed-pitch propellers. Performance was so mediocre that the PGs were dubbed "pigs." (National Soaring Museum)

The XPG-2A substituted a 200-horsepower Ranger to improve performance to at least tolerable levels. The principal differentiating features were three forward inlets and twin exhaust pipes on the starboard side. This second example was built by Army personnel and included a landing light in the nose. (San Diego Air & Space Museum)

Sensenich two-blade wooden props to a CG-4A. The "packaged power units" were nacelles containing the engine, oil tanks, and fuel tank installed under the wings inboard of the struts. Each powerplant unit weighed 738.32 pounds, oil and fuel bringing it to 1,135.82 pounds. With another 40.93 pounds of instruments and controls, all this added 2,312.57 pounds to the glider's empty weight.[3]

Following several test flights at Newark Air Base during early July 1943, delivery was on the 8th during a flight to Wright Field under its own power—albeit very slowly and at low altitude.[4] The Clinton County team tested the XPG-2 during the first half of August 1943. At a loaded weight of 8,500 pounds, the aircraft flew at 81 mph with a range of 250 miles.

Performance of the aircraft was improved later in 1943 by Ridgefield, bringing their contract to $54,000.00. They substituted 220-horsepower L-440-7 Rangers with the Sensenich propellers to make the XPG-2A. A second example (42-77062) was created by Army personnel at the Glider Mechanics Technical School, Sheppard Field, Texas, in 1943 as a student exercise.[5] Waco may have formalized the design as they identified it as Model 2-RZR.[6] As the data below indicates, some performance figures fell below the values accepted as guarantees by Northwestern.[7]

In August 1943 the Glider Branch stated that the XPG-2A design was suitable for production. It was demonstrated to several interested activities in spring 1944. Typical of the whole glider program, one organization expressed a need for the capability while another insisted there was no requirement. Interest in the powered gliders ebbed and flowed, so it was August 1944 before a headquarters in the ETO requested kits to convert a dozen CG-4As, while a Wing in the South Pacific also expressed an interest. The UK-based unit planned to use the airplanes in a bulk freight delivery scheme within the Isles to reduce workload on C-47s.

Table 12-03	
XPG-2A Specifics (G = guarantee)	
empty weight	5,690 lbs
payload weight (normal)	3,310 lbs
gross weight	9,000 lbs
maximum takeoff weight	9,950 lbs
maximum takeoff weight	10,000 lbs
maximum speed	100 mph (G 105)
maximum range speed	82 mph
maximum range	295 mi
endurance	3.6 hrs (G 4.0)
maximum rate of climb	290 fpm (G 300)
service ceiling	6,400 ft (G 7,150)
single engine	0 ft
stall speed	52.5 mph (G 49)
takeoff over 50-foot obstacle	3,450 ft (G 3,000)
landing over 50-foot obstacle	1,145 ft (G 1,500)
fuel/oil capacity	120/10 gal

The end of war in Europe and looming terminus of WWII also spelt the end of powered glider ambitions. Ultimately, just 10 of the PG-2As were delivered as the contract quantity was repeatedly cut. This example suggests that the UK acquired at least one of these aircraft. (The Peter M. Bowers Collection/The Museum of Flight)"

The installation appeared suitable for production, this coming in the form of field modification of existing CG-4As. Kits were to be produced for the conversions as well as aircraft converted States-side. The first of the Northwestern production PG-2A airplanes is shown. (National Archives)

In February 1945 actions began to convert 60 CG-4As already allocated the ETO to PG-2As. Materiel Command was also to produce 18 kits minus engines, as the ETO had spare Rangers already on hand, for in-theater conversion. However these were later regarded as spares. Northwestern was given the work under a 22 March letter contract. The existing XPG-2A (Aerotruck N.A.C.-1 to Northwestern) was flown to Wold-Chamberlain on 6 April 1945 to assist their efforts. On 4 August 1945 the quantity on order was reduced to 20, and soon after to 10 with 5 spare engineless kits.[8] The first was delivered in July and the last in September, with at least one shipped to Europe.

Northwestern was also paid to convert a CG-4A with Jacobs R-755-9 radial engines of 245 horsepower and 102-inch prop to become the XPG-2B (Waco Model 2-YZR). However, the effort was dropped in 1945 and the engines went to the third and final powered glider effort.

The XPG-2C is also referenced in a table of design characteristics provided by Waco in fall 1944.[9] Whether it was built or was just a design study is unclear. It was to have 315-horsepower Jacobs R-755-E engines with geared drives for the 114-inch propeller. Identified as Model 2-XZR, the following data were provided. It would certainly have been the best performer of the "pigs."

During spring 1944, when the glider program was in an ebb, Waco sought work by proposing it convert a CG-15A with engines. The firm was given a $125,000.00 contract at the end of 1944 or beginning of 1945 to install two 245-horsepower R-755-9 engines on a modified XCG-15A (44-90986) to give the Army the XPG-3 (Model 2-YEU). (This serial immediately precedes those of the only two identified XCG-15As, and so it is reasonable to assume 44-90986 was never completed as a XCG-15A.) The engines turned 102-inch Hamilton Standard constant speed props, and electric starters were installed.[10] (All previous PG incarnations lacked starters and constant speed props, with one consequence that the engines had to be "hand-propped.") Like the XPG-2, each nacelle was installed under a wing between the fuselage and strut, although the base of the nacelle joined the strut and the two auxiliary stiffening struts between the main strut and wing were discarded. Two additional struts was added joining the nacelle to the fitting of the main lift strut and fuselage. The wingspan was expanded slightly by 8.3 feet to 70.5 feet so it had about 60 square feet on the baseline CG-15A wing area. All this increased the CG-15A empty weight of 2,360 pounds to 6,385 pounds and the design weight by 2,100 pounds to 10,100 pounds.[11]

Testing of the XPG-3 began on 2 April 1945 and first flight occurred on the 25th. This showed the design to be satisfactory, although performance was marginal. In powered flight the aircraft achieved 116 mph cruise with a range of about 300 miles.[12]

Table 12-04

XPG-2B Specifics (estimated, not built)	
empty weight	6,184 lbs
payload weight (normal)	1,621 lbs
gross weight	9,000 lbs
maximum takeoff weight	10,309 lbs
maximum speed	112.5 mph
maximum range speed	70 mph
maximum range	531 mi
endurance	2.67 hrs
maximum rate of climb	598 fpm
service ceiling	15,000 ft
single engine	0 ft
stall speed	52.5 mph
takeoff over 50-foot obstacle	1,587 ft
landing over 50-foot obstacle	1,145 ft
fuel/oil capacity	120/10 gal

Table 12-05

XPG-2C Specifics (likely not built)	
empty weight	6,360 lbs
payload weight (normal)	1,445 lbs
gross weight	9,000 lbs
maximum takeoff weight	10,309 lbs
maximum speed	130 mph
maximum range speed	70 mph
maximum range	610 mi
endurance	2.08 hrs
maximum rate of climb	1,063 fpm
service ceiling	21,500 ft
single engine	8,000 ft
stall speed	52.5 mph
takeoff over 50-foot obstacle	917 ft
landing over 50-foot obstacle	1,145 ft
fuel/oil capacity	120/10 gal

Table 12-06

Waco Aircraft XPG-3 Specifics	
empty weight	6,385 lbs
payload weight (normal)	2,500 lbs
gross weight	10,100 lbs
takeoff weight	10,500 lbs
maximum speed	121 mph
maximum range speed	79 mph
maximum range	507 mi
endurance	2.67 hrs
maximum rate of climb	568 fpm
service ceiling	8,400 ft
single engine	0 ft
stall speed	55 mph
takeoff over 50-foot obstacle	3,000 ft
landing over 50-foot obstacle	1,100 ft
fuel/oil capacity	120/10 gal

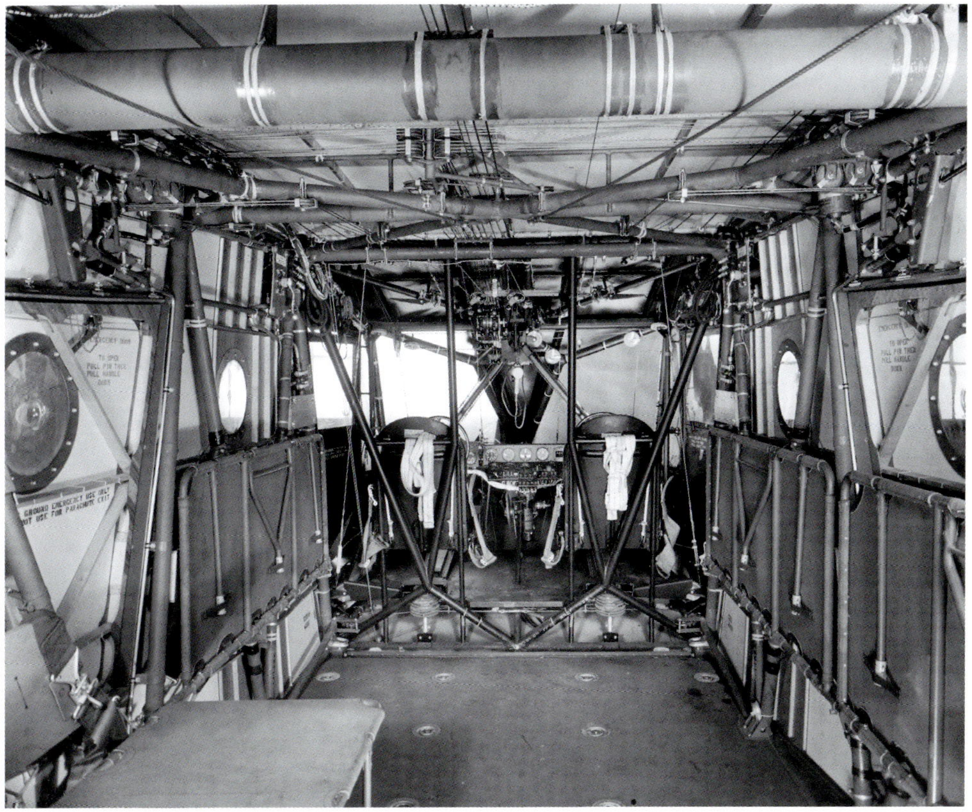

This interior shot of the XPG-3 includes the cockpit controls with added instruments and levers overhead. It also reveals controls and hose plus cable runs at the wing root suggesting a person was required at the this station during at least engine start. While the power installation intruded little into the interior of the glider, the added weight significantly impacted payload capability. (National Museum of the United States Air Force)

Waco also developed an installation of two 245-horsepower Jacobs radials for the CG-15A as the XPG-3, shown at CCAAF. Performance was slightly improved at 116-mph cruise and 300 mph range. (National Soaring Museum)

Table 12-07	
Waco Aircraft XPG-3A Specifics (estimated, not built)	
empty weight	6,400 lbs
payload weight (normal)	1,405 lbs
gross weight	9,000 lbs
takeoff weight	10,500 lbs
maximum takeoff weight	12,371 lbs
maximum speed	137 mph
maximum range speed	79 mph
maximum range	592 mi
endurance	2.08 hrs
maximum rate of climb	1,045 fpm
service ceiling	18,500 ft
single engine	5,000 ft
stall speed	55 mph
takeoff over 50-foot obstacle	1,049 ft
landing over 50-foot obstacle	1,020 ft
fuel/oil capacity	120/10 gal

Table 12-08	
Chase Aircraft XPG-4 Specifics (estimated, not built)	
empty weight	9,770 lbs
payload weight (normal)	6,427 lbs
gross weight	15,000 lbs
maximum takeoff weight	16,197 lbs
maximum speed	170 mph
maximum range speed	155 mph
maximum range (10% reserve)	658 mi
endurance (10% reserve)	1.64 hrs
maximum rate of climb	850 fpm
service ceiling	15,000 ft
single engine	5,000 ft
stall speed	60.9 mph
takeoff over 50-foot obstacle	1,348 ft
landing over 50-foot obstacle	1,356 ft
fuel/oil capacity	200/20 gal

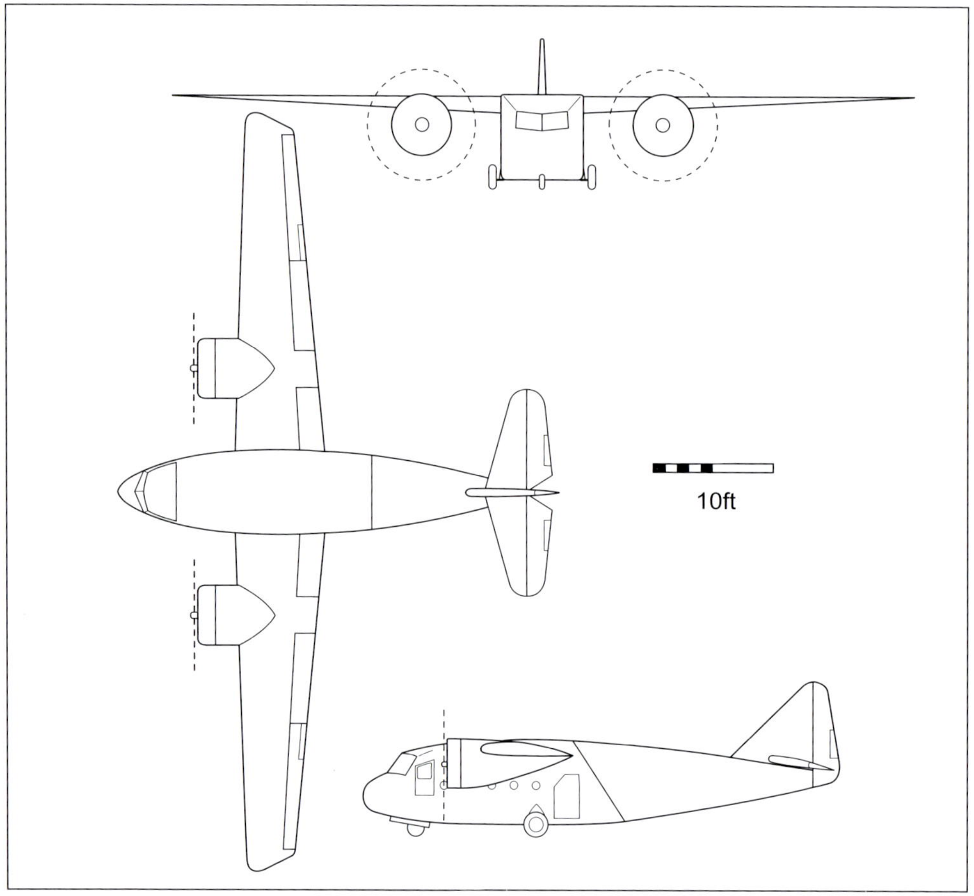

Other powerplants were considered for PG installation as well as other gliders. Chase drew up a specification for the XPG-4 based on addition of two 550 horsepower radials added to the XCG-14A. Nothing came of this. Note the windscreen arrangement does not match the XCG-14A as built, suggesting the original drawing upon which this art is based was either simplified or represented an altered configuration. (Author)

A second pair of Jacobs packs, using the 315-horsepower R-775-E and gear-driven 114-inch props, was procured for possible installation on XCG-15A 45-5277 (although a CG-4A is also mentioned as the planned recipient). A pair of nacelles was priced at $14,000.00, and the entire XPG-3 effort cost $126,000.00. Tentatively designated the XPG-3A (Model 2-XEU), the modification was underway in April 1945 for a planned May flight, but there is no evidence it was completed.[13]

Non-Fliers (XPG-4, XCG-10A, Others, Experiments)

Presumably under USAAF direction, Chase Aircraft prepared a specification for a powered version of their XCG-14A glider identified as XPG-4 or Chase MS-5. They

The "pigs" lingered longer than one could account for given their meager performance and payload. Yet, efforts were made to address these issues with further resources like the addition of JATO rockets. This image shows the XPG-3 taking off with two under-wing bottles generating their characteristic smoke trail. (The Peter M. Bowers Collection/ The Museum of Flight)

planned to mount two 600-horsepower Pratt & Whitney (P&W) R-1340-AN-1 Wasp radials direct-driving Hamilton Standard constant speed, two-blade propellers. Although money was set aside for the conversion, this fell to the axe.[14]

At the Army's behest, Laister-Kauffmann developed plans in 1944 to add engines to the XCG-10A (then still in development, although the XCG-10 was extant) as the LK-12. This would be achieved by inserting a 4.7-foot wing segment of parallel leading and trailing edges with a 1,200-horsepower (P&W) R-1830-92 Twin Wasp engines, plus fuel and oil tanks on both sides, increasing wing area by 11.4 percent.

The engines were to be mounted ahead of the wing segment on 4.7-foot span detachable steel truss nacelle segments that would integrate nacelle and wing structure. The segments would contain tanks for a total a 400 gallons. These segments would be inserted between the centersection and next outboard wing panel per side, effectively increasing the wing area by 11.4 percent. The nacelle and wing segments were expected to add 6,500 pounds, plus 945 pounds more in structural enforcement, to ensure carriage of the same 12,000-pound payload as the XCG-10A. Hence, the empty weight of the aircraft was projected to rise by 7,445 pounds to 19,200 pounds and gross could be 30,000 to 34,000 pounds.[15]

The LK-12 proposal was formally submitted in fall 1944, but the Air Forces had lost interest. The modification would make it a cargo aircraft with an entirely different set of specifications for which the aircraft would require even more costly changes.

During October 1944 there were discussions between the USAAF and Waco regarding adding a pair of P&W R-985-ANI Wasp Junior engines to a CG-13A, but this also came to naught.

With the miserable performance, any idea of using the powered gliders for routine transport flights without tow appeared impractical. Various propellers and constant speed control were tested. Tests using JATO to improve takeoff performance of the XPG-2A and XPG-3 were conducted, but these suffered the same limitations as the rockets used for deceleration and only improved one part of the performance limitations. There was also discussion of mounting two Ford PJ131 pulsejet engines from the JB-2 missile to the CG-4A. The jets, which might have been jettisonable, was expected to provide 125 mph speed to 100 miles range.[16] However, nothing came of this either.

Set Aside

The powered glider concept was codified in a May 1945 document proposing the characteristics of such an aircraft. This was endorsed as late as an August 1945 requirements conference, although it was pointed out the aircraft meeting the characteristics were essentially light transports and so redundant. However, during this period it appeared certain to many that the war would be won with the weapons on hand or in the "pipeline." Consequently, the powered glider concept was shelved for later application, if required. The program had been dealt a severe blow in July of that year when it was assessed as having no tactical value. In December, the Deputy Commander, USAAF, killed any idea of adopting metal powered gliders on the grounds that shortages of aluminum and higher priority work made it infeasible. The entire effort had consumed $246,000.00.

Navy work on bomb gliders (glider bombs, or GLOMB as they referred to them) began with an LNS-1 to test autotow systems while permitting a safety pilot aboard. This example, apparently at the Naval Aircraft Modification Unit plant in Johnsville, Pennsylvania, has a rig on the nose above the normal towline attach point just ahead of the skid and what appears to be an added elevator trim tab (none on the baseline Schweizer). This could be for line angle sensing and so this may be the initial GLOMB testbed. (National Soaring Museum)

13

Sacrificial Lambs — Bomb Gliders

As the U.S. military began working with towed aircraft and gliders, their thoughts naturally turned to roles beyond transporting personnel and equipment. If an unmanned glider fitted with explosives could be made to self-stabilize behind a tug, it could be towed to a target area and released. Provided the same autopilot features, and remote or autonomous guidance, the glider could potentially be directed to hit a target with much greater accuracy than conventional bombing techniques and without risking manned attack aircraft. If towed by a fighter—aircraft usually possessing much excess power in cruise flight—the fighter pilot could egress the area quickly and defend himself effectively. High-value but heavily defended and point targets like capitol ships and submarine pens might be more efficiently engaged by such weapons than mass bomber formations or squadrons of dive-bombers.

Both the USN and AAF launched programs to explore the potential of such bomb gliders through technology development and practical experimentation. The work leveraged off other autopilot, remote piloting, and autonomous guidance efforts for unmanned aircraft, ballistic and glide bombs, and missiles. Given the greater uncertainties with a completely autonomous missile, the glider approach appeared logical, with lower technical risk and cost.

Navy Progress

Glider bombs were pursued most vigorously by the Navy. This was a spin-off of their powered assault drone or "aerial torpedo" work, underway since 1936. The inspiration came in December 1940 from Lieutenant Commander Del Fahrney, then head of the Special Designs Branch at BuAer, who wrote a proposal to explore the glider option. Envisioned was a glider towed under automatic stabilization to within glide range of a target by a fighter or transport aircraft. A television camera in the nose of the glider would provide an image of the target to which the remote pilot would guide the aircraft via radio control from a "mother ship" aircraft nearby. Gliders offered less costly airframes, and tow could be by the aircraft that also contained the remote controller—conceivably the pilot and so a one-man operation. It was also felt the glider might provide supplemental fuel to the tow ship. The Naval Aircraft Factory and Fahrney were then deep into development of remote control and TV guidance systems for the powered drones. The towline indicators developed in the UK provided input to an autopilot system. Hence, all elements appeared to be in hand. Fahrney always envisioned initial development with a safety pilot aboard the glider who, at a minimum, was required to land the glider at the end of the test. (In the USN's drone program an operator on the ground controlled the aircraft for takeoff, transferring control to the airborne operator once up and away, then resumed control for the landing. Only manual landings are found in GLOMB literature.)

The BuAer concurred with Fahrney's proposal on 25 March 1941 and directed the NAF on 19 April to take up the project. Work would begin with two-seat training gliders and progress to unmanned ships up to 15,000 pounds GW (practical for fighter tow) while work to reduce the size of the electronic gear was conducted concurrently. Radar was considered a potential future guidance system for operations during periods of darkness when the TV was ineffective. Added to the team was Commander Barnaby, then Assistant Chief Engineer at the NAF. Barnaby coined the moniker "GLOMB," ("glider bomb") for the notional weapon. It was formally titled Project George.

To begin the work, NAF was authorized on 19 April 1941 to buy two Schweizer LNS-1 trainers to test radio control. However, progress in the first years was slowed by parallel work on the drones and basic equipment development that commanded the lion's share of the NAF resources. Another personality joining the team was Lieutenant Molton B. "Molt" Taylor, USN, who, by early 1943, was the lead officer on the project and greatly helped accelerate the effort.[1] Fahrney departed BuAer in June 1943, leaving leadership of guided weapons to Lieutenant Commander Grayson Merrill. However, Fahrney was assigned to command the Naval Aircraft Modification Unit in Johnsville, Philadelphia, under the Naval Air Material Center (NAMC) formed on 14 July 1943 that also included the NAF. Fahrney was relieved at NAMU by Barnaby in June 1944.

Tests were conducted in early March 1942 with an LNS-1s controlled during towed takeoff and towed flight. This showed that remote controlling the glider under tow from the tow plane was impractical.[2] Focus then shifted to automatically stabilizing the glider on takeoff and tow. However, natural stabilization was soon judged likely unobtainable. In attempting to devise an autotow system, the NAF built upon prior work with drone autopilots and the "angle-of-dangle" measuring device. Like the Army system, the autotow system sensed towline orientation and change from a nominal state that caused hydraulic actuators to displace control cables and correct the glider's attitude. Tests were performed with the LNS-1s and an NAF-developed autotow system, and another from the W. L. Maxson Company of New York City. The former was ultimately selected for use.[3] Release commanded from the tug transferred control from the autotow to gyros and remote control. Trials from June-September 1942, still with a safety pilot although it got to the point he did not touch the controls, showed good progress on all aspects of the system including autotow, remotely controlled free-flight, and targeting. Bomb arming could also be commanded via radio.

The very low wing loading of the LNS-1 gliders, long wingspan, and single center wheel made them cumbersome for the autopilot testing. It was found they developed "periodic slackness in the towline," as might occur if the glider dived down slightly on high tow, that played havoc with the stabilization system. It interpreted this as an attitude change when sensing the altered angle-of-dangle. Heavier gliders with drag more like an airplane suffered the slackness only momentarily and this was tolerable. Furthermore, the Navy men found that a low tow was less prone to the occasional towline slackness and so this was adopted as standard operating procedures.[4]

In seeking a more representative testbed, during spring and summer 1942 the NAF adopted a Great Lakes BG-1 (9512), an antiquated radial-engine biplane. This was employed in early trials of radio control and TV transmissions, including simulated tow, remote radio release from the tug, and glide to targets. It was then towed by a Douglas TBD-1 Devastator torpedo bomber to test a potential system, the drone flying on tow via the auto system. More extraordinary, on 20 May the BG-1 was remotely maneuvered into place to snag a towline streaming from the TBD-1, presumably using the system as the F4Fs had done earlier in the month (Chapter 11).[5] The BG-1 tests ultimately proved satisfactory with releases from 3-9 miles from the target and five "hits" out of seven runs.

The BG-1 results sparked the interest of the CNO, especially in light of the results of the recent Battle of Midway where entire squadrons of planes were sacrificed in attacks on enemy aircraft carriers. Consequently, while awaiting suitable gliders for the trials, BG-1 9508 was modified in June 1942 with its engine removed, the tow and TV equipment installed plus lead ballast, but a seat and controls retained for a safety pilot.[6] Onboard pilot for the BG-1 trials was Lieutenant (jg) E.R. Dare. The use of a Grumman J2F Duck amphibian as the tow plane was disappointing, with poor climb performance of the combination.[7]

The development of radio control and television transmission of instrument panels for aircraft installation was also facilitated by its use in high-risk high-speed diving structural tests of otherwise manned fighter and attack aircraft. This, by necessity, included radio control of all phases of flight, bringing the Navy to an unprecedented and unique level of knowledge and skill in these remote piloting capabilities. The Radio Corporation of American (RCA) television equipment proved most suitable, and other radio telemetry of instrument values were also perfected.[8]

The makeshift and hazardous BG-1 operations only persisted through November. More representative gliders had been found for the experiments in the 3-place trainers, most notably a Taylorcraft TG-6 acquired from the Army in exchange for an LNE-1, and three more obtained from the AAF in October 1942.[9] NAF modifications rendered them XLNT-1s. Changes included a revised main undercarriage that increased the distance between tires for greater ground stability, added nose gear, all the glider bomb electronics gear installed in the cockpit with external antennae. Some had a wind-driven turbine hanging off the port fuselage aft of the wing and main gear struts. It appears a conventional landing gear was too unstable for tow off the ground under automatic control.

All the preliminary work was translated to an LNT-1 and the GLOMB work finally gained momentum. Additionally, Captain Richard Figley visited Wright Field on 6 February 1943 to observe what the Army had achieved in glider autotow and autopilots. He reported their device for measuring and translating angle-of-dangle to be superior to the British model.[10] However, the final Navy GLOMB models did not have "feeler" bars evident above the towline attachments, suggesting that an internal sensing of towline attach fitting motion was ultimately devised.

By spring 1943, the XLNT-1 autotow was performing very well, the glider following along dutifully from takeoff through cruise even in turbulence, although a safety pilot remained onboard. The big success came on 4 April 1943.[11] Released from five miles out and 5,000 feet altitude, the glider could be easily directed at the target via the television picture. A range of 20-miles seemed practical as did one-man operation by the tow pilot. In fact, the flight seemed so effortless that automatic guidance seemed entirely practical should it be developed.[12]

Also evaluated under autotow were British Hotspur and Horsa transport glider, Waco LRW-1, plus LNR-1 and LNP-1 3-place trainers. Apart from the learning experience of the GLOMB conversions, these aircraft were also evaluated as potential basis for GLOMB production.[13] The two Hotspur were to be modified for GLOMB but with a radar homing ("super-sniffer") system and expended in terminal tests, as directed on 25 January 1943.[14] While GLOMB flights were performed with the Hotspurs, the fatal glides into targets do not appear to have been executed.

The LRW-1 was flying under autotow between April and June 1943 in support of the USMC glider program (Chapter 9). This, again, met with completely satisfactory results even when the tug maneuvered or the combination encountered adverse weather. The LRW-1 testing continued, to include flights with several people and 144 gallons of fuel aboard, towed by a F4F-3. This combination required 2,000 feet to get off and tow was at 85 mph with 700 fpm rate of climb. The team found the flight went easier with the autotow flying as opposed to the pilot.[15]

Seeking a more practical platform for the GLOMB tests, the Navy adapted several of the Army three-place Taylorcraft trainers it had labeled LNT-1. Evident are the significant modifications with added nose gear, revised main gear, electronics boxes in the forward cockpit, and numerous added antennae. The setting is also NAMU, Philadelphia. (National Museum of Naval Aviation)

While the XLNT-1 GLOMB design appeared practical, it was not without its difficulties. This aircraft, suffering a nose gear collapse, reveals the wind-driven turbine on the port side of the glider. It clearly was not operationally suitable as it could accommodate little explosives in the crowded cockpit and meager remaining payload weight. (Air Force Flight Test Center)

Testing with the LNTs continued apace. To determine the feasibility of a tug drawing fuel from a towed glider, trials were ordered by BuAer on 1 July 1942. These were to be accomplished at Norfolk with a Consolidated PB2Y-1 Coronado. The tests were finally flown in July 1943 with water pumped from the glider through a hose attached to the towline.[16]

The Navy acquired a pair of Hotspur gliders from Canada for GLOMB tests. They were modified for autotow but also with terminal guidance via radar. This Hotspur, photographed at NAMU, has a modification to the nose that includes a recessed device below the normal line attach point, and protrusions on both sides of the nose that may be antennae or antennae mount points. (National Soaring Museum)

While GLOMB tests performed on other gliders were instructive, it was clearly desirable to concentrate on a single type for development and training. Subsequently, further tests planned for the Hotspur and LRW-1 were directed to be performed on XLNT-1s, the aircraft that consistently appeared most suitable for further GLOMB development.[17] Also, despite the encouraging progress, all the GLOMB equipment remained experimental and none had been tested as a representative and integrated whole.[18] It was time to work towards a finalized system.

With the LNT-1 appearing the best platform for the GLOMB tests, six more were acquired from Army stocks in September 1943.[19] The seven from the training base were also likely transferred to GLOMB work. Modifications to XLNT-1s were performed at NAMU.[20] An additional 25 of the gliders were directed to the Navy on 15 December 1943. Six were equipped with a 12-Volt Block I television and "supersonic" radio control gear, five with the Block I TV and frequency modulated (FM) control equipment, 12 identified as LNT-2 were given 24-Volt Block III TV and FM control, 8 LNT-2 with a 24-Volt system for testing homing systems, and 12 LNT-1s prepared for use by the Training Task Force to prepare GLOMB pilots.[21]

The radio remote control and TV transmit/receiver from RCA for targeting also coalesced to the suitably functional Block I design that fit into the XLNT-1 and a control aircraft as small as a trainer. Further refinements were already in work. In general, on release from tow the system transferred from autotow to a gyro-stabilized flight under remote control and directed to the target. The glider was either directed all the way to the target by reference to the TV image with a few adjustments, or locked into a stabilized flight path. It appears from descriptions that the TV image was only available after release. By fall 1943, these capabilities were ready for service trials and three XLNT-1s were authorized by BuAer on 3 September to be expended in destructive tests.

The first GLOMB terminal test and first unmanned "no-pilot solo" or "Nolo" flight (name again thanks to Barnaby), was at NAS Patuxent River on 17 September 1943.

These are examples of the expertly assembled ground support equipment for preparing an experimental XLNT-1 GLOMB for launch. In the background of the right hand image appears to be the prototype XLRA-1 and a Horsa glider. The left hand picture has an XLNT-1 in the background, tipped back on its tail. (Air Force Flight Test Center)

This may be a no-pilot solo (NOLO) autotow flight of an XLNT-1 as photographed from a chase airplane. A television camera appears to be positioned to image out the nose glazing. After much effort the Navy had the glider flying dutifully on tow without intervention, from takeoff to release. (National Museum of Naval Aviation)

The glider carried a live 325 pound depth charge armed by remote signal. The XLNT-1 (36429) was pulled by a Vultee SNV-1 Valiant (12963) whose pilot also flew the XLNT-1 after release.[22] The 20-mile flight was in turbulence, but without problem. After 35 minutes, release was at 3,000 feet altitude and 3.0 miles upwind of the target—an area off Bloodsworth Island in the Chesapeake Bay—the tug aligning the glider with the target before release. Unfortunately, following castoff the TV image became just a black blot and the target could not be discerned. Because of observers near the site who might be at risk, the pilot, Lieutenant Taylor, was forced to command a GLOMB spiral descent into the bay, well short of the target, where the depth charge exploded on impact (electrical impact switch to fuse). Most likely the magnetic field of the GLOMB, altered by installation of the depth charge, disrupted the delicate TV gear, although this could have been corrected if fine adjustments had been made in the final flight configuration.[23]

A second XLNT-1 destructive test was attempted before the 28th but also met with failure. An auxiliary power supply packed in near the release point and the glider crashed.[24] Despite these setbacks, BuAer was convinced GLOMB was "completely practical and is potentially a very effective weapon."[25]

The only other GLOMB terminal test was conducted at NAS Lakehurst, New Jersey, on 25 February 1944 against a 30x50-foot sand pit. With the radio and Block I television gear in the XLNT-1 (67803), only 228 pounds of sand bags representing explosives brought the glider to full weight. The entire test was conducted as an "expeditionary operation," with the aircraft and all gear and personnel flown to Lakehurst, the mission executed and cleaned up, and the team departing after six hours. With no 'dry' pass, glider release was at 4,500 feet altitude and 4.0 miles upwind of the target. After a three-minute flight, the GLOMB,

This series of photos shows the XLNT-1 GLOMB terminal test at Lakehurst, New Jersey. Released from the tug, the glider was directed via remote control, by reference to a TV image, to impact a sand pit four to five miles away.

The non-explosive impact was just 23 feet from the center of the pit. (National Soaring Museum)

controlled by Lieutenant Taylor, struck within 23 feet of the target center (the control plane then 5.0 miles away) and with enough momentum to trip an arming circuit.[26]

Although not entirely successful due to continuing limitations of the early TV systems, the promise shown in these XLNT trials was clear. They also demonstrated that a tow pilot could direct the GLOMB after release such as a fighter pilot would do on a combat mission. Even before the final XLNT tests, the NAF proposed a production GLOMB on 10 August 1943 with a 3000-pound glider hauling a 4,000-pound bomb for a gross of 7,000-7,500 pounds. With a Grumman F6F-3 Hellcat fighter as tug and mother ship, a 350-mile combat radius was envisioned.[27] For naval operations, such range suggested launch from an aircraft carrier. On 25 March 1944, BuAer declared that GLOMBs should be operable from carriers, and directed NAF to perform catapult trials of a glider and tow plane combination.[28]

The two aircraft were initially catapulted separately to develop the proper technique. This may account for an XLNT-1, without electronics gear, fitted with a trestle protruding from the nose and a hook at its apex. These were reported on 14 April and entailed three launches of the singular NAF XN5N-1 monoplane (1521) with an LNT-1 behind.[29] Further catapult tests saw four shots conducted with a F4F-3 (3990, piloted by Lieutenant Commander Heap) at Pax River's shore-based cat. The fighter was launched off with the glider in tow from the tailhook mount (hook removed). Because the XLNT-1 (42-58561, piloted by Major Figley, Lieutenant Ryan, and Captain Reilly) did not have the nose gear addition, its tail was placed in a raised trough and the tail wheel held back with a frangible restraint (0.25-inch cotton line). On one shot the glider had 400 pounds of ballast but this was replaced in subsequent launches by two passengers (no GLOMB gear). Minor alterations to reinforce the glider's structure were necessary to withstand the launch loads, and the towline release mechanism was also modified, bringing total weight to 1,200 pounds. The towline was 100 feet of 0.44-inch steel cable, a small canvas drogue parachute taped to the glider's nose so as to be easily pulled free and keep the line from whipping. The combination was launched via the H.E-1 and XH IV catapults with end speeds up around 74 mph and maximum acceleration 2 g.

The structure projecting from the nose of this XLNT-1, that lacks a nose gear, suggests a modification for catapult on its own. The hook on the end might have held the catapult shuttle bridle. It is known such tests were performed. (National Soaring Museum)

On one launch the glider pilot tried to remain below the tug's wake during the takeoff but buffeting forced the left wing to drag on the ground until the tug climbed above the LNT-1. On another launch the front canopy of the glider flew open and the pilot released soon after. In general, however, catapulting a fighter with glider in tow was entirely practical.[30]

Going Mainstream

In initially laying out the plans for production GLOMBs, the Navy sought to have them serve a dual purpose as Marine Corps cargo gliders supporting their amphibious glider ambitions as well as guided bombs. As related in Chapter 6, requirement was initially addressed in a 29 June 1942 BuAer document that called for an aircraft that could carry fuel, freight, or explosives. The subsequent 29 September directive sought three types. These initially leveraged off the VLR types under contract and the NAF's XLRN-1, but GLOMB applications were never realized.

As NAF testing provided more clear insight into GLOMB characteristics, requirements for a production glider bomb evolved from the summer 1942 outline. Released in August 1943, these specified a 3,000-pound empty weight glider with a 4,000-pound explosive payload and 400-mile radius of action when deployed by a Hellcat fighter. They could be towed at 150 mph whereas the LNT-1 was limited to 100 mph, somewhat slow for the fighter-bombers envisioned as the mother ship.[31] Autotow, remote control, and television systems were to be installed along with accommodations for the warhead. GLOMB proposals were submitted in September 1943 from six companies and contracts were negotiated with three in November.

Pratt, Read and Company was to build 100 LBE-1, the initial three as XLBE-1, under a September 1943 contract. A mockup of the glider was inspected on 5-6 June 1944. The glider had fixed landing gear, split dive flaps, and a glazed portion of the nose of the TV camera. A ram air turbine under the nose, with variable pitch fan, generated electrical power. This was felt superior to a small gasoline engine.[32] The three prototypes had a cockpit for

If the GLOMB was to be a naval weapon, it would need to be launched from an aircraft carrier. Hence, catapult tests of a F4F-3 towing a manned XLNT-1 was conducted in late spring 1944. The glider (lacking a nose gear) has its tail raised via a trestle to prevent an abrupt pitch-over during initial acceleration. A small parachute is lightly taped to the nose to stabilize the tow rope after glider release and the Wildcat's arresting tailhook was removed to accommodate the towline release mechanism. (National Soaring Museum)

Another NAF GLOMB concept also had fixed and faired landing gear with spacious forward fuselage for the bomb. The podded fuselage with twin booms permitted the bomb to be loaded through the aft end, possibly without crane. The raised aft end of the model's fuselage has a wind turbine attached. (Air Force Flight Test Center)

a safety pilot. In the missionized configuration the pilot station would be replaced with mounts for a 4,000 pound bomb case sans fins.

The first LBE was delivered in May. The first flight from Patuxent River that month was behind a Lockheed PV-1 Ventura that required 6,800 feet of runway. The glider safety pilot could perceive so little through the distortion of the molded canopy that he would have been in dire straits had the autotow malfunctioned. Six 1,000-pound JATO bottles on the PV-1 reduced the takeoff to 3,800 feet.[33]

Piper Aircraft was also to build 100 LBP-1 gliders, the first three as XLBP-1

The Pratt, Read XLBE-1 appeared a conventional tricycle gear aircraft except for lacking and engine. Split and perforated dive flaps are evident as is the wind turbine under the nose and towline release on the nose. The pilot station for the manned testbed is visible with the canopy removed. (Air Force Flight Test Center)

A fit check of a 4,000-pound bomb casing in the incomplete XLBE-1 reveals much. The underlying steel tube frame is evident along with the complexity of control runs, electrical wiring, and other mechanisms. Some of the wood structure is also apparent. (National Archives)

The Naval Aircraft Factory apparently performed initial concept design for the GLOMB, as they had done for the transport gliders. All the concepts had fixed undercarriage and had to accommodate a bomb casing. This design looks much like the eventual LBE-1 glider. (Naval Aviation Archives, above Air Force Flight Test Center)

The first completed XLBE-1, 85290, is photographed with a person in the cockpit that contains a yoke controller. The transparency in the nose was to permit television camera imaging. The mount projecting above the mid fuselage was to hold a multi-prong antenna. (Air Force Flight Test Center)

that also took a 4,000-pound weapon. The actual engineering work for the wooden glider was performed by Designed for Industry and the construction undertaken in Cleveland, Ohio, by a team lead by Dick Barber. The rest of the work was performed in Lock Haven.[34] The glider had the dimensions of a light plane (span 33.0 feet) but clearly designed as an unmanned and expendable aircraft. All surfaces were fully cantilevered; the lines clean for high-speed tow. The wing featured spoilers. The fixed tricycle gear included main gear posts under the wing with spring shock absorbers. The forward fuselage was set low for ease of bomb loading into the nose and a window above the towline attach fitting facilitate the TV vision. Beneath the nose was a mount for the wind-driven generator.

The mockup of the LBP-1 was inspected on 3 April 1944.[35] The first XLBP-1 was transported via truck to Fort Dix, New Jersey, where it first flew behind an F4F in January 1945. This aircraft appears to have been fitted with an anti-spin parachute pack in the tail.

Taylorcraft Aviation was contracted to build 25 LBT-1 (at least the first as an XLBT-1) designed for a 2,000 pound bomb. (It was also observed that using stacked charges, the explosive load would be expanded by 66 percent.[36]) It looked much like their modified LNT-1 except for more durable construction and cleaner lines on the nose, with a simplified canopy, that ended in a port for the TV camera. A wind turbine was mounted off the port side. The aircraft still used spoilers like the LNT-1, but eschewed flaps. Perforated dive brakes on the aft fuselage normally lay aligned with the airflow but could be rotated 90 degrees. Maximum takeoff weight was 5,000 pounds, tow speed to 240 mph, and landing speed 120 mph. Sink speed was 2,200 fpm, with 260 mph dive speed and capable of 5-g pull-outs.[37]

The first XLBT-1 was flown by Taylorcraft in early March 1944.[38] Al Barber, Taylorcraft test pilot, frequently flew as safety pilot in the LBT-1 when acceptance trials began in April after delivery that month to NAMC. A second machine, fully equipped with autotow, remote control, and TV systems, was handed over in October. A third, devoid of the electronics, was passed to the Test and Evaluation Unit established in Traverse City. Michigan.[39] Aircraft four through nine went to Traverse City without electronics while 10 through 25 were fitted with the special gear at the Ohio plant before following to Michigan in March 1945.[40] The LBT-1 was commonly towed aloft and controlled by a Wildcat or a Ventura. Flight tests, mostly by Barber, extended well into 1945. This was punctuated by an accident at Traverse City on 23 July 1945. The Ventura was laboring to climb, barely clearing the end of the runway. At 40 feet the towline accidentally released and the safety pilot of the LBT-1 (85269) had nowhere to go but into a wooded area where he was seriously injured.[41]

The LBT-1 was also subjected to catapult trails. These included launches with a tug from NAMC's field cat. However, additional work was performed with aircraft 85266 at the NAF's Muston Field. The glider was itself launched at up to 4,000 pounds from the H2-1 catapult. The shuttle cock bridle (pendant) attached to two points under the fuselage approximately half way between the main and nose gear. The holdback shackle was attached to a fitting under the glider aligned with the two main gear aft posts. They used a ½-inch diameter and 9.9-foot long tensioned holdback angled at 5 degrees.[42] As with the XLNT-1, these tests may have been a prelude to launches in combination with a fighter shot off and the glider in trail.

Examples from each of the three companies were ready for testing on or before 1 January 1945 and all were flying in April. As with so many wartime projects, production orders were placed for all three GLOMB designs before the system had proven itself, for a total 100 of each. Although the initial Taylorcraft order was small, it was expanded to 50 LBT-1s in June 1944.[43] This was extended again to 100 gliders. (The record shows Bureau

The prototype Piper XLBP-1 is poised to begin the takeoff roll under tow. A TV camera aperture is above the towline attachment while the bag beneath likely contains the drogue parachute to stabilize the line after release. The face of the pilot is barely visible far back in the cockpit and buried amongst gear. (Air Force Flight Test Center)

The low-slung XLBP-1 was purpose-built for ease of bomb loading, likely through the belly where removable panels are evident. Note the shock mounts for the main gear struts, perforated dive flaps, the wind turbine under the nose, and the spin recovery parachute under projecting from the fuselage rear end. The antenna above the fuselage was common to all three purpose-built GLOMBs. (Air Force Flight Test Center)

Taylorcraft's XLBT-1 GLOMB (the first, 85265, shown) was clean, like the others, for high speed. This angle emphasizes the wind turbine and perforated dive brake panels that rotate 90 degrees into the airflow. Note the towline attach point on the nose and the flat optical panel at the forward end of the canopy for the TV camera imaging. (National Archives)

Set for a catapult shot from a land-based H2-1 catapult in Philadelphia, XLBT-1 85266 was clean, like the others, for high speed. The bridle to the catapult shuttle and holdback shackle are shown attached to the glider, all tensioned such that the nose strut is fully compressed. The safety pilot station is visible through the open door and the GLOMB electronics boxes are seen forward of this. (National Museum of Naval Aviation)

Numbers assigned for only an additional 35 LBT-1s, so perhaps the 50 is a mistaken 60 or contracts for the full number were never formalized.) However, the slow progress by the manufacturers and dwindling enthusiasm in the Department compelled the CNO to order on 23 September 1944 cancellation of all GLOMBs production beyond a total of 100.[44] Hence, all the GLOMB contracts were reduced to 85 each in November 1944 and 35 each in February 1945. The Taylorcraft contract was cancelled in October 1944. Only the initial 25 were completed. The LBP-1 has been described as an alternate production source for the LBE-1.[45] Its contract was cancelled on 8 June 1945 owing partially to problems landing the fully loaded aircraft. The three prototypes were collected in Lock Haven and scrapped, along with all existing production parts. The Pratt, Read contract was finally terminated on 14 August 1945 with only the three XLBE-1s delivered. A fourth was 90 percent complete at cancellation but finished in Johnsville.[46]

Commander in Chief of the United States Fleet expressed the view that canceling GLOMB was premature and, given the combat success of the radar-homing Bat missile, urged the system be adapted to the gliders. On 29 May 1945 he directed that three LBE-1s be so modified.[47] However, this could not be accomplished on the proposed schedule and it fell away at the end of the war.[48]

Air Forces Parallel

The USAAF pursued guided weapons programs to reduce losses from mass bomber raids taking out point targets. Their focus was on manually or autonomously directed

Although flown and relatively successful, as exemplified by this landing XLBP-1, the GLOMB program was ultimately cancelled. By fall 1944 deployment of significant numbers was so far in the future as to appear operationally insignificant for the ongoing war. Only a handful of the three types were completed. (Air Force Flight Test Center)

free-fall bombs or bombs with aero surfaces for minimal glide such that the release aircraft could remain outside flak range of a heavily defended target. However, some effort was expended on exploring bomb gliders.

Any unmanned towed glider would face the same need for autotow from takeoff as the Navy GLOMBs, and the USAAF appears to have worked on this problem. The Air Forces also explored towed gliders to serve as targets, supplementing or replacing drones and other towed devices like sleeves. The earliest towed target of this period was from Bristol Aeronautical who was under a 3 December 1941, $25,000.00 fixed-price contract to develop and produce 10 C-1 towed target gliders to be delivered from December 1941 to February 1942. The contract was amended to 12 gliders and $30,000.00, the 13 for $33,918.00.

The C-1s were slow in emerging and being tested, with deliveries in January through August 1942. Another 25 gliders were orders on 13 February 1943 for $26,250.00. This was cancelled on 13 July after nine articles were delivered for a loss of $13,680.38. The Army was dissatisfied with Bristol's performance and had found a radio-controlled model that satisfactorily served their purpose. However, another report has it that the AAF spent $76,000.00 for 21 target gliders.[49]

To assist C-1 development and gather other fundamental data on naturally stabilized towed gliders, a very rudimentary model of approximately five foot span was built for wind tunnel tests and towing behind a jeep (to include figure eight turns). This work was performed at NACA Langley in the early months of 1942. Towline attach points, tail surface area, and wing dihedral could be altered quickly and testing repeated. It was noted "it seems that there is a very small range in which successful tow can be made."[50] Tests with this and like models plus the C-1 continued into 1943. Through this expedient, means for naturally stabilizing the aircraft on tow were identified, to include the importance of placing the towline attach point ahead of the center of gravity.

Possibly as part of the automatic tow effort, a Frankfort XTG-1 training glider was modified for radio control. To improve ground stability during the takeoff roll, wheel landing gear was added on the sides of the fuselage and it retained the original all-moving tail surfaces. The towline hook mechanism was modified for electrical release. The cockpit was filled with electronics and an antenna protruded from the nose.

Bristol Aeronautical Corporation of New Haven, Connecticut, built 21 C-1 tow target gliders for the Army during 1943 before a radio-controlled article was adopted. This was a simple aircraft shape but wings supported by guy wires and with skids under the fuselage and wings. The wooden target (seen here at moment of release) measured 35.0 feet in span, 33.0 feet in length, and stood 6.3 feet high. (National Museum of the United States Air Force)

"Working to find a means to naturally stabilize an unmanned glider on tow, the USAAF and NACA joined forces for experiments during 1942 and 1943. Among the work was this rudimentary glider of a few feet span, with the "side force fin" above the wing centersection, which could be towed behind a jeep and quickly modified. The BG-2A marking is not believed to have anything to do with bomb gliders. (National Archives)"

A parachute filled what had been the windscreen to permit recovery of the valuable aircraft if radio-guided landing proved impractical (if even contemplated). Under the project direction of Captain Adam Stolzenberger, the modified glider was taken to the Eglin Field proving grounds for testing during 1943. There it was lost in a spin after the parachute failed to deploy. Some reports suggest spin or flutter trials were the principal purpose of the testing.[51]

The US Army Air Forces had their own bomb glider development program. This required autotow and remote control for the aircraft. Among the first experiments along these line was flight testing of this heavily modified XTG-1 trainer with radio control, an almost all-moving vertical tail, and a recovery parachute in the nose. (National Archives)

Some of the "innards" of the XTG-1 converted as a remotely piloted aircraft are revealed in this image of the wrecked glider. During tests in Florida during 1943 that reportedly included spins, the aircraft impacted the ground. Note the recovery parachute still packed. (Charles Day Collection)

The research work and feasibility studies by the Engineering Division's Equipment Laboratory supported a January 1942 decision to move quickly in acquiring bomb gliders. A development program was established as a radio-controlled bomb glider project MX-197.

The Air Forces began the process of acquiring bomb gliders with an order for ten XBG-1 aircraft. These were to be provided by the Fletcher Aviation Corporation of Pasadena, California, under an $87,250.00, 5 March 1942 contract. The glider was developed by removing the R-985 engine from the piloted PQ-11A and PQ-11B aerial targets and installing remote control systems. Ten of the wooden PQ-11s had been completed (sharing the same serial number as the XBG-1s) before the order was cancelled. The PQ-11s were themselves redesign of the CQ-1 drone control aircraft. Fletcher had completed a single metal YCQ-1A (41-38984) in 1942 with R-985, but a

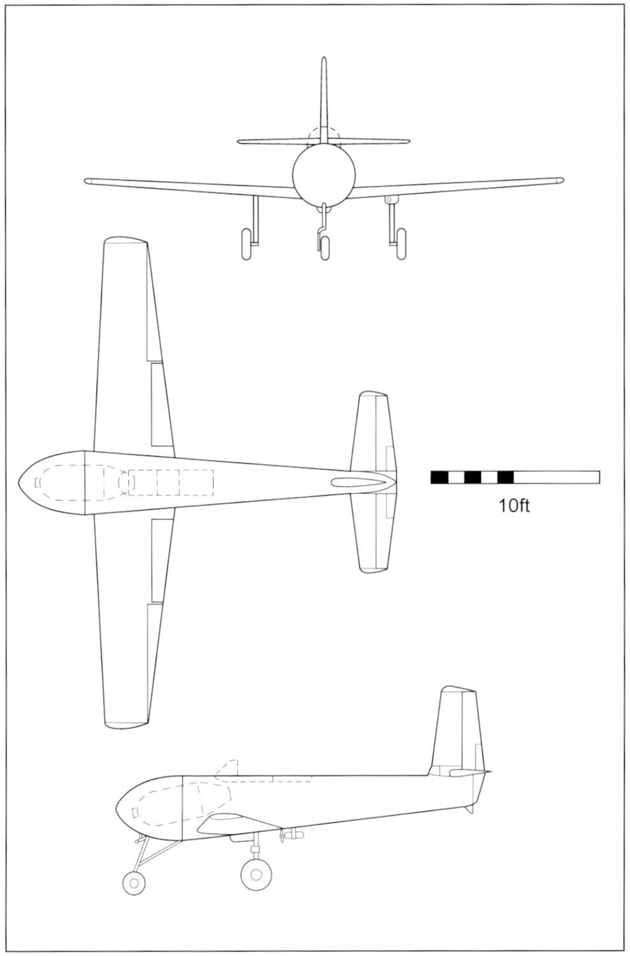

Table 13-01	
Fletcher Aviation XBG-1 Specifics (estimated, not built)	
span	30.0 ft
wing area	125 ft^2
length	23.3 ft
height	10.4 ft
empty weight	1,616 lbs
loaded weight	3,700 lbs
maximum dive speed	286 mph
stall speed	77 mph
glide ratio	10:1

The Fletcher Aviation Corporation of Pasadena, California, took a contract to built 10 of these BG-1 bomb gliders. The otherwise rudimentary aircraft was to have a television camera and radio remote control, with electrical power provided by the wind-driven turbine beneath the fuselage. Piloting gear, including the windscreen, could be installed for ferry missions, but the interior would normally be configured to take a 2,000-pound bomb as shown. (Author)

subsequent pre-production order was cancelled. The CQ-1 was itself a redesign of the unsuccessful Fletcher FBT-2 wooden trainer with R-769 engine developed by Wendell S. Fletcher who headed the company that also included Frank P. and Maurice C. Fletcher. For the CQ-1, in addition to the engine swap, a turtle deck was eliminated and landing gear altered from conventional to tricycle.[52] Consequently, the PQ-11 airframes were on hand for a second metamorphosis and delivered in May 1942.

The wood BG-1 was to carry a 2,000-pound AN-M34 warhead in the 3.9-foot wide fuselage. Landing gear would remain fixed and flaps would be electrically actuated.[53] Upon release as much as 11.0 miles from the target, the operator aboard the towing bomber would guide the glider into the objective via reference to a TV image. Maximum gross weight was to be 3,700 pounds.[54]

The first XBG-1 was completed in April 1942, albeit in a manned configuration for flight testing and likely lacking all other remote control gear. This actually appears to have been a wood CQ-1A with full sliding canopy versus the simple windscreen and overturn bar planned for the final manned configuration. The engine and cowling had been removed and replaced with a wooden nose fairing. Three piloted tow and

The basis for the Fletcher BG-1 bomb glider was the firm's CQ-1A drone control aircraft. This was a simple and quickly manufactured design that began life as an all-wood trainer hopeful. The sole example of this type, the YCQ-1A is shown at Wright Field. (National Museum of the United States Air Force)

This photo shows an example XBG-1 during flight tested at Muroc in a manned configuration. The BG-1 removed the CQ-1A's engine and added an aerodynamic nose plug. The fitting on the belly was meant for a ram air turbine. (National Museum of the United States Air Force)

free-flights tests were conducted from the dry lakebed at Muroc AAB on the 26th and 27th. Mr. Browne of Fletcher piloted the glider while Lieutenant Colonel Dent and Lieutenant Decker piloted the B-23 tow plane. Tests up to 3,800 pounds gross weight were satisfactory, although the c.g. was too far forward at the heaviest weight. Maximum rate of descent was 1,700 fpm at 115 mph with ¼ flaps.[55]

Stall tests were performed at Mines Field on 23 August 1942 with a CQ-1A drone control aircraft (41-38930) fitted with a mockup of the television guidance system fairing under the left wing.[56]

By June 1942, conversion of the PQ-11s was well underway, with five aircraft accepted that month and reportedly all delivered by the end of the month.[57] These featured installation of a 3-axis compact hydraulic servo unit, electric motor throttle control, propeller pitch control and flap control, SCR-549 television transmitter, radio equipment,

The YCQ-1A was flown on 23 August 1942 to check for altered stall behavior with several proposed shapes intended to represent the television camera installation on the BG-1. These were evidently on the port wing of the wooden airplane. This pair of images reveals two of the installations. (National Archives)

Table 13-02	
Fletcher Aviation XBG-2 Specifics (estimated, not built)	
span	45.0 ft
wing area	208 ft²
length	23.3 ft
empty weight	2,431 lbs
loaded weight	6,531 lbs
stall speed	84 mph
glide ratio	10.9:1

bomb arming equipment, tow cable solenoid release mechanism, and wind-driven generator under the belly. Further manned flight testing at Muroc was planned as well as remote flight at Biggs Field, El Paso, Texas, with a 1,000-pound bomb to avoid an overloaded condition.

Fletcher was also awarded a letter contract on 1 April 1942 for development of three wood XBG-2s for $83,000.00. This glider was to use two fuselages and outer wing panels of the XBG-1 joined by a new wing center section and horizontal tail, four main gear struts, and the TV fairing under the inboard wing on the centerline or in the starboard fuselage nose. A 2,000-pound bomb was to be installed in each fuselage.[58]

Extensive work appears to have been conducted with the XBG-1 and baseline PQ-11A, but an Engineering Division memorandum of 9 June 1943 reported that, ultimately, the flight characteristics proved unsatisfactory. They recommended canceling the XBG-1 and XBG-2 programs.[59] The XBG-2 contract was terminated on 8 September 1942 with none completed and Fletcher paid $16,546.56.[60]

Cornelius Aircraft Corporation submitted a proposal on 28 January 1943 for a bomb glider capable of carrying a 4,000-pound bomb. This was resubmitted on 8 May with a recommended cost of $92,958.60 for a single flight example to be delivered six months after agreement. This was a tailless design of 28.8-foot length and forward-swept wings spanning 53.0 feet, very similar to their XFG-1 fuel glider (Chapter 11). The "electrical eye" in the nose would be uncovered then the towline was released and capable of 25-degrees tilting motion. Other equipment would include electric servos, bomb arming

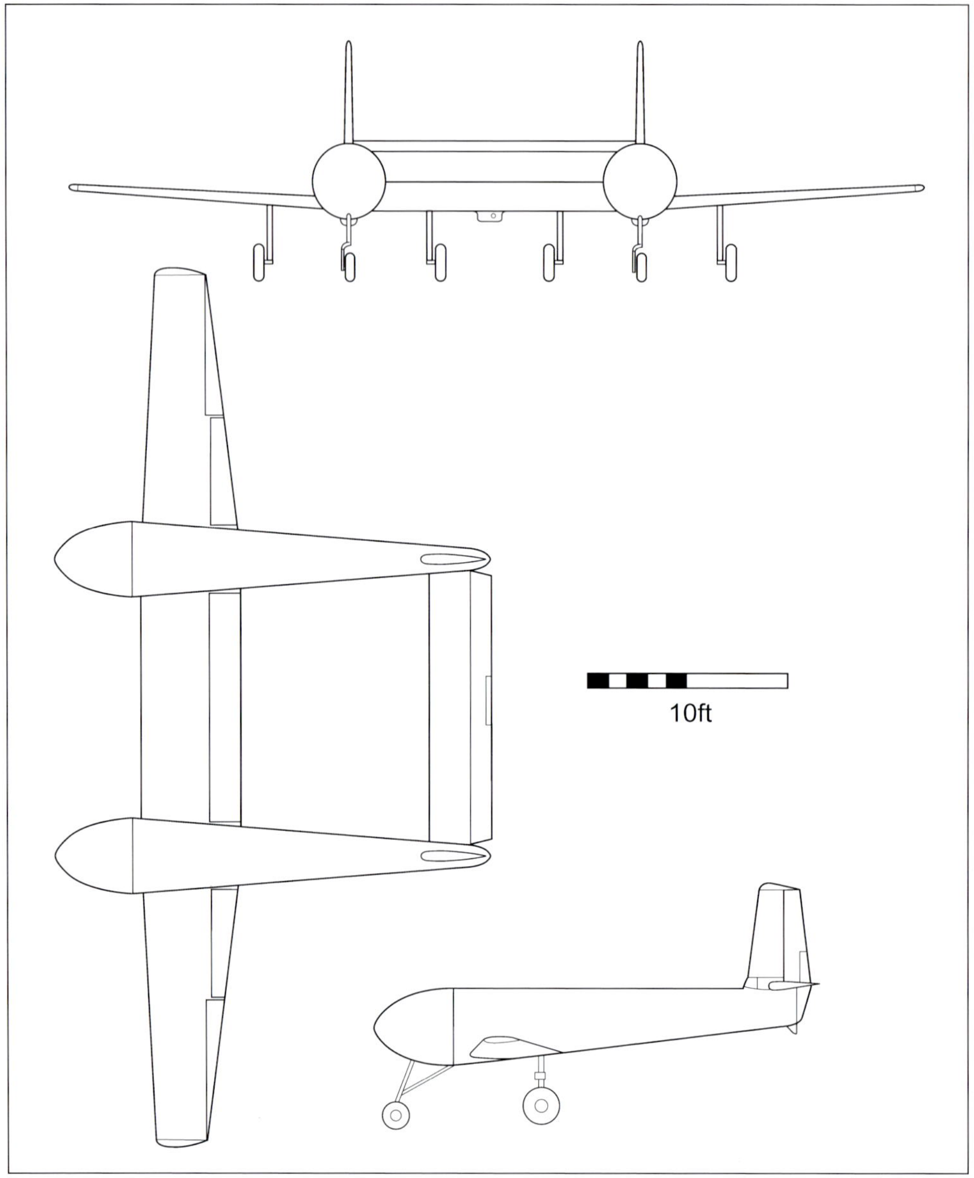

Fletcher also contracted to develop the XBG-2 bomb glider and deliver three. Based upon the XBG-1 by joining two with a common center wing and horizontal, it was very unusual. However, work only progressed to 20 percent complete before the project was abandoned, flight characteristics judged via analysis to be unsuitable. (Author)

mechanism, radio transmitter, battery, and wind-driven generator. A tripod landing gear would be jettisoned after tow off.[61]

The Aircraft Laboratory worked with Cornelius to achieve a glider of suitable stability and control. The Lab desired examples for flight test of the unusual configuration.

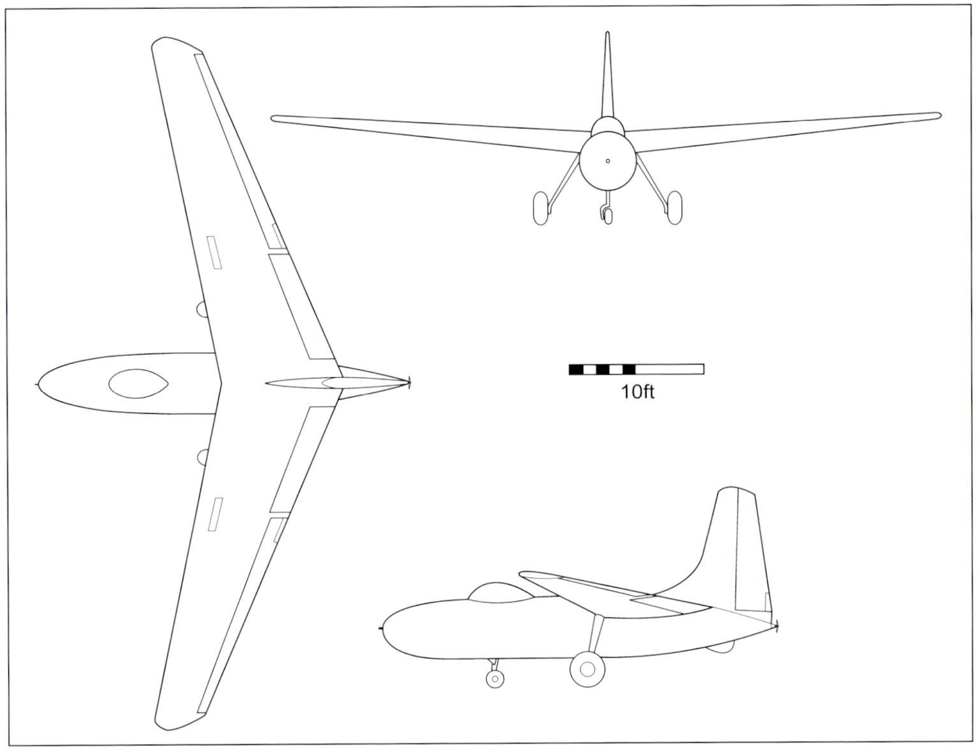

Cornelius Aircraft Corporation also conceived a bomb glider design that won an Army contract for one example. The tailless, forward-swept wing design with fixed undercarriage and aft wind turbine was innovative. Although there was interest in pursuing the project for its engineering value alone, it was shortly terminated. (Author)

These images of period drawings show how the XBG-3 was proposed to be operated. The optionally piloted feature is clear, the canopy deleted for the combat tow behind a bomber, the bridle towline attachment apparent adopted because of the television camera in the nose.

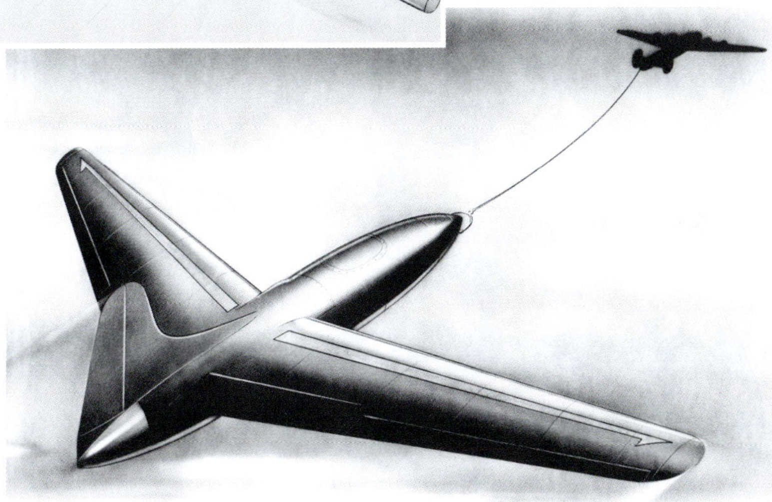

Bomb loading employs hand-cranked winches at four points. (National Archives)

Cornelius was contracted for one XBG-3 in 1943, but that order was also cancelled the same year before delivery.[62]

There appears to nave been another bomb glider project executed by the Engineering Division and identified only as MX-166. They built a "flying mockup" experimental glider capable of hauling a 2,000-pound bomb and fabricated of wood. Grossing 3,400 pounds and with 144 square foot wing area, it is known to have had a conventional tail, and the towline attachment point was 9.7 feet ahead of the c.g. The glider was shipped to Muroc on 10 December 1943 and was, at least temporarily, lost in transit. This work was to provide data for a glider capable for carrying a 10,000-pound bomb.[63]

Fade Out

Ultimate failure of the USAAF bomb glider program to produce any fieldable weapons may be linked to several factors. They simply did not prove necessary given the tremendous rate of bomber production and steady erosion of enemy fighter forces. It was found that dragging a glider consumed so much excess power that the "mother ship" would likely be unable to carry internal bombs if a flight of any practical range was planned. Natural stability on tow was possible but a careful balancing act that could be upset in turbulence. Additionally, the remote sensing of a target and radio control of the aircraft left much to be desired. Even the free-fall guided bombs were proving poor in combat. All this suggested mission success rate would be quite low.

The more promising Navy effort was ultimately doomed by its initial slow progress in the shadow of the drones, ending any chances it would contribute to the war. The drone program did yield a fielded weapon that saw a few unsuccessful war shots. GLOMB results simply arrived too late and the gliders continued to suffer problems, especially in light of the final Traverse City accident in July 1945. A review the following month resulted in program cancellation soon after. The larger GLOMB gliders, as discussed in Chapter 9, had already been eliminated. The system was clearly not going to be required in bringing the war to a successful conclusion and more practical guided weapons were already in the wings. The Traverse City team had concluded in April 1945 that the LBT-1 system was unsuitable for carrier operations—a requirement dictated by the CNO as the war moved into a more mobile phase for the U.S.—owing to "logistics difficulties, complicated operations and control equipment, etc."[64]

Additional tow planes were qualified as they became available. This included the Fairchild C-82A Packet with the challenge of attaching the tow rope to the twin booms. This 1946 image shows a CG-15A towed behind the Packet in a very high-tow position. (National Archives)

14

Postwar Momentum

Following Japan's surrender and the sudden end to the Second World War, orders for more than 4,000 cargo transport gliders were abruptly cancelled. At the end of hostilities many hundreds of CG-4As were disposed of overseas, scrapped or burned, instead of bothering to hauling them back home. Many hundreds more were scrapped States-side without having been shipped. An enormous surplus was offered for sale, still crated, at just $50-200 apiece. The principal attraction was the excellent crates with thousands of board-feet of high-quality lumber, or the boxes left intact to serve as sheds.

Dedicated glider pilot training and Flight Officers disappeared entirely. Some of the few glider pilots that remained in the service transformed to power pilots, and glider flying became just another qualification for a rated officer. Although the assumption for a time was that gliders would remain part of airborne operations, the number of operational gliders and pilots declined precipitously. There was little grief over these developments within the Army Air Forces since gliders and glider pilots had been simply tolerated during the war. Gliders had never been popular even with airborne troops.

The wartime gliders offered utility lacking in powered transports. While efforts to add powerplants to the gliders yielded anemic airplanes, it was suggestive of the tactical transports so urgently needed. This production PG-2A was, based upon markings, photographed in or after 1947 and so more properly a G-2A. (The Peter M. Bowers Collection/The Museum of Flight)

Carrying On

A momentous change was creation on 18 September 1947 of the United States Air Force (USAF) as a separate service. A June 1948 aircraft designation shuffle that removed the "C" from the former "CG" for the combat gliders. Hence, the CG-4As retained in the postwar period became G-4A, in addition to G-15As and G-13As. A few XPG-2As survived long enough to be redesignated PG-2A on 18 November 1946[1] and G-2As in June 1948, while the XPG-3 became G-3.

The equally dramatic drawdown of U.S. forces left gliders largely neglected. Postwar plans included requirements for 1,059 G-4As or equivalent lift per airborne division, with the expectation of one division at 60 percent strength or 750 gliders. War strength could demand 6,000 gliders per year.[2] As things wound down in fall 1945, the intent was to ensure retention of tooling and jigs to permit a rate of 300 Wacos per month at any

Gliders were one means for artic rescue and resupply. Here a CG-4A operates on an ice runway. It has a multitude of skids under the nose, lacks mid-fuselage skids, and has high-floatation main gear tires with a small skid plate replacing the tail wheel. The interior has been insulated. (National Soaring Museum)

future date. However, the political and fiscal realities were such that no action was taken to realize such production or reserves.

Although consideration was given to postwar production of the G-15A, the low production rate would have meant a prohibitively high cost. Additionally, Waco suffered profound labor strife following the war that undermined profitability, and it soon liquidated. The lack of production meant the gliders were bound to disappear over time owing, if for no other reason, to attrition. Experience had shown that attrition was greater for gliders than airplanes, even in training.

Some improvements were made to the existing glider fleet plus efforts at standardizing configurations. Postwar G-15As were seen with a trio of fairings under the noses that were likely streamlined reinforcing skids. Trials with the glider towed by a Fairchild C-82A Packet were performed in 1946. This new twin-boom airlifter was suitable for towing gliders up to 15,000 pounds.

Six G-15As (45-5520 and -5276 observed) and two Douglas C-54 tugs were modified at Wright-Patterson AFB in 1947 (prior to September) to support arctic rescue. The gliders had a gas heater in a "heater bump" fairing above the cabin, a gasoline tank inside, insulation, added radios, and an all-metal belly to withstand impact from snow and ice. The Skymasters were winterized, given long-range fuel tanks and additional radios, and carried glider pick-up gear. These were felt necessary after B-29s were stationed in Alaska to perform weather reconnaissance ahead of any combat operations. At any one time, a trio of gliders and one tow plane would be stationed in Alaska to react if a bomber went down in the wilderness. The glider could land nearby, take the crew aboard, and be snatched out while the heater kept the men from freezing.[3] Prior to this, at least one G-15A was devoted to artic rescue, fitted with skis in place of the fuselage skids (45-5399 observed).

One notable rescue was performed on 13 December 1948 but with a G-15A fitted with neither heater nor skis. A C-47 had suffered fuel exhaustion and crash-landed on the frozen Stewart River in Alaska. As planned, the glider landed on the ice, the crew erected the pick-up rig, everyone clambered aboard, and the C-54 snatched the lot to safety.[4] A similar attempt in late 1948 while trying to retrieve downed C-47 and B-17 aircrew in Greenland left two G-15As with (heaters equipped but without skis) wrecked on the ice. One was rendered non-airworthy when its tow ropes snapped during two

For operations on snow, this CG-15A has been fitted with a ski undercarriage, both main and tail. Artic rescue remained a priority for several years with continuing flights to and from Europe via Greenland and similar locales. B-29s were also performing weather reconnaissance in Alaska and so increasing the potential need. (National Museum of the United States Air Force)

This is one if six G-15As modified for Artic climates with a heater in a dorsal fairing and what is likely an exhaust in the forward corner of the fuselage. The ends of the sheet metal belly can be seen bent up the base of the glider while unseen is interior insulation. This glider has an angle-of-dangle input rod projecting from the nose, its forward stabilizing struts are extended, pilot doors removed, and high-flotation tires installed. (National Museum of the United States Air Force)

Although high-volume production of the CG-10A was approved, the USAAF struggled to balance this against competing requirements. A row ensued with Ground Forces Command who saw the glider as the answer to many of its airborne assault ills. After frustrating delays, production was ordered, but the sudden end of the war meant the quantity was cut to the point only ten of the YG-10As, like that shown here, were delivered. (National Museum of the United States Air Force)

snatch attempts, on the last the line recoiling back to badly damage the aircraft. The other got airborne before the towline broke and the pilot crash landed back on the ice. A JATO-equipped C-47 finally brought everyone out.[5]

The development and test work that introduced changes to the G-15As carried on in other aspects of combat gliders, albeit at a peacetime pace. The XCG-14A continued to be flown for a few years after the war, collecting data for another generation of gliders, should they be funded. Flight testing by the AAF occurred as late as June 1948 and by Chase as late as October 1948 after the government bailed the aircraft to the company. Some unclear modifications apparently occurred during this period. The glider was declared excess materiel on 16 December 1949.[6]

Plans for the CG-10A (Chapter 8) were dramatically sidetracked by the end of hostilities, postwar budget cutting, and advent of the C-82A. Here, again, there was a profusion of conflicting direction as to reducing the numbers, stretching out production, or immediate termination. In May 1945, Army Ground Forces had sought 139 CG-10As, sufficient to meet the heavy equipment transport demands of an airborne division in a single lift.[7] The numbers was reduced to ten YCG-10As on 19 October 1945, then to three gliders on 12 February 1946 in a decision that effectively terminated the contract. The AGF efforts in November 1945 to reconstitute the production were disapproved. Elements of the 100 gliders were already under construction by subcontractors. The converted 41-61100 was inspected at the new Louisville plant in April 1946. The first of the YCG-10As was delivered in St. Louis on 5 October 1945, the second on 9 February 1946, and the last on 1 April 1946. Because of the investment to get to this point in the program, and the termination fees, these were among the three most expensive aircraft purchased by the USAAF to that time at roughly $1,100,000.00 apiece. A total $11,000,000.00 had been expended on the Laister-Kauffman program.

Some of the YCG-10As survived through June 1948 to become YG-10As, but appear to have been scrapped soon thereafter. The whole affair ended badly with an extensive investigation of company claims for final payments, suits against the company by vendors who had not been paid in the interim, and great political pressure in Washington. Laister-Kauffmann filed for bankruptcy.

Experiments Continue

Major Floyd Sweet spent his wartime Army service in gliders. This was wise use of manpower as he had been a pre-war glider flight instructor; an occupation he continued in uniform before joining the glider development team in Ohio. He came to lead this work in the immediate post-war period. (National Soaring Museum)

Army glider test activities moved in November 1945 from Clinton County AAF to Freeman Field in Seymour, Indiana. On 19 February 1946, the engineering activities were moved to the Aircraft Projects Section, Engineering Division. The following month they moved back to Wright Field with Major Floyd Sweet, Captain Marion A. Miller, and Lewis J. Stowe principal players in the postwar glider work. Workload dropped significantly as urgency dissipated and the glider force was trimmed to a shadow of its former self. However, at least for several years, it was assumed that gliders would have some role in future airborne warfare. Improvements in the equipment were pursued.

The deceleration devices trials continued after the war, likely in support of new gliders in development for which such things were encouraged in specifications. The bazooka-fired spike was seen being tested beyond late 1947, and CG-15 plow tests earlier. Further efforts were made to develop suitable rocket bottles. This sought lightweight (apparently on the order of 50 pounds) devices producing 1,200 pounds of thrust for 4 seconds that could be made to fire either forward or aft as selected by the pilot. An 8,000-pounds thrust unit with 3-second duration weighing 46.9 pounds appeared promising at the end of 1946. Yet, the rockets were not adopted as standard kit.[8]

Trials towing "crippled" aircraft was continued for a time until this, too, disappeared. It saw such unusual spectacles as a prop-driven bomber towing a jet fighter and a helicopter being dragged (presumably in autogyration) by a transport. Snatch experiments also continued, to include a Sikorsky R-5 helicopter picking up items.

Gliders also served in less martial experiments not directly associated with their intended purpose. At least two TG-32s were modified and used in June-September 1946 to collect data on developing thunderstorms, and possibly later. The gliders were given dive brakes for the tests, in addition to special weather instruments, and were required to descend rapidly into thunderclouds. This Thunderstorm Project was based at Pinecastle

Testing of the tube-fired spike to rapidly decelerate the glider was resumed in 1948 as evidenced by this pair of photos with an experimental installation on a U.S. Air Force G-15A. A steel cable is attached between the spike and the nylon line stored in the bottom housing. The images appear to show spike loading and results following a landing (tape having secured temporary line routing). (National Archives)

Tow tests were continued after the war as benefits were seen in aiding stricken aircraft or extending the range of fighter aircraft and helicopters. Here a Lockheed P-80 is towed behind a B-29 during flight testing in 1947. The hook-up was apparently via snatch and with an unusually short line from what is evidently an added member projecting from the P-80 nose. (National Museum of the United States Air Force)

AAB in Pinecastle, Florida. Modifications included extensive instrumentation plus a hole in the nose that permitted ice crystals to enter and stick to a rolling tape drawn into the aircraft to be closely photographed, before melting, for determination of particle size.[9]

Two LNE-1s (TG-32s) were modified and operated by the Southern California Soaring Association, under government, Department of Defense, and academia funding for atmospheric research. Changes included cameras, sensitive atmospheric instruments, barograph, radio, oxygen system, cockpit insulation, new bubble canopies and added side doors, and sealing the inboard aileron. In 1951 and 1952 they were employed in flights to around 40,000 feet in studying mountain lee waves over the Sierra Nevada Mountains in California. These exceptionally hazardous endeavors claimed one of the aircraft, although the pilot survived.[10] The flights set two world records.[11] In 1955 the remaining aircraft was used for jet stream research.

At least two Pratt, Read TG-32s were modified for postwar research flights into thunderstorms. The cockpit and forward fuselage of one of these gliders is shown, with special instruments, scientific equipment, and a pilot oxygen system evident. (National Soaring Museum)

Postwar, the United States Air Force followed up on Navy and Luftwaffe testing of short and rigid tow systems. Its advantages included the ability to taxi with the glider in tow and greatly reduce the pilot tasks during flight. This is demonstrated at Wright Field as a C-46 pulls a CG-15A on a rigid tow bar arrangement during 31 June 1947. (National Museum of the United States Air Force)

Rigid Tow

The U.S. investigated the German glider experience of the recent war and especially their extensive experimentation, paying the personnel formerly involved to document the work. Among this last was the use of a rigid tow bar instead of a tow rope hundreds of feet long. Some work had been performed along these lines in the U.S. during the war. The Navy had conducted tow with lines reduced to as little as 25 feet and then to a rigid bar (Chapter 11). Further work along these lines in America during 1946-48 was initially also sponsored by the USN.

Wright Field first considered rigid tow experiments in May 1946 after the Third Air Force's Airborne Division performed field trials with a rigid tow system. However, it was November before definite action was taken and equipment fabricated, apparently following the Navy pattern. At the tug end was a ball and socket. At the glider end was a standard fitting but on a universal joint. The bar was 4.0 feet long and weighted approximately 100 pounds. It had a spring-loaded telescoping section with 4-inches of travel for damping longitudinal motion and stress relief. Position lights were added to the horizontal stabilizer of the tug to help the glider pilot maintain position during night operations.

On the tug side of the rigid tow bar system was a ball and socket installation in the end of the transport, here a C-46 with surrounding fairing. The glider-side of the rigid tow system reveals the universal joint ahead of the fitting into the release mechanism. Also seen is the telescoping section for stress relief, a chord for ship-to-ship intercom, and the taut cable likely for a tug-end release. (National Soaring Museum)

Rigid tow of the CG-15A behind a C-82 required a triangular truss arrangement with attachment to the tug at the end of each boom. It appears there is a rotating interface at the crossbar and the angled tubes to the tow bar. For a tricycle gear aircraft, the glider airborne first and pulling the tug's tail up was less critical that for a tail wheel airplane. (National Archives)

The flight tests in June-October 1947 employed a CG-15A (45-12758) and CG-4A behind a C-46F (44-78708, CD-708). Other trials employed another CG-15A (45-55276) and a C-47 (42-23918), while tests were also performed with 45-55276 behind a C-82A (44-23004). In the later case the bar was at the apex of a triangular truss attached to the end of each of the transport's tail booms.

Trials with the CG-15 behind the C-46 were encouraging. Flight in weather and turbulence did not prove any more fatiguing than in a twin-engine trainer. The tug could tow the glider down on a night or instrument approach and release it at about 50 feet above the runway. The glider could then land on the sod beside the runway as the tug landed on the pavement. Alternatively, the glider could make S-turns to kill speed and land behind the tug on the runway. The combination could even taxi together, including negotiating turns. Additionally, the rigid bar provided a more reliable interphone connection between the two aircraft.

The design was not without some concerns. The CG-4A behind the C-46 was not as good a combination because the glider's aileron control was too slow during takeoff, in addition to other undesirable characteristics. Unlike common practice with a towline, if the glider lifted off before the tow plane it would lift the tug's tail wheel off the ground and produce directional instability. So, while promising, the rigid tow system was not adopted as standard practice by the USAF.

Fighter-Glider Composites

The German use of *Mistel* composite aircraft, or a fighter physically attached in combination with an unmanned or unpowered aircraft, including gliders, was likely unknown to the Allies when they began considering a similar approach with cargo gliders. However, there were pre-war precedents that also offered inspiration. If a fighter propelled the glider below its fuselage in "pick-a-back" fashion, tow difficulties would be eliminated and the fighter could remain in the area after release to protect the LZ. This was in contrast to a transport or bomber that could only turn for home, the transport being slow, unarmed, and unarmored. The fighter combination could also execute evasive action more effectively. Additionally, the glider pilots would not have the exhausting tow flying during the trek to the objective and so would arrive more fresh. Flight in instrument conditions was more feasible. There was also a possibility the power required to haul the glider would be less than on a towline, increasing range and reducing engine overheat potential. Fuel for the flight could be drawn from a tank within the glider, allowing the fighter full fuel to loiter after glider release. Pick-a-back could also provide a means to ferry gliders to the theater, saving the enormous freight volume, time, and cost.

Of course, such ideas were not the province of Germany alone, although they were more inclined to expend resources on such marginal pursuits. An example of the ideas offered in America during the dire period of 1942 was a compound aircraft concept from Ford Motor Company engineer Charles D. Koch. He conceived a glider-pursuit composite with the fighter attached atop a glider that was filled with fuel to give the fighter extended range across the vast Pacific distances. The glider also had bombs so that when the pursuit aircraft reached its destination it could release the glider to descend onto and destroy a target. Koch's idea was rejected as infeasible, although the fuel and bomb gliders were the subject of later experimentation as already described.

A similar composite was proposed by Lieutenant Colonel Anthony B. Harris, USAAF, in Fall 1941 as a means of ferrying fighters. Although ignored, he promoted the idea again in August 1943 with respect to gliders after the discouraging experiences of the North Africa and Sicily glider lifts. Harris, an Airborne officer, also envisioned a 200-foot wingspan glider with nine single-engine fighters attached. However, his initial idea was a Lockheed P-38 Lightning mounted above one of the British large-capacity Hamilcar gliders.[12]

Assigned in England, Harris contacted the RAF and General Aircraft, Ltd., manufacturer of the Hamilcar, receiving encouragement and offers of assistance. After studying the two aircraft together at Netheravon in August 1943, it appeared possible that a P-38 above each wing would be required. The glider wings would need additional bracing, and fuel tanks within the wings. With a single P-38 above the fuselage, it was expected a C-47 would still be required to assist takeoff by towing the combination aloft with the P-38 engines contributing. During the flight to the objective, the combination would be flown by the glider pilot who would have control of the P-38's engines, and the fighter would have its flight controls locked. Some initial engineering and flying with the P-38 in a high-drag configuration suggested the concept was feasible, the engines not at risk of overheating.

The UK Ministry of Aircraft Production initially endorsed a flight test by the USAAF provided British resources were not required. By February 1944 preliminary design of the necessary hardware and aircraft modifications had been performed but approval to proceed with flight testing had still not been granted. Detailed design work was undertaken at Lockheed Overseas Corporation at Langford Lodge, Northern Ireland. Their proximity to Belfast and the Short Brothers works meant the team could consult the personnel who had created and operated the Short-Mayo pre-war composite.[13] A single-point and dual-point attachment was explored. There was certainly interest within the European Theater for capabilities offered by the P-38+Hamilcar composite.[14]

Subsequent analysis by British and American elements cast grave doubts on the ability of a single P-38 to haul the Hamilcar without engine overheat, adequate stability and control of the combination, and success of the inflight separation. The "Over-Under" project was a long-shot without considerable engineering. Invasion of the continent appeared imminent so time may already have run out to support that operation. Consequently, the P-38+Hamilcar composite was shelved while more promising combinations were studied. Consequently, the effort was suspended by summer 1944 with advice that it be further developed in the States with proper engineering resources. Design was 90 percent complete and hardware 50 percent, and a flight had been anticipated for mid-May.

The Glider Branch took up the project in July 1944, assisted by other Materiel Command elements and Harris. In short order the analysis deemed the P-38+Hamilcar combination infeasible. It also appeared that the aerodynamic interference between the aircraft meant the fighter had to expend more power than in towing flight. However, a P-38+XCG-10A hybrid appeared more feasible for demonstrating the concept, although the useful load of the glider would be compromised. The matter was set aside awaiting specific direction from Air Staff. This was not forthcoming.[15]

Harris did not forget Materiel Command's comment on the XCG-10A and raised his proposal again in a February 1946, suggesting the North American P-82 Twin Mustang be substituted for the Lightning. Although no requirement then existed for such hybrids, it was felt the feasibility should be explored through a flight test. The Luftwaffe's *Mistel* trials with gliders were known by this time. Following the wartime difficulties of transporting disassembled gliders overseas in enormous crates and then assembling them in the hundreds for operations, the composite had the additional attraction for the US in permitting long-range deployment of a fully assembled glider that could perhaps contain fuel transferable to the fighter in flight. However, the press of more practical work in the fiscally constrained postwar environment meant no project was established. Claims that a P-38+Hamilcar composite was finally flown by the U.S. Army in December 1949 are almost certainly erroneous.

Charting a Course

In early 1944, Wright Field urged rejuvenation of glider development work to address criticisms from operators in support of what they were then calling "airphibious" operations. They considered an all-metal model of clean aerodynamic design and increased efficiency. With resources like sheet aluminum by then more plentiful, it was possible to contemplate all-metal gliders that were more durable and might have a broader role. There was also the concept of making the glider easily converted with engines. Prior to the winning of air superiority the aircraft would be flown with engines, after they could fly as gliders. However, on 6 July 1944 the Dayton team urged that such efforts be held in abeyance until data from actual combat employment of the original model gliders was obtained from the ETO.[16]

A Luftwaffe Me 109 drags a DFS 230 glider along in a composite "Mistel" configuration. Although the Americans considered such a concept during the war, the U.S. Army did not seriously address it until postwar. Some effort was expended analyzing a P-38 affixed atop a Hamilcar glider, but the work ultimately led nowhere. (National Museum of the United States Air Force)

By 1945 the U.S. Army had gained sufficient experience with gliders to appreciate their potential and deficiencies. In January of that year, even given the looming production of the CG-10A, the Army Ground Forces made clear the need for improved assault gliders.[17] Reflecting this sentiment, the Deputy Chief of Air Staff proclaimed on 30 March 1945 that "all present types of gliders are considered to be obsolescent, because they deteriorate rapidly, and are inflexible in that they can be used only as gliders."[18]

As the U.S. Army contemplated the future of the glider force in the postwar period, they chose to consider them more as assault aircraft in keeping with their role as it had evolved during the conflict. They continued from the assessment of mid-1944 that the wartime gliders had very limited capabilities and were wasteful as single-mission aircraft. The CG-4A was already considered obsolete at that time, yet remained the dominant combat glider. It was also evident that the cost of the final evolution of these aircraft, as represented by the XCG-10A and CG-13A, compared with their likely high loss rate during assault landings, would probably be uncomfortably great. The example of the powered glider as *ersatz* tactical transports suggested that money was best spent on a rugged powered aircraft in a peacetime economy. Parachuting heavy equipment from transport airplanes remained exploratory, and accuracy of paradrop still relatively poor.

Meetings at the beginning of 1945 endorsed these improvement efforts and provided general guidelines to be pursued. Highlights included all-metal gliders in the 6,000-pound and 12,000-pound payload classes with quickly detachable power units. By spring, this had been refined to an 8,000-pound capacity aircraft possessing a 24.0x7.5x6.0 feet cabin (length x width x height), and another carrying 16,000 pounds in a 30.0x9.2x7.1-foot cabin. Number of troops transported was abandoned as a classification basis. Being limited to the 75 mm howitzer was unacceptable, larger weapons being then required. The gliders were to have tricycle undercarriage, low fuselage floor, and rear loading ramp. Such an aircraft seemed feasible except for replicating the very short landing performance of the extant gliders. Troop Carrier Command cautioned that gliders must not run ahead of the ability to tow them.

The evolving perspective on combat gliders was reflected in a statement by Brigadier General A.R. Maxwell on 27 November 1946, then Chief of the Requirements Division, Office of the Assistant Chief of Air Staff for Operations, when he said, "We are interested in replacing gliders as military equipment since they are too bulky and difficult to ship. ... It is hoped that some day a helicopter can be developed to take its place, but it is possible that gliders will always be with U.S. for some missions. ... The assault transport is not a glider with engines, but is envisioned as something halfway between a C-47 and a helicopter." This view was enforced during August 1947 with an AAF headquarters recommendation that a light assault transport be developed during fiscal year 1949. If this proved a suitable replacement for the light glider, a medium assault transport program should follow in 1951. Advanced glider work should continue in the interim to ensure adequate military capability.[19]

Hence, focus during late 1945-1946 was on more durable and long-lived gliders that might be adapted with power units. These might not be inexpensive aircraft to procure. Those performing the service trials on the XCG-10A recommended an aluminum variant in spring 1945, and this was seriously considered. The manufacturer reworked the LK-12 concept in response, stating the change would cost $1,244,000.00 and take 18-24 months. It was not taken up.

Since the glider had little utility beyond actual combat employment, and potentially hundreds were required to support the airborne forces in wartime, the AAF faced the problem of maintenance and storage of these many idle aircraft. One idea was that steel tube gliders could be built without covering and stored for long periods. An emergency combat need would prompt covering with fabric and immediate employment. A few would be periodically prepared for training and exercises to keep depot skills fresh.[20] The idea had merit, but the service was keen to move away from fabric, and the growing complexity of the gliders bespoke some continuing maintenance demands. The transport and assembly of large gliders could consume weeks and so make rapid response by airborne units meaningless.

Towing in instrument conditions remained impractical, despite extensive development work, greatly limiting tactical value. While the rigid tow bar tests appeared promising, other work appeared less adaptable or operationally suitable. Radar was considered briefly but dismissed as the weight, volume, and power demands of then-current units were prohibitive and use for close-in formation impractical. Even with an autopilot, flight in weather would make deicing a requirement, over-taxing the simple power generation systems aboard the glider.[21]

The XCG-17 experience prompted postwar speculation about similar designs as the USAAF considered all-metal gliders. In February 1946, Fairchild Aircraft proposed a glider derived from its C-82 Packet twin-engine transport.[22] Likewise, it was suggested using surplus Curtiss C-46 Commando twin-engine transports, hundreds of which moldered away in storage, as gliders. The idea appears to have been first proposed in August 1947.[23]

Analysis of both proposals was not promising. While possible, neither conversion would yield a practical assault glider. For the C-46, some 8,100 pounds of ballast would have been permanently mounted to keep the c.g. within limits, giving an empty weight of 27,850 pounds. With a 38,129-40,000-pound GW, depending upon payload, only the four-engine B-29 or C-74 were suitable tugs, requiring 9,800-12,000 feet takeoff distance to clear a 50-foot obstacle. Any manner of steep, low-speed descent for a short landing on unprepared field was out of the question. During the war the C-46 had been frustrating to onload/offload given the slanting deck of the conventional gear airplane and the height of the cargo door from the ground. The capabilities did not compare well with the tactical gliders the USAAF was then contemplating, and the Engineering Division advised against the conversion. A modest $7,500.00 would be required to convert a C-46 to glider prototype and a projected $5,250.00 for 'production' examples. Yet, while cheap, they were so much cast-off junk not coming near to filling Airborne's need. Nothing more came of either proposal.[24]

Formulation of requirements for new gliders began during spring 1945 by Air Technical Services Command. With cancellation of all glider contracts in the immediate postwar period, especially the CG-10A, a de facto freezing of capabilities resulted. By the end of the 1945 the Army had committed to the simultaneous acquisition of gliders with 8,000 pounds useable load and a model of 16,000 pound capacity. They were to be all-metal, aerodynamically clean for high-speed tow, feature tricycle landing gear, and be loaded from the rear. Even with all-metal construction, the mission demanded added attention to crashworthiness in the nose, mandating welded steel tube structure in this area. Cockpits would be more like transport aircraft to ensure against fatigue on long missions. They were to be fitted with full dual controls, emergency escape doors, and removable armor plate. No radio installation was anticipated, only the intership intercom being specified. Flaps and dive brakes were expected to achieve the desired descent rate. Acceleration and deceleration devices such as rockets were to be accommodated. Facilities for paratroop static line jumps were to be included. Troop seats would fold up to allow unobstructed cargo loading. The rear cargo opening was to match the full dimensions of the cargo compartment. There remained the requirement for the aircraft to be broken down into easily transported loads. Simplicity, low cost, inexpensive materials, ease of production, use and storage in adverse conditions, and maintainability were all emphasized.

The C-82 was the preferred tug. However, its performance towing the envisioned heavy glider was projected to be marginal. More powerful engines for the aircraft were being considered. This offered a new prospect for a transport aircraft undergoing significant upgrade to support the glider tow mission, but it did not occur.[25]

The Aircraft Laboratory had designed an all-metal, twin-boom, rear-loading glider designated ATSCD519. The conceptual installation of a pair of P&W R-985-AN1 Wasp Junior engines yielded the ATSCD531.[26] Although this was not taken beyond the drawing board, the notion arose again in spring 1946 with the advent of the Light and Heavy Glider, Assault programs. These included the stated goal of the all-metal gliders readily converted with engines. The improved aerodynamics and load-bearing capability of the metal gliders permitted more powerful engines to be mounted. These would not be "pigs."

New Gliders

Postwar, the aircraft engineering and acquisition functions were separated again with ATSC becoming Air Materiel Command (AMC) on 6 March 1946 and based at what had become Wright-Patterson AFB, joining two nearly contiguous bases. The Engineering Division prepared representative model specifications for the two envisioned gliders. This would help companies prepare proposals and guide the evaluation board. It included a concept representing the 8,000-pound capacity design, identified as ATSC Design No. 559. It featured a lifting aft fuselage and drop-down ramp for cargo onload/offload. The aircraft would still be capable of being broken down for shipment. Provisions would be included for acceleration and deceleration devices, and installation of armor plating at the pilot positions. All this underlay formulating the Military Characteristics for the light glider.

Characteristics were also published for the powered version of this glider, with conversion in eight hours. In addition to the tabulation below, the aircraft was to have provisions for twin .30 cal or a .50 machine gun flex-mounted at the copilot station. A navigator and radio operator station was to be an option. The engine nacelles were to contain fuel tanks, as well as a cabin tank and jettisonable external tanks supporting ferry operations.[27]

After these Characteristics for the 8,000-pounds capacity glider were released, initial bids were welcomed. Of the 21 firms solicited, only three sent proposals. Bell Aircraft Corporation submitted their Model D-44 with clam shell rear cargo doors and a proposed price of $4,111,876.23. Douglas Aircraft Company offered the DS-1028 with swing-aside tail at $1,912,459.00. Hughes Aircraft Company sent in the Model 31 with swing-aside tail for $2,473,629.00. Evaluation of these offerings began in April and was completed by 14 June.

Table 14-01

3 January 1946 Military Characteristics for Glider, Assault, Light[26]

span	81.6 ft (ATSC 559)
fuselage length	52.3 ft (ATSC 559)
height	21.7 ft (ATSC 559)
floor height	2.0 ft (ATSC 559)
maximum weight	15,000 lbs (ATSC 559)
useful load	8,000 lbs, 10,000 alternate
limit speed	120% of tow speed
towing speed	200 mph, 180 acceptable
stall speed, flaps	45 mph, 55 acceptable
sink speed, 70-90 mph	1,750 fpm, 1,500 acceptable
landing ground roll, hard surface	180 ft, 250 acceptable
capacity	2 pilot, troops/litters as many as can be carried
cargo compartment and rear opening	7.6 wide x 6.5 high x 24.0 long ft

Table 14-02

Powered glider, Light Assault Specifics

useful load	4,000 lbs
maximum operational range	1,000 mi, 600 acceptable
maximum ferry range	3,000 mi, 2,400 acceptable
maximum rate of climb, sea level	800 fpm, 600 acceptable
service ceiling	15,000 ft, 12,000 acceptable
single engine	5,000 ft, 3,000 acceptable
takeoff distance over 50 ft obstacle	1,200 ft, 1,500 acceptable (unprepared field)

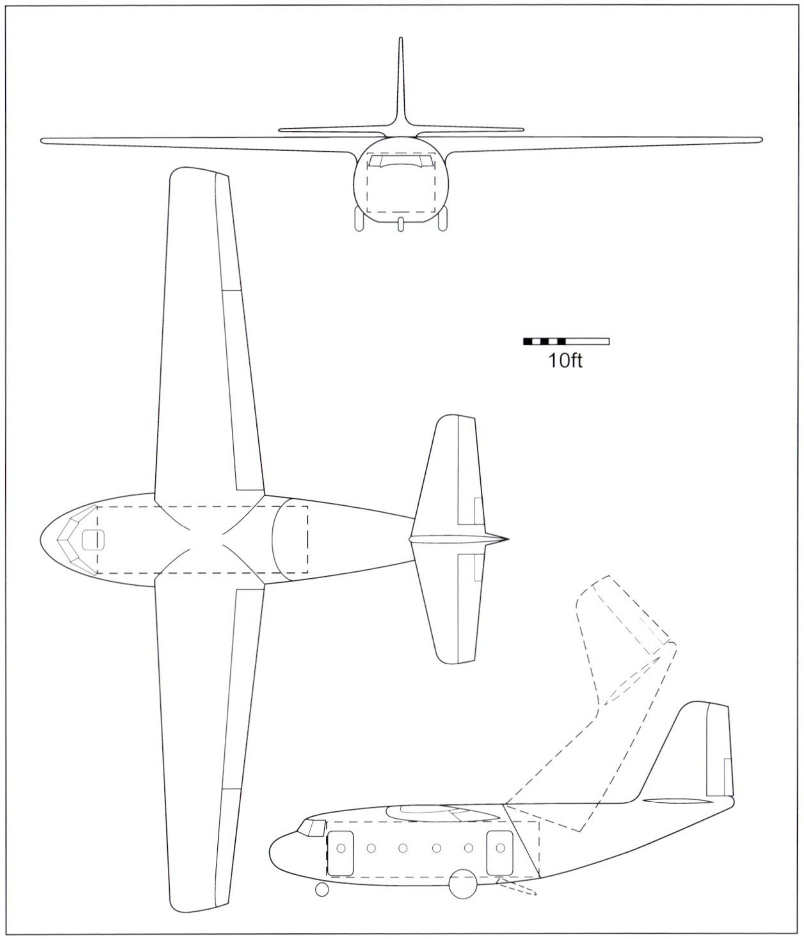

In the final year of the war thoughts had turned to more durable and efficient combat gliders. This evolved to light and heavy models of 8,000 and 14,000 pounds useful load, respectively. Air Technical Services Command performed conceptual design of these that included this all-metal 8,000-pound glider with a lifting tail for cargo compartment access. (Author)

This concluded that the Douglas design was the winner, in addition to being the low bidder, while Bell came in last.[28]

In initially contemplating the all-metal and tricycle-gear glider at the end of the war, Engineering Division had considered yet another evolution of the Chase glider as the XCG-14B with aluminum covering. This was one reason testing continued on the XCG-14A after WWII. This never congealed into a formal program during the war years. Chase Aircraft, having cut its teeth with gliders, was most enthusiastic to compete for any new efforts. At AAF encouragement, they made an offer to convert the XCG-14A to a metal airframe XCG-14B, estimating $859,000.00 for the work. When a formal program to develop metal gliders was kicked off, Chase submitted proposals in December 1945 and the following January, estimating $1,233,606.00. Created before release of the Characteristics, the notional design did not match requirements of the 8,000-pound capacity glider.

Having performed so well with the XCG-14A, Chase was given a 24 January 1946 letter contract for a XCG-18 even before formal bids had been received from other competitors or an evaluation performed. Its design would be altered to match the 8,000-pound specification. The later request to award a contract to Douglas for the XCG-19 was also approved. Perhaps it was felt advisable to have a firm with the resources and experienced of Douglas, long a leader in commercial and military transport aircraft, take on the ambitious glider development employing traditional semi-monocoque stressed-skin, metal construction, in addition to the less experienced firm. Chase also lacked production capacity.

The USAAF urged Douglas to adopt the upward swinging tail in place of their proposed swing-aside design. Regardless, Troop Carrier (Third Air Force) passed along word that they strongly felt both features were tactical non-starters and recommended clam shell type doors in the aft fuselage. The twin-boom C-82 had clamshell doors at the aft end of its level-deck center-pod fuselage, and this was being duplicated in the follow-on Fairchild C-119. While not tactical transports, the utility of these designs were demonstrable. Additionally, Lew Stowe of the Glider Branch championed a system that eliminated the clamshells, instead featuring an upper door

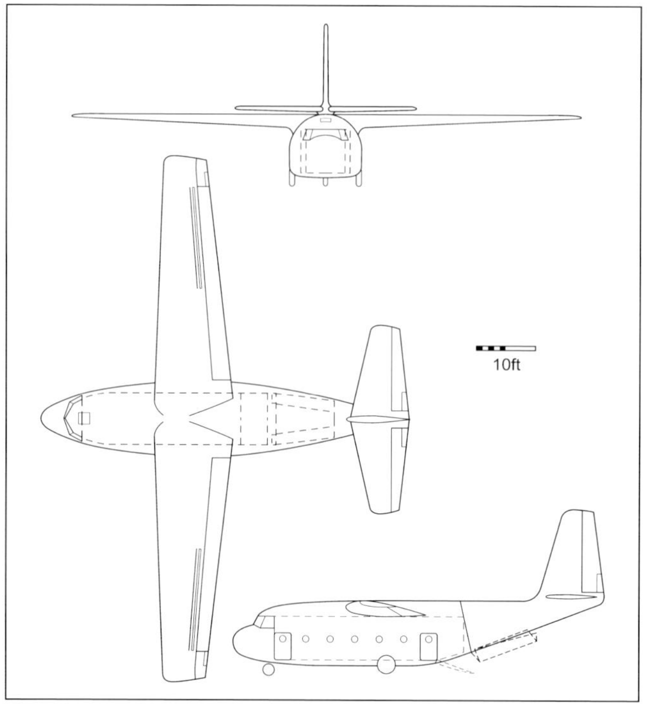

Like the 8,000-pound useful load, all-metal glider, ATSC also conducted conceptual design work for the 16,000-pound requirement. Realizing the lift tail might be impractical on this scale and combat conditions might render it ineffectual, a doors and ramp arrangement was adopted. Landing flaps were part of these designs from the outset. (Author)

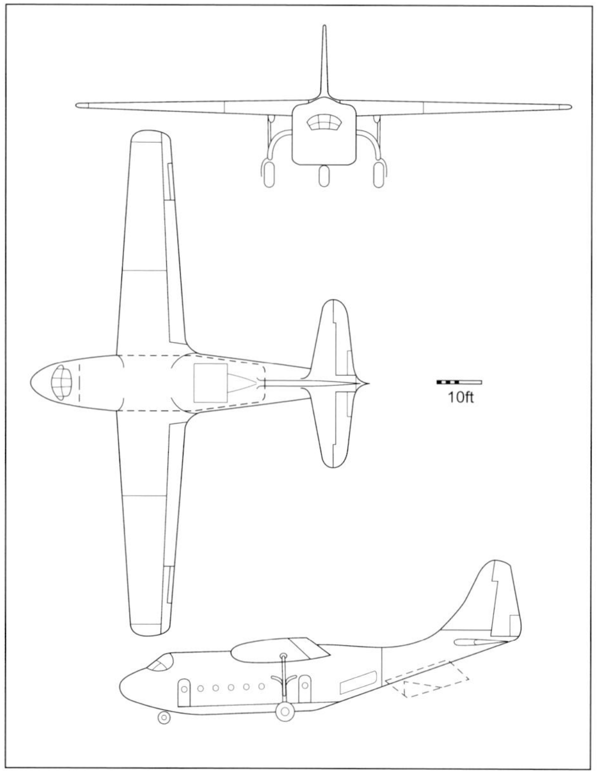

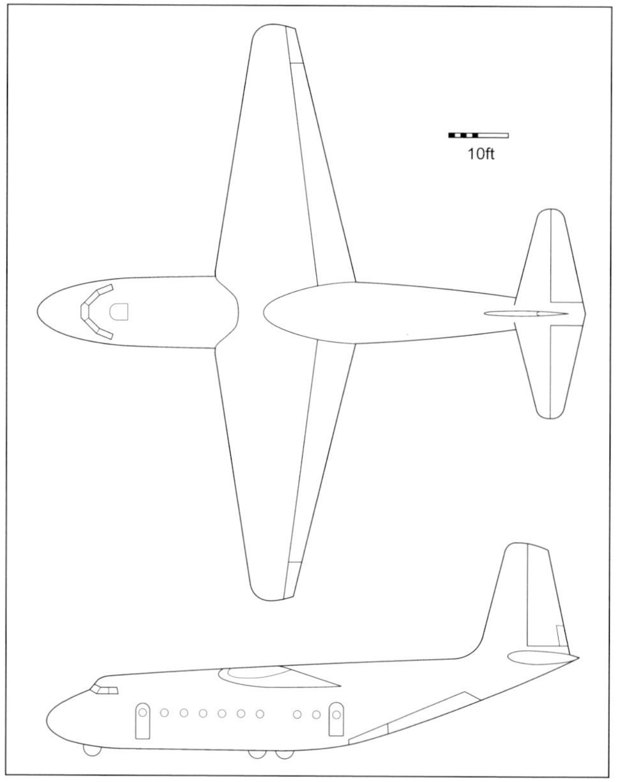

The competitors for the 16,000-pound glider included these entrants. Bell's D-45 (left) featured a podded fuselage with aft clamshell doors. Douglas' DS-1029 (center) and Hughes' Model 32 (right) used the recommended doors and ramp arrangement. (Jay Miller Collection photo, Author drawings)

Table 14-03	
13 December 1945 Military Characteristics for Glider, Assault, Heavy[32]	
span	95.5 ft (ATSC 555)
fuselage length	68.6 ft (ATSC 555)
height	29.6 ft (ATSC 555)
floor height	2.6 ft (ATSC 555)
limit speed	120% of tow speed
stall speed, flaps	55 mph, 65 acceptable
towing speed	190 mph, 180 acceptable
landing ground roll, hard surface	250 ft, 500 acceptable
sink speed, 70-100 mph	1,750 fpm, 1,500 acceptable
useful load	16,000 lbs
maximum weight	28,000 lbs (ATSC 555)
capacity	2 pilot, troops/litters as many as can be carried
cargo compartment and rear opening	8.7 wide x 7.9 high x 35.0 long ft

Table 14-04	
Powered glider, Assault, Heavy Specifics	
takeoff distance over 50 ft obstacle	2,000 ft, 2,300 acceptable (unprepared field)
maximum rate of climb, sea level	800 fpm, 600 acceptable
maximum ferry range	4,000 mi, 3,000 acceptable
maximum operational range	750 mi, 800 acceptable
service ceiling	15,000 ft, 12,000 acceptable
single engine service ceiling	5,000 ft, 3,000 acceptable
useful load	9,000 lbs

Table 14-05	
Chase Aircraft XCG-18A Specifics (G = guarantee)	
span	86.3 ft, 95.7 ft YG-18A
wing area	706.5 ft^2
fuselage length	53.4 ft
height	19.9 ft
empty weight	6,900 lbs
loaded weight	14,900 lbs
maximum loaded	16,900 lbs
maximum tow speed	180 mph (180 G)
stall speed (flaps)	58 mph (57 G)
THP to tow at 139 mph	450 hp (470 G)
rate of descent, 70-90 mph	1,200 fpm (1,500 G)
capacity	2 pilots and 32 troops or 24 stretchers
landing ground roll, paved	580 ft (450 G)
cabin dimensions (long x wide x high)	24.2 x 7.7 x 6.5 ft

An airshow appearance by the XCG-18A offers a good look at the all-metal glider. The pronounced waves and buckling of the exterior skin emphasize that it is not a stressed skin—the interior framing carrying all the flight loads. Note the tow rope sensing arm projecting from the nose. (National Museum of the United States Air Force)

opening into the aft fuselage and an adjacent drop-down ramp hinged to the floor.[29]

A meeting was convened on 28 June 1946 to resolve the cargo opening issue. The participants decided the most expedient and practical design was folding doors opening down and out from the bottom of fuselage. Clam shell doors were suitable for aircraft with twin-boom tails. By that time, however, the USAF had contracted with Chase for the XCG-18 that had an upward swinging tail for a 7.7 x 6.5 foot opening, and Engineering Division recommended revising that design.[30]

Even before the first aircraft had been completed, there was pressure to buy 13 of the light gliders for service trials, and the 1947 defense budget had a line item for this acquisition. Given the fiscal constraints of the period, this was rejected despite the many benefits early procurement offered.[31]

The Engineering Division also prepared a concept representing the 16,000-pounds capacity glider identified as ATSC Design No. 555. It was essentially an expanded version of 559 but with folding doors opening downward and out from the bottom of fuselage plus loading ramp. Their representative specification mentioned retractable undercarriage and the ability to land gear-up on skids. A tow rope position indicator was also noted as a standard instrument, but the document did not mandate an autopilot.

Provisions for the powered variant were identical to the smaller aircraft but for the characteristics.

The characteristics for the heavy glider were circulated to 22 firms of which four submitted proposals. Bell offered the Model D-45 with clam shell doors and bid $5,196,656.38. Chase had their MS-3 concept at $2,867,045.62. Douglas showed their DS-1029 with swing open doors, proposing to develop it for $3,490,874.00. Hughes' Model 32 could be had for $2,838,631.52. Results of the competitive evaluation were summarized on 8 July 1946. The Chase design was judged the best with a Figure of Merit of 843.7 out of 1,000 (Douglas 827.4, Hughes 783.9, Bell 749.8), as well as being the low bidder. All were judged suitable for conversion to power aircraft.[33] Chase would be source of the heavy XCG-20.

Chase XCG-18, XCG-18A, & YG-18A

Chase's 24 January 1946 letter contract was followed by a 26 June 1946 fixed-price contract for $1,550,000.00. The company was to provide a static test airframe and flight test aircraft, the XCG-18.[34] No mockup was required, possibly because the XCG-14A was considered a flying mockup of the new aircraft. Chase relocated to larger facilities at the Mercer County Airport in Ewing Township (West Trenton), New Jersey, during late 1946 to build the

The interior of the XG-18A looks much like the WWII gliders, with welded steel tube framing, except that they are tied by longerons to which are riveted unstressed aluminum sheeting. The tube and canvas seating for the 32 troopers is deployed. Note the handles on both sides of aft opening to pump down the ramp and pump up the cargo door. (National Archives)

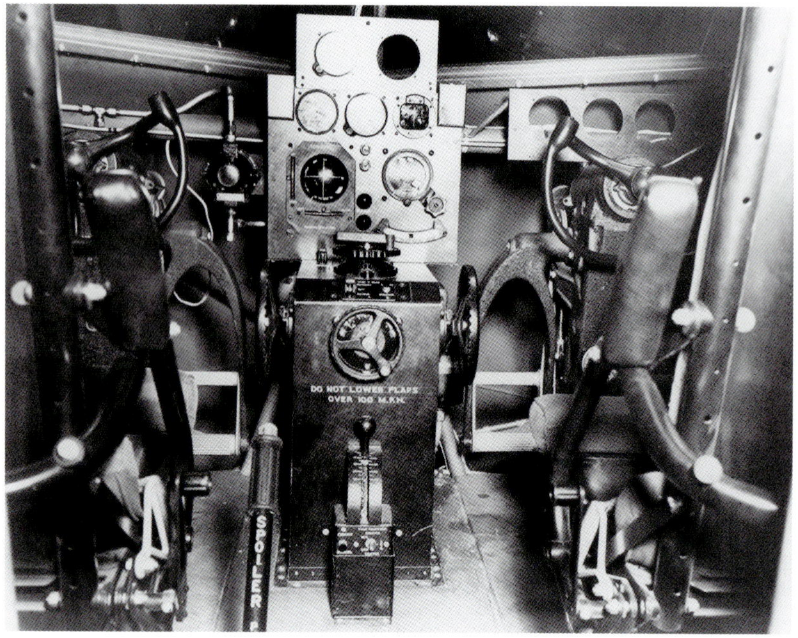

The cockpit of the XG-18A was spares and utilitarian, consistent with the mission of the glider. The tow rope position indicator is prominent, as is the gyro horizon. Three axis trim wheels, spoilers and flap handles, and the center-mounted tow release handles are evident. (National Archives)

aircraft. The project was coded MX-877 and first flight (delivery) planned initially for June 1947.

With the move to meet the 8,000-pounds capacity requirements during the latter half of 1946, a new $1,725,000.00 contract for two XCG-18A (MS-6A Avitruck) gliders was signed on 3 January 1947. The same serial numbers were retained, the static article now becoming a flight test airframe. A static article was ultimately built, delivered in June 1948, and tested to destruction.[35] Contract value increased to $1,770,000.00 with engineering changes, and eventually reached $224,293.00, with first flight slipped to December 1947. With the alterations engendering the increases, the design drifted far from the XCG-14A or modestly redesigned XCG-14B to an entirely new, larger aircraft. The move initially from the lifting tail with 7.7 by 6.5 foot opening to "bomb bay" doors jelled eventually as the more simple cargo door lifting into the aft fuselage and loading ramp dropping down from the bottom.

The design changes were reflected in shifting numbers. As originally contracted, the aircraft was to have an empty weight of 6,900 pounds, design weight of 14,700 pounds, and alternate load weight of 16,900 pounds. All these figures increased by 3-8 percent. Understandably, projected landing distance increased by half to 450 feet with normal braking. The 180-mph towing speed dropped by 13 percent. Tail height increased from 17.6 feet by 11 percent.

The XCG-18A was the world's first all metal transport glider. It retained the welded steel tube fuselage structure but with duralumin sheeting skin. Areas of compound curves like the nose failing and eyebrow fairing were formed of noninflammable plastic. The nose also featured downview windows at the pilots' knees to aid in maintaining a view of the LZ during turns. (This would be a feature of future tactical transports intended for assault landings.) The wing and tail were conventional metal structures, the wings fitted with Fowler flaps and spoilers. Towline attachment was at the apex of the nose. The main landing gear, with hydraulic brakes, was fixed but the nose gear was electrically retractable. The nose gear could be retracted on the ground if desirable to change the slope of the cargo floor (although presence of the gear doors would seem to make this challenging).[36] Twin skids under the nose protected the fuselage during a nose-gear up landing or should the gear fail. An HRU-28a auxiliary power unit (APU) was located under the cockpit, providing electrical power and battery charging, particularly powering the flaps and gear. There was a troop door forward of the ramp on both sides of the fuselage, a small door adjacent to each pilot station, and an emergency escape hatch under the wings on both sides. The loading ramp and cargo door were interlocking and hydraulically operated in an up-swept aft fuselage. A loading support jack ahead of each corner of the loading ramp stabilized the fuselage for heavy equipment loading. A total 30 troops could be seated in the cabin or 24 litters accommodated. Troop seats were aluminum tube and canvas affairs that folded down from the sidewalls. A third row of seats could be erected on centerline.

Table 14-06	
Chase Aircraft YG-18A Specifics	
span	95.7 ft
length	61.7 ft
height	22.2 ft
empty weight	7,500 lb
loaded weight	16,000 lbs
maximum GW	16,900 lbs
maximum tow/dive speed	216 mph
horsepower to tow 160 mph	612 hp
stall speed (flaps)	62 mph
maximum sink rate	1,500 fpm
capacity	2 pilots, 32 troops
cabin dimensions (long x wide x high)	24.2 x 7.7 x 6.5 ft

The first XCG-18A finally flew on 18 December 1947 behind a C-46E. The two prototypes were supplemented on 5 March 1948 with a $2,663,848.40 contract for five slightly altered YCG-18As for further testing, soon becoming YG-18As. These had a larger wing for more ready conversion with engines. The first of these flew on 24 June

One of the five YG-18As is towed aloft behind a C-82, nose gear yet to be retracted. Changes from the XG-18A were slight. Interestingly, the tow rope attachment to the transport appears to be under the fuselage. Testing of the seven Chase gliders was thorough and ran approximately two years and the last was scrapped nearly four years after first flight. (The Peter M. Bowers Collection/The Museum of Flight)

As originally planned, the new generation of gliders was to be convertible to power. Hence, the second YG-18A was modified with twin engines to become the YC-122. This configuration endured as a dozen production airplanes while the G-18A faded away. (National Museum of the United States Air Force)

1948.[37] As in 1947, the 1948 defense budget had funding for CG-18s at 147 aircraft. Again, this was premature but never reoccurred.

Flight testing and evaluations continued into 1949. The glider flew very well. Testing included landing with the nose gear retracted. The biggest criticisms was inadequate rate of descent, suggesting greater spoiler dimensions, and excessive landing ground roll unless very heavy braking was employed.[38] With only differential braking for landing directional control (no nose wheel steering), control was inadequate. Frustratingly, towline intercom systems continued to prove balky with only a radio suitable for inter-ship communications, and the tow rope position indicator and gyro-horizon were inadequate for blind flying. It general, the YG-18A was suitable for tactical air assault mission and much superior to prior combat gliders.[39]

Table 14-07	
Douglas Aircraft XCG-19 Specifics (estimated, not built)	
span	85.0 ft
wing area	885 ft^2
fuselage length	61.0 ft
height	24.0 ft
empty weight	6,340 lbs
loaded weight	14,340 lbs
overload weight	18,340 lbs
maximum tow/dive speed	200 mph
capacity	2 pilots, 30 troops or 26 litters
cabin length x width x height	24.8 x 7.7 x 6.5 ft

By the end of 1947 the USAF became serious about exploring the powered option for the XCG-18A as an experimental assault transport. After a series of estimates and proposed funding options were discussed throughout 1948, the decision was made to convert one of the XG-18As as powered YC-122 and build two more as entirely new airplanes. The 30 June 1948 supplemental agreement for this work was at $1,011,786.08. Although these were initially conceived as gliders with rapidly installed or removed power "packages," the design eventually evolved to meeting all the standards of a purposed-built airplane.

The second YG-18A was converted with a pair of 1,350-horsepower Pratt & Whitney R-2000-11 engines to become the YC-122 that first flew on 18 November 1948. Stroukoff was then able to demonstrate his personal conviction that a successful airplane should also be a good glider. The twin made a nice companion to its glider counterparts, which it could tow. The two pre-production YC-122As were built in 1949 with the same engines. One was soon re-engined with 1,450-horsepower Wright R-1820-101s. In 1949 this powered design entered limited production with nine built as the 34,400-pounds gross weight YC-122C. Their performance was marginal, particularly with a single-engine out. These 12 machines were operated through 1957 as a fine example of a tactical transport. The glider, however, was not carried forward.

Douglas XCG-19

The second project in pursuit of the 8,000-pound all-metal glider was the Douglas Aircraft Company Model 1028. The $1,966,197.00 contract was awarded on 11 January 1946 under MX-878, although amended on 8 November following further negotiations. It called for a wind tunnel model, mockup, two gliders, and engineering data.

The XCG-19 had the appearance of a conventional, tricycle-gear tactical airlifter with slotted flaps, save for the lack of engines. The original fold-aside aft fuselage to facilitate cargo onload/offload was altered in detail design to doors opening out and down from the aft fuselage, and a loading ramp with 6.8-feet additional cargo floor length. Landing distance with normal braking was projected to be 298 feet.

Douglas had the mockup about 60 percent complete, due for inspection in January 1947, and estimated first flight was in December. However, Air Forces budget limitations compelled the service to down-select in December 1946 to either the XCG-18 or XCG-19. The latter, less advanced in development, was axed on 16 January 1947.

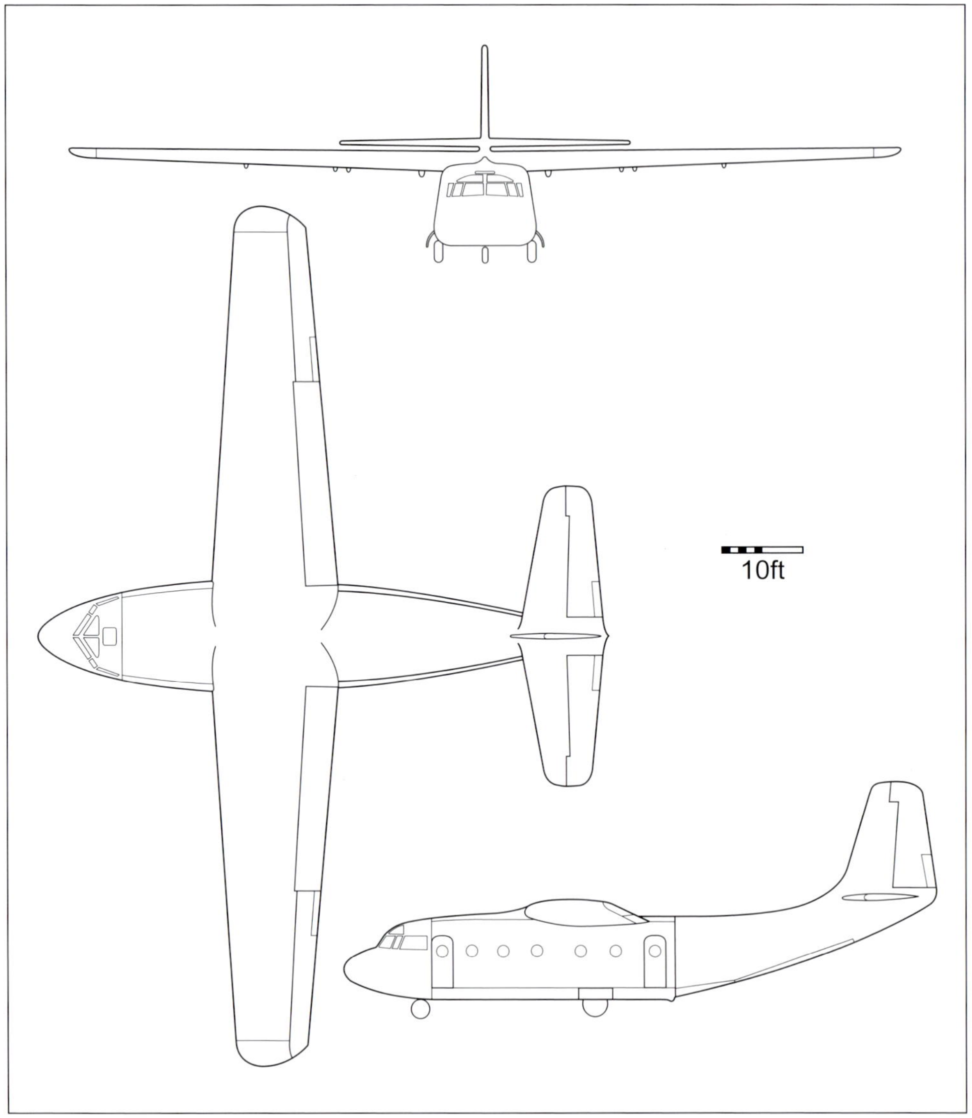

Douglas was contracted to develop a competing 8,000-pound useful load, all-metal glider in the immediate postwar period. The XCG-19, featuring cargo door and loading ramp, was well along in initial design (shown here) when fiscal pressures compelled the USAAF to make an early down-select to a single contractor. The Douglas project was cancelled. (Author)

Chase XCG-20 & XG-20

It was 10 October 1946 before approval to proceed with a contact to Chase was obtained for the heavy glider. The Air Forces was prepared to sign a contract in December 1946, but this was held up due to uncertainty in congressional appropriations for research and development. That issue was to be resolved after the New Year, but matters slipped even further. A $3,200,000.00 letter contract (up from an originally projected $2,870,000.00) was issued on 26 April 1947 under MX-879 for wind tunnel model, mockup, and two XCG-20 gliders of which one would also serve as a static test article. There was also a proposal in fall 1947 to procure six service test machines at $4,500,000.00, but this was held in abeyance due the immature state of the design. Three quarters of a million dollars per glider also gave pause. The 1948 defense budget had a line item for 13 heavy gliders, but this soon vanished.

Chase moved ahead with the design work and the mockup inspection was performed on 17 December 1947. The mockup and wind tunnel results suggested the XCG-20 would be more successfully converted to a powered aircraft, and final negotiations for the contract presented an opportunity.[40] With such a configuration gaining greater appeal, the formal $3,653,186.00 cost-plus-fixed-fee contact signed on 4 March 1948 ordered one prototype of the glider (43 percent of contract value) and an XC-123 powered variant. The change from two gliders to one was another indication of shifting emphasis. The XC-123 specification stated the airplane should be capable of being towed as well as towing.

The original delivery of the XCG-20 was to be October 1948, and February 1949 for the XC-123. However, design changes intruded as new ideas were applied and matters stretched out. Wingspan increased by 7.8 feet, length by 2.6 feet, height 3.5 feet, and weight grew by 5,000 pounds.[41]

Built entirely of metal with conventional construction (eschewing the welded steel tubes outlined in the original proposal), the XG-20 was a substantial aircraft so far removed from the WWII combat gliders that a crew chief had to be added to the complement. The nose was reinforced with steel tubing and carried over the downview windows from the XCG-18A. It featured hydraulically actuated slotted flaps, spoilers, and fully retractable landing gear with differential braking. The nose gear, with dual wheels, was steerable. A pad under the nose, aft of the nose gear well, served as a skid for landing with the nose gear up. Instead of nose gear doors that opened to the sides like the XCG-18A that could be easily damaged operating on rough terrain or interfere with a tow bar, the XG-20 had a door that slid aft along the belly. The hydraulic pump was electrically powered via an APU that also supplied electrical power in addition to a battery. While the interphone was included, no radio was specified. The towline attached at the nose apex and cockpit instruments included a tow rope position indicator.

The fuselage was set low to the ground and, from the earliest days of the design, the up-turned aft fuselage opening was created by an upward opening cargo door and loading ramp, like that adopted for the XCG-18A.[42] A pulley at the forward end of the cargo compartment allowed assistance in pulling loads aboard by a truck, the cable or chain running out the back of the aircraft or a nose opening.[43] A port side forward crew door was joined by an aft troop door on both sides of the fuselage. The pilot side window could also be jettisoned as an emergency exit.

The XG-20 could accommodate 60 fully equipped troops in sidewall and optional centerline canvas seats. It could operate up to a maximum gross weight of 70,000 pounds However, no tow plane existed that could haul such a load aloft. Consequently, the aircraft was limited to 40,000-pound as a glider. Not surprisingly, aerial pickup was not intended.

The XCG-20 was developed coincident with the XCG-18, also under the company moniker Avitruck. Construction ran from June 1948 through January 1950, six months longer than the powered XC-123. Reflecting the slow pace of aircraft development in the postwar period and general neglect of gliders, delivery of the XG-20 was in 1949. First flight followed on 26 April 1950. By the end of that year the program had cost $3,877,453.64 of which $2,313,932.18 was for the glider.

A very clean aerodynamic design was another benefit of the all-metal, semi-monocoque structure of the XG-20. The low fuselage lent the aircraft a low gradient loading ramp. Note the tow rope position sensing arm projecting from the nose with "Remove Before Flight" streamer fluttering from it. (National Archives)

Table 14-08	
Chase Aircraft XCG-20 Specifics (G = guarantee)	
span	110.0 ft
wing area	1,223.22 ft^2
fuselage length	77.1 ft
height	32.6 ft
empty weight	17,495 lbs
loaded weight	33,495 lbs
overload weight (impractical)	70,000 lbs
maximum tow/dive speed	190 mph (200 mph G)
maximum THP to tow 140 mph	(910 hp G)
stall speed, flaps	(65 mph G)
maximum sink rate, 100 mph, flaps	(1,500 fpm G)
landing ground roll, paved	(362 ft G)
capacity	2 pilots, 60 troops or 50 litters16,000 lbs (alternate 20,000)
cabin length x width x height	35.0 x 9.2 x 8.2 ft

The XG-20 could carry sixty troops, with some seated on the loading ramp as shown. The interior appears like any tactical transport seen in the second half of the 20th century, except for lacking insulation blankets on the fuselage interior. The fully retractable main landing gear (unique for an American military glider) required gear wells that protruded into the cabin. (National Archives)

The cockpit of the XG-20 shared much in common with the smaller XG-18A. The unusual yoke on the port side allows pilot "stick" forces to be measured during flight test. Note the wind shield wipers; something unknown on previous gliders because of limited onboard power. (National Archives)

One of a kind, the only XCG-20 is shown under tow, with its undercarriage left down, behind a C-54. The peak of combat glider technology, interest had decidedly turned away from such aircraft during the four years it was under development. It was the last of a breed. (San Diego Air & Space Museum)

The XG-20 was subjected to a brief but thorough flight test before itself being converted to power. This was the XC-123A with four turbojet engines in twin nacelles. While this configuration was not carried forward, the conversion and flight before the sole XG-20 was completed is indicative of the rapidly fading interest in assault gliders. (American Aviation Historical Society)

Only one of the gliders on contract was completed as such, the other converted to power. The twin recips made for a very worthy transport airplane, the XC-123. This design was produced in large numbers and multiple configurations as the USAF's first truly effective tactical transport. (San Diego Air & Space Museum)

The glider was beat into the air by the XC-123 on 14 October 1949 powered by two 2,200-horsepower Pratt & Whitney R-2800-83 radials. Perhaps as an indication of the Air Force's growing disinterest in gliders, the XG-20 was subjected to a thorough but brief flight test in summer 1950 before being modified with a pair of twin turbojet engine pods—four General Electric J47-GE-11s. It flew in this form (XC-123A) on 21 April 1951 as the USAF's first jet transport. Chase was soon subsumed by the Kaiser-Frazer Corporation who won a contract to build 300 C-123s, only to have this opportunity withdrawn and Fairchild contracted for the production. The reciprocating engine variant had gained favor and was manufactured in considerable numbers as a very successful first generation tactical transport.

Extinction

The XG-20 in 1950 was America's last new combat glider. The excruciatingly slow pace of work on this and the XG-18A, in contrast to many other weapons undergoing rapid development, reflected the low priority of the work. While fine efforts matching goals, no production of either type was undertaken. An apparent postwar notion was that gliders could be rapidly acquired and deployed if 'the worst happened'—echoing the misperceptions of 1941.

The powered glider was sustained through the last American experience with military gliders. This suggested the desire for true tactical transports, although the powered gliders were not practical substitutes. Such airplanes, descendents of the wartime transport gliders, and refined airdrop techniques would be much more operationally flexible than gliders, powered or otherwise. After more than a decade seeking such warplanes, development efforts were bearing fruit with operationally suitable transports like the C-123 with low fuselage and aft loading ramp. A June 1951 test at Eglin of the G-18A and XG-20 against the C-82, C-122, C-123, and C-125 concluded that "Assault transports

The Korean War offered the next opportunity to employ gliders, but they were passed by. Although training with gliders to that time, the airdrop capabilities of aircraft like this Fairchild C-119C Flying Boxcar suitably met combat needs. The time of the glider had passed. (San Diego Air & Space Museum)

can accomplish the assault mission better than gliders even though they do not quite match the landing performance of the glider." The report also recommended that "The use of gliders be discontinued and that assault transports be used."[44] Although few and under-appreciated for many years, these airplanes made off-field delivery of vehicles, guns, and materiel possible. Unlike gliders, they could self-deploy to the combat theater and fly at greater speeds with less vulnerability than a tug-glider combination.

The technology and tactics of parachute delivery of cargo had also greatly matured since the war. High-altitude paratroop drops with improved parachutes allowed some measure of silent insertion of airborne troops. Likewise, helicopters were rapidly reaching a state where they could insert significant forces and materiel precisely, if not silently, and also extract personnel. However, these could not self-deploy to a distant theater as could the tactical transport (and still cannot today). As these assets looked more promising, investments in gliders waned in concert with interest. Although it would be decades before the transport airplanes and helicopters approached the volume and lift capabilities of the mass glider landings of WWII, their mission flexibility, responsiveness, and cost effectiveness were indisputable. And, no one was eager to return to those days when "single-mission" gliders delivered troops and equipments under the guns of the enemy with dismaying casualties.

The winter of 1947 saw the largest airborne exercise since the war with a mass drop of 2,200 82nd Airborne Division paratroops at Fort Campbell, Kentucky. The next day just 24 gliders were landed with heavy equipment. A small number of G-15As, enough to carry a single regiment, remained to support the last operational exercise that included them, April 1949 at Fort Bragg, North Carolina.[45] As the new decade dawned, the sun was setting on American military gliders. The aircraft complement then consisted of one XG-20, four G-18As, 34 G-15As with 81 more stored, and 6 G-4As with 28 stored. The Fourteenth Air Force was operator of any requirement for the gliders and they maintained just 18 in combat-ready status.

The two combat airdrops of an airborne regiment during the Korean War were supported by parachute delivery of heavy equipment that included jeeps, trucks, and howitzers. These showed the feasibility of operations without gliders.[46] The 'handwriting on the wall' had been evident for some time. By fall 1950, the Army and USAF had agreed the gliders were defunct. An April 1952 statement of the Joint Airborne Troop Board was clear; "gliders, as an airborne capability, are obsolete, and should no longer be included in airborne techniques, concepts, and doctrine, or in reference thereto."[47] Cargo gliders were a product of their time, and their time had passed.

The last YG-18A was sent to reclamation in November 1951.[48] The glider lift capability was deleted from airborne assault tactics in 1953, and the USAF struck G-types from their order of battle on 31 August 1957. This was belated since by then they were long gone. Gliders were abandoned by most other nations as well. The USSR retained the capability until 1965.

For better or worse, the humble Waco CG-4A was the aircraft that delivered almost all American personnel to battle who went in gliders. Hastily developed with little understanding of how it would be employed, it had many deficiencies. These were dealt with over time during a remarkable production program that ensured aircraft were on hand when needed. (National Soaring Museum)

15

Retrospective

In Sum

Introduction of combat gliders to the United States armed forces during the Second World War was exceedingly difficult. Development and production of these machines was characterized by fluctuating demand and evolving requirements in one of the nation's most turbulent aeronautical undertakings. This was due principally to the pressures for fielding gliders rapidly and the uncertainties associated with what was an entirely new concept for the Allies who had to evolve strategy and tactics as the weapons arrived. However, this enormous program, and the gliders' contribution to victory, was subsequently little appreciated.

Almost all involved in the procurement, at all levels, initially assumed combat gliders would be simply enlarged sailplanes which were seen as rudimentary flying machines. These winged trailers could be built quickly for their likely single mission. Employing wood as the principle structural components would ease the burden on more traditional aircraft materials suppliers while employing a lesser-tapped element of the nation's industry. That these were all misperceptions would be made clear only through a lengthy and trying period of procurement, test, and combat.

For safety and practicality, the combat gliders were essentially unpowered transport aircraft that required much the same attention and care as their powered brethren. The design and manufacturing criteria for such requirements were not pre-existing, and no great effort was made to establish them. Using plasticized wood in such a large way for aircraft production required experimentation, new tools, and workforce training. Employing small companies introduced the complexities of these firms expanding in want of financing, shop space, manpower, and training on the basis of often meager experience, contract values, and under wartime economic conditions. The inexperience of the military with such equipment made for many requested design changes. All these factors mitigated to create programs characterized by much delay, cost overruns, and a discouraging number of failures.

The glider was transformed into an instrument of war because the Germans had demonstrated its potential and established a new dimension of modern warfare. The Allies hastened to catch up while their tactics for airborne warfare were still maturing. This meant that, in time, some of the procured gliders were found unnecessary and others wanting. Consequently, the initial concept of a silent assault was eventually abandoned for mass landings from low altitude. Although first looked upon askance, the airborne teams came to realize the value of the equipment and munitions the gliders could deliver to the battlefield under fire. This led to requests for more capable gliders and, during the last year of the war, for all-metal tactical aircraft. While far from loved by the Air Forces or airborne operators, the glider was at least appreciated.

Despite the difficulties, the U.S. built and deployed in just a few short years a glider force greater than the sum of all other nations combined. The initial rush to procure tactical gliders saw contracts placed for 11,814 aircraft in 1941 through 1943, of which about 10,000 were delivered. In developing the cargo glider, the U.S. Air Forces worked with 16 companies and 22 basic contracts. It expended \$6.2 million through 31 October 1944, and more the next year. Ten of these contracts were cancelled, all but two because of poor contractor performance. An interim program in 1944 and final effort in 1945 saw nearly 5,000 additional gliders delivered of 8,150 ordered. The U.S. also experimented with many advanced models and associated equipment. The Army and Navy together contracted for 39 glider types, flew 23 of them, and placed 11 types into production. The Americans ultimately expended approximately $327 million ($4.12 billion in today's dollars).

While the glider program succeeded in equipping the service to deliver airborne forces directly into combat, these were almost exclusively with the Waco CG-4A. This single model was built in numbers exceeded by only a few airplane types during the war. The nearly 15,928 military gliders included 14,644 combat types, almost exclusively CG-4As, of which 9,723 were deployed overseas. Of these, more than 6,000 were shipped to the ETO, 2,303 to the MTO, 515 to CBI and Pacific Theater, and 746 supplied to the UK. Approximately 4,500 CG-4As saw combat, this roughly corresponding to the number of combat sorties—a remarkably small number compared with other mass-produced warplanes, only because if the unique character of the glider mission. This compares with totals of 5,935 military gliders built in Great Britain and 3,995 in Germany. From 4 gliders delivered in 1941, 1,601 were acquired in 1942 and 6,243 in 1943.[1]

Much of the investment in gliders was spent on experimental gliders and development. The proliferation of projects during 1943 and 1944 were burdens on companies already engaged in high rate production and the government offices administering the numerous contracts. Yet, considering the nature of the companies performing the work, lack of combat experience with the cargo gliders, and the uncertainties inherent with this new weapon system in an environment of rapidly evolving doctrine and tactics, the measures appeared reasonable if burdensome. They inevitably contributed to the general haste, complexity, confusion, and turbulence prevalent throughout the glider program. General Arnold, responding to such criticisms, growled that he had never said war was cost effective. It was only through perseverance, dedication, goodwill, and a national motivation that the American glider corps achieved the lofty results that it did in such a brief period.

After August 1944 it was clear the defeat of Germany was only a matter of maintaining the pressure for a sufficient time. The materiel on hand was more than adequate for the task. Japan presented other challenges, although slowly being choked to death. However, gliders would likely contribute little to that campaign. Consequently, many developmental glider programs and tests were terminated or run to completion without follow-up. Most production contracts were cancelled or dramatically scaled back.

Despite the slowdown, the latecomer United States had several advanced combat gliders in development or early fielding at the end of the war. These matched or exceeded the capabilities and manufacturing excellence of anything built abroad. Some of these were large and reusable gliders, exceeding 25,000 pounds gross weight, making large strides in the evolution of tactical airlift.

The Army trained approximately 6,500 glider pilots to fly gliders during the war and converted around 500 power pilots, all more than any other nation. This was one of the most extraordinary flight training undertakings by the U.S. military. It was a massive endeavor to train thousands of citizen soldiers in a short period on a new aircraft type only then being manufactured for a mission yet to be fully defined. Executed at a time of unprecedented military expansion, the program was chaotic and wasteful. However, it ultimately met requirements.

The Army had 1,106 training gliders built for the mission, of which seven types were produced. Of these, 750 were 3-place converted light planes that were more suitable to the required training than sailplanes. It spent $3,586,727.10 for 1,172 training gliders acquired between May 1941 and July 1943. The Navy acquired an additional 97 trainers

The Waco CG-13A was developed based on requirement provided by the airborne forces and seeking a much more practical combat aircraft than the CG-4A. However, the more careful development added time and ultimately the combat teams were dissatisfied. Hence, adherence to more common procurement practices, even at an accelerated pace, meant much time expended and ultimately a small production run when Ground Forces judged the glider unsuitable. (National Museum of the United States Air Force)

Germany built 200 of the Messerschmitt Me 321 Gigant (Giant) during 1941 and 1942, ostensibly to support the invasion of the British Isles. The largest glider ever built, it was ponderous and required considerable resources to deploy. While it contributed to combat resupply missions, it was largely impractical and a reflection of German tendency to disperse effort among many "wonder" weapons—a predilection the Americans largely avoided to their credit. (National Museum of the United States Air Force, insert National Soaring Museum)

for $1,405,962.94, of which 76 were of one type. All were declared surplus before training was completed.

Following the war the military training gliders were sold, rejuvenating the American soaring sport in hiatus since 1941. This, however, undercut the war-expanded glider industry. Only Schweizer survived.

A TG-4A acts as the centerpiece for a War Bonds gala soon after the U.S. entered the conflict. For this brief event the glider pilots were seen as warrior heroes. However, most Americans were little aware of the glider program during and after WWII. (National Soaring Museum)

The second XLRA-1 Invader prototype sits awaiting its fate at the end of the program. It shows further evolution of the canopy design. Although a true tricycle undercarriage was called for, a compromise is evident in the wheels added to the tail and wing skids. (National Soaring Museum)

Naval Post-Mortem

More than two years of effort had seen more than $30 million spent and the labor of hundreds of people expended on the abortive naval glider program. Of 260 cargo gliders on order, 5 had been delivered. For these meager transports over $7.5 million was spent. Unlike some military programs wherein at least engineering and training value can be considered an outcome following cancellation, little can be perceived as deriving from the Department of the Navy's glider undertaking. The best that can be said is that the misstep did not cost lives or excessive treasure, and did not significantly impact other vital war efforts.

No one ever undertook amphibious gliders development approaching what the U.S. Navy achieved. The Germans did some work with floating gliders. This included some motorboat tows in 1943 with a DFS 230 glider on twin floats. They found the water resistance on the submerged rope made tow to takeoff impossible.[2] This, however, was not the American experience. The concept simply had little military value.

Along with glider acquisition, hundreds of marines and sailors were tied up in the abortive amphibious glider effort. In contrast to other efforts at home and abroad, the sea service judged wisely when to cut their losses and move on. By that time the training gliders were of no further use even to the Army. (National Archives)

Would gliders have actually been useful in marine combat in the Pacific? It appears doubtful. At the time the cancellation decision was made the only large-scale combat experience in amphibious warfare had been the Guadalcanal and Tulagi landings—unopposed and so not comparable to was to come. The distances were too large, the volume of Japanese defensive fire too great, and gliders too vulnerable and cumbersome to unload on the beach. Even inland landings would have exposed isolated groups of infantrymen to determined Japanese assault. By the time gliders had been ready for action their dubious value would have been made clear by the increasingly costly island campaign. Sea landings were providing effective in an island-hopping campaign so lethal as to render amphibious gliders unsuitable.

Legacy

The United States Army expended considerable effort in developing a large glider corps to deliver airborne troops to landing zones as part of major offensives. Only a few types were built in quantity and just the CG-4A committed to battle. Besides these principal efforts, there were the many lesser-known projects to improve the safety and efficiency of glider operations, plus exploring other missions. Few of the unusual experimental aircraft and modifications that flew, and little of the other developmental testing, was translated into fielded capabilities. However, they illustrate the expansive vision of the U.S. armed forces during WWII and the extent of testing undertaken for what were essentially a sideshow to American training and glider combat, itself an often under-reported chapter in military aviation.

The Allies had come a long way in just a few years of hard work. The American glider experience was a mixed one and quite unlike any other program in Air Force history to that time. It varied from rescue and casualty evacuation, airhead seizure, small-scale resupply, to enormous airborne operations in concert with paratroops. The scope of these combat operations outstripped anything accomplished by the other combatant nations. The hastily assembled capability, revolving around the humble Waco, was far from ideal. However, it was the right weapon for the period and strategy.

The glider was naturally tied to a tow aircraft. Hence, the glider's combat potential required two aircraft and aircrew. Recovery and reconditioning of the glider proved impractical. A low-cost machine, the Wacos were still costly to ship and assemble, difficult to maintain and employ, and closely associated with airborne forces that were husbanded for unique circumstances. Regardless, it proved itself in relatively accurate delivery of high-value materiel that could not be guaranteed by paradrops. Although reputed as the most hazardous means of entering combat, they were demonstrably no more dangerous for pilot or troops than that of the transport pilots and paratroops, and glider insertion no more costly than coastal landings and paratroop drops. In the circumstances of WWII, American gliders contributed to a successful combination of weapons and capabilities. Different circumstances might have generated different results. The larger gliders that were in development were openly questioned as to their operational practicality. Certainly the more powerful transports to tow these machines were only just becoming available at the end of the war.

The glider was part and parcel of the American airborne forces that grew and matured during WWII. While the glider faded, their role in guiding the development of vertical envelopment and the aircraft supporting that mission is undeniable. This image, with Brigadier General Anthony McAuliffe of the 101st Airborne division addressing a gathering of personnel the day before the Holland landings, says much to the tremendously capable team built on that foundation which played such a vital role in the eventual victory. (United States Department of Defense)

The legacy of the WWII gliders and the few that followed was the impetus to develop tactical transports. The "missing link" was the XG-20 glider that became the C-123 airplane, with cargo loading and rugged construction for off-field landing evident here (is it the airplane or glider?). These attributes were reflected in three generations of American tactical transports to this day. (San Diego Air & Space Museum)

As vital to the airborne mission as the gliders themselves were the tow planes. Supply of the C-47 and training of aircrew for the towing mission had to come along in parallel. That success is another story of hard work and dedication. (San Diego Air & Space Museum)

Partners Britain and the U.S. built airborne capabilities and skills unmatched anywhere. There is little doubt that gliders were significant contributors to successful airborne assault in WWII, which were themselves vitally important in unhinging enemy defenses. However, it will probably be forever debated whether the gliders were necessary and truly essential to the success of the Normandy invasion and other large-scale operations. Certainly they contributed to sowing confusion, and the materiel they carried in helped disrupt enemy ability to respond effectively to coastal landings or river crossings. There were decisive effects from insertion of elite forces behind enemy lines as elements of larger offensives, as witnessed in Burma.

The Americans may have done more with gliders, such as emergency 'motorless transport' to compensate for the lack of true tactical airlift. Only a few *coup de main* actions, stealthily and precisely inserting commandos, were attempted, in contrast to British efforts. However, training ensured the potential was there should commanders chose to employ it. Far from being the "silent wings" they are so often credited as being, the CG-4A flight under tow was extremely noisy for the occupants. The fuselage fabric beat like a drum so loudly that conversation was impossible. The low altitude tow by transports were deafening for those below, rendering any element of surprise moot.

It is not surprising that the U.S. Army and Air Forces commanders were hesitant to employ a new weapon that was largely unproven until the last year of the war. Even then the efforts required to use gliders were great and the vulnerability of glider and tow ship an unanswered concern. However, the Americans did avoid the trap of developing many experimental types and fielding a diversity of aircraft. They pragmatically stuck with what could be put into production quickly and built in large numbers, and which *worked*. Its imperfections were to be expected with a new

A graphic symbol of the close relationship between British and American airborne teams is this Horsa bearing markings of both nations. Photographed on 30 May 1944, the glider appears to have come to a bad end during the large training maneuvers preceding the Normandy invasion. Horsas and Wacos were readily swapped between the allies with little regard for markings or even complete accounting. (National Museum of the United States Air Force)

The pinnacle of US Army glider development was the Laister-Kauffmann XCG-10A with tricycle landing gear and rear loading doors. Its 12,800-pound payload and cargo compartment dimensions allowed it to carry much larger vehicles and guns than previous gliders. Yet, in the last year of the war and after, the all-wood "Trojan Horse," with fabric covering control surfaces and on the wings aft of the main spar, was criticized for its short service life. A product of the war, it was discarded with the end of hostilities. (National Soaring Museum)

weapon quickly conceived and developed in a total-war environment. Development projects that bogged down were usually quickly euthanized.

By mid-1944, the role and utility of cargo transport gliders was clear. Yet, some in the Air Forces leadership remained unimpressed. They considered early "disposable" models, which had emphasized wooden construction, to be cost ineffective. The finish of the CG-4A had to be carefully maintained and the wood monitored to prevent attack by the elements—drying with delamination, or rotting with mold. Focus had also turned from solely transport of airborne troops to the airlift of equipment like trucks and large-caliber guns. The cargo glider had to mature further if it were to have a future. Eyes had turned in that direction by the end of the war and this was pursued after, but morphed into the tactical transport that supplanted the glider.

Despite the weapon's limitations and the suspicion by some, the Americans and British were stand-out users of gliders during the conflict. Although the original innovators in introducing airborne warfare, the Soviets were late in building combat gliders. They then limited this to about 700 in two principal types. Apart for a small role in one poorly executed airborne assault, they were isolated to bold but small-scale resupply efforts, particularly for partisans. After abandoning airborne operations following Crete, the Germans used gliders routinely as flying workshops, for medical evacuation, and most prominently for resupply of hard-pressed or isolated units. They also executed a few bold commando operations with gliders. Through the last days of the war, Germany continued using the DFS 230 but also the more advanced Gotha Go 242 and the enormous Messerschmitt Me 231 Gigant for urgent logistics flights. Many of these were one-way missions for machine and pilot as resources grew scarce and the situation ever more desperate. Losses were horrendous.

It is only that the U.S. got started late and fought hard on the battlefield that advanced American gliders were not produced in large numbers nor fielded. Given the mixed results with the British Hamilcar and the ill-conceived German Me 321, there was considerable doubt whether the larger gliders were operationally practical. Fortunately, the opportunity to test them in combat expired with the end of the frightfully destructive conflict. Still, the innovation of the U.S. designs and excellence of the manufacturing stands toe-to-toe with that of Germany and Great Britain.

American cargo glider development, especially experiments with new models, lost momentum in the final year of the war.[3] Compared with the breakneck speed of the CG-4A development and production, the CG-13 and CG-10 were plodding affairs. The XCG-4 contract was let in June 1941 and the first flight article was airborne 11 months later, and found suitable in June 1942. Production had been ordered in January 1942, the first Letters of Intent issued in February, and the initial production gliders delivered in September 1942—15 months from initiation. In truth, these later programs included all the development steps normally expected yet at an accelerated wartime pace. Thorough review, testing, and adjustment before committing to a production configuration would avoid the glaring deficiencies of the earlier Wacos and other gliders projects that failed miserably. The CG-13A was a year before early production articles were available for operational test. Yet, another six months transpired before the warfighters concluded this large glider was unsuitable and production was stopped. The derivative CG-15 took seven months from delivery of an aerodynamically representative airframe to a production contract, and five more to delivery of production articles. Interestingly, the Germans began the war in this manner yet ended in the frenetic, many faceted efforts that marked the initial American efforts.

Postwar glider work, carrying on wartime programs, was even slower in the face of waning budgets and priority. Interest had definitely turned to endeavors with more potential utility. Yet, during this period, the peak of combat glider ambitions took form as the outstanding XCG-18A and XCG-20. There was simply no longer a compelling mission for them. The glider as a means of transporting soldiers into combat disappeared in the United States and soon everywhere else.

Gliders reappeared in the U.S. military decades after the Army discarded its last tactical glider. These were limited to sailplanes for cadet flight orientation and test pilot training. Airplanes with the aspects of powered gliders were built in small numbers for covert missions. These eventually morphed into unmanned aircraft of similar attributes. Bomb gliders were never again pursued, but glide bombs and other gliding munitions and decoys were acquired and employed in combat by many

Another company of D-Day soldiers pose for a snapshot before boarding their gliders (note towlines on the ground). While not always eager for the glider ride, it carried them into battle more reliably than parachute jumps and with more gear. Below is the shoulder patch of the glidermen troops. (National Soaring Museum, bottom Author)

nations. The wartime services program in this field directly contributed to these postwar guided weapon programs.

Gliders and glider pilots contributed immensely to the combat successes that won the war. The outstanding legacy of the WWII combat glider experience was the national will to create and employ a new and costly weapon during a frantic time and in such overwhelming numbers. More inspiring were the citizen soldiers who flew into battle aboard the thousands of fabric-covered gliders, fighting against tyranny that threatened to engulf the world. Especially noteworthy are the thousands of mostly enlisted men who volunteered for the hazardous glider piloting duty and then fought with such exemplary valor. Among them were 208 killed in action and 138 in accidents. As the last of these men now pass away, those who benefit from their feats of arms can but honor their memory.

Glider pilots were an odd bunch; part Air Forces, part grunt. A bit older than the average military aviator, most were motivated by the chance to see action, flight pay, and the thrill of flight. The USAAF never fully embraced the Flight Officers and their mission. (National Museum of the United States Air Force)

Acronyms and Abbreviations

AAA All American Aviation
AAB Army Air Base
AAF Army Air Field
AFB Air Force Base
AGF Army Ground Forces
AMC Air Materiel Command
APU auxiliary power unit
ATSC Air Technical Services Command
AWOL Away Without Leave

BuAer Bureau of Aeronautics
BuNo Bureau Number

CAA Civil Aeronautics Administration
cal caliber
Cat Catalina
CBI China-Burma-India theater of operations
CCAAF Clinton County Army Air Field
c.g. center of gravity
c/n construction number
CNO Chief of Naval Operations
CO commanding officer
Corporation Corporation
CPT Civilian Pilot Training

D.C. District of Columbia
DZ drop zone
ETO European Theater of Operations
FO Flight Officer

fpm feet per minute
ft feet, foot
FTC Flying Training Command

G guaranteed
g acceleration due to gravity
gal gallon, gallons

GATC General Airborne Transport Company
GE General Electric
GLOMB glider bomb
G.P. Glider Pilot
GW gross weight

hp horsepower
hrs hours

Inc. Incorporated
inc. including

JATO Jet-Assisted Take-Off
jg junior grade
Jr. Junior

L.A. Los Angeles
lbf pounds force
lbs pound, pounds
L/D lift/drag
L-K Laister-Kauffman
LZ landing zone

max. maximum
MCAS Marine Corps Air Station
mi mile, miles
min. minimum
Mk. Mark
mm millimeter
mph miles per hour
Mr. Mister
MTO Mediterranean Theater of Operations

NAC Northwestern Aeronautical Corporation
NACA National Advisory Committee for Aeronautics

NAF Naval Aircraft Factory
NAMC Naval Air Material Center
NAMU Naval Air Modification Unit
NAS Naval Air Station
No. number

PM Prime Minister
psf pounds per square foot
P&R Pratt & Whitney
RAF Royal Air Force

s/n serial number

TCC Troop Carrier Command
THP thrust horsepower
TV television

UHF Ultra High Frequency
UK United Kingdom
U.S. United States
USA United States of America
USAAC United States Army Air Corps
USAF United States Air Force
USAAF United States Army Air Forces
USN United States Navy
USMC United States Marine Corps
USSR Union of Soviet Socialist Republics

VHF Very High Frequency
VE-Day Victory in Europe Day
VJ-Day Victory over Japan Day

WWI World War One
WWII World War Two

Appendix: Glider Summaries

U.S. Army Appropriated Training Gliders of WWII

Model	Type	Seats	Serial (Registra.)	Date Bought	Price ($)	Owner	Owner Locale
TG-1A	Frankfort Cinema IIB	2	42-57159 (NC34208)	7-4-42	1,610.00	St. Louis Soaring Association	St. Louis, Missouri
			42-57198 (NC34209) *tie-ups uncertain*	6-27-42	1,300.00	Lewis School of Aeronautics	Lockport, Illinois
TG-1B	Frankfort Cinema IIB	2	42-57164 (NX29101)	6-24-42	1,107.50	Frankfort Sailplane Co.	Joliet, Illinois
			42-57169		1,132.50		
			42-57190 (NR34202)	6-30-42	1,970.00	G.W. Blaisdell	Kalamazoo, Michigan
			42-57203 *tie-ups uncertain*	7-21-42	1,720.00		
TG-1C	Frankfort Cinema IA	1	42-57173 (NC34243)	6-29-42	2,150.00	Purdue Glider Club	West Lafayette, Indiana
			42-57184 (NC34242)	6-29-42	1,610.00	Southwest Soaring Club, Inc.	Phoenix, Arizona
			42-57186 (NX18476) *tie-ups uncertain*	?	?	reported	spurious ?
TG-1D	Frankfort PC-2 (modified) Cinema I	?	42-57179 (NR34227)	6-29-42	1,205.00	Delber N. Lewis	Anderson, Indiana
TG-2	Schweizer SGS 2-8	2	42-46632	4-4-42	2,000.00	Buffalo Soaring Society	Buffalo, New York
			42-46633	4-4-42	1,600.00	Elmira Area Soaring Corp.	Elmira, New York
			42-46634		1,600.00		
			42-57160	4-22-42	1,700.00	Capt. E.F. Knight	Minneapolis, Minnesota
			42-57161	5-8-42	1,800.00	Twenty-Nine Palms Air Academy	Twenty-Nine Palms, California
			42-57162	7-4-42	880.00	Hudson Valley Glider Club	Wurtsboro, New York
	cancelled		42-57163 *tie-ups uncertain*	4-14-42	2,000.00	2Lt. Leeds Mitchell, Jr.	Chicago Illinois
TG-2A	Schweizer SGS 2-8	2	42-46890	6-26-42	2,870.00	Jaycee Glider Patrol	Chicago, Illinois
			42-46891		2,870.00		
			42-47370		2,570.00		
			42-57189 (NC22443)		2,720.00		
			42-57196	6-30-42	3,340.00	Federal Security Agency (NYA)	Chelsea, Michigan
			42-47201	7-7-42	2,840.00	NYA for Michigan	
			42-57205 (NC20642) *tie-ups uncertain*	8-11-42	2,075.00	Elmira Area Soaring Corp.	Elmira, New York
TG-4B	Laister *Yankee Doodle* LK-10, Bob Sparling *Bluebird*	2	42-57191 (NC26497)	7-4-42	920.00	Laister-Kauffman Aircraft Corp.	St. Louis, Missouri
TG-12A	Bowlus-Du Pont Utility M1PU3	?	42-57200 (NR15314)	7-6-42	1,975.00	Orvil Leigh Smith	Elmira, New York
TG-13A	Briegleb Sailplane Co. BG-8 or modified BG-6	2	42-57158 (NX33636)	6-30-42	1,150.00	Milsoubee School of Engineering	Milsoubee, Alabama
			42-57180 (NC18299) *tie-ups uncertain*	6-27-42	1,950.00	Milsoubee Glider Club	
TG-14	Herman and Henry Stieglemeier S-24 *The Stick*	1	42-57183 (NX15539)	6-29-42	850.00	Herman J. Stiglmeier	Inglewood, California
TG-15	Franklin PS-2	1	42-57174 (NC456Y)	6-30-42	890.00	XYZ Soaring Club of Michigan	Detroit, Michigan
			42-57177 (N15194)	6-29-42	920.00	Randolph B. Meeker	Birmingham, Michigan
			42-57178 (NC443Y)		1,000.00	Dallas Wise	Detroit, Michigan
			42-57187 (NC4474)		580.00	Harold Edgar	Wausoon, Ohio
	Continued next page		42-57194 (NC12184)	7-4-42	650.00	John M. Phelan	Brooklyn, New York
			42-57199 (NC11181)		530.00	Schenectady Gliding and Soaring Association	Schenectady, New York

TG-15	Franklin PS-2 *Continued from previous page*	1	42-57206 (NC455Y)	8-11-42	525.00	Elmira Area Soaring Corp.	Elmira, New York
			42-57207 (NC11186) *tie-ups uncertain*		525.00		
TG-16	Authur Schultz A.B.C. Sailplane,	1	42-57172 (NC15774)	7-15-42	1,450.00	Donald B. Doolittle	Penn Yan, New York
	ABC Glider		42-57202	6-29-42	1,660.00	A.B.C. Glider Club	Detroit, Michigan
TG-17	Stevens-Franklin, Stevens Tech *Gull Wing Franklin*	1	42-57193 (NC12186)	7-10-42	1,050.00	Th. P. Pfeiffer & P. Sutherland	Brooklyn, New York
TG-18	Midwest Gliders	1	42-57166	6-24-42	1,370.00	Joe Steinhauser	Chicago, Illinois
	MU-1		42-57167	6-24-42	1,120.00		
			42-57176 (NC26499)	6-30-42	1,160.00	Soaring Club of Michigan	Detroit, Michigan
TG-19	Karl Schweyer *Rhonsperber*, builder Emil Lehecka	1	42-57165 (NC17898)	6-24-42	2,120.00	Joe Steinhauser	Chicago, Illinois
TG-20	Göppingen Gö-1 Schempp-Hirth *Wolf*	1	42-57168	6-24-42	1,370.00	Joe Steinhauser	Chicago, Illinois
			unknown (NC14829?)	6-30-42			
			42-57175 (NC11643)		1,360.00	XYZ Soaring Club of Michigan	Detroit, Michigan
			42-57195 (NC20676)	7-4-42	1,350.00	Stephen J. Bennis	Glendale, Long Island, New York
			42-57204 (NC20647)	8-11-42	1,050.00	Elmira Area Soaring Corp. (built by Leonard Parker)	Elmira, New York
			unknown (unknown)	7-6-42	1,010.00	Laister-Kauffman Aircraft Corp.	St. Louis, Missouri
TG-21	Notre Dame ND-1, student project	1	42-57170 (NR29108)	6-24-42	1,550.00	University of Notre Dame	Notre Dame, Indiana
TG-22	Emerson Mehlose and J. Laister *The Dean*	1	42-57181 (N11391)	6-30-42	840.00	Lawrence Institute of Technology	Highland Park, Michigan
TG-23	Louis Harper and Stan Corcoran Cinema	1	42-57192 (N18133)	6-30-42	1,275.00	Fred R. Thacher	Frankfort, Michigan
TG-24	Göppingen Gö-5 / Schempp Hütter H-17	1	42-57185 (NC1305)	6-30-42	1,000.00	George W. Law	Natley, New Jersey
TG-25	Plover	1	42-57182 (N18959)	6-29-42	790.00	Franklin E. Velcott	Glendale, California
TG-26	Universal Glider Co. Utility, Blackhawk Glider Club *BT-2*	2	42-57188 (NC18462)	6-30-42	1,760.00	James C. Baker	Detroit, Michigan
TG-27	Grunau 8, builder Daniel Sanborn	2	42-65552 (NX16029)	5-6-42	1,790.00	Associated Glider Club of Southern California	San Diego, California
TG-28	Haller-Hirth Kassel 20 Hawk Junior	1	42-65555 (NC13134)	6-14-42	500.00	James P. Spurgeon	San Diego, California
TG-29	Volmer Jensen VJ-10	2	42-65553 (28375)	6-11-42	2,005.00	Temer Johnson	South Glendale, California
TG-30	Mel Smith & Joe Stazneck *Bluebird*	2	42-65554 (NR19991)	6-11-42	1,550.00	Joseph Satasnook	Santa Monica, California
TG-31	Aero ITI G-2	1	42-57171 (NC19965)	6-29-42	1,090.00	Aero Industries Technical Institute	Los Angeles, California

U.S. Army Procured Training Gliders of WWII

Type	Make	Seats	Year Acquired	No. Acquired	Serial Numbers(s)	Notes
XTG-1/ TG-1A	Frankfort	2	1942-1943	3/40	X 41-29609/11, A 42-52884/923	Xs with registered NC34204/6
TG-2/TG-2/ TG-2A	Schweizer	2	1942-1943	3/26/12 ?	X 41-29612/14, 42-8708/25, -46632/34, -53014/20	SGS 2-8, up to 12 A from Navy as LNS-1 5 Aug 1943 likely unserialed
XTG-3/ TG-3A	Schweizer	2	1942-1943	3/111	X 42-14702/4, A 42-57924/98, -53097/131, rest unknown	X SGS 2-12, A SGS 2-12A
TG-3A	Air Gliders	2	1943	1	42-91974, cancelled -91975/2023	contract cancelled
XTG-4/ TG-4A	Laister-Kauffman	2	1942	3/150	X 42-14705/7, A 42-43679/753, -53022/96	LK-10A and B *Yankee Doodle Two*
XTG-5/ TG-5	Aeronca	3	1942	0/253	X 42-68302/5 (possibly none of the s/n's applied), 42-57229/478, 43-12493/5	conversion of L-3, X contract cancelled, 3 to Navy as XLNR-1 and returned later
TG-6	Taylorcraft	3	1942	253	42-58561/810,former LNT-1 43-12496/8	conversion of L-2B as ST-100, 25 to Navy as LNT-1 and 3 returned later, 10 later to Navy as XLNT-1 for bomb glider testing
XTG-7	Orlik II (Eagle)	1	1942		42-53519 (NA23727)	Polish glider, bought 8-27-41 from Dr. Wladyslaw St. Zbikowski of Detroit, Michigan, for $2,700
TG-8	Piper	3	1942	253	43-3009/258, 43-12499/501	conversion of L-4, c/n G-1/250, three to Navy as XLNP-1 and returned later
XTG-9	Briegleb Sailplane Co.	1	1942	3	42-62603/5	Model BG-6 bought 5-29-42, cost $650 each for two and $750 for third
uncertain	"swamp glider"	?	1941	3	uncertain	bought 12-18-41 for 7,500.00 from Prigg Duct Works, Miami, Florida
XTG-10	Wichita Engineering	2	1942	0	42-57197	contract cancelled due to poor company performance,3 ordered, one given serial number
XTG-11	Göppingen 3 Minimoa	1	1941	1	42-53518 (NC1306)	bought for $2,000.00 from Chester J. Decker, East St. Louis. Illinois, 9-10-41, evaluated at CCAAF
XTG-12	Bowlus	2	1942	1	X 42-96830/32	Model XBM-5, only first NX28386 accepted,contract cancelled due to poor manufacturer performance
XTG-13	Briegleb	2	1942	1	42-96829	Model BG-8, A NX33636 flown, contract cancelled due to poor manufacturer performance
TG-32	Pratt, Read & Co.	2	1943	73	43-39509/78,-43329/31	Model G-1, from Navy LNE-1, 73 transferred 5 Aug 1943
XTG-33	Taylorcraft	1	1944	1	42-58562	TG-6 modified for prone pilot research

U.S. Army Cargo Gliders

Type	Make	Seats / Payload (lbs)	Year Contracted / Delivered	No. Delivered	Serial Number(s)	Notes
XCG-1	Frankfort	8 / -	1941/-	0	41-29615 assigned	Model TCC-4-1, failed static test, contract cancelled
XCG-2	Frankfort	15 / -	1941/-	0	41-29616 assigned	Model TCC-2-1, contract cancelled
XCG-3/ CG-3A	Waco (Commonwealth production)	9 / 2,000	1941/1942- 1943	1/100	X 41-29617, A 42-43518/617	Model NYQ, X 8-seat, production curtailed, training only
XCG-4/XCG-4A/ XCG-4B/XCG-4C & G-4C	Waco	15 / >3,700	1941/1942- 1945	2/13,909/ 1/(35)	X 41-29618, X-A, 42-53534, B 42-46394, C unknown	Model NZR, many alterations, B from Timm (1943) with all-wood fuselage, C for Navy rigid towbar on CG-4As
CG-4A & G-4A	Waco (produced by 16 firms)	15 / >3,700	1941/1942- 1945	13,906	see supplemental summary that follows	
XCG-5	St. Louis	8 / -	1941/1942	1	41-29619	Model SL-5, failed static test, contract cancelled
XCG-6	St. Louis	15 / -	1941	0	41-29620 assigned	Model SL-6, contract cancelled
XCG-7	Bowlus	8 / 2,000	1941/1942	1	41-29621, Douglas s/n1360 static, 1359 flier	Model BM-3, built by Douglas, failed static test, some flight test, contract cancelled
XCG-8	Bowlus	15 / 3,600	1941/1942	1	41-29622, Douglas s/n 1361	Model BM-2, built by Douglas, failed static test, some flight test, contract cancelled
XCG-9	AGA	32 / -	1942/-	0	42-56607/8 assigned	Model G-5, poor contractor performance, contract cancelled
XCG-10	Laister- Kauffman	30 / 10,000	1943	2	X 42-61099/100	Model LK-11, some evaluation
XCG-10A/YCG-10A/ YG-10A	Laister-Kauffman	42 / 12,650	1943-1946	(2)/3	X-A 42-61099/100 converted, Y 45-44450/2, -44453/9 cancelled	Model LK-11-A, extensive evaluation,cancelled at end of war
XCG-11	Snead & Co.	30 / -	1942/-	0	none apparently assigned	poor contractor performance, contract cancelled
XCG-12	York then Read-York	30 / 8,283	1942/-	0	none apparently assigned	failed static test, poor contractor performance, contract cancelled
XCG-13/XCG-13A/ YCG-13/YCG-13A/ CG-13A & G-13A	Waco (Northwestern & Ford production)	30 / 10,000 Ford examples seated 40	1942/1943– 1945	2/2/3/134	X 43-28245/6, X-A (43-28245), Y 43-43864, -43915, Y-A 43-43865, -43914, -43916, A43-43866/913, -43917/63, 44-85942/78	production examples with significant changes from prototypes, halted in favor of more CG-4As & undesirable characteristics, some deployed
XCG-14	Chase	15 / 4,000	1943/1944	1	44-90989	Model MS-1, seeking high-speed tow
XCG-14A	Chase	24 / 5,000	1943/1945	1	44-90990	Model MS-1B, 2nd prototype with many changes, too late in war
XCG-15/XCG-15A/ CG-15A & G-15A	Waco	16 / 3,975	1943/1944–1945	1/2/427	X 43-37082 (CG-4A), X-A 44-90987/8, A 45-5276/660, -12743/84, -12785/13232 cancelled	Model NEU, further development of CG-4, XCG-15 was CG-4A modification, deployed
XCG-16/ XCG-16A	General Airborne Transport Co.	42 / 10,000	1943/1944	1	44-76193, A-76194 not completed	Model MC-1A, commercial development, 1st prototype MC-1 (NX21757) crashed, won government contract, testing unsatisfactory
XCG-17	(Douglas)	42 / 15,000	1944	2	41-18496 (1944), 53-16229 (1946)	USAAF modification of DC-3/C-47 as glider, evaluation only
XCG-18 (not built), XCG-18A, YCG-18A/ YG-18A	Chase	30 / 8,000	1946-1948/1948	2/5	X-A 46-506 -067, Y-A 47-640/4	development of XCG-14A, Model MS-6A Avitruck, all metal, 47-641 converted to powered C-122
XCG-19	Douglas	30 / 8,000	1946	0	N/A	Model 1028, cancelled due to budget in favor of XCG-18
XCG-20 & XG-20	Chase	60 / 16,000	1946/1949	1	47-787	Model MS-3A all metal stressed skin, C-123 powered version
Hotspur Mk. II	General Aircraft	8	1943	2	including British HH553, BT770	GAL 48, evaluation and test
AS.51 Horsa	Airspeed	25 / 7,000	1943-1945	>300	including British DP425, DP765 in US	acquired from Britain, all but a few operated there
Hamilcar	General Aircraft	- / 17,500	1944	1	HH975	GAL 49, evaluation and test

CG-4A Production Summary

Company	Total Built	Serial Number(s)
G & A Aircraft	627	42-43784/843, -57527/618, -79426/545, 43-36809/7008, 45-13233/387, cancelled were 45-13388/682
Babcock Aircraft	60	42-47392/441, -57517/26
Cessna Aircraft	750	42-61101/460, 61821/2210, cancelled 42-61461/820, -62211/600
Ford	4,190	42-77015/8014, 43-39579/0778, 45-5976/6700, -15143/6239, 16242/263, -16266/272, -16274/409, -16412/4, cancelled 45-16240/1, -16264/5, -16273, -16410/1, 45-16415/7142
General Aircraft	1,112	42-45647/721, -73596/749, 43-19674/957, 43-40779/1278, 45-17243/341, cancelled 45-17342/742
Gibson Refrigerator	1,078	42-46552/611, -46619/31, -52853/81, -55785/844, -68306/335, -73750/4112, 43-41279/778, 45-27936/48, -27962/71, cancelled 45-27949/61
Laister-Kauffman Aircraft	310	42-43649/78, -73516/95, 43-42129/228, 45-17143/242
National Aircraft	1	42-52852
Northwestern Aeronautical	1,510	42-43754/83, -56643/96, 43-27254/469, -36609/708, -42229/728, 45-5661/975, -13683/949, -14034/43, -14094/121, cancelled 42-56697/702, -13950/4033, -14044/93
Ward Furniture	7	42-46612/18
Pratt, Read	956	42-52777/851, -56108/607, 43-41779/2128, 45-26436/66, 45-26467/7935
Commonwealth Aircraft	1,470	42-53132/281, -74313/612, 43-42829/3328, 45-14543/5062, cancelled 42-53282/331
Ridgefield Manufacturing	156	42-46917/36, -58074/109, 43-36709/808
Robertson Aircraft	170	42-43628/47, -78795/844, and 43-42729/828
Timm Aircraft	434	42-46322/551, -62609/812, cancelled 42-62813/3349
Waco Aircraft	1,075	42-78923/9422, 43-37009/508, 45-5201/75

United Kingdom CG-4A Hadrians (incomplete)

25 Hadrian Is serialed FR556/80. FR559 and 560 lost at sea. FR580 provided to Canada.

1,070 Hadrian IIs serialed FR581/778, KH871/992, KH994/7, KK569/789, KK792/968, NP664, VJ120/65, VJ198/222, VJ239/84, VJ313/49, VJ368/413, VJ735/81, VJ821/47, VK573/609, VK623/55, and VK874/7. KH871/997 provided to Canada. Deployed to India included KH871/922.

Also mentioned in literature are KK791, and KK969-992. Reported as allocated but not taken up are VJ426/59, VJ481/520, VJ538/59, VJ583/628, VJ650/87, VJ712/31, VJ850/76,VJ890/908,VJ912/51, VJ986/99, VK127/59, VK183/222, VK261/303, VK321/69, VK392/431, VK467/87, VK491/527, VK555/71, VK661/93, VK712/47, VK777/83, VK786/829, and VK841/74.

Tie-ups between the RAF serials and American are few. Known serials are:

42-36715, 36731, 39579, 39587, 39599, 39854, 39856, 39859/61, 39863/5, 39868, 41981, 42236 (KH947 to RCAF), 42900, 43665/6, 45659 (FR564), 45660 (FR565), 45661 (FR566), 45662 (FR567), 45663 (FR568), 45664 (FR569), 45665 (FR570), 45666 (FR571), 45667 (FR572), 45668 (FR573), 45669 (FR574), 45670 (FR575), 46489, 46491/3, 46622/3, 47411, 52860, 52873, 52878, 52880, 52881, 52858, 53233, 53236, 55786, 56129, 56168, 56214, 56240, 56331, 56361, 56366, 56375, 56377/81, 56383, 56388, 56398, 56403, 56407/8, 56414, 56417, 56421, 56424 (KH944 to RCAF), 56440, 56455, 56458, 56532, 56561, 56568, 56570, 56573/4, 56596 (FR661), 56598 (FR662), 56601 (FR663), 56603 (FR664), 56605 (FR665), 56606 (FR666), 57535, 57536/42, 57563, 61318 (FR557), 61327 (FR558), 61897 (5561M instructional airframe), 62193, 62706, 62710/1, 62713, 62717, 62720, 62745, 62769, 62775, 62694, 62697, 73575, 73883, 73890, 73912, 73931, 73934, 73976, 73997, 74027, 74069, 74089, 74094/7, 74109, 74346, 74374, 74403/4, 74408, 74431, 74468, 74478/9, 74482, 74496, 74512/6, 74518, 74523, 74524 (KH945 to RCAF), 74525/7, 74553, 74573, 74608, 74612, 77065, 77067, 77131, 77341, 77363, 77561, 77802, 77804/5, 77807, 77816, 77822, 77825, 77844, 77869, 77875, 77877, 77882, 77898, 77906/7, 77909/10, 77926, 77928/9, 77932, 77938/9, 77940/1, 77952, 77965, 77972, 77976, 77978/9, 78004, 78012, 78797, 78811/3, 78115, 78818/20, 78824/5, 78827/8, 78830/1, 78833/4, 79027, 79217, 79291, 79306, 79311, 79313, 79315, 79317, 79339, 79345, 79349/50, 79361 (KH946 to RCAF), 79388, 70409, 79439, 79446/7, 79529, 79537, 79542	**43**-19721, 19764, 10769/70, 19779, 19829, 19898, 19903/4, 19907, 19909, 19920, 19932/3 19939, 36699/700, 36710, 36738 (FR667), 36739 (FR668), 36740 (FR669), 36741 (FR670), 36763/4, 36766, 36770, 36780, 36783, 36801/6, 36808, 36971/2, 36989, 37253, 37312, 37373, 37479, 37484, 39579, 39598, 39603, 39662, 39697, 39744 (5241M instructional airframe), 39760/79, 39773, 39776/7, 39849, 39857, 39862, 39874, 39876, 39878, 39919, 40004/24, 40026/36, 40037 (FR673), 40237, 40245, 40247, 40261, 40274 (FR671), 40275/9, 40280/2, 40284/7, 40322, 40340, 40348, 40352, 40406, 40466, 40472, 40480/2, 40502/6, 40512/21, 40953 (5071M instructional airframe), 40599, 40629/30, 40632/5, 40663, 40700, 40703, 40707, 40724/7, 40733/4, 40769/77, 40849, 40951, 40956, 40957 (FR679), 40966, 40968, 40981, 41053, 41061, 41099, 41103, 41113/4, 41121, 41126, 41129/30, 41220, 41248, 41262, 41265, 41267/73, 41384, 41387, 41486, 41503, 41515, 41518, 41541, 41561, 41779/82, 41785, 41787/9, 41833, 41834/6, 41838/9, 41843/4, 41868 (FR659), 41879 (FR660), 41908/10, 41912, 41914, 41916, 41918, 41931, 41935, 41944/5, 41961/2, 41980, 41982, 41987/8, 42001, 42014, 42018/19, 42022/23, 42078/82, 42084/88, 42097, 42133/7, 42140 (FR778), 42142/3, 42146, 42161, 42170, 42172, 42178/80, 42214/6, 42229, 42231/4, 42628, 42638/41, 42666/7, 42708, 42716, 42781/2, 42845, 42849, 42857, 42859, 42865, 42867, 42873, 42875, 42882, 42885, 42891, 42894, 42897, 42903, 42906, 42919, 42923, 42925, 42930, 42932, 42933, 42935, 42937, 42943, 42945/6, 42948, 42953, 42955, 42957, 42965, 42967, 42971, 42974, 42981, 43050/2, 43111/4, 43153, 43161/62, 43164/83, 43210, 43212/5, 43218/20, 43222, 43228, 43260/2, 43265, 43267, 43297/8, 43321, 43325/8, 43738/41	**45**-6129, 6168

U.S. Navy/Marine Corps Gliders of WWII

Type	Make	Seats / Payload (lbs)	Year Contracted / Delivered	No. Delivered	Bureau Number(s)	Notes
XLNE-1/ LNE-1	Pratt, Read	2 / -	1941	2/74	X 31505/6, 31507/80,cancelled 31581/85 34115/34	first X NX41803, 73 transferred to Army 5 Aug 1943 as TG-32
XLNP-1	Piper	3 / -	1942	3	36425/27 Army 43-3065, -3070, -3075	as Army TG-8
XLNR-1	Aeronca	3 / -	1942	3	36422/24 Army 42-57452, -57461/2	as Army TG-5
LNS-1	Schweizer	2 / -	1942	12	02979/80, 04380/89, cancelled 26426	SGS 2-8, as Army TG-2, unknown number transferred to Army
XLNT-1/LNT-1/LNT-2	Taylorcraft	3 / -	1942-1943	3+7/25 inc. 12 -2	XLNT-1 36428/30 Army 42-12496/98, 67800/06, LNT-1 87763/87 inc. Army 42-58561	as Army TG-6
XLRA-1/LRA-1	Allied	12 / -	1943	2/0	11647/8, cancelled 31403/12	amphibian, 100 production cancelled
XLRA-2	Allied	12 / -	1943	0	31413/502	as XLRA-1 but tricycle landing gear, cancelled
LR2A-1	Allied	12 / -	(1942)	0	31503/4	high-wing design with floats, not formally ordered
XLRQ-1/ LRQ-1	Bristol G & A	13 / -	1943	2/0	11651/2, cancelled 33715/814	amphibian, cancelled
XLRG-1		24 / -	1942	0	none	amphibian, 40% scale version from AGA flown, cancelled
XLRH-1/LRH-1	Snead and Co.	24 / -	1942	0/0	11649/50, production 31586/635	amphibian, poor contractor performance, all cancelled
XLRN-1	Naval Aircraft Factory	80 / 18,000	1944	1	36431/32	cargo/GLOMB, only 36431 completed, cancelled
XLR2N-1	Naval Aircraft Factory	24 / 12,000	1944	0	none	cargo/GLOMB amphibian, cancelled with little progress
LRW-1	Waco	15 / >3,700	1942	13	37639/48 (ex 42-61938/9, -61943, -61945/7, -61950/3), 44319 (ex 42-45653), 69990/1 (ex 42-52784/5)	as Army CG-4A, 10 returned to Army 5 August 1943
LR2W-1	Waco	16 / >3,700	1943 ?	(2)	85094/5	purportedly CG-15A
Hotspur II	General Aircraft	8	1943	6	unknown	loan from Canada, evaluation and test
Horsa	Airspeed	25	1943 ?	1	including British H6765	evaluation

Miscellaneous U.S. Gliders of WWII

Type	Make	Seats / Payload (lbs)	Year Contracted/ Delivered	No. Delivered	Serial Number(s)	Notes
C-1	Bristol	none	1942	21	unknown	tow-target gliders
XAG-1	Christopher	8 / -	1943	0	44-84153/4	Model CB-1, armed/armored assault glider, concept dropped, contract cancelled
XAG-2	Timm	8 / -	1943	0	44-90991/2	Model XAG-2, as above
XFG-1	Cornelius	1 / 677 gallons	1944-1945	2	44-28059/60	Model CFG-1, towed fuel tank glider, manned prototypes, cancelled
XPG-1	Northwestern	15 / 1,700	1943	1	43-27315	CG-4A with two 125-hp Franklin 6AC-298 engines installed as kit
XPG-2, XPG-2A, PG-2, XPG-2B cancelled,XPG-2C notional ?	Ridgefield	15 / 3,310	1943, 1945	2/10	X 42-58090, X-A 42-58090, -77062, A 45-14034/43,B 45-14044 cancelled, C N/A	CG-4A with two 175-hp Ranger L-400-7 engines installed as kit. B with 245-hp Jacobs R-755-9 cancelled. C likely notional with 315-hp Jacobs R-755-E
XPG-3, XPG-3A	Waco	16 / 2,500	1945	1	X 44-90986, X-A unknown	CG-15A with two 245-hp Jacobs R-755-9 engines installed as kit. XPG-3A with 315-hp R-775-E likely not completed
XPG-4	Chase	20 / 6,427	N/A	0	none	notional conversion of XCG-14A, two 600-hp P&W R-1340-AN-1
XBG-1	Fletcher	1 for test / 2,000 bomb	1942	10	42-46892/901	Model 17, from PQ-11 target, radio-controlled bomb glider, cancelled
XBG-2	Fletcher	1 for test / 2 2,000 bombs	1942	0	42-46902/4	Model 16, cancelled
XBG-3	Cornelius	0 / 4,000 bomb	1943	0	42-46911	Model CBG-1, cancelled
MX-166	Engineering Division, USAAF	0 / 2,000 bomb	1943	1	unknown	little known
MX-334	Northrop	1	1943	3	none	Model N-12, unpowered mockup of XP-79 rocket fighter
MX-324	Northrop	1	1943	1	none	small rocket motor added to MX-334
JB-1A	Northrop	1	1944	1	none	unpowered aero shell of Model NS-16 missile
XLBE-1/LBE-1	Pratt, Read	1 for test / 4,000 bomb	1941	3/0	85290/92, 85293/389 all cancelled	glider-bomb, only three completed
XLBP-1/LBP-1	Piper	1 for test / 4,000 bomb	1941	3/0	85165/7 c/n 1/3, 85168/264 all cancelled	glider-bomb, only three XLBP-1s completed
XLBT-1/LBT-1	Taylorcraft	1 for test / 2,000 bomb	1941	1 ?/25	85265 ?/85266//89, 44320/54 other not known, all but first 25 cancelled	glider-bomb, 25 completed, first XLBT-1?

Endnotes

Chapter 1

[1] Grim, J. Norman, *To Fly the Gentle Giants, The Training of U.S. WW II Glider Pilots*, xix.

[2] *Development & Procurement of Gliders in the Army Air Force, 1941-1944*, Army Air Forces Historical Studies: No. 47, 3.

[3] *The Glider Pilot Training Program: 1941 to 1943*, Army Air Forces Historical Studies: No. 1, 2. This is the preeminent source of information on the Army glider pilot training effort.

[4] Spaatz, Carl, "Glider Training", Routing and Record Sheet, Comment 1, 22 September 1941, Henry Harley Arnold file frame 965.

[5] Echols, Oliver P., "Glider Training", Routing and Record Sheet, Comment 8, 30 December 1941, Henry Harley Arnold file 968.

[6] *Glider Project Books*, Vol. I, microfilm frames 88, 109, and 273. There had previously been little offered as documented evidence that the gliders were considered expendable from the first.

[7] "Military Characteristics of Aircraft," no author stated, memorandum, 12 February 1941.

[8] "Military Characteristics of Aircraft," no author stated, memorandum, 21 July 1941.

[9] Schweizer, Paul A., *Soaring Through the 20th Century*, 88.

[10] Wolfe, K.B., Lieutenant Colonel, "Assignment of Type Symbol "G" for Gliders," 5 June 1941.

[11] Dwiggins, Don, *On Silent Wings: Adventures in Motorless Flight*, 67.

[12] *Glider Project Books*, Vol. I, 104.

[13] Dent, F.R., Jr., Major "Final Report of Major F.R. Dent, Jr., Air Corps, on Trip to England," letter, 9 December 1941, p. 2, Henry Harley Arnold file 910.

[14] *Glider Project Books*, Vol. I, 98, and 137.

[15] *Glider Project Books*, Vol. I, 186.

[16] Spaatz, Carl, Brigadier General "Army Glider Program," memorandum, 2 December 1941, Henry Harley Arnold file 925-932.

[17] Spaatz, Tab A.

[18] Ibid.

[19] Hanley, T.J., Jr., Colonel, "Glider Program," memorandum, 3 March 1942, Henry Harley Arnold file 822.

[20] Hanley, T.J., Jr., Colonel, "Procurement of Gliders for Army Glider Program," 27 January 1942, Henry Harley Arnold file 860.

[21] Cooley, John B. Lieutenant Colonel. "Transport Airplanes for Glider Program," 4 February 1942 and Comment dated 23 February, Henry Harley Arnold file 857-858.

[22] Spaatz, Tab B.

[23] "Hanley, "Glider Program."

[24] Barringer, Lewin B., "Report on Glider Program," memorandum, 7 May 1942, Henry Harley Arnold file 1139, is among the earliest documents mentioning the 30-place glider.

[25] Wood, Karl D., Professor, Purdue University, letter to General Arnold, 11 September 1941, Henry Harley Arnold file 964, relates work performed that summer at Wright Field assisting Major Dent related to troop-carrying glider, particularly takeoff, performance, and stability and control of towed gliders, and especially selection of suitable towing cables and shock absorbers.

[26] *Glider Project Books*, Vol. I, 110, and Material Division, "A Study of Eight and Fifteen-Place Towed Troop-Carry Gliders," no author stated, memorandum, 25 November 1941.

[27] Materiel Division, "Performance of the C-47 Airplane While Towing Gliders," no author stated, memorandum, 19 November 1941.

[28] Unknown to the Allies, at least initially, German glider pilots were Luftwaffe personnel usually with minimal ground combat training except for those closely tied to special forces units.

[29] Lough, Maxon S., Colonel, 3rd Endorsement 18 August 1941 to Spaatz, Carl, Brigadier General, "Organization of Glider Units," 7 July 1941, Henry Harley Arnold file 896.

[30] Johnson, Davenport, Major General, "Gliders" letter, 13 February 1942 and 1st Endorsement by Lieutenant Colonel John B. Cooley, 6 March 1942.

[31] Echols, Oliver P., Brigadier General, "Experimental Glider Procurement," 28 November 1941, in response to a query from Bowlus, Henry Harley Arnold file 923.

[32] Day, Charles L., *Silent Ones: World War II Invasion Glider Test and Experiment*, 9-10, plus XCG-3 and XCG 4 captions.

[33] Grim, 115.

[34] Brown, Robert Vance, *The Navy's Transport Glider Program 1941-1943*, 7. This is the principal source regarding the Navy glider program referenced for this book. Citations include the text as well as microfiche frames of appended reference material.

[35] Devlin, Gerard M., *Silent Wings: The Story of the Glider Pilots of World War II*, 68, and Updegraph, Charles L., Jr., *Special Marine Corps Units of World War II*, 48. This requirement was never materially addressed in the experimental models and there is no evidence it was a feature specified to the contractors.

[36] Brown, 7.

[37] NAS Patuxent River began operations as the new Naval Air Test Center on 29 June 1943, supplanting and eventually replacing NAS Anacostia in the crowded D.C. area.

Chapter 2

[1] *Glider Project Books*, Vol. I, 186. However, Henry Harley Arnold file 1113 has Twining, N.F., Colonel, "Glider Pilot Training," letter, 15 May 1942, that instructed "All privately owned gliders in the continental United States that are considered satisfactory types shall be secured by purchase or condemnation immediately and shall be overhauled commercially, for use not later than July 1, 1942." This direction likely came from Arnold himself as he penned on a memo regarding acquiring training aircraft for the glider pilot training, with respect to light plane, "Go out and get those owned by private individuals – Do not wait for production HHA," this in Air

Forces Flying Training Command, "Plan for Training Glider Pilots," memorandum, 9 May 1942, Henry Harley Arnold file 1124.

2 Note that the civil registration codes of the period used N for the United States of America with a following C for Standard, L Limited, R Restricted, and X Experimental.

3 *Glider Project Books*, Vol. III, 763.

4 The available documentation may also be incomplete. It is known that a Bowlus Baby Albatross was also operated by the service yet not found in the literature. Blacksten, Raul, "Clio Whispers," *Bungee Chord*, Winter 2003-4, 12.

5 The Army also acquired another high-performance German glider, a Kranich (Crane) 2-place. In June 1944 the Aircraft Laboratory was seeking to resume assembly of the aircraft if free shop time could be found, and the CCAAF crowd was interested in operating it. How the service came by the glider and its ultimate fate in unclear. Corriveau, A.L., "Progress Report on Foreign Gliders," memorandum, 11 July 1944.

6 *Glider Project Books*, Vol. III, 763, lists the Laister-Kauffman acquisition separately for unclear reasons. Only unpublished summaries found in archives attribute this to a special effort, but also claim the firm built three TG-20s. This last is not consistent with the official record. See also the letter by Matthew E. Rodina, Jr., dated 6 July 1982 and found in the glider records at the National Museum of the United States Air Force that summarizes information from official Aircraft History Cards.

7 *Request for Model or Type Designation Change of Status of Equipment*, "Airplane, Training Glider, Model XTG-1," form, 7 July 41.

8 *Request for Model or Type Designation Change of Status of Equipment*, "XTG-1-FR Glider," form, 1 August 1945.

9 Blacksten, 13.

10 *Request for Model or Type Designation Change of Status of Equipment*, "Airplane, Training Glider TG-2," form, 10 December 1941.

11 Schweizer, 89.

12 *Glider Project Books*, Vol. III, 744. Most accounts have just 110 for which serials are recorded.

13 *Army Aircraft Characteristics, Production and Experimental*, Report No. TSEST – A2, 46.

14 Schweizer, 89.

15 *Glider Project Books*, Vol. III, 726.

16 *Glider Project Books*, Vol. I, 173.

17 *Glider Project Books*, Vol. III, 715.

18 *Glider Project Books*, Vol. I, 124.

19 *Glider Project Books*, Vol. III, 766, and 844.

20 Ibid, 716.

21 Blacksten, 14.

22 Briegleb, Gus, "Gus Briegleb's Two-Place, The Briegleb Two-Place Sailplane," *Soaring*, July-August 1943, 9.

23 These are shown in *Glider Project Books*, Vol. III, 761, as TG-13As two-seaters purchased in June 1942 from private owners. This suggests the gliders may have been some other Briegleb product or conversions of the BG-6, especially as they were acquired in June 1942 at which point Briegleb was still obligated to deliver the BG-8s to the government.

24 Day, 63.

25 *Development & Procurement of Gliders in the Army Air Force, 1941-1944*, 71.

26 Peek, Chet, *The Taylorcraft Story*, 155.

27 Ibid.

28 Peperell, Roger W., *Piper Aircraft, The Development and History of Piper Designs*, 44.

29 *Glider Project Books*, Vol. I, 93.

30 Brown, 246, and *Glider Project Books*, Vol. III, 709.

31 Byard, Jeff, "What Ever Happened to all the TGs?," *Bungee Chord*, Spring 1998, 11, and Grim, 109.

32 Simons, Martin, *Sailplanes, 1920-1945*, 244.

33 Sallada, H.B., Captain, "Glider Program," 24 June 1942, Henry Harley Arnold file 1113.

34 Simons, Martin, *The World's Vintage Sailplanes 1908-45*, 174.

35 Brown, 209.

36 Whelan, Robert F., *Exploring the Monster, Mountain Lee Waves: The Aerial Elevator*, 42. Of course this date, related by a principal participant, conflicts with the later truncation of the order, suggesting this was a formality that followed an earlier stop-work order.

37 Brown, 209.

38 Ibid, 246.

Chapter 3

1 Kuter, L.S., Brigadier General, "Glider Pilot Training," memorandum, 10 June 1942, Henry Harley Arnold file 1103.

2 Ibid.

3 Conley, Manuel, "Silent Squadrons," *American History*, June 1983, 16.

4 Buffkin, Ronald M., Major, *Assault Gliders: A Reexamination*, 3, and Huston, James A., Major, *The Airborne Team 1941-1945*, 160, and Larson, George A., "D-Day Glider Attack, The Waco CG-4A Glider," *Airborne Quarterly*, 67.

5 Huston, 54.

6 Meyers, E.B., Major General, "CG-4A Gliders in Storage," memorandum, 30 March 1944, Henry Harley Arnold file 1040.

7 The Americans were aware the British Army pilots were sergeants. The "First Pilot" was more thoroughly trained and responsible for takeoff and landing while the "Second Pilot" was only responsible for flight on tow.

8 Huston, 55.

9 Bagley, Mark B., *The G Stands for Guts, A Glider Pilot Remembers WWII*, 87. This was down from an original 45 gliders per squadron, probably as the 15-place glider became the standard, Huston 12. However, by September 1943 the calculus was four gliders to every tow plane, probably accounting for attrition, Huston 46. All such numbers remained goals never achieved or sustained. The uncertainty was also a product of inadequate planning given the unknown demands expected of the airborne team, lack of large unit tactics training, and general immaturity of the combat elements.

10 *The Glider Pilot Training Program: 1941 to 1943*, 74.

11 Craven, Wesley F., and Cate, James L., *The Army Air Forces in World War 2, Volume V Men and Planes*, 624.

12 Grim, 240.

13 Craven and Cate, 624.

14 Holcomb, Thomas, Major General, "Glider Training," memorandum 24 June 1942.

15 Brown, 160, and Updegraph, 52, disagree on the number of officers, (26 by Brown and 20 Updegraph), one perhaps being a typographical error.

16 Grim, 7.

17 Sallada.

18 Brown,161.

19 On 8 July 1942, Rear Admiral J.H. Towers, Chief of the Bureau of Aeronautics, and requested "one each of the early production models of the troop and cargo carrying gliders being developed by the U.S. Army Air Forces, be assigned to the Navy for such tests and studies as may be found desirable in the glider program." In exchange, he proposed to "transfer to the Army, from production contracts, one of each of the glider models being developed by the Navy, for the same purpose." Arnold agreed on 3 August 1942. Towers, J.H., Rear Admiral, "Glider Models – Procurement of for Tests," letter to Commanding General, Army Air Forces, 9 July 1942, Henry Harley Arnold file 1086, and reply Arnold, H.H., Lieutenant General, "Glider Models – Procurement of for Tests," letter to Chief of the Bureau of Aeronautics, 3 August 1942, 1090.

20 Updegraph, 53.

Chapter 4

1 *Glider Project Books*, Vol. III, 719-720.

2 Most material from *Glider Data Book, MX-114*.

3 Ordway, Jr., F.I., "Army Glider Program," correspondence, 27 January 1942, Henry Harley Arnold file 868.

4 *Glider Project Books*, Vol. I, 115.

5 Ibid, 123.

6 *Glider Project Books*, Vol. III, 776.

7 Ibid.

8 Echols, Oliver P., "Glider Production Facilities," memorandum, 17 January 1942, Henry Harley Arnold file 865.

9 *Glider Project Books*, Vol. I, 126, Vol. III, 771.

10 *Glider Data Book, MX-114* reported a three-seat row behind, two seats behind that, and an eighth seat in the rear. However, this information appears to date from 15 August 1941 and based on early design information.

[11] *Glider Project Books*, Vol. I, 115.

[12] *Glider Project Books*, Vol. III, 777, and 784.

[13] Ibid, 715.

[14] *Glider Data Book, MX-114*, and R*equest for Model or Type Designation Change of Status of Equipment*, "Airplane, Troop Glider, XCG-6," form, 7 July 1941. Laminar flow refers to smooth flow of the air close to the wing surface for more of the length aft of the leading edge than the turbulent flow to which the laminar flow transition to at some point, for less drag. While the plywood-covered D-section promised the very smooth surface from the leading edge to the spar to promote laminar flow, the transition to fabric aft of that was unlikely to do so if such was expected. The objective was innovative but challenging, the technology classified, and so likely not realized. Likewise, the slotted flaps were an unusually advanced feature for the glider.

[15] Day, 88.

[16] *Glider Project Books*, Vol. I, 115.

Chapter 5

[1] Huston, 54.

[2] Conley, 15.

[3] *Glider Project Books*, Vol. III, 776.

[4] This apparently began with a note from Arnold to his chief of Air Staff, Brigadier General Spaatz, on 18 August 1941, seeking to initiate development, Henry Harley Arnold file 939.

[5] This contrasts with the British and Soviets who expended valuable resources on the impractical endeavor of turning a light truck and light tank into temporary gliders. These met with various measures of success but were not carried to production, yet both manufactured large-capacity cargo gliders.

[6] Dunham, S.W., "Report on Detachable Wings for a ¼-Ton Liaison Truck (Jeep)," memorandum, 21 November 1941.

[7] *Glider Project Books*, Vol. I, 113.

[8] *Glider Project Books*, Vol. III, 776.

[9] Flutter is an unstable oscillation of a portion of the aircraft or control surface that can grow to catastrophic levels. The instability is induced by unsteady air loads interacting with elastic deformation of the structure or control surface rotation at like frequencies (resonance). On the face of it, it appears unlikely the dorsal addressed flutter. It is more likely the rudder extension did this with mass ahead of the hinge line, although such extensions are also used to lighten rudder forces.

[10] *Glider Project Books*, Vol. I, 139.

[11] Meyers.

[12] *Gli*

[13] *Glider Project Books*, Vol. III, 738.

[14] Ibid.

[15] *Glider Project Books*, Vol. III, 739-742.

[16] *Glider Project Books*, Vol. I, 742.

[17] Holley, Jr., Irving Brinton, *United States Army in World War 2, Special Studies, Buying Aircraft, Matériel Procurement for the Army Air Force*, 373, and *Glider Project Books*, Vol. I, 264, and Vol. III, 713.

[18] *Glider Project Books*, Vol. I, 139.

[19] Perrin, Edwin S., Brigadier General, "Gliders," letter, 11 April 1944, Henry Harley Arnold file 1037.

[20] Meyers.

[21] McKee, William F., Colonel, "Past Difficulties in Determining Glider Requirements," memorandum, 3 October 1944, Henry Harley Arnold file 1017-1018.

[22] McKee, William F., Colonel, "Deterioration as Affecting CG-4A Glider Requirements," memorandum for Deputy Chief of Air Staff, 25 May 1944, Henry Harley Arnold file 1034.

[23] Echols, Oliver P., Major General, "Glider Requirements Versus Production," letter, 23 March 1945, Henry Harley Arnold file 997.

[24] Snodgrass, Raymond J., *The AAF Glider Program, November 1944 – January 1947*, Army Air Forces Historical Studies: No. 217, 57.

[25] Ibid, 62.

[26] Ibid, 58.

[27] Timberlake, Patrick W., Brigadier General, "Glider Production After V-E Day," memorandum, 24 March 1945, Henry Harley Arnold file 994.

[28] Snodgrass, 63.

[29] *Glider Project Books*, Vol. III, 741.

[30] Ibid, 198, and 250.

[31] Ibid, 198.

[32] Grim, 100.

[33] Snodgrass, 78.

[34] Ibid 204-205, and 283-284.

[35] Lindley, John M., "A Great Experience, Villaume Builds Gliders in World War II," *Ramsey County History*, Winter 2007, 24.

[36] *Glider Project Books*, Vol. III, 753-754.

[37] Ibid, 709, and 729.

[38] Grim, 111.

[39] *Glider Project Books*, Vol. III, 730-731.

[40] "Glider Tactics and Technique," AFM No. 3, 24 January 1944, 18.

[41] *Glider Project Books*, Vol. I, 274.

[42] Ibid.

[43] Grim, 181.

[44] *Glider Project Books*, Vol. VI, 602-603.

[45] Craig, H.A., Brigadier General, "Availability of CG-4A Gliders in the Maxton-Camp, Mackall, North Carolina, Area," memorandum, 3 November 1943, Henry Harley Arnold file 1056.

[46] *Glider Project Books*, Vol. I, 273-274.

[47] Littel, E.G., Major, "Report of Brigadier General Junius W. Jones, Air Inspector, on Synopsis of Investigation of Crash of CG-4A Glider at Lambert Field, St. Louis, Missouri, 1 August 1943," memorandum, 23 October 1943.

[48] Interview with author. The experiment with charges to blow off the aft fuselage of the CG-4A is corroborated by a personal account in Wood, Alan, *History of the World's First Glider Forces*, 268. See also Larson, George A., *Aerial Assault Into Burma*, 25.

[49] Butler, C.T., Flight Officer, "Ludington-Griswold, Inc, Modified Nose for the CG-4A Glider," memorandum, 24 August 1943.

[50] Devlin, 126.

[51] *Glider Project Books*, Vol. I, 72, and 281.

[52] Day, 79.

[53] Bagley, 142.

[54] Connor, Sara Witter and Day, Charles L., "The Ah Da Wa Gam Cardboard Box," 2-3. The one glider with the "paper" nose and floor, tested at Clinton County in early 1944, was called the "snow glider" for uncertain reasons. The floor was so limited in terms of point loading that the gliders were almost exclusively employed for personnel transport.

[55] Davidson, Norman, Major, "Armor Plate Requirement CG-4A Glider," memorandum, 31 May 1945.

[56] Hockett, H.E., Lieutenant Colonel, "Armor Plate Requirement CG-4A Glider," memorandum, 14 June 1945.

[57] Grim, 268-269.

[58] Pearcy, Arthur, *Lend-Lease Aircraft in World War 2*, 130-131, and Wood, Alan, 187, are the source of lend-lease information. Yet, Snodgrass, 138, credits only 746 airframes provided to Britain.

[59] Todd, R., Squadron Leader, British Air Commission, "Forms 263A for CG-4 Gliders," letter, 11 October 1944.

[60] Welsh, W.L., Air Marshall, letter to Major General Barney M. Giles, 29 March 1944, Henry Harley Arnold file 1029.

Chapter 6

[1] Although the Army considered glider shipment to theater from the earliest days of pursuing their program, the Navy appears to have neglected this aspect. Towing thousands of miles to the war zone was impractical, either by air or on the surface. While detachable wings were mentioned in a very early missive (Brown microfiche 8, frame 41), and the experimental contracts called for trailers to move the gliders (wings detached), there is no indication that further breakdown for shipment was considered.

[2] While flaps could be used to assist in descent, they appeared likely to be damaged upon water contact. None of the photographs the author has examined of the experimental floatwing gliders show flaps extended during water operations.

[3] The planing hull is shallow for less drag and greater speed. The steps allow an aircraft to more easily separate from the water on takeoff.

[4] Brown microfiche 7, frame 11.

[5] Aeromold had been proportionately owned by Greenport Basin & Construction Company and two owners of Bristol Aircraft, Warren and Patterson. These men worked up the bid for both companies.

Brown microfiche 7, frame 27, and 32. The new entity was actually Aeromold personnel and assets, and the Navy was surprised to learn it was this organization with which it had negotiated a contract rather than the Virginia "Bristol" that was believed to have more assets upon which to build. However, the Connecticut "Bristol" insisted it had brought along the plastic bonded mold knowledge and expertise of the Virginia organization and was essentially the same company. Still, its resources were meager by comparison to the Virginia firm, and the USN had committed.

6 This advance was predicated on Bristol securing a bond to cover the government against loss. When this was not forthcoming, the firm agreed to a joint account. Banks had hesitated to back the company that had been in business less than a month with cash assets of just $1,000 and only leased facilities. Although working on C-1 tow targets for the Army, they had no engineering offices or facility for building a large glider. Based on these discoveries, there was initial hesitation to proceed with the contract, but the urgency of war prevailed. Brown, 51-62.

7 Refer to the Appendix for bureau numbers. The record shows BuNos 11653/4 which do not appear to be associated with the follow-on 100-aircraft order. The association of these two numbers remains unclear. Andrade, 201.

8 Brown, iv.

9 Figley, Richard E., Major, *Flight Tests of XLRQ-1 Glider, Project George*, Memorandum Report No. 8-43, 24 August 1943, 1, and Cassagneres, Ed, "Bristol XLRQ-1 Glider Story," *AAHS Journal*, Summer 2003, 124.

10 Brown, 109.

11 Ibid, 184.

12 Ibid, 186.

13 Brown microfiche 10, frame 37.

14 Figley, 1.

15 Brown, 163.

16 Summary of *Status Report* 7/1/43, 56.

17 Bristol Aeronautical Corporation, *Aircraft Characteristics, LRQ-1*.

18 Brown, 185.

19 Gallagher, William E, "The U.S. Navy's WWII Floatwing Assault Gliders," *National Soaring Museum Historical Journal*, Vol. 25 No. 2, 2003, 6.

20 Such a contract covers actual costs plus a reasonable profit but usually has a cap above which the contractor must accept a loss. In the present day, such contract forms are considered inappropriate for new aircraft development.

21 Brown, 27.

22 Ownership of the company was vested in four member of the Breed family. Brown microfiche 7, frame 40.

23 Brown, 239.

24 Ibid, 238.

25 Ibid, 205.

26 Ibid, 243.

27 Ibid, 50, and 63.

28 Ibid, 64.

29 The Navy also seems to have had the notion gliders could be built quickly and cheaply. Witness Winston, R.A., Lieutenant, "Large-Capacity Gliders Towed by Airplanes and Their Possible Employment in Naval Aviation," memorandum, 12 January 1942, in Brown microfiche 8, frame 65, (Lieutenant Winston was on Commander Fahrney's staff) and Thomas, Charles S., letter, 28 May 1942, Brown microfiche 8, frame 91, both which expected the wooden structures to be built cheaply and quickly from plasticized plywood laid into simple molds employing moderately skilled and under-employed labor in furniture and cabinetry shops.

30 Allied's original price had been $25,000 for each glider and this was reduced only after persuasion by Navy officials.

31 Brown, 203.

32 Ibid, 233. The LRA-2 designation is mentioned, described as having a jettisonable two-wheel main gear assembly.

33 Sallada, 2.

34 Wehle, John, Lieutenant Colonel, "A Study of Military Gliders and Their Use in the Marine Corps," undated (summer 1942).

35 Brown, 106.

36 Brown microfiche 10, frame 36.

37 Brown, 246.

Chapter 7

1 No military employed women glider pilots, and certainly no women pilots in combat.

2 The British and apparently also Germans continued to employ lines of hemp or other common rope materials, and accounts would suggest they suffered more frequent breaks.

3 Spencer, Leon B., "Glider Tow Ropes, WWII Military Gliders," paper, 7 June 2003, 1.

4 Arnold, H.H., General, letter to Devers, Jacob L., Lieutenant General, 1 August 1943, Henry Harley Arnold file 1025-1026.

5 Ibid, and Barringer, Lewin B., "Report on Glider Program," memorandum, 7 May 1942, Henry Harley Arnold file 1140. Barringer recommends "that serious consideration be given to the great advantages of towing most of them across."

6 Suggestions in some references that the Rebecca was aboard gliders is surely erroneous. The power and dedicated monitoring requirements, plus the top secret nature of the set, would have made this prohibitive. No personal accounts of such equipment aboard the gliders have come to light nor photographs of the Rebecca antennae on gliders.

7 Grim, 243.

8 Spencer, Leon B., "WWII U.S. Army Air Forces Glider Aerial Retrieval System," paper, undated, 2. How the glider flew with only a dummy pilot is unclear, and this may be muddled.

9 Lewis, W. David and Trimble, William F., *The Airway to Everywhere, A History of All American Aviation, 1937-1953*, 111.

10 Ibid.

11 Day, 52.

12 Thoms, Keith H., *Interim Heavy Airlift: Sea Base Logistics Glider Concept*, NSWCDD/TR-06/52, January 2007, 7-8.

13 Lewis, 113.

14 This was extended in 1943 to experimental snatching of personnel, conceivably downed aircrew members, in what later became the Fulton Recovery System also used to grab film canisters from satellites and unmanned aircraft from under parachute descent.

15 Day. 53.

16 "Glider Tactics and Technique," 3.

17 *Glider Project Books*, Vol. I, 116, and Vol. II, 602.

18 McKee, "Past Difficulties in Determining Glider Requirements."

19 Harris, Anthony A., Lieutenant Colonel, "Pick-a-Back Method for Glider Propulsion," memorandum, 15 February 1946, 7.

Chapter 8

1 *Glider Project Books*, Vol. I, 134.

2 Curtis, Edward P., Major "Large Capacity Transport Gliders," memorandum, 10 December 1941, Henry Harley Arnold file 917.

3 Smith, L.T., Lieutenant Colonel, "Large Capacity Transport Gliders," letter, 8 February 1942, Henry Harley Arnold file 914 and similar documents in this period.

4 *Glider Project Books*, Vol. I, 134.

5 Ibid, 136.

6 Weaver, W.R., Major General, "Military Characteristics of Aircraft," memorandum, 8 February 1942.

7 There is some confusion in the literature as to the number of personnel for which the XCG-9 was to accommodate, seen as both 30 and 32, possibly because of an assumption the pilot and copilot was added to any "troop," "seat," or "place" figure. However, *Request for Model or Type Designation Change of Status of Equipment*, "Airplane, Transport Glider, XCG-9," form, 30 July 1942, is specific about "thirty-place (including pilot and copilot)."

8 Barringer, Lewin, "A.G.A. Aviation Corporation Troop Glider," undated note, Henry Harley Arnold file 943. Barringer says his flights were on 6 November which contradicts Brown, 64, that says 16 November, one possibly being a typographical error.

9 *Glider Project Books*, Vol. I, 135.

10 *Operational and Tactical Suitability of the XCG-10A Glider*, no author stated, 12 February 1945, 8.

11 Ibid, 9.

12 Ibid, 17, and 19.

13 Timberlake, Patrick W., Brigadier General, "Glider Production After V-E Day," memorandum, 24 March 1945, 994.

14 Giles, Barney M., Lieutenant General, "Requirement for CG-10A Gliders," memorandum, 31 January 1945, Henry Harley Arnold file 1000.

15 Timberlake, 994.

16 Giles, 999.

17 Ibid, 995.

18 *Request for Model or Type Designation Change of Status of Equipment*, "Airplane, Transport Glider, XCG-11," form, 30 July 1942.

19 *Resume, XCG12 Gliders*, York Aircraft Company, in *Glider Project Books*, Vol. VI, microfilm frame 461.

20 Ibid, 481.

21 *Glider Project Books*, Vol. I, 282, and *Development & Procurement of Gliders in the Army Air Force, 1941-1944*, 40.

22 *Glider Project Books*, Vol. I, 137 and Vol. II, 548 and conjoined pages give a thorough if convoluted history of this program's death throes.

23 Read-York, Inc., "Contract X 535 ac-40197," letter to Colonel Paul H. Kemmer, 2 November 1943, in *Glider Project Books*, Vol. I, microfilm frame 556.

24 *Glider Project Books*, Vol. III, 781.

25 *Request for Model or Type Designation Change of Status of Equipment*, "Glider, Transport, AAF Model XCG-13," form, 5 January 1945.

26 *Glider Project Books*, Vol. III, 782.

27 Day, 93.

28 *Request for Model or Type Designation Change of Status of Equipment*, "Waco 30 Place Glider, YCG-13," form, 15 January 1944. Confusion over the designation of the first gliders on contract abound. Records of serial numbers indicate the initial contracts built the XCG-13s and XCG-13As mentioned in the text. However, the Army studies referenced lists these as YCG-13 and YCG-13A machines. The contractual records make clear there were no separate contracts for any such machines.

29 "Performance of CG-13," no author stated, 15 December 1943, Henry Harley Arnold file 1051.

30 Ibid.

31 Snodgrass, 99.

32 Ibid, 137. The page also gives a total program cost of $6,165,000, although this conflicts with the source's earlier statement on page 100 that Northwestern alone was paid $6,305,339.09.

33 Pearcy, 131, is the source of the serials.

34 "Test Report of Half Scale Prototype," part of initial Airborne Transport, Inc. proposal, located in National Archive files.

35 Kemmer, Paul H., Colonel, USAAF, "42-place Glider Proposal – Airborne Transport, Inc.," memorandum, 28 December 1942.

36 Echols, O.P., Major General, "Airborne Transport, Incorporated," memorandum, 16 February 1943.

37 *Development & Procurement of Gliders in the Army Air Force, 1941-1944*, 43.

38 "Resume of Happenings on XCG-16 Glider Project," no author stated, 16 October 1944.

39 Without official support it is unlikely the design team acquired sufficient data on the NACA laminar flow airfoil to incorporate it in the aircraft, and this feature is not mentioned in subsequent specifications or other documentation.

40 Haig, H.A., Brigadier General, "Requirement for Aircraft—Gliders, Transport," Memorandum, 4 October 1943.

41 *Glider Project Books*, Vol. I, 284.

42 Cook, Orval R., Colonel, USAAF, "Meeting on Bowlus-Criz Glider Production," memorandum, 2 November 1943.

43 Morgan, W.M., Colonel, USAAF, "Criz Glider," memorandum, 21 October 1943.

44 Branshaw, E., Major, General, U.S. Army, "Information Leaks Concerning Criz Glider," memorandum, 13 November 1943.

45 *Glider Project Books*, Vol. I, 284.

46 *Request for Model or Type Designation Change of Status of Equipment*, "General Airborne Transport Company glider, model designation MC-2," form, 18 November 1943 assigning the XCG-16 denotes the Model as MC-2. This may have been an error or reflects preliminary information. None of the subsequent formal documentation used MC-2.

47 *Glider Project Books*, Vol. I, 284, Vol. III, 831.

48 *Model Specification, Glider, Cargo and Troop Transport, Towed, A.A.F. XCG-16 + G.A.T.C. MC-1A*, Report No. M-100, General Airborne Transport Company, 4 December 1943, Revision 2, 26 April 1944.

49 "Resume of Happenings on XCG-16 Glider Project."

50 Meyers, B.E., Major General, "Status of XCG-16 (Criz Bowlus) Glider," memorandum, 6 May 1944, Henry Harley Arnold file 1024.

51 "Resume of Happenings on XCG-16 Glider Project."

52 Echols, Oliver P., Major General, "Status of the XCG-16 Glider," memorandum, 5 October 1944, Henry Harley Arnold file 1016.

53 Roberts and Monahan, Majors, *Preliminary Report of the Test of Operational and Tactical Suitability of the XCG-16 Glider*, rough draft undated but likely end of October 1944, and Zell, John H., Captain, *Comparison of Model Specification Requirements of General Airborne Transport Company's XCG-16 Glider with Actual Flight Test Values*, 27 October 1944.

54 *Request for Model or Type Designation Change of Status of Equipment*, "General Airborne Transport Company Model XCG-16A Glider, AAF Serial No. 44-76194)," 16 November 1944.

55 *Model Specification, Glider, Cargo and Troop Transport, Towed, AAF XCG-16A + G.A.T.C. MC-1B*, Report No. M-100A, General Airborne Transport Company, 25 August 1944.

56 Ober, Jon H., Captain, "Development of Glider Type Aircraft," memorandum, 6 July 1944.

57 Hawks, Charles R., Major, *Progress Report, Contract No. W33-038 AC-1666, General Airborne Transport Company, Model XCG-16*, 5 December 1944.

58 Christopher Engineering Company, "New Design of Improved Glider," no author stated, letter, 19 September 1942.

59 Moore, C.K., Colonel, "Glider, Transport," memorandum, 10 October 1942.

60 Kowalski, Jr., Frank, Captain, "Gyro-Glider," letter, 10 September 1941, Henry Harley Arnold file 953.

61 Curtis, Edward P., Major, "Gyro-Glider," memorandum, 3 November 1941, Henry Harley Arnold file 948.

62 Coates, Steve with Carbonel, Jean-Christophe, *Helicopters of the Third Reich*,. 74-75.

63 *Glider Project Books*, Vol. I, 134.

64 "Military Characteristics of Aircraft," no author stated, memorandum, 19 April 1944.

65 Wilson, R.C., Colonel "Glider Developments." memorandum, 8 August 1944.

66 Chase Brothers, *General Specification for Transport Glider MS*, 21 November 1942.

67 Stroukoff, Michael, *Model Specification Contract W33-038 AC-1206 Glider, Cargo and Troop – Transport Towed, Army Air Forces Model Designation XCG-14*, 10 June 1944.

68 Carroll, F.O., Brigadier General, "Glider Developments," memorandum, 2 September 1944.

69 Several sources stated first flight was on the 4th, and one gave location as Newark AB, Delaware. *Chase / Stroukoff*, http://1000aircraftphotos.com/HistoryBriefs/Chase.htm.

70 Giles, Barney M., Major General "Priority for CG-14 Glider Engineering and Breakdown Tests," 11 November 1943, Henry Harley Arnold file 1052 and Craig, H.A., Brigadier General, "CG-13 Glider Requirements," 23 December 1943, frame 1049.

71 Ober, Jon H., Captain, "Development of Glider Type Aircraft." memorandum, 6 July 1944.

72 Nikiforoff, Paul, *Model Specification Glider, Cargo and Troop – Transport, Towed, Army Air Forces Model Designation XCG-14A Chase Model MS-1A*, 25 January 1945.

73 Popowich, George, "Phase II Tests on the XG-14A Glider, USAF No. 44-90990," memorandum, 23 August 1948.

74 Kaden, George, "Performance of the XCG-14A Glider," memorandum, 30 October 1946 and Pfeiffer, H.H., *Flight Test Report, Report A 110*, Chase Aircraft Company, 15 October 1948.

75 Sauers, William F., Captain, *Memorandum Report No. TSEAL2-4565-3-1, Glider Development Conference*, 26 April 1945, 4.

76 Taylor, H.A., *Airspeed Aircraft Since 1931*, 103.

77 Letter to British Air Commission, no signatory given, 5 January 1942, Henry Harley Arnold file 902.

78 *Glider Project Books*, Vol. I, 118.

79 Warren, John C., Dr., *Airborne Operations in World War II, European Theater*, USAF Historical Studies: No. 97, 19, 22, and 224.

80 Esvelin, Philippe, *D-Day Gliders: The American Gliders of D-Day*, 31.

81 Snodgrass, 59.

82 Huston, 71-72.

83 *History Leading up to Assault Glider Contracts*, undated summary and copied correspondence, approximately March 1943. Brown,

96, reveals Admiral Towers, chief of the Navy's Bureau of Aeronautics, expressed a desire on 13 June 1942 for an amphibious glider of capacity less than 12 for tow from a carrier deck. This and discussions with the Army may be the roots of this unusual requirement.

84 Nagel, F., Christopher Aircraft Company, "Eight Place Assault Glider XAG-1," letter, 21 December 1942, and *Request for Model or Type Designation Change of Status of Equipment*, "Airplane, Assault Glider XAG-1," form, 20 March 1943.

85 Brown, J.M., Christopher Aircraft Company, "Change Order on Contract W35ac37433," letter, 24 September 1943.

86 Timm Aircraft Corp., *Specification, Model XAG-2*, Report No. 248-A, 1 March 1943.

87 Huston, 72.

88 *Development & Procurement of Gliders in the Army Air Force, 1941-1944*, 56.

89 Kemmer, Paul H., Colonel, USAAF, "Contract No. W535AC-37433 XAG-1 Assault Glider Cancellation for Default," memorandum, 16 October 1943.

90 Smith, George F., Colonel, letter to Christopher-National Aircraft Products Company, 11 February 1948.

Chapter 9

1 Brown, 99.

2 Ibid,125-126.

3 Ibid ,130.

4 Ibid, 96.

5 *History Leading up to Assault Glider Contracts*.

6 Wehle.

7 Brown, 145.

8 Ibid, 146.

9 Ibid, 169.

10 Brown, 120, words of Admiral Ernest M. Pace, Jr., Director of the Material Division within the Bureau of Aeronautics.

11 This was ostensibly at no loss to the government, but the Navy agreed to reimburse Snead up to $180,000 for expansion of the Orange plant. Brown, 115.

12 This must have been a contractor test to verify predictions as the static article had yet to be delivered to the NAF. Brown, 117.

13 Brown, 245.

14 Figley, Richard E., Captain, *Memorandum Report No. 2-43, Experimental Cargo Line, Project George*, 20 January 1943, 1.

15 Summary of *Status Report* 7/1/43, 56.

16 Figley, 7.

17 Ibid, 1-2.

18 Brown, 170.

19 Figley, 7, and Brown microfiche 9, 58.

20 Only a C-47 with modest payload could tow a fully loaded CG-4A. A reviewer of the Figley report appended a comment noting that the CG-4A was a "universally horrible example" and not indicative of the Navy models in the wings that would require much less effort by the tug (Brown microfiche 9, 97), although no source for this conclusion is provided and it was clearly only an expectation.

21 This was relearned after the war when some former GIs attempted to form commercial freight companies using towed gliders. Profits were elusive. All American Aviation also demonstrated such operations by flying live lobsters in a TG-3A from Hull, Maine, to Teterboro, New Jersey over five days in October 1945 using snatch. Lewis and Trimble, 116. While it is true that such monetary "bean counting" is largely neglected during combat operations, fiscal economies are a consideration on a more national and strategic scale.

22 Brown, 175.

23 Fahrney, Delmar S., Rear Admiral, *The History of Pilotless Aircraft and Guided Missiles*, 460.

24 Grim, 116.

25 Summary of Status Report 7/1/43, 56, and Barnaby, R.S., Naval Aircraft Factory, "Long Distance Glider Towing Using Autotow Equipment," memorandum, 18 June 1943, and Brown microfiche 10, 3.

26 Summary of *Status Report* 7/1/43.

27 Brown microfiche 10, 11.

28 Brown, 233.

29 Ibid, 245-246.

30 Doodwin, Hugh H., Captain, "Naval Gliders – Allocation of," memorandum, 13 July 1943.

31 Bristol Aeronautical Corporation, "Disposition of LRQ-1 Glider," letter to Major B.B. Price, 4 August 1943, and Breed, III, Richard E., Allied Aviation Corporation, "Allied Invader Glider Allocated to Army," press release, 21 September 1943.

32 Cassagneres, 124.

33 Bristol, Disposition of LRQ-1 Glider".

34 Kemmer, Paul H., Colonel, "Disposition of LRQ-1 Glider," letter to Bristol Aeronautical Corporation, 16 August 1943.

35 Patterson, A.L., Bristol Aeronautical Corporation, telegram to Lieutenant Colonel B.B. Price, 17 September 1943.

36 Gallagher, 6.

37 Brown, 243.

38 Ibid, 243 and 247.

39 Andrade, John M., *U.S. Military Aircraft Designations and Serials 1909 to 1979*, 200.

40 Brown, 209.

41 Ibid, 244.

42 Brown, 210.

43 Trimble, William F., *Wings for the Navy: A History of the Naval Aircraft Factory, 1917-1956*, 271.

44 Fahrney, 458.

45 This may account for two additional XLRQ-1 BuNos, 11653/4, found in the literature. However, their contiguity with the original two XLRQ-1 numbers appears to argue against this.

46 Ibid, 189.

47 Ibid, 210.

48 The Navy is also said to have acquired two CG-15As from the Army as LR2W-1s, likely just for trials as potential GLOMBS given the late date these were available (end of 1944). Andrade, 201 and Lynch, Tim, *Silent Skies, Gliders at War 1939-1945*, 79. However, the source for conclusion these were CG-15s is unclear.

49 Ideas like hauling engines and serving as a towed fuel tank dated from at least December 1941, as expressed in Winston, "Large-Capacity Gliders Towed by Airplanes and Their Possible Employment in Naval Aviation."

50 Trimble, 271.

51 Fahrney, 458.

52 Trimble, 272.

53 Summary of *Status Report*, 56.

54 *Air Force and Moment for XLRN-1 Glider*, Report No. 665, Aerodynamical Laboratory, 22 April 1943, Figure 3.

55 Summary of *Status Report*.

56 Fahrney, 461.

57 "Fuel Transfer Diagram, Proposed, (XLRN-1)," drawing, 29 October 1942.

58 Fahrney, 458, reports the first flight was on the 19th. However, Pearl, W.W., "XLRN-1 Glider #36431 – Report of Flight Tests at NAS Patuxent River, Md. 11/7/44 & 11/9/44," 14 November 1944, is very clear as to the sequence of events and specifically names the eighth run on the 25th as the "first actual flight."

59 Trimble, 272-273.

60 Summary of *Status Report* and Barnaby, Ralph, letter to William K. Horn, 16 December 1977.

61 Fahrney, 459.

Chapter 10

1 Mrazek, James E., *The Glider War*, 273.

2 Huston, 214.

3 Warren, 19.

4 Output from this facility totaled over 4,000 gliders by the end of April 1945. This included 200 assembled from 450 that arrived with some of their crates misplaced. Furthermore, in this and other theaters, crates had been damaged and the gliders degraded by water intrusion. Spencer, Leon B., "26th Mobile Reclamation and Repair Squadron," 8 and B1.

5 Buffkin, Ronald M., Major, *Assault Gliders: A Reexamination*, 40.

Chapter 11

1 Huston, 74.

2 *Glider Project Books*, Vol. VI, 655. In the case of the Laurinburg-Maxton test, the aircraft settled onto a submerged tree, impaling the fuselage. The glider was wrecked during the attempted recovery.

3 A series of photographs of the CCAAF operations board from March 1945, found at the National Archives, shows 16 foot target glider stability study work underway.

4 *Army Aircraft Characteristics, Production and Experimental*, 49a.

5 Trimble, 273 and Reilly, Robert V., 1st Lieutenant, USMCR, *Salvage of a Disabled Aircraft by Towing as a Glider, Project George*, Memorandum Report No. 5-43, 18 May 1943.

6 Figley, 7.

7 Figley, R.E., Captain, *Investigation of Short Glider Towlines*, Memorandum Report Mo. 2-43, 20 January 1943.

8 "Status Report, Aircraft (Gliders)." 10 May 1942.

9 Greene, Frank L., "The "Wildcat" Story," *AAHS Journal*, Winter 1961, 237-238. This suggested the towed airplane required an electric propeller or a hydraulic pump that could be operated electrically. Battery endurance also had to be of suitable duration for this operation.

10 Ibid, 238.

11 Ibid and Fahrney, 447.

12 Ibid and Fahrney, 448.

13 Kemmer, Paul H., Colonel, "TI-1570 - C-47 Conversion to Glider," memorandum, 14 December 1943.

14 "Jet" was adopted because the device generated a jet of exhaust gases for the reaction motor. With some initial Army funding, JATO production began in early 1942 followed by production by developer AeroJet Engineering Corporation of Azusa, California. The standard unit was the solid propellant 12AS-1000 D-1 unit; a steel bottle approximately 0.8 feet in diameter, 3.0 feet long, and weighing 205 pounds. It operated for about 12 seconds delivering 1,000 pounds-force of thrust, or about the equivalent of 330 horsepower at 90 mph. Several bottles could be attached externally and ignited electrically. The fittings could be made to drop the empty motor after exhaustion.

15 Grim, 243.

16 Smith, N.Y., Col, "Chase Plow Deceleration Tests on CG-4A Glider," memorandum, 16 June 1945.

17 Bauer, R.C., 1st Lieutenant, "Type A-3A Automatic Pilot Installation in CG-4A Glider," memorandum, 28 June 1943.

18 Day, 48.

19 Lowell, Arthur L., 1st Lieutenant, "Progress Report on Development of Bellows Flaps for Gliders," memorandum, 7 December 1941.

20 Robbins, E.M., Colonel, "Request for Bellows Flap Installation on XTG-3 Glider," memorandum, second endorsement, 24 April 1943.

21 Much of the details within this section is derived from Matthews, Henry, *Chronology of MX-324, America's First Rocket Airplane, X-Planes Monograph-1*, that is, in turn, derived from official documents.

22 These were not formally considered aircraft and so were given no other designation or serial numbers (although the national stars-and-bars insignia was applied). Since they were also to fly under military auspices, they received no registration numbers either.

23 Matthews, 38.

24 Ibid.

25 Although many accounts state the program began in late 1943 (see Anderson, Fred, *Northrop, An Aeronautical History*, 70), the well-researched Fahrney, 800-802, makes clear the JB-1 began the same time as the JB-2, July-September 1944, in response to the initial German V-1 attacks. Additionally, Meredith, R.A., Lieutenant Colonel, "Development of Guided Missiles for Artillery Employment," 22 July 1944, Henry Harley Arnold file 362, and similar documents in this file, makes clear that summer 1944 was the birth of such efforts.

26 The range is given as 650 or 670 miles by many sources and likely drawn from the specification based upon projected engine performance and fuel quantity. Echols, O.P., Major General, "Progress Report to 15 November 1944, on JB-2 and JB-1 Robot Bombs," memorandum, 18 November 1944, Henry Harley Arnold file 324, gives expected range with satisfactory engine at 400 miles at 450 mph. The 200-mile figure (Anderson, Fred, *Northrop, An Aeronautical History*, 70 and Gunston, Bill, "Northrop's Flying Wings," *Wings of Fame*, Volume 2, 30) may reflect actual fuel consumption and volume.

27 Accounts frequently identify the JB-1A as the jet-powered element of the program. However, Northrop photograph captions reveal the glider bore this designation, possibly as a Northrop creation. It is also seen as JB-1a in their documentation. However, Echols, O.P., Major General, "Progress Report to 3 January 1945 on JB-2 and JB-1 Robot Bombs," memorandum, 5 January 1945, Henry Harley Arnold file 321, uses the JB-1A designation when referring to the JB-10, and so this may also have been a temporary means to distinguishing the turbojet and pulsejet missiles.

28 Pape, Garry R. and Campbell, John M., *Northrop Flying Wings, A History of Jack Northrop's Visionary Aircraft*, 105, gives the year as 1943, but this appears inconsistent with initiation of the program in September 1944.

29 Conversation with Gerald Balzer, former long-time employee of Northrop, quoting personal knowledge derived from oral history.

30 Pape, 105. However Fahrney, 819, makes clear this system could not have been available before October 1944.

31 Northrop, John K., "The Development of All-Wing Aircraft," 35th Wilbur Wright Memorial Lecture, The Royal Aeronautical Society, 29 May 1947, 497.

32 Cully, George and Parsch, Andreas, *Designations of U.S. Air Force Projects*, http://orbat.com/site/andreas/U_S_ per cent20Air per cent20Force per cent20Projects.htm.

33 Mention is also found for a American Aviation "tanker glider" in a 25 May 1943 teletype message, *Glider Project Books*, Vol. I, 103. This was mentioned in relation to Richard Du Pont who had previous associated with All American Aviation. Nothing more is known of such a project that may have been competing with Cornelius for the contract.

34 Stewart, W.H., Cornelius Aircraft Corporation, *Model Specification, Fuel Glider, Army Air Forces Model Designation XFG-1, Cornelius Model Designation CFG-1*, Report No. 102-A, 15 January 1944.

35 Chambers, Joseph R. and Chambers, Mark A., *Radical Wings & Wind Tunnels, Advanced Concepts Tested at NASA Langley*, 55-6.

36 "XFG-1 Flight Test Program," no author stated, memorandum, 5 September 1945.

37 Papana, Alex, *Spin Test of the XFG-1 #44-29060 Flown on the 5 September 1945*, report, undated.

38 *Request for Model or Type Designation Change of Status Equipment*, "XFG-1-CR, Glider, Fuel," form, 22 November 1946.

39 Dent, "Final Report of Major F.R. Dent, Jr., Air Corps, on Trip to England," 911.

40 On 11 July 1944 the Hamilcar was still disassembled and in disrepair, and the Army was seeking a civilian firm to assemble, repair, and place the craft in flying order. Witness Corriveau, A.L., "Progress Report on Foreign Gliders," memorandum, 11 July 1944. Photographs of the CCAAF operations board during March 1945, found at the National Archives, shows the Hamilcar listed and indications five of seven flights had been performed. The memorandum also appears to repudiate claims the glider was "towed over" from Britain—a feat that would surely have been more prominently acclaimed.

41 Day, 109, notes that it was also demonstrated during postwar flights, but on 110 says it was previous flown for two years at CCAAF. The Corriveau, "Progress Report on Foreign Gliders," memo and Moyers, Frank N., Colonel, teletype to Commanding Officer, Rosecrans Field, St. Joseph, Missouri, 12 April 1945, appear to disagree.

Chapter 12

1 Sauers, William F., Captain, *Memorandum Report No. TSEAL2-4565-3-1, Glider Development Conference*, 26 April 1945, Appendix 4, Miller, Marion A., 1st Lieutenant, The Status of Powered Gliders Today, 53. Although presented as if describing an actual hardware program and not just a study, a clearly incorrect date of early 1945 is given and no other source mentions this effort. An attempt to fly with one engine producing a strong yaw from off-centerline thrust appears an unusual if not unwise step.

2 Gassner, A.A., Jenter Corporation, *Weight and Performance Data, Proposal, Engine Installation Glider CG-4A, Engine Ranger Model 6-440C-2*, Report No. 110-A, 8 March 1943.

3 Isen, S., Ridgefield Manufacturing Corporation, *Actual Weight Group, Engine Nacelle Installation, Ranger Model 6-440C-2 in Glider Model CG-4A, A.A.F. Project XPG-2, Contract AC 26597*, Report No. 116, 12 July 1943.

4 *Glider Project Books*, Vol. III, 731.

5 *Request for Model of Type Designation Change of Status or Equipment*, "Airplane, Misc., Glider Powered, AAF Model XPG-2A" form, 4 May 1944.

6 Arcier, A. Francis, The Waco Aircraft Company, "Change to Exhibit "A" Performance Data on Light Transports Derived from CG-4A and CG-15A Gliders," letter, 12 October 1944.

7 *Model Specification, Glider, Cargo and Troop Transport, Powered, Army Air Force Designation – PG-2A, Northwestern Aeronautical Corp. Designation "Aerotruck"-N.A.C.-1" Army Air Force Contract No:- W535ac26936*, Engineering Report No. 1010, no author stated, 5 March 1945.

8 *Project Record – PG-2A Glider, Northwestern Aeronautical Corporation, Contract W535 AC-29636*, no author or date given, but includes data through 15 October 1945.

9 Arcier.

10 Sauers, unnumbered page.

11 *Characteristics, XPG-3*, 15 November 1946, with hand corrections.

12 Larkin, W., The Waco Aircraft Company, *Model Specification, Airplane, Transport (Cargo) Light, Army Air Forces Model Design XPG-3A, Waco Model Designation 2-YEU*, Report No. 1575, 17 April 1944.

13 Sauers.

14 Protasewich, P., Chase Aircraft Company, Inc., *Model Specification, Airplane, Glider, Cargo Transport, Powered, Chase Model MS-5*, Report No. 200, 12 November 1945.

15 Bouton, I., Laister-Kauffmann Aircraft Corp., *Estimated Performance of Model LK-12*, 9 June 1944, and *Preliminary Weight Estimate of the LK-12*, 14 June 1944. The latter document is clear that there would no additional metal content to the aircraft besides these powerplant segments and attachment fittings. This contradicts Sauers, unnumbered page, that the LK-12 was to be all-metal. That was a separate proposal, as clarified by Snodgrass 37-38.

16 Sauers, 57.

Chapter 13

1 Molt Taylor would go on to found Aerocar Corporation after the war and build his famous flying car.

2 Fahrney, 449, and 456.

3 Ibid, 450.

4 Ibid.

5 Fahrney, 447, and Greene, 237.

6 Fahrney, 450-451.

7 Ibid, 442.

8 Ibid, 439.

9 Ibid, 452, and 457.

10 Ibid, 454.

11 Trimble, 269, and *Status Report*, 4 April 1943. Trimble probably read the Status Report as an unmanned flight when, in fact, the report reads "... the LNT-1 had been taken off and towed automatically without assistance from the safety pilot." This only says the safety pilot made no inputs, not that he was absent. The first clearly stated Nolo flight is described later.

12 Fahrney, 456.

13 Trimble, 269.

14 Fahrney, 455, and 459.

15 Ibid, 460.

16 The glider and tug types, and location of the test, are not clear from the source, Fahrney, 461.

17 Ibid, 463.

18 Ibid, 453.

19 Ibid. These were presumably drawn from the seven acquired earlier in the year for training (Chapter 3). What became of the seventh is unclear.

20 Ibid, 457. On 463 Fahrney says NAF did the work.

21 Ibid, 459. This sums to 43. However, Fahrney also says on 457 that 34 TG-6s were converted. With the original three XLNT-1s for training returned to the AAF (Chapter 9), the seven for training likely passed along for GLOMB work, one from the Army in exchange for a LNE-1 in addition to three more, another six, and then the added 25, the available airframes appear to be 42. So, the available information appears incomplete.

22 Figley, Richard E., Major, *XLNT-1 GLOMBs, Expendable Tests, Project George*, Memorandum Report No. 9-43, 28 September 1943, clearly reports that this also marked the first GLOMB Nolo flight. On the surface it appears unwise to have proceeded to an armed flight (unmanned) to terminate on a target without having first flown an unarmed Nolo mission. However, without a safety pilot, landing under radio control, while conceivable, appears problematic and none are described in the literature.

23 Ibid.

24 Fahrney, 462.

25 Ibid, apparently quoting a Bureau document.

26 Figley, Richard E., Major, *XLNT-1 GLOMBs Expendable Tests*, Memorandum Report No. 1-44, 26 February 1944.

27 Fahrney, 461.

28 Ibid, 464.

29 Ibid.

30 Figley Richard E., Major, *Catapulting an Airplane with a Glider in Tow, Project George*, Memorandum Report No. 7-43, 25 June 1943 and Summary of *Status Report* 7/1/43, 56.

31 Ordway, III, Fredrick I. and Wakeford, Ronald C., *International Missile and Spacecraft Guide*, 180.

32 Ibid.

33 Fahrney, 466.

34 Peperell, 72.

35 Fahrney, 466.

36 Ibid, 463.

37 Trimble, 270.

38 Fahrney, 464.

39 Traverse City was then serving as the test site of USN guided weapons programs.

40 Fahrney, 464-465.

41 Ibid, 465.

42 This information was derived from the captions of photos located at the National Museum of Naval Aviation.

43 Fahrney, 464.

44 Ibid, 465.

45 Swanborough, Gordon and Bowers, Peter M., *United States Navy Aircraft Since 1911*, 597.

46 Fahrney, 466.

47 Friedman, Norman, *US Naval Weapons*, 201.

48 Fahrney, 466.

49 *Development & Procurement of Gliders in the Army Air Force, 1941-1944*, 59. A Navy source, reviewing Bristol's War Department contracts, says the initial contract was 19 November 1941 and amended to 13 gliders at $33,918, the later cost-plus-fixed-fee contact for 25 dated 13 March 1943 and a subcontractor performed most of the work. Brown microfiche 10 frame 10-11.

50 Carroll, F.O., Colonel, "Stability Tests of Towed Gliders," memorandum, 18 March 1942.

51 Charles Day communication, 2006.

52 Andrade, 98, and 157.

53 "Radio Controlled Bomb Gliders Types XBG-1 and XBG-2," no author, memorandum 9 June 1943.

54 Wileman, E.E., Fletcher Aviation Corporation, *Glider, Radio – Controlled (Bomber)*, Report No. 115A, 13 February 1942.

55 Dent, Jr., Fred R. Lieutenant Colonel, "Flight Tests of the Fletcher XBG-1 Glider," memorandum, 2 May 1942.

56 Browne, L.W., "Flight Test – TV Installation, Mines Field," memorandum, 23 August 1942. The existence of any CQ-1As contradicts available data suggesting none were completed.

57 *Glider Project Books*, Vol. III, 809.

58 Fletcher Aviation Corporation, "Specification 116A, Fletcher Model 16, Bomb Glider, Radio Controlled," 20 January 1942.

59 Leet, Jack, Captain, USAAF, "Memorandum Report No. ENG-50-884," 9 June 1943.

60 *Glider Project Books*, Vol. I, 185.

61 Abbeman, John F., The Cornelius Aircraft Corporation, "Proposal for Cornelius Model CBG-1 Gliders, related Equipment and Data," letter, 8 May 1943.

62 Perkins, Courtland D., "Report of a Conference on the Procurement of a Tailless, Swept-forward Wing Glider," memorandum 18 March 1943.

63 Berry, J.R., 1st Lieutenant, "Detail Design of a Glider to Carry a 2000-Pound Bomb," memorandum, 13 January 1943 and Bogert, H.Z., Colonel, USAAF, "Shipment of Glider, MX-166," memorandum, 6 June 1944.

64 Fahrney, 465.

Chapter 14

[1] *Request for Model of Type Designation Change of Status or Equipment*, "XPG-2A-RI, Glider, Power" form, 18 November 1946.

[2] Snodgrass, 64.

[3] Notes by Ed Kaminiski accompanying photo in National Museum of the United States Air Force.

[4] Photo caption of image archived at the National Museum of the United States Air Force.

[5] Grim, 288 and Frisbee, John L., "Valor: Greenland Rescue," *Air Force Magazine*, March 1998, and Farmer, Edward J., "Stranded," *Air & Space*, September 2011, 38-43.

[6] *Air Force Developmental Aircraft*, April 1957, 98.

[7] Huston, 195.

[8] Bonner, L.G., Dr., Technical director, Allegany Ballistics Laboratory, *Notes on a Meeting at ABL, December 3, 1946, to Discuss the Status of the Glider Trust Unit, 4-ES-1200, T-21*, 11 December 1946.

[9] Note accompanying photograph archived at the National Museum of the United States Air Force and conversation with Seán Roberts, then test pilot and later Director of the National Test Pilot School.

[10] Simons, 244.

[11] Whelan, Robert F., *Exploring the Monster, Mountain Lee Waves: The Aerial Elevator*, 163.

[12] Harris, Anthony B., Lieutenant Colonel "The Fighter-Glider Combination," 27 August 1943.

[13] This composite had a Short S.20 *Mercury* twin-engine floatplane mounted above a Short S.21 *Maia* C-class four-engine flying boat, detachable in flight. This greatly extended the range of the smaller aircraft.

[14] Harris, Anthony B., Lieutenant Colonel, "The Lightning-Hamilcar Combination," 3 February 1944.

[15] Carroll, F.O., Brigadier General, "Over-Under Project, P-38/Hamilcar Combination," memorandum, first endorsement remarks, 2 August 1944.

[16] Ober, Jon H., Captain, "Development of Glider Type Aircraft," memorandum, 6 July 1944.

[17] Huston, 194.

[18] Snodgrass, 22.

[19] *Air Force Developmental Aircraft*, 98-99.

[20] Eaker, Ira C, Lieutenant General, "Glider Requirements," Routing and Record Sheet, 6 December 1945. While a fine idea in concept, fabric work is neither simple nor quick.

[21] Crawford, A.R., Brigadier General, "Glider Development Program," memorandum, 14 November 1946. This missive establishes that the highest levels of the AAF were opposed to powered gliders. The General pointed out the mere name "is a misnomer" and pursuit of such aircraft would compete with airplanes.

[22] Thieblot, A.J., Fairchild Aircraft, "Development of Gliders," letter, 15 February 1946.

[23] Doubleday. T.C., Colonel, "Surplus C-46A and D Aircraft," memorandum, 6 August 1947.

[24] Dutt, D.L., Brigadier General, "Surplus C-46A and D Aircraft," memorandum, first endorsement, 22 September 1947.

[25] *Guest Lecture of the New Development Division, Command and Staff Course, AAF School, Maxwell Field, Alabama*, "ND54 – New Special Aircraft, Transports Gliders, and Liaison Airplanes," no author or date. Manuscript has notation "Rec'd 6-25-46" and is clearly early postwar.

[26] Engineering Division, *Representative Model Specification for Glider – Assault, Light, 8,000 Pounds Useful Load*, no author stated, 1 February 1946.

[27] Sauers, Appendix 1, 3-7.

[28] Air Materiel Command, *Informal Design Competition, Glider, Assault*, Light, no author stated, memorandum, 14 June 1946.

[29] Day, Charles L., "Glider Legacy in the U.S. Air Force," paper, undated but approximately 2009.

[30] Miller, M.A., "Conference on Light Assault Glider Loading Apertures," memorandum, 8 July 1946.

[31] Crawford, A.R., Brigadier General, U. "Procurement of Glider, Assault, Light," memorandum, 6 December 1946.

[32] Engineering Division, *Representative Model Specification for Glider – Assault, Heavy, 16,000 Pounds Useful Load*, no author stated, 1 February 1946 plus Errata Sheet.

[33] Air Materiel Command, *Informal Design Competition, Glider, Assault, Heavy*, no author stated, memorandum, 30 August 1946.

[34] *Chase / Stroukoff*, http://1000aircraftphotos.com/HistoryBriefs/Chase.htm.

[35] *Air Force Developmental Aircraft*, 98, and 103.

[36] *Handbook of Flight Operating Instructions, USAF Series YG-18A Gliders*, T.O. No. 09-80CAA-1, 18 January 1949, 3, and Brigman, Leonard, ed., *Jane's All the World's Aircraft, 1948-49*, 237c.

[37] *Air Force Developmental Aircraft*, 100.

[38] Hauder, Jr., George H., *Memorandum MCRFTP-2188, Phase II Tests on the XG-18A Glider, USAF No. 46-067*, 1 February 1949.

[39] Compton, Louis J., Colonel, *Report of Test of Project No. AB 748 YCG-18 Medium Glider*, 27 October 1949.

[40] Smith, George F., Colonel, "Assault Transport Development Program," 22 January 1948, in Bagwell, Margaret C., *Case History of the C-123 Airplane (26 April 1945 – 7 September 1951)*, microfilm frames 129-130.

[41] Kramer, H.A., Chase Aircraft Co., Inc., *Glider Initial Weighing, Report No. P-3058*, 12 April 1950.

[42] Sherman, A., Chase Aircraft Co., Inc., *Estimated Characteristics and Performance of the Chase Aircraft Co. Assault Heavy Glider Model MS-3*, Report No. 151, 1 June 1946.

[43] *Model Specification, Glider, Cargo and Troop Transport, Towed*, Report No. 3001 Revision C, no author stated, 3 April 1950.

[44] Boatrer, B.L., Major General, *Interim Report on the Comparative and Tactical Evaluation of Assault Transport Aircraft and Gliders*, approximately 30 June 1951, 13-14.

[45] Lynch, 186.

[46] Galvin, John R, *Air Assault: The Development of Airmobile Warfare*, 260-1. Drops of 75 mm howitzers were made during *Market* but this was an almost experimental effort. Each gun was broken down into six parachute bundles dropped from beneath a C-47, the wheels for the gun carriage dropped out the cargo door. Collecting, unpacking, and assembling these components was exceptionally more laborious compared with glider delivery. Buffkin, 42. Yet, it was successful under those circumstances. Huston, 226. (The British dropped such guns and jeeps, supported by many parachutes, from the bomb bays of bombers.) Today, even larger weapons are airdropped combat-ready on parachute platforms.

[47] Galvin, 264.

[48] *Air Force Developmental Aircraft*, 100.

Chapter 15

[1] Holley, 552 and 558.

[2] Nowarra, Heinz J., *German Gliders in World War II*, 165-166.

[3] The British had few such program underway, apparently having decided they had what was needed in the near-term and there was no compelling long-term need.

Bibliography

Books

Abel, Alan, Abel, Drina Welch and Matt, Paul, *Piper's Golden Age*, Wind Canyon Books, Brawley, California, 2001.

Allard, Noel E. and Sandvick, Gerald N., *Minnesota Aviation History 1957-1945*, MAHB Publishing, Chaska Minnesota, 1993.

Anderson, Fred, *Northrop, An Aeronautical History*, Northrop Corporation, Los Angeles, California, 1976.

Andrade, John M., *U.S. Military Aircraft Designations and Serials 1909 to 1979*, Midland Counties Publications, Leicester, UK, 1997.

Bagley, Mark B., *The G Stands for Guts, A Glider Pilot Remembers WWII*, Hellgate Press, Ashland, Oregon, 2008.

Bickers, Richard Townshend, *Military Air Transport Airlift: The Illustrated History*, Osprey Publishing Ltd., London, 1998.

Bowers, Peter M., *Of Wings & Things, Volume 1: 1972-1979*, Flyer Media, Lakewood, Washington, 2000.

Brigman, Leonard, ed., *Jane's All the World's Aircraft, 1945-1946*, Sampson Low, Marston, and Company, Ltd., London, 1947. Also years 1946-47, 1947-48, 1948-49, 1949-50, 1950-52, 1952-53, and 1953-54.

Carpenter, D.M. and D'Alessandro, P.V., *JB-1A Thunderbug, WWII Flying Wing Bomb*, Jet Pioneers of America, 1997.

Chambers, Joseph R. and Chambers, Mark A., *Radical Wings & Wind Tunnels, Advanced Concepts Tested at NASA Langley*, Specialty Press, North Branch, Minnesota, 2008.

Chatterton, George, *The Wings of Pegasus: The Story of the Glider Pilot Regiment*, The Battery Press, Inc., Nashville, Tennessee, 1982.

Chinnery, Philip D., *Air Commando*, St. Martin's Press, New York, 1997, pp. 8-15.

Coates, Steve with Carbonel, Jean-Christophe, *Helicopters of the Third Reich*, Schiffer Publishing, Ltd., Pennsylvania, 2002.

Craven, Wesley F., and Cate, James L., editors, *The Army Air Forces in World War 2, Volume V□Men and Planes*, The University of Chicago Press, Chicago, Illinois, 1955.

Dank, Milton, *The Glider Gang: An Eyewitness History of World War II Glider Combat*, J. B. Lippincott Company, New York, 1977.

Davis, Larry, *C-47 Skytrain in Action*, Aircraft Number 149, Squadron/Signal Publications, Carrollton, Texas, 1995.

Day, Charles L., *Silent Ones: World War II Invasion Glider Test and Experiment*, 2001.

De Chant, John A., *Devilbirds, The Story of Marine Corps Aviation in World War II*, Harper & Brothers Publishers, New York, 1947.

Devlin, Gerard M., *Silent Wings: The Story of the Glider Pilots of World War II*, W. H. Allen & Co., London, 1985.

DFS 230 "Hochbein, Robbe" DFS 331 und Ka 430, Luftfahrt History Heft 11, Luftfahrt History Impressum, Neunkirchen, Germany, 2004. (German)

Dwiggins, Don, *On Silent Wings: Adventures in Motorless Flight*, Grosset & Dunlap, Inc., New York, 1970.

Esvelin, Philippe, *D-Day Gliders: The American Gliders of D-Day*, Heimdal, Bayeux, France, 2001.

Fahey, James C., *U.S. Army Aircraft, 1908-1946*, Ships and Aircraft, New York, 1946.

Fahey, James C., *USAF Aircraft, 1947-1956*, Air Force Museum Foundation, Inc., Wright-Patterson AFB, Ohio, November 1978.

Flying Through the Years, no author stated, Northrop Corporation, 1971.

Forsyth, Robert, *Mistel: German Composite Aircraft and Operations, 1942-1945*, Classic Publications, Ltd., England, 2001.

Francillon, René J., *McDonnell Douglas Aircraft Since 1920: Volume I*, Putnam Aeronautical Books, London, 1995, pp. 334-337.

Friedman, Norman, *US Naval Weapons*, Conway Maritime Press, London, 1983.

Galvin, John R, *Air Assault: The Development of Airmobile Warfare*, Hawthorn Books, Inc., New York, 1969.

Glines, Carroll V., *Those Legendary Piper Cubs, Their Role in War and Peace*, Schiffer Military History, Atglen, Pennsylvania, 2005.

Gregory, Barry, *Aircraft of Airborne Forces*, Blandford Press, London, 1998.

Grim, J. Norman, *To Fly the Gentle Giants, The Training of U.S. WW II Glider Pilots*, AuthorHouse, Bloomington, Indiana, 2009.

Gunston, Bill, *The Illustrated Encyclopedia of the World's Rockets & Missiles*, Salamander Books Ltd., London, 1979.

Hemmings, John, *Silent Approach: The Operations of the Glider Pilot Regiment in World War II*, The Book Guild Ltd., Sussex, England, 1999.

Holley, Jr., Irving Brinton, *United States Army in World War 2, Special Studies, Buying Aircraft, Matériel Procurement for the Army Air Force*, Center of Military History, United States Army, U.S. Government Printing Office, Washington, D.C., 1989.

Isby, David, *C-47/R4D Units of the ETO and MTO, Osprey Combat Aircraft #54*, Osprey Publishing Ltd., Oxford, UK, 2005.

Jarrett, Philip, ed., *Aircraft of the Second World War: The Development of the Warplane 1939-45*, Putnam Aeronautical Books, London, 1997.

Knickerbocker, W. D., *Those Damned Glider Pilots*, Static Line Books, College Park, Georgia, 1989.

Knott, Richard C., *The American Flying Boat, An Illustrated History*, Naval Institute Press, 1988, Annapolis, Maryland.

Larson, George A., *Aerial Assault Into Burma*, Xlibris, 2008.

Lewis, W. David and Trimble, William F., *The Airway to Everywhere, A History of All American Aviation, 1937-1953*, University of Pittsburgh Press, Pittsburgh, Pennsylvania, 1988.

Lloyd, Alan, *The Gliders*, Leo Cooper, Great Britain, 1983.

Lowden, John L., Silent Wings at War: Combat Gliders in World War II, Smithsonian Institution Press, Washington, D. C., 1992.

Lynch, Tim, *Silent Skies, Gliders at War 1939-1945*, Pen & Sword Books, Barnsley, South Yorkshire, United Kingdom, 2008.

Maloney, Edward T., *Northrop Flying Wings*, World War II Publications, Coronal del Mar, California, 1990.

Mankau, Heinz and Petrick, Peter, *German Gliders in World War II*, Schiffer Military History, Schiffer Publishing, Ltd., Pennsylvania, 2010.

Masters, Charles J., *Glidermen of Neptune: The American D-Day Glider Attack*, Southern Illinois University, 1995.

Matthews, Henry, *Chronology of MX-324, America's First Rocket Airplane, X-Planes Monograph-1*, HPM Publications, Beirut, Lebanon, 1995.

Maynes, S.W., *The "G" is for Guts, An American Glider Pilot's Story*, BookSurge, 2006.

Morrison, Alexander, *Silent Invader: A Glider Pilot's Story of the Invasion of Europe in World War II*, Airlife Publishing Ltd., London, 1999.

Mrazek, James E., *Fighting Gliders of World War II*, St. Martin's Press, Inc., New York, 1977.

Mrazek, James E., *The Glider War*, St. Martin's Press, Inc., New York, 1975.

Nowarra, Heinz J., *German Gliders in World War II*, Schiffer Military History Vol. 48, Schiffer Publishing, Ltd., Pennsylvania, 1991.

Ordway, III, Fredrick I. and Wakeford, Ronald C., *International Missile and Spacecraft Guide*, McGraw-Hill Book Company, New York, 1960, p. 180.

Pape, Garry R. and Campbell, John M., *Northrop Flying Wings, A History of Jack Northrop's Visionary Aircraft*, Schiffer Publishing Ltd., Atglen, Pennsylvania, 1995.

Pape, Garry R., Campbell, John M. and Campbell, Donna, *The Flying Wings of Jack Northrop, A Photo Chronicle*, Schiffer Publishing Ltd., Atglen, Pennsylvania, 1994.

Pearcy, Arthur, *Lend-Lease Aircraft in World War 2*, Motorbooks International, Osceola, Wisconsin, 1996.

Peek, Chet, *The Taylorcraft Story*, Three Peaks Publishing, Norman Oklahoma, 1992.

Peperell, Roger W., *Piper Aircraft, The Development and History of Piper Designs*, Air-Britain Ltd, England, 1996.

Perna, Dr., Albert F., *The Glider Gladiators (of World War II)*, Pine Hill Press, Freeman, South Dakota, 1970.

Ross, Jr., Rank, *Guided Missiles: Rockets and Torpedoes*, Lothrop, Lee & Shepard Co., Inc., New York, 1951.

Schultz, Jake, *A Drive in the Clouds, The Story of the Aerocar*, Flying Books International, 2006.

Schweizer, Paul A., *Soaring Through the 20th Century*, Schweizer Books, Elmira, New York, 2004.

Seth, Ronald, *Lion with Blue Wings*, Panther Books, August 1959.

Shannon, Kevin and Wright, Stephen, *One Night in June: The Story of Operation Tonga, the Initial Phase of the Invasion of Normandy, 1944*, Wrens Park Publishing, 2000.

Sherrod, Robert, *History of Marine Corps Aviation in World War II*, Presidio Press, San Rafael, California, 1980.

Simons, Martin, *Sailplanes, 1920-1945*, EQIP Werbung & Verlang GmbH, Germany, 2001.

Simons, Martin, *The World's Vintage Sailplanes 1908-45*, Kookabura Technical Publications Pty. Ltd., Melbourne, Australia, 1986.

Smith, Claude, *The History of The Glider Pilot Regiment*, Leo Cooper, London, 1992.

Swanborough, Gordon and Bowers, Peter M., *United States Military Aircraft Since 1909*, Putnam Aeronautical Books, London, 1989.

Swanborough, Gordon and Bowers, Peter M., *United States Navy Aircraft Since 1911*, Naval Institute Press, Annapolis, Maryland, 1990.

Taylor, H.A., *Airspeed Aircraft Since 1931*, Putnam and Company, Ltd., London, 1970.

Trimble, William F., *Wings for the Navy: A History of the Naval Aircraft Factory, 1917-1956*, Naval Institute Press, 1990, Annapolis, Maryland.

Updegraph, Charles L., Jr., *Special Marine Corps Units of World War II*, History and Museums Division, Headquarters, U.S. Marine Corps, Washington, D.C., 1977.

Van Wagner, R. D., *Any Place, Any Time, Any Where: The 1st Air Commandos in World War II*, Schiffer, Atglen, PA, 1998.

Waldron, Alec, *From Pacifist to Glider Pilot*, Woodfield Publishing, West Sussex, UK, 2000.

Whelan, Robert F., *Exploring the Monster, Mountain Lee Waves: The Aerial Elevator*, Wind Canyon Books, Brawley, California, 2000.

Williams, Nicholas M., *Aircraft of the United States' Military Air Transport Service, 1948-1966*, Midland Publishing Ltd., Leicester, England, 1999, p. 169.

Wood, Alan, *History of the World's Glider Forces*, Patrick Stephens Limited, England, 1990.

Wright, Lawrence, *The Wooden Sword*, Elek Books Ltd., London, 1967.

Articles

Arnold, H.H., General, "The Aerial Invasion of Burma," *The National Geographic Magazine*, August 1944, pp. 129-148.

Balzer, Gerald, "The Aircraft of Jack Northrop," *AAHS Journal*, Spring 1981, p. 86.

Berry, Peter, "The Transatlantic Flight of a CG-4A," *AAHS Journal*, Winter 1992, p. 320.

Blacksten, Raul, "Clio Whispers," *Bungee Chord*, Winter 2003-4, pp. 11-14.

Bodie, Warren M., "Thunderbolt," *Wings*, Special Edition No. 1, 1981, pp. 28-29.

Bowers, Peter M., "Breezing Along with the Breeze!: The U.S. WWII Glider Program," *Wings*, December 1989, pp. 10-21.

Bowers, Peter M., "Burnelli's Flying Fuselages Pt. II," *Airpower*, January 2002, pp. 54-55.

Briegleb, Gus, "Gus Briegleb's Two-Place, The Briegleb Two-Place Sailplane," *Soaring*, July-August 1943, pp. 9-10 and back cover.

Byard, Jeff, "What Ever Happened to all the TGs?," *Bungee Chord*, Spring 1998, pp. 8-11.

Cassagneres, Ed, "Bristol XLRQ-1 Glider Story," *AAHS Journal*, Summer 2003, pp. 123-128.

Cole, Merle T., Major "The Paramarines: Organization and Training of USMC Parachute Troops, 1940-1944," *AAHS Journal*, Winter 1989, pp. 242-249.

Conley, Manuel, "Silent Squadrons," *American History*, June 1983, pp. 12-21.

Connor, Sara Witter, "Wisconsin's Flying Trees: The Plywood Industry's Contribution to World War II," *AAHS Journal*, Fall 2009, pp. 162-170.

Connor, Sara Witter, "Wisconsin's Flying Trees, The Plywood Industry's Contribution to World War II," *Wisconsin Magazine of History*, Spring 2009, pp. 16-27.

Connor, Sara W. and Day, Charles L., "Primary Light Airplane Gliding School at Janesville, Wisconsin," *AAHS Journal*, Spring 2011, pp. 62-69.

Day, Charles L., "The XCG-17 Glider," *Friends Journal*, Winter 2005/2006, pp. 13-15.

Dean, Jack, "Payload," *Wings*, October 1989, pp. 36-55.

Downie, Don, "Glider Pilot," *Wings*, December 1989, pp. 38-55.

Farmer, Edward J., "Stranded," *Air & Space*, September 2011, pp. 38-43.

Fisher, Scott M., "Just Follow the Rope: WWII Glider Pilots Remember," *Flight Journal*, February 2002, pp. 76-86.

Frisbee, John L., "Valor: Greenland Rescue," *Air Force Magazine*, March 1998, pp. unknown.

Gallagher, William E, "The U.S. Navy's WWII Floatwing Assault Gliders," *National Soaring Museum Historical Journal*, Vol. 25 No. 2, 2003, pp. 2-6.

"Glider Pick-up from Sea of Mud at Zon. Holland," no author stated, *The "Pick-Up"*, July 1945, p. 2.

Goyer, Robert M., "The Rise and Fall of the Cargo Glider," *Air Classics*, September 1991 (Part I), pp. 22-29 and 82-83, October 1991 (Part II), pp. 43-49.

Greene, Frank L., "The "Wildcat" Story," *AAHS Journal*, Winter 1961, 223-246.

Grim, Norman, "Army Glider Construction During World War II: From the Pudgy Three Seaters to the Gentle Giants," *AAHS Journal*, Winter 1989, pp. 298-307.

Grim, J. Norman, "Training WW II Glider Pilots in Arizona," *Arizona Flyways*, October 1994, pp. 14-15.

Gunston, Bill, "Northrop's Flying Wings," *Wings of Fame*, Volume 2, 1996, pp. 24-37.

Herr, Allen, "On the Edge of Greatness: The Aviation Career of Charles D. Koch," *AAHS Journal*, Fall 1985, pp. 233-234.

Holcomb, Mal, "The Nine Day Wonders," *Wings*, September 1981, pp. 8-19.

Johnson, E.R., "Vertical Envelopment," *AAHS Journal*, Fall 2003, pp. 182-189.

Keillor, Lynn, "That Old Crate," *Air & Space*, June/July 2011, pp. 56-59.

Kelleher, C.J., "Patrick the Porcine Pelican," *Soaring*, July 1967, pp. 32-33.

Larson, George A., "Alliance Army Air Forces Base and the Training of Airborne Crews," *Airborne Quarterly*, Fall 1998, pp. 18-24.

Larson, George A., "D-Day Glider Attack, The WACO CG-4A Glider," *Airborne Quarterly*, Winter 1999, pp. 65-68.

Larson, George A., "The Glider in World War II: The Waco CG-4A Combat Glider," *AAHS Journal*, Winter 2001, pp. 270-279.

Larson, George A., "Last Parachute and Glider Operation of WWII, Appari, Luzon, Philippines, 23 June 1945, Task Force 'Gypsy'," *Airborne Quarterly*, Summer 2005, pp. 37-41.

Larson, George A., "Operation Market-Garden," *Airborne Quarterly*, Spring 1999, pp. 18-24.

Larson, George A., "Silent Warriors: The Untold Story of the Waco CG-4A Glider in Combat," *Combat Aircraft*, January-February 2001, pp. 172-177.

Larson, George A., "Silent Winged Warriors," *USAF Yearbook 2001*, 2001, pp. unknown.

Lindley, John M., "A Great Experience, Villaume Builds Gliders in World War II," *Ramsey County History*, Winter 2007, pp. 22-27.

Meakin, Bob, "Utah Gliding History 1927-1950, Part III – 1939-1950," *AAHS Journal*, Summer 2002, pp. 94-107.

Nicholas, William H., "Gliders—Silent Weapons of the Sky," *The National Geographic Magazine*, August 1944, pp. 149-160.

Ochadlick, Paul, "Taylorcraft: A Complex Classic," *Air Enthusiast*, No. 45, 1992, pp. 52-55.
"On a Wing," no author stated, *Air Force Magazine*, March 1999, p. 77.
Ornauer, Richard L., "The Dover AFB Museum's CG-4A Cargo Glider," *AAHS Journal*, Fall 1997, p. 232.
Ostrowski, David W., "The Trojan Horse from St. Louis," *AAHS Journal*, Fall 1992, pp. 190-201.

"Pilotless Aircraft," no author stated, *Naval Aviation News*, January 1946, pp. 19-21.

"Radio Robots," no author stated, *Naval Aviation News*, date unknown, pp. 1-6.
Riding, Richard, "Bowlus Twin-Boomers," *Aeroplane Monthly*, May 1990, pp. 268-270.

Schrader, Richard K., "Douglas' Deadly Gliders," *Air Classics Special* "Son of Fabulous Flying Flops!," Vol. 1, 1990, pp. 64-71.
Sciuttim W.J., "The First Air Commando Group August 1943 – May 1944," *AAHS Journal*, Fall 1968. pp. 178-186.
"Sea-Going Gliders: Experiment in Failure," (no author stated), *Air Classics Special* "Flying Oddballs," Vol. 3, 1992, pp. 10-15.
Seydel, Carie A., Captain, "Silent Wings of History," *Airman*, April 2003, pp. 44-48.
"Shangri-La Rescue Made by Air Pick-up," no author stated, *The "Pick-Up"*, July 1945, pp. 1-2.

Thoms, Keith H., Berry, Gerald and Jett, Lee, "Austere Recovery of Cargo Gliders," *JFQ*, 1st Quarter 2008, pp. 134-139.
Thoms, Keith H., "Snatch Pickup of Gliders from Naval Vessels," *Naval Engineers Journal*, #2 2009, pp. 63-77.
"Transport Gliders: The Rise and Demise of a Weapon System," no author stated, *Air Enthusiast*, Part I, March 1972, pp. 126-134 and 163, Part II, April 1972, pp. 207-216, Part III, May 1972, pp. 250-253, Part IV, June 1972, pp. 318-322.
"Troop Carrying Glider," no author stated, *Aero Digest*, January 1942, p. unknown.
"Troop Transport Glider Gets Detachable Engines," no author stated, *Aero Digest*, June 1943, pp. 173 and 334.

"War Gliders," no author stated, *Life*, 7 September 1942, pp. 52-57.
Wehle, John, Lieutenant Colonel, USMC, "Glider," *Flying*, February 1943, pp. unknown.

Studies

Airborne Operations in the Mediterranean Theater, 1942-1945, no author stated, USAF Historical Studies: No. 74, USAF Historical Division, Research Studies Institute, Air University, September 1955.
Air Force Developmental Aircraft, no author stated, Air Research and Development Command, United States Air Force, April 1957, compilation of brief program histories and aircraft characteristics assembled at request of Congress.

Bagwell, Margaret C., *Case History of the C-123 Airplane (26 April 1945 – 7 September 1951)*, Historical Office, Office of the Executive Assistant Deputy Commanding General, Air Materiel Command, Wright-Patterson AFB, March 1952
Brown, Robert Vance, Lieutenant Commander, USNR, *The Navy's Transport Glider Program 1941-1943*, Monographs in the History of Naval Aviation, Volume XX, Deputy Chief of Naval Operations (Air), Naval Aviation History Unit Op-519B, U.S. Navy, November 1944. (The author possesses a hardcopy of the main body of this report in addition to a copy of the full report on microfiche. The differences in these two documents are only in formatting, suggesting perhaps the hardcopy is a near-final draft or copy from which page numbers are drawn for this portion of the document.)
Buffkin, Ronald M., Major, U.S. Army, *Assault Gliders: A Reexamination*, Thesis, U.S. Army Command and General Staff College, Fort Leavenworth, Kansas, 1991.

Development & Procurement of Gliders in the Army Air Force, 1941-1944, no author stated, Army Air Forces Historical Studies: No. 47, Assistant Chief of Staff, Intelligence, Historical Division, September 1943.

Fahrney, Delmar S., Rear Adm., USN (Ret.), *The History of Pilotless Aircraft and Guided Missiles*, unpublished manuscript, undated.

The Glider Pilot Training Program: 1941 to 1943, no author stated, Army Air Forces Historical Studies: No. 1, AAF Historical Office, Headquarters, Army Air Force, March 1946.

Huston, James A., Major, U.S. Army, *The Airborne Team 1941-1945*, Historical Division, Special Staff, U.S. Army, 1948.

Noetzel, Jonathan C., Lieutenant Colonel, *To War on Tubing and Canvas: A Case Study in the Interrelationships Between Technology, Training, Doctrine and Organization*, Thesis, School of Advanced Airpower Studies, Air University, Maxwell Air Force Base, Alabama, May 1992.

Snodgrass, Raymond J., *The AAF Glider Program, November 1944 – January 1947*, Army Air Forces Historical Studies: No. 217, Historical Office, Intelligence Department, Air Materiel Command, Wright Field, November 1947.

Taylor, Joe G., Dr., *Air Supply in the Burma Campaigns*, USAF Historical Studies: No. 75, USAF Historical Division, Research Studies Institute, Air University, April 1975.

Warren, John C., Dr., *Airborne Operations in World War II, European Theater*, USAF Historical Studies: No. 97, USAF Historical Division, Research Studies Institute, Air University, Maxwell Air Force Base, Alabama, September 1956.
Wehle, John, Lieutenant Colonel, USMC, "A Study of Military Gliders and Their Use in the Marine Corps," paper, undated (summer 1942).

Reports

Air Force and Moment for XLRN-1 Glider, Report No. 665, no author stated, Aerodynamical Laboratory, Department of Aeronautics, Navy Yard, Washington, D.C., 22 April 1943.
Army Aircraft Characteristics, Production and Experimental, Report No. TSEST – A2, no author stated, ATSC, United States Army, 1 April 1946.
Boatrer, B.L., Major General, *Interim Report on the Comparative and Tactical Evaluation of Assault Transport Aircraft and Gliders*, Air Proving Ground, Eglin AFB, approximately 30 June 1951.
Bouton, I., Laister-Kauffmann Aircraft Corporation, *Estimated Performance of Model LK-12*, 9 June 1944. *Preliminary Weight Estimate of the LK-12*, 14 June 1944
Bouton, I., Laister-Kauffmann Aircraft Corporation, *Preliminary Weight Estimate of the LK-12*, 14 June 1944.

Compton, Louis J., Colonel, *Report of Test of Project No. AB 748 YCG-18 Medium Glider*, Army Field Forces Board No. 1, 27 October 1949.

Driscoll, B.J., Lieutenant, USAAF, Materiel Command, Engineering Division, *Memorandum Report on Performance Tests, XPG-2 Glider, Ridgefield Manufacturing Corporation*, 23 August 1943.

Figley Richard E., Major, USMC, *Catapulting an Airplane with a Glider in Tow, Project George*, Memorandum Report No. 7-43, Naval Aircraft Factory, Philadelphia, Pennsylvania, 25 June 1943.
Figley, Richard E., Captain, *Experimental Cargo Line, Project George*, Memorandum Report No. 2-43, 20 January 1943, Naval Aircraft Factory, Philadelphia, Pennsylvania.
Figley, Richard E., Major, *Experimental Cargo Line, Project George*, Memorandum Report No. 4-43, Naval Aircraft Factory, Philadelphia, Pennsylvania, 22 May 1943.
Figley, Richard E., Major, *Flight Tests of XLRQ-1 Glider, Project George*, Memorandum Report No. 8-43, Naval Aircraft Factory, Philadelphia, Pennsylvania, 24 August 1943.
Figley, R.E., Captain, USMC, *Investigation of Short Glider Tow Lines*, Memorandum Report Mo. 2-43, Naval Aircraft Factory, Philadelphia, 20 January 1943.
Figley, Richard E., Major, *XLNT-1 GLOMBs, Expendable Tests, Project George*, Memorandum Report No. 9-43, Naval Aircraft Factory, Philadelphia, Pennsylvania, 28 September 1943.
Figley, Richard E., Major, USMC, *XLNT-1 GLOMBs Expendable Tests*, Memorandum Report No. 1-44, Flight Test Section, Engineering Department, Naval Aircraft Factory, Philadelphia, Pennsylvania, 26 February 1944.
Figley, Richard E., Major, *XLRA-1 Glider – Final Demonstration Report, Project George*, Memorandum Report No. 10-43, Naval Aircraft Factory, Philadelphia, Pennsylvania, 19 October 1943.

Gassner, A.A., Jenter Corporation – Aircraft Division, *Weight and Performance Data, Proposal, Engine Installation Glider CG-4A, Engine Ranger Model 6-440C-2*, Report No. 110-A, 8 March 1943.
Glider Project Books a.k.a. *"Glider Report"* written in 6 Volumes by the Procurement Division for General Echols and delivered in November 1943. Acquired on microfilm from the Archives Branch of the Albert F. Simpson Historical Research Center, Air Force Case History Files, Air Force Historical Research Agency, Maxwell AFB, Alabama, (Microfilm Roll A2057-A2059, Reel 3826-3827, Index 1530)

Hawks, Charles R., Major, USAAF, *Progress Report, Contract No. W33-038 AC-1666, General Airborne Transport Company, Model XCG-16*, 5 December 1944.
Hauder, Jr., George H., *Memorandum MCRFTP-2188, Phase II Tests on the XG-18A Glider, USAF No. 46-067*, 1 February 1949.

Isen, S., Ridgefield Manufacturing Corporation, *Actual Weight Group, Engine Nacelle Installation, Ranger Model 6-440C-2 in Glider Model CG-4A, A.A.F. Project XPG-2, Contract AC 26597*, Report No. 116, 12 July 1943

Kramer, H.A., Chase Aircraft Co., Inc., *Glider Initial Weighing, Report No. P-3058*, 12 April 1950.

Larkin, W., The WACO Aircraft Company, *Model Specification, Airplane, Transport (Cargo) Light, Army Air Forces Model Design XPG-3A, WACO Model Designation 2-YEU*, Report No. 1575, 17 April 1944.

Memorandum Report No. MCR EOA-5-67, Engineering Inspection of the Chase XG-20 Heavy Assault Glider, no author stated, Headquarters, Air Material Command, Wright Patterson AFB, Dayton, Ohio, 23 March 1951.

Model Specification, Glider, Cargo and Troop Transport, Powered, Army Air Force Designation – PG-2A, Northwestern Aeronautical Corporation Designation "Aerotruck"-N.A.C.-1" Army Air Force Contract No:-W535ac26936, no author stated, Engineering Report No. 1010, no author stated, 5 March 1945.

Model Specification, Glider, Cargo and Troop Transport, Towed, Report No. 3001 Revision C, no author stated, 3 April 1950.

Model Specification, Glider, Cargo and Troop Transport, Towed, A.A.F. XCG-16 + G.A.T.C. MC-1A, Report No. M-100, no author stated, General Airborne Transport Company, 4 December 1943, Revision 2, 26 April 1944.

Model Specification, Glider, Cargo and Troop Transport, Towed, AAF XCG-16A + G.A.T.C. MC-1B, Report No. M-100A, no author stated, General Airborne Transport Company, 25 August 1944.

Ober, Jon H., Captain, USAAF, "Development of Glider Type Aircraft," Memorandum, 6 July 1944.

Operational and Tactical Suitability of the XCG-10A Glider, no author stated, Report of Army Air Forces Board, Orlando Florida, Project No. 4107DH452.1, 12 February 1945.

Papana, Alex, Test Pilot, *Spin Test of the XFG-1 #44-29060 Flown on the 5 September 1945*, report, undated,

Pfeiffer, H.H., *Flight Test Report, Report A 110*, Chase Aircraft Company, Inc., 15 October 1948.

Popowich, George, Air Material Command, *Memorandum Report on Rigid Tow Bar for Gliders*, TSFTE-2107, Wright Field, Ohio, 3 November 1947.

Project Status Report, Army Air Forces Model XCG-18A, Chase Model MS-6A, no author stated, Chase Aircraft Co., Inc., 15 July 1947.

Protasewich, P., Chase Aircraft Company, Inc., *Model Specification, Airplane, Glider, Cargo Transport, Powered, Chase Model MS-5*, Report No. 200, 12 November 1945.

Reilly, Robert V., 1st Lieutenant, USMCR, *Salvage of a Disabled Aircraft by Towing as a Glider, Project George*, Memorandum Report No. 5-43, Naval Aircraft Factory, Philadelphia, Pennsylvania, 18 May 1943.

Reilly, Robert V., 1st Lieutenant, USMCR, *Test of Gar Wood Training Glider Winch, Project George*, Memorandum Report No. 6-43, Naval Aircraft Factory, Philadelphia, Pennsylvania, 21 June 1943.

Roberts and Monahan, Majors, Army Air Forces Board, *Preliminary Report of the Test of Operational and Tactical Suitability of the XCG-16 Glider*, rough draft undated but likely end of October 1944.

Sauers, William F., Captain, Air Corps, Air Technical Services Command, Engineering Division, Headquarters, *Memorandum Report No. TSEAL2-4565-3-1, Glider Development Conference*, 26 April 1945. Includes Appendix 1 "Military Characteristics of Aircraft (Proposed), Powered Glider – Medium," and Appendix 4, Miller, Marion A., 1st Lieutenant, Air Corps, "The Status of Powered Gliders Today," all in Bagwell, Margaret C., *Case History of the C-123 Airplane (26 April 1945 – 7 September 1951)*.

Sherman, A., Chase Aircraft Co., Inc., *Estimated Characteristics and Performance of the Chase Aircraft Co. Assault Heavy Glider Model MS-3*, Report No. 151, 1 June 1946.

Stewart, W.H., Cornelius Aircraft Corporation, *Model Specification, Fuel Glider, Army Air Forces Model Designation XFG-1, Cornelius Model Designation CFG-1*, Report No. 102-A, 15 January 1944.

Thoms, Keith H., *Interim Heavy Airlift: Sea Base Logistics Glider Concept*, NSWCDD/TR-06/52, Naval Surface Warfare Center, U.S. Navy, Dahlgren, Virginia, January 2007.

Thoms, Keith H., *Interim Heavy Airlift: Sea Base Processing of Logistics Gliders*, NSWCDD/TR-07/7, Naval Surface Warfare Center, U.S. Navy, Dahlgren, Virginia, October 2007.

Timm Aircraft Corporation, *Specification, Model XAG-2*, Report No. 248-A, 1 March 1943.

Wileman, E.E., Fletcher Aviation Corporation, *Glider, Radio – Controlled (Bomber)*, Report No. 115A, 13 February 1942.

White, Karl H., *Estimated Performance – Initial Flight – XLRN-1 Towed by PBY-5A*, Report No. 52, 1 October 1943, Naval Aircraft factory, Philadelphia, Pennsylvania.

White, Karl H., Naval Aircraft Factory, *Revised Performance Estimate – XLRN-1 Towed by PBY-5A*, Report No. 100, 7 July 1943.

Zell, John H., Captain, USAAF, *Comparison of Model Specification Requirements of General Airborne Transport Company's XCG-16 Glider with Actual Flight Test Values*, 27 October 1944.

Manuals

Aircraft Inspection and Maintenance Guide for CG-4A Gliders, AN 09-40CB-2, Army Air Forces, 5 October 1944.

Erection and Maintenance Instructions for Army Model CG-4A Glider, T.O. No. 09-40CA-2, Army Air Forces, Revised 30 April 1945.

Erection and Maintenance Instructions for Army Model CG-13A Glider, OO-20A-2-CG-4A, Army Air Forces, 16 November 1943.

Erection and Maintenance Instructions for Army Model CG-15A Gliders, AN 09-40CC-2, Army Air Forces, 30 January 1945.

Handbook of Flight Operating Instructions, USAF Series YG-18A Gliders, T.O. No. 09-80CAA-1, 18 January 1949.

Pilot's Flight Operating Instructions for Glider, Army Model CG-4A, AN 09-40CA-1, Army Air Forces, Revised 20 June 1945.

Pilot's Flight Operating Instructions for Glider, Army Model CG-13A, AN 09-40CB-1, Army Air Forces, Revised 20 June 1945.

Pilot's Flight Operating Instructions for Glider, Army Model CG-15A, AN 09-40CC-1, Army Air Forces, Revised 15 December 1944.

Pilot's Handbook for Army Model CG-10A Glider, AN 09-15AB-1, Army Air Forces, 24 September 1945.

Pilot Training Manual for the CG-4A Glider, AAF Manual No. 50-17, Headquarters AAF, Office of Flying Safety, March 1945.

Pilot's Notes for Horsa I Glider, 2nd Edition, Air Ministry, January 1944.

Correspondence

Abbeman, John F., The Cornelius Aircraft Corporation, "Proposal for Cornelius Model CBG-1 Gliders, related Equipment and Data," letter to Commanding General, Army Air Forces, 8 May 1943.

Air Forces Flying Training Command, "Plan for Training Glider Pilots," memorandum for General Arnold, 9 May 1942, Henry Harley Arnold file frame 1124.

Arcier, A. Francis, The WACO Aircraft Company, "Change to Exhibit "A" Performance Data on Light Transports Derived from CG-4A and CG-15A Gliders," letter, 12 October 1944.

Arnold, H.H., General, Commanding General, Army Air Forces, letter to Lieutenant General Jacob L. Devers, Commanding General, European Theater of Operations, 1 August 1943, Henry Harley Arnold file frame 1025-1026.

Arnold, H.H., Lieutenant General, "Glider Models – Procurement of for Tests," letter to Chief of the Bureau of Aeronautics, 3 August 1942, frame 1090.

Barnaby, Ralph, letter to William K. Horn, 16 December 1977.

Barnaby, R.S., Naval Aircraft Factory, "Long Distance Glider Towing Using Autotow Equipment," memorandum, 18 June 1943.

Barringer, Lewin, "A.G.A. Aviation Corporation Troop Glider," undated note, Henry Harley Arnold file frame 943.

Barringer, Lewin B., Glider Specialist, "Report on Glider Program," memorandum for Commanding General, Army Air Forces, 7 May 1942, Henry Harley Arnold file frame 1139-1140.

Bauer, R.C., 1st Lieutenant, USAAF, "Type A-3A Automatic Pilot Installation in CG-4A Glider," memorandum, 28 June 1943.

Bennett, T.C., "Strength Requirements – XLRN Glider," Naval Aircraft Factory, 13 July 1943.

Berry, J.R., 1st Lieutenant, USAAF, "Detail Design of a Glider to Carry a 2000-Pound Bomb," memorandum, 13 January 1943.

Bogert, H.Z., Colonel, USAAF, "Shipment of Glider, MX-166," memorandum, 6 June 1944.

Branshaw, E., Major, General, U.S. Army, "Information Leaks Concerning Criz Glider," memorandum, 13 November 1943.

Bristol Aeronautical Corporation, "Disposition of LRQ-1 Glider," letter to Major B.B. Price, USAAF, 4 August 1943.

Brown, J.M., Christopher Aircraft Company, "Change Order on Contract W35ac37433," letter, 24 September 1943.

Browne, L.W., "Flight Test – TV Installation, Mines Field," memorandum to Ted Woolsey, 23 August 1942.

Butler, C.T., Flight Officer, USAAF, "Ludington-Griswold, Inc, Modified Nose for the CG-4A Glider," memorandum, 24 August 1943.

Carroll, F.O., Brigadier General, USAAF, "Glider Developments," memorandum, 2 September 1944.

Carroll, F.O., Brigadier General, USAAF, "Over-Under Project, P-38/Hamilcar Combination," memorandum, first endorsement remarks, 2 August 1944.

Carroll, F.O., Colonel, USAAC, "Stability Tests of Towed Gliders," memorandum, 18 March 1942.

Clark, Lawrence B., Major, USMC, "Recommendations of Board of Officers Ordered to Study the Glider Situation," 11 November 1942.

Cook, Orval R., Colonel, USAAF, "Meeting on Bowlus-Criz Glider Production," memorandum, 2 November 1943.

Cooley, John B., Lieutenant Colonel, Assistant Air Adjutant General, "Transport Airplanes for Glider Program," 4 February 1942 and Comment dated 23 February, Henry Harley Arnold file frame 857-8.

Corriveau, A.L., "Progress Report on Foreign Gliders," memorandum, 11 July 1944.

Craig, H.A., Brigadier General, Acting Chief of Air Staff, "Availability of CG-4A Gliders in the Maxton-Camp, Mackall, North Carolina, Area," memorandum for Lieutenant General J.T. McNarney, 3 November 1943, Henry Harley Arnold file frame 1056.

Craig, H.A., Brigadier General, Acting Chief of Air Staff, "CG-13 Glider Requirements," 23 December 1943, Henry Harley Arnold file frame 1049.

Craige, L.C., Brigadier General, "Informal Design Competition, Glider, Assault, Heavy," 30 August 1946.

Crawford, A.R., Brigadier General, Deputy Chief Army Air Forces, "Glider Development Program," memorandum, 14 November 1946.

Crawford, A.R., Brigadier General, U.S. Army, "Procurement of Glider, Assault, Light," memorandum, 6 December 1946.

Christopher Engineering Company, "New Design of Improved Glider," no author stated, letter, 19 September 1942.

Curtis, Edward P., Major, Secretary of the Air Staff, for Chief of the Army Air Forces, "Gyro-Glider," memorandum for the Assistant Chief of Staff, 3 November 1941, Henry Harley Arnold file frame 948.

Curtis, Edward P., Major, Secretary of The Air Staff, "Large Capacity Transport Gliders," memorandum for the Assistant Chief of Staff, G-3, 10 December 1941, Henry Harley Arnold file frame 917.

Davidson, Norman, Major, USAAF, "Armor Plate Requirement CG-4A Glider," memorandum, 31 May 1945.

Davidson, Ralph, Captain, USN, "Glider, Fuel and Explosive Carrier; Construction of," Bureau of Aeronautics, 22 June 1943.

Dent, F.R., Jr., Major, "Final Report of Major F.R. Dent, Jr., Air Corps, on Trip to England," letter to the Assistant Chief of Staff, G-2, 9 December 1941, p. 2, Henry Harley Arnold file frame 910-911.

Dent, Jr., Fred R. Lieutenant Colonel, "Flight Tests of the Fletcher XBG-1 Glider," memorandum, 2 May 1942.

Doodwin, Hugh H., Captain, USN, "Naval Gliders – Allocation of," memorandum, 13 July 1943.

Doubleday. T.C., Colonel, USAAF, "Surplus C-46A and D Aircraft," memorandum, 6 August 1947.

Dunham, S.W., Materiel Division, Experimental Engineering, "Report on Detachable Wings for a ¼-Ton Liaison Truck (Jeep)," memorandum, 21 November 1941.

Dutt, D.L., Brigadier General, USAAF, "Surplus C-46A and D Aircraft," memorandum, first endorsement, 22 September 1947.

Eaker, Ira C, Lieutenant General, Headquarters Army Air Forces, "Glider Requirements," Routing and Record Sheet, 6 December 1945.

Echols, O.P., Major General, USAAF, "Airborne Transport, Incorporated," memorandum, 16 February 1943.

Echols, Oliver P., Brigadier General, Chief, Materiel Division, "Experimental Glider Procurement," 28 November 1941, Henry Harley Arnold file frame 923.

Echols, Oliver P., Brigadier General, Chief Materiel Division, "Glider Production Facilities," memorandum for Chief of the Army Air Forces, 17 January 1942, Henry Harley Arnold file frame 865.

Echols, Oliver P., Major General, Assistant Chief of Air Staff, "Glider Requirements Versus Production," letter to the Secretary of Air Staff, 23 March 1945, Henry Harley Arnold file frame 997.

Echols, Oliver P., Chief, Materiel Division, "Glider Training", Routing and Record Sheet, Comment 8, 30 December 1941, Henry Harley Arnold file frame 968.

Echols, O.P., Major General, "Progress Report to 15 November 1944, on JB-2 and JB-1 Robot Bombs," memorandum for Chief of Air Staff, 18 November 1944, Henry Harley Arnold file frame 324

Echols, O.P., Major General, "Progress Report to 3 January 1945 on JB-2 and JB-1 Robot Bombs," memorandum for Chief of Air Staff, 5 January 1945, Henry Harley Arnold file frame 321.

Echols, Oliver P., Major General, Assistant Chief of Air Staff, Materiel and Services, "Status of the XCG-16 Glider," memorandum for Chief of the Air Staff, 5 October 1944, Henry Harley Arnold file frame 1016.

Fahrney, D.S., Captain, USN, "XLRN-1 Gliders," Naval Aircraft Modification Unit, 12 February 1944.

Fahrney, D.S., Captain, USN, "XLRN-1 Gliders," Naval Aircraft Modification Unit, 24 March 1944.

Giles, Barney M., Major General, Chief of Air Staff, "Priority for CG-14 Glider Engineering and Breakdown Tests," 11 November 1943, Henry Harley Arnold file frame 1052.

Giles, Barney M., Lieutenant General, for Commanding General Army Air Forces, "Requirement for CG-10A Gliders," memorandum for the Chief of Staff, 31 January 1945, Henry Harley Arnold file frame 999-1002.

Haig, H.A., Brigadier General, U.S. Army, "Requirement for Aircraft—Gliders, Transport," memorandum, 4 October 1943.

Hanley, T.J., Jr., Colonel, "Glider Program," memorandum for the Assistant Chief of Staff, G-3, 3 March 1942 Henry Harley Arnold file frame 822.

Hanley, T.J., Jr., Colonel, Assistant Chief of the Air Staff (for the Chief), "Procurement of Gliders for Army Glider Program," 27 January 1942, Henry Harley Arnold file frame 860.

Harris, Anthony A., Lieutenant Colonel, Air Corps, "Pick-a-Back Method for Glider Propulsion," memorandum, 15 February 1946, 7.

Harris, Anthony B., Lieutenant Colonel, USAAF, "The Lightning-Hamilcar Combination," 3 February 1944.

Harris, Anthony B., Lieutenant Colonel USAAF, "The Fighter-Glider Combination," 27 August 1943.

Harrison, F. Lloyd, Commander, USN, "XLRN Glider – Manufacture of – N.A.F. Schedule No. 2666," Naval Aircraft Factory, 14 July 1943.

Hockett, H.E., Lieutenant Colonel, USAAF, "Armor Plate Requirement CG-4A Glider," memorandum, 14 June 1945.

Holcomb, Thomas, Major General, "Glider Training," memorandum for the Chief of Naval Operations, 24 June 1942.

Johnson, Davenport ,Major General, "Gliders" letter to Chief of the Army Air Force, 13 February 1942 and 1st Endorsement by Lieutenant Colonel John B. Cooley, Assistant Air Adjutant General, 6 March 1942

Jones, R.F., Commander, Utility Squadron Five, "Gliders and Glider Training; Request for," 26 April 1942, and endorsements.

Kaden, George, USAAF, "Performance of the XCG-14A Glider," memorandum, 30 October 1946

Kemmer, Paul H., Colonel, USAAF, "Contract No. W535AC-37433 XAG-1 Assault Glider Cancellation for Default," memorandum, 16 October 1943.

Kemmer, Paul H., Colonel, USAAF, "Disposition of LRQ-1 Glider," letter to Bristol Aeronautical Corporation, 16 August 1943.

Kemmer, Paul H., Colonel, USAAF, "TI-1570 - C-47 Conversion to Glider," memorandum, 14 December 1943.

Kemmer, Paul H., Colonel, USAAF, "42-place Glider Proposal – Airborne Transport, Inc.," memorandum, 28 December 1942.

Kowalski, Jr., Frank, Captain, "Gyro-Glider," letter to Director, New Weapons Division, 10 September 1941, Henry Harley Arnold file frame 953.

Kuter, L.S., Brigadier General, Deputy Chief of Air Staff, "Glider Pilot Training," memorandum for the Chief of Staff, 10 June 1942, Henry Harley Arnold file frame 1103.

Lauder, John T., Lieutenant, USNR, "Report of Conference Held 27 April 1944 at NAMC. Bldg. 75 – XLRN-1 Gliders, Surface Coating," Naval Air Material Center, 6 May 1944.

Leet, Jack, Captain, USAAF, "Memorandum Report No. ENG-50-884," 9 June 1943.

Letter to British Air Commission no signatory given, 5 January 1942, Henry Harley Arnold file frame 902.

Littel, E.G., Major, HQ, AAF Materiel Command, "Report of Brigadier General Junius W. Jones, Air Inspector, on Synopsis of Investigation of Crash of CG-4A Glider at Lambert Field, St. Louis, Missouri, 1 August 1943," memorandum to Commanding General, Army Air Forces, 23 October 1943.

Lough, Maxon S., Colonel, for Chief of Infantry, 3rd Endorsement 18 August 1941 to Brigadier Spaatz, Carl, General, "Organization of Glider Units," 7 July 1941, Henry Harley Arnold file frame 896.

Lowell, Arthur L., 1st Lieutenant, Air Corps, "Progress Report on Development of Bellows Flaps for Gliders," memorandum, 7 December 1941.

The Major General Commandant to The Chief of Naval Operations, "Glider Program," 1 October 1941.

Materiel Division, "Performance of the C-47 Airplane While Towing Gliders," no author stated, memorandum, 19 November 1941.

Material Division, "A Study of Eight and Fifteen-Place Towed Troop-Carry Gliders," no author stated, memorandum, 25 November 1941.

Maxwell, Alfred R., Brigadier General, "Military Characteristics of Aircraft, Glider, Assault, Heavy," Headquarters Army Air Forces, 13 December 1945.

Maxwell, Alfred R., Brigadier General, "Military Characteristics of Aircraft, Glider, Assault, Light," Headquarters Army Air Forces, 3 January 1946.

McKee, William F., Colonel, Acting Assistant Chief of Air Staff, Operations, Commitments & Requirements, "Deterioration as Affecting CG-4A Glider Requirements," memorandum for Deputy Chief of Air Staff, 25 May 1944, Henry Harley Arnold file frame 1034.

McKee, William F., Colonel, Acting Assistant Chief of Air Staff, Operations, Commitments & Requirements, "Past Difficulties in Determining Glider Requirements," memorandum for the Chief of Air Staff, 3 October 1944, Henry Harley Arnold file frame 1017-1018.

Meredith, R.A., Lieutenant Colonel, Assistant Ground Adjutant General, "Development of Guided Missiles for Artillery Employment," 22 July 1944, Henry Harley Arnold file frame 362.

Meyers, E.B., Major General, Deputy Assistant Chief of Air Staff, Materiel, Maintenance & Distribution, "CG-4A Gliders in Storage," memorandum for the Chief of Air Staff, 30 March 1944, Henry Harley Arnold file frame 1040.

Meyers, B.E., Major General, Deputy Assistant Chief of Air Staff, "Status of XCG-16 (Criz Bowlus) Glider," memorandum for Chief of Air Staff, 6 May 1944, Henry Harley Arnold file frame 1024.

"Military Characteristics of Aircraft," no author stated, memorandum, 19 April 1944.

"Military Characteristics of Aircraft," no author stated, memorandum to Assistant Chief of Air Staff, Materiel, Maintenance and Distribution, 12 February 1941.

"Military Characteristics of Aircraft," no author stated, memorandum to Deputy Chief of Staff (Air), 21 July 1941.

Miller, M.A., "Conference on Light Assault Glider Loading Apertures," memorandum, 8 July 1946.

Moore, C.K., Colonel, USAAF, "Glider, Transport," memorandum, 10 October 1942.

Morgan, W.M., Colonel, USAAF, "Criz Glider," memorandum, 21 October 1943.

Moyers, Frank N., Colonel, Air Corps, Chief, Aircraft Laboratory, teletype to Commanding Officer, Rosecrans Field, St. Joseph, Missouri, 12 April 1945.

Nagel, F., Christopher Aircraft Company, "Eight Place Assault Glider XAG-1," letter, 21 December 1942.

Ober, Jon H., Captain, USAAF, "Development of Glider Type Aircraft," memorandum, 6 July 1944.

Ordway, Jr., F.I., Major, Assistant Executive, Material Division, "Army Glider Program," correspondence to Chief of Army Air Forces, 27 January 1942, Henry Harley Arnold file frame 868.

Ostrander, Jr., J.E., Commander, Engineering Division, "Additional Procurement of 12- and 24-Place Gliders," Bureau of Aeronautics, Navy Department, Washington, D.C., 7 October 1941.

Patterson, A.L., Bristol Aeronautical Corporation, telegram to Lieutenant Colonel B.B. Price, 17 September 1943.

Pearl, William W., Project Engineer, "Report of Conference 8/16/44 Between Captain E. Rounds, USNR of NAS Patuxent River, Lieutenant R.J. Ryan, NAMU and Mr. W. Pearl, NAMU at NAS Patuxent River Md. on First Flight of XLRN-1 Gliders," Naval Aircraft Factory, memorandum, 18 August 1944.

Pearl, W.W., "XLRN-1 Glider #36431 – Report of Flight Tests at NAS Patuxent River, Md. 11/7/44 & 11/9/44," Naval Aircraft Factory, 14 November 1944.

Pearl, W.W., Project Engineer, Naval Aircraft Factory, "XLRN-1 Glider – Report of Flight Tests at NAS Patuxent River, Md. 10/24 and 10/25/44," memorandum, 30 October 1944.

Pearl, W.W., "XLRN-1 Rudder Control System," Naval Aircraft Factory, 25 April 1944.

"Performance of CG-13," no author stated, 15 December 1943, Henry Harley Arnold file frame 1051.

Perkins, Courtland D., "Report of a Conference on the Procurement of a Tailless, Swept-forward Wing Glider," memorandum 18 March 1943.

Perrin, Edwin S., Brigadier General, Deputy Chief of Air Staff, "Gliders," letter to AG/AS Operations, Commitments & Requirements, 11 April 1944, Henry Harley Arnold file frame 1037-1038.

Popowich, George, Air Material Command, "Phase II Tests on the XG-14A Glider, USAF No. 44-90990," memorandum, 23 August 1948.

"Radio Controlled Bomb Gliders Types XBG-1 and XBG-2," no author, memorandum, 9 June 1943.

Ramsburgh, J.S., Lieutenant Commander, USN, "BuAer Project Order 180-43 – Design and Manufacture of One Static Article and Two Flight Articles of the Model XLRN-1 Glider – Increase of," Bureau of Aeronautics, Washington, D.C., 23 May 1943.

Read-York, Inc., "Contract X 535 ac-40197," letter to Colonel Paul H. Kemmer, 2 November 1943, in *Glider Project Books*, Vol. VI, microfilm frame 556.

Reggig, James C., letter to Everett Cassagneres, 3 April 1970, regarding the XLRQ-1 glider experience.

Robbins, E.M., Colonel, Engineering Division, "Request for Bellows Flap Installation on XTG-3 Glider," memorandum, second endorsement, 24 April 1943.

Rodina, Jr., Matthew E., letter to Bob Storck, 6 July 1982, summarizing research on Army training gliders.

Sallada, H.B., Captain, USN, "Glider Program," 24 June 1942.

Schmidt, H., Acting Commandant U.S. Marine Corps, "Military Gliders," 9 October 1942.

Seifert, W. M., Lieutenant Commander, USNR, "XLRN-1 Airplane," Naval Aircraft Modification Unit, 15 October 1943.

Seifert, W. M, Lieutenant Commander, USNR, "XLRN-1 Gliders," Naval Aircraft Modification Unit, 13 April 1944.

Sexton, W.R., Chairman General Board, USN, "Glider Program," 17 January 1942.

Smith, George F., Colonel, Engineering Division, "Assault Transport Development Program," 22 January 1948.

Smith, George F., Colonel, letter to Christopher-National Aircraft Products Company, 11 February 1948.

Smith, L.T., Lieutenant Colonel, Executive Assistant, "Large Capacity Transport Gliders," letter for the Chief of the Air Corps to Chief of Air Staff, 8 February 1942, Henry Harley Arnold file frame 914.

Smith, N.Y., Colonel, USAAF, "Chase Plow Deceleration Tests on CG-4A Glider," memorandum, 16 June 1945.

Spaatz, Carl, Brigadier General, "Army Glider Program," memorandum for the Chief of Staff, 2 December 1941, Henry Harley Arnold file frame 925-32.

Spaatz, Carl, Chief of the Air Staff, "Glider Training", Routing and Record Sheet, Comment 1, 22 September 1941, Henry Harley Arnold file frame 965.

Sparks, Harold, letter to Everett Cassagneres, 21 March 1978, regarding the XLRQ-1 glider experience.

Stroukoff, Michael, *Model Specification Contract W33-038 AC-1206 Glider, Cargo and Troop – Transport Towed, Army Air Forces Model Designation XCG-14*, 10 June 1944.

Stroukoff, M., *Proposal for Design and Construction of Chase Model MS-3 Glider*, Chase Aircraft Company, 18 November 1946.

Thieblot, A.J., Fairchild Aircraft, "Development of Gliders," letter, 15 February 1946.

Thomas, Charles S., Bureau of Aeronautics, letter to Frank M. Folsom, 28 May 1942, Brown microfiche 8 frame 91.

Thorton, T.H., "Memorandum for Captain R.S. Barnaby," Naval Aircraft Factory, Philadelphia, 18 May 1944.

Timberlake, Patrick W., Brigadier General, Acting Chief of Air Staff, "Glider Production After V-E Day," memorandum for Chief of Air Staff, 24 March 1945, Henry Harley Arnold file frame 994.

Todd, R., Squadron Leader, British Air Commission, "Forms 263A for CG-4 Gliders," letter, 11 October 1944.

Towers, J.H., Rear Admiral, "Glider Models – Procurement of for Tests," letter to Commanding General, Army Air Forces, 9 July 1942, Henry Harley Arnold file frame 1086.

Towers, J.H., U.S. Navy, "Memorandum to the Secretary of the Navy," undated.

Twining, N.F., Colonel, Secretary, Air Staff, "Glider Pilot Training," letter to Commanding General, Air Forces Flying Training Command, 15 May 1942.

Weaver, W.R., Major General, USAAC, "Military Characteristics of Aircraft," memorandum, 8 February 1942.

Welsh, W.L., Air Marshall, British Joint Staff Mission, Officer of the Combined Chiefs of Staff, letter to Major General Barney M. Giles, Chief of Air Staff, 29 March 1944, Henry Harley Arnold file frame 1029.

White, Karl H., "XLRN Glider – Drafting Section Conference on Specification for Installation of Auxiliary Power Plant," Naval Aircraft Factory, 15 February 1943.

Wilson, R.C., Colonel, USAAF, "Glider Developments." memorandum, 8 August 1944.

Winston, R.A., Lieutenant, "Large-Capacity Gliders for Naval Use," 12 January 1942.

Winston, R.A., Lieutenant, "Large-Capacity Gliders Towed by Airplanes and Their Possible Employment in Naval Aviation," memorandum for Admiral Horne, 12 January 1942.

Wolfe, K.B., Lieutenant Colonel, Engineering Section, "Assignment of Type Symbol "G" for Gliders," memorandum, first endorsement, 5 June 1941.

Wood, Karl D., Professor, Purdue University, letter to General Arnold, 11 September 1941, Henry Harley Arnold file frame 964.

Worton, W.A., USMC, "Board of Officers to Study the Glider Program," 20 October 1942.

"XFG-1 Flight Test Program," no author stated, memorandum for Colonel Frank N. Moyers, 5 September 1945.

Other Documents

Air Materiel Command, *Informal Design Competition, Glider, Assault, Heavy*, no author stated, memorandum, 30 August 1946.

Air Materiel Command, *Informal Design Competition, Glider, Assault, Light*, no author stated, memorandum, 14 June 1946.

Allard, Noel, "Northwest Aeronautical and the WWII Glider Program," paper, undated but approximately 2009.

Allard, Noel, "Troop Glider Manufacturing in the Twin Cities," paper, undated but approximately 2009.

Bonner, L.G., Dr., Technical Director, Allegany Ballistics Laboratory, *Notes on a Meeting at ABL, December 3, 1946, to Discuss the Status of the Glider Thrust Unit, 4-ES-1200, T-21*, 11 December 1946.

Breed, III, Richard E., Allied Aviation Corporation, "Allied Invader Glider Allocated to Army," press release, 21 September 1943.

Bristol Aeronautical Corporation, *Aircraft Characteristics, LRQ-1*, no author stated, date unknown (after 17 September 1943).

Characteristics, XPG-3, no author stated, 15 November 1946.

Chase Brothers, *General Specification for Transport Glider MS*, 21 November 1942.

Connor, Sara Witter and Day, Charles L., "The Ah Da Wa Gam Cardboard Box," paper, undated but approximately 2009.

Day, Charles L., "CG-4A Glider Communications Systems," paper, undated but approximately 2009.

Day, Charles L., "Glider Legacy in the U.S. Air Force," paper, undated but approximately 2009.

Day, Charles L., "CG-4A Quick Connect and the Griswold Nose Protection Device," paper, undated but approximately 2009.

Day, Charles L., "The USAAF XCG-3 and XCG-4," article, undated but approximately 2009.

Day, Charles L., "Voo Doo was my Name, Flying was my Game," article, undated but approximately 2009.

Day, Charles L. and Spencer, Leon B., "Development and Use of the Waco CG-4A Cargo Glider Deceleration Parachute," paper, December 2003.

Engineering Division, Air Technical Service Command, *Representative Model Specification for Glider – Assault, Heavy, 16,000 Pounds Useful Load*, no author stated, 1 February 1946 plus Errata Sheet.

Engineering Division, Air Technical Service Command, *Representative Model Specification for Glider – Assault, Light, 8,000 Pounds Useful Load*, no author stated, 1 February 1946.

Fletcher Aviation Corporation, *Specification 116A, Fletcher Model 16, Bomb Glider, Radio Controlled*, 20 January 1942.

"Fuel Transfer Diagram, Proposed, (XLRN-1)," drawing, 29 October 1942.

Glider Data Book, MX-114, Copy Number 9, August 1941, collection of period, non-standard glider project information sheets, stored at National Archives, pages unnumbered.

"Glider Program," Status Report, Bureau of Aeronautics, 1 July 1943.

"Glider Tactics and Technique," AFM No. 3, Army Air Forces, 24 January 1944.

Guest Lecture of the New Development Division, Command and Staff Course, AAF School, Maxwell Field, Alabama, "ND54 – New Special Aircraft, Transports Gliders, and Liaison Airplanes," no author or date. Manuscript has notation "Rec'd 6-25-46" and clearly early postwar.

Henry Harley Arnold file. Microfilm Reel 28167 provided on CD Rom from the Archives Branch of the Albert F. Simpson Historical Research Center, Air Force Case History Files, Air Force Historical Research Agency, Maxwell AFB, Alabama, collection of correspondence and other documents.

History Leading up to Assault Glider Contracts, undated summary and copied correspondence, approximately March 1943.

Lowden, John L., *A Brief History of the Combat Glider in World War II*, undated paper.

Nikiforoff, Paul, *Model Specification Glider, Cargo and Troop – Transport, Towed, Army Air Forces Model Designation XCG-14A Chase Model MS-1A*, 25 January 1945.

Northrop, John K., "The Development of All-Wing Aircraft," 35th Wilbur Wright Memorial Lecture, The Royal Aeronautical Society, 29 May 1947, printed in 1947 proceedings pp. 481-510.

Project Record – PG-2A Glider, Northwestern Aeronautical Corporation, Contract W535 AC-29636, no author or date given, but includes data through 15 October 1945.

Request for Model or Type Designation Change of Status of Equipment, "Airplane, Assault Glider XAG-1," form, 20 March 1943.

Request for Model of Type Designation Change of Status or Equipment, "Airplane, Misc., Glider Powered, AAF Model XPG-2A" form, 4 May 1944.

Request for Model or Type Designation Change of Status of Equipment, "Airplane, Transport Glider, XCG-9," form, 30 July 1942.

Request for Model or Type Designation Change of Status of Equipment, "Airplane, Transport Glider, XCG-11," form, 30 July 1942.

Request for Model or Type Designation Change of Status of Equipment, "Airplane, Troop Glider, XCG-6," form, 7 July 1941.

Request for Model or Type Designation Change of Status of Equipment, "Airplane, Training Glider, Model XTG-1," form, 7 July 41.

Request for Model or Type Designation Change of Status of Equipment, "General Airborne Transport Company glider, model designation MC-2," form, 18 November 1943

Request for Model or Type Designation Change of Status of Equipment, "General Airborne Transport Company Model XCG-16A Glider, AAF Serial No. 44-76194)," form, 16 November 1944.

Request for Model or Type Designation Change of Status of Equipment, "Glider, Transport, AAF Model XCG-13," form, 5 January 1945.

Request for Model or Type Designation Change of Status of Equipment, "Waco 30 Place Glider, YCG-13," form, 15 January 1944.

Request for Model or Type Designation Change of Status Equipment, "XFG-1-CR, Glider, Fuel," form, 22 November 1946.

Request for Model of Type Designation Change of Status or Equipment, "XPG-2A-RI, Glider, Power" form, 18 November 1946.

Request for Model or Type Designation Change of Status of Equipment, "Airplane, Training Glider TG-2," form, 10 December 1941.

Request for Model or Type Designation Change of Status of Equipment, "XTG-1-FR Glider," form, 1 August 1945.

Resume of Happenings on XCG-16 Glider Project, no author stated, 16 October 1944.

Spencer, Leon B., "Death of General Don F. Pratt," paper, June 2006.

Spencer, Leon B., "Glider Tow Ropes, WWII Military Gliders," paper, 7 June 2003.

Spencer, Leon B. "They Flew into Battle on Silent Wings," paper, undated.

Spencer, Leon B., "The Wizards of Crookham Common, A Concise History," paper, undated.

Spencer, Leon B., "WWII U.S. Army Air Forces Glider Aerial Retrieval System," paper, undated.

Spencer, Leon B., "26th Mobile Reclamation and Repair Squadron," paper, undated.

Stanley, Max, "The Flying Wings," *Society of Experimental Test Pilots Twenty-Fourth Symposium Proceedings*, 24-27 September 1980, pp. 237-56.

Summary of various *Status Report* of Navy development programs reproduced in unknown document with dates hand-written beside some entries, found within files of the Naval Aviation Archives.

Type Designation Sheet, Airplane – Glider, TG Training, U.S. Army summary document, undated.

Type Designation Sheet, Airplane – Glider, CG Troop, U.S. Army summary document, undated.

York Aircraft Company, *Resume, XCG12 Gliders*, in *Glider Project Books*, Vol. VI, microfilm frame 461.

Internet

Chase/Stroukoff, http://1000aircraftphotos.com/HistoryBriefs/Chase.htm.

Cully, George and Parsch, Andreas, *Designations of U.S. Air Force Projects*, http://orbat.com/site/andreas/U_S_ per cent20Air per cent20Force per cent20Projects.htm.

U.S. Military Rockets and Missiles, website, www.designation-system.net/dusrm/app1/, 2006.

Video

Silent Wings, The American Glider Pilots of WWII, produced, directed, and written by Robert Child, Inecom Entertainment Company, 2007.

Suicide Missions: Silent Wing Warrior, The History Channel, A&E Television Networks, New York, 1999.

Index

30 mm guns 133
65TC Defender 27
75 mm field gun 63-64, 100, 114, 120, 135, 137-138, 220
breakdown for airdrop 260
105 mm howitzer 116, 120-122, 125, 127
redesigned for airborne transport 114
155 mm howitzer 116-117
A-20A Havoc 174
A-25 Shrike *97*, 171
A-28 Hudson 44
A-29 Hudson 44
A-44, XA-44 188
A.B.C. Glider 242
Addison Point 49
Aerojet 177, 182
Aeromold Corporation 85, 252
aeromold process 71
Aeronca Aircraft Corporation 27-28, 31, 160, 243, 246
AG-1
serials 247
specifics 141
XAG-1 133, 141-*142*, 143, 247
AG-2
serials 247
specifics 143
XAG-2 141-142, *143*
A.G.A. Aviation Corporation 65, 69, 90-91, 114-115, 141, 244
Airborne Command 42-43, 120, 129, 141-142
airborne forces 9, 236
American 14, 43, 157
airborne (airphibious) tactics 9, 43, 114, 160
Airborne Transport Incorporated 127-128
Aircraft Laboratory 10, 13, 62, 128, 133, 141, 176, 182, 210, 221, 249
airdrop, parachute delivery 9, *167*-168, 228-229, 234, 260
Air Gliders Incorporated 25, 243, 247
Air Materiel Command (AMC) 221
Airspeed Limited 138, 189, 244, 246
Air Technical Services Command (ATSC) 10, 118, 137. 220-222
Air Transport Command 42, 46
Akron 173
Alaska 214
Albert Criz Company 129
Aldis lamp 103
All American Aviation (AAA) 105-106, 173
Alliance 27
Allied Aviation Corporation 85, 88-90, 92-93, 149, 151-152, 246
Allied glider integration 10, 113-114, 157, 161-162, 167-168, 236
America, American
see United States of America
Anheuser-Busch 71
aquaplane
see gliders, amphibious
Arcier, A. Francis 80
Arizona 176
Arkansas 42, 48, 71, 111
Army Air Forces Board 130-131
Army Ground Forces (AGF) 11, 41, 120, 125, 141, 143, 215, 220
Arnhem 165, 167
Arnold, Henry "Hap", General 10-*11* 13-15, 23, 27, 34-35, 51, 65-66, 128-129, 131, 141, 143, 167, 232
seeks civilian expertise 12-13
Astoria 70
Athens 168
Australia 72, 159-160
automatic stabilization 199-200, 202
autonomous guidance 198-200
autopilots 149, 167, 172, 179, 198, 200, 220
A-3 Automatic Pilot 179-*180*
D-1 117, 123, 126, 129, 179, 181
autotow 149, 152, 154, 167, 179, 200, 204-207
auxiliary power unit (APU) 142, 153, 177, 224, 226

B-17 Flying Fortress *17*, 96, 116, 119, 125, 128, 130, 169, 171, *174*, 214
B-23 *15*, 105-*106*, 125, 174, 209
B-24 Liberator 61, 165, 171, 176-177
B-25 171
B-29 *17*, 175, 186, 188, 214, *216*, 220
BA-100 25
Babcock Aircraft Corporation 65, 69, 245
Babcock, Verne C. 69
Barber, Al 206
Barber, Dick 206
Barberton 25
Barnaby, Ralph S., Lieutenant, Lieutenant Commander, Commander, and Captain *18*-19, 83, 90, 149, 151, 153-*154*, 174, 199-200, 202
Barringer, Lewin B., Major 12-*13*, 22, 27, 29, 58, 114, 141, 143
Barstow 183
Bastogne 168
Bat missile 207
Battle of the Bulge 168
BD-1 174
Beech Aircraft Company 66, 69
Belfast 219
Bellanca Aircraft Corporation 48
Bell Aircraft Corporation 174, 221-223
bellows flaps *181*-182
Beverly Hills 26
BG-1 (airplane) 200
BG-1 *210*
serials 247

specifics 209
XBG-1 208-209, 247
BG-2
serials 247
specifics 210
XBG-2 210, 247
BG-3
serials 247
XBG-3 211, 187, 247
BG-6 21, 26, 241, 243, 249
BG-8 26, 241, 243, 249
Biak 126
Big Flats 23
Biggs Field 210
blitz landing 43, 98-99
Bloodsworth Island 202
Blossom, Howard 116
BM-5 25
XBM-5 243
Boeing Airplane Company 66, 69-70, 96, 174
bomb gliders (USAAF) 207-211, 247
see also glider bombs (GLOMB, USN)
Bowlus-Du Pont Utility 26, 241
Bowlus Sailplane Company 25-26, 57-58, 90, 243, 244, 249
Bowlus, William Hawley 25-26, 57-59, 127-128
Bowman Field 43
Breed, Richard E., III 89
Briegleb Sailplane Corporation 21, 26-27, 241, 243, 249
Briegleb, William G. "Gus" 26
Brisbane 72, 159
Bristol 85
Bristol Aeronautical Corporation 85-87, 89, 92-93, 151-152, 207-208, 246-247, 252
Bristol Aircraft Corporation 85, 252
Britain, British *see Great Britain*
Bromley Engineering Company 66, 71
Bronx 135
Brown, Joseph M. 141
Browne 209
Browning, Frederick, General 114
BT-13 37, 173
BT-15 Valiant 37
Bureau of Aeronautics (BuAer) 16, 19, 83, 85, 89, 91-92, 145-148, 151-152, 199-203
Burke, Walter F. **89**
Burma 159-161, 169, 236
Burma Road 176
Burnelli, Vincent J. 128
Butler, Francis 71
Buxton, Jay 29

C-1 towed target 207, 247, 252
C-46 Commando 17, 96, 114, 119, 125, 167, 171, 188, 217-218, 224
glider concept 220
C-47 Skytrain 14-15, 17, 38-40, 43, 45-46, 63, 94-95, 96-97, 101, 102-103, 116, 118-119, 127, 130, 133, 139-140, 145, 156-157, 160-161, 164, 170-171, 175, 177, 193, 214-215, 218-220, 236, 244, 255
airdrop from 116, 164, 167
modification as glider 176
modification for towing 95, 98
snatching gliders 107-108, 110, 125
C-53 Skytrooper 38
C-54 Skymaster 114, 119, 146, 167, 171, 176-177, 188, 214, 228
C-60A Lodestar 39, 42, 171
C-74 120, 220
C-81, XC-81D 173
C-82 Packet 212, 214-215, 219, 221-222, 225, 228
engine change for towing considered 220
glider concept 220
C-119 Flying Boxcar 222, 229
C-122, YC-122 225
C-123 228, 236
XC-123 226, 228
C-125 228
California 13, 25-26, 34, 41, 58-59, 71, 127-128, 130, 143, 183, 208, 216
Camalaniugan Airfield 126, 169
Camp Mackall 119
Canada 79, 98, 201, 245-246
Cardenas, Bob, Captain 75, 171
Cardinal C-2 56
Caribbean Air Forces 15
Catalina *(see PBY-5)*
Cessna Aircraft Corporation 65-66, 69-70, 146, 174, 245
CG-1
serials 244
specifics 53
XCG-1 12, 52-53, 244
CG-2
serials 244
specifics 53
XCG-2 12, 52-53, 244
CG-3
model A 38, 51, 54-55, 71, 189, 244
serials 244
specifics 54-55
XCG-3 12, 18. 50-51, 53-54-55, 56, 61, 63, 107, 244
CG-4 39
ambulance (litter) conversion 76-77, 168
armor for 79
assembly 99, 157, 161-162, 164, 256
British operation of 61, 67, 79, 157-158, 161, 232, 245
Celluweld floor 77, 251
center of gravity control 106
deceleration parachute 76-77, 78, 164, 177, 180
description 63-64, 110
deterioration 67-68, 99, 105, 109-110, 159-160, 163, 237, 256
disposal at end of war 213
ditching 171-172
droppable undercarriage 72, 159
early serviceability issues 39, 43, 72
engineering equipment sized to fit 160
explosives to breakup following landing 75, 251
field modifications 74-75, 109
fighter intercept of 103
flight hours 109
flying workshops 79, 109
glide ratio 98
ice runway operation 214
landing damage 105, 109, 163, 168
landing distance 72, 98
landing light 74, 100, 149, 193
late delivery of initial examples 39, 43, 66, 69-70
long tows 98, 164
losses 158, 161, 167-169
model A C, 7, 11, 16-17, 38-40, 42-45, 46-47, 49, 51-52, 54-55, 60-61, 63-64, 66, 68, 70, 79-80, 94-95, 101, 102-103, 104-105, 106, 113-116, 119-120, 122-125, 134-135, 138-141, 149, 156-157, 158-169, 170, 172, 174, 176, 179, 180-181, 189-193, 195, 197, 213, 218, 230, 232, 234, 236-239, 244, 246-247
model B *(see XCG-4B)*
model C 174
Navy considers adopting 146
noise in flight 236
nose protection devices 75-76, 77, 79, 163, 167, 173, 177-178, 180-181
obsolete by mid-1944 220
over-speed hazard 95
pack animals transported 161
payload weight 101
production costs 66, 69-71, 109
production end decisions 67-68
production establishment 65, 69-71 237
productions hours and materials 66
production numbers 61, 65-71, 81, 120
production subcontracting 66, 69-71
prone pilot modification 182
quadracycle landing gear 77
radio 74, 97
reconditioned 68, 71, 234
recovery efforts 61, 108-110, 163, 165, 167-168, 234
redesign to carry jeep 62-63
Robertson in-flight breakup 44, 72-73, 158
serials 244-245
ship to theaters 66, 157, 161, 232
shipping crates 64-65
snatch of 106-107, 108, 110
specifics 62, 65
specifications adopted 74
storage difficulties 67-68
surplus offered for sale 213
tail bracing 72, 157
throw-over control column 64, 72
tow speed 101
training losses 61
transport difficulties 68
unusual feats 99
upgrades 64, 71, 79
wrecked by winds 61, 157, 162
XCG-4 12, 51, 53-56, 59, 61-62, 63, 72, 192, 237, 244
XCG-4A 63, 72, 172, 244
XCG-4B 77, 244
see also G-4A and G-4C
CG-5
serials 244
specifics 56
XCG-5 12, 56-57, 244
CG-6
serials 244
specifics 56
XCG-6 12, 56, 244
CG-7
serials 244
specifics 58
XCG-7 12-13, 57, 58-59, 128, 244
CG-8
serials 244
specifics 59
XCG-8 12, 57, 59, 128, 244
CG-9
serials 244
XCG-9 69, 114-115, 244
CG-10 Trojan Horse 237
all-metal variant considered 220
final costs 215
model A 120, 215, 220
production plans 120, 125, 215, 220
serials 244
specifics 119
XCG-10 115-116-117, 128-129, 197, 244
XCG-10A 116, 117-118, 120, 197, 219-220, 237, 244
YCG-10A 114, 120, 131, 215, 244
see also G-10A
CG-11
specifics 121
XCG-11 120-121, 244
CG-12
specifics 122
XCG-12 121-122, 244
CG-13 17, 95, 237
Britain acquires 126
combat experience 126
deceleration parachute 126
dissatisfaction with 125, 237
experiments to improve 124, 126
model A 117, 120, 124-125, 126, 130-131, 169, 179, 220, 232, 237
serials 244
specifics 126

XCG-13 *14*, 116, 122-*123*, 129, 177, 244
XCG-13A 123, *125*-126, *169*, 197, 244
YCG-13 123, 125, 244
YCG-13A 114, *124*-125, 244
see also G-13A
CG-14
serials 244
specification 134
specifics 135, 137
XCG-14 *17*, 134-135, *136*, 196, 244
XCG-14A Avitruck 135, *137*-137, 196, 215, 222-224, 244
XCG-14B 138, 222, 224
CG-15 *17*, *80*, 114, 123, 215, 237
model A *80-81*, 120, 125, 134, *169*, *178-179*, *180-181*, 191, 195-196, 212, 218, 244, 247
operation on snow *214*
serials 244
specifics 81
XCG-15 79-81, 244
XCG-15A 80, 172, 195-196, 244
see also G-15A
CG-16
metal elements proposed 131
Operational and Tactical Suitability testing 130
serials 244
specification 129
specifics 133
XCG-16 *17*, 120, 129-*130*, *131-132*, 133-134, 244
XCG-16A *131*
see also MC-1
CG-17
serials 244
specifics 177
XCG-17 *17*, *176-177*, 220, 244
CG-18
pilot production considered 223, 225
powered variant *225*
serials 244
specifics 223
XCG-18 222-223, 244
XCG-18A Avitruck *223*-226, 237, 244
YCG-18A 224, 244
see also G-18A
CG-19
specifics 227
XCG-20 226-*227*, 244
CG-20
pilot production considered 226
powered variant 226-*227*
serials 244
specifics 227
XCG-20 Avitruck 222, 225, *228*, 237, 244
see also XG-20
Chandler, C.C. 128
Chanute Field 63
Chapman, Randy 116
Chase Aircraft Company Incorporated 134-135, 196, 215, 222-226, 228, 244, 247
Chase Brothers 134
Cherry Point 148
Chesapeake Bay 202
Chicago 129, 159
Chidlaw, Benjamin W, Brigadier General 142
Chin Hills *160*
China 161, 176
Chindits 160
Christopher Aircraft Company 133, 141, 143, 247
Christopher, Arthur B. 141
Christopher Engineering Company 133
Christopher-National Aircraft Products Company 143
Churchill, Winston 10
Cinema 47, 242
model IA 22, 241
model II 23
model IIB 22, 47, 241
model PC-2 22, 241
Civil Aeronautics Administration (CAA) 11, 22-23, 26-27, 30, 35, 39-40, 42
Civilian Pilot Training (CPT) 39-40, 49
Clark, Irving 71
Cleveland 179, 206
Clinton Country Airport 16
Clinton Country Army Air Field (CCAAF) 16-*17*, 22, 55, 59, 75-77, *78*-79, 97, 107-108, 116-117, 123, 125, 130, 135, 138, 173-174, 176, 178-179, 182, 188-189, 192-193, 196, 215, 243, 249
Columbia Aircraft Corporation 71
Commonwealth Aircraft Incorporated 55, 69, 71, 244-245
Condor Field 34, 41
Connecticut 29, 75, 85, 208, 252
Consolidated Aircraft Corporation 19, 176, 201
contract types, procurement 11, 25, 52, 66, 88, 92, 120-121, 252
Convair 188
Coral Sea 159
Corcoran, Stanley "Stan" R. 22, 47, 242
Corey, Warner R., Lieutenant Colonel 75
Cornelius Aircraft Corporation 186-187, 210-211, 247
Cornelius, George W. 187
CQ-1 208-209
model A 209
YCQ-1A 208, *209-210*
Crete 10, 161, 237
Criz, Albert 127-129
Crookham Common 161, 165
Crosby, Harry 183-*185*, 186
Cub *(see J-3 Cub)*
Cuddyback Lake 127
Curtiss Electric 174
Curtiss-Wright Corporation 11, 85, 92, 96-97, 114, 120, 173, 175
Curtiss-Wright Technical Institute 25

Dare, E.R., Lieutenant (jg) 200
Dayton 10-11, 13, 25, 54, 63, 133, 186, 219
DC-3 38, 145, 176, 244
DC-4 146
DC-65 Tandem 27
Dearborn 125
deceleration devices 221
bazooka-fired spike 178-*179*, 215-*216*
Chase Plow 178
plow blades 142, 178-179, 215
see also rockets, glider boost and deceleration
Decker, Chester "Chet" R., Lieutenant 13, 22, 105, 176, 209, 243
Deep River 29
Deland 69
Delaware 70, 105, 254
Delaware River 87, 89
Del Rio 43
Denbo, R.W., Lieutenant Commander 174
Dent, Fred R., Jr., Major, and Colonel *13*, 15, *20*, 23, 33-*34*, 52, 62, 71, 107, 114-115, 127-128, 133, 141, 189, 209, 248
De Ponti, Angelo "Shorty" *71*
De Ponti Aviation Company 71
Design for Industry 206
Detroit 24, 66
DFS 230 *9*, 133-134, 219, 234, 237
Dichman, Ernest W., Colonel 13
Dobodura 159
Dodd, D.O. Major 176
double (dual) tow 39, 42, 96-*97*, 148, 160, 168-*169*, *170*-171
Douglas Aircraft Company 14, 38, 57-59, 95, 105, 114, 145-146, 155, 174, 176, 200, 214, 221-223, 225, 244
Douglas, Donald 57
Driscoll, Bernie 182
drone, unmanned airplane (Navy) 18, 199-200
Dundalk 85
Du Pont, Felix, Major 13
Du Pont, Richard C. 12-*13*, 22, 105-106, 127-128

Eagle Farm AB 72, 159
Eagle Mountain Lake 48-49, 151
Eben Emael 10
Echols, Oliver P., General 11
Edenton 49
Edo Aircraft Corporation 90-91
Eglin Field 149, 186, 208, 228
Eindhoven 165
Elmira 13, 20, 23, 33-34, 79
Elmira Area Soaring Corporation School 33
El Paso 210
El Segundo 58-59
Elwood 70, 141, 143
Engineering Division 13, 182, 208, 210-211, 220-223, 247
English Channel 161, 177
Epworth, Lincoln 121
Eureka, radar transmitter (AN/PPN-1A) and radio Beacon (CRN-4) 103
Evenrude 86
Ewing Township 223

F4F-3 Wildcat 89-90, 174, 200, 203-*204*, 206
F6F-3 Hellcat 202, 204
Fa 223 133
Fa 225 V1 auto-gyro 133-*134*
Fahrney, Delmar S., Lieutenant Commander, Commander, and Captain 18, 149, 151-152, 199-200
Fairchild Aircraft 212, 214, 220, 222, 228-229
FBT-2 209
FG-1 The Goose 187
serials 247
specifics 188
spin model 187
XFG-1 *187-188*, 210, 247
Fighter Command 171
fighter-glider composite (Over-Under project)
advantages 218
P-38+Hamilcar combination studied 219
P-38+XCG-10A combination studied 219
prior concepts and examples 218-219
Figley, Richard E., Lieutenant, Captain, and Major 18, 87-88, 148-149, 153, 200, 203
Firestone Tire and Rubber Company 69, 91
Fletcher Aviation Corporation 208, 210, 247
Fletcher, Frank P. 209
Fletcher, Maurice C. 209
Fletcher, Wendell S. 209
Flight Officer (FO) 36, 239
rank established 42
floatwing
see glider, amphibious 83
Florida 18, 21, 49, 69, 131, 148-149, 171, 216
flutter described 250
Flying Training Command (FTC) 21, 34, 37-38
contracts with civilian pilot training schools 21
Focke-Achgelis 133
Foote, Jack C. 71
Ford Motor Company 48, 65-66, 68, 70, 81, 125, 197, 218, 244-245
Fort Benning 15
Fort Bragg 229
Fort Campbell 229
Fort Dix 206
Fort Smith 71
Fort Walton Beach 149
Fort Worth 49
France, French 110, 168
Frankfort (city) 22
Frankfort Sailplane Company 22-23, 37-38, 52-53, 207, 241, 243-244
Franklin 18-19, 192, 241-242

Freeman Field 215
Fw 200 103

G-1 29, 243
G-2A 213
G-3 213
G-4A 214, 244
intent to retain postwar production capacity 213-214
postwar numbers 213-214, 229
see also CG-4
G-4C 174, 244
see also CG-4
G-10A 244
YG-10A production curtailed 215
see also CG-10
G-13A 213, 244
see also CG-13
G-15A 213-214, 216, 229
configured for artic rescue *214*
see also CG-15
G-18A Avitruck 225, 228-229
conversion with engines 225
specifics 224
XG-18A *224*-225
YG-18A 224-*225*, 228, 244
see also CG-18
G-20
XG-20 226-*227*, 228-229, *236*, 244
see also CG-20
G & A Aircraft Incorporated 65, 69, 91, 93, 114, 145, 147, 245-246
Gabel, Ernest, Lieutenant Colonel *128*
Garges, J.P. Donald "George" 85
Gar Wood winch *48*
Gassner, A.A. 71
Gates, Artemus L. 148
Gee, SCR-717C 103
General Airborne Transport Company (GATC) 129-131, 244
General Aircraft Corporation 65, 69-70, 219, 245
General Aircraft Limited 189, 244, 246
General American Transport Corporation 129
General Electric (GE) 179, 185
Georgia 15
German, Germany 16, 34, 81, 105, 110, 140, 163, 168, 188, 234
fighter-glider composite (Mistel) 218-*219*
glider pilots 248
gliders 18, 21-22, 133-134, 161, 178, 232
introduces gliders to combat 9-11, 231
observes Soviet gliders 10
reduces glider role 10, 237
U.S. applies glider experience postwar 217
Gibson Refrigerator Company 65, 70, 245
Giles, Barney M., Major General 129
GL-1 11
GL-2 *10*-11
GL-3 *11*
Glen Rock 22
glider bombs (GLOMB, USN) 18, 149, 151, 198-207, 246-247
catapult tests 203
concept 198
explosives or freight gliders 152, 204
production type requirements 204
requirement to operate from aircraft carriers 203, 255
tricycle landing gear required 200
see also bomb gliders (USAAF)
glider-borne infantry, gliddermen *C*, 9, *47*, 96, 103, 158-159, 161, 165
losses 61, 105, 141, 158, 163-165
Glider Branch (Washington) 13
Glider Branch (Ohio) 13, 15-16, 65, 74-75, 121-122, 126-128, 171, 176, 179, 193, 219, 222
experimental work 14-15
Glider Equipment Company 35
Glider Mechanics Technical School 193
Glidermen *(see glider-borne infantry)*
glider obstacles 105
Glider Pick-up Mechanism 109
Model 40 105-*106*, 107-108
Model 80 107
Model 120 107
Model 160 107, 119
see also snatch
glider pilots, Army 15-16, 111
additional duties 110
capabilities assessed 42-43, 46
combat exposure 110
combat preparedness 110
converted airplane pilots 46, 168
copilot lack 110, 162, 164-165, 168
hazardous duty pay 110
fate at end of war 213
losses 61, 105, 141, 158-159, 161, 163, 165, 167-168, 238
number of 14, 21, 34, 36-37, 39-40, 42-43, 161-162, 164-165, 168, 232
qualifications 34-36, 40
parachutes for 110, 162, 165
recruitment 34-36
skills envisioned 14
training 21, 33-46, 232
wings *36*, 42, 159
glider pilots, USMC
recruitment 47
number of 19, 47, 49
trainers of 28, 47-49
Glider Pilot Regiment (UK) 10, 164-165
gliders, amphibious 16, 83, 133, 145-146
carrying flying boat engine 83, 152
catamaran twin hull concept 83-84, 90
concept development of 83, 234
floatwing concept 83-84
German experience 234
outboard motor 83, 85, 89-91
tow from carrier deck considered 146
gliders, assault (airland)
characteristics 141
concept 141,
launch from aircraft carrier sought 141, 146
see also AG-1 and AG-2
gliders, military
advantages in combat 9
armament proposed for 16, 114, 127, 142
armor 141, 220-221
attrition greater than airplanes 214
blind flying (instruments) 179-189
cargo winch 80
commercial airline interest 15
disassembly for transport 58, 64, 114, 116-117, 120, 125, 129, 218-220, 252
downview windows 63, 118, 123, 224, 226
electrical system in 23, 80, 97, 116, 123, 129, 137, 153, 169, 200, 204, 210, 220
expendable aircraft 58, 72, 74, 108-110, 181, 186, 220, 237, 248
flaps on 80, 114-115, 120, 123, 129, 135, 141-142, 153, 169, 181, 220, 224-225, 250, 252
glide ratios 12, 176
hazard compared 234
inclement weather towing 98, 148-149, 179, 220, 225
inefficient as "cargo trailers" 148, 150, 176, 255
interphone with tug 74, 96, 98, 137, 149, 162, 218, 225-226
largest 152, 232
manpower intensive 149
mass assault operations 99-105, 158-168
night operation 103, 148-149, 157, 160-161, 164
parapacks 116, 123
practicality of large gliders 220, 237
radios in 22, 24, 27, 40, 114, 120, 123, 142, 225
seeking higher tow speeds 114
tactics development 14-16, 40, 43, 161, 168, 231
uneconomical as tactical transports 220, 229, 237
wing loading and airspeed match to tug 12, 63, 80, 114, 123, 133, 200
gliders, powered 191-197, 228, 257
rocketed assisted takeoff 197
tow-assisted takeoff 192
gliders, trainers
accommodating parachutes 23, 11, 25
acquisition 11, 14, 53
Army appropriation of civilian gliders 13, 21-22
certification 11
eliminating metal from 23, 25, 28
initial five experimental 13, 21
number of 14, 21, 42, 232
overall cost of 232
side-by-side instruction 25, 30
storage of 42
Glider Unit 13, 63
Globe Corporation, Aircraft Division 52
Go 242 178, *189*, 237
Göppingen
Gö-1 22, 242
Gö-3 Minimoa 22, 243
Gö-5 242
Gotha 189, 237
Gould Aeronautical Division 28
Gould Aviation Company 28
Gould, James A. 29
Grasshopper 27
Great Britain, British 19, 40, 44, 79, 105, 109, 146, 161, 164-165, 168, 181, 193, 199-200, 219
combat experience with gliders 157-168, 236
develops glider corps 10-11
gliders developed by 15, 75, 79, 113, 138-140-141, 145, 189, 219, 237, 250
glider pilots 15, 33, 110, 250
glider operation techniques 96
U.S. considers towing to 98, 253
Great Lakes Aircraft Corporation 200
Greece, Greek 167-168
Greenland 214
rescue attempt 214
Greenport Aeronautical Corporation 85, 90, 252
Greenville 70
Griswold, Roger W., II 29, 75
Gross, Frank A., Dr. 25
Ground Forces Command 215
Grumman Aircraft 48, 85, 87, 89, 174, 200, 203
Grunau 242
Guadalcanal 167, 234
Guymon, Vernon M., Lieutenant Colonel 47-*48*, 49
gyro-glider 133-134

Hadrian 79, 161
Mk. I 79, 98, 245
Mk. II 79, 245
serials 245
Hamilcar 114, 161, 219, 237, 244
demonstrated in U.S. *189*, 257
U.S. seeks 140
Hamilton Standard 195
Hammond Instruments Company 185-186
Harpers Lake 183, 185
Harris, Anthony B., Lieutenant Colonel 219
Harvey 47
Hawthorne 183
Haywood-Wakefield Furniture Company 70
Heap, Lieutenant Commander 203
Heinemann, Ed 58
helicopters 220, 229
Hengist 79, 138
Himalaya Mountains 176
Hirth, Wolf 22
Hitler, Adolf 10, 159
Hoekstra, Harold D. 27

Holcomb, Thomas, Major General 16, 19
Holland 44, 109, 165, 167-168, 235
Hollophane beacon lamp *(see Aladis lamp)*
Horsa 75, 79, 103, *113*, *138*, *139-140*, *146*, 157, 164, 168, 179, *202*
aft fuselage removal 140
AS.51 Mk. I 115, 189, 244
AS.58 Mk. II 138
combat use by U.S.A. 140, *161*-162, *236*
demonstrated in U.S.A. 138, 146, 148, *189*
Navy autotow tests with 200
numbers in U.S. service 140-141, 165
production in U.S. for Army considered 114-115, 145-146
production for USN considered 145
serials 244, 246
specifics 140
UK production for U.S.A. considered 140
U.S. Army acquires 138-139
Hotspur, GAL.48 *15*, 138, 179, 244
demonstrated in USA 148, 151, *189*
Navy autotow tests with 200-*201*, 202
serials 244, 246
Houghton, Rovel S. 178
Hughes Aircraft Company 221-222
Hutchens, Lieutenant 118
Hutchinson 69

Illinois 3, 33, 47, 63, 117, 129, 185
India, Indian 160, 176, 245
Indiana 22, 37, 70, 141, 215
Iron Mountain 66, 70, 125
Italy, Italian 95, 159, 164, 167

J2F Duck 48, 87-90, 200
J-3 Cub 27, 105-*106*
Jack Heintz Company 179
Jacobs Aircraft Engine Company 195-196
Japan, Japanese 16, 68, 159-161, 175-176, 186, 213, 232, 234
invasion of 120, 169, 232
Jaquith, E.K. 87
JB-1 185-*186*, 257
model A 185-*186*, 257
specifics 186
JB-2 197, 257
JB-10 186
JE-1 Pacemaker 48
jeep
carried in glider 52-53, 59, 62-*63*, 114, 120, 122, 127, 133, 135, 137-138, 161
flying jeep concept 62
Jenter Corporation 65, 71
Jersey City 90-91
Jet-Assisted Take-Off (JATO) 177-178, 182, 197, 205, 214, 256
jet engines 185-186, 197
JN-4 *11*

John H. Wilson Glider School 36
Johnson, Davenport, Major General 15
Johnsville 198, 200, 207
Joliet 22, 37
Kaiser-Frazer Corporation 228
Kansas 55, 69
Kansas City 55, 71
Karnow, Paul 83
Kauffman, John R. 24
Kenosha 121-122
Kentucky 43, 120, 229
Kershaw 44
King, Ernest J., Rear Admiral 149, 151
Klemin, Alexander 91
Knox, Frank 16, 146, 151
Koch, Charles D. 218
Korean War 229
Kowalski, Frank, Jr., Captain 133-134

L-1 37, model A Vigilant 37-*38*
L-2B 27-28, 243
L-3B 27, 243
L-4 27-28, 37, 243
L-5 110
Lae 159
Laister, John "Jack" W. 24, 115-116, 241, 242
Laister-Kauffman Aircraft Corporation (L-K) 22, 24, 33, 65, 70, 114-115, 119-120, 129, 197, 215, 237, 243-245, 249
Lakehurst NAS 18, 188, 202-203
Landis, Reed, Colonel 11
LaMont, J.B. *14*
Lambert Field 71-72
Lamesa 36
laminar flow airfoil 58, 127, 250
Langford Lodge 219
Langley Memorial Aeronautical Laboratory 84, 91, 183, 187-188, 207
Laurinburg-Maxton AAB 11, 16, 44-*45*, *46*, 75, 98, 119, 138, 149, 171-171, 178
LBE-1
serials 247
XLBE-1 204-*205*, 207, 247
LBP-1
serials 247
XLBP-1 205, *206-207*, 247
LBT-1 206-207, 211
catapult tests *206*
production orders 206-207
serials 247
XLBT-1 *206-207*, 247
Lee, Arthur 178
Lee, William C., Major General 44
Lend-Lease 68, 79
Leonard, Parker 29
Lewis School of Aeronautics 33, 47-48
Link trainer 37, 42
Lipa 169

Litchfield, Burnham 89
LK-10 Yankee Doodle Two 24, *33*, 241, 243
LK-12 197, 220
LNE-1 *18*, 29-30, 47-48, *49*, 152, 173, 200, *234*, 243, 246, 258
postwar atmospheric research, use in 216
serials 246
specifics 29
XLNE-1 *29*-30
LNP-1
autotow tests with 200
serials 246
XLNP-1 27, *30*-31, 246
LNR-1
autotow tests with 200
serials 246
XLNR-1 27, *31*, 243
LNS-1 23, *30*, 47-*48*, 152, *198*, 200, 243, 246
LNT-1 200-*201*, 202-204, 206, 243, 246
autotow tests with 200
catapult tests, 203-*204*
modifications for GLOMB tests 200
serials 246
XLNT-1 27, 31, 48, 152, 200-*201*, *202-203*, *204*, 206, 243, 246, 258
LNT-2 202
Lockbourne 39
Lock Haven 27, 206
Lockheed Aircraft 39, 44, 183, 205, 216, 219
Lockheed Overseas Corporation 219
Lockport 33, 47
Long Island 70
LORAN 103
Los Angeles (L.A., city) 58, 127
Los Angeles, U.S.S. (dirigible) *18*
Louisville 120, 215
Lowell Airport 70
L.P.R. Corporation 181
LRA-1 Invader 92
post-cancellation 151
serials 246
specifics 90
XLRA-1 *85*, *88-89*, 90, *147*, *149*, 151, *202*, *233*
LRA-2 92, 252
serials 246
XLRA-2 92
LR2A-1
serials 246
specifics 92
XLR2A-1 92-*93*
LRG-1
specifics 90
subscale flight model 90, 114
XLRG-1 90-91, *92*, 114-115, 145
LRH-1
serials 246
specifics 90
XLRH-1 90-*91*, 93, *144*-145, *148*

LRN-1
serials 246
specifics 154
XLRN-1 116, *152-154*, 204
LR2N-1, XLR2N-1 152
LRQ-1 93
post-cancellation 151
serials 246, 256
specifics 88
XLRQ-1 83, 85-*86*, *87*, *89*-90, *147*, 149, *151*-152
LRW-1 49, *146*, 148-149, 151-152
autotow tests with 200, 202
serials 246
LR2W-1 246, 256
Lubbock 39, 42, 46, 102
Ludington Airplanes 28
Ludington, C.T. 29
Ludington-Griswold Incorporated 75-76, 109
Luftwaffe 167, 217, 219, 248
Luzon 169

M-22 light tank 119
Malloney, Frank, Senator 151
Mallory, Eschol M., Lieutenant 47
Malta 10
Manhattan 135
Manila 176-177
March Field 128-129
Martin, Glenn L., Company 142
Maryland 18, 85
Massachusetts 70
Masters Field 148
Materiel Command 10-11, 15, 26, 33, 37-38, 42, 52, 63, 68-69, 71, 74, 115, 128-131, 134-135, 141, 192, 195, 219
Materiel Division 10-12, 65, 125, 133, 181-182
Maxton 16
Maxwell, A.R., Brigadier General 220
MC-1 *128-129*, 130
crash of 128
half scale flying model *127*
infringement on Burnelli lifting body patent 128
model A 129
model B 131
origins 127
production proposed 128-129
specification 127, 129
stall and spin characteristics 128
McAuliffe, Anthony, Brigadier General *235*
McCain, John S., Rear Admiral 148
McClure, W.H., Lieutenant Commander 174
McDonald, E.F., Commander 48
Me 109 219
Me 321 *232*, 237
Mercer County Airport 223
Merrill, Grayson, Lieutenant Commander 200
Messerschmitt 232, 237
Meyers, John 183

Miami 21, 148
Michigan 24, 65-66, 70, 125, 206
Middleton 27
Midway, Battle of 200
Midwest Gliders 105, 242
Miller, Marion A., Captain 215
Minimoa *(see Göppingen Gö-3)*
Mines Field 59, 209
Minneapolis 71, 171
Minnesota 71
Missouri 56, 71, 133, 141
Mitchell, General 149
Mitscher, Marc, Captain 16
Mojave Desert 58
Morocco 157
Morrison, Howard *128*
Motorless Flight Institute 47
MS glider *134 see also CG-14*
Muroc AAB 58, 173-174, 183, 185-186, 209-211
Murphy, Mike, Major, and Lieutenant Colonel *43*, 141, 171, 177-178
Mussolini, Benito 133
Mustin Field 89, 206
MX project number
  definition 12
  MX-114 12, 181
  MX-151 186
  MX-166 211, 247
  MX-197 208
  MX-200 173
  MX-205 113
  MX-285 113
  MX-294 181
  MX-296 179
  MX-324 Rocket Wing 182-183, *184-185*, 186, 247
  MX-325 141
  MX-334 182-183, *184*, 186, 247
  MX-365 182
  MX-416 186
  MX-543 185
  MX-877 224
  MX-878 225
  MX-879 226

N3N-3 48
N5N-1, XN5N-1 48, 173, 203
Nadzab 126, 159
Nagel, Felix 133
National Advisory Committee for Aeronautics (NACA) 84, 86, 173, 183, 188, 205, 207
National Aircraft Corporation 65, 70, 141, 245
National Airport 131, 149
National Bureau of Standards High Voltage Laboratory 57
natural stabilization 200, 211
Naval Aircraft Factory (NAF) 16, 18, 48, 83-85, 87, 89-91, 147-149, 151-152, 154, 172, 199-200, 203-206, 246
Naval Air Modification Center (NAMC) 200, 206
Naval Air Modification Unit (NAMU) 151-152, 198, 200-202
Netheravon 219
Nevada 183
Newark 137
Newark Air Base 193, 254
New Guinea 159
New Haven 85, 88, 151, 208
New Jersey 18, 22, 71, 90, 137, 188, 202-203, 206, 223
Newkirk, James, Lieutenant *128*
New York 13, 20, 23, 33-34, 70, 121, 135
New York City 91, 121-122, 200
Nichols Field 177
Nijmegen 165
nolo, no-pilot solo 202, 258
Noorduyn 160
Norfolk 148, 201
Normandy 43-44, 77, 110, 134, 140-141, 159-160, 162, 164, 177-178, 236
North Africa 95, 98-99, 102, 157, 219
North American Aviation 48, 173, 219
North Carolina 16, 44-45, 49, 92, 119, 229
Northern Ireland 219
Northrop Aircraft Incorporated 182-183, 185, 247
Northrop, John A. "Jack" 182-183
Northwestern Aeronautical Corporation (NAC) 13, 65, 68-69, 71, 81, 123, 125-126, 192-195, 244-245, 247
Northwest Airlines 71

O-49 14, 35
Ohio 10, 13, 17, 25, 27, 39, 81, 173, 179, 186-188, 206, 215
Okinawa 177
Oklahoma 49, 187
Operation
  Bughole 159
  cancelled 159, 164, 167-168
  Dragoon 164-165
  Freshman 157
  Fustian 157
  Husky 157
  Ladbroke 157
  Manna 168
  Market-Garden 77, 165, 167-168
  Neptune 162-163
  Red 46
  Repulse 168
  Thursday 160-161
  Varsity 81, 110, 126, 168-169
Orland 131
Orange 91, 145, 255
Oxnard Army Flight Strip 130

P-38 Lightning *17*, 171, 183, 185-186, 219
P-39 174
P-40 72, 92, 151
P-47 Thunderbolt 61, 135, 137, 171, 172-173, *174*
P-51 *17*, 61, 173
P-61A 173
P-79
  XP-79 182, 185
  XP-79B 185
P-80 *216*
P-82 Twin Mustang 219
Panama Canal Zone 15
Papana, Alex 184-185, 188
paratroops 9, 229
  U.S. 10, 14
  marine 17, 19, 152
  jumps from gliders 171, 221
Parker, John E. *14*, 71
Parker skid 75
Parris Island, MCAS 30, 47-48
Pasadena 208
Patterson, Albert L. "Pat" 85, 252
Patuxent River, NAS 18, 153, 155, 202-203, 205
PBY-5A Catalina 19, *49*, 86-88, 90, 146, 148-149, 153, 171, 173, *189*
PB2Y-1 Coronado 201
Pearl Harbor 13, 33
Pennsylvania 16, 27, 69, 198
Pensacola 18
PG-1
  serials 247
  specifics 192
  XPG-1 *191-192*, 247
PG-2
  model A *194*-195, *213*
  production 193-194
  serials 247
  specifics 193-195
  UK acquired 194
  XPG-2 190, *192-193*, 195, 247
  XPG-2A Aerotruck *193*, 197, 213, 247
  XPG-2B 195, 247
  XPG-2C 195, 247
PG-3
  serials 247
  specifics 196
  XPG-3 81, *195-196*, *197*, 213, 247
  XPG-3A 196, 247
PG-4
  specifics 196
  XPG-4 *196*-197, 247
Philadelphia 16, 18, 90, 114, 148-149, 151, 173, 200-201, 207
Philadelphia Navy Yard 86-89
Philippines, The 81, 160, 169, 177
pickup *(see snatch)*
Pinecastle 216
Pinecastle AAB 215-216
Piper Aircraft Corporation 27-28, 30-31, 37, 105-106, 205, 243, 246-247
Pitcairn-Larson Autogiro Company, Incorporated 69, 90
Pitts, Y.A., Colonel 11
Poland, Polish 21
Porterfield Aircraft Company 65, 71
Porterfield, E.E., Jr. 71
Port Moresby 159
PQ-11 208-210
Pratt & Whitney (P&W) 197
Pratt, Don, Brigadier General 177
Pratt, Read & Company, Incorporated 18, 28-30, 49, 65, 71, 75, 79, 146, 204-205, 207, 216, 243, 245-247
Pratt, Read Piano Company 29
PRG-1 29-30
Price, Bruce B., Major and Colonel 13-*14*, 15, 33
Prigg Duct Works 243
Project George *(see glider bombs (GLOMB))*
prone pilot position 182, 243
Prüffling (Graduate) *18*
PS-2 18-*19*, 241-242
PT-1W 56
PT-17 Kaydet 37
PV-1 Ventura 205-206

R4D 145
R-5 215
R5D 146, 153, 155
radar 102-103, 158, 199-200, 207, 220
Radio Corporation of America (RCA) 200, 202
Raleigh-Durham 44
Ranger Engines 192-193
Read, Robert C. 121
Read-York Incorporated 122, 244
Rearwin Aircraft and Engines, Incorporated 55, 71
Rebecca airborne radar beacon transceiver 102, 253
refueling, in flight from glider 153, 186, 188, 199, 257
  tests 201
Reilly, Robert V., Lieutenant, Captain, and Major 18, 87, 151, 153, 203
Remagen 168
remote (radio) piloting 152-154, 188, 198-200, 204, 206-208, 211, 247
  systems 202
Republic Aviation 90, 121, 173
Rhine River 46, 81, 165, 168
Ridgefield (city) 71
Ridgefield Manufacturing Corporation 65, 71, 192-193, 245, 247
Ridgeway, General 43
Rietherman, Alfred 187-188
rigid tow bar 174, *217-218*, 220, 244
River Meuse 10
Roach Lake 183
Roberts, Seán 259
Robertson (city) 71
Robertson Aircraft Corporation 65, 71-73, 245
Robertson, William B. 71
Robinson, Barnette, Captain 47
rockets, glider boost and deceleration 125, 177-*178*, 215, 221

Rogers Dry Lake 58
Rommel, Erwin, Field Marshall 161
Rommel's Asparagus (Rommel-spargel) 161, 165
Royal Air Force (RAF) 15, 19, 79, 98, 140, 219, 245
Royal Canadian Air Force (RCAF) 79, 148
Russia, Russians *(see Union of Soviet Socialist Republics (USSR), Soviets)*
Ryan Aircraft 25
Ryan, R., Lieutenant 18, 153, 203
Sailplane Corporation of America 27
sailplanes, sport 18
  acquired for training 11
  eliminated as trainer 39, 42, 48
Salo, George 87
San Antonio 43
San Fernando 25, 58, 127
San Francisco 57
Saybrook 75
SB2C Helldiver 97, 173, *175*
Schemp, Martin 22
Schultz, Arthur B. 105
Schweizer Aircraft Corporation 13, 20, 23-25, 30, 34, 41, 47-48, 198, 200, 241, 243, 246
Schweizer Ernest 23
Schweizer Paul 23
Schweizer William 23
Scott Field 117
Scotland 79, 98
Sensenich 193
Seymour 215
SGS 2-8 20, 23, 30, *41*, 47, 241, 243, 246
SGS 2-12 243
Shawnee 49, 153
Sheppard Field 42, 98, 193
Shoop, Richard, Captain *128*
Short Brothers 219
Short-Mayo 219, 258
Sicily, airborne invasion of 44, 157-159, 161-162, 219
Sierra Nevada Mountains 216
Sikorsky 215
Simmons Company 121-122
Smith, Don 185
Smith, Lee 27
snatch, glider pick-up 42, *106-107*, 108, 110, 119, 125, 140, 148, 161, 171, 174, 214-215, 255
  dual pickup 105, 108
  early demonstrations 105
  in-flight snatch 174-*175*
  night 108
  origin 105
  see also Glider Pick-up Mechanism
Snead & Company 90-91, 93, 120-121, 145, 147-148, 244, 246, 255
SNJ-2 48
SNV-1 Valiant 202
Soaring Society of America 13, 18
South Carolina 44, 47-48
Southern California Soaring Association 216
South Lowell 70
South Plains AAB 39, 102
Spaatz, Carl, General 13-14, 33-34
Sparks, Harry C. 87-88
Spartan Aircraft Company 187-188
SR-10 Reliant 105-106, *174*
ST-100 27, 243
Stainhauser, Joe 47
St. Louis (city) 24, 44, 57, 72, 74, 115, 117, 133, 141, 158, 215
St. Louis Arena 116
St. Louis Aircraft Corporation 56-57, 244
St. Louis Car Company 56
St. Paul 71
Stanley, Bob 29
Stanley Mountains 159
Stanton, Charles I. 27
Stanton-Taylorcraft 27
Stark, Harold R., Admiral 19
  restrains USMC glider program 19
static tests, described 22
Stearman 37, 69-70
steel tubing, as glider construction material 22-24, 29, 54-55, 63-*64*, 77, 120-121
Steinway & Sons, Piano Manufacturers 70, 121
Stewart River rescue 214
Stinson 14, 35, 37-38, 105-106, 173-174
Stinson Field 43
Stolzenberger, Adam J., Captain 188, 208
Stowe, Lewis "Lew" J. 215, 222
Stroukoff, Michael 134, 225
Stuttgart 42, 48, 111
Sundstedt, Hugo, Captain 121
swamp gliders 21, 243
Sweet, Floyd J., Captain, and Major *75*, 79, *215*

tactical airlifters
  developed as alternative to gliders 220
  postwar descendents of combat gliders 114, 220, 225-229, 232, 236-237
  tandem towing 118, *170*, 176-*177*
Taylorcraft Aviation Corporation 27-28, 31, 173, 200-201, 206-207, 243, 246-247
Taylor, Molton B. "Molt", Lieutenant 200, 202-203, 258
TBD-1 Devastator 200
TBF 174
telemetry, radio 183, 185, 200
television (TV) 152-154, 199-200, 202-206, 209-210
Tennessee 44
Texas 25, 36, 39, 42-43, 48-49, 98, 102, 193, 210
TG-1 42, 52
  model A 22-*23*, *37-38*, 42, 241, 243
  model B 22, 241
  model C 241
  model D 22, 241
  serials 243
  specifics 23
  XTG-1 22, 243
  XTG-1 modified for remote control 207-*208*
TG-2 *13*, *15*, 23, *32*, *35*, *41*, 48, 241, 243, 246
  model A 241, 243
  serials 243
  specifics 23
  XTG-2 *20*, 23, *34*, 243
TG-3 *13*, *15*, 23
  model A 23, *24*, 243, 255
  serials 243
  specifics 23
  XTG-3 23, 25, 105, 181, 243
TG-4 *15*
  model A *24*, 116, *233*, 243
  model B 24, 241
  serials 243
  specifics 24
  XTG-4 24, 243
TG-5 "Descender" 27-*28*, 31, *36-37*, *160*, 243, 246
  serials 243
  specifics 27
  XTG-5 27, 243
TG-6 27-*28*, 31, *39*, 173, 182, 200, 243, 246, 258
  serials 243
  specifics 27
  XTG-6 172
TG-7, XTG-7 21, 243
TG-8 27-*28*, 30-31, 105, 243, 246
  serials 243
  specifics 28
  XTG-8 27
TG-9, XTG-9 21, 26, 243
TG-10
  specifics 25
  XTG-10 *25*, 243
TG-11, XTG-11 21-22, 243
TG-12
  specifics 26
  model A 26, 241
  XTG-12 25-*26*, 127, 243
TG-13
  model A 27, 241, 249
  specifics 27
  XTG-13 *26*, 243
TG-14 241
TG-15 241
TG-16 242
TG-17 242
TG-18 242
TG-19 242
TG-20 22, 242, 249
TG-21 242
TG-22 242
TG-23 242
TG-24 242
TG-25 242
TG-26 242
TG-27 242
TG-28 242
TG-29 242
TG-30 242
TG-31 242
TG-32 152, 215-216, 243
  modified for postwar atmospheric research 216
  serials 243
TG-33
  XTG-33 172-*173*, *182*, 243
Thunderstorm Project 215-216
Timm Aircraft Company 71, 141-143
Timm Aircraft Corporation 65, 71, 77, 85, 90, 244-245, 247
Timm, Otto 71
Timm, Wallace 71
Tinian 175
Tito, Marshall 159
Titusville 49, 152
Tokyo 177
Towers, John H., Rear Admiral 19, 146
towed targets 172-*173*, 207-*208*
towing power-off airplanes 173-*174*, *175*, 200, 215-*216*
towline 95-96, 148, 160, 169, *238-239*
  attachment 11, 49, 75-76, 95-*96*, 172, 207, 224, 226
  material 11-12, 16, 95, 105, 203, 252
  multi-point attachment 138, 172, 176, 183, 186
  parachute *32*, 203-*204*, 206
  recovery 104-105
  shortened 173-174, 217
Tow Rope Position Indicator 117, 137-138, 179-*180*, 199-200, 226
  Tow Cable Angle Indicator 179
  tow rope position arm 126, 169, *180-181*, 200, 223, 227
Traverse City 206, 211
triple tow 171
Troop Carrier Command (TCC) 39, 42-43, 46, 79, 96, 110, 158, 164, 220, 222
Troy 52, 81
Tucson 176
tug aircraft 43-44, 96, 171, 234
desire to use fighters 114, 171
numbers 13-14, 38
Tulagi 234
Tulsa 187-188
Tunisia 157
Twenty-Nine Palms (location) 26-27, *35*, 58, 79
Twenty-Nine Palms Air Academy 34, 40-*41*

UC-64 Norseman 160
UC-77 Airmaster 174
UC-81D 174
Union of Soviet Socialist Republics (USSR), Soviets 159, 250
  German glider operations in Russia 10
  introduces military gliders 9, 237
  last operating gliders 229

United Kingdom *(UK, see Great Britain)*
United States of America (U.S.)
begins glider program 10, 171
civil aircraft registration codes 249
Congress 16, 47
demise of military gliders 229
glider industry 11-12, 21, 24, 37, 51, 120
glider operational details 95-111, 148
glider orders cancelled at end of war 213, 232
initial glider concepts 11-12, 14, 231
number of gliders ordered and delivered 231-232
overall cost of glider program 231-232
Universal Glider Company 24, 242
U.S. Air Force (USAF)
8,000-pound class Light Assault Gliders developed 220-225
12,000-pound class Heavy Assault Gliders developed 220-227
alternatively powered gliders 220
created 213
effort at glider standardization 214
glider designations changed 213
U.S. Army
airborne forces organization 13, 40, 42-43, 250
U.S. Army 8-place gliders 11, 14, 61, 113
acquisition 11, 52-53-4, 56-57, 114
number of 13-14, 65
specifics 12
specifications 11-12
U.S. Army 15-place gliders 11, 14, 38, 61, 113
acquisition 11, 52-54, 56-57, 114
advanced model for improved efficiency 134
number of 13-14, 65
specifics 12, 134
specifications 11-12
U.S. Army 30-place gliders
number of 14
origins of 114
specifics 114
U.S. Army 60-place gliders 133
U.S. Army Air Corps (USAAC), U.S. Army Air Forces (USAAF)
8,000-pound class Light Assault Gliders conceived 220-*221*, 222
12,000-pound class Heavy Assault Gliders conceived 220-*222*, 223
all-metal gliders considered 220
alternatively powered gliders 220-222
antipathy toward gliders and glider pilots 15, 42, 68, 213, 236-237, 239
artic rescue with gliders 214
budget for gliders 14
combat experience with gliders 157-169
develops glider corps 11
difficult glider development and procurement 15-16, 231
early towing tests 207-208
existing gliders consider obsolete late war 220, 237
glider designations 12
glider test and evaluation care 114, 237
glider testing 16, 171-175
landing zone preparation 102-103
late war and postwar course for gliders 219-220
organizations supporting glider procurement 13
rear loading concepts advocated 220-223
U.S. Marine Corps (USMC) 105
air troops 16, 19
Division of Aviation 19
glider development 16, 83, 152
number of gliders 19
paratroops 16, 19, 152
U.S. Navy (USN)
12-place gliders developed 16, 19, 83-85, 90, 92, 151
24-place gliders developed 19, 83-84, 90, 93, 152
considers adopting Horsa 145-146
early experiments 18
freight or explosives gliders 152, 204
gliders transfer to Army 151-152
initiates glider program 17
misperceptions about gliders 145, 252
overall program results and cost 234
production continuation considered 151
production expansion considered 146,
program difficulties 145-146, 234
program reconsidered 146
tugs limitations 146
Utility (glider) 105

Van Nuys 71, 143
Vertical Spin Tunnel 187
Villaume Box and Lumber Company 71
Vinet, Camille "Cammy" 105
Virginia 84-85, 91, 148, 183, 252
VLN, Class 28, 84, *see gliders, amphibious*
VLR, Class 204
Vultee 37, 173, 202

Waco 7, 38, 40, 42-43, 46, 49, 51, 53, 55, 60-63, 65, 70-71, 73, 75, 79-81, 95, 114, 116, 122-123, 140-141, 146, 148, 151, 159, 161-168, 191, 193, 195-197, 230, 232, 234, 236-237, 244-247
background 52-53
liquidation 214
War Department 21, 24, 30, 42, 51, 55, 58, 68-69, 84, 120, 125
directs glider procurement from small firms 12, 65, 84, 114, 231
prohibits glider flying 11, 33
rejects gliders prewar 11
Ward Furniture Manufacturing Company 65, 71, 245
Warren, George W. 85, 93, 151, 252
Washington, D.C. 10-13, 15, 22, 27, 36, 65, 70-71, 120, 128-129, 131, 133, 141-142, 149, 215
Weaver Aircraft Company 53
Wehle, John, Major, and Lieutenant Colonel 19, 47-48, 145, 147
Wesel 105, 168
West, Ben, Captain *14*
West Trenton 223
Whitehead Aircraft Corporation 24
Whittingham *14*
Wichita 69-70
Wichita Engineering Company 25, 243
Wichita Falls 25
Williamson, Hugh S. 89
Willow Grove 69
Wilmington (Ohio) 16-17, 39, 59, 116, 125, 133, 176, 188-189
Wilmington (Delaware) 105
Winston-Salem 92
Wisconsin 121
W.L. Maxson Company 200
Wold-Chamberlain Airport/Field 71, 192, 195
wood as glider construction material 11, 51, 54, 63, 84-85, 115, *205*, 231, 252
aluminum substitute considered 197, 219
care required 120, 237
largest wood aircraft 116, 152
Wood, Karl D., Professor 248
World War I (WWI) 17
Wright Aircraft Engines 89
Wright Field 10, 13, *15-16*, 22, 24-25, 27, 34, 38-39, 52-53, 58-59, *62*, 65-66, 71, 75-76, 97, 105, 116, 120, 123, 127-129, 134, 137, 140-143, 151, 174, 177-178, 182, 188, 193, 200, 209, 215, 217, 219, 248
Wright-Patterson AFB 214, 221

XCALR-200A 182-*184*

Yankee Doodle 24, 241
York Aircraft Corporation 121-122, 244
York, Holcomb 122
Yugoslavia 159

About the Author

William J. Norton is a flight test engineer, instructor, and a writer. His experience has come to focus on development testing of new and modified aircraft, a great deal of this at the Air Force Flight Test Center, Edwards AFB, California. For 20 years, Bill did much the same things during a career as a U.S. Air Force officer where he also served as aircrew on test aircraft. He has contributed to such programs as the RQ-4 Global Hawk, MQ-9 Reaper, X-47B, F-22A Raptor, F-35A Lightning, CV-22 Osprey, C-17A Globemaster III, AGM-129 Advanced Cruise Missile, F-15E Strike Eagle, C-23A Sherpa, and many others. Bill holds a Masters of Science degree in Aeronautical Engineering. He has penned a dozen aviation books, scores of magazine articles, plus numerous technical papers and reports. Bill is a pilot with a number of civil aeronautical ratings including glider, has restored and operates a De Havilland DHC-1 Chipmunk, and has built a Rutan Long-EZ. Bill resides in California's Mojave Desert.